GEORGE ELIOT

GEORGE ELIOT
The Emergent Self

RUBY V. REDINGER

THE BODLEY HEAD
LONDON SYDNEY
TORONTO

*Grateful acknowledgement is made to the following for permission
to reprint previously published material:*

Columbia University Press and Routledge and Kegan Paul Ltd:
Scattered excerpts from *Essays of George Eliot*,
edited by Thomas Pinney (1963)

Oxford University Press (Oxford, England, New York)
and The Clarendon Press: Scattered excerpts from
George Eliot: A Biography by Gordon S. Haight.
Copyright © 1968 by Oxford University Press

Oxford University Press, Oxford, England:
Scattered excerpts from *Edith Simcox and George Eliot*,
edited by K. A. MacKenzie.
Copyright © 1961 by Oxford University Press.

Frederick Ungar Publishing Co.: Scattered excerpts from
The Life and Works of Goethe by George Henry Lewes.
Copyright © 1965 by Frederick Ungar Publishing Co.

Yale University Press: Scattered excerpts from
George Eliot and John Chapman, edited by Gordon S. Haight (1940)
and scattered excerpts from *The George Eliot Letters*,
7 volumes, edited by Gordon S. Haight (1954-1955)

For Pam—again

CONTENTS

Acknowledgements

O NE REGRETTABLE CONSEQUENCE OF THE LONG SPAN OF TIME this study has consumed in my own life is that several individuals who wished me well while it was in progress are no longer here to see it in its final form. I am thinking particularly of my mother and father, Maude and Elber Redinger; Marie B. Garvin; Nancy (Harriet) Carran —and also of Joby, Judy, and Teddy. In my mind too are grateful memories of my esteemed graduate professor of many years back, John De Lancey Ferguson (who more recently gave me an invaluable set of books when I could not afford to buy it—the Gordon S. Haight edition of George Eliot's *Letters*), and of my long-time friend and erstwhile publisher, Hiram Haydn, who helped direct my manuscript to Knopf.

I also acknowledge with gratitude the moral support given me by friends with whom I am still in contact: Peggy Charlier, Doris Bidwell, Ruth Ballou, Margaret Counts, Neva Goldberg. In a special category is Jo (Mrs. Hayden) Monroe, who not only cheered me onward but typed the entire manuscript from what was occasionally abominably rough copy. I am also deeply appreciative of the patient interest expressed by my colleagues in the English Department of Baldwin-Wallace College, as well as by many students, especially those who participated in the George Eliot Seminar (Winter 1974).

As I review these heartfelt acknowledgments, I am convinced that any book which achieves publication is the result of an indefinable kind of collaboration. With this in mind, my final tribute is twofold: first, to my editor and publisher, Robert Gottlieb, who shares my interest in (although not necessarily all my views on) George Eliot and who has made the transition from manuscript to print as exciting and as painless as possible; second, to George Eliot herself, who occasionally has annoyed or disturbed me but has never bored me.

RUBY V. REDINGER
Berea, Ohio

Preface

THE EMERGENCE OF GEORGE ELIOT AS A GREAT NOVELIST AND A great person is the subject of this book. Although these two unfoldings had different beginnings, they eventually coincided, especially at that time when George Eliot was gradually overcoming her resistance to the forces of creativity and producing her first stories. As it was also at this time that she forged the literary techniques she was to use with increasing skill and subtlety in proceeding from novel to novel, these early works receive here the most concentrated attention. Analysis of the later novels belongs more properly to the realm of literary criticism that is independent of biographical connotation.

My choice of "emergent" as the key word in my subtitle is in part homage to George Henry Lewes, who was the first to use the term to signify an unpredictable result arising from known sources. The word served as a constant reminder to me that even the most exhaustive verbal analysis of any form of creativity is at best incomplete, for inevitably lacking is that elusive quality which makes a dynamic process more than the sum total of its components.

R. V. R.

Prologue

Geoge Eliot came into being on 4 February 1857, already a mature woman of thirty-seven and if not an equally mature writer of fiction, at least one who was jubilantly beginning to break the bonds which had long imprisoned her creativeness. Symbolic birth though this was, more than a mere name was born. For the reading public, it soon became the personality of the George Eliot novels: that omniscient, brooding spirit, with its distinctive blend of force and gentleness, of compassion and sardonic humor, encompassing yet transcending the manifold life of its own creation. For the woman who bore the pseudonym, it was first—as she herself called it—no more than "a tub to throw to the whale in case of curious inquiries"; but gradually it evolved into another self, her writing self, which arched over the not always harmonious selves of Mary Ann Evans,* Marian Evans, Marian Lewes, and even Mrs. John W. Cross. Slowly and naturally, without deliberate effort, she grew into that self, so that even the most intimate of her friends who knew her only during her late years rarely, if ever, had glimpses of the impulsive and bitterly frustrated person she had once been; whereas many of those who had known her best in the earlier years were inclined to think the George Eliot role a pose. George Henry Lewes alone had reason to know her as one whole person, for she began to live with him as his wife two years before she began to write fiction, and from then on, her active writing career coincided exactly with her life with him.

Her contemporary readers were intent upon divorcing "George Eliot" from "that woman," who lived with Lewes without benefit of

* She was baptized Mary Anne but did not write the final e after 1837. In 1850 she adopted Marian, with which she signed almost all personal letters until 1880, when she reverted to Mary Ann.

legal marriage. They made the name inviolate; nevertheless, the perpetuation of the George Eliot legend has had unfortunate consequences also, the least important of which has been to create an awkward problem for librarians and biographers. Under which of her several names should her work be catalogued? "George Eliot," presumably—yet George Eliot did not do, for one example, the English translation of Ludwig Feuerbach's *Das Wesen des Christentums*, the only work to which she signed the name Marian Evans. And by what name should she be called in biographical studies of earlier phases of her life? George Eliot literally never had a childhood, so that to speak of her as having been too tomboyish to please her mother is as unconvincing as it is to refer to Mary Ann Evans (or Marian Lewes or Mrs. John Cross) as the author of the George Eliot novels.

A far more serious disadvantage of the legend is that in clouding over the details of her real life it also obscures the significance of her relatively late start at creative writing. True, by 1857 she had produced an impressive amount of good writing, but all of it nonfiction—translations, book reviews, essays. Yet she had always been possessed of a fervent desire to write fiction. "Always" is her own word, used in a lengthy Journal entry she made to summarize the miraculous (as they seemed to her) events pertinent to her first published fiction, *Scenes of Clerical Life*: "It had always been a vague dream of mine that some time or other I might write a novel. . . . But . . . as the years passed on I lost any hope that I should ever be able to. . . ." However, she did write, not just one novel but a series of novels, each one arising out of her innermost being. This is of special interest, as it is far more usual for a young person to express himself creatively and then lose the desire for such expression, or the creativeness itself, with maturity. Although George Eliot was unable to write even when youth, talent, and opportunity were present, creativity did not wither within her, but stayed alive and mysteriously protected, so that when it finally burst forth, it did so with as much vigor and freshness as if she had been in the spring of her life.

An exploration of the causes of her long period of frustration and her release from it provides considerable insight into her career as a writer; it also illumines, as individuated in her, the unfolding self—its power and uncanny strategy, whether or not it leads, as in her instance, to the tangible production of genius. Now that there is the advantage of hindsight, it is easy to think—as did Henry James—that "in one way or another, in the long run, her novels would have got themselves written. . . ." Yet the more one is aware of the depth and power of her frustration, the more remarkable does it seem that she triumphed over it. That triumph was not achieved by one leap into fiction writing: rather, hers was a gradual and tenuous history, which might well have been fatally interrupted at any time during the period of her writing. For hers was not the self to come forward in an instant, like Athena, full-armed. There were latent powers to be awakened, and their awakening came as a result of the subtly continuing, modulating force of her writing present upon her buried past.

It would be of inestimable value in understanding the nature of George Eliot's talent—its restrictions as well as its scope and power —if her earliest life could be reconstructed with more than problematic certainty. In her later years, her thoughts went back more and more frequently to her childhood, or what she herself called "the primal passionate store" of all her future life; but other than the factually unreliable kind embedded in the novels, she left only a meager account of it. On her fifty-first birthday, Lewes gave her "a Lock-up book for her Autobiog[raphy]." Unfortunately, if ever she used this book for its designated purpose, she saw to it that it was indeed locked up permanently.

As George Eliot's fame increased, others urged her to write an autobiography, the most insistent being John W. Cross, her husband for the last eight months of her life and destined to be her most reverential biographer. She stayed firm in her refusal to do so, although on one occasion she did make a small admission to him: " 'The only thing I should care much to dwell on would be the absolute despair I suffered, and a knowledge of this might be a help to some other struggler,'—adding with a smile, 'but, on the other hand, it might only lead to an increase of bad writing.' " At the time, Cross no doubt believed her reluctance to write her own life stemmed from her unwillingness to reopen for public view her life with Lewes. If this was indeed part of the reason, Cross would have realized too that as the relationship had long been public knowledge, she might well have used an autobiography to vindicate it, for gossip had either ignored or distorted the facts which made it seem impossible for Lewes to obtain a divorce from his legal wife, Agnes. Cross must have been puzzled also by her reference to "absolute despair"; he had never witnessed her in despair, other than the understandable kind over the death of Lewes, and the memories she passed on to him were mellowed ones, transfigured not only by time but by her own hard-earned sympathy for others and transcendence over personal unhappiness. One can easily imagine how her beautiful contralto voice must have evoked for him a golden past, with little trace of the meaner alloys of hurt and fury which had tormented her for almost all the years preceding her life with Lewes.

Nonetheless, Cross persisted (and he is seldom given due credit for this persistence) in his belief that the world was owed, if not an autobiography, then the nearest thing to it. He dedicated himself to providing this by allowing her life—or as much of it as he deemed proper —to be revealed through her own letters. It was difficult, even cour- ageous, work; unfortunately, in doing it he added to, rather than dispelled, the most obscuring elements of the George Eliot legend. His reasons for deliberately doing so were more complex than is com- monly granted. True, he was a far more typical son of his age than she its daughter, so that he felt bound to honor the many Victorian euphemisms and verbal taboos; but this was perhaps the least of the forces which motivated his drastic editing of her letters. Of much greater importance were more personal reasons, such as his idolatry of her as George Eliot, which (as happened to many other sensitive young men of the day) began with his reading of *Romola* before he met her, and was heightened to almost religious fervor by the awesome gravity of the events that inevitably transformed their casual friendship into a deeply intimate one. These events moved George Eliot herself, shortly after their marriage in May of 1880, to describe the history of their association as "something like a miracle-legend."

The history had begun in Rome on a spring day eleven years earlier, when Cross, his mother, and one of his sisters went by invitation to visit George Eliot and George Henry Lewes in their rooms at the Hotel Minerva. There, no doubt because of George Eliot's known preference for conversing with only one person at a time, Lewes entertained Cross and his sister on one side of the room, while George Eliot and Mrs. Cross sat talking on the sofa across from them. Cross, however, was impatient over this strategy and strained to overhear that conversation in which he was not sharing, for already he "was better acquainted with George Eliot's books than with any other literature. And through the dimness of these fifteen years"—he wrote commemorating this momen- tous meeting—

> and all that has happened in them, I still seem to hear, as I first
> heard then, the low, earnest, deep musical tones of her voice. I still
> seem to see the fine brows, with the abundant auburn-brown hair
> framing them, the long head broadening at the back, the grey-blue
> eyes, constantly changing in expression, but always with a very
> loving, almost deprecating, look at my mother, the finely formed,
> thin, transparent hands, and a whole *Wesen* that seemed in com-
> plete harmony with everything one expected to find in the author
> of "Romola."

At the time of this meeting, she was fifty, famous, and—as Cross's description testifies—at last "in complete harmony" with herself as George Eliot. This was as Cross was always to know her: assured but becomingly unassuming, calm and serenely poised, her bearing marked by what Oscar Browning (another young man who knew her during her late years) recorded as "kindly and majestic grace." Cross himself at this time was thirty, well established in his banking career yet also drawn to literature and the arts, devoted to his sisters but to his mother above all other women. It was no accident that one of the most vivid details in Cross's memory of this first meeting was that "very loving, almost deprecating, look" he saw George Eliot bestow upon his mother. In time to come, she and his mother were to be inextricably joined for him in hallowed association—an important factor which guided Cross in his preparation of George Eliot's *Life*.

A second meeting occurred several months later, when George Eliot and Lewes visited the Cross home at Weybridge. Of this Cross remembered: "A day did the work of years. Our visitors had come to the house as acquaintances, they left it as lifelong friends." Mutual sympathy effected the sudden change. The Crosses were concerned over the approaching confinement of Cross's sister with her first child, and Cross himself was about to leave for America on a business trip; and the Leweses were anxious because of the illness of Thornton, George Henry's son. "And the sequel of that day greatly intensified the intimacy. For within a month my sister had died in childbirth, and her death called forth one of the most beautiful of George Eliot's letters [apparently not preserved]. A month later Thornton Lewes died."

However, there was not much occasion for frequent meetings until the Leweses in 1877 moved to their country home, Witley Heights in Surrey, near enough to Weybridge for Johnnie—as Cross was by then affectionately called by both Lewes and George Eliot—to walk over on Sundays. He thus became one of the very few persons allowed to break in upon the "dual solitude" so zealously safeguarded by George Eliot during all her years with Lewes. Together the three had happy times—talking, reading, singing, walking, and even, under Cross's tutelage, playing lawn tennis and badminton. Before long, however, there was a desperate note underlying the gaiety, for once again an ominous "shadow of trouble" had appeared "on both our houses. My mother was in her last illness, and Mr. Lewes was constantly ailing, though none of us then thought that he would be taken first. But the sharing of a common anxiety contributed to make our friendship much more intimate." Probably Lewes himself knew that his illness was fatal, although he made it easy for his companions to forget his bouts with pain, for "the moment the pain ceased the extraordinary buoyancy of his spirits returned. Nothing but death could quench that bright flame." It would seem that Lewes's valiant efforts to conceal the seriousness of his condition deceived even George Eliot. She was unprepared and shocked to the core of her being when death came for him on 30 November 1878.

For five months she saw no one other than for strict necessity; then suddenly, on the twenty-second of the following April, she sent Cross an urgent message: "I am in dreadful need of your counsel. Pray come to me when you can—morning, afternoon, or evening." Thus goes the version Cross gives of her summons. The complete letter restored by Gordon Haight throws a different light on their relationship:

Tuesday/ ½ past 11.

Dearest N.

I am in dreadful need of your counsel. Pray come to me when you can—morning, afternoon, or evening. I shall dismiss anyone else.

You will probably not get this till the Greek Kalends, for I never know where you are. If I address you at Cornhill, you will be at the club, if I address you at the club, you will be at Weybridge, and if I address you there you will be gone on a distant visit.

Your much worried
Aunt.

Was her pique justifiable; had he been deliberately eluding her? There are other signs that he was almost overwhelmed by the growing intimacy which had taken root in the protective make-believe aunt-nephew relationship.

But his response to this letter was as prompt as she had desired, and while she had not feigned her need for his counsel concerning financial matters, one can assume that the talk quickly became personal, for to Cross this visit marked the beginning of their final relationship: "From this time forward I saw George Eliot constantly. My mother had died in the beginning of the previous December,—a week after Mr. Lewes; and as my life had been very much bound up with hers, I was trying to find some fresh interest in taking up a new pursuit." The new pursuit was the reading of Dante, in which George Eliot joined him, helping him master the Italian. "In the following twelve months we read through the 'Inferno' and the 'Purgatorio' together; not in a *dilettante* way, but with minute and careful examination of the construction of every sentence. The prodigious stimulus of such a teacher (*cotanto maestro*) made the reading a real labor of love. . . . The divine poet took us into a new world. It was a renovation of life." Soon they were going together "very frequently to the National Gallery, and to other exhibitions of pictures, to the British Museum sculptures, and to South Kensington. This constant association engrossed me completely, and was a new interest to her. A bond of mutual dependence had been formed between us . . . and on the 9th April it was finally decided that our marriage should take place as soon, and as privately, as might be found practicable." They were married on 6 May 1880, at St. George's, Hanover Square, with very few people present. Charles Lewes, George Henry's oldest and only surviving son, gave George Eliot away.

If grief over death had brought her and Cross together, their companionship after marriage was by no means a solemn affair. There was illness, to be sure; Cross was stricken by a fever during their Continental honeymoon, and she was seriously ill shortly after their return to England. But both recovered, she with what for her was remarkable resiliency. Otherwise they settled down in the attractive Chelsea house provided by Cross at 8 Cheyne Walk, overlooking the river, and soon had established the same enriching routine which had long formed the structure of her life with Lewes—reading, discussing, walking, and concert-going. All that was lacking was her daily cloistered session at writing, which had been sometimes debilitating, sometimes exhilarating. If no longer driven by the urge to create new imaginary lives, she was unusually preoccupied with thoughts of her own childhood and planned with Cross "a visit to Warwickshire, that she might renew the sweet memories of her child-days." It is as if she intuitively knew that her life had completed its cycle and had made only an illusory fresh start.

Her death on 22 December 1880 came with shocking suddenness, so that Cross began that very night to write hurried notes to a few of her closest friends to spare them the pain of first learning of it in an impersonal newspaper account. To one such letter he could not resist adding: "And I am left alone in this new House we meant to be so happy in. . . . I am stunned." His sorrow was no doubt deepened by the season, for his mother also had died in December, two years earlier. Yet it had been this death which had released him for marriage with George Eliot, for it is unlikely that he would ever have married as long as his mother lived. George Eliot became indeed a mother figure to him, but an ideal and hence a safe one, her children being of the mind and not the flesh.

Thus it was with a doubled sense of loss that Cross set himself to the task of going through the papers that had so abruptly come into his possession, and then of collecting as many of George Eliot's letters as possible by means of painstaking correspondence and personal interviews. His reading of the early letters was his first introduction to the woman who had been other than George Eliot; and he must have been often startled as he came upon angry, bitter, defiant words flung out in the heat of unmastered feeling. No doubt he was troubled by what he found, although on reflection he must have realized that these unhappy letters illumined what had formerly perplexed him. Now he could see there had been no exaggeration when she had spoken of her early but long-lived despair as "absolute." He must have recalled with renewed significance how deeply pained she had been when during his first meeting with her he had felt "obligated to admit that, with all my admiration for her books, I found them, on the whole, profoundly sad."

Why should anyone as wise as George Eliot be painfully surprised to learn that her readers found the overall tone of her novels melancholy? Cross deliberately set the memory of his comment and her response very near the end of his *Life*, rather than in his otherwise detailed account of that first meeting. The letters had instructed him: the somber tone of her novels was an unavoidable residue of her early life. Furthermore, its detection by others signified to her a kind of failure, as if she had permitted some accent of her personal unhappiness to enter into the voice of George Eliot, whose function it was to transcend the personal. Cross's very next sentence is expiation for his insight: "But sadness was certainly not the note of her intimate converse."

Above all, the letters would have helped Cross understand her reluctance to leave an autobiography. How in autobiographical form could she have explained the difference between Marian Evans and George Eliot, as well as the strange necessity which linked the two? Had she not been the often egotistic, uncontrolled, and suffering Marian Evans, she could not have written the particular novels she did; it is also probable that had George Eliot not come into existence, she would have written *no* novels. Certainly she was not possessed of a dual or split personality, yet there was a subtle dichotomy about her life when seen entire which had either to be clarified or concealed. Rightly or wrongly, Cross felt it necessary to thrust the essential Marian Evans out of sight—at least, that is the actual result of his work. To him it would have seemed that if he allowed Marian Evans to reveal the whole of herself as present in her unedited letters, he would risk nullifying the one theme which most persistently threads its way through all the novels: that salvation can come only through the achievement of selflessness and awareness of other-than-self, the same theme which led the American philosopher Josiah Royce to speak of George Eliot as a great religious teacher although he was quite aware she herself was an agnostic:

> Religious knowledge and life come to us then . . . [George Eliot] teaches, through the influence of individual souls, whose sympathy and counsel awaken us to a new sense of the value of life, and to a new earnestness to work henceforth not for self, but for the Other than self. This Other, as you see, is always at least negatively infinite; it takes in this philosophy the place of the supernatural. You know not its boundaries. This grand ocean of life stretches out before you without discovered shore. You are brought to the strand.

Will you embark? To embark and lose yourself is religion; to wait
on the shore is moral starvation.

George Eliot did not wait on the shore, She did, however, embark
on the grand ocean in a secure if not always comfortable vessel—her
writing—an aid not granted to any one of her struggling heroines, as
it also had been withheld from Marian Evans. It is clear that in
beginning her life with Lewes she had hoped to repudiate and obliter-
ate her past, so that she could sanction his admonishing their friend
Barbara Bodichon: "But, dear Barbara, you must not call her Marian
Evans again: that individual is extinct, rolled up, mashed, absorbed
in the Lewesian magnificence!" This was before "George Eliot" had
become much more than a pseudonym, and of course his remark is a
half-joking reminder that in all but the legal sense her name had been
changed. Yet his language is too forceful not to suggest that he and
she had agreed "Marian Evans" was extinct as a self as well as a name.
Gradually, as her writing more and more absorbed her and she discovered that "Looking Inward" inevitably becomes "Looking Backward" (her own titles, in that order, for the two quasi-autobiographical
chapters in *The Impressions of Theophrastus Such*), she came to the
recognition that her unwanted past had been a necessary apprenticeship to what she called her "true vocation" of novel writing. It was
thus with conviction that she wrote to the Swiss painter and friend
D'Albert-Durade, who had known her during the year after her father's
death when she was miserably adrift, without home or any prophetic
sign that the "true vocation" lay ahead: ". . . my books are deeply
serious things to me, and come out of all the painful discipline, all
the most hardly-learnt lessons of my past life." This was in 1859. By
the time her friendship with John Cross had become intimate, twenty
years later, she had achieved total harmony with all the phases of her
early life and reminisced to him accordingly.

Little wonder, then, that Cross was unprepared for the Marian
Evans he met in her letters. Furthermore, he saw even George Eliot
through his own ideal image of her, as his final tribute to her indicates:

> For she had the distinctively feminine qualities which lend a
> rhythm to the movement of life. The quick sympathy that under-
> stands without words; the capacity for creating a complete atmos-
> phere of loving interest; the delight in everything worthy—even the
> smallest thing—for its own sake; the readiness to receive as well as
> to give impressions; the disciplined mental habit which can hold in
> check and conquer the natural egoism of a massive, powerful per-
> sonality; the versatility of mind; the varied accomplishments—these
> are characteristics to be found more highly developed among gifted

women than among gifted men. Add to these the crowning gift of
genius, and, in such companionship, we may possess the world
without belonging to it.

From one point of view, this is a rapturous eulogy of someone not
wholly concretized in reality; from another, there is a touch of defensiveness about it, especially concerning her femininity, and certainly
at least one item reveals that the early letters had made their impact
on Cross: "the disciplined mental habit which can hold in check and
conquer the natural egoism of a massive, powerful personality."

Cross's most effective method of deflecting attention from the time
when the egoism of that "massive, powerful personality" was not yet
disciplined was silently to omit telltale passages and occasionally whole
letters. He applied these methods not only to the early letters, but to
her later frank references to such a time. To give one mild example,
the rhetorical question she put to Barbara Bodichon in 1859—"I am
a very blessed woman, am I not? to have all this reason [Lewes and her
writing] for being glad that I have lived, in spite of my sins and sorrows—or rather, by reason of my sins and sorrows. I have had no time
of exultation. . . ."—is rendered by Cross quite simply as: "I am a
very blessed woman, am I not, to have all this reason for being glad
that I have lived? I have had no time of exultation. . . ." This in itself
is relatively unimportant. When almost all such references are eliminated, however, her personality is distorted; evidence of her growing
awareness of the significance of her past is removed; and the somber
tone of her novels remains a mystery, as it had been for a long while
to Cross himself.

Understandably, such careful censoring took considerable time, and,
besides, the work placed Cross under great psychological strain. It is
clear that he approached his project reluctantly and finally resolved
to undertake it largely because he was aware—so he told Edith Simcox
in January 1881—that "if he did not some one else would. . . ." He
had reason to be uneasy over what that someone might do, especially
as no one but himself possessed the necessary primary materials. So
he set himself to the task but by the end of March 1882 became quite
ill and was forbidden all emotional excitement, his sisters assuming
(perhaps rightly) that the source of such unwanted excitement was his
work on the George Eliot *Life*. He wavered, but then rallied to his
project, this time not to leave it until completed.

His achievement was no doubt a disappointment to Edith Simcox.
Because of Cross's seeming vacillation, she had cherished a growing
hope that she would be the one destined to bring the George Eliot
Life to fruition. Consciously or not, Edith had prepared herself for
this momentous work from the time of her first meeting with George

Eliot on 9 December 1872, when, at twenty-eight, Edith was already a remarkably independent individual whose way of thinking and many socially minded activities certainly shatter the stereotyped image of the Victorian female, particularly a spinster. Edith was adamantly uninterested in marriage unless she happened to find an ideal counterpart to Garibaldi or John Stuart Mill, with either of whom—so she confessed in her autobiographical writing—she might "have been predisposed to fall femininely in love. . . ." She does admit too that in adolescence her infatuations were for older women. As fate would have it, when she first visited George Eliot—the occasion arising from her desire to review *Middlemarch*—she fell very much in love with the novelist, who was then at the peak of her fame and had only to write *Daniel Deronda* to bring her novel writing to its somewhat perplexing close. In George Eliot's presence, Edith did her utmost to conceal her adoration (although not always successfully). When alone, she gave release to her pent-up emotion by writing in her journal-like "Autobiography of a Shirt Maker" about what she herself called "The Love Passion of My Life."

No doubt well aware of Edith's real feeling for her, George Eliot was both attracted and repulsed by it, perhaps seeing in the younger woman something of her own earlier rebellious and searching self, and perhaps also drawn to her because of her two Oxford-educated brothers (to the end of her life George Eliot valued the sister-brother relationship most highly). In any event, Edith was soon granted informal admittance to the Leweses' home, by then the Priory. From the first she was charmed by George Henry Lewes, but she was early jealous of Cross, as if she had a premonition of the important role he would soon play in George Eliot's life. In the end she was to work harmoniously with Cross, if not with complete openness concerning her own letters to and from George Eliot. And it was she who, only two days after George Eliot's funeral, "set off on what must have been at once a pious pilgrimage and a fact-finding tour of the Nuneaton-Coventry region." (In 1885 she again went to Warwickshire in order to talk with Maria Lewis, Caroline Bray, and Sara Hennell.)

One can only conjecture what was lost or gained by Edith's not having done the *Life*; it is certain, however, that she would have been far less timorous in her requests for information and letters than Cross was to be. As late as 1884, Charles Lewes told Edith that she ought to offer Cross her own George Eliot letters, as the latter "does not like to ask—apparently is afraid of being refused, or of being expected to print all that are shown to him, instead of using them at his discretion." An interesting revelation of Cross's diffident method of collecting material, this is also a prophetic warning that there still may be unsuspected gaps in the extant correspondence. For Edith did not give her letters to Cross, nor have they been found; so one can read even the Gordon Haight *Letters* without realizing that Edith was more than a slight acquaintance who occasionally made formal calls at the Priory.

Although she might have been more zealous in gathering information, Edith would have been as protective of her subject as Cross, if in a different way and for different reasons. This is seen in her admission that she did not, any more than Cross, want "too many letters given *in extenso*, not enough to challenge criticism of Her as a letter writer." In fact, she seems to have agreed with most of Cross's procedure, and, although personally jealous of him, had frequent and amicable talks with him about his progress. She also took up his suggestion that she do a magazine article on George Eliot, even if she set to work on this without enthusiasm, feeling that the necessary "self-suppression strangled . . . the utterance of the 'passion' she [George Eliot] used to wish for in my writing." The result—"George Eliot, A Valedictory Article" (*The Nineteenth Century*, May 1881)— is a creditable and dignified essay.

Cross meanwhile struggled on, doing his best to overcome both inner and outer resistances. His external obstacles were stronger and more manifold than can now be readily realized. There were others besides himself and Edith Simcox who were concerned with protecting George Eliot against what they considered to be the vulgar curiosity of the general public. And then there were a few most interested in protecting themselves—notably, Herbert Spencer. Unwittingly, George Eliot herself was to be the greatest stumbling block of all, although Cross never admitted this. First, there was her well-known desire for privacy, of which there had been signs years before either she or anyone else could have predicted the fame ahead of her. Early cut off from a free exchange of ideas within her own family, she became absorbed in letter writing, especially to her teacher and good friend, Maria Lewis. It is not surprising, therefore, to find that the extant correspondence opens with a letter to Maria. Obviously this letter—written when George Eliot was seventeen, literarily precocious, and in desperate need of a confidant—had been preceded by others, but these have been lost; and also missing are many later letters in this important correspondence. As Edith Simcox learned, it was during what she calls the "Strauss time"—between 1844 and 1846—that George Eliot somewhat ruthlessly recalled her letters from Maria and then gave them to Sara Hennell. What, if anything, happened to these letters in transit cannot now be known.

Later, when fame was becoming a near probability and there was still serious reason for George Eliot's preserving her incognito (although by this time—September 1859—her camouflage was being sorely tried by the absurd Liggins imposture), she responded with understandable exasperation to Charles Bray's argument that those actively seeking to learn of her identity were only doing her the honor still being done Shakespeare (specifically, Bray was referring to the efforts of one Mr. Bracebridge, who happened to be an archeologist). "I entirely differ from you," she wrote back to Bray, "in your view of such conduct as Mr. Bracebridge's and fail to see any parallel between it and that of the investigators into the personal history of Shakspear: I am not yet an 'archäological' subject."

Less understandable is her further rejection of personal letters in February 1861, by which time *The Mill on the Floss* had been published and her incognito worn thin. On the eighth of that month she wrote Sara Hennell that she had delivered over the "Strauss letters" to Mary Marshall, Sara's cousin. According to Haight's interpretation, these were letters written by George Eliot to Sara during the translation of Strauss. When Sara had returned them to George Eliot is not known; nor is it known why Sara wanted these letters back. It is possible that when she briefly visited with the Leweses only three weeks earlier, Sara had been made to feel with new certainty how estranged she now was from her friend of the Strauss translating days. If by any chance Sara's request for the letters was only halfhearted in the hope that George Eliot would refuse it, she must have been dismayed by the decisive response sent her:

> Miss Marshall called yesterday and I delivered over to her the "Strauss letters." I have not read them since you gave them to me, years ago, and I would rather not know what is in them since I have not the right to destroy them. The knowledge would only give a more definite repugnance to the idea of their falling into other hands after your death.
>
> I have destroyed almost all my friends' letters to me, simply on that ground—because they were only intended for my eyes, and could only fall into the hands of persons who knew little of the writers, if I allowed them to remain till after my death. In proportion as I love every form of piety—which is venerating love—I hate hard curiosity; and unhappily my experience has impressed me with the sense that hard curiosity is the more common temper of mind.

As late as 28 November 1880 (less than a month before her death), George Eliot wrote Caroline Bray on the same subject, employing the same uncompromising phrase, "hard curiosity":

> I think you are quite right to look over your old letters and papers and decide for yourself what should be burnt. Burning is the most reverential destination one can give to relics which will not interest

any one after we are gone. I hate the thought that what we have looked at with eyes full of living memory should be tossed about and made lumber of, or (if it be writing) read with hard curiosity.

In his presentation of this letter, Cross omits these remarks, as well as George Eliot's somewhat ominous conclusion to her paragraph: "I am continually considering whether I have saved as much as possible from this desecrating fate."

As a final warning guide, Cross would have noted her statement in *The Impressions of Theophrastus Such*:

> In all autobiography there is, nay, ought to be, an incompleteness which may have the effect of falsity. We are each of us bound to reticence by the piety we owe to those who have been nearest to us and have had a mingled influence over our lives, by the fellow-feeling which should restrain us from turning our volunteered and picked confessions into an act of accusation against others, who have no chance of vindicating themselves; and most of all by that reverence for the higher efforts of our common nature, which commands us to bury its lowest fatalities, its invincible remnants of the brute, its most agonizing struggles with temptation, in unbroken silence.

In fact, the whole of this strange chapter ("Looking Inward") in this strange last book of George Eliot's is an indirect confession of her simultaneous fear of revealing herself in writing to be read by others and her desire to do so—the twin psychic forces which had long played a futile game of tug-of-war within her. Finally, through a complex of circumstances, the desire proved stronger than the fear. But that this had been a near-Pyrrhic victory is indicated by the very existence of this chapter, in which she expresses acid contempt for uninhibited self-revealment: "This *naïve* veracity of self-presentation is attainable by the slenderest talent on the most trivial occasions. The least lucid and impressive of orators may be perfectly successful in showing us the weak points of his grammar." In the same passage, she is giving sophisticated, if oblique, homage to Rousseau, whose *Confessions* had early captivated her. They too—so says Theophrastus, in effect—had been written with "*naïve* veracity of self-presentation," but out of far more than "the slenderest talent," so that what he "unconsciously enables us to discern" about himself is of far greater worth than "the weak points of his grammar."

One of the first readers in England to appreciate the psychological, as well as literary, significance of Rousseau's autobiography, George Eliot was at once perceptive of the uncertain line drawn within it between subjective and objective truth and also admiring and envious of the freedom and spontaneity which had made such uncertainty possible. While she had not been able to grant herself such freedom in her novels, she was willing for Theophrastus to admit: ". . . I too may be so far like Jean Jacques as to communicate more than I am aware of."

It is improbable that Cross in reading this chapter was fully aware that it contains the essential clue to George Eliot's long struggle against what she had described to him as "absolute despair" concerning her writing. Nor, in reconstructing her life, did he have to work with the totally unbroken silence recommended by the disenchanted Theophrastus Such. But he must have realized as he read and reread the autobiographical material at his disposal that he had only fragments and broken images of the "massive, powerful personality" he had learned to accept as a living, daily companion. Some of the missing fragments were irrevocably gone, notably, George Henry Lewes's letters, which at George Eliot's request were buried with her. Some within his reach Cross ignored, perhaps in scrupulous deference to what he imagined would have been George Eliot's wishes. When Edith Simcox did not volunteer her letters, for example, he apparently did not ask for them, no doubt being well aware that they were passionate ones. Nor did he accept the ones offered him by John Chapman. He did approach Herbert Spencer, who had corresponded with George Eliot for twenty-seven years, but Spencer at this time was adverse to making public his early relationship with her and refused to cooperate, even declining Cross's invitation to write a sketch of George Eliot as he had known her. (However, he later did write copiously and sympathetically about George Eliot in his *Autobiography*.)

Faced with such obstacles—both self-imposed and objectively real ones—Cross moved at a slow pace. The *Life* was not ready for print until four full years after George Eliot's death, his Preface being dated —by coincidence or otherwise—December 1884, and the three volumes appearing early in 1885. In this Preface he announces his plan and purpose:

> With the materials in my hands I have endeavored to form an *autobiography* (if the term may be permitted) of George Eliot. The life has been allowed to write itself in extracts from her letters and journals. Free from the obtrusion of any mind but her own, this method serves, I think, better than any other open to me, to show the development of her intellect and character.
>
> In dealing with the correspondence I have been influenced by the desire to make known the woman, as well as the author. . . .
>
> By arranging all the letters and journals so as to form one connected whole, keeping the order of their dates, and with the least possible interruption of comment, I have endeavored to combine a narrative of day-to-day life, with the play of light and shade which

only letters, written in various moods, can give, and without which
no portrait can be a good likeness.

After this promising beginning, Cross adds a qualification stunning
to any scholar who honors objectivity: "Each letter has been pruned
of everything that seemed to me irrelevant to my purpose—of everything that I thought my wife would have wished to be omitted." As
already suggested, his work was a worshipful, not scholarly, activity,
and he very much wanted the public to see his subject as he had seen
her. Yet his Preface is as uneasy as it is modest, as if he himself suspected he had not allowed the true nature of her art to stand fully
revealed: "The intimate life was the core of the root from which
sprung the fairest flowers of her inspiration." Having given generous
thanks to all those who contributed letters and information, Cross
accepts full responsibility for his "sins of omission or commission,"
and one can believe that his concluding deprecating statement is a
sincere one: " . . . it is in no conventional spirit, but from my heart,
that I bespeak the indulgence of readers for my share of this work.
Of its shortcomings no one can be so convinced as I am myself."

THOSE FIRST READERS OF CROSS'S *Life* WHO HAD COME WITHIN
range of George Eliot's rich and compelling personality recognized immediately that he had obliterated it. They could not of course be certain about the omissions, but they sensed them (" 'It is not a Life at
all,' exclaimed Gladstone. 'It is a Reticence in three volumes.' "). William Hale White ("Mark Rutherford"), who had known her best and
had been in love with her during her Bohemian days as subeditor of
the *Westminster Review*, was so incensed by the impression of near-
suffocating respectability engendered by the *Life* that he was moved
to write a letter to the *Athenaeum* to say so, concluding:

> I do hope that in some future edition, or in some future work, the
> salt and spice will be restored to the records of George Eliot's en-
> tirely unconventional life. As the matter now stands she has not
> had full justice done to her, and she has been removed from the
> class—the great and noble church, if I may so call it—of the In-
> surgents, to one more genteel, but certainly not so interesting.

Reactions differed, however. Oscar Browning, who had not known
her during the *Westminster* days, had more sympathy for Cross's
reticence, for in the prefatory Note to his *Life of George Eliot* he
admits: "I have had access to a considerable number of unpublished
letters, but I have only thought it desirable to print four of them."

Later on he justifies his procedure in a tantalizingly suggestive passage:

> No attempt will be made to relate new facts in her life. The life written by her husband must remain for a long time the received and invariable account. To relate new facts imperfectly verified, and uncorrelated with the whole story of the life, might gratify an unhealthy curiosity, but would conduce to misconception. Some day, perhaps, George Eliot will undergo the fate of Goethe. We shall know how she spent every week of her existence, and how far the scenes of her novels, even the most sensational, are records of her own trials and experiences.

Still later, after stating that "she had a strong, passionate nature," Browning conjectures that "Perhaps some of the more passionate scenes in her novels are transcripts from her own experiences." His suggestions cannot be lightly dismissed (although they cannot be used as facts), for he was writing out of "a friendship of fifteen years, and a deep and unswerving devotion to her mind and character." Both his own book and her letters to him indicate that this was no one-sided friendship; until her relationship with Cross deepened, she talked more freely to Browning about herself and her writing than to anyone else except Lewes.

Edith Simcox's reaction to Cross's published work is another reminder that there were those in George Eliot's closest circle who awaited the *Life* in breathless fear that it would reveal the very facets of her nature and life which have had to be so laboriously resurrected in the twentieth century. Edith of course read the work with mixed feelings, all of them intense; soon her essential reaction was one of relief, which even allowed room for faint praise of Cross's method: "the blasphemers"—she wrote in her "Autobiography"—"I think will be at a loss for anything to take hold of and the invention of the arrangement is good." And a few days later she recorded: "Saw Mrs. Congreve [who had also loved George Eliot "lover-wise"] yesterday who shares my feeling of relief." By then, Edith was taking a more condescending view of Cross's achievement; she added: " . . . I am not sure that the book will give a very true or complete picture to those who did not know Her at all. Its value to me seems to be that it gives the world as much as it deserves and is not likely to misuse."

At the outer fringe of this circle stood Henry James, who had unequaled knowledge of George Eliot's fiction but only a surface personal acquaintance with her and who consequently arrived at a conclusion very different from Oscar Browning's conception of her life outside her novels. James was almost alone in expressing complete satisfaction with the *Life*. He was aware—as the opening of his review of it makes clear—that this was a minority opinion, and his account of his reasons for holding it leads ingeniously into criticism of the novels. The elements which disappoint readers of the *Life* stem, not from Cross, but from the same source which gave rise to the artistic deficiencies in the novels. James accepted Cross's portrait of George Eliot without question, for it seemed to justify his own view of her work—a view, incidentally, not free of ambivalence, for he had learned much about his own craft from a close study of hers, even if he was not eager to admit his indebtedness. Then too he was almost wholly dependent upon Cross for insight into her personality, as he had known her only in the relatively formal setting of the Sunday receptions at the Priory, where—so his reports to his brother William reveal—he was made welcome but not noticeably encouraged to advance beyond the bounds of polite friendship.

James's imperfect knowledge of George Eliot as an individual is evident throughout his essay. This would not matter in itself were it not so glaringly present and misapplied in his final, most telling remarks:

> What *is* remarkable, extraordinary—and the process remains inscrutable and mysterious—is that this quiet, anxious, sedentary, serious, invalidical English lady, without animal spirits, without adventures or sensations, should have made us believe that nothing in the world was alien to her; should have produced such rich, deep, masterly pictures of the multiform life of man.

To see the large assumption implied in these words as the result of the *Life* alone is to overlook the subtle complexity of James's review, which, for reasons of his own, he deftly manipulated to serve several purposes close to him. His was not a typical reaction, and its potency lay unfolded in the future. He was to become the acknowledged Aristotle of the novel form, so that still today unsuspecting readers react not to the George Eliot novels themselves but to James's carefully structured version of them.

Of less importance to literary criticism and history but of great aid in sustaining the George Eliot legend were the more usual reactions from those who had known and loved her through her novels only, and so had eagerly awaited the *Life* for an intimate revelation of the woman behind the pseudonym. When finally they encountered the *Life*, the most astonishing (and to some, disillusioning) revelation it seemed to offer was her hypochondriacal preoccupation with physical ailments. As one contemporary American reviewer put it:

> If any admirer of George Eliot's writings expected to find in these volumes much which would throw new light on the genesis and processes of her genius, he is doomed to disappointment. . . . The pangs of childbirth are usually considered the most dreadful phys-

ical torments entailed on women for the sin or indiscretion of Eve. In reading this biography we are made to believe that they are slight in comparison with the pangs of bookbirth. . . . Throughout the work one gets the general impression that he is following . . . the life of an invalid. . . . Her spiritual health, when we recur to her novels, seems strangely at variance with the almost constant physical ill health which she ruefully records in her letters.

This analogy between childbirth and bookbirth at least goes to the heart of the matter by implicitly relating George Eliot's physical disturbances to her writing (as indeed many of them were), and it is true that there are frequent references to them in her correspondence. More often than not, these references were used as excuses for not having answered letters as promptly as she had intended. This alleviating context is usually lost in Cross's shortened versions. Accentuating the seemingly ponderous emphasis upon physical complaints is Cross's omission of some of her pithiest observations on people, including herself, because he deemed them too caustic or too racy in expression. Further, the deletion of salutations and endings, done to give the effect of an uninterrupted account, not only eradicates many softening and informal touches; it also obscures the interestingly careful use of her several different names. Thus, as Edith Simcox had predicted, the final product of Cross's devoted service did not give a true or complete picture to those who had no other means of knowing her. Unless they were astute enough to fill in the blanks, even her most faithful and enthusiastic readers were forced to the disappointing conclusion that here was the real George Eliot—a humorless, sententious, and chronically ailing Sibyl.

Perhaps the most harmful, although indirect, influence of Cross's *Life* was upon the English-writing novelists who came of age, literarily speaking, within the first two decades of the twentieth century. Already natural rebels against the Victorian age, their symbolic parent, almost all of them accepted the legend as it had been hermetically sealed by the *Life* and assumed without further investigation that George Eliot had nothing to say to them. Consequently, she was more ignored than scorned. "Her centenary," lamented Blanche Colton Williams, "created scarcely a ripple. Insufficient money was subscribed for even the modest memorial alcove in the Gulson Library [Coventry]. . . . Sir Francis Newdigate [whose family had long been intimately associated with her] gave oak for the panels. . . . No worthy book appeared by way of commemoration." Such neglect during that year, 1919, is understandable, for by then the methods of and the taste for prose fiction were being reshaped by the first impact of the writings of D. H. Lawrence, James Joyce, and Virginia Woolf.

The last-named of that impressive triumvirate was a notable exception to the general indifference toward George Eliot. Virginia Woolf occupied a unique position between the old and the new in literature. No one could have been more dissatisfied with the inherited traditional tools of fiction, and she was destined to become a radical, if severely controlled, experimenter in her own writing. Yet through her father, the brilliant and eccentric Sir Leslie Stephen, she was more naturally linked to the literary past than any of her contemporaries of equal stature. Sir Leslie's first wife was Minny (Harriet Marian) Thackeray, who died suddenly in 1875, but whose sister, Anne, stayed close to the Stephens for many years. Both sisters had followed George Eliot's career with intense interest—perhaps a little jealous of its rivalry with that of their father—and had called upon her, although Anne, who also became a respected writer on her own, had the better chance to know her personally. Sir Leslie himself knew George Eliot and exchanged letters with her when she appealed to him for advice on the Cambridge life of Daniel Deronda. In 1888 he contributed an article on her to the *Dictionary of National Biography*, and in 1902 he wrote a full-length biography of her for the newly initiated English Men of Letters series. Perhaps because he was tired and overworked when he undertook the second project, his account is largely perfunctory and even curiously antagonistic, as if he were suspicious of both the idolatry given her as a person and the critical esteem given her novels during her lifetime.

This somewhat unsatisfactory book by her father, no doubt augmented by the verbal, as well as written, reminiscences by Anne Thackeray, may have first turned Virginia Woolf's alert attention to George Eliot. Or perhaps she did not need such impetus. It is possible that from her own reading of the novels she felt drawn toward a kindred spirit, for although she looked into a Bergson-like universe of flux and undulating outlines which presumably George Eliot had never seen, there are several amazing similarities between the writing temperaments of these two women novelists. Apparently, Virginia Woolf did her most consistent and serious reading of the novels during the George Eliot centenary, for it was on 14 September 1919 that she wrote her close friend Lytton Strachey: "Altogether, I find it very hard to settle to my book, which is, at this moment, the complete works of George Eliot. But you have never read them. I wish you had because then perhaps you would explain the whole puzzle." As she does not designate a novel, and as the novels themselves are not necessarily puzzles until contemplated in relation to the *Life*, one might infer that it was the *Life* Virginia Woolf was actually reading, for by then it was included in most sets of George Eliot's "complete works." Certainly she knew it well by the time she came to write her essay on George Eliot (now printed in *The Common Reader*, First Series). Despite its brevity, this is as perspicacious as any interpretation could be when forced to rest its case on the biographical data provided by what Virginia Woolf called "the sad soliloquy in which Mr. Cross condemned . . . [George Eliot] to tell the story of her life."

The opening of her essay makes it clear that Virginia Woolf had by no means resolved to her own satisfaction the perplexity she had confessed to Strachey:

> To read George Eliot attentively is to become aware how little one knows about her. It is also to become aware of the credulity, not very creditable to one's insight, with which, half consciously and partly maliciously, one had accepted the late Victorian version of a deluded woman who held phantom sway over subjects even more deluded than herself. At what moment, and by what means her spell was broken it is difficult to ascertain. Some people attribute it to the publication of her *Life*.

Having her own novels to write, Virginia Woolf could not afford the time to pursue the puzzle. And as she was alone in her recognition that the *Life* was somehow not in harmony with the novels, it was left to modern French writers—who were disturbed by neither distorted nor full knowledge of George Eliot's personal life—to continue the serious evaluation of her as a novelist. Proust admired and owed something to her; Gide, although often impatient with her, bothered to read her in English and gave her grudging respect; as a young girl, Simone de Beauvoir found in Maggie Tulliver a heroine with whom she could identify; and perhaps in part for this reason, Sartre drew an illustrative point from *The Mill on the Floss* for his definitive essay *Existentialism*. These writers did not have to "rediscover" George Eliot, for their country had accepted her as an important novelist from the beginning of her career; even if her last novels were considered inferior to the earlier ones, her prestige remained high and she was never erased from the literary mind. There is some irony in this, for it was to France, as opposed to England, that many young British and American writers were to turn during the early part of this century for fresh literary inspiration. Hence it is not impossible that, in a roundabout way, George Eliot's influence upon the English novel was less interrupted than it seemed to be.

By now George Eliot has been reinstated in "the great tradition" of English novelists, although exactly where, no one seems quite certain. The dispersing of the legend was begun by Gordon S. Haight's *George Eliot and John Chapman* and still more importantly by Haight's seven-volume edition of her letters, which largely rectifies Cross's *Life* by restoring wherever possible his omissions and reviving the original expressions to supplant his often fastidious and sometimes misleading substitutions. However, even in Haight's edition, as in Cross's, the extant letters begin with a single one for 1836 and then leap to the few for 1838 and 1839. It is not until the 1840's, when she was over twenty, that the correspondence is frequent and sequential enough to provide a clear, if seldom whole, view of her life. From then on until the death of her father in 1849, Haight augments the epistolary record by including comment from her friends the Brays and the Hennells; but these people had not known her as either child or adolescent.

So one must still go back to Cross, for his "Introductory Sketch of Childhood" remains the only "primary" source of biographical information about this very important formative period of her life. As such it is of value. The compressed data and somewhat confused chronology he supplies, however, as well as his implicit interpretations, need to be untangled and judged with care. There is no reason to suppose that the same impulses which destroyed the objectivity of his editing of the letters were not at work here. Cross states in his Preface that he is indebted chiefly to Isaac Evans, George Eliot's brother, for the facts of her childhood, yet he does not give as much space to actual facts as to a general discussion of England in the first quarter of the nineteenth century and to a glance at the novels for their seeming autobiographical content.

Cross's intention throughout is transparent: to persuade the reader that Mary Ann Evans was a happy child in a happy home. His rosy picture does not tally with even the few facts he does offer, nor with what now can be learned from George Eliot herself in her letters. Unfortunately, there is no empirical way to verify, disqualify, or correct Cross's Sketch as there proved to be for a goodly number of the letters. It must be accepted as it stands; even then it yields, when closely examined, more than at first appears—and perhaps more than Cross realized or would have desired.

ONE

The Primal Passionate Store

To HELP THE READER ENVISAGE THE EVANS FAMILY AS A whole, Cross constructs a detailed but purely imaginary portrait, vaguely placing it in 1824, when Mary Ann would have been five years old:

> Anyone, about this time, who happened to look through the window on the left-hand side of the door of Griff house, would have seen a pretty picture in the dining-room on Saturday evenings after tea. The powerful middle-aged man with the strongly marked features sits in his deep leather-covered arm-chair, at the right-hand corner of the ruddy fireplace, with the head of "the little wench" between his knees. The child turns over the book with pictures that she wishes her father to explain to her,—or that perhaps she prefers explaining to him. Her rebellious hair is all over her eyes, much vexing the pale, energetic mother, who sits on the opposite side of the fire, cumbered with much service, letting no instant of time escape the inevitable click of the knitting-needles,—accompanied by epigrammatic speech. The elder girl, prim and tidy, with her work before her, is by her mother's side; and the brother, between the two groups, keeps assuring himself by perpetual search that none of his favourite means of amusement are escaping from his pockets.

Obviously, much of this picture comes from *The Mill on the Floss*, although in that novel Tom (Isaac) and Maggie (Mary Ann) have no sister but, rather, a neat and ladylike cousin, Lucy Deane. Also, the mother is clearly not Mrs. Tulliver, but Mrs. Poyser from *Adam Bede*; nor does the father's appearance suggest Mr. Tulliver. Possibly he is Adam Bede grown older, or perhaps he is Caleb Garth from *Middlemarch*. Cross has simplified the family structure, and in this he might be considered justified, for shortly after Mary Ann's birth, it had been arranged for the two children from Robert Evans's first marriage to leave home. For that matter, had anyone looked through the window on a weekday rather than Saturday, he would have seen only the father and mother, for by 1824 all three children were away to boarding schools, although they did sometimes come home on weekends.

If not overwhelmed by these qualifications, one can accept the picture for what Cross intended it to be—a cozy domestic scene in the life of a small and closely knit family.

Yet it is possible that with unknowing accuracy Cross, by his imaginary grouping of the people, symbolized not so much this family's unity as its tensions and potential discord. From this scene one would not guess, for instance, that Mary Ann and Isaac were the "inseparable playfellows at home" that Cross tells us they were, for here they are apparently indifferent to one another and engrossed in unrelated interests. In position, Isaac is the center of the group, thus standing between Mary Ann and her mother; he is also supremely self-sufficient, as if confident of approval without having to strive for it. The elder girl (Chrissey) too is contentedly self-absorbed, although one senses that Cross did not know what else to do with her, just as a third child would have been most inconvenient in the Tulliver family. Mary Ann alone is aggressively demanding attention, gaining by her efforts, however, not only her father's attention but her mother's disapproval.

The portrait suggests that the mother—Christiana Pearson Evans—was the dominant force of the family, but Cross gives a disappointingly meager account of her. Concerning her background, he says only that she came of "a race of yeomen, and her social position was therefore rather better than her husband's" and that she had three married sisters, "all living in the neighbourhood of Griff . . . and probably Mr. Evans heard a good deal about 'the traditions in the Pearson family.'" Her age at the time of her marriage to Robert Evans in 1813 is unknown: Cross makes no mention of her birth date, and even Gordon Haight wavers between 1788 and 1785. If the real date lies within these three years, she would have been twenty-five or over when she married. This relatively late age for marriage in those pre-Victorian days, as well as her having married slightly beneath her social station, suggests that she married primarily to escape spinsterhood—a dreadful fate then for a dependent woman, and especially so had she been forced to live upon the charity of her three married sisters.

But if the course she chose spared her this humiliation, it could not have been a wholly joyous or easy one for her. In acquiring the desired status of a married woman, she also acquired two young stepchildren, Robert, then eleven, and Frances Lucy (Fanny), eight. Christiana quite properly began producing her own children, her first child and namesake (called Chrissey) being born in 1814, Isaac following in two years, and Mary Ann coming three and a half years after him, on 22 November 1819. Then Christiana, who would have been between thirty-one and thirty-four, must have decided that she had had enough of childbearing; perhaps too much, for she never recovered from the debilitating effects of giving birth to Mary Ann. Although she was to live to within a few days of her twenty-third wedding anniversary, she apparently did so in a state of semi-invalidism, thus withdrawing in a way common to women who do not really desire the families they produce. It would seem that Christiana did not languish on the couch or otherwise withdraw herself in a physical sense. Rather, she effected an exodus of the children, so that one by one they were sent away from home, the reason always being the irreproachable one of their mother's enfeebled health.

As Cross relates, "shortly after her last child's birth she became ailing in health, and consequently her eldest girl, Christiana, was sent to school at a very early age, to Miss Lathom's at Attleboro. . . ." (Indeed Chrissey, only five, was young to be sent off to boarding school, and Mary Ann was to be no older when it came her turn to go.) In fact, Mary Ann must have started school in infancy, for as soon as Chrissey was gone, she and Isaac "spent some part of their time every day at the cottage of a Mrs. Moore, who kept a dame's school close to Griff gates." Another drastic change occurred at about the same time: "Shortly after the last child's birth, Robert, the son, became the agent, under his father, for the Kirk Hallam property, and lived there with his sister Frances. . . ."

It is thus clear that Mary Ann's birth signaled withdrawals and removals which could not have meant happiness to everyone concerned—and certainly not to her when she was old enough to realize their close association with her own coming into the world. However, as a result of the reduced size of the family, one change did occur that was to bring her happiness: "when the baby girl was only four months old, the Evans family removed to Griff, a charming red-brick, ivy-covered house on the Arbury estate. . . ." This house was to be Mary Ann's homestead for twenty-one years, the first five of which were to pass without further momentous change within the family. No doubt this explains why Griff was always to hold a place of such deep significance in her memory, for those first few years were to prove the only period of security and relative happiness that she was to know until her mature life with George Henry Lewes.

The reduced household also explains why the psychic pattern

which was to direct her course throughout life was formed almost
exclusively by her relationship with her mother, her father, and—
most observably—with Isaac. The others who might have been
shaping influences had been removed from her emotional ken, and
one senses that in her adulthood her feeling for those others (with
the possible exception of Chrissey) was without deeply entangled
roots in the past. Robert, for instance, is rarely mentioned in her
extant letters, although there are occasional glimpses of him acting
in brotherly service to her, especially when he—and not Isaac—came
to stay with her when their father died and she was otherwise alone.
No doubt it was this act and comparable ones that she had in mind
when after his death in 1864 she wrote to Robert's own son (also
Robert) what probably she wished she could say in truth about Isaac:
". . . all my memories of your father were those of unbroken kindness and generous brotherliness on his part toward me." Perhaps too
these words were prompted by the fact that this third Robert of the
family had been one of the few Evanses to make friendly overtures to
her and Lewes.

Oscar Browning claims that her half sister, Fanny, "had great influence over her younger sister [Mary Ann]," although he does not
clarify his meaning. The claim is credible, for Fanny was the only
one of the family to approach George Eliot even remotely in intellectual interests. When, for instance, George Eliot was creating a family
crisis by refusing to attend church, Fanny let it be known that she too
had traveled the road to unorthodoxy, having read "by stealth" both
Hennell and Strauss, and of the two preferring the more radical
Strauss because his views were nearer to her own. But she had "no
idea of making herself singular and obnoxious by an avowal of her
opinions" and considered her half sister "very foolish not to keep her
notions snugly to herself." At the time, Fanny's attitude probably
seemed sheer hypocrisy to George Eliot, who was then intent upon
asserting her views openly; yet not long after this she too, with equal
deliberation although differently motivated, was to resolve never to
make herself "singular and obnoxious by an avowal of her opinions."
Not surprisingly, Fanny alone of the immediate family accepted
George Eliot's relationship with Lewes.

It seems likely that Fanny's "great influence" went in the direction
of tempering her sister's idealism with that shrewd practicality which
eventually was to make George Eliot as keen a business woman as
she was sensitive artist. But there is little reason to believe that a
strong emotional tie existed between the two women, perhaps because
Fanny's life had not been one to mold a warmly affectionate nature,
although it might well have equipped her with practical wisdom and
worldly tolerance. She had been three when her mother died, eight

when her father remarried, and but fourteen when she moved (or, rather, was *re*moved) to Kirk Hallam with her brother, apparently as his housekeeper, so that her position must have become difficult when he married. Fanny did finally gain a home of her own in marrying Henry Houghton, but she bore him no children. When he died in 1864 (only two months after Robert's death), she was again alone and living in a home not hers, that of Robert's widow. Apparently, however, during the early years she had kept some watch over the little Mary Ann, for it was she who had surprised Cross by telling him that Mary Ann had been slow in learning to read. As Cross thus reveals that he had talked with Fanny in preparing the *Life*, one wonders why he did not acknowledge her in his Preface along with Isaac. And as it is improbable that she would have given him only one small item of information, one wonders too if he had not found cause— a caustic tone, facts ill fitting his intent?—to "edit" her remarks.

If much of George Eliot's relationship with Fanny can be conjectured only, the relationship between Mary Ann and her full sister, Chrissey, can be established with even less certainty, although Cross makes it sound simple. As George Eliot herself had told him that she had had Chrissey continually in mind while delineating Celia Brooke, he concluded that the relationship between the real sisters had been "somewhat like that described as existing between Dorothea and Celia in 'Middlemarch'—no intellectual affinity, but a strong family affection." But a child does not place much stock in the presence or absence of "intellectual affinity," and while Cross's neat summation is probably generally speaking an accurate description of the later relationship of the two sisters, it casts no light on the important childhood one. That is the peculiar problem here: everything known about George Eliot and Chrissey is known about them as mature women, when the inexorable flow of life had buried, but not eradicated, childhood tensions and fears.

Chrissey does not overtly appear in either of George Eliot's two most obvious re-creations of her childhood—*The Mill on the Floss* and the "Brother and Sister" sonnet sequence. Her absence from the poem is less surprising, for these sonnets celebrate the time between Mary Ann's third and fifth years, when Chrissey was home from school only infrequently. According to Cross, even when she was home, being "the chief favourite of the [maternal] aunts, as she was always neat and tidy . . . [Chrissey] used to spend a great deal of her time with them, whilst the other two were inseparable playfellows at home." This association of Chrissey with the Pearson sisters, who —again according to Cross—"are, no doubt, prototypes of the Dodsons in the 'Mill on the Floss,' " inevitably brings to mind Lucy Deane of that novel, the pretty cousin whom as a child Maggie pushes into the mud because Tom was giving her admiring attention, with whom Tom is later futilely in love, and from whom as a young woman Maggie takes (or almost takes) her fiancé. George Eliot's evocation of the past—but a past transformed by her own deepest wishes —was a highly emotional experience for her. As she wrote, her sister was in her mind whether or not she wished her there, for Chrissey was ill and died even while she was planning and beginning to write *The Mill on the Floss.*

Granting the possibility that Chrissey does appear in a dreamlike role in the *Mill,* one must remember that a dream belongs to the dreamer alone; there is no reason whatever to assume that she was ever more than an imagined threat to Mary Ann, who, as Cross admits, was "very jealous in her affections . . . knowing 'all the wealth and all the woe' of a preeminently exclusive disposition." It is unlikely that the ladylike older girl had been eager to share Isaac's boyish activities as Mary Ann so passionately tried to do. The two growing sisters do not seem to have been close. Although they were at school together for eight years, at the end of which time Mary Ann was sent to school in Coventry while Chrissey presumably returned home to stay, there are no allusions to girlhood memories involving her sister either in George Eliot's reminiscences to Cross or in her extant letters. Chrissey was perhaps too "meek and passive," as George Eliot described her to Maria Lewis, to gain the loving respect of her impulsive and strong-willed younger sister until much later.

What Cross calls a "strong family affection" developed after Chrissey's marriage in 1837, when she embarked on a wretched course of childbearing, child-burying, illness, and acute financial distress. Widowed in 1851, Chrissey had by then borne nine children, five of whom had died by the time of her own death in 1859. Her health declining, she became increasingly dependent upon Isaac. George Eliot accused him of being miserly in his aid to their sister and exerted herself to intervene in Chrissey's behalf, although she was by this time working and living in London. As a result, Chrissey found herself in the middle of a tug-of-strong-wills and apparently submitted to the wishes of whichever one happened to be present. George Eliot lost dominion when she eloped with Lewes, although she still had plans for helping Chrissey in the future.

Although the dynamics created by Chrissey's rare presence at Griff in the early days might be personified by Lucy Deane in the *Mill,* the real Chrissey of later time is surely echoed in Gritty Moss of the same novel, described as "a patient, prolific, loving-hearted woman," who with eight living children regrets "that the twins had not lived," and who is humiliatingly dependent upon her brother, Tulliver (Book I, chapter 8). In fact, Chrissey may well be the progenitor of the long line of "prolific" women in George Eliot's fiction who are loving but debilitated mothers, ranging from Milly Barton in the first of the *Clerical Scenes* to Gwendolen's mother in the last novel, *Daniel Deronda*. But the child Chrissey hardly exists in the George Eliot records. Even Cross unintentionally slights her when, obviously meaning Isaac and Mary Ann, he states: "The boy was his mother's pet and the girl her father's."

Ignoring the fact that Chrissey needed accounting for, Cross took this otherwise symmetrical distribution of parental affection directly from the *Mill*—although in a later passage in his Sketch he warns the reader that the autobiographical representation in this novel is "so mixed with fictitious elements and situations that it would be absolutely misleading to trust to it as a true history." He makes this wise admonition largely to reassure his readers that the trouble which developed between the real brother and sister was not nearly so serious as that between Tom and Maggie Tulliver; and yet he himself often draws promiscuously on the *Mill* for autobiographical data, thus unfortunately establishing a pattern to be followed by all later biographers. Not that this procedure would have been wholly wrong if applied with caution, for the novel is certainly autobiographical and more profoundly so than if it were only a literal transcription of George Eliot's childhood. As suggested earlier, on at least one level its meaning is dreamlike, both in its manifest and its latent content, representing a kind of compromise between the thrust of forbidden wishes and the writer's censor. Hence its importance as a possible route to understanding George Eliot as both person and writer—but hence also its easy deceptiveness.

T HE FEW KNOWN FACTS OUTSIDE *The Mill on the Floss* uphold the first part of Cross's assertion—that Isaac was his mother's pet—far more conclusively than the second half of it—that Mary Ann was her father's. Cross diligently suppressed all evidence hinting at trouble between father and daughter. The Haight edition of the letters reveals, on the other hand, that as she grew into young womanhood, the relationship between them became increasingly strained and uneasy. Their wills clashed, their temperaments clashed, their ideas clashed. If ever her father had been proud of Mary Ann's precocity (as Cross says he was), the pride was soon supplanted by hostile suspicion toward the large world of the mind which she had opened for herself. Rather than acknowledge her independence of thought, Rob-

ert blamed her heretical views on her closest friends, the Brays and
the Hennells.

What emotion Robert Evans may have felt when this youngest child
entered his already complex household is hidden behind the characteristically laconic notation in his Journal, where—again characteristically—the vital statistic appears in the midst of recorded business
transactions: "Nov. 22, 1819.—Mary Ann Evans was born at Arbury
Farm, at five o'clock this morning." It is quite possible that as an infant she aroused his astonishment and even awe, if only because she
had come into his life eighteen years after his first child, when he
himself was forty-six. For the same reason, he must have seemed somewhat remote to the child, so that even casual attention from him might
well have appeared in the light of extraordinary favor. "In my earliest
remembrance of [my father]"—says the partially autobiographical
Theophrastus Such—"his hair was already grey, for I was his youngest
. . . child; and it seemed to me that advanced age was appropriate to a
father, as indeed in all respects I considered him a parent so much to
my honour, that the mention of my relationship to him was likely to
secure me regard from those to whom I was otherwise a stranger. . . ."
Also like Robert Evans, the father of Theophrastus was a staunch
Conservative:

> To my father's mind the noisy teachers of revolutionary doctrine
> were, to speak mildly, a variable mixture of the fool and the
> scoundrel; the welfare of the nation lay in a strong government
> which could maintain order; and I was accustomed to hear him
> utter the word "government" in a tone that charged it with awe,
> and made it part of my effective religion,—in contrast with the
> word "rebel," which seemed to carry the stamp of evil in its syl-
> lables, and, lit by the fact that Satan was the first rebel, made an
> argument dispensing with more detailed inquiry. ["Looking Back-
> ward"]

This is the same dogged conservatism which would set her father,
and then Isaac, against her in the 1840's, when she became a rebel
against orthodoxy in both religion and politics; here it is recalled with
tolerant amusement and without reference to the anguish it had cost
her. Cross was wholly captivated by the nostalgic tone and after
quoting the passage above, complacently added that "it is the key to a
great deal in the mental attitude of the future thinker and writer.
It is the foundation of the latent Conservative bias." Not only is
it questionable whether George Eliot had a "latent Conservative bias,"
but Cross had to twist time curiously to effect the association, for
Theophrastus Such was her last published writing, and it is unduly
stretching the power of figurative language to refer to anything in
that work as a "key" to the author's future attitude.

Robert Evans was no country parson (as Theophrastus's father was) but a land agent, apparently a competent and successful one. However, although authoritative in his work, Cross admits that he had "a certain self-distrust, owing perhaps to his early imperfect education, which resulted in a general submissiveness in his domestic relations. . . ." It is evident from the painful frustration he later caused his daughter by his inability to make decisions concerning matters of vital importance to her that this was no minor weakness. It seems clear that without Christiana, Robert Evans could only flounder, until his lack of self-assurance had hardened into stubborn evasiveness. But it is probable that, like most dependent people, he inwardly chafed under the domination as long as it lasted, even though his nature demanded it. If, as Isaac said (and George Eliot confirmed this), anecdotes which they had heard from their father were written into *Adam Bede,* one can imagine that he found satisfaction in talking somewhat boastfully to his youngest children about his earlier adventures and feats of physical prowess before the Pearson family entered his life. Yet Christiana's death would have been a devastating blow to him, and it is possible that the "alarming illness of my dear Father" (referred to in George Eliot's first extant letter) was brought on by the realization that his wife was about to leave him. She died only a month later, whereas Robert lived for another twelve years.

After the marriages of Chrissey and Isaac left him alone with his youngest daughter, Robert Evans proposed that he hire a housekeeper, an offer she promptly rejected (perhaps to his chagrin), although at that time domestic chores were odious to her. The years that followed until his death were in many ways the unhappiest of George Eliot's life, not only because of external circumstances but because of her own inward drive to thrust her will upon her father's. Her rebellious test of his affection and her own power took the form of openly breaking with the family religion and refusing to attend church with him. This pained and angered him, as she must have anticipated. But instead of decisively ousting her as he threatened, or granting her the right to her own thinking, which he showed no inclination of doing, he vacillated until turning finally to Isaac for instruction. As a result, she was denied both self-righteous martyrdom and forgiveness, and had little choice but to return to the same surroundings and dull round of duties.

This humiliating experience of abortive rebellion was to be a crucial one for her, especially as she had time to reflect upon the alarming extent to which her own strident aggressiveness had brought about the family tempest. From this was forged the first and most difficult lesson in tolerance which was to endure for the remainder of her life—that the highest form of tolerance is to endure intolerance.

Furthermore, she made the disconcerting discovery that it had been easier to cast out God the Father than to sever her emotional tie to her father of the flesh. This discovery was to dictate the tacit premise of all the novels, the primary importance of human relationships; the supernatural—in no matter what specific religious form—remains present only as seen and felt by the characters.

The more immediate result of this momentous experience was that her deliberate dedication to her father, in giving him companionship and nursing him through his long final illness, took the place of the orthodox religion she had put aside. Understandably then her father's death, although long expected, left her for a while spiritually as well as physically homeless. Shortly after George Eliot had found a newly significant personal life through both Lewes and her writing, she was to pay her father her most enduring tribute in the character of Adam Bede, which was not meant to stand as a realistic portrait of Robert Evans but arose out of what she had heard about him as a young man—her father as she had never known him. It is as if she wished to restore in the eyes of the world what she herself had cause to suspect her father lacked: manliness, especially in decisive thought and action within his own home. Adam is, above all else, manly.

Outside her fiction too she stood a zealous guard over what the world should think of her father. When her identity as George Eliot began to be known and readers became curious about her obscure background, nothing annoyed her more than to be referred to as a "self-educated farmer's daughter," for to her this was blasphemy against what she called her "piety towards his memory." "My father did not raise himself from being an artisan to be a farmer," she wrote severely to the Brays, who perhaps had themselves originated the rumor as a well-meaning way of emphasizing the magnitude of her achievement. " . . . he raised himself from being an artisan to be a man whose extensive knowledge in very varied practical departments made his services valued through several counties." Again manliness is subtly stressed: Robert Evans did not rise from one vocational class to another, but from an artisan to a *man*. The Brays did not take the hint much to heart, for upon meeting Nathaniel Hawthorne in 1860, a few months after her letter, their report to him was not very much improved: "The Adam Bede lady," they told him, "was the daughter of a steward, and gained her exact knowledge of English rural life by the connection into which this origin brought her with the farmers." They had known Robert Evans best when he was in his seventies, no longer active in his work, and when the chief vigor of his mind expressed itself in stubbornness and seeming ingratitude toward his daughter. Their memory of "the old man," as they privately called him, had not been transfigured by his death into an object of piety as had his daughter's.

After reading George Eliot's letters, Cross too would have been aware of the less attractive side of the older Robert Evans, as well as of his daughter's short-lived stand in defiance of him. But as he was equally aware of both the hard-earned lesson that came to her through the defiance and her transformed memory of her father, he would have wished to expose neither the origins of the defiance nor the need for transformation. One can imagine what a touching moment it was for both George Eliot and Cross when in the last year of her life she presented him with her childhood copy of *The Linnet's Life*, bearing the inscription: "This little book is the first present I ever remember having received from my father. Let any one who thinks of me with some tenderness after I am dead, take care of this book for my sake." Nothing more would have been required to persuade Cross to remove from her letters all passages written in a spirit contrary to this inscribed memento.

O F GEORGE ELIOT'S FEELINGS FOR HER MOTHER, THERE remains no memento as substantial as even a children's book. Cross is strangely unhelpful here, although he stresses the grief she felt over her mother's death. (For some reason or other, Cross places this in the summer of 1836, whereas it apparently occurred on 3 February of that year.) Cross's assertion that "to a highly wrought, sensitive girl of sixteen such a loss seems an unendurable calamity" is quite credible. But his following statement can be flatly refuted: "Many references will be found in the subsequent correspondence to what she suffered at this time, all summed up in the old popular phrase, 'We can have but one mother.'" Even in the Haight edition of the extant letters, only two contain mention of a mother obviously her own, the first (already noted) referring to what was to prove to be the temporary illness of Robert Evans and the fatal one of Christiana; and the second in an 1859 letter to Sara Hennell, in which George Eliot gives an account of the source of some of her material for *Adam Bede*, mentioning in passing that her father had left Derbyshire "six or seven years before he married my mother."

In both the Cross and the Haight editions, letters for the two years following the mother's death are missing, Haight having discovered only one—that of 26 May 1838—before Cross's of 18 August in that year. Yet this is the period when one would expect to find the most frequent and spontaneous references to her mother. Furthermore, one would expect to find such letters directed to her teacher-friend Maria Lewis, who was closer to the family as a whole than any other correspondent of George Eliot's then or later. Were these unhappy and self-incriminating letters? Whatever they were, they had a strange fate, the reasons for which can be only conjectured.

When Edith Simcox called upon Maria Lewis during the second phase of her pilgrimage, in 1885, she already knew Miss Lewis had long ago lost possession of George Eliot's earliest letters, and during this visit Edith found out why. Miss Lewis told her that "when Marian asked to have her letters back she [Maria Lewis] said she would lend them her, but must have them returned; then Marian did not return them and told Miss Lewis . . . that Mr. Bray said they were the property of the writer or to that effect." Four years earlier, Edith had learned that these letters to Miss Lewis (or most of them) had been given for safekeeping to Sara Hennell. Edith implies that at this time she saw some of them, but she gives no account of their contents. Obviously, someone withdrew these letters from the chance of publication. Who, and why? And why did George Eliot want the letters back?

Apparently this matter was out of Cross's control, or was something he did not care to pursue. We know that he was aware of their omission because he calls attention to this major gap in his version of the George Eliot letters. But aside from letters themselves, he must have discarded much information about Christiana gleaned from her son and her stepdaughter, not to mention George Eliot. As a result, there is no objective evidence about George Eliot's memory of her mother. Cross's somewhat groping attempt to sum up her feeling for her mother in the old popular phrase, "We can have but one mother"—which, incidentally, he appropriated from one of George Eliot's own letters—loses the impact he intended while gaining new significance when seen in its original context, an 1858 letter to Sara Hennell written upon news of the death of Sara's mother:

> I enter so deeply into everything you say about your mother. To me that old old popular truism "We can never have but one mother" has worlds of meaning in it, and I think with more sympathy of the satisfaction you feel in at last being allowed to wait on her, than I should of anything else you could tell me. I wish we saw more of that sweet human piety that feels tenderly and reverently towards the aged.

If personal memory is involved here (and it is not wholly clear that it is), the last sentence suggests George Eliot's nursing of her father rather than her mother, for Christiana was between fifty and fifty-three when she died, and although not young for the time, she was not "aged" in the same sense as Robert Evans, who died at seventy-six. Aside from this, the "worlds of meaning" in the old popular truism (is not a slightly derogatory sense in the word "truism" also eliminated by Cross's substituting "phrase"?) suggest not only much meaning but several levels of meaning. One might add: " . . . and I am happy to have had the mother I had"; but a different person might involuntarily think: " . . . and I am sorry to have had the one I had."

Because of the serious ways in which the family changed in response to Christiana's wishes—whether expressed openly as requests or negatively in the form of psychosomatic illness is immaterial—it is easy to accept Cross's statement that she "was a woman with an unusual amount of natural force." For the same reason, it is difficult to assent to the whole of his claim that "Hers was an affectionate, warm-hearted nature, and her children, on whom she cast 'the benediction of her gaze,' were thoroughly attached to her." Her children would presumably have been thoroughly attached to her in their infancy, but if they remained so as they entered childhood they must have suffered for it, since they were kept away from her. Isaac had the least cause to feel rejected, for he alone was privileged to stay at home until he was eight—which bears out Cross's assertion that he was his mother's favorite. In Mary Ann's case, even if she had cause to be aware of special attention from her father, this would not have been adequate compensation for her instinctive recognition that she occupied at best second place in the affections of her mother, the fountainhead of her very life. There is no reason not to accept the essence of Cross's description of her nature as a child: "she showed, from the earliest years, the trait that was most marked in her all through life, namely, the absolute need of some one person who should be all in all to her, and to whom she should be all in all. Very jealous in her affections . . . [she was] of a preeminently exclusive disposition. She was affectionate, proud, and sensitive in the highest degree." Such an ardent nature would have difficulty finding happiness in ideal circumstances. To have to adjust to a mother's rejection could have been enough to scar it for life.

Interestingly, the phrase quoted by Cross to emphasize Christiana's maternal love—"the benediction of her gaze"—comes from Sonnet III of "Brother and Sister," in which the mother is seen stroking down the girl's tippet, setting the boy's frill, and admonishing them to keep to the trodden ways:

> Then with the benediction of her gaze
> Clung to us lessening, and pursued us still
> Across the homestead to the rookery elms . . .

The wording—especially "clung" and "pursued"—suggests that both boy and girl are as eager to escape their mother's gaze as they are her fussing, for slight as the scene is, it conveys the overprotectiveness of an essentially rejecting mother. Something of the same impression is suggested by the only known reference to Christiana outside the brief sonnet scene and Cross's Sketch. In her memoir of George Eliot written for Cross's 1887 edition of the *Life*, Mrs. John Cash (nee Mary Sibree) states: "Mrs. Evans (Miss Lewis tells me) was a very serious, earnest-minded woman, anxiously concerned for the moral and religious training of her children. . . ." This is a disappointingly indirect and general observation, and again one wonders why Cross did not appeal to Maria Lewis herself for information. But for what it is, it fits in with the "Brother and Sister" scene, whereas the other "facts" offered by Cross raise conflicting images of Christiana.

Neither of these references evokes the vivid Mrs. Poyser of *Adam Bede*, although no one has seriously questioned Cross's statement that the real Christiana was "a shrewd practical person, with a considerable dash of the Mrs. Poyser vein in her." If so, why did she not leave a more individualized memory in the minds of those who had known her—and why did those who had known her not eagerly come forward with examples of her shrewd practicality and her pithy sayings? One wonders too why Isaac made no mention of having recognized his mother in Mrs. Poyser, although he was quick to say that he knew the novel must have been written by his sister because it contained anecdotes told them by their father. George Eliot was justifiably proud of Mrs. Poyser as an original creation, so that when one reviewer assumed her sayings were drawn from remembered proverbs, she was annoyed enough to make a flat denial of this to her publisher, John Blackwood: "I have no stock of proverbs in my memory, and there is not one thing put into Mrs. Poyser's mouth that is not fresh from my own mint." Since she was both scrupulously honest in giving credit where it was due and quickly indignant over the slightest suggestion that she had borrowed without acknowledgment, it seems strange that she did not mention her mother here as the source of Mrs. Poyser's epigrammatic speech.

Nonetheless—in the words of Blanche Colton Williams—"though caution would not ascribe to the real woman too much of the one imagined [Mrs. Poyser], family tradition acknowledges the identity." As caution would surely not ascribe to the real woman Mrs. Poyser's verbal brilliance, it is of some importance to view this character shed of that peculiar glamour. In this light she emerges as a woman who dominates through verbal criticism with such force that the reader is surprised when reminded that she is pale and not vigorous in health,

presumably having been weakened by childbearing. She is, if anything, over-anxious about her children (who, however, are but blurs
in the novel), and the mother role seems to weigh heavily upon her.
Her concern over Adam might be called loving, but she is motherly
toward neither Dinah nor Hetty, and the latter especially suffers from
this, for she is in great need of mothering and totally dependent upon
Mrs. Poyser for it. However, Hetty is made to occupy an unhappily
anomalous position in the household, where as a poor relation she
is treated as neither a real member of the family nor yet quite a
servant; and she is the object of Mrs. Poyser's harsh judgment even
before she has given cause for censure.

In basic personality, Mrs. Poyser is thus much closer to the less attractive Mrs. Tulliver than first appears. Mrs. Tulliver is also a
woman of an unusual amount of natural force, which, however, is
directed (often with grimly ironic results) into subterranean channels
because she is seemingly overshadowed by her husband—even though
his bluster is proved by events to be more self-destructive than
dominating. She too is essentially critical (especially of her daughter), but as her criticism is usually in the form of egocentric complaining, she seems to inhabit a world much smaller than that of
Mrs. Poyser. She too impresses one as enervated, although hers seems
more a sickness of spirit than of body. If in deference to "family tradition" Mrs. Poyser is to be retained as providing some insight into
Christiana Evans, then those traits, however modified, that she shares
with Mrs. Tulliver are bound to be her most important contribution.
Of the two, Mrs. Tulliver is by far the more significant mother figure,
if only because she is the mother of Maggie, with whom George Eliot
identified as a child and young woman more spontaneously and un-
reservedly than with any other of her heroines.

A still more revealing mother-daughter relationship remains, that
between Gwendolen Harleth and her mother in *Daniel Deronda*. In
this final mother figure, Mrs. Davilow, are repeated the traits of joylessness, over-anxiousness, and passive acceptance of mysterious illness,
so that it seems likely that these characteristics, although not Mrs.
Poyser's verbal genius, were drawn from life. In one respect, however,
Mrs. Davilow differs markedly from both Mrs. Poyser and Mrs. Tulliver: she is too admiring and too much in awe of her brilliant daughter to be openly critical of her and has, in fact, lovingly spoiled her.
One can readily believe that although Gwendolen's creator disapproved of her pampered egotism and saw to it that she was harshly
punished for it, as much wishful thinking as conscious planning went
into the molding of the background to "The Spoiled Child" (Book
I of *Daniel Deronda*).

Unintentionally, Cross suggests that the real mother was essentially critical of her youngest daughter, for in the only two references in his Sketch which bring together Christiana and Mary Ann, the former is expressing disapproval. In the first reference (already noted in the family portrait), she is vexed by the child's unruly hair. And in the second, by her passion for books, for after Mary Ann had somewhat tardily mastered reading, "she read everything she could lay her hands on, greatly troubling the soul of her mother by the consumption of candles as well as of eyesight in her bedroom." Probably the child was far more affected by the apparent begrudging of candles than concern over her eyesight, especially as there is no evidence that the Evanses' financial circumstances demanded strict economy. Perhaps some feeling-memory of this time surged into her consciousness during her stay in Switzerland many years later, after the death of her father, when she was made acutely sensitive to every gesture toward her by her awareness that she no longer had a home. "I have a large lamp and five bougies always in my room," she wrote to Charles and Caroline Bray, "2 on the mantelpiece two on my piano and one on my dressing-table." What was more, Mme D'Albert-Durade (whom she quickly took to calling "Maman") had scolded her when she found her reading by a single bougie. Was it childish to talk about such things? No doubt—"but to me it is so blessed to find any departure from the rule of giving as little as possible for as much as possible."

Significantly, the affectionate attention given George Eliot by the D'Albert-Durades evoked not only her gratitude but the ever-ready sense of unworthiness which inevitably completes the psychic pattern of basic deprivation. Half-bragging, half-apologizing, she told the Brays that she was being made a "spoiled child." Then later, when about to leave Switzerland, she wrote them: "I . . . shall return to you more of a spoiled child than ever. Indeed I think I am destined to be so to the end—one of the odious swarm of voracious caterpillars, soon to be swept away from the earth by a tempest."

George Eliot would not be swept away by a tempest as Maggie Tulliver was, nor would she be so harshly chastened by life itself as Gwendolen Harleth. Yet she was to endure many years in the ominous presence of some undefined inner threat, which she came to call "egotism," and under the burden of which all her major feminine characters were to struggle before they either triumphed or succumbed to it. (Rosamond Lydgate, who successfully imprisons her husband within her own narrow self-centeredness, is the only exception here.) When we realize her conviction of unworthiness and her predisposition to self-punishment, it is less surprising to learn that she was slow to accept the happiness and success which came to her in later life. Indeed, it is a tribute to a basically healthy ego that she was able to permit them even to enter her life.

Her earliest guilt was probably reactivated by her growing awareness of her role in her mother's prolonged illness, and then still more consciously reinforced by her being called home—putting an end to her official schooling—to nurse her mother during her final illness. Even the most loving nursing of a parent is an experience which releases unsuspected hostility in far more normally balanced individuals than she was. This new impetus to guilt would have reinforced her ambivalence for her mother, and the conflict must have been augmented yet again during her life with her father, when as his housekeeper she set herself up (consciously or not) as Christiana's rival.

George Eliot's unnatural reticence concerning her mother, as well as the rarity of a satisfactory mother among her fictional characters, suggests that she did not easily come to terms with her unresolved feelings for her mother. But her attempt to do so may well have been a motivating, although untraceable, force in the private quest that led her from novel to novel once she was free to write fiction. One relatively late (but not specifically dated) poem discloses that she had finally succeeded in penetrating the commingled guilt and hostility to recapture the ecstatic memory of her first love for her mother. This poem, "Self and Life," is in the form of a dialogue and is one of her most personal utterances. In the second stanza "Life" speaks:

> I was thy warmth upon thy mother's knee
>   When light and love within her eyes were one;
> We laughed together by the laurel-tree,
>   Culling warm daisies 'neath the sloping sun;
>
>   We heard the chickens' lazy croon,
>   Where the trellised woodbines grew,
>   And all the summer afternoon
>   Mystic gladness o'er thee threw.
>   Was it person? Was it thing?
>   Was it touch or whispering?
>   It was bliss and it was I:
>   Bliss was what thou knew'st me by.

This is a remarkable recall of symbiotic love; the child is not distinct from the mother, but an actual part of her sentient being—"thy warmth upon thy mother's knee." Memory of this organic union evokes also the "mystic gladness" that had accompanied it, and the "we" functions as if singular: *We* laughed, *we* culled the daisies, *we* heard.

But (in memory at least) the bliss was abruptly and harshly dispersed. In the third stanza, "Self" speaks out with a painfully earned identity through an awareness of its separateness from "Life" and hence by implication from the mother:

> Soon I knew thee more by Fear
> And sense of what was not,
> Haunting all I held most dear;
> I had a double lot:
> Ardour, cheated with alloy,
> Wept the more for dreams of joy.

The normal awakening to the experience of feeling separate and hence cast out from the source of life is shock enough for the infant. But the trauma here described suggests something more. Perhaps the young Mary Ann sensed that Christiana was, in effect, aiding the natural process more than was required; and then perhaps later, her first feeling of having been thrust away was intensified by her dawning recognition that Isaac, and not she, was the center of her mother's world.

Significantly, love and fear are also important thematic elements in the sonnets which compose "Brother and Sister," her tribute to her childhood relationship with Isaac. Here the sequence is reversed, at least in actual wording, for in Sonnet V she remembers

> The fear, the love, the primal passionate store,
> Whose shaping impulses make manhood whole.

This is only one of several indications that at about the age of three Mary Ann had attached herself to her brother, and had already been schooled in still deeper lore than she was to learn with him, since she had been taught to fear rejection and hence love itself. It was inevitable, of course, that she should turn to Isaac with all the passion and exclusiveness of her nature, for he was literally the only accessible one left on her emotional horizon and also the greatest threat to her hold on both her father and mother. In fairness to Isaac, it should be remembered that she demanded that he be all in all to her—father and mother, as well as playmate—without granting him occasion to accept or refuse this difficult role. It was no more his fault than hers when later their widely differing temperaments, as well as circumstances, forced him to reject it. Unfortunately for her, the growing gap between them had the same emotional connotation as the earlier rejection, thus stirring the live embers of the smoldering original.

In 1873, when she was fifty-four, George Eliot wrote to John Blackwood in response to a letter from him in which he had described his son and daughter on a picnic: "I hope that the brother and sister love each other very dearly: life might be so enriched if that relationship were made the most of, as one of the highest forms of friendship." Then she added, "A good while ago I made a poem, in the form of eleven sonnets after the Shakespeare type, on the childhood of a brother and sister—little descriptive bits on the mutual influences in their small lives. This was always one of my best loved subjects." This is her first mention to her publisher of the existence of the "Brother and Sister" sonnets, which had been written over the summer of 1869.

It is not wholly surprising that she had not sought immediate publication for this autobiographical work, which she might have felt reluctant to submit to an undiscriminating audience as it obviously had great personal meaning for her, relating not only to her past but to her love for Lewes. Yet it is possible that she had not at first thought of restricting its circulation, for she did publish it in *The Legend of Jubal and Other Poems,* in 1874, when presumably she might have been almost as sensitive about it. Also, just before writing it, she had been having phenomenal success in marketing her poems: under 24 May 1869, for example, she recorded in her Journal the sale of the relatively short "Agatha" to the *Atlantic Monthly* for £300 (then the approximate equivalent of 1,500 American dollars). While this in itself could not have provided the inner motivation which she needed for any writing, whether poetry or prose, it no doubt spurred her on to express in poetic form ideas and feelings already in her mind. As it is true that she was keenly alert to all possibilities of legitimate financial reward, it seems probable that with the good fortune of "Agatha" fresh in mind, she would not at first have thought of withholding even "Brother and Sister" from publication. But an odd coincidence occurred which perhaps caused her to give the matter a second thought.

In that same summer in which she had completed the sonnet series, Harriet Beecher Stowe had also written for the *Atlantic Monthly* her strangely prejudiced but sensationally effective essay, "The True Story of Lord Byron's Life." This immediately re-ignited the gossip about Byron's alleged incestuous love for his half sister Augusta

Leigh (although that had not been Mrs. Stowe's aim, which was, rather, to vindicate Lady Byron). Even before this article made its public appearance in the September issue of the *Atlantic,* Mrs. Stowe, who had recently opened a correspondence with George Eliot, sent the latter a copy. She thus received it but a few weeks after she had completed the sonnets.

The arrival of this essay and the furor it so quickly produced in both America and England—which was to be shortly again re-aroused by Mrs. Stowe's longer treatment in her book of 1870, *The Vindication of Lady Byron*—might have caused George Eliot to keep "Brother and Sister" private. She was moved to strong distaste for Mrs. Stowe's handling of the subject because it reopened the Byron–Augusta Leigh scandal, despite the fact that when she first read Mrs. Stowe's essay, her sympathy was with Lady Byron. Her earliest expression of this to Caroline Bray, however, is oddly wavering:

> I, in my total ignorance of the inner facts, was more prepared to feel with Lady Byron, than you seem to be, who know much of her through her intimate friends. Byron and his poetry have become more and more repugnant to me of late years. . . . As to this story, I cannot help being sorry that it seemed necessary to publish what is only worthy to die and rot. After all Byron remains deeply pitiable, like all of us sinners.

It would seem that further absorption of the "inner facts" made her more decisive, not necessarily in shifting her sympathy to Byron, but in feeling morally indignant over the publicity being given to the theme of incest. By now George Eliot felt a genuine friendship for Mrs. Stowe, and respected her highly as a writer since reading *Uncle Tom's Cabin* in 1852, a book which helped determine her own first approach to fiction. But these facts did not deter her from telling Mrs. Stowe directly, although in mild terms, of her disapproval: "For my own part I should have preferred that the 'Byron question' should not have been brought before the public, because I think the discussion of such subjects is injurious socially. But with regard to yourself, dear friend, I have felt sure that . . . you were impelled by pure, generous feeling."

Eight years later she presented the same reasoning on the same subject to Sara Hennell in much more forceful language:

> In my judgment the course [Mrs. Stowe] took was socially injurious. . . . I have no sympathy with self-vindication or the becoming a proxy in vindication deliberately bought at such a price as that of vitiating revelations—which may even *possibly* be false. To write a cruel letter in a rage is very pardonable. . . . We poor mortals can hardly escape these sins of passion. But I have no pity

to spare for the rancour that corrects its proofs and revises and lays
it by, chuckling with the sense of its future publicity.

This seems a harsh reversal of her assurance in 1869 to Mrs. Stowe
that she believed the latter had been led to write on Byron by "pure,
generous feeling." Clearly her feeling of revulsion had grown rather
than diminished over the years, and clearly, too, that feeling was her
reaction to the fact that the revelations had become public property
and not to *what* had been revealed. One senses that the matter had a
morbid fascination for her and that there was some force at work beneath the surface which even she did not wholly recognize or understand.

Some close association between the "Byron question" and her
own brother-and-sister theme is evident, for in the 1873 letter to
Blackwood in which she tells him of her sonnet series, immediately
after remarking that their theme had always been one of her best
loved subjects, she adds without transition: "And I was proportion-
ately enraged about that execrable discussion raised in relation to
Byron. The deliberate insistence on the subject was a worse crime
against Society than the imputed fact." It was perhaps this uneasy
association in her own mind that led her to describe the brother-sister
relationship to Blackwood as "one of the highest forms of friendship."
Actually, she meant an elemental love and fear that provide what in
the sonnets she calls "the primal passionate store" of the individual.

"Friendship," as either word or concept, has no place in the context
of the sonnets she wrote about herself and Isaac, the first of which
begins:

> I cannot choose but think upon the time
> When our two lives grew like two buds that kiss
> At lightest thrill from the bee's swinging chime,
> Because the one so near the other is.

The two children were not, in fact, as alike as the two buds in this
opening image. There were, first of all, the obvious differences of
sex, age, and size:

> He was the elder and a little man
> Of forty inches, bound to show no dread,
> And I the girl that puppy-like now ran,
> Now lagged behind my brother's larger tread.

And there were also less obvious but more fateful differences between
the two, those of temperament and interests. These are present only
implicitly in the sonnets, for it was clearly George Eliot's conscious
intention to suppress the negative aspects of the relationship (they
had already erupted a decade earlier in *The Mill on the Floss*).

Ages can be ascribed to the children fairly specifically with the help of Cross, who states (as George Eliot herself does figuratively) that "Brother and Sister" belongs to the "budding time of life—from the age of three to five." At the most she would have been five and Isaac eight, for at these respective ages the two were sent to separate schools, and the final sonnet opens ominously: "School parted us." It is possible that a still earlier summer is being recalled than the one immediately preceding their going off to school. "Forty inches" —an oddly specific detail inserted at some sacrifice of poesy—would be quite short for an eight-year-old boy, and Cross says with a definiteness which suggests he heard from George Eliot herself that her fourth year "was the time when the love for her brother grew into [her] affections." Whatever the actual time, it was of short duration when measured by an adult, as the concluding couplet of Sonnet IX acknowledges with some pathos:

> His years with others must the sweeter be
> For those brief days he spent in loving me.

George Eliot's later entries in her Journal while she was at work on the sonnets suggest that she composed the series in three sets (Sonnets I–V, VI–VIII, IX–XI), with approximately two weeks intervening between the first and second sets and again between the second and third. This is borne out by the fact that each set has its own tone and approach to the basic theme. Despite these differences, the first eight sonnets may be read as a true sequence, and Sonnet XI is a logical enough conclusion to this sequence; Sonnets IX and X, on the other hand, seem misplaced and were perhaps added as afterthoughts—very important afterthoughts.

As would be expected, Sonnets I–V are introductory in nature. They depict a leisurely scene, that of the children starting off from their home and mother, carrying rod and line and a basket of food; the time element is generalized so that it could be any summer morning. By virtue of his sex, age, and size, the brother is the leader, and the sister the trusting, worshipful follower.

> I thought his knowledge marked the boundary
> Where men grew blind, though angels knew the rest.
>
> If he said "Hush!" I tried to hold my breath;
> Wherever he said "Come!" I stepped in faith. [Sonnet I]

The memory of things seen on these summer mornings brings with it an ecstasy not unlike the earlier bliss (evoked later) of "Self and Life."

> The firmaments of daisies since to me
> Have had those mornings in their opening eyes,
> The bunched cowslip's pale transparency
> Carried that sunshine of sweet memories,

And wild-rose branches take their finest scent
From those blest hours of infantine content. [Sonnet II]

On and on they go, until out of their mother's sight and alone in an enchanted world of their own. Sonnet V states the overt theme of the series:

Thus rambling we were schooled in deepest lore,
And learned the meanings that give words a soul,
The fear, the love, the primal passionate store
Whose shaping impulses make manhood whole.

This (so George Eliot thought in 1869) was the seed-time of all her after life, and especially did she see it as the source of her power to love as a mature woman, for only love can beget love.

My infant gladness, through eye, ear, and touch,
Took easily as warmth a various food
To nourish the sweet skill of loving much.

For who in age shall roam the earth and find
Reasons for loving that will strike out love
With sudden rod from the hard year-pressed mind?
Were reasons sown as thick as stars above,

'Tis love must see them, as the eyes see light:
Day is but Number to the darkened sight.

More than mere love for the brother is meant here; it is the larger love of being, of life itself, that is engendered by his presence—at least when, as a sonnet later in the series discloses, there is no need to fear his anger. Indeed, even the fear has been accepted as an important and necessary part of the primal store of shaping impulses.

It is in this sense—perhaps the very sense which George Eliot feared would be misunderstood—that "Brother and Sister" is a love poem. A tribute to the generative power of childhood love, it is, furthermore, a chastened tribute, one that she could not possibly have managed had she not earlier written *The Mill on the Floss*, in which memory was at work much less guardedly. Her belief is Wordsworthian: "The child is father of the man." Understandably, Wordsworth was her favorite modern poet, and certain lines from his own great tribute to childhood, the "Ode on Intimations of Immortality from Recollections of Early Childhood," might well have been hovering in her mind as she wrote her sonnets—for instance, these lines:

But for those first affections,
Those shadowy recollections,
Which, be they what they may,

> Are yet the fountain-light of all our day,
> Are yet a master-light of all our seeing;
> Uphold us . . .

Here the similarity ends. She lacked Wordsworth's poetic genius, of course, and also his idyllic view of childhood, his nostalgic yearning to return to it, and even his conviction that with its passing, "there hath passed away a glory from the earth."

"Childhood," she had written to Sara Hennell in 1844, "is only the beautiful and happy time in contemplation and retrospect—to the child it is full of deep sorrows, the meaning of which is unknown." She was then twenty-five, her intellectual outlook had undergone a revolution, Isaac was married, and she was living alone with her father; despite these external changes, no great new feeling had come to assuage or take the place of the mysterious sorrows of childhood, so that she was not yet capable of seeing it in retrospect. To Sara she had added, no doubt flippantly, what proved to be an accurate prophecy: "All this dear Sara, to prove that we are happier than when we were seven years old, and that we shall be happier when we are forty than we are now, which I call a comfortable doctrine and one worth trying to believe." It is improbable that she really believed this, yet at the end of 1857, when she was nearing forty, she wrote in her Journal: "Few women, I fear, have had such reason as I to think the long sad years of youth were worth living for the sake of middle age." At last, through what in the same Journal entry she calls "the blessedness of a perfect love and union" with George Henry Lewes, had come a feeling strong enough to supplant the old tortuous ones, and she was beginning to be able to look back as well as inward. Together she and Lewes shared a "dual solitude" remarkably like that portrayed in the first five sonnets of "Brother and Sister."

As the series moves into the second set of sonnets, however, a shadow is cast over the relationship between the children, although the sustained tone of serenity makes it seem nothing more than a momentary obscuring of the sun. These three sonnets (VI–VIII) command special attention as they relate the only specific episode in the series. Sonnet VI retains the general time setting, but makes it clear that the children have arrived at the "brown canal," where they have come to fish. The sister sits on the bank, absorbing through her senses the sights, sounds, and fragrances around her, happily unaware that near-disaster is at hand.

> Unknowing how the good I loved was wrought,
> Untroubled by the fear that it would cease.

> Slowly the barges floated into view,
> Rounding a grassy hill to me sublime

With some Unknown beyond it, whither flew
The parting cuckoo toward a fresh spring-time.

The wide-arched bridge, the scented elder-flowers,
The wondrous watery rings that died too soon,
The echoes of the quarry, the still hours
With white robe sweeping on the shadeless noon,

    Were but my growing self, are part of me,
    My present Past, my root of piety.

Except for the opening pronoun—"*Our* brown canal"—the brother is absent from this sonnet, and the sister contentedly in her world alone. A curiously similar atmosphere of dwelling apart from all others is conveyed in an 1861 Journal entry George Eliot made after she and Lewes had returned home from a "white bait" dinner party at Greenwich, which had been given by John Blackwood in her honor and to which he had also invited several other special friends: "The chat was agreeable enough, but the sight of the gliding ships darkening against the dying sunlight made me feel chat rather importunate. I think, when I give a white bait dinner I will invite no one but my second self, and we will agree not to talk audibly." Not even Lewes was to be invited—as not even the brother's presence is felt in Sonnet VI.

With the fifth line of Sonnet VII the time abruptly becomes specific in such a way as to suggest that the preceding sonnets have been gradually leading up to this episode, which might thus be considered the heart of the series:

One day my brother left me in high charge,
To mind the rod, while he went seeking bait,
And bade me, when I saw a nearing barge,
Snatch out the line, lest he should come too late.

Proud of the task, I watched with all my might
For one whole minute, till my eyes grew wide,
Till sky and earth took on a strange new light
And seemed a dream-world floating on some tide—
A fair pavilioned boat for me alone,
Bearing me onward through the vast unknown.

Sonnet VIII reveals that she almost paid a great penalty for her day-dreaming:

But sudden came the barge's pitch-black prow,
Nearer and angrier came my brother's cry,
And all my soul was quivering fear . . .

Then, miraculously, not only did she succeed in lifting the line out of the way of the barge, but on the hook was a silver perch, so that her "guilt that won the prey, / Now turned to merit, had a guerdon rich / Of hugs and praises." Her "triumph reached its highest pitch / When all at home were told the wondrous feat. . . ." This was pure glory, for only the brother could have done the telling. Nevertheless, although the joy of hearing him praise her to others relieved her of the "quivering fear" of his anger, she stayed uneasily aware of her "guilt."

> In secret, though my fortune tasted sweet,
> I wondered why this happiness befell.

Almost as if she had voiced her disturbing question, she was given a simple explanation.

> "The little lass had luck," the gardener said:
> And so I learned, luck was with glory wed.

This brief story holds much significance in revealing the less happy side of the brother-sister relationship, and in bringing together those very elements which were most intimately associated with her writing. To begin with, Sonnet VIII strengthens the impression given in Sonnet VII that the girl willingly surrenders to a dream world which is independent of her brother; it is even stressed that the fair pavilioned boat is coming for her alone. If this interesting fact were not recorded in these sonnets, it would be easy to agree with Blanche Colton Williams that imagination came to her aid as compensation when Isaac lost interest in playing with her: "Proud, sensitive, bitter, she wandered about Griff, refashioning her world into what she would have liked it to be; the development of her imagination begins with Isaac's relinquishing her companionship."

To the contrary, the child Mary Ann (at least as George Eliot remembered her childhood self) already had developed imagination before her separation from Isaac, and it was most productive when she was at peace and happy. Admittedly memory has many faces, as well as levels, and although its origins are in the past, it is inevitably modulated by conditions existing at the moment of recall. It is possible that there was a time when George Eliot herself believed that her imagination had come into being to fill a deficiency in real life, as suggested by her remarks to Maria Lewis in a letter written when she was just past nineteen: "When I was quite a little child I could not be satisfied with the things around me; I was constantly living in a world of my own creation, and was quite contented to have no companions that I might be left to my own musings and imagine scenes in which I was chief actress." It is understandable that she should not have mentioned her brother here, for he was still too integral a part of her life to allow her to see him through memory. And as she was at this time under the spell of Evangelicalism, she would not have dared associate imagination (at worst a form of lying, and at best, an egoistic discontent with life as it is) with happiness and contentment. Yet her comment to Maria Lewis corroborates the evidence in the sonnets that she was highly imaginative at an early age; and the sonnets indicate further that at least in 1869 George Eliot remembered her imagination as having been active when she was at her happiest with Isaac. This is an important clue to understanding her writing block and its eventual dissolution. Had her imagination not held an autonomous position in her ego but functioned primarily as a defense against the various threats to her ego, it would have flourished during her unhappiest years and collapsed when she regained happiness and emotional security. Fortunately, her strongest defenses were against imagination itself, so that when they were broken down, it was at last free, and she was to be at her most creative during her happiest years.

However, to insist that her earliest imaginative life was independent of her brother is not to deny that he was a necessary accessory to it. Apparently his comradely presence was needed to give her security enough to float away on the wings of her own phantasies. Even George Henry Lewes, who later provided the comradely presence, became aware he should not try to enter the private world which was the source of her writing.

Of course the great difference between Lewes and the brother of the sonnets is that the latter was totally unaware that his sister inhabited a world different from his own. His angry demand—as in the silver-perch episode—that she return to the real world, his world, caused her very soul to be consumed with fear, the boundless kind of terror which is disproportionate to the reality because it is fed by inner guilt. By luck (so the gardener called it) her wrong-doing ended in extraordinarily good fortune which brought her approval and praise, while still leaving her feeling of guilt unappeased. Had luck not intervened and the consequence been outright failure, she would have had the misery of bearing her brother's unrelenting anger but the cold comfort of "knowing" that she had received the punishment she deserved. Which is the lesser of the two evils—to fail and earn deserved disapproval, or to succeed and earn praise which one is convinced is undeserved?

This simple little story exposes an important part of the psychic dilemma which for many years prevented George Eliot from writing creatively. It is not necessary to prove that the episode did actually occur or that, having occurred, it is related with objective accuracy. Even if she invented it to serve as an exemplum in "Brother and Sister," it clearly discloses that in her own mind guilt and daydreaming were associated, and that this association was in turn linked with her brother. Such associations alone would have been a formidable obstacle to the writing of fiction; they were further strengthened by a nearly equal fear of failure and of success. What might have been a challenging obstacle became a solid impasse before which her creative power was rendered inert. That she was fully aware of her failure is evident from her frequent allusions to it; it would have taken almost super-human self-knowledge for her to have detected that the far less rational fear of success was giving insidious support to the more understandable fear. Yet, interestingly enough, her own often-repeated explanation of her frustration, the element which she told Cross she would dwell upon if she were to write an autobiography—"the absolute despair I suffered from of ever being able to achieve anything"—is broad enough to cover both fears.

In the spring of 1854 she had expressed herself similarly, although more specifically, to Caroline Bray in a letter which begins with reference to "various aches" that had kept her in bed the day before: "My troubles are purely psychical—self-dissatisfaction and despair of achieving anything worth the doing." By implication she here discounts what she had already achieved, which would have seemed considerable to anyone else—the translations of Strauss and Feuerbach, and substantial work on the *Westminster Review*; obviously for her, "anything worth the doing" lay in a different kind of writing. It was not until 1861, when she had proved to herself several times over that she could write fiction, that she began to see her despair as unrealistic in that it had prevented her from even *trying* to succeed. In making a last entry in the Journal she had begun in 1849, she recalls how she had felt then: "What moments of despair that life would ever be made precious to me by the consciousness that I lived to some good purpose! It was that sort of despair that sucked away the sap of half the hours which might have been filled by energetic youthful activity." But then she admits, "and the same demon tries to get hold of me again whenever an old work is dismissed and a new one is being meditated." By this time, *Scenes of Clerical Life, Adam Bede, The Mill on the Floss,* and *Silas Marner* were all published. Her new onslaught of despair was over the need to begin the actual writing of *Romola,* which she had delayed by long months of intensive study into background material.

It is evident that repeated success had done little to allay her propensity to despair. It had, in fact, brought into play the second fear which had kept her in deadlock for many years, but which had had no reason to assert itself until the unanticipated and phenomenal success of *Adam Bede.* Those who knew her identity expected her to receive this success with joy; they were surprised and dismayed to see her become anxious and increasingly melancholy. Both John and William Blackwood plied her with reasons why she should be glad and grateful over the reception given the novel. The happiest response she could muster was this, written to William: "Yes—I *am* assured now that 'Adam Bede' was worth writing—worth living through long years to write. But now it seems impossible to me that I shall ever write anything so good and true again. I have arrived at faith in the past, but not at faith in the future." Years later, Edith Simcox in a conversation with Mrs. Richard Congreve learned how at the great success of *Adam Bede* George Eliot

> was unhappy and—"you will hardly be able to believe this"—irritable: it was for Mr Lewes's sake that She struggled with the melancholy moods. . . . The fact that She needed in some ways as much forbearance as she showed is a point to be remembered on Mr Lewes's side—he was not a mere recipient.

Indeed, Lewes gave her far more than forbearance, for again it was his intuitive understanding which saved her; he came to realize that success threatened her almost as direly as failure would have done. By the time she was writing *Romola*, he had extended his role to include not only offering her the usual forms of encouragement and "critical" approval, but also guarding her against seeing or hearing all outside criticism, the good as well as the bad. He explained this in no uncertain terms to Sara Hennell, who had sent them a report of some unfavorable criticism she had heard or read, but which he caught sight of in time to "mislay" her letter so that George Eliot would not see it.

> After the publication of "Adam Bede" Marian felt deeply the evil influences of talking and allowing others to talk to her about her writing. We resolved therefore to exclude everything as far as we could. No one speaks about her books to her, but me; she sees no criticisms. The sum total of success is always ascertainable, and she is not asked to dwell on the details.
>
> Besides . . . there is a special reason in her case—it is that excessive diffidence which prevented her writing at all, for so many years, and would prevent her now, if I were not beside her to encourage her. A thousand eulogies would not give her the slightest confidence, but one objection would increase her doubts.

"Diffidence" only partially connotes her complex pattern of despair, but it effectively carried Lewes to the heart of the matter. The "thousand eulogies," arising from sheer luck, would be meaningless to her; but one word of negative criticism would shatter her tenuous self-confidence, for it would seem to confirm her own conviction that she *should* fail. In an attempt to give her some sense of progress so that she would continue to write, Lewes proclaimed each new work superior to the preceding one, although as his own Journal entries reveal, he did not always believe this to be true. None too friendly observers considered his zealous guard over what she saw and heard about her work an absurd form of pampering; those who were close enough to her to realize how vulnerable she was to attacks of despair were impressed with how right he was and how necessary to her was his deliberately created role.

Although it is unlikely that George Eliot composed the silver-perch episode with the conscious intention of symbolizing her writing life, possibly as she planned the telling of it some recognition passed through her that she was doing just that. In the opening of Sonnet VII, which begins the episode, the only lines in the whole of "Brother and Sister" that might be called an allusion to her writing occur:

> Those long days measured by my little feet
> Had chronicles which yield me many a text:

Inevitably by the time of the sonnets, whatever surged up from her deepest self pertained to her writing in some way or other, for it was there that she most truly lived and had her being.

It is possible too that she recognized that when finished, Sonnets VI–VIII revealed more of the separateness of brother and sister than harmony between them, for the third and final set of sonnets opens with a reaffirmation of their closeness, the time element again generalized:

> We had the selfsame world enlarged for each
> By loving difference of girl and boy:

Then follows a new description of the brother-sister relationship, one that might more naturally have come in the introductory sonnets, for here it interrupts the sequence thus far established. Now the brother is his sister's loving protector, admonishing himself whenever they approach a new adventure or game:

> "This thing I like my sister may not do,
> For she is little, and I must be kind."

Because he willingly places kindness to her before his own desires and interests, his total character is ennobled:

> Thus boyish Will the nobler mastery learned
> Where inward vision over impulse reigns,
> Widening its life with separate life discerned,
> A Like unlike, a Self that self restrains.

This is why his later "years with others must the sweeter be" for having loved his little sister.

This sonnet so clearly reflects George Eliot's own ideal—the voluntary holding back of self for the sake of other selves—that one doubts whether the "boyish Will the nobler mastery learned," and suspects, rather, that she is projecting her own painful lesson. She credits a seven- or eight-year-old boy with what she had achieved only after living for many years under the burden of. a self which had refused to submit to "inward vision" until she had gained inner poise through adult love and the unconscious therapy of creative writing. Perhaps this sonnet was written in compensation for having permitted a glimpse into the brother's hostility in the preceding sonnets, and perhaps too it is a subtle preparation for the significant sonnet that follows (the tenth), although the latter has no logical connection with it and even refutes much of its meaning.

This penultimate sonnet reveals that it was the sister who saw to it that they inhabited "the selfsame world" and that she did this by giving up her own world (including her dream world) in order to enter her brother's:

> His sorrow was my sorrow, and his joy
> Sent little leaps and laughs through all my frame;
> My doll seemed lifeless and no girlish toy
> Had any reason when my brother came.
>
> I knelt with him at marbles, marked his fling
> Cut the ringed stem and made the apple drop,
> Or watched him winding close the spiral string
> That looped the orbits of the humming top.

In effect, she obscured the "loving difference of girl and boy," which the preceding sonnet had celebrated; to make sure of having and holding her brother's companionship, she identified with him. No doubt this also explains her slowness in learning to read. Had her brother shown a marked interest or ability in reading (and it seems reasonable to assume that he did not; George Eliot's very last letter to him suggests that he had always been drawn to an active, outdoor life), she would not have dared outstrip him in mastery of reading, as she was soon to do when they were no longer playfellows. Isaac himself told Cross that his sister's difficulty in learning to read "was not from any slowness in apprehension, but because she liked playing so much better." If Isaac had specified playing with *him*, he would have been nearer the truth. When she could no longer have him as intimate playmate, she turned to reading with a vengeance: "Books now became a passion with the child; she read everything she could lay hands on. . . ." One suspects that it was through this avid reading, chiefly of novels, as her retrospective letters to Maria Lewis reveal, that she attempted to fill the gap created in her life by Isaac's absence.

How closely her early reading was related to imagination is suggested by an episode which was perhaps the first outward sign of her desire to write. Cross acknowledges Edith Simcox to have been the first to recount the episode, and it is from her Valedictory essay that he quotes:

"Somewhere about 1827 a friendly neighbor lent 'Waverley' to an elder sister of little Mary Ann Evans. It was returned before the child had read to the end, and, in her distress at the loss of the fascinating volume, she began to write out the story as far as she had read it for herself, beginning naturally where the story begins with Waverley's adventures at Tully Veolan, and continuing until the surprised elders were moved to get her the book again." Miss Simcox has pointed out the reference to this in the motto of the 57th chapter [Book Six] of "Middlemarch":

> They numbered scarce eight summers when a name
>   Rose on their souls and stirred such motions there
> As thrill the buds and shape their hidden frame
>   At penetration of the quickening air:
> His name who told of loyal Evan Dhu
>   Of quaint Bradwardine, and Vich Ian Vor,
> Making the little world their childhood knew
>   Large with a land of mountain, lake, and scaur,
> And larger yet with wonder, love, belief
>   Towards Walter Scott, who, living far away,
> Sent them this wealth of joy and noble grief.
>   The book and they must part, but, day by day,
>   In lines that thwart like portly spiders ran,
>   They wrote the tale, from Tully Veolan.

It is possible of course that this sonnet is the sole source of the anecdote. Edith was ever keenly on the watch for the slightest bit of personal revelation in all of George Eliot's writings, and *Middlemarch* especially she knew almost by heart. That possibility does not necessarily detract from the value of the anecdote, for the sonnet was surely inspired by an experience independent of the *Middlemarch* chapter, to which it is only vaguely applicable. Interestingly, except for the use of "they" (perhaps a poetic license to fit the Garth children, who figure in the chapter), it brings to mind "the little world" of "Brother and Sister," and the bud image quite specifically recalls the opening of the latter. It is even possible that the *Middlemarch* sonnet was originally composed for "Brother and Sister" (which was written when George Eliot was at work upon the novel) but then put aside when she decided that the sonnet series should pertain only to the time before fiction had entered her life.

Of greater importance is the fact that according to both the sonnet and Edith Simcox's account, the child wrote out that portion of the Scott novel which she had already read. A normally imaginative child might have felt the urge to continue the story, but without the desire

to repossess in visible form the part already known. It is probable
that the reproducing of the original from memory was a far more
creative act than either the child-author or the surprised older spec-
tators could have realized. Thus it seems that when following the trail
already cut by someone else's imagination, the eight-year-old Mary
Ann Evans could compose with spontaneity and fluency—as suggested
by "lines that thwart like portly spiders ran." There is little doubt that
had she been psychically free to translate the visions of her own
imagination into outward form, she would have been a natural writer
from a very early age.

But by the time of the Scott episode, identification with her brother
had already strengthened her guilt over giving free play to her imagination. This masculine identification was to be a strong component in
her psychic make-up and thus destined to play a vital role in both her
personal and creative life. It was also one of the first facets of her
personality to be buried under the George Eliot legend by Cross's
example (soon followed by others) of over-protesting her femininity.
She was indeed feminine, yet neither wholly nor effortlessly so. Once
born a woman, she was automatically forced into a mold which set
rigid limits to her developing manlike qualities, even though they
might have been struggling for expression. But by 1928 Virginia
Woolf could make a candid generalization upon her own delightful
hero-heroine, Orlando:

> Different though the sexes are, they intermix. In every human being
> a vacillation from one sex to the other takes place, and often it is
> only the clothes that keep the male or female likeness, while under-
> neath the sex is the very opposite of what it is above. Of the com-
> plications and confusions which thus result every one has had
> experience. . . .

But in George Eliot's time, one had to be all-man or all-woman—or
at least pretend to be in public. As hers was an extraordinarily powerful nature, it is little wonder that for the many years during which
she was caught between the need for and fear of both masculine aggressiveness and feminine passivity, her sense of identity was blunted
and her sense of unworthiness augmented. Where in the great family
of man-woman did she belong?

In relation to her art, it is impossible to overestimate the importance of her bisexual identification, although this alone need not
have produced her writing block. Substantial evidence indicates that
similar twofold identification has occurred in a considerable number
of other writers, some of them the most prolific and of the highest
stature—Dostoevsky, Henry James, and D. H. Lawrence are three
richly varied instances. In George Eliot the effect was to barricade her

imagination for a long while, for the expression of imagination—that is, its work of re-creation outside the psyche—depends first upon a passive acceptance of its offerings.

I
F GEORGE ELIOT HAD BEEN ABLE TO BELIEVE IN A PAGAN OR Christian muse, she could have freed her imagination as many before her had done by shifting the responsibility for its workings to a source outside herself. As it was, she eventually did aid its release—admittedly in a somewhat haphazard because unknowing way—by growing into the "George Eliot" pseudonym and freeing a "second self" for writing, but not her whole self from the old fears. It was this limiting factor which was to help forge her style. Even when at last able to be attentive to inspiration, she still could not be completely passive before it. She had to convince herself—and her reader as well—that she was in complete control of its content by analyzing and commenting upon it, thus often concealing the fact that her writing proceeded from a strong and luxuriant imagination, and just as often forcing the reader into an intellectual, rather than aesthetic, response. Most modern literary criticism dismisses the analysis and commentary in her writing as the result of a lamentable propensity to teach and preach. Her contemporary Anthony Trollope was more perceptive in recognizing that they were intimately related to imagination itself:

> Her imagination is no doubt strong, but it acts in analysing rather than in creating. Everything that comes before her is pulled to pieces so that the inside of it shall be seen, and be seen if possible by her readers as clearly as by herself.

It was of course her defense against it, not imagination itself, that was doing the analyzing, yet Trollope was right in seeing that in her writing the analyzing cannot be separated from the very act of creation and so is an integral part of her art.

Sonnet X in "Brother and Sister" makes explicit George Eliot's own awareness of her need to control her power of imagination and also her conception of the source of that need. In contrast to the lucid simplicity of the first eight lines (in which the sister "becomes" the brother), the remaining six are expressed in tortuous language and syntax:

> Grasped by such fellowship my vagrant thought
> Ceased with dream-fruit dream-wishes to fulfill;
> My aery-picturing fantasy was taught
> Subjection to the harder, truer skill

> That seeks with deeds to grave a thought-tracked line,
> And by "What is," "What will be" to define.

Thus is her identifying with her brother rationalized and excused: in entering his world, she has penalized herself by sacrificing her own precious one of imagination. Her immolation, although far less violent, is not unlike Maggie's drowning with Tom—locked in one another's arms. It was George Eliot of course who decided that Tom could be drowned only if Maggie drowned also. It is quite possible that the deepest motive for the writing of "Brother and Sister" was one of expiation for *The Mill on the Floss,* which of all George Eliot's novels reveals most clearly her need for justification.

Sonnet XI abruptly ends the leisurely movement of scenes and action:

> School parted us; we never found again
> That childish world . . .

The physical separation from home and Isaac proved to be traumatic, although there is no indication of this in the sonnets, unless it be a displaced one in the "quivering fear" of the silver-perch episode. But in 1880 George Eliot told Cross

> that what chiefly remained in her recollection about this very early school-life was the difficulty of getting near enough the fire in winter to become thoroughly warmed, owing to the circle of girls forming round too narrow a fireplace. This suffering from cold was the beginning of a low general state of health; also at this time she began to be subject to fears at night—"the susceptibility to terror"—which she has described as haunting Gwendolen Harleth in her childhood.

George Eliot was to suffer from cold for the rest of her life, and her death resulted from an illness which began with her having caught a chill. As for the other, more tormenting suffering, Cross leads the reader to identify its cause with Isaac, for to describe the night terrors, he quotes (although changing the verb form) the words from Sonnet VIII which describe the sister's intense reaction to her brother's anger: "she was not unhappy except at nights; but she told me that this liability to have 'all her soul become a quivering fear,' which remained with her afterwards, had been one of the supremely important influences dominating at times her future life."

" . . . in every parting," George Eliot was to write in "Amos Barton," "there is an image of death." This association of parting and death signifies the residual strength of the shock of her first parting from her family. Even though she joined Chrissey at school, she could interpret her having been sent away only as a deliberate withdrawal of love, as indeed would most five-year-old children. But this was a second experience of rejection, the first having been with her mother; and as Isaac had to some extent helped her to recover from her first loss, his absence would have been felt with double intensity. Such early basic experiences do not become lifeless relics in the self; they lie in wait for the slightest cue from the outside world to spring into action again. Without doubt these were the chief sources of the lasting sadness which marked her facial expression, the cast of her thought, and the prevalent tone of her novels. Those who knew her only near the end of her life assumed that this was an impersonal sadness born of her extraordinary insight into and compassion for humanity. Perhaps so, but not until very late. Only four years before her death she wrote to Sara Hennell:

> It is remarkable to me that I have entirely lost my *personal* melancholy. I often, of course, have melancholy thoughts about the destinies of my fellow-creatures, but I am never in that *mood* of sadness which used to be my frequent visitant even in the midst of external happiness.

If by then her personal sadness was gone, she remained as insatiable in her need for love as ever, for no amount of it could redeem the original loss. This explains how she could endure what to most others would have been a surfeit of demonstrative worship from the young men and women who (often quite literally) sat at her feet. Far from showing jealousy of these adorers, Lewes encouraged them and made no secret of his own worship. One senses that the more public aspect of his devotion to her was yet another self-appointed role which grew out of his understanding that what he had told Sara Hennell about George Eliot and her writing could be said also about her reaction to love. A thousand protestations would leave her unmoved (and one gains the impression that the adoration touched only the surface of her feelings), but the withdrawal of only one of the worshippers would have reactivated the old doubt of self-worth. A remarkable instance of this occurred when one day Maria Congreve went to visit George Eliot after not having seen her for a while. She told Edith Simcox

> how on seeing her again after an interval, her heart was palpitating so violently that to avoid a painful breaking down she forced herself into a calm that seemed cold; she tried to talk in common fashion. Mr. Lewes was there, and then—the Darling, my sweet Darling, rushed out of the room in tears. Mr. Lewes signed to Mrs. Congreve not to follow her and with a breaking heart she sat through his call, and afterwards, though she guessed the Darling had been pained by her seeming coldness, she dared not ask her for she thought too she did not wish it to be thought. After a while she,

the dearest, spoke of it and then it could all be told. I said, were you
not very happy to think that she could care so much for your love?

Thus the early loss and lack of love formed a more important part
of her "present Past" than the mother's early love. George Eliot's
awareness of the dynamic continuance of negative as well as positive
factors into adult life is evident (although she chose to ignore this
darker side of childhood in "Brother and Sister") in several instances
in her work and letters. One of the most telling is the otherwise
incomprehensible motto she supplied for Book II, chapter 20, of
Middlemarch:

> A child forsaken, waking suddenly,
> Whose gaze afeard on all things round doth rove,
> And seeth only that it can not see
> The meeting eyes of love.

This is an oddly fragmentary bit of verse; stranger still, the chapter
it heads has nothing to do with a child, but concerns a young married
woman and her older husband: Dorothea is at the bleak dawn of
realizing there is no real love between herself and Casaubon.

The seemingly uncaused sadness and the unending need for love
were no doubt the remnants of the more violent night terrors, about
which—despite their importance in her life, admitted to Cross—
George Eliot was apparently reticent. Except for Cross's Sketch, there
is no record of them in reported conversations or in her letters, unless
(and this seems likely) they are obliquely alluded to when she wrote to
Sara Hennell in 1844 about the deep sorrows of childhood, "the meaning of which is unknown. Witness colic and whooping-cough and
dread of ghosts, to say nothing of hell and Satan, and an offended Deity
in the sky who was angry when I wanted too much plum cake." Nor
is there any trace of it in her fiction until, as Cross notes, the appearance of Gwendolen Harleth in her last novel. Perhaps the fact of having given expression to this series of terrorizing experiences in the
portrayal of Gwendolen freed her to talk about them to Cross.

Probably too she was most willing to talk about them when she felt
most secure. One feels certain that she discussed them with Lewes in
conversations now irrevocably lost, and it is even possible that he had
such talks in mind when he wrote in his *Problems of Life and Mind*
how "the terror felt in darkness . . . raises images of robbers, wild
beasts, ghosts or demons, as probably present. . . ." Before this discussion he had stated that emotions, including terror, "do not spring
up uncaused as products of the subjective factor alone. . . ." But to the
five-year-old child abruptly removed to school, the objective factor
would have seemed to be Satan or an offended Deity, for the real cause
was physically absent. It is possible that the actual source of these

attacks still puzzled the adult George Eliot, and that her associating the sister's quivering fear with her brother's anger was an attempt to explain rationally what still eluded her. By the time Gwendolen appears in *Daniel Deronda*, she was ready to describe the nature of the terror more specifically, but without explaining its origin. When alone or confronting a wide scene of solitude, Gwendolen suffers "an undefined feeling of immeasurable existence aloof from her, in the midst of which she was helplessly incapable of asserting herself." When someone joins her, however, she quickly recovers "her indifference to the vastness in which she seemed an exile; she found again her usual world in which her will was of some avail . . ." (Book I, chapter 6). One major difference between Gwendolen and her creator is that the former had suffered no rejection or fundamental deprivation. Quite the opposite —she was "the spoiled child." Used to having her own way, she is all the more terrorized by her feeling of helplessness and inability to assert her will. She is, in effect, being punished for her aggressive will to control.

Although George Eliot does not ever say so explicitly, it is psychologically understandable that Gwendolen felt ashamed of these attacks and exerted herself to conceal them from her family, as it would seem the child Mary Ann did, for she appeared unchanged when she was brought home for occasional visits. According to Cross, "Mr. Isaac Evans's chief recollection of this period is the delight of the little sister at his home-coming for holidays, and her anxiety to know all that he had been doing and learning." "Anxiety" is a telltale word here, whoever supplied it, suggesting that underneath the eager welcome lay the dread question: was Isaac's new life taking him still farther away from her? Even her hope that they would again share the summers was shattered by what Cross calls "a deeply felt crisis": when she was about seven, "her brother had a pony given to him, to which he became passionately attached. He developed an absorbing interest in riding, and cared less and less to play with his sister." However, life went on, and there is one more glimpse of the two together in comradely fashion, this when she was between nine and thirteen: "On coming home for their holidays the sister and brother began . . . the habit of acting charades together before the Griff household and the aunts, who were greatly impressed with the cleverness of the performance; and the girl was now recognized in the family circle as no ordinary child."

The final glimpse of them in this period is on Chrissey's wedding day, not long after the mother's death: "One of Mr. Isaac Evans's most vivid recollections is that on the day of the marriage, after the bride's departure, he and his younger sister had 'a good cry' together over the break-up of the old home-life. . . ." Apparently, then, it was the time between 1825, when both Mary Ann and Isaac went off to school, and

1837, when their sister was married, that was meant in these lines from Sonnet XI:

> Yet the twin habit of that early time
> Lingered for long about the heart and tongue;
> We had been natives of one happy clime,
> And its dear accent to our utterance clung . . .

From then on the differences between the brother and sister, which had always existed but which the sister had long refused to recognize, became more outwardly marked. Cross attempts to make light of them, but they were serious:

> For instance, all that happened in real life between the brother and sister was, I believe, that as they grew up their characters, pursuits, and tastes diverged more and more widely. He took to his father's business, at which he worked steadily, and which absorbed most of his time and attention. He was also devoted to hunting, liked the ordinary pleasures of a young man in his circumstances, and was quite satisfied with the circle of acquaintance in which he moved. After leaving school at Coventry he went to a private tutor's at Birmingham, where he imbibed strong High-Church views.

Meanwhile, his sister had absorbed "ultra-Evangelical tendencies" and of course attempted to convert Isaac to them. This new and final attempt on her part to force him into her world was unsuccessful, and his marriage in 1841 took him out of her ken of control. These no doubt were "the dire years whose awful name is Change" noted in Sonnet XI; yet as she was writing this sonnet in 1869, it seemed to her that even in the dire years their souls had been "still yearning in divorce." But change "pitiless shaped them in two forms that range / Two elements which sever their life's course."

Sonnet XI—and hence the whole of "Brother and Sister"—ends with a couplet which softens the harshness of the preceding lines:

> But were another childhood-world my share,
> I would be born a little sister there.

The "But" prevents this from being read as merely a nostalgic wish. It says, in effect: despite the pain I experienced as a little sister, I would be one again—although, of course, there can be no "again."

TWO

Root of Piety

IN THE SUMMER OF 1838, THE BROTHER AND SISTER TOGETHER visited London for a week. Their childhood world was long past, but they were of an age to have made the trip a gay adventure—she nineteen, and he twenty-two—and they were without chaperone ("that seems rather Irish," she later admitted to Maria Lewis, perhaps indulging in a wistful bit of boasting once the trip was over). But while in London, she had seen to it that the visit was a dolorous affair. Every day they "worked hard at seeing sights," yet she refused to be interested in any of them except hospitals and churches, and even a Sunday afternoon visit to St. Paul's aroused her indignation "towards the surpliced personages . . . who performed the chanting . . . their behavior being that of schoolboys, glad of an opportunity to titter unreproved." Isaac invited her to the theaters, but she declined and "spent all her evenings alone, reading." As for shopping, "the chief thing she wanted to buy was Josephus's 'History of the Jews'; and at the same bookshop her brother got her this he bought for himself a pair of hunting sketches." When not otherwise occupied, they held "animated argument," she attempting to convert her brother to Evangelicalism; for she, "as she now was, could not rest satisfied with a mere profession of faith without trying to shape her own life—and, it may be added, the lives around her—in accordance with her convictions. The pursuit of pleasure was a snare; dress was vanity; society was a danger." One can imagine Isaac buying the hunting sketches as a symbolic gesture of self-defense; at least he remembered the incident vividly enough to relate it to Cross almost half a century later.

Obviously, this is no longer the little sister who loved playing with her brother above all else and who had found her root of piety in fantasy and in delighting in the sun and breeze and waters of the brown canal while in his presence. More than years appear to lie between that child and the young woman who accompanied her brother to London. When the surface differences are penetrated, the same passionate nature is revealed, yet now a large part of its force was directed against that to which it had earlier inclined—the sheer joy in living and the will to assert itself. What is fortunate is that this force had found an outlet—no matter what kind, no matter how temporary—other than the subliminal one of night terrors.

The most obvious explanation of the startling change is that for years she had been under the spell of Evangelicalism. The time of her subjection to this restrictive and pleasure-denying religion has usually been regarded as a lamentable detour which postponed the unfolding of her creative genius. But had the influence of Evangelicalism been thus wholly negative, one would expect that when release from it came, her creativeness would also have been freed. With the one exception of an abortive attempt to start a novel, it was to be almost fifteen years after her decisive break with Evangelicalism before George Eliot was able to write fiction. As a matter of fact, there are signs to suggest that Evangelicalism provided a many-leveled protective shelter against her growing burden of self, without which her talent might well have been permanently damaged rather than merely held in check.

On one level, this religion offered her some compensation for the lost intimacy with Isaac, for God was to be known, not through dogma or creed, but intimately and directly by the individual who had achieved the state of conversion and thus was receptive to the mystic experience of losing all sense of self in union with the Absolute. Evangelicalism made no easy promise that the experience of conversion would occur. The preparatory program was a rigorous one, demanding of the individual unceasing self-probing, self-confession, and self-denial. Hence all responsibility rested with the individual seeker. He alone (with God introjected into his conscience) could judge his own triumphs and defeats by measuring the temptations he had resisted and those to which he had succumbed. Although he was to master, Stoic-like, all desire for worldly pleasure until the desire itself disappeared, he was not at liberty to withdraw from the world. Rather, he was to be ever busy doing good, approaching the souls of others by supplying materialistic need but preaching to them also, for by definition he was to Evangelize.

All the while the convert himself was to remain emotionally uninvolved and without even a sense of satisfaction over having performed his duty. Only through constant introspection could he keep himself informed as to whether he had failed or succeeded in sustaining his dispassionate role. This curiously rigid but nonsectarian and individualistic religion remained both out of and in this world, making its reconciliation between worldly and other-worldly action in much the same way as even Krishna in the *Bhagavad Gita* explains the Yoga of Action to the puzzled but receptive Arjuna. Through this reconciliation—calling for the threefold path of self-renunciation, self-examination, and disinterested altruism—Evangelicalism became an individual ethic and, if not an actual social philosophy, the most widespread humanitarian movement in England during the first half of the nineteenth century.

If later—as indicated in *Middlemarch*, for example—George Eliot became implicitly critical of the simple program of charity thus inaugurated by Evangelicalism, her eager participation in it during her younger years, starting in her schooldays, had been a mainstay of her life. Long after she had left their Coventry school, the Misses Franklin remembered her "not only as a marvel of mental power, but also as a person 'sure to get something up very soon in the way of a clothing-club or other charitable undertaking.' " This kind of activity became even more meaningful to her after her mother's death and Chrissey's marriage, when "the entire charge of the Griff establishment devolved" on her and she became, according to Cross, "a most exemplary housewife." Perhaps she derived some satisfaction from this position through thinking that it made her father and Isaac somewhat dependent upon her. Otherwise, the constant household chores caused her life to seem trivial and made serious inroads on the time she wanted to give to study, for as Cross says, "she was always prosecuting an active intellectual life of her own." She had, in fact, outlined for herself a course of study which would eventually make her one of England's most learned women, but at the time the only fruit it bore was to emphasize with painful clarity her alienation from those with whom she lived. And for what was she preparing herself?

She was already tormented by a sense of large but undefined destiny, and no doubt her proud and admiring teachers had fired her smoldering ambition. Yet there was no sign to give her reason to think that her position in life would ever be other than that of spinster housekeeper in a provincial setting. Even Cross admits that "it requires no great effort of imagination to conceive that this life . . . was, as a matter of fact, very monotonous, very difficult, very discouraging." Directly apropos and without identification, he quotes the embittered words of Daniel Deronda's talented mother: "You may try, but you can never imagine what it is to have a man's force of genius in you, and yet to suffer the slavery of being a girl." Cross quickly adds that this point of view "will always be corrected by the other point of view which she [George Eliot] has made so prominent in all her own writing—the soothing, strengthening, sacred influences of the home life, the home loves, the home duties." Perhaps so. However, she had to achieve the larger life before she could see the good in the one she had escaped, and then only through mellowed memory, for in the earlier life she had had little cause to feel the home loves which transform home duties into sacred influences. She herself in 1840 called hers "a *walled-in* world."

Her philanthropic work up through the 1840's took her into a larger, if not a particularly cheerful, world by giving her a sense of purpose and usefulness; and also, more literally, by giving her entry into homes both higher and lower than would otherwise have been open to her. In these she absorbed atmosphere and fact which were patiently to await re-creation in fiction. Similarly, the more subjective phase of Evangelicalism admitted her to a larger spiritual home than she might have found for herself, one that encompassed even the night terrors, thus somewhat counteracting the sense of rejection which had given rise to them. The demand for self-renunciation, rather than thwarting her, provided a welcome sanction to her own desperate efforts to curb the forces within her which she feared without knowing why. For a time at least she had some defense against the eruptions of what in *Daniel Deronda* she was to describe as that "great deal of unmapped country within us which would have to be taken into account in an explanation of our gusts and storms" (Book III, chapter 6). But, interestingly, the heroine of that novel, Gwendolen Harleth, is given no such defense, although she too is subject to attacks of terror and her greatest fear too is of herself. She could not make use of the "spiritual fetters" which temporarily sustained her creator, for she had no consciousness of them,

> having always disliked whatever was presented to her under the name of religion, in the same way that some people disliked arithmetic and accounts: it had raised no other emotion in her, no alarm, no longing; so that the question whether she believed it had not occurred to her, any more than it had occurred to her to inquire into the conditions of colonial property and banking, on which . . . the family fortune was dependent. [Book I, chapter 6]

Gwendolen's "undefined feeling of immeasurable existence aloof from her" signified only a "vastness in which she seemed an exile," because "this fountain of awe within her had not found its way into connection with the religion taught her or with any human relations" (Book I, chapter 6).

The "or" in the last phrase is arresting: it shifts emphasis from the spiritual to the temporal, suggesting that the root of piety might be nourished by a deeply meaningful human relationship, not as a substitute for but an equivalent of a given religion. And in the course of the novel Gwendolen does discover just that in her unique relationship with Daniel Deronda. George Eliot's own final position was that of finding religious value in humanity. The fact that this had also been her first instinct, at least as memory gave form to "Brother and Sister," is one reason why after her loss of faith, not only in Evangelicalism but in the existence of God, she could find spiritual fulfillment in the human world alone. She was spared the tortuous despair which afflicted most of her contemporaries who also found it necessary to face the consequences of there being no God. In fact, she was never again to ally or identify herself wholly with any one doctrine or movement, whether religious, philosophical, or social. Was her Evangelical period the one exception in her life? Had she found in her relationship to God a satisfactory adjustment to what she admitted to Cross was "from the earliest years, the trait that was most marked in her all through life, namely, the absolute need of some one person who should be all in all to her, and to whom she should be all in all"?

The answer to both questions is probably not. It is unlikely that she ever realized the mystic state of conversion. The references to God in her early letters are in a tone of self-reproach, as if she were guiltily aware that she had failed to close the distance between Him and herself. Certainly she had intellectual understanding of the essential mystic experience; for example, in a letter of 1840 she wrote to Maria Lewis: "Why do we yearn after a fellow mortal but because we do not live and delight in conscious union with Him who condescends to say, 'Ye shall no more call me Baali or Lord, but ye shall call me Ishi, my husband.' " A few sentences later she reveals the very human reason why she had raised and answered this question. She had been struggling to rid her mind of the image of a young man who had attracted her and she felt that she had been fairly successful in doing so "in consequence of entire occupation and, I trust in some degree, desire and prayer to be free from rebelling against Him whose I am by right, whose I would be by adoption."

At this time of her life she was as incapable of a pure mystic experience as she was of creative writing, and for much the same reason. Both mysticism and art require passive receptiveness on the part of the subject, so much so that he or she becomes as one with the object of his "knowing." Such receptiveness (a large part, if not the whole, of empathy) implies a loss of the sense of self through the opening of its boundaries so as to admit the object. It is evident that George Eliot eventually came near to this goal; otherwise the novels would not have been written, nor would she have impressed those people whom she chose to befriend with what Oscar Browning called "her burning power of sympathy." That she herself recognized this to have been both a difficult and an uncommon achievement is suggested by her observation in *Daniel Deronda*: "Receptiveness is a rare and massive power, like fortitude . . ." (Book X, chapter 6).

In her Evangelical days she indeed struggled to lose the sense of self, but too hard and in the wrong way. Because they were based on fears, her attempts at self-renunciation led to greater restrictedness of self, not release. "I find," she wrote in the letter describing her London trip with Isaac, "as Dr. Johnson said respecting his wine, total abstinence much easier than moderation." In her own view of herself she had no alternative to total abstinence but total depravity—a complete surrender to sensualism, egoism, pride, vanity, ambition. There was also another form of abstinence at work, that from people. She had not recovered from her traumatic departure from home at the age of five. As she was to remark about Gwendolen Harleth (although the observation is curiously unnecessary to illumine Gwendolen's character): "At five years old, mortals are not prepared to be citizens of the world, to be stimulated by abstract nouns, to soar above preference into impartiality . . ." (Book I, chapter 3). Oscar Browning discovered that even at her first boarding school, Miss Lathom's, "The memory of Mary Ann Evans still lingers about the place 'as an awkward girl, reserved and serious far beyond her years, but observant and addicted to the habit of sitting in corners and watching her elders.' " Was she watching out of curiosity—or in wariness, anticipating another betrayal? Her childhood was thus over too soon, but this is also to say that a part of her remained arrested in it, a condition which helps to explain the uneven pace of her later emotional development. Because of her unusual intellect, her need to withdraw was soon cloaked by a precosity which must have successfully frightened her contemporaries away. According to a note made by Sara Hennell:

> Miss Shaw says she remembers Mary Anne at a children's party at her mother's—about 9 or 10 years old, she thinks. M.A. sat apart from the rest, and Mrs. Shaw went to her and said, "My dear, you do not seem happy; are you enjoying yourself." "No, I am not," said M.A. "I don't like to play with children; I like to talk to grown-up people."

By the time she was approaching sixteen and was at the Misses Franklin's school, her obvious mental superiority lessened her need for a more dramatic withdrawal, and "Her school fellows loved her as much as they could venture to love one whom they felt to be so immeasurably superior to themselves. . . ."

George Eliot's learned distrust of the permanency and sincerity of human relations led her to God. She was far too intellectually sophisticated to hold the concept of an anthropomorphic god, yet her own concept attributed to Him qualities which corrected the deficiences she found in human beings. He was eternal, firm but loving and kind, understanding, and forgiving when right motives and honest confession were present. In the same letter describing her London visit, she commented on a marriage:

> I trust that the expected union may ultimately issue in the spiritual benefit of both parties; for my part when I hear of the marrying and giving in marriage that is constantly being transacted I can only sigh for those who are multiplying earthly ties which though powerful enough to detach the heart and thoughts from heaven, are so brittle as to be liable to be snapped asunder at every breeze.

Three years later she wrote less stiltedly but more specifically to her Uncle Samuel Evans (a devout Methodist):

> I feel increasingly that nothing but the enjoyment of God's favour, walking in the light of His countenance, and daily progressing in fitness for His presence and the companionship of the saints in light, can give real satisfaction. Our earthly friends disappoint us and often wound us by coldness, and there is in every cup enough of bitterness to make him who drinks it feel the need of patience, faith, and hope.
>   You ask me about my own state and express a hope that I am running the way of God's commandments. I must answer that I am often, very often stumbling, but I have been encouraged to believe that the mode of action most acceptable to God, is not to sit still desponding, but to rise and pursue my way.

If her uncle was astute, he must have realized that his niece was further from God than ever, that her real feeling was over the bitterness in the human cup, and that a new note of self-assertiveness had appeared. Indeed, she was already in the process of rejecting God, and only a few months after this letter she was to refuse to attend church for fear of committing what had become her new cardinal sin— hypocrisy. She had been quite safe in giving God some human attributes, for she had by no means originated them and they were more or less acceptable to even the most orthodox of believers. But unknowingly she had also thrust upon God human demands. She had wanted response—actual *presence, companionship, demonstrations of love*— but she had found none; she had been too long deprived of the human love she desired to accept any form of love on faith alone. She could read over and over that the Lord had said "Ye shall call me Ishi, my husband," but she could not hear the words; whereas the image of the real man, despite her efforts to banish it, lingered disconcertingly in her mind. God had failed her and, being for her more phantom-like than real, He could be rejected with comparative ease.

Her struggle to believe in Him and in the accompanying Evangelical tenets still served her well for a time by converting her fears into categorical imperatives. The command to love God above all else rationalized the fear of seeking the "brittle" human relations that snap asunder so easily. The blocking fear of both success and failure became translated into a new sequence: Ambition and love of praise are sins because they demand worldly involvement . . . hence confess them and then throttle them. A helpful frame of reference, but also a precariously fragile one, especially as the exhortation to examine the self minutely inevitably brought into consciousness a disturbing flotsam of self-knowledge. Thus it is doubtful that Evangelicalism could have held her within its fold for a dozen or so years were it not for a human as well as a religious significance. The religion was not "taught" her in the usual sense. Rather, she absorbed it as part of a warm human relationship, the first—and for many years, the only—meaningful relationship she experienced outside the troubled ones within her immediate family.

IN 1828, WHEN SHE WAS NINE OR SO, MARY ANN BECAME A boarding student at Mrs. Wallington's school in Nuneaton, with Chrissey. There, as a matter of course, she met Maria Lewis, then about twenty-eight and the head governess. The impact of this meeting was dynamic and long-lasting for both despite the difference in age. Maria Lewis, in Cross's words, "became then, and remained for many years after Mary Ann Evans's most intimate friend and principal correspondent. . . ." Cross adds that at the school

> the growing girl soon distinguished herself by an easy mastery of the usual school-learning of her years, and there, too, the religious side of her nature was developed to a remarkable degree. Miss Lewis was an ardent Evangelical Churchwoman, and exerted a strong influence on her young pupil, whom she found very sympathetically inclined. But Mary Ann Evans did not associate freely with her schoolfellows, and her friendship with Miss Lewis was the only intimacy she indulged in.

As not even an unusually precocious child of nine is likely to select her own religion, and as reasons later were to conspire to place Maria Lewis in an unfavorable light, her "strong influence" has been interpreted to mean that she "inculcated in the impressionable young girl a most painful form of Evangelical piety that frowned on every kind of worldly amusement." However, no religion can be inculcated without sympathetic response on the part of the recipient; nor can Maria

Lewis's influence be evaluated without considering Mary Ann's yearning for an intimate and exclusive relationship. The child turned to her teacher not for religion but for love; and finding it, she saw the teacher's religion through the glow of her own love.

As Maria Lewis quickly won the approval of Robert and Christiana Evans and became a frequent visitor at Griff, Cross's adjective "ardent" in describing her as an "Evangelical Churchwoman" must be taken to mean devout and unswerving, but without emotional demonstration. The Robert Evanses were as mild and conservative in the expression of their religious sentiments as in their political thinking. It would therefore seem likely that Maria had always been as Edith Simcox found her in 1885—"a 'good churchwoman' of a sober sort," who in fact was convinced that her erstwhile pupil's "fall into infidelity was due to the overexcitement, fostered by the Methodist Franklins [whose school George Eliot entered after leaving Mrs. Wallington's, but who actually were Baptists] and the Aunt [Mrs. Samuel Evans, for a while a Methodist preacher], leading to a reaction." Edith had also heard that Christiana had held up the "virtuous cultivated young lady . . . as a model of imitation to her aspiring little daughter." One wonders to what extent Christiana realized that the cultivated young lady was in many ways fulfilling the role she herself had earlier relinquished. For although Maria Lewis told Edith that she had been "like an elder sister" to both Chrissey and Mary Ann, it is clear that she was more compellingly drawn to the younger one—perhaps because she sensed that she was more needed by her, as well as because of her brilliance—and that at least in the earliest years of the association she served as a mother figure. When in 1874, after George Eliot had been long famous, Maria wrote her, "not many knew you as intimately as I once did," she was not boasting beyond the truth. She alone had been in a position to give testimony to the unhappiness which lies embedded in Cross's Sketch despite his valiant effort to gloss over it. She had found the child—so she told Edith—"very loveable, but unhappy, given to great bursts of weeping; finding it impossible to care for childish games and occupations." Then Edith adds on her own, "it is of course significant that as a mere child, the governess should have been her friend rather than any schoolfellow."

Because of the strange history of George Eliot's letters to Maria Lewis, there are serious gaps in the extant correspondence, so that the relationship is never seen in its entirety either in time or depth. The most significant loss is that of the earliest letters. Probably letter writing started when George Eliot left Mrs. Wallington's in 1832 for the Misses Franklin's school; but even Edith Simcox reported that the earliest letters she saw were from 1836, although (as already noted) only one letter from that year is now published. The year 1836 was of course a

crucial one because of the death of Christiana Evans. The following
year Chrissey married and left Griff, so that by 1838, when the extant
letters begin to form a coherent sequence, it was with an intensified
sense of her own loneliness and isolation that George Eliot turned to
Maria as her sole confidante. The salutation of the first 1838 letter
reads "Dear Miss Lewis"; that to the second is "My dear Friend," and
to the third "My very dear Friend," which it remains until she gives
Maria the flower name "Veronica."

Brief as the extant correspondence is, it discloses subtle divisions
reflecting changes of tone, content, and even writing style. As the
vitality in the relationship ebbs (for George Eliot, at least), the letters
become shorter, lighter, more casual, and more relaxed. Thus the first
segment of letters—those from 1838 through part of 1840—are the
most personal and intense, even if their somewhat forbidding style
does much to obscure these qualities. Some small part of this style was
no doubt artificial, the result of an effort to impress as well as please
a former teacher. As that teacher, Maria Lewis has been blamed for the
more painful aspect of it, especially the Johnsonian English. But aside
from the questionable matter of what the style might have been without the external influence of Maria Lewis, the basic elements present
in it were to remain constant to the end of George Eliot's writing days,
emerging most clearly in the *Westminster Review* essays, but extending also into the novels in the distinctive commentary which accompanies the narrative. The same psychological necessity which was
shaping her character (and hence destiny) in her Evangelical days was
also forging her style. Her prime need then as later was to conceal her
strong and important but self-forbidden aggressive tendencies. For
this purpose the long and usually well-balanced sentence served her
well, protectively enveloping the pith of the content, which is often
caustic, cynical, or sarcastic—even if at times rendered almost incomprehensible by an excessive burden of meaning. Often for the same reason the early letters are studded with quotations from the Bible, and
less frequently, the most respectable English classics. These quotations
are always applicable, often ingeniously so, and never merely pedantic;
they also conveniently shift the responsibility for their message from
the writer to their source. That source was to broaden considerably
over the years, but the use of references continued. The texts of the
novels are not interrupted by such quotations, but they are certainly in
evidence, especially as mottoes heading the chapters of the later works.

All style is based upon negative elements in that it is formed by the
selection (and thus also rejection) of structures and words available in
a given language and known to the user. However, one part of this
selecting-rejecting process is conscious and one part is not; and some

of it (especially that which is unconscious) is determined by motives which have nothing to do with writing, whereas some proceeds from the deliberate effort to achieve certain effects. It is impossible to know whether the unconscious element in the evolution of George Eliot's style was greater than commonly occurs in writing. In view of her unusually strong need for certain defenses—a need which comes most clearly to light during her Evangelical days—it might be at least conjectured that this was so. What is more certain is that she paid a price for the style which emerged as her own, for as it was being shaped, it was also determining she would never be a true wit or a genuine poet. There is abundant evidence that she possessed a keen, often biting, sense of humor, and there is equal evidence that she was capable of poetic sentiment. But by the time either the humor or the poesy reached paper, it had been transformed in the psychic workshop of her style so that it emerged expanded, lacking the unique kind of brevity requisite both for the brilliant joke and the poem, liberating much meaning while leaving it unexpressed. Except for the few unrelieved dramatic scenes in the novels, the only kind of brevity possible for George Eliot was that of condensation, which usually resulted in too heavy a burden of explicit content to be tolerated by either wit or poetry.

Needless to say, her mature style is freer of superfluities, more assured, and more efficient than in the earliest letters, in which the style is not yet pliable enough to fulfill all that she demanded of it. Her defenses overflow into content—unnecessary apologies for egoism, statements of exaggerated modesty, protestations of unworthiness. Even the grim prudery and piety are often defensive in nature. Undoubtedly these were also aimed at eliciting reassuring responses from Maria, who for a considerable length of time responded as desired. Any expression of disapproval from her would have ended the correspondence, as eventually it was to end the relationship. At no time are the letters from neophyte to religious monitor; they are from friend to friend, with only an occasional explicit reminder that the writer is the younger of the two. Such remarks as "I dare say . . . I shall scribble much nonsense but remember our letters were to be mere conversation, and if you were chatting with a silly girl of nineteen you would think yourself bound to excuse a considerable deal of froth" are rare and soon disappear altogether. More telltale is the fact that the writer has greater interest in talking about herself than in hearing news about her correspondent (although she dutifully asks for it, and no doubt Maria supplied it, for she too was having an unsettled time during the letter writing). That Maria encouraged such talk of self becomes clearer as the letters proceed, for the earliest form of apology for egotism finally gives way to remarks such as: "So much for self of which I believe you wish me to speak and so I will not even ask pardon."

Maria's importance to the young writer was not that of one actively involved in her life, but of a firm backdrop against which she could toss off her feelings and thoughts without the least fear of ruffling it. The danger implicit in the young girl's tacit assumption that as long as she herself knew she was sincere, a trusting friend could not possibly find reason to criticize or rebuke her, was to manifest itself (more disastrously for Maria than for herself), yet it gives to these earliest letters their peculiar value. "I generally let my feelings flow to the end of my pen as soon as I begin to write to you," she told Maria in 1840, and there is no reason to doubt the truth of this.

Because these letters are the least guarded of the extant ones she was ever to write, they clearly and often naïvely reveal the young George Eliot's serious inner strife and turmoil. As a good Evangelist, she did not dare dwell upon her anguish for fear of seeming self-pitying. But secure in her knowledge that Maria was already well aware of her fundamental unhappiness, she was safe in alluding to it in statements which could pass as impersonal. "I think," she wrote Maria in 1839, "there are few who know much of mental conflict that would not choose external trial in preference to it." How near she was to the breaking point is indicated by her susceptibility to hysterics. When once she ignored her own good advice to herself to abstain totally and attended a dancing party, she confessed to Maria that

> when I had been there some time the conviction that I was not in a situation to maintain the *Protestant* character of the true Christian, together with the oppressive noise that formed the accompaniment to the dancing, the sole amusement, produced first headache and then that most wretched and unpitied of afflictions, hysteria, so that I regularly disgraced myself.

Probably the scene she created did bring the startled dancers to a temporary halt and she may have felt some satisfaction as well as the disgrace she professed. Certainly there is no humility in her conclusion: "One good effect of a temporary annoyance and indisposition will be to render me more decided in rejecting all invitations of a dubious character."

There were calmer times, when renunciation brought a masochistic glow of pleasure sufficient to inspire her to poetry. Shortly after the London visit she sent Maria

> some doggrel [*sic*] lines, the crude fruit of a lonely walk last evening, when the words ["knowing that shortly I must put off this my tabernacle"—2 Pet. I. 14] of one of our martyrs occurred to me. You must be acquainted with the idiosyncrasy of my authorship, which

is that my effusions, once committed to paper, are like the laws of the Medes and Persians that alter not. My attempt at poetry will serve to amuse you, if no more, and you love a laugh so well that it would be ungenerous to withhold the occasion of one.

This first allusion to authorship, although far more heavy-handed, anticipates the juxtaposition of not quite credible modesty and unyielding self-assurance with which she would later respond to John Blackwood's criticism of her first fiction. The poem itself—"Farewell" —reveals a subtler contradiction. In it she takes leave of everything in "this bright, lovely world" with one exception, the Bible: "To thee I say not, of earth's gifts alone, / Farewell!" What the poem actually discloses is a sad reluctance to part from the known world of the senses; and even the reason for the sweeping farewell—Heaven—is conceived as a place of sensual delight: "There shall my newborn senses find new joy, / New sounds, new sights my eyes and ears employ . . ." Somewhat surprisingly, reading is included among the natural objects which appeal to the senses (not the intellect), and her negative tribute to books (no doubt novels, now sternly censored by herself) indicates the intensity with which she had read them:

> Books that have been to me as chests of gold,
> Which, miser like, I secretly have told,
> And for them love, health, friendship, peace have sold,
> Farewell!

Presumably Maria assured her that "Farewell" had not made her laugh, for it appeared in the *Christian Observer*, January 1840, under the initials M.A.E. The scrupulous editor was perturbed over the lurking worldliness in this poem about other-worldliness and added an admonishing reminder that M.A.E. would not need even the Bible in the New Jerusalem: "The Bible is god's gift, but not for heaven's use." The conflict underlying the poem was to emerge more openly a year or so later when she wrote Maria about the natural sky: "The beautiful heavens that we have lately enjoyed awaken in me an indescribable sensation of exultation in existence and aspiration after all that is suited to engage our immaterial nature; but I feel that this is not pure, not chastened, and therefore not to be indulged."

Ambition was stirring too, as indicated by her having sought publication of her "doggrel lines." "Farewell" apparently had a lasting meaning for George Eliot as her first work to appear in print. Understandably, she never included it in her collected work; yet forty years later she remembered its publication well enough to mention it to Cross, who diligently searched for and found it in the old issue of the *Christian Observer*. But the restrictions which she had imposed upon herself, as well as the Evangelical framework, left her only a very narrow scope for ambition; whatever she did would have to be construed as a "good work." Finally she lighted upon a project of ponderous scholarship, one in which imagination could have no place but which would require a disciplined submission to facts. In March 1840, she outlined her plan to Maria. She would draw up a series of perpendicular columns that would

> successively contain, the Roman Emperors with their dates, the political and religious state of the Jews, the bishops, remarkable men and events in the several churches, ... the aspect of heathenism and Judaism toward Christianity, the chronology of the Apos-(tolical) and Patristical writings, schisms and heresies, General Councils, eras of corruption ... and ... possibly an application of the Apocalyptic prophecies. ...

This chart would break off at 606, "when Mahommedanism became a besom of destruction in the hand of the Lord, and completely altered the aspect of Ecclesiastical Hist[or]y." As she told Maria, it was an "airy project," by which she meant that it was as yet in her head only, although she had already explored the possibilities of publication. She had been "encouraged to believe that it will answer my purpose to print it. The profits arising from its sale, if any, will go partly to Attleborough Church and partly to a favorite object of my own. Mrs. Newdegate is very anxious that I should do thus. ..." She thereby outlined the contents of an ecclesiastical chart and simultaneously exhibited a pattern that she was to use frequently years later. Her desire for publication was successfully rationalized, and she had made it appear that the source of motivation was external rather than within herself.

Even so, she did not get on with the work, and when a few months later a more industrious compiler appeared in print with a chart which rendered hers superfluous, she admitted that hers was still an "airy vision." She confesses to Maria that she imparts this news "without one sigh," but she perhaps over-protests: "I console all my little regrets by thinking that what is thus evidenced to be a desideratum has been executed much better than if left to my slow fingers and slower head." Her fingers had indeed been slow. The procrastination no doubt proceeded from several causes—her already crowded schedule, her disturbance over Isaac's engagement, her lack of a deeply felt interest in the project. Yet it is also possible that this was one of the first instances in which her fear of success as well as of failure was doing its insidious work by throttling her will to act.

Although she had done nothing to bring her idea for the ecclesiastical chart to fruition, she had become increasingly absorbed in language study, and as she considered this "laboriously doing nothing," she made lightning progress in it. "I am beguiled by the fascinations that the study of languages has for my capricious mind," she wrote to Maria in May 1840, "and could e'en give myself up to making discoveries in the world of words." She admitted that the "fascinations" were not unmixed with romantic sentiments for her tutor: "My pilot too is anything but uninteresting, all external grace and mental power, but 'Cease ye from man' is engraved on my amulet." Her interest in words survived her interest in the man, and over a year later she writes Maria of a discovery most writers make during their apprenticeship: words are obstacles as well as essential tools and must in part be transcended. "When a sort of haziness comes over the mind making one feel weary of articulated or written signs of ideas does not the notion of a less laborious mode of communication, of a perception approaching more nearly to intuition seem attractive?" Then she adds:

> Nathless I love words; they are the quoits, the bows, the staves that furnish the gymnasium of the mind. Without them in our present condition, our intellectual strength would have no implements. I have been rather humbled in thinking that if I were thrown on an uncivilised island and had to form a literature for its inhabitants from my own mental stock how very fragmentary would be the information with which I could furnish them. It would be a good mode of testing one's knowledge, to set one's self the task of writing sketches of all subjects that have entered into one's studies, entirely from the chronicles of memory.

This would seem to be an exploratory statement. It is doubtful whether she realized how her subject had shifted by the end of her paragraph—from "perception approaching more nearly to intuition" to "the gymnasium of the mind" and "intellectual strength." Was intuitive perception desirable only as a means of grasping recorded fact; were the "sketches" written "entirely from the chronicles of memory" to provide only a literature of information? Quite likely she had been drifting toward a "shadowy conception" of writing a novel, as is implied by one sentence in her 1857 summary-statement "How I Came to Write Fiction": "It had always been a vague dream of mine that some time or other I might write a novel, and my shadowy conception of what the novel was to be, varied, of course, from one epoch of my life to another." She surely would have considered her Evangelical years as "one epoch" in her life, and it is clear that she was more excited about something besides what she actually wrote out for Maria, for she added, " . . . I can fancy you shaking your head and saying to yourself 'This poor girl's brain is fast losing its little specific gravity and is flying off to Milton's Limbo to keep company with all "the unaccomplished works of Nature's hand, abortive monstrous or unkindly mixed." ' " The next morning she was uncertain that her retraction had been emphatic enough and so added a postscript: "I have reopened my letter, my dear friend, conscious that it was written in an evening's delirium to which I am subject, and which this 'sober-suited morn' has dissipated."

She did not yet dare admit openly to herself, let alone to Maria, that she was even dreaming of writing fiction. In an earlier letter to Maria —that of 16 March 1839—she had ruthlessly censored almost all imaginative literature, and her intellectual stand on that matter had not changed. This letter is of special interest in that it reveals how widely read she was in fiction. More importantly it is, with some translating, an astonishingly accurate prophecy of the kind of fiction she herself was eventually to write. Apparently she and Maria had agreed upon a set topic for discussion—the expedience of reading works of fiction—but before plunging into her negative arguments, she makes a few reservations. She does not intend to "legislate" for the compulsively omnivorous reader, and she does not mean to repudiate "standard works whose contents are matter of constant reference, and the names of whose heroes and heroines briefly and therefore conveniently describe characters and ideas. Such are Don Quixote, Butler's Hudibras, Robinson Crusoe, Gil Blas, Byron's Poetical romances. . . ." These, *always providing our leisure is not circumscribed* by duty within narrow bounds, we should I think qualify ourselves to understand." Then, of course, there is the inevitable problem of Shakespeare: he "has a higher claim . . . on our attention but we have need of as nice a power of distillation as the bee to suck nothing but honey from his pages."

Aside from these qualifications, what reasons could possibly exist for the reading of fiction? Does the mind require discipline? Then better to read history. Entertainment? Relaxation? But

> "Truth is strange—stranger than fiction." When a person has exhausted the wonders of truth, there is no other resort than fiction; till then I cannot imagine how the adventures of some phantom conjured up by fancy can be more entertaining than the transactions of real specimens of human nature, from which we may safely draw inferences. . . . The real secret of the relaxation talked of is one that would not generally be avowed; but an appetite that wants seasoning of a certain kind cannot be indicative of health. Religious novels are more hateful to me than merely worldly ones. They are a sort of Centaur or Mermaid and like other monsters that we do not know how to class should be destroyed for the public good as soon as born. . . . Domestic fictions as they come within the range of imitation seem more dangerous. For my part I am ready to sit down and weep at the impossibility of my understanding or barely knowing even a fraction of the sum of objects

that present themselves for our contemplation in books and in life. Have I then any time to spend on things that never existed?

The real premise for this attack upon fiction was an acknowledgment of its tremendous power, which she had already personally felt.

> I am I confess not an impartial member of a jury in this case for I owe the culprits a grudge for injuries inflicted on myself. I shall carry to my grave the mental diseases with which they have contaminated me. When I was quite a little child I could not be satisfied with the things around me; I was constantly living in a world of my own creation, and was quite contented to have no companions that I might be left to my own musings and imagine scenes in which I was chief actress. Conceive what a character novels would give to these Utopias. I was early supplied with them by those who kindly sought to gratify my appetite for reading and of course I made use of the materials they supplied for building my castles in the air. But it may be said, "No one ever dreamed of recommending children to read them. . . ." I answer that men and women are but children of a larger growth; they are still imitative beings. . . . We are active beings too. We are each one of the Dramatis personae in some play on the stage of life—hence our actions have their share in the effects of our reading.

Memory has many faces, and this one is in part a defense against the hurt over Isaac's "desertion." As a little child she had been "quite contented to have no companions," a theme which she was to re-emphasize in a sonnet she wrote and copied out for Maria a few months after the essay-letter. In this poem she tells how "Oft, when a child, while wand'ring far alone, / That none might rouse me from my waking dream," or disperse her fanciful visions with "a disenchanting earthly tone," she would imagine that she saw in the distance an unusually charming spot, only to discover upon reaching it that it was no different from any other. Hence the moral:

> To my poor thought, an apt though simple trope
> Of life's dull path and earth's deceitful hope.

Yet despite the conspicuous absence of Isaac from the sonnet and the memory as recorded in the letter, both anticipate the stricture on imagination which was to appear in "Brother and Sister"—that imagination is egotistical and delusional. Nonetheless, it continued to torment her and became one of the major "sins" needing confession. "My imagination is an enemy," she told Maria a year after having written the sonnet,

> that must be cast down ere I can enjoy peace or exhibit uniformity of character. I know not which of its caprices I have most to dread —that which incites it to spread sackcloth "above, below, around,"

or that which makes it "cheat my eye with blear illusion, and beget strange dreams" of excellence and beauty in beings and things of only "working day" price.

Confession was not effective. She could explain very well why she *ought* to trample down imagination, but she had not yet touched upon the reason for her fear of it; nor had she yet stumbled upon the truth that imagination could be something more than egocentric daydreaming, that it was a power which could, at the right touch, ally itself with and thus reinforce sympathy and empathy. To her at this time imagination implied an admission of dissatisfaction ("I could not be satisfied with the things around me"), a turning away from reality ("I was constantly living in a world of my own creation"), and exhibitionism ("I was chief actress"). The first two factors were self-evident faults to her; it is improbable that she was aware of the significance of the words—or should one say form of art?—she chose by which to express figuratively her concept of the daydream: acting, drama. The same figure of speech thrusts itself forward at the end of the passage, although the subject of daydreams has been put aside: "We are each one of the Dramatis personae in some play on the stage of life." An image so commonplace as to be trite, yet in her instance the comparison comes near to revealing why she was so determined to seal off her imagination. Being an actress implies walking fearlessly on a stage and "dramatizing," and it also implies having an audience. The crucial point does not concern literal acting, although there is the reference to her having impressed the Griff household and the aunts by acting charades with Isaac. For whatever reason, Cross inserts this brief note immediately after his introduction of Maria Lewis, and one wonders if her new-found friendship with Maria had not given her a confidence which temporarily broke through her growing self-repression. Be that as it may, it is probable that the charade-acting did not continue beyond one holiday; it does not tally with other anecdotes of this period which stress her dislike of fun and normal entertainment. The fragment becomes intriguing, however, if considered along with the fact that Gwendolen Harleth is acting out a tableau when she has the one attack of terror that justifies George Eliot's explaining its origin and nature in the detail she does.

More illuminating because more traceable are the remarkable and seemingly nonrational changes which her attitude toward music—or, rather, toward the performance of it—underwent. After remarking that she "very early became possessed with the idea that she was going to be a personage in the world," Cross relates: "When she was only four years old she recollected playing on the piano, of which she did not know one note, in order to impress the servant with a proper no-

tion of her acquirements and generally distinguished position." Yet
by the time she reached the Misses Franklin's school, she was no longer
capable of being a fearless performer, although then she both knew
and loved music. For this evidence Cross quotes from a reminiscent
essay by "a lady whose mother was at school with Mary Ann Evans":

> Her enthusiasm for music was already very strongly marked, and
> her music-master, a much-tried man, suffering from the irritability
> incident to his profession, reckoned on his hour with her as a
> refreshment to his wearied nerves, and soon had to confess that he
> had no more to teach her. In connection with this proficiency in
> music, my mother recalls her sensitiveness at that time as being
> painfully extreme. When there were visitors, Miss Evans, as the best
> performer in the school, was sometimes summoned to the parlor
> to play for their amusement, and though suffering agonies from
> shyness and reluctance, she obeyed with all readiness, but, on being
> released, my mother has often known her to rush to her room and
> throw herself on the floor in an agony of tears.

That her excessive shyness was the not unusual defense against a
strong aggressive tendency is indicated by its hardening into contemptuous disdain for all those who *did* perform. Hence her caustic description of the choir of St. Paul's. Three months after the London visit, she
listened to an oratorio in Coventry—"the last I think I shall attend,"
she wrote Maria, and then attempted to mitigate her high-handed
attitude by absurd professions of her own inadequacy:

> I am not fitted to decide on the question of the propriety or lawful-
> ness of such exhibitions of talent and so forth because I have no
> soul for music. . . . I am a tasteless person but it would not cost me
> any regrets if the only music heard in our land were that of strict
> worship, nor can I think a pleasure that involves the devotion of all
> the time and powers of an immortal being to the acquirement of an
> expertness in so useless . . . an accomplishment can be quite pure
> or elevating in its tendency.

Describing the same oratorio to a younger friend, Martha Jackson, she
felt no need to guard against appearing intolerably critical and was
still more vehement in her denunciation:

> I think nothing can justify the using of an intensely interesting and
> solemn passage of Scripture, as a rope-dancer uses her rope, or as
> a sculptor the pedestal on which he places the statue, that is alone
> intended to elicit admiration. . . . I ask myself can it be desirable,
> and would it be consistent with millenial [*sic*] holiness for a human
> being to devote the time and energies that are barely sufficient
> for real exigencies on acquiring expertness in trills, cadences, etc.?

The only argument that seems to me to have any speciousness in favor of such exhibitions of skill is, that without them we should never have an opportunity of appreciating the beautiful powers of the human voice when carried to their highest point of improve-ability. But by once admitting such reasoning we disarm ourselves of every weapon against opera dancing, horse racing, nay, even against intemperance. . . .

Biographers who have taken note of these remarks have been non-plussed by them. In the words of Sir Leslie Stephen: "The religious theory is . . . characteristic; but it is singular that a woman who was to find one of her greatest delights in music, and who was already skilled in the art, should think herself devoid of the capacity." Sir Leslie did not enjoy being nonplussed, and he dismisses the matter somewhat flippantly—"possibly, the singing at Coventry was out of tune"—although he had seen the letter to Martha Jackson (not printed by Cross), which makes it doubly clear that it is not the *quality* of the performance which is being criticized. In fact, it is not far-fetched to believe that the better the performance, the more vituperative would have been her reaction.

Even Cross was puzzled:

The above remarks [to Maria] on oratorio are the more surprising because, two years later, when Miss Evans went to the Birmingham festival, in September, 1840, previous to her brother's marriage, she was affected to an extraordinary degree, so much so that Mrs. Isaac Evans—then Miss Rawlins—told me that the attention of people sitting near was attracted by her hysterical sobbing. And in all her later life music was one of the chiefest delights to her, and especially oratorio.

Then without further transition he quotes this bit about Maggie and music from *The Mill on the Floss*:

Not that her enjoyment of music was of the kind that indicates a great specific talent; it was rather that her sensibility to the supreme excitement of music was only one form of that passionate sensibility which belonged to her whole nature, and made her faults and virtues all merge in each other—made her affections sometimes an impatient demand, but also prevented her vanity from taking the form of mere feminine coquetry and device, and gave it the poetry of ambition. [Book VI, chapter 6]

Time and time again Cross reveals great sensitivity and intuitive sure-ness in selecting passages from the novels which most certainly do seem to apply to George Eliot personally, and this instance is no exception. But he leaped ahead too far in time to make this passage pertinent in the 1838–40 context into which he attempts to force it, for it contains words and ideas that she could not at this period have admitted described her: "passionate sensibility," "vanity," "poetry of ambition." Still, Cross is to be thanked for spotlighting this passage by quoting it where he does, for the inclusion of those very words signifies how the "sins" she was struggling with at this time were unified in her love of music and thus explains why her conflicting reaction to it roused the deepest forces within her being.

As George Eliot herself makes clear in her indignant remarks to both Maria Lewis and Martha Jackson, this reaction was not to the music itself but to the necessarily exhibitionistic nature of the performance of it, a small but important qualification that both Sir Leslie Stephen and Cross overlooked. It seems likely that her strong defense against this was first broken through at the oratorio she attended in Birmingham with her brother and future sister-in-law, when, as Cross was informed, she gave way to "hysterical sobbing." Obviously she was moved by more than the music alone. The intensity of her response was no doubt provoked by hearing the oratorio in the presence of Isaac and Sarah Rawlins, whose approaching wedding would mean for her not only the final loss of Isaac but removal from beloved Griff. Unlike her earlier hysterics at the dancing party, this experience was a true release, a catharsis. Of it she wrote to Maria her first natural statements about music (without mentioning her emotional reaction): "I heard the Messiah on Thursday morning at Birmingham and some beautiful selections from other Oratorios of Handel and Haydn on Friday. With a stupid, drowsy sensation produced by standing sentinel over damson cheese and a warm stove I cannot do better than ask you to read if accessible Wordsworth's short poem on the Power of Sound with which I have just been delighted." As Gordon Haight suggests in his note to the last sentence, "Stanzas 13 and 14 representing all sounds as thanksgiving to the Creator must have appealed particularly to GE." But these stanzas would have told her nothing new; there are quieter lines in the poem which must have stood out to her with unique meaning in this dawn of her new and more harmonious way of thinking and feeling. In Stanza X, for example, Wordsworth reminds one that the sounds of life are music too ("To life, to *life* give back thine ear: / Ye who are longing to be rid / Of fable . . . "), but so diverse and vast in scope that he asks in Stanza XIII:

> Ye wandering Utterances, has earth no scheme,
> No scale of moral music—to unite
> Powers that survive but in the faintest dream
> Of memory?

This was what she now was beginning consciously to seek, to become a unified sensibility, her powers liberated and at peace with one another—what Maggie had to a certain extent achieved through music in the passage to which Cross calls attention. Even earlier, when only thirteen, Maggie had had "an ear straining after dreamy music that dies away and would not come near to her; a blind, unconscious yearning for something that would link together the wonderful impressions of this mysterious life, and give her soul a sense of home in it" (Book III, chapter 5).

The Birmingham experience was a lasting one. Not surprisingly, "especially oratorio" (as Cross says) became George Eliot's favorite form of music and music itself "one of the chiefest delights to her." She was never again to regress to the bondage of disgust over musical performance, and her last novel, *Daniel Deronda*, is saturated with music, not merely descriptions of its sounds but minute observation of what the discipline of its performance meant to several of the major characters. Music also became increasingly intertwined with her personal life until the very end, although it is doubtful that she herself ever performed without exerting restraint. While she played the piano often, it was only for herself or her most intimate friends. The same was true of singing. In recalling her singing voice, Herbert Spencer— one of her closest friends when she boarded with the Chapmans in London—*thought* that it was "of rather low pitch" and "naturally strong," but then he adds: "On this past point I ought to have a more definite impression, for in those days we occasionally sang together; but the habit of subduing her voice was so constant, that I suspect its real power was rarely if ever heard."

Music provides a relatively direct example of the prohibitive fear of exhibitionism because it normally requires a live audience, whereas imagination—the kind in which the daydreamer is the central character—holds only an imagined audience and so, rationally speaking, should be safe from this restriction. Unfortunately, the human psyche is not this simple: what is imagined can be more compelling than that which is externally present especially when it is accompanied by an urge for expression. Still more certain, the dreamer is not at liberty to select his audience: it must consist of those he most *wishes* to please, not those he feels most capable of pleasing. In actual theater, an approving and empathetic audience does much to ensure a satisfactory performance. Similarly, the private audience in imagination is a large part of the source of the unique kind of courage needed to convince the artist, in whatever medium, that he can breathe life into a seemingly arbitrary array of inanimate material. Thus a chasm separates the would-be but frustrated artist from the productive one—perhaps an even greater chasm than that between the non-artist and the artist: a rich fantasy life, talent, and even the conscious desire to execute may be meaningless without the inner sanction liberated by the private audience. The yet-untested writer might sit forever before blank paper, unconvinced that to put down marks on that paper might not merely despoil it. Or if he should make an attempt, he discovers that what he had most needed is suddenly gone, just as the dreamer's censor at times most annoyingly switches off all the lights and sound effects at the very moment of dénouement in the ego drama.

Figuratively speaking, George Eliot sat so poised for many years. Who had been her first imagined audience? All evidence would point to Isaac or possibly on a still deeper level her mother; but the influence of Isaac, like that of music, is more traceable. Even Cross, whether by conscious association or not, states in the sentence immediately following the anecdote of her pounding on the piano at the age of four to impress the servant: "This was the time when the love for her brother grew into the child's affection." As we know through her own idealized recollection in "Brother and Sister," this was also the time when she not only thought it necessary to give up her world of imagination to gain Isaac's companionship, but (according to her memory) earned his anger whenever she slipped into this world of her own accord. As her audience, he would have been at worst disapproving and at best wholly indifferent. This may well account for the unexpected intensity of her reaction against her own novel reading as recorded in her earlier memory and written to Maria: "I shall carry to my grave the mental diseases with which they [novels] have contaminated me." Somewhat understandably, this sentence so startled Cross that he deleted it. It is also in the same tone as the surprising line in "Farewell," which was written only a few months after the letter to Maria: "And for [books, I] love, health, friendship, peace have sold. . . ." It is clear that at this time she thought of novel reading as having fed her enemy, imagination.

When the force of her fear is considered, her victory over it must be seen as a great achievement. In time she no longer thought of imagination as merely self-centered wishful thinking; rather, it became for her the power to discern, empathize with, and reproduce the actual drama of the real world. This view of the function of imagination is apparent in much of her *Westminster* reviewing, but it is stated most explicitly in the "False Testimonials" chapter of *Theophrastus Such*. Here she criticizes the popular *mis*conception that imagination is "a very usual lack of discriminating perception . . . unchecked by the troublesome need of veracity." A truly fine and genuine imagination —she continues—"is always based on a keen vision, a keen consciousness of what *is*, and carries the store of definite knowledge as material for the construction of its inward visions." She had been remarkably near this concept even in 1840, when she wrote Maria that imagination was her enemy because it at times caused her to see "excellence and beauty in beings and things of only 'working day' price." Yet this is exactly what she was to ask her reader to do with her in "Amos Barton."

In 1840 she could not trust this glimmering of vision. Then imagination was the deadly enemy because she associated it with egotism; it pampered that major sin and kept it alive, despite her rigorous efforts to smother it and its offspring such as ambition and love of praise. She conscientiously obeyed the Evangelical command to confess, although as early as 1839 it is clear that she was uneasily aware her confessions touched nothing vital within her. In a letter of that year she wrote Maria:

> The self-deceptive practice of substituting confession for amend-ment is not peculiar to the disciples of the Pope—I am continually detecting myself in its commission. . . . There is a species of frank-ness and candor very inconsiderately lauded, which often has its source in either a proud indifference to censure, a deadness to moral distinctions, or still more frequently an ostentatious affecta-tion of humility. This for myself. No one ought to wince more under the application of that probe than myself.

She was equally candid in writing to her Aunt and Uncle Samuel Evans, but tuned her confessions to their more emotional form of piety. Somewhat earlier in the same year she had told her aunt:

> I feel that my besetting sin is the one of all others most destroying, as it is the fruitful parent of them all, Ambition, a desire insatiable for the esteem of my fellow creatures. This seems the centre whence all my actions proceed. This seems the great stumbling block in my path Zion-ward. . . . I make the most humiliating and appalling confessions with little or no corresponding feeling.

A year later she reiterated this in a somewhat different vein: "I earnestly desire a spirit of childlike humility that shall make me willing to be lightly esteemed among men; this is the opposite of my besetting sin, which is an ever struggling ambition."

Small wonder that confession for her at this time held none of the therapeutic value it undeniably had for many adherents of Evangeli-calism, for confession—like the ego drama of imagination—requires an audience. And although within the framework of her professed religion she had an omniscient one in God, it is as doubtful that she was ever convinced He heard *her* word to Him as it is that she ever heard a word from Him spoken directly to her. It is not improbable that Isaac had stepped into her private inner world as her confessor, and that his indifferent or disapproving presence nullified the effectiveness of her confession much as it blocked her imagination; for what she most needed in these unhappy years was inner defense against him, not an abject display of her faults. Near the end of her life, when she had come to terms with her bitterest memories through writing, she was to remark in *Daniel Deronda*:

> It is hard to say how much we could forgive ourselves if we were secure from judgment by another whose opinion is the breathing-medium of all our joy; who brings to us with close pressure and immediate sequence that judgment of the Invisible and Universal which self-flattery and the world's tolerance would easily melt and disperse. In this way our brother may be in the stead of God to us, and his opinion, which pierced even to the joints and marrow, may be our virtue in the making. [Book VII, chapter 7]

In contrast, at the beginning of her writing career—long before this deeper recognition could occur and shortly after she had experienced the regenerative power of confession between herself and Lewes of what they then thought to be their wasted lives—she had made an almost contradictory statement:

> The impulse to confession almost always requires the presence of a fresh ear and a fresh heart: and in our moments of spiritual need, the man to whom we have no tie but our common nature, seems nearer to us than mother, brother, or friend. Our daily familiar life is but a hiding of ourselves from each other behind a screen of trivial words and deeds, and those who sit with us at the same hearth are often the farthest off from the deep human soul within us, full of unspoken evil and unacted good. ["Janet's Repentance," chapter 16]

This observation has its own significance in the linking of mother, brother, and friend—as well as in the omission of sister.

B<small>Y THE TIME</small> G<small>EORGE</small> E<small>LIOT HAD FACED THE DISCOURAGING</small> fact that she was unmoved by her own confessions, Maria Lewis was the only friend close enough to be the recipient of more meaningful confidences, but by then she had mentally moved too far away from the older woman to give them to her. In fact, George Eliot kept her changed attitude to herself. Indeed, almost as if in some compensation to Maria for this secrecy (which, strictly judged, was a form of duplicity, as she perhaps later realized), she initiated a new stage in their relationship which on the surface seemed to signify a still closer intimacy but which actually intensified the screen between them. In October of 1840, inspired by the fact that Martha Jackson had bestowed upon her the flower name of Clematis (meaning Mental Beauty), she consulted her newly acquired floral dictionary and gave to Maria the name Veronica (Fidelity in Friendship).

The letters change in tone almost immediately, and remarks such as this one of 11 March 1841 are not uncommon: "Your letter this morning, my Veronica, was sweet to me as the early incense of the jasmine, and sent a thrill from my heart to my finger ends. . . ." The letter ends: "Your affectionate, / Clematis." The adoption of make-believe names gave the friendship a new impetus which temporarily put Evangelicalism aside. How soon and willingly Maria entered into the new current of feeling is suggested by a quotation from one of her letters with which George Eliot begins hers of 20 May 1841: "Is there no quiet lane in my Clematis's vicinity whose banks rival the intensest sapphire of the firmament from the luxuriance of my emblems, admonishing her to emulate the fidelity of which their name and colour are the representatives?" The answer read: "Yes, my Veronica, there is such a lane, and I have not only gazed at and gathered your bewitching namesakes, but I have talked of you more than, considering one's friends are multiplicands of self, an honest eschewing of egotism would allow. Last evening I mentioned you to my neighbour who is growing into the more precious character of a friend. . . ."

This must have been most gratifying to Maria when she received it, yet the whole of the long letter contains several warning signals: the neighbor was Mrs. Pears, Charles Bray's sister, and it was through her that George Eliot (now living on the outskirts of Coventry) was to make the acquaintance of the Brays and the Hennells, who would supplant Maria's role in her life. Although she was preoccupied emotionally and physically with Isaac's approaching marriage, there is no sign of her anguish, no confession, no otherwise self-revealing remarks. Rather, she expresses concern over Maria's problems in seeking a new position and concludes with an apology for not writing more and a hint that Maria need not respond at length: "I have a world more to say . . . but I really think even your affection will not make the task of deciphering my letter easy. . . . Adieu my dear Veronica. Write me a scrap when you have time and then you shall hear again from your / Clematis."

The next letter begins with a matter-of-fact excuse for not having written sooner: "The whole of last week was devoted to a bridesmaid's duties, . . ." but closes with a small revelation of her turmoil: "Write my dear Veronica . . . and you shall hear again if she still live from /

your faithful and affectionate, / Clematis." In the following letter, written ten days after her brother's marriage, she states in an offhand way: "By the bye I have not yet told you that Isaac is married, that I officiated as bridesmaid and that the pair are now in Scotland . . ." and ends with the kind of light apology that was becoming typical: "This is not a letter . . . it is a hybrid between that and a note and is half folly and half feeling with a little matter of fact and so a good type of its parent." It was too much to expect Maria to remain an unruffled backdrop for the shift in relationship signaled by the change in tone and content of these letters. She was no longer the confidante but, rather, the one in need of reassurance. In the letter responding to the news of Isaac's marriage, Maria asks for advice, the specific nature of which can be only conjectured, and receives some pious guidance that once might well have been written by herself to her young friend: "In reply to the query at the close of your letter I give an unhesitating No! unless very rare conditions be annexed. Your feelings on the subject are such as God approves."

Protestations of affection continue, but they betray the fact that Maria is no longer the center of George Eliot's emotional life:

> How should I love to join you at Margate now that you are alone! A few days of conversation would I believe set my crazy body right. In consequence of its slight ailments I have of late felt a depression that has disordered the vision of my mind's eye, and made me *alive* to what is certainly a *fact* though my imagination when I am in health is an adept at concealing it, that I am *alone* in the world. . . . I mean that I have no one who enters into my pleasures or my griefs, no one with whom I can pour out my soul, no one with the same yearnings the same temptations the same delights as myself.

But had not Maria been led to think of herself as just that—the one to whom the writer of this letter could pour out her soul? Apparently the letter aroused doubts in Maria as to her own right to express herself spontaneously, for three weeks later George Eliot writes in obvious response to some apologetic remark: "There is another truth I would have you enter on your creed which does not seem yet to be there—viz. that to receive the mere *outpouring of feeling* from you is my chief consolation under inability to assist you more validly. Ergo *never* apologize for details about yourself. . . ." And in the postscript to this letter she adds an answer to an equally obvious question:

> Yes, I firmly believe our love is of a nature not to be changed by place or time, and though my path on earth should lie between the tropics and yours should still remain among these bleak latitudes, I humbly hope and pray that when the poor modicum of

three score years and ten or far less is consumed we shall enter
on a condition whose moral elements are all congenial to love. . . .

That this exaggerated declaration did not convince Maria is suggested by remarks in George Eliot's next letter: "I want a letter from
you all about yourself with a retraction of a very ambiguous reply to
my statement of accounts between us. You do not really mean to refuse
me a visit at least at Christmas?" The remainder of this letter is given
up to the quoting of verses ("My head and heart are both so sadly that
I am reduced to copying to fill my sheet") and an unabashed expression of delight in the October weather ("Delicious Autumn! my very
soul is wedded to it, and if I were a bird I would fly about the earth
seeking the successive autumns"). It closes: "I will sicken you or infect
you . . . so dearest Veronica, I will assure you that you are continually
sharing my warmest love and deliver you by a good bye from more of
this trash." A letter written two weeks later concludes with an abrupt
postscript: "May I call you Maria? I feel our friendship too serious
a thing to endure even an artificial name. And restore to me Mary
Ann." Without questioning the sincerity of the reasoning, one senses
that Maria (as Veronica) had been too demanding and that George
Eliot was withdrawing.

Restoring the real names produced in Maria an effect opposite to
what had been desired, for in her next letter George Eliot makes no
effort to conceal her annoyance:

> You are veritably an overreaching friend, my dear Maria, not
> content with my scribbling a couple of sheets to every quarter of the
> moon, you even insist on dictating the subjects of the same, and the
> one you now impose on me is at once so sterile, so incomprehensible
> and so unfascinating that I should be quite justified in refusing to
> descant *thereon*. If you complain that my letters become increasingly
> illegible, just take into consideration the necessary effect of having
> to write a few pages almost daily. This has been the case with me of
> late, and I am likely to be more and more busy, if I succeed in a
> project that is just now occupying my thoughts and feelings.

Any explanation of the "project" is almost insultingly absent, and
she even resents Maria's expressed fears over her health which, however, she is forced to admit she herself has "been culpable in raising
from a foolish habit both in writing and discourse of saying *all* the
truth. What mortal has not occasionally headaches? and if there are
exceptions in this case, I am sure there are none who have not sometimes heartaches." Then follows the unusual admission for George
Eliot of enjoying the blessings of both good health and prosperity, and
this is concluded by a sentence which was no doubt meant to reflect

unfavorably upon Maria's sobriety: "Not that a wise and grateful reception of blessings obliges us to stretch our faces to the length of one of Cromwell's 'Barebones,' nor to shun that joyous bird-like enjoyment of things . . . that is distinct from levity and voluptuousness." She closes with "Love and *practically* remember / Your Affectionate / Mary Ann."

Maria did not respond to this letter, and would perhaps have been spared much future pain had George Eliot not repented and written her—although, considering the circumstances, her opening is somewhat cruel: "Like a true friend, my ain dearie, I am delighted to plunge you in blushes for not writing to me on Saturday by sending you a second packet within the week." Ostensibly this letter was written to inclose information concerning a position as governess she thought might interest Maria. But it also contains what might be construed as an apology: "Tell me what you think of the matter [the position] to-morrow, if possible and also tell me that you forgive my —something between brusquerie and confusion in my last letter."

To this Maria did reply, apparently questioning the desirability of her as yet unsettled Christmas visit. After allowing "eight or nine" days to elapse, George Eliot wrote back: "Think—is there any *conceivable* alteration in me that would prevent your coming to me at Christmas? I long to have a friend such as you are I think I may say alone to me, to unburthen every thought and difficulty—for I am still a solitary, though near a city." This seemed a promise of the renewal of the old intimacy, and Maria could not resist it. Besides, it is possible that she had by now detected (or learned from some source) the drastic change in religious views which underlay the change in tone of the letters and had some hope of guiding her erstwhile pupil back into the fold.

Although it is not clear that she visited specifically on Christmas Day, it is known from Robert Evans's Journal that she was present on that fateful Sunday, 2 January 1842, when George Eliot announced her decision not to attend church: "Went to Trinity Church in the forenoon. Miss Lewis went with me. Mary Ann did not go. I stopd the sacrament and Miss Lewis stopd also." Had Maria's presence—symbolizing as it did all that she was rejecting—goaded her into this defiant stand? Or had she dared assume that Maria, as trusting friend, would accept even this and serve as an intermediary between herself and her shocked and indignant father? It is probable that Maria did help mollify Robert Evans at least temporarily, for she remained until (or returned on) January 14, when he recorded: "Miss Lewis is here and she is waiting to go by the Mail to Nuneaton to take possession of her new school at Nuneaton." Although she could not accept George

Eliot's position uncritically, she had no intention that it should rupture the friendship. There is no sign that they were involved in bitter argument during the January visit (or visits). In fact, the next letter to Maria, that of 18 February, indicates that whatever talk had passed between them had cleared the way for George Eliot to drop all pretense and to cease to couch her thoughts (and hence somewhat distort them) in Evangelical terms.

This letter amounts to a manifesto of an almost complete transvaluation of principles, although the introduction has an innocent appearance until seen in the context of the entire letter:

> How go you for society, for communion of spirit, the drop of nectar in the cup of mortals? But why do I say the drop? The mind that feels its value will get large draughts from some source if denied it in the most commonly chosen way.

The mind that feels its value: this strikes a decidedly different note from that of the self-depreciating modesty of the earlier letters. Ten lines of her own poetry follow, significantly in tribute to sympathy— the first important reference in her correspondence to the power which eventually was to be uniquely associated with her both as person and novelist. The significance is made still more apparent by the comment that follows the poem:

> Beautiful ego-ism! to quote one's own. But where is not this same ego? The martyr at the stake seeks its gratification as much as the court sycophant, the difference lying in the comparative dignity and beauty of the two egos. People absurdly talk of self-denial—why there is none in Virtue to a being of moral excellence—the greatest torture to such a soul would be to run counter to the dictates of conscience, to wallow in the slough of meanness, deception, revenge or sensuality.

Then, no doubt as a shock absorber for Maria, she adds somewhat anti-climactically: "This was Paul's idea in the 1st chapter of 2d Ep[istle] to Timothy (I think that is the passage)." It is; but if the thought actually had an external source it was, as Gordon Haight notes, more likely to have been Charles Bray's *Philosophy of Necessity*.

More likely still was that her new insight had been gained through personal experience, for she was in the midst of what with grim humor she was to call the "Holy War," the complex reverberations of her having refused to attend church. Her unusual association of "the martyr at the stake" and the "court sycophant" was based on subterranean logic, although she probably did not realize it at the time. (Later, she was to become increasingly aware of the different levels of meaning in the seemingly casual choice of words. "Watch your own speech," she says in *The Mill on the Floss* [Book VI, chapter 6], "and notice how it is guided by your less conscious purposes. . . .") On the one hand, she had maintained her defiant stand and had some reason to think of herself as a martyr. Only a short time before this letter to Maria she had written less restrainedly to Mrs. Pears about her position: "For my part, I wish to be among the ranks of that glorious crusade that is seeking to set Truth's Holy Sepulchre free from a usurped domination. We shall then see her resurrection!"

These are the proud words of a martyr. But on the other hand she had to face Isaac's insinuations that by her association with her new free-thinking Coventry friends, the Brays, she was making herself ineligible for a respectable marriage and hence was a financial drain on the family—in effect, a sycophant. Caroline Bray reported to her sister Sara Hennell that Isaac was saying

> that his sister had no chance of getting the one thing needful—
> i.e. a husband and a settlement, unless she mixes more in society,
> and complains that since she has known us she has hardly been any-
> where else; that Mr. Bray, being only a leader of mobs, can only
> introduce her to Chartists and Radicals, and that such only will
> ever fall in love with her if she does not belong to the Church.

Added to this was the humiliation of having to await her father's unreasonably delayed decision as to whether to break up the Foleshill Road house which she had managed for him or to retain it and invite her back to live with him. All things considered, the comments in the letter to Maria which reveal the personal basis of her re-evaluation of egoism are a calm understatement:

> I have had a weary week and you have the fag end. At the beginning
> more than the usual amount of *cooled* glances, and exhortations
> to the suppression of self-conceit. The former are so many hail-
> stones that make me wrap more closely around me the mantle of
> determinate purpose—the latter are needful and have a tendency to
> exercise forbearance that well repays the temporary smart.

But she was too impressionable by nature, too vulnerable to experience and keenly perceptive of it, to remain psychologically static in such an atmosphere. In coming to recognize the naturalness of egotism within herself, she was on the verge of recognizing (and respecting) its inevitable presence in everyone else. The clue to her nearness to this revelation lies in the simple fact that her comment on egotism follows her poem on sympathy: once fearless self-identity has been achieved, the boundaries of self can be opened to other-than-self. She had at last evaluated herself by her own untrammeled conscience, the very taskmaster which had made her a good, if struggling, Evangelist. She was by no means the first or last strong-minded individual to be cast outside Evangelicalism by the force of the inexorable dialectic emanating from its own center.

George Eliot was to suffer more and gain still more wisdom from the Holy War, since it heightened in intensity and lasted almost eight weeks after this 18 February letter to Maria. However, she was also to find a more sympathetic audience in Mrs. Pears and Charles and Caroline Bray. Maria was supporting her out of affection, and perhaps too from some intimate knowledge of certain personality problems within the family. Indeed, it is a tribute to Maria that the letter is so freely and honestly written. But Maria could not even pretend to offer the moral and intellectual approval and understanding which were forthcoming from these new friends. According to the letters now in print, George Eliot did not write again to Maria until 27 May 1842, when her trouble had been resolved except for lingering echoes in her own mind. This is an affectionate-seeming letter and includes a friendly invitation as of old, but it reveals nothing of her own state of mind. It is also the last letter to Maria in the extant correspondence.

In 1885 Maria told Edith Simcox that the correspondence had continued to near the time of Robert Evans's death in 1849, although she admitted that it had "dropped into a matter of friendly notes; she still visited—which is how the Brays knew her as 'the squinting Miss Lewis'—in spite of the dissuasion of clerical employers. She refused to give up her old pupil and the hope of influencing her for good!" The exclamation point is of course Edith's and signifies her reaction to Maria's naïve assumption that she might possibly have realized her hope. For even her great love for George Eliot had not blinded Edith to the fact that within the frail body and underlying the compassionate gaze was an iron resistance to control without her own full consent, as is also implicit in the revealing comment in *Daniel Deronda* about "the repulsion that most of us experience under a grasp and speech which assume to dominate" (Book V, chapter 6). But Maria Lewis had persisted in again overreaching herself, this time in a way which could end only in disaster for herself. "M(ary) A(nn) came this morning," Caroline Bray wrote her sister Sara as late as 3 January 1847. "She is rejoiced at your coming, but she is going to have a stupid Miss Lewis visitor for a fortnight, which will keep her busy at home." Could the unflattering adjective have been picked up from the reluctant hostess herself?

Maria's fault was merely the very human one of failing to recognize that she had outlived her purpose in this particular relationship, which perhaps was the most important one in her long and probably lonely life. There was no open quarrel and apparently the correspondence went on smoothly, if innocuously, so that it must have come as a cruel jolt to her when George Eliot abruptly demanded her letters back. Maria's own explanation of this to Edith Simcox was that George Eliot had written her that an anonymous friend had suggested "that Miss Lewis's friendship was not disinterested." Edith accepted this as a "true reminiscence" because of the "hurt tone" in which Maria had related it. Nevertheless, Edith pursued her inquiry with a second visit to Caroline Bray and Sara Hennell, when Sara said that she thought the rift between the two had been "gradual, incompatibility of opinions, etc., that Miss Lewis had been finding fault, governess fashion, with what was imprudent or unusual in Marian's manners and that Marian always resented this." All this was no doubt true. But probably, too, George Eliot had some feeling that as long as Maria possessed the letters she also possessed a hold over her which she could no longer tolerate. As her friendship with Sara Hennell had by this time reached an emotional pitch, she was perhaps uneasily remembering the Veronica letters. Also she may have developed some guilt feelings over her lack of utter frankness with Maria concerning her break with the religion which had first brought them together. Then again, perhaps she simply wanted to bring what had become an annoying relationship to an end with finality and as little unpleasantness as possible.

Maria complied with the request for the letters, and although understandably hurt, she harbored no grudge. When in 1874, after fifteen years of fame, George Eliot learned her whereabouts and wrote her what must have been an affectionate letter, enclosing £10, Maria responded:

> As "George Eliot" I have traced you as far as possible and with an interest which few could feel; not many knew you as intimately as I once did, though we have been necessarily separated for so long. My heart has ever yearned after you, and pleasant it is truly in the evening of life to find the old love still existing.

She so treasured her letter from George Eliot that she allowed Cross to make a copy of it for himself only upon his promise that he would not use it in the *Life*. After this first overture, George Eliot sent Maria a letter with money once or twice each year, the last, as indicated by her Journal, being only a month before her own death. And when Maria read the *Life*, she wrote feelingly to Cross:

> Such memories! Your work has marvellously brought out the doings and changes of the thirty years of silence between us, and the end almost unhinged me, bringing back the old sadness. What it must have been to you to pen it all!

WITH THE RETURN OF HER LETTERS TO MARIA, GEORGE Eliot must have felt that she had at last successfully concluded the Evangelical epoch of her life, which had, in the person of Maria, disconcertingly overlapped the new epoch signaled by her Coventry life. Yet from the earlier one she was to take with her much that would help shape her future life and work, even if this fact was to be obscured from her for some time. What she most consciously took from it was bitterness. The bitterness came from within herself, of course. But that she at first directed it against the world-and-life view she had rejected is suggested by Herbert Spencer's recollection that the "throwing off of her early beliefs left her mind in an attitude of antagonism which lasted for some years." Certainly her *Westminster Review* essays —especially "Evangelical Teaching: Dr. Cumming" (1855) and "Worldliness and Other-Worldliness: The Poet Young" (1857)—reveal how determined she was at this time to expose the hypocrisy she had come to detect in certain exponents of many of the beliefs she had once tried to live by. True, her target is ever the perversion of religious ideas by the individuals under attack, and not the ideas themselves. Yet she boldly gave "Evangelical Teaching" first place in the title of her scathing essay on Cumming, and it was her own "proposition" (which the publisher, John Chapman, accepted) that she should dissect Edward Young, whom she had frequently quoted admiringly to Maria. "Amos Barton" is also an offshoot of this antagonism.

Silently awaiting the dispersal of this bitterness was the fund of her intimate knowledge of both the objective and the subjective phases— as well as the strengths and weaknesses—of Evangelicalism. Eventually she would draw upon this unique store of information and deeply lived experience. She was making ready for so doing in 1856 when she wrote her essay "Silly Novels by Lady Novelists," in which she unsparingly ridicules the lack of realism in the popular Evangelical novel, dubbed by her "the *white neck-cloth* species . . . intended as a sort of medicinal sweetmeat for Low Church young ladies; an Evangelical substitute for the fashionable novel. . . ." Then with sudden nonsatiric seriousness she pauses to observe: "The real drama of Evangelicalism —and it has abundance of fine drama for any one who has genius enough to discern and reproduce it—lies among the middle and lower classes. . . ." It is probable that when she wrote this remark she was the only person in England with the requisite genius and knowledge to produce such a work of fiction. She shortly was to do just that in the third and most powerful of the *Clerical Scenes*, "Janet's Repentance."

Less tangible than George Eliot's knowledge of and final respect for Evangelicalism, but of greater importance to her art as a whole, were other elements which had arisen out of the configuration of her experience within that religion and made an indelible mark upon her. Several of these elements were to determine the structure of her fiction, such as the various defenses and compromises which resulted in her extraordinary style, and her lasting insistence that she be the overall commentator, rather than chief actress, in her novels. Too, she was never to swerve from her idea of what made worthwhile reading as she had described it in the 1839 letter to Maria: "the transactions of real specimens of human nature, from which we may safely draw inferences." At the time she had meant this to be a description of "truth" in contrast to "fiction" as she then conceived it. Gradually, however, as her conception of the scope and power of the imagination was enlarged, this became a directive for the kind of fiction she was to write. Add to this demand for veracity the Evangelical demand for the close scrutiny of motives and the probing for hidden ones, and one has come close to describing the unique realism that was to be hers—psychological rather than philosophical, and analytic rather than dramatic. By now this mode of realism seems relatively commonplace; but both she and her first readers had to wait until she initiated it to realize the possibility of its existence.

Such writing would not have become a possibility had not certain disparate elements within her nature begun their slow travel toward one another, to merge finally into a liberating whole. Perhaps what spearheaded this progress was the element of confession. From "Mr. Gilfil's Love Story" on, the dynamic power of the right confession made to the right person was to be important thematic material. Underlying even this was her personal frustration over confession during the Evangelical days. Without such experience, she might not have been haunted by the need to continue the effort to confess, which was to be a vital force in her motivation to write. When we remember that her earliest concept of imagination would broaden to include sympathy (just as confession for her came to include memory), it is clear that in the Evangelical period preparation was being made for the synthesis of the necessary components of creativity. True, the synthesis was as yet far from completed, and it is little wonder that for many years she looked back upon this time with both bitterness and the conviction that it had been a sterile period in her life. Possibly, however, she also had it in mind when in *Silas Marner* she observed: "Our consciousness rarely registers the beginning of a growth within us any more than without us; there have been many circulations of the sap before we detect the smallest sign of the bud" (Part I, chapter 7).

THREE

The Dire Years

ONE OF THE STRANGEST FACTS SURROUNDING THE RECALL OF the letters to Maria Lewis is that George Eliot did not keep them herself but gave them to Sara Hennell. Intentionally or not, the handing of the letters to Sara was a symbolic gesture. For although George Eliot was to be close to both Charles and Caroline Bray, it was Sara, Caroline's sister, who would continue Maria's role on a more sophisticated level and hence provide the one stable relationship in the otherwise confused and many-sided Coventry epoch.

When the most decisive event of this period—the Holy War—had its beginning, the intimacy with Sara had not yet started. This war ostensibly revolved around religion; in reality it was a family crisis, a result of the eruption of the smoldering antagonisms of three major participants—sister, brother, father. And although it had its dramatic opening on that January Sunday when George Eliot refused to attend church, its actual cause lay in the growing rift between her and Isaac, which was augmented by the problem of living arrangements thrust upon them by his engagement to Sarah Rawlins. Even before that, the home life at Griff had been broken up by the death of the mother and Chrissey's marriage to Edward Clarke, a surgeon practicing at Meriden. In the letters to Maria there are signs that George Eliot conscientiously attempted to create a new home life. She hired and managed servants, cooked, and saw to it that Isaac had birthday parties; but her allusions to these activities are rarely cheerful. On 20 May 1839, for example, she told Maria: ". . . my writing to you just now is an act of unmixed selfishness, undertaken as a delassement after a day of disagreeable bustle in preparing for a party met to celebrate Isaac's twenty third birthday." Significantly, this remark is followed immediately by her admission that confession has been for her but a substitute for amendment, thus revealing the closeness between her family troubles and her haunting need to confess. Cross apparently recognized this association, for he neatly disposed of it by deleting the entire paragraph.

By the next May, the threatening prospect of Isaac's engagement had shocked her into the realization that the very chores which bored her were—as far as outer circumstances indicated—her only reason for being. "I will only hint," she wrote Maria, "that there seems a probability of my being an unoccupied damsel, of my being severed from all the ties that have hitherto given my existence the semblance of a usefulness beyond that of making up the requisite quantum of animal matter in the universe." The alternatives which would be forced upon her by Isaac's marriage were unattractive: to remain at Griff, but with her sister-in-law supplanting her as feminine head of it; or to leave the beloved homestead and make a new home for herself and her father. The indirectness of her manner of informing Maria of the engagement suggests that plans had stayed unsettled enough to give her hope that they were, as she told Maria, but "prospects that may yet after all pass by as the scenery of a Diorama."

Isaac himself appears to have been undecided, for two months later Maria is told that "Isaac is in Paris! There has been a mist of suspense thrown around our prospects lately. My brother's marriage is at present uncertain, so I know not what will be our situation." Of course some of the "mist of suspense" may have emanated from Sarah Rawlins, yet it seems more likely that Isaac's dilemma arose over uncertainty as to where to make his home if he did marry, especially as his father failed to take an authoritative stand on the matter. Within another two months the engagement was decisively on again, and its renewal was celebrated by the Birmingham visit during which the momentous attendance at the music festival occurred. No matter what George Eliot may have felt about her brother's marriage, she had some reason at this time to be relieved and even happy over a new plan concerning her future. "My prospects," she wrote Maria, "have been long fluctuating so as to make it unsafe for me to mention them; now I believe I may say that I am not to be dislodged from my present pedestal or resign my sceptre. The secession has devolved on another and the *flutterer* is to leave the nest. . . ."

But this plan was soon discarded—understandably, as Isaac was to assume major responsibility for their father's business. Near the end of the month, Maria is being asked for a "timely promise that you will spend your holidays chiefly with me, that we may once more meet among scenes which now I am called on to leave them, I find to have *grown in* to my affections." Another five months passed before she wrote to another friend: ". . . we are undergoing one of the chief among the minor disagreeables of life—that of moving. To me it is a deeply painful incident—it is like dying to one stage of existence, henceforth nothing will have the charm of old use and wont which makes the days pass so easily—at least until novelty has merged once again into habit." According to her father's Journal, she preceded him to the new home, Bird Grove, in Foleshill Road, Coventry, and with help from Isaac moved in the furniture on a stormy March day.

As her intimacy with the Brays and Sara Hennell increased, novelty did merge into habit. But she was never again to feel attached to a house as she had to Griff—the later Priory and Witley Heights not excepted. As late as 1874, upon receiving some photographs of Griff from Isaac's daughter Edith, she responded:

> Dear old Griff still smiles at me with a face which is more like than unlike its former self, and I seem to feel the air through the window of the attic above the drawing room, from which when a little girl, I often looked towards the distant view of the Coton "College" [the workhouse that figures in "Amos Barton"]—thinking the view rather sublime.

Her sense of exile in England was to grow with the years and became apparent to the friends of her later life. "Indeed," Oscar Browning was led to observe, "it is difficult to understand why George Eliot, who was always most happy and most productive under the circumstances of foreign life, should have lived so much in England, except that her husband was a confirmed Londoner."

Some bitterness was no doubt mingled with her sadness over leaving Griff, for during the difficult period of waiting, she had at least twice been given the tantalizing hope that it would not be necessary. Underlying Isaac's indecisiveness had of course been that of their father. When George Eliot first announced the engagement to Maria, she added, "I desire to imitate my beloved father's calm endurance and humble gratitude and be quite free from anxiety respecting my destination." But as the months of uncertainty went on and there came from him no authoritative word, his "calm endurance" became a source of humiliation for her. As a dependent single woman, she was in no position to determine her own destiny, as Isaac could his. If her father did not assume decisive responsibility for it, who would? Besides, she must have been made to feel that she alone was the chief obstacle to a simple resolution of the problem of who should live where and perhaps to the marriage itself. Surely it was no mere coincidence that this frustrating time of waiting was also the time when she was fast preparing herself to reject another father, God.

ONE OF THE MOST REVEALING ACCOUNTS (AND THE ONLY firsthand one) of George Eliot's loss of faith is that by Mrs. John Cash (nee Mary Sibree), who lived with her family in Foleshill Road only a few minutes' walk from Bird Grove. Both Mary, then sixteen, and her seventeen-year-old brother, John, were the first of the many intelligent and sensitive young people to be profoundly influenced by a personal relationship with George Eliot. In writing to Cross as he was preparing the *Life*, Mary stated that her five years of intimacy with George Eliot formed "the most important epoch in my life." Further evidence of the importance of this period to Mary is that she was dissatisfied with her contribution to the *Life* when it appeared in print, and wrote out a fuller version of her "scattered reminiscences," which Cross obligingly included as an appendix to the second edition. Hence, Mary's total account is in two instalments, and although there are no blatant contradictions between the two, there are subtle shifts in emphasis which suggest that George Eliot's association with the Sibrees was a complex one leading (despite Mary's omission of unpleasant details) to unhappy consequences.

There was much in the Sibree family to touch George Eliot's deepest feelings. She must have been irresistibly drawn to Mary and John because of their close brother-sister relationship, and their father and mother would have come inevitably into her emotional orbit as parent figures. On the surface, at least, the family symbolized what she had wished her family to be, so that acceptance by them would have meant much to her. At first she was warmly welcomed by both the father, minister of the nearby Independent Chapel, and the mother, a pious churchwoman, because she had been recommended to them as one who would be likely to ask Mrs. Sibree's help in organizing an Evangelical charity project. She had not been their neighbor long before they were shocked to learn—according to Mary—not from George Eliot but through a mutual friend "the information that a total change had taken place in this gifted woman's mind with respect to the evangelical religion, which she had evidently believed in up to the time of her coming to Coventry. . . ."

Upon learning that her unorthodoxy had become known, George Eliot was immediately more concerned over the danger of losing Mrs. Sibree's friendship than with defending her new views. As Mary recalled, "To Miss Evans's affectionate and pathetic speech to my mother, 'Now, Mrs. Sibree, you won't care to have anything more to do with me,' my mother rejoined, 'On the contrary, I shall feel more interested in you than ever.' " However, it is clear that Mrs. Sibree was reserving her final judgment; she told Mary that "she thought argument and expostulation might do much" to reconvert their new neighbor, and it was no doubt this hope of hers which motivated the often emotional discussions between her husband and George Eliot.

Although temporarily tolerant, Mrs. Sibree from the start openly disapproved of the close association which rapidly developed between her daughter and George Eliot when the latter began to tutor Mary in German. This fact is not made clear in Mary's first communication to Cross. But in her second one, she relates that when George Eliot inquired whether the lessons were to continue, Mrs. Sibree said to her, "You know, with your superior intellect, I cannot help fearing you might influence Mary, though you might not intend to do so. But . . . her father does not agree with me: he does not see any danger. . . ." Thus the weekly tutoring proceeded for nearly two years, fortunately for Mary, who during this time needed an older friend to whom she could trustingly confide her own wavering orthodoxy. George Eliot encouraged such confidences as being spiritually healthful for her young friend "but," so Mary emphasizes, "with no attempt to directly unsettle my evangelical beliefs, confining herself in these matters to a steady protest against the claim of the Evangelicals to an exclusive possession of higher motives to morality—or even to religion." On this second point, the living example of George Eliot herself must have been more persuasive than any amount of verbal argument, for the release from Evangelicalism had, without in the least weakening her individualistic sense of morality, humanized her to a degree which was "traceable even in externals,—in the changed tone of voice and manner,—from formality to a geniality which opened my heart to her. . . ." Although Mary could discern for herself this progressive change, it must also have been discussed between them. George Eliot told her that for Evangelicalism "she had at one time sacrificed the cultivation of her intellect, and a proper regard to personal appearance. 'I used,' she said, 'to go about like an owl, to the great disgust of my brother; and I would have denied him what I now see to have been quite lawful amusements.'"

The Rev. Sibree was apparently more intrigued by and attracted to this unfolding personality than alarmed over the state of her soul; and that George Eliot was in turn drawn to him is suggested by the amount of personal feeling she invested in her arguments with him. In her second account of these arguments, Mary expands her version of one:

> The evening's discussion with my father, to which I have referred in my previous communication in the "Life," is now vividly

present to my mind. There was not only on her part a vehemence
of tone, startling in one so quiet, but a crudeness in her objections,
an absence of proposed solution of difficulties, which partly distressed and partly pleased me (siding as I did mentally with
my father), and which was in strange contrast to the satisfied
calm which marked her subsequent treatment of religious differences.

Upon my father's using an argument (common enough in those
days) drawn from the present condition of the Jews as a fulfilment
of prophecy, and saying, "If I were tempted to doubt the truth of
the Bible, I should only have to look at a Jew to confirm my faith
in it." "Don't talk to me of the Jews!" Miss Evans retorted, in an
irritated tone; "to think that they were deluded into expectations
of a temporal deliverer, and then punished because they couldn't
understand that it was a spiritual deliverer that was intended!" To
something that followed from her, intimating the claim of creatures
upon their Creator, my father objected, "But we have no claim
upon God." "No claim upon God!" she reiterated indignantly; "we
have the strongest possible claim upon Him."

I regret that I can recall nothing more of a conversation carried
on for more than two hours; but I vividly remember how deeply
Miss Evans was moved, and how, as she stood against the mantelpiece during the last part of the time, her delicate fingers, in which
she held a small piece of muslin on which she was at work,
trembled with her agitation.

Mary associates another memory with this discussion, but as she does
so thirteen pages later, one suspects that it and its significance had not
surged into her mind before her consciousness was stimulated by the
actual writing of the memoir. In this strangely delayed passage, she
relates how at some unspecified time she and George Eliot were talking
about the authenticity of various claims one person might make upon
another.

One claim, as she regarded it, from equals to each other, was
this, the right to hear from the aggrieved, "You have ill-treated me;
do you not see your conduct is not fair, looked at from my side?"
Such frankness would, she said, bring about good understanding
better than reticent endurance. Her own filial piety was sufficiently
manifest; but of the converse obligation, that of the claim of child
upon parent, she was wont to speak thus strongly. "There may be,"
she would say, "conduct on the part of a parent which should
exonerate his child from further obligation to him; but there cannot be action conceivable which should absolve the parent from
obligation to serve his child, seeing that for that child's existence
he is himself responsible."

To this Mary adds what probably she had not perceived in her teens: "I did not at the time see the connection between this view and the change of a fundamental nature marked by Miss Evans's earlier contention for our 'claim on God.' The bearing of the above on orthodox religion I did not see."

Thus stand revealed facts which can also be conjectured from George Eliot's letters as restored by Gordon Haight—that underlying her rebellion against her spiritual father lay the rebellion against her earthly father. Her real emotional struggle was over the latter. When that struggle with the real father was seemingly overcome (it was to reappear in different form) and her intellect free to take command, all friction was removed from the path which led inevitably to the second rejection. She might have abandoned only Evangelicalism; instead, she was driven to attack the very heart of Christian orthodoxy—her belief in God. Her worried friends realized this, and as she with appealing candor professed dissatisfaction with her own conclusions, they felt no hesitation "in asking her to receive visits from persons of different persuasions, who were judged competent to bring forward the best arguments in favour of orthodox doctrines." Willingly she complied, yet each visitation ended in defeat for the would-be missionary. A Baptist minister with a reputation as "an original and interesting preacher" exclaimed after his interview with her: "That young lady must have had the devil at her elbow to suggest her doubts, for there was not a book that I recommended to her in support of Christian evidences that she had not read."

During this time when there were outward signs that she would welcome reconversion, she had no difficulty in maintaining friendly relations with the Sibrees. Mary eagerly recorded her impressions of their interesting young neighbor in letters to her brother, John, who was in residence at Halle University in Germany. In her second communication to Cross, Mary quotes generously from these letters, and one passage in particular (in a letter dated 28 October 1842— an arresting date because it is the same year of both the last extant letter to Maria Lewis and the Holy War) reveals that there had been changes in more than religious beliefs. After remarking that George Eliot now seemed "more settled in her views than ever," Mary proceeds to tell John the substance of the remainder of a conversation which took place between their mother and Miss Evans, the latter

pleading for works of imagination, maintaining that they perform an office for the mind which nothing else can. On the mention of Shakespeare, she praised him with her characteristic ardour, was shocked at the idea that mother should disapprove the perusal of his writings, and quite distressed lest, through her influence, I should be prevented from reading them. She could be content were she allowed no other book than Shakespeare; and in educating a child, this would be the first book she would place in its hands.

A paragraph later Mary adds that her mother, although an ardent admirer of Shakespeare, objected that there were "things" in each of his plays offensive to her. This objection, responded George Eliot, "was as reasonable as the objection to walk in a beautiful garden, 'because toads and weeds are to be found in it.'" To appreciate the drastic reversal of viewpoint, one has only to set this record against the letter to Maria Lewis of 1839 in which she condemns almost all "works of imagination" and gives Shakespeare but faint praise by saying that "we have need of as nice a power of distillation as the bee to suck nothing but honey from his pages"—very much what Mrs. Sibree in fact was saying.

Of course Mary also wrote her brother details about George Eliot's growing skepticism, and when he returned from Germany he gave the intriguing neighbor her first lessons in Greek. The spirited and intellectually frank letters which George Eliot wrote him in 1848 (perhaps the most so of her life) show that John and she had a meaningful companionship. A revolutionary year for many individuals, as well as countries, 1848 proved especially so for John, who was then deciding to take the momentous step of leaving the clergy, for which he had been trained. To what extent George Eliot may have influenced him can be only surmised, but when by letter he made clear to her his final decision, she responded:

> You have my hearty and not inexperienced sympathy, for . . . I have gone through a trial of the same genus as yours, though rather differing in species. I sincerely rejoice in the step you have taken—it is an absolutely necessary condition for any true development of your nature. It was impossible to think of your career with hope while you tacitly subscribed to the miserable etiquetter . . . of sectarianism. Only persevere—be true, firm and loving—not too anxious about immediate usefulness to others—that can only be a result of justice to yourself. Study *mental hygiene*—take long doses of "dolce far niente," and be in no great hurry about anything in this "varsal world"! Do we not commit ourselves to sleep, and so resign all care for ourselves every night? lay ourselves gently on the bosom of nature or God? A beautiful reproach to the spirit of some religionists and ultra-good people.

Soon after this, John returned to Germany and immersed himself in the study of Hegel, one result of which is still well known—his 1849 translation of Hegel's *Lectures on the Philosophy of History*.

Although in her second memoir Mary refers to her brother's difficult decision and George Eliot's recognition that it was a courageous one, she makes no mention of the fact that George Eliot was in actual correspondence with him when he made it. She concludes her reminiscences with a paragraph which begins: "More than twenty years elapsed before I had again the privilege of seeing George Eliot, and that on one occasion only, after her final settlement in London." (More specifically, on 2 March 1873, when as Mrs, John Cash she and her daughter called on George Eliot during one of the famous Sunday soirees.) Thus it seems reasonable to assume that, whether by coincidence or not, at the very time George Eliot and John were exchanging letters over his dilemma, the former's relationship with the elder Sibrees was severed far more definitely than Mary implies.

Mary does not hint that any unpleasantness occurred. Yet there must have been something of a serious nature, for when George Eliot was sojourning in Switzerland after the death of her father in 1849, Mary wrote to ask her to send letters to her under the address of Rosehill (the home of Charles and Caroline Bray) because she feared her father would object to their corresponding. This George Eliot refused to do, indirectly telling Mary so in a letter to the Brays: "Please to give my love to her and tell her that I cannot carry on a correspondence with anyone who will not avow it." In the same letter she reveals the surprising fact that Mary's father had recently gone out of his way to call upon her as he traveled through Switzerland: "Mr. Sibree called. . . . I cannot say that I was in the least obliged to him as from the terms in which we are, it could be nothing else than a piece of impertinent curiosity." In her next letter to the Brays, she added a few scathing comments about his visit: he had looked "silly," had brought with him his brother ("a vulgar-looking man, exceedingly oily, pitted with small-pox"), and had made stupid conversation. However, "I received him very politely indeed with my usual hypocrisy, begged him to sit down etc." Still later she wrote that even Mary—otherwise "a sweet good girl"—had

> a strong leaven of Sibreeanism in her which I have tended to nourish by shewing a very strong interest in her. Sibreeanism is that degree of egotism which we call bad taste but which does not reach to gross selfishness—the egotism that does not think of others, but would be very glad to do them good if it did think of them—the egotism that eats up all the bread and butter and is ready to die of confusion and distress after having done it.

The sarcasm betrays her hurt: the Sibrees' wary attitude toward her had reactivated the old sense of rejection. The hurt was superficial, however, compared to what it might have been had she not been almost simultaneously welcomed into a family far more congenial to her new thoughts and temperament, that of Charles and Caroline Bray.

Only a year or so before George Eliot and her father moved to Bird Grove, Charles Bray, a successful ribbon manufacturer, had purchased a nearby property called Rosehill, a fine house with a large, shaded lawn. In summer, a huge bearskin was spread under an acacia tree. Here many provocative conversations took place, for Bray, a free-thinker and courageous reformer, attracted friends of diverse and unconventional interests. As he modestly observed in his autobiography, "every one who came to Coventry with a queer mission, or a crochet, or was supposed to be a 'little cracked,' was sent up to Rosehill"; yet some of his guests were truly distinguished, such as Thackeray and Emerson. For the first time in her life George Eliot found herself in an intellectually stimulating atmosphere other than the one vicariously provided by books. Soon, so Mary wrote in her first memoir, "Mr. and Mrs. Bray and Miss Hennell [Sara], with their friends, were *her* world; and on my saying to her once, as we closed the garden-door together, that we seemed to be entering a paradise, she said, 'I do indeed feel that I shut the world out when I shut that door.'" Thus associated with George Eliot, Rosehill had an emotional significance for Mary Sibree. (Quite fittingly, she and her husband were quick to buy it in 1857, when Bray was forced to sell it.)

Important as the intellectual companionship George Eliot found at Rosehill was, probably its greatest value to her lay in the fact that she was accepted warmly and non-critically, with none of the silent disapproval she increasingly sensed with the Sibrees or the stultifying lack of understanding she felt within her own home. She could at last be herself. Bray's recollection makes clear that it was not yet a harmonious self:

> . . . I consider her the most delightful companion I have ever known; she knew everything. She had little self-assertion; her aim was always to show her friends off to the best advantage—not herself. She would polish up their witticisms, and give them the *full* credit of them. But there were two sides; hers was the temperament of genius which has always its sunny and shady side. She was frequently very depressed—and often very provoking, as much so as she could be agreeable—and we had violent quarrels; but the next day, or whenever we met, they were quite forgotten, and no allusions made to them.

Although it is doubtful that such uninhibited behavior was good for her as it dissipated her psychic and potentially creative energies, it was the inevitable reaction to having cast off the rigid bonds she had imposed upon those same energies under the guise of Evangelicalism.

Somewhat amusingly, she had first been brought to Rosehill by the unsuspecting Mrs. Pears (Charles's sister), who according to Bray thought "that the influence of this superior young lady of Evangelical principles might be beneficial to our heretical minds." It did not take Charles and Caroline long to recognize that their new friend was not only extraordinary but had already gone far in seeking freedom of thought in religious opinions. They were especially impressed to learn that she had bought for herself and read the second edition (August 1841) of Charles Hennell's *An Inquiry Concerning the Origin of Christianity*, a pioneer work in the attempt to separate the historical facts from the myths surrounding the rise of Christianity. This book had great meaning to the Brays. The author was Caroline's brother, and he had, in fact, undertaken his study at her request.

Immediately after her marriage to Charles Bray in 1836, Caroline had become alarmed over the extent of her husband's unorthodox views on religion. Writing in his old age, Bray gave an understanding account of his young wife's predicament: "She had been brought up in the Unitarian faith, and, as might be expected in a young person of one-and-twenty, religion with her was not a question of Biblical criticism, but of deep feeling and cherished home associations. . . ." As a young man on his honeymoon, however, he had not been possessed of such wisdom. At that time he thought he "had only to lay my new views on religious matters before my wife for her to accept them at once. Consequently I had provided myself with Mirabeau's 'System of Nature,' Volney's 'Ruins of Empires,' and other light reading of that sort to enliven the honeymoon. But . . . I only succeeded in making my wife exceedingly uncomfortable." Miraculously after such a honeymoon the marriage survived, but, still disturbed, Caroline "referred the critical part of the matter to her elder brother, Charles C. Hennell, who had already gone very fully into the subject, and had come out completely convinced on the Unitarian stand-points." Somewhat reluctantly, Charles Hennell began a reinvestigation of the subject and concluded with results quite different from those of his first study. The embodiment of his research—the *Inquiry*—gave far greater support to Bray's rationalistic view on religion than to Caroline's inherited ones.

Caroline was persuaded by her brother's new findings. Being of meticulous conscience, she immediately suggested that it was hypocritical to continue the outward observance of religious ceremonies in which she and her husband no longer believed. For a while, Bray insisted upon following a more pragmatic approach to the problem, believing as he did "that the National Religion ought to be supported for the good of the poor, and for those who, like them, had nothing else to fall back upon." But finally to him too it appeared that "the service was a complete sham" and impossible to countenance "for the sake even of an indirect social benefit." Consequently, very soon after their move into Rosehill, the Brays "discontinued the habit of attending any place of worship."

All this George Eliot would have learned soon after her first meeting with the Brays, for intimacy sprang up quickly between them, and their talk as Charles Bray remembered it "went over all subjects in heaven or earth." She would have been deeply moved to discover that the writing of the *Inquiry* had been a family project— a brother's response to a sister's expressed wish—and when she met Charles Hennell, as she soon did at Rosehill, she judged him to be "a model of moral excellence." She was equally impressed by Charles Bray's zealous humanitarianism and his wife's natural kindness and sensitiveness. These people, deemed dangerously heretical by almost everyone in the neighborhood except herself, must have seemed living examples of her own dawning conviction that virtue and sectarian religion were separable. In a letter of 1840 she had admitted to Maria Lewis that years earlier she had been considerably troubled by finding "a very amiable atheist" in a novel (*Devereux*) by Bulwer-Lytton, because the portrayal gave rise to "the impression that religion was not a requisite to moral excellence." She had of course intended this comment as criticism of a writer's irresponsible use of material; yet the seed had taken root more firmly than she realized, so that when the restraining force of Evangelicalism was removed, it came into full bloom. By the time she met the Brays and the Hennells, religion to her meant a reverence for life and one's fellow beings which emanated from within the self and was independent of external creed and commandment. It was to remain so throughout her life.

Mrs. Bray, so George Eliot told Mrs. Sibree, "is the most religious person I know." Although she was to enjoy a greater comradeship with Charles Bray than with his wife, and a more intense emotional and intellectual relationship with Sara, she was to have for Cara (as Caroline was called by everyone close to her) an unswerving tenderness and respect. When in 1854 she eloped to the Continent with Lewes, it was Cara's hesitation to voice approval of her action which hurt her more than the slander of those who had far greater power to determine her future as a novelist. And back in 1841, the gentle Cara's firm view concerning the role of conscience in determining whether or not one should attend church worked its influence upon her. The argument appealed to her own highly developed conscience, and also provided her with what she was in need of without realizing it—a platform upon which to take her stand against her father. A few lines of a letter Cara wrote her sister Mary not long after George Eliot had refused to attend church with her father on that momentous first Sunday of 1842 show that Cara was somewhat uneasily aware of her influence:

> The poor old gentlemen [Robert Evans], it seems, has been quite puzzled about this new case of conscience, and has not known how to act. Miss Rebecca [Franklin] and Mrs. Pears have a little enlightened him by telling how wrong he has been, and how the world would condemn him. He expressed a fear that Mrs. Bray had influenced his daughter, but Miss Rebecca said she did not think Mrs. B. had shown any disposition to proselytize—so Satan has all the credit, and it is well he should perhaps.

THERE IS LITTLE DOUBT THAT AT THE TIME GEORGE ELIOT took the defiant step of refusing to attend church, she was totally unaware of the hostile aggressiveness implicit in it. She saw it, rather, as an act conforming to the dictates of her own conscience. But that those around her sensed some deeper layer of motivation is indicated by the serious consequences the otherwise simple gesture evoked. Bewildered, the father appealed to Isaac for help—or perhaps Isaac's mediating role was a self-appointed one. Certainly it was not a comfortable one. It is understandable why he, who had never entered the world of his sister's thoughts, believed this new attitude could be but an aberration caused by some external influence such as her new friends, the Brays, for had he not only a few years earlier been forced to listen to her Evangelical proselytizing? So now he and his father agreed that it would be best to send her off to the neutral Chrissey, at Meriden, where it was to be hoped she would come to her senses, and where shortly "Isaac," as the troubled father noted with significant emphasis in his Journal under 25 February 1842, "called . . . and *schooled* Mary Ann."

An experience that was both crucible and whetstone for her genius followed, although at the time she could think of it as only the former. Isaac's schooling had negative results. With a tactlessness which amounted to cruelty, he harped on his sister's peculiar marriage problem, blaming this too upon the Brays, as Cara reported in a letter to Sara:

> It seems that brother Isaac with real fraternal kindness thinks that his sister has no chance of getting the one thing needful—i.e. a husband and a settlement, unless she mixes more in society, and complains that since she has known us she has hardly been any-

where else; that Mr. Bray, being only a leader of mobs, can only introduce her to Chartists and Radicals, and that such only will ever fall in love with her if she does not belong to the Church.

Isaac had aroused his sister's sense of unworthiness and linked it with money (this was to be a lasting association). She had been made to feel that her staying single was an act of selfishness which placed a financial burden on the entire family. And so she wrote the one extant letter to her father (not, of course, published by Cross):

> From what my Brother more than insinuated and from what you have yourself intimated I perceive that your establishment at Foleshill is regarded as an unnecessary expence having no other object than to give me a centre in society. . . . I am glad at any rate this is made clear to me, for I could not be happy to remain as an incubus or an unjust absorber of your hardly earned gains which might be better applied among my Brothers and Sisters with their children.

As her father had intimated also that he intended to sell Bird Grove and move alone into a cottage which he owned at Packington, she added: "I should be just as happy living with you at your cottage . . . or any where else if I can thereby minister in the least to your comfort. . . ." She also admits that she is aware she has unintentionally given him pain. Otherwise, it is by no means a contrite or humble letter. Its opening makes clear that it is not to be taken as a sign that the convictions which caused the upheaval have weakened:

> I wish entirely to remove from your mind the false notion that I am inclined visibly to unite myself with any Christian community, or that I have any affinity in opinion with Unitarians more than with other classes of believers in the Divine authority of the books comprising the Jewish and Christian Scriptures. I regard these writings as histories consisting of mingled truth and fiction. . . . Such being my very strong convictions, it cannot be a question with any mind of strict integrity . . . that I could not without vile hypocrisy and a miserable truckling to the smile of the world for the sake of my supposed interests, profess to join in worship which I wholly disapprove. This and this *alone* I will not do even for your sake. . . .

She would have expected her father to show Isaac the letter and it was perhaps essentially written for him. Yet she must have known from past experience that neither her father nor Isaac would care a fig for her reasoning or the nicety of her conscience. One senses that it was with a feeling of futility that she concludes her high-flown self-vindication:

> I do not hope to convince any other member of our family and probably not yourself that I am really sincere, that my only desire is

to walk in that path of rectitude which however rugged is the only
path to peace, but the prospect of contempt and rejection shall not
make me swerve from my determination so much as a hair's breadth
until I feel that I *ought* to do so.

Her sincerity was not questioned. But for Isaac and her father sincerity
was not in itself the first and all-inclusive principle of action which she
at this time thought it to be. However, Isaac was impressed by her
explanation of motives—or perhaps he belatedly realized to what a
serious pass things had come as he watched his father carry on plans to
break up Bird Grove and heard his sister resolve, as Cross relates, "to
go into lodgings at Leamington, and to try to support herself by
teaching"—an unenviable course of action for any woman at that time.
For a while there was a lifting of tension, so that Cara could report to
her sister Mary:

> You will be glad to hear that Miss Evans' affairs seem coming
> round all right again. I met her in the street yesterday with a face
> very different from the long dismal one she has lately worn, and she
> tells me of a letter from her brother Isaac . . . saying that great
> minds are never ashamed of owning that they have been in fault;
> that since she did not wish to set herself up against the family, and
> only wished for liberty to act according to her present convictions,
> he thought that she had been treated very harshly; that the sending
> her away was entirely the father's doing, not from economy, but
> because he could not bear the place after what had happened; and
> ended with begging that she would go to him at Griff, not doubting
> but that Mr. Evans would send for her back again very soon.

George Eliot acquiesced to the plan indicated in Cara's letter and
went to Griff on 23 March.

Once there, she found "abundant and unlooked-for blessings,"
as she wrote a week later to Mrs. Pears. She was treated with "delicacy
and consideration from all whom I have seen," and what pleased her
most was that "my acquaintances of this neighbourhood seem to seek
an opportunity of smiling on me, in spite of my heresy." In these
happier circumstances, the return of Isaac's comparative friendliness
being not the least, her mood softened and she confessed to Mrs. Pears
that "on a retrospection of the past month, I regret nothing so much as
my own impetuosity both of feeling and judging." This thought was
eventually to take total possession of her. But when she first announced
it, she was not yet ready to acknowledge the value of the lesson learned.
Her future was still disturbingly uncertain, for she had little reason
to share Isaac's confidence that their father would soon welcome
her back to his home. All she knew was that he continued to have
alterations made on his cottage at Packington, where, presumably, he

planned to live alone. "I expect," she confided to Mrs. Pears in the midst of her otherwise optimistic report, "the ancient difficulty of being compelled to *worm* out the intentions of others. . . . I must have a *home*, not a visiting place." Then comes the real reason for the letter: "I wish you would learn something from my Father, and send me word how he seems disposed."

On 20 April she writes (still from Griff) to Cara in the same strain, but much less patiently and in a mood which she herself described as "extraordinarily dense and selfish," the result being another letter which Cross ignores completely, whereas he gives at least a telescoped version of the preceding one to Mrs. Pears. Although Isaac's wife, Sarah ("whose affection in spite of my excommunicated state I have been happy enough to win"), had spoken up in her behalf, and even her father "said that I had better return to him after a time," he still did not specify the time and continued to seem "bent . . . more determinedly than is usual with him, on leaving Foleshill." By now she is ready to be outspoken about the real effort it had cost her to stay at Griff. She had come in the first place only

> in compliance with my Father's wish that I should retire for a time from a neighbourhood in which I had been placed on the very comfortable pedestal of the town gazing-stock and to be very plain but not less true, made a fool of by announcing my departure to everyone connected with me. . . . I must have a settled home if my mind is to become healthy and composed, and I shall therefore write to my Father in a week and request his decision. It is important, I know, for him as well as myself that I should return to him without delay, and unless I draw a circle round him and require an answer within it, he will go on hesitating and hoping for weeks and weeks. It was a sacrifice in the first instance to take up my abode with any of my family, and though I have every kindness here, there are feelings which are incommunicable that render it impossible for me to continue long an adjunct to a family instead of an integral part.

If such a letter to her father was necessary, it has not survived; nor is there a direct account of her return to Bird Grove, which occurred before 1 May, as indicated by a note made by Cara: "Miss Evans spent the day here, and I delighted her beyond measure by letting her read some of C. C. [Hennell]'s letters in 1837 concerning the progress of his investigations when writing the 'Inquiry.' " As this was possibly her first day back (a letter of 30 April is still addressed from Griff) and as her Aunt and Uncle Samuel Evans were then visiting at Bird Grove, her rushing off to the Brays was perhaps a much-needed act of assertion after four months of compliance, suppressed indignation, and finally self-blame. Even Cross, anxious as he was to make light of this upheaval, admits that she returned home and was gladly received by her father only "through the intervention of her brother, the Brays, and Miss Rebecca Franklin"—to which he should have added at least Sarah Evans, Mrs. Pears, and Maria Lewis.

It was not an easy life she returned to. Although she may have been defiantly assertive during the first few days, she soon outwardly complied with what her father most desired: "Went to Trinity Church," he recorded 15 May: "Mary Ann went with me to day." Not only had she been denied the satisfaction of the martyr; she was forced into seeming duplicity. Despite her ignominious position (or perhaps because of it), her thought and feeling underwent a slow and painful but dynamic change. Now stripped of what little glamour it may originally have had for her, the defiant act dictated by her conscience appeared no more than an outburst of the very egotism she had sought for years to discipline. She had been made aware of half this truth even while in the midst of the Holy War, and had written to Maria Lewis her momentous discovery that all human action springs from egotism, that of the martyr at the stake as well as that of the court sycophant. To this she had added, "the greatest torture to such a soul [that of the martyr] would be to run counter to the dictates of conscience. . . ." Yet here she was now, a would-be martyr who had apparently chosen to put aside her conscience almost as readily as she had put aside Evangelicalism.

No law forced her back to her father, and certainly he, rather than exerting any pressure for her return, had stayed obstinately silent to the end. It is clear that she had seriously considered going off on her own, but was afraid to take this step. This was not merely because she would have hated a governess's life; as a matter of fact, almost any new environment might well have provided her with more satisfaction than that offered by the outwardly static life she resumed. Had her father ordered her to leave him, she indubitably would have done so without hesitation and perhaps without deep regret. Her fear was of a different and more anxiety-producing sort, and is stated directly in her 28 February letter to her father: "I fear nothing but voluntarily leaving you." It is probable that at the time of writing she herself was unaware of the total meaning of this fear. Implicit in her expression of it is her dawning realization that, no matter how sincere, her stand for conscience had been both in cause and effect an act of aggression against her father, and that to leave him voluntarily would have been but a continuation of that act.

Her habitual self-probing did not allow her to escape the full implication of that curious fear. Had she weakened, or was she being inconsistent? Even when writing that letter she had known there was no hope of returning to her father and simultaneously continuing to live solely by the light of her own conscience. But she knew too that she was being neither weak nor inconsistent. Rather, she had discovered within herself a force—an independence of spirit—stronger and more compulsive than conscience, even her own rigorously trained conscience. At first she recoiled from the discovery. Then eventually (and fortunately for her future psychic development) she assimilated and absorbed it into her total being, although a residue of the initial shock of revelation stayed with her forever. Twenty-five years later she was to say in Oscar Browning's hearing that the "collision with her father, which she thought might have been avoided, caused her regret to the end of her life." And she made a still later reference to it to Cross: ". . . in the last year of her life she told me that, although she did not think she had been to blame, few things had occasioned her more regret than this temporary collision with her father, which might, she thought, have been avoided with a little management."

She had, in fact, reached this conclusion a year and a half after returning to Bird Grove—a short time in one sense, yet a long time for brooding upon the matter. In October of 1843 she wrote in response to a letter from Sara Hennell, who by then had supplanted Maria Lewis as her confidante:

> . . . I will tell you as briefly as possible my present opinion which you know is contrary to the one I held in the first instance. . . . The first impulse of a young and ingenuous mind is to withhold the slightest sanction from all that contains even a mixture of supposed error. When the soul is just liberated from the wretched giant's bed of dogmas on which it has been racked and stretched ever since it began to think there is a feeling of exultation and strong hope. We think we shall run well when we have the full use of our limbs and the bracing air of independence, and we believe that we shall soon obtain something positive which will not only more than compensate to us for what we have renounced, but will be so well worth offering to others that we may venture to proselyte as fast as our zeal for truth may prompt us. But a year or two of reflection and the experience of our own miserable weakness which will ill afford to part even with the crutches of superstition must, I think, effect a change. Speculative truth begins to appear but a shadow of individual minds, agreement between intellects seems unattainable, and we turn to the *truth of feeling* as the only universal bond of union. We find that the intellectual errors which we once fancied were a mere incrustation have grown into the living body and that we cannot in the majority of causes [cases?], wrench them away without destroying vitality.

The whole of this important declaration is couched in guardedly impersonal terms, as if the bitterness still smoldered too near the sur-

face for her to trust herself to describe in other than general terms
what had been an extremely personal and painful experience:

> The results of non-conformity in a family are just an epitome of
> what happens on a larger scale in the world. An influential mem-
> ber chooses to omit an observance which in the minds of all the
> rest is associated with what is highest and most venerable. He can-
> not make his reasons intelligible, and so his conduct is regarded as
> a relaxation of the hold that moral ties had on him previously.
> The rest are infected with the disease they imagine in him; all the
> screws by which order was maintained are loosened, and in more
> than one case a person's happiness may be ruined by the confusion
> of ideas which took the form of principles.

Much of this statement strikes the keynote to the broad tolerance
which manifests itself in the novels. If not yet psychically free to write,
she had unknowingly made a more decisive move toward that freedom
than if she had actually begun a novel (as she was to do, unsuccessfully,
a few years hence). Near the time of the letter to Sara, she made a
pertinent comment to Mary Sibree: "My dear child, the great lesson
of life is tolerance." To this Mary adds: "In the proverb, 'Live and let
live,' she saw a principle involved, harder to act upon, she would say,
than the maxims of benevolence,—I think, because bringing less
credit with it." Mary's somewhat naïve conclusion suggests that she
missed an important distinction intended by George Eliot: it is far
easier to live by readymade maxims, which can be indiscriminately
applied without regard for change or individual differences, than to
live by a lesson wrung from life itself so that it must be revitalized
over and over again in order to keep pace with an ever-changing
existence.

More and increasingly controlled experience would be needed
before George Eliot could master spontaneous tolerance, but she
had already been afforded new insight into the dynamics of the self
in its relationship to other selves. Genuine tolerance can occur only
when the tolerant one keeps back his views, not out of hypocrisy
or superiority, but with a desire to enter into the feelings underlying the views of another and thus to arrive at the *"truth of
feeling"* she had emphasized in her letter to Sara as the only possible
"universal bond of union." Most important is the power of the
motivating desire, which must be more compelling than its natural
competitor—the desire to express one's own views aggressively, even
when aggression is camouflaged by the appeal to a scrupulous conscience. At last she had made the discovery which had eluded her
for many years of anguish: that the conscious suppression of self can
lead to greater release from the burden of self than the most drastic
attempts to reduce the latter by venting it outward, whether in the

form of an attack of hysterics at a dancing party or a high-minded refusal to attend church.

This was also the release needed for the development of her extraordinary capacity for empathy, although that was to prove a still more gradual process. Even Mary seems to have sensed its first appearance, for she relates the otherwise insignificant incident of George Eliot's telling her "of a visit from one of her uncles in Derbyshire [Samuel Evans], a Wesleyan, and how much she had enjoyed talking with him, finding she could enter into his feelings so much better than she had done in past times, when her views seemed more in accordance with his own. . . ." This emergent power is also indicated by Charles Bray's coupling her lack of self-assertiveness with her aim "always to show her friends off to the best advantage"; yet his allusion to the "shady side" of her temperament (especially the "violent quarrels") reveals that the self-suppression still was not mastered sufficiently to be depended upon at all times. She had always given sympathy unstintingly in the form of charitable deeds, but, as she told Mary, the more passive kind (nearer to empathy) could tax her: " 'They [servants] come to me,' she used to say, 'with all their troubles,' as indeed did her friends generally,—sometimes, she would confess, to an extent that quite oppressed her." Mary herself had demonstrably been drawn to that power even while it was more latent than active.

By the time George Eliot was in Switzerland (1849–50), this receptive force within her was exerting an even more magnetic effect upon the people around her. One senses her own growing awareness of this and that it was with a kind of impersonal awe, rather than lack of modesty, that she wrote the Brays about a fellow lodger. Mme de Ludwigsdorff, who "has told me her troubles and her feelings, she says, in spite of herself—for she has never been able in her life to say so much even to her old friends—it is a mystery she cannot unravel." Gordon Haight notes here: "A good example of the future novelist at work collecting material." Perhaps so. But except for background, she was rarely to collect material by so calculating a method. The empathy most vital to the novels was to reach toward characters of her own creation, arising more out of the deepening levels of memory than out of contemporary life. And as this empathy would occur without total self-identification, so would the distance between these characters and herself evolve into the personality of "George Eliot," puzzling some readers almost as much as Cross's *Life*.

Psychic phenomena defy verbal description; if it is attempted, the results are usually misleading. Hence it seems paradoxical to state that the most remarkable quality about George Eliot's empathy— which was necessarily based on passive receptiveness—was its outward-going strength. But that is what impressed the people close to her in her fully mature years. Arresting testimony is seen in Oscar Browning's choice of words in explaining why Lewes was drawn to her: "[He] was evidently subdued by her large commanding nature, and her *burning power of sympathy*." Her aggressiveness had lost none of its native force through rechanneling; the great difference was that finally it was free to emerge in a form unhampered by guilt feelings.

Simultaneously, this unique process of transformation gave her new ego strength, a new sense of identity. Almost as a corollary she became, without arrogance, a law unto herself, and in a far more inclusive way than is implied simply by living according to individual conscience. After her voluntary return to her father, she would never again submit to external pressure—whether man-made law or public opinion—as a reason for action. This is most apparent, of course, in her alliance with Lewes, obliquely adumbrated in the early 1840's when she told Mary Sibree that she thought the stringency of the marriage laws which made divorce almost impossible had an injurious effect upon wives "because they knew their own position to be invulnerable." Years later, when Cara Bray was reluctant to express approval of the elopement with Lewes because of the lack of a formal tie, thus rendering the union (so Cara thought) impermanent, George Eliot calmly explained, rather than defended, her position:

> If we differ on the subject of marriage laws, I at least can believe of you that you cleave to what you believe to be good, and I don't know of anything in the nature of your views that should prevent you from believing the same of me. . . . We cannot set each other quite right on this matter in letters, but one thing I can tell you in few words. Light and easily broken ties are what I neither desire theoretically nor could live for practically. Women who are satisfied with such ties do *not* act as I have done—they obtain what they desire and are still invited to dinner.

Indeed it is highly improbable that she would have entered into marriage with Lewes had he been conventionally eligible.

This same demand for unforced commitment was to underlie her approach to fiction. The novel—she was to recognize—has only potential form, and no prescribed technique by which that form is to be realized. So much freedom is disastrous for many writers. Yet for George Eliot it was not only a stimulating challenge but a necessity. Her *Westminster Review* essay of October 1856—the pitiless exposé of the absurdities in "Silly Novels by Lady Novelists"—concludes with a succinct statement which shows how carefully she had measured the dangers inherent in the peculiar formlessness of the novel:

> No educational restrictions can shut women out from the materials of fiction, and there is no species of art which is so free from rigid

requirements. Like crystalline masses, it may take any form, and yet be beautiful; we have only to pour in the right elements— genuine observation, humour, and passion. But it is precisely this absence of rigid requirement which constitutes the fatal seduction of novel-writing to incompetent women. Ladies are not wont to be very grossly deceived as to their power of playing on the piano; here certain positive difficulties of execution have to be conquered, and incompetence inevitably breaks down. Every art which has its absolute *technique* is, to a certain extent, guarded from the intrusions of mere left-handed imbecility. But in novel-writing there are no barriers for incapacity to stumble against, no external criteria to prevent a writer from mistaking foolish facility for mastery.

Although the "we" in the second sentence is an editorial one, it had a far more personal connotation than readers could have known, for she finished this essay-review on 12 September and began writing "Amos Barton" on 23 September. The sureness of touch with which she handled the subject matter of "Silly Novels by Lady Novelists" shows that she had been thinking concretely of the form she would give her own fiction, as well as of the pitfalls she was determined to avoid.

B UT IN 1843, ALTHOUGH GEORGE ELIOT HAD GAINED NEW insight into herself and was struggling courageously to become "the self that self restrains," her feelings still betrayed her by rushing out in every possible direction in search of love. As Bray remembered her at this time, "She was of a most affectionate disposition, always requiring some one to lean upon. . . ." Indeed, it would seem that she early leaned upon him quite literally, for Maria Lewis spoke to Edith Simcox, no doubt with pained disapproval, of Marian's "walking about with Charles Bray 'like lovers.'" Such conduct transgressed the accepted propriety of the times and may or may not have signified that she was emotionally attached to Bray. Probably she was as yet incapable of maintaining a wholly impersonal relationship with anyone with whom she was brought into relatively close contact, man or woman. She herself was well aware that her own clamoring feelings were the cause of her unhappiness, and she sought to allay them by finding some work which would allow her to forget herself. Executing an ecclesiastical chart would satisfy her no longer. Yet creative writing was still closed to her—perhaps fortunately, for either she would have failed miserably in it and thus added to her despair, or it would have brought her face to face with the self she was attempting to escape. So she turned to translating, although even this was not to provide the serene refuge she thought she desired.

As early as April 1842, when she was "visiting" Griff, she proposed to the Reverend Francis Watts that he oversee a translation of Vinet's *Liberté des Cultes* she wished to make. She was acquainted with Watts because he had been one of the freer-thinking ministers called in by Mrs. Sibree to "persuade" her back into the faith. Obviously he had not been successful, but the two had emerged from the contest of wills with respect for one another. "I should like to set about the translation immediately," she wrote him, "as I have need of an occupation that would occasionally withdraw me from myself." She was sincerely interested in Vinet's book, the theme of which—that man's capacity for heroic action was not dependent upon his beliefs in an afterlife—was a confirmation of her own evolving ideas. But the wording in the first two extant letters to Watts suggests that her deepest motive in seeking such an arrangement was to establish a more personal relationship with him. In the first letter she exhibits the abject humility which often appears in her earliest letters to Maria Lewis (but which, one can be sure, had been absent when she argued with him): "I am aware of my inadequacy, with the inexperience and ignorance of twenty-two years, to judge on a subject so difficult. . . ." A later sentence, although no less humble, makes a response from him obligatory: "I venture to send you an echantillon that you may judge whether I should be in danger of woefully travestying Vinet's style, and if you approve of my project I shall be delighted if you will become foster-father to the work, and arrange for its publication."

Apparently Watts urged her on with the translation, for in the second letter to him, she wrote:

> When my sister has left me [Chrissey and her family were staying at Bird Grove because Edward Clarke was in the midst of serious financial difficulties] . . . I shall be at leisure and will gladly translate a new section should you think it desirable, for I shall proceed *con amore* now that you encourage me to hope for the publication of the memoir. I confess my spirits were flagging at the idea of translating four hundred pages to no purpose.

In this same letter, which was written three months after the first, a passage occurs that is both enigmatic and revealing of the personal feelings involved:

> A friend has given some admonitions that led me to fear I have misrepresented myself by my manner. . . . It gives me much pain to think that you should have received such an impression, and I

entreat you to believe that the remembrance of you, your words and looks calls up, I will not say humble, but self-depreciating reflections and lively gratitude. I am always inclined to make a father-confessor of you, perhaps because I augur that you have no heart for inflicting heavy penances, though I fear even you will say that I deserve them when I tell you that my affections have been disturbing forces which have shaken my intellect from a steady direction to the object you and my better self would make my pole-star, but this will not I trust shall not be so again.

It does not seem that her affections had shaken her intellect because of Watts himself, unless she was being very circumspect; it is however clear that she took pleasure in telling him that this had happened.

It is also clear that she persisted in wanting to add to the role of father-confessor (which perhaps he had unwittingly assumed during their argumentative talks concering religion) that of foster father to her work. This pattern she was to repeat until her deep wish for this kind of relationship with a man was satisfied by her union with Lewes. Despite her serious planning for the Vinet translation, it was several months after her initial proposal that she suddenly discovered she could not procure the needed books and so asked Watts for the loan of his. He sent them to her, and she responded:

I will not worry you with long letters, but I wish to express fully what I think in reply to a question of yours. If we should be so happy as to get one of Vinet's works published I beg you to understand that I consider myself *your* translator and the publication as yours, and that my compensation will be any good that may be effected by the work, and the pleasure of being linked to your remembrance.

Apparently in her enthusiasm—or perhaps at Watts's suggestion—she had now expanded her project to include works by Vinet other than *Liberté des Cultes.*

Despite these favorable auguries, no Vinet translation materialized. In February of 1843 she returned Watts's volumes, writing him: "I hope I am not too rash in committing your valuable books to the railway without a guardian, but I am ashamed to retain them longer, and I feel that I need the excuses of being engaged in a translation of a part of Spinoza's works for a friend and of having had some family trials for not returning them before." Yet, as Cara Bray was to make known, the Spinoza translation was undertaken at George Eliot's sole request, and she had had fewer family trials than usual over the months of her correspondence with Watts. What had happened? Did she sense reluctance on his part? Perhaps he had become uneasily aware of the deep yearning within her which she could articulate only in the guise of formidable intellectual projects. He may have withdrawn by pleading too much work of his own and even illness within his family, for her letter concludes:

> I hope you are equal in bodily health to your arduous occupations and that you have the comfort of seeing Mrs. Watts and your dear little girl quite well. It will be a satisfaction to me to know that the parcel has arrived quite safely, but I beg you only to tax your goodness for the most laconic note that can serve the purpose.

The Spinoza piece is uncertain: perhaps it was the *Tractatus Theologico-Politicus,* which would have thrilled her with its call to freedom; or perhaps it was Part I of the *Ethics,* the whole of which was to absorb her later. More certainly, the friend for whom this translation was begun was Cara, who wrote about it to Sara: "Spinoza came (from Dr. Brabant) and looked so temptingly easy that I grieved to let Mary Ann carry it off, for I am sure I could understand his Latin better than her English; but it would disappoint her." Cara's remark indicates how well aware the Rosehill people were that Mary Ann needed an occupation to take her out of herself. It also introduces a figure, Dr. Robert Brabant, who was to become a far more significant foster father in her emotional life than Francis Watts.

The Spinoza translation was also abortive, for she was soon involved in a set of circumstances which led to her monumental translation of David Friedrich Strauss's *Das Leben Jesu* (*The Life of Jesus*). This work came to her with curious and even—as events unfolded—humiliating indirection. The translation was unofficially commissioned by Joseph Parkes, a London free-thinker and friend of both Brabant (who knew Strauss personally) and Charles Hennell, whose *Inquiry* had evoked a congratulatory letter from Strauss. It fell to Charles to find a translator. He turned first to his learned sister Sara, but she, according to the version in her 1899 memoir of her brother, considered the task to be beyond her, "both for its labour and difficulty." Then Charles, so Sara continues,

> had recourse to Miss Brabant, who at once took it up, being herself a fairly good German scholar, and as having besides always at hand her father to give her any needful help; while on my own part I voluntarily undertook, as a general security against inaccuracy, to revise scrupulously her manuscript under comparison with the original.

What Sara neglected to mention is that Charles and Elizabeth Brabant (better known as "Rufa," the nickname given her by Coleridge because of her red-gold hair) were in love and wished to marry, although Dr. Brabant opposed the marriage because Charles was tubercular. Nonetheless, after Rufa had translated only two chapters of the Strauss, she resolved to marry Charles despite her father's opposition, the doctor became reconciled, and preparations for the wedding were made.

Understandably, Rufa had no wish to be encumbered with the translation on her honeymoon, and it was at this point, according to Charles Bray, that "Miss Evans was persuaded by Mr. Hennell to undertake the completion of it." George Eliot's real feelings concerning her role as substitute-translator can only be conjectured. It is not improbable that she was at this time in love with Charles Hennell. An extreme view which appears in at least two biographies is that they were actually engaged and that she was jilted when Rufa appeared. Gordon Haight has called this a "preposterous fiction," for it seems clear that Rufa and Charles were engaged before he met George Eliot. However, Charles and Rufa's engagement would not have precluded George Eliot's being in love with Charles. Emotionally vulnerable as she was during these years and welcome as an intimate at Rosehill, she could hardly have remained a passive onlooker as she watched him admirably fulfill his relationship as a brother. Charles treated his sisters without condescension, shared their interests, and made their intellectual and family life as one. Perhaps her increasingly frequent, intense presence determined Rufa to marry Charles quickly; Rufa was shrewd enough to sense that she had a dangerous, if unacknowledged, rival who was quite capable of being the aggressor in following the dictates of her heart. If so, Rufa won—and George Eliot was left with translating Strauss, a task which was to fill the better portion of two and a half years of her life, was to be always arduous, and near the end, was to cause her sheer agony.

Just before this work was under way, she was invited to join a party which traveled to London to see Charles and Rufa married on 1 November 1843. This occasion was to have consequences which would remove Charles Hennell from her mind, had he ever been there with significant meaning. Always laconic in describing personal matters, Charles Bray says merely:

> In November, 1843, we went to London to be present at Charles Hennell's marriage with Miss Brabant at Finsbury Chapel, where W. J. Fox, one of the most eloquent preachers of the day, was officiating minister. Miss Evans went with us, and was one of the bridesmaids, and she afterwards paid a visit to Dr. Brabant, the bride's father, at Devizes, in order to cheer him upon the loss of his only daughter.

Bray fails to mention, although he must have known it, that this pleasant-sounding visit ended disastrously. In inviting her to his home, the doctor had acted unwisely. Yet even if she had been knowledgeable enough to sense the potential danger in the situation, she probably would have been unable to resist rushing into a relationship for which she had been longing as "daughter" to a "father" who would appreciate, respect, and use the whole of her power to work (Brabant had made a dilatory translation of parts of *Das Leben Jesu*). Unlike the cautious Reverend Watts, the doctor filled his role to perfection. "What name do you think I have been baptized withal?" she wrote Cara the day after her arrival at Devizes. "Rather a learned pun, Deutera, which *means* second and *sounds* a little like daughter."

And he had already insisted that she consider his library *her* room. "I am in a little heaven here," she wrote again to Cara, adding almost a fortnight later, "Dr. Brabant being its archangel. . . ." How really to describe him? There was not time enough "to tell of all his charming qualities. We read, walk and talk together, and I am never weary of his company." She had written to her real father "to beg for a longer leave of absence. . . ."

There were also lesser angels on the scene. "Mrs. Brabant [who was blind] is a most affectionate amiable being, . . ." she admitted to Cara. Mrs. Brabant's sister, Miss Hughes, somewhat annoyingly (and no doubt with a significance that the young worshipper did not yet understand) was "advising" her to go home "by Cheltenham and Birmingham"; but she hoped that she had "yet three weeks to consider about the matter." Even Rufa's appearance for a leavetaking visit and apparently without her new husband was not too disturbing. Deutera could afford to be generous. As she wrote Cara: "I have been very glad to resign part of my interest in her papa for a week . . . consoling myself with the prospect of being a pis aller by and bye." Had Cara dared express some skepticism of the doctor's saintliness? "He really is a finer character than you think. Beautifully sincere, conscientious and benevolent. . . ." And just as she is writing, the doctor himself appears to take her for a walk "as a reward for the good character" she has given him. The letter ends in a flurry of excited anticipation: "I hardly know what I am writing."

Paradise was to end with rude abruptness. The affectionate and amiable Mrs. Brabant, perhaps incited by a barrage of jealous observations from her sister, told the young votary in no uncertain terms to get out and that if she ever re-entered the house, Mrs. Brabant would leave instantly. Meanwhile the beautifully sincere, conscientious, and benevolent doctor stayed passive, intervening for the honor of neither side. Years later, Rufa, who was perhaps a little jealous herself, accused him of "unmanliness in the affair," and of having "acted ungenerously and worse, towards Miss E. for though he was the chief cause of all that passed, he acted towards her as though . . .

the fault lay with her alone." Rufa also asserted in this confidence to John Chapman that "the Doctor liked her [George Eliot] extremely, and said that so long as she had no home she must consider his house as her permanent home." (Apparently George Eliot intimated to Brabant that she had regained no "real" home after the Holy War.) Aside from her own father as the "chief cause," Rufa ascribed the trouble to George Eliot's inability to follow "the required conventionalisms." In recording this private conversation with Rufa and its consequences, Chapman himself speculated whether George Eliot had acted "in the simplicity of her heart and her ignorance of (or incapability of practicing)" the necessary conventionalisms. By the time of his talk with Rufa in June 1851, he had reason to wonder about the real nature of his new assistant, for only two months earlier she had been driven out of his own home by a situation similar to (although much more complex than) the one at Devizes in 1843.

Inexcusably or not, George Eliot had been unarmed against the domestic tragi-comedy which ousted her from the Brabant household, and her feelings for the doctor were to stay vulnerable for many years to come. Although no doubt hurt by his failure to defend her against his hostile womenfolk, she decided that she had as much right to his translated notes from Strauss as his own daughter would have had. She did not ask him for them herself, but requested Sara to gain them for her through Rufa. But when she had the notes in hand, the urgency was gone. She read one paragraph and put them aside, having discovered, as she told Sara, that to read another person's translation was too much "like hearing another piano going just a note before you in the same tune you are playing." She might easily have anticipated this result; the real value of the notes to her lay simply in possessing them.

Three years later, when her Strauss labor was over, she and the doctor exchanged letters (now extinct) which caused new alarm to the Devizes women. They lost no time in reporting this ominous renewal of correspondence to Rufa, who in turn lost little time asking Sara to investigate. To Sara's inquiry, probably solicitous and admonishing in tone, George Eliot responded hotly: "Pray convince her [Rufa] and every one concerned . . . that I am too inflatedly conceited to think it worth my while to run after Dr. Brabant or his correspondence. If I ever," she continues, for the moment a traitor to those ecstatically happy letters from Devizes, "offered incense to him it was because there was no other deity at hand and because I wanted some kind of worship pour passer le temps. I always knew that I could belabour my fetisch if I chose, and laughed at him in my sleeve." Yet in this same letter she was forced to admit that she *had* renewed correspondence with him ("as a favour *conferred* by me rather than *received"*), for Sara well knew that only a week earlier George Eliot had had a copy of her Strauss translation bound at her own expense and sent to him. No doubt it was this gesture that had precipitated the letter writing; she could hardly have expected him to accept her offering without any acknowledgment whatsoever.

Apparently some correspondence continued between them, and apparently again the letter writing was not allowed to remain a private matter. As late as 28 February 1847, she wrote Sara with the usual defensive sarcasm now reserved for references to him: "I never *meant* to write to Dr. B. on family matters—I merely said in my vicious, hyena fashion that I should like to send him an anathema maranatha." In the same letter she reveals that she had asked Sara to mail back his copy of Spinoza, which she had borrowed from Cara all of four years earlier: "I certainly should have been delighted if the Spinoza parcel could have been sent at a high pitch of velocity to Devizes and found its mark somewhere about Dr. B's ear, so as to give a salutary bruise to his Nos. 6 and 7 [uncomplimentary phrenological symbols]. . . ." She still wanted the Spinoza, but not his copy; and she begged Sara to "take the trouble to ask Mr. Chapman to get me a copy of the same edition if possible—Mind, I really want this. . . ." Brabant was not offended. Sara wrote her mother on 5 August that Mary Ann "had a most affectionate invitation from Dr. B. a few days ago to go to Germany with him!" There were to be others in the party, and Sara thought the trip "would have been the most delightful thing in the world for her, and just now she could conveniently leave her father." But George Eliot wrote back simply, thanking him and saying it was impossible to accept.

Although there is no further news of him during her Coventry life, the intrepid doctor made a point of seeing her when she was living with the Chapmans at 142 Strand, where he was an occasional lodger. After one such visit she wrote Cara that the "house is only just exorcised of Dr. Brabant." But the next day she wrote to Charles Bray quite differently of this visit, revealing that she had spent considerable time in the doctor's company, he having "very politely" taken her "to the Crystal Palace, the theatre, and the 'Overland Route.'" Possibly she never wholly exorcised Brabant until she re-created him, or a part of him, in the dusty Casaubon of *Middlemarch*.

She was well armed by the presence of George Henry Lewes when the ubiquitous doctor reappeared—by coincidence or otherwise—in their railway carriage after their elopement to the Continent in the summer of 1854. He "kindly exerted himself" to arrange a meeting in Cologne between her and the man to whose work she had given so much time and anguish, Strauss himself. But she rather wished that the interview had not occurred: it was a melancholy affair, with

Strauss looking "so strange and cast-down. . . ." More ironically, the two were prevented by the language barrier "from learning more of each other than our exterior which in the case of both would have been better left to imagination." She modestly ascribed this barrier to her "deficient German," thus indirectly revealing that Strauss's English must have been equally deficient. Disappointing though the meeting may have been, it seems highly appropriate that Dr. Brabant initiated it—the last recorded appearance of the doctor in the life of his Deutera.

AFTER THE RETURN FROM DEVIZES, THE TRANSLATING OF Strauss had not proceeded smoothly. In 1845—just a little over a year after the ill-fated visit—it was interrupted by another emotional adventure: she went to the perilous brink of becoming engaged to a man who presumably was near her own age (twenty-five) or perhaps even younger. The young man remains unidentified, but the strange progress of this brief affair, which lasted not much longer than a week, is recorded by Cara Bray in a newsy letter to Sara:

I must give you some account of a matter which has been much in our thoughts this last week relating to Mary Ann: she wished me to tell you and has often said "How I wish Sara were here, for she knows what would be for my good!" I may as well say at the beginning though that it has all come to nothing. She says she was talking to you about a young artist she was going to meet at Baginton. Well, they did meet and passed two days in each other's company, and she thought him the most interesting young man she had seen and superior to all the rest of mankind; the third morning he made proposals through her brother-in-law Mr. Hooton [Houghton]—saying, "she was the most fascinating creature he had ever beheld, that if it were not too presumptuous to hope etc. etc., a person of such superior excellence and powers of mind," etc., in short, he seemed desperately smitten and begged permission to write to her. She granted this, and came to us so brimful of happiness;—though she said she had not fallen in love with him yet, but admired his character so much that she was sure she should: the only objection seemed to be that his profession—a picture-restorer—is not lucrative or over-honourable. We liked his letters to her very much—simple, earnest, unstudied. She refused anything like an engagement on so short an acquaintance, but would have much pleasure to see him as a friend etc.

So he came to see her last Wednesday evening, and owing to his great agitation, from youth—or something or other, did not seem to her half so interesting as before, and the next day she made up her mind that she could never love or respect him enough to marry him and that it would involve too great a sacrifice of her mind and pursuits. So she wrote to him to break it off—and there it stands now. Poor girl, it has been a trying, exciting week to her and she seemed quite spiritless this morning; and we cannot help feeling that she has been over-hasty in giving it up. And yet—and yet—one does not know what to advise.

The young man's agitation is not surprising. Without benefit of explanation, he had been abruptly cast down from one superior to all mankind to one who could not be respected, let alone loved, enough for marriage. His downfall was obviously the result of psychological reasons on her side rather than factual ones, for his youth and occupation would have been as clearly known in Baginton as at Foleshill a few days later. Cara's nonplussed "or something or other" is more illuminating if only because of its ambiguity. Probably George Eliot herself could not have put the reason more precisely. There was panic in her withdrawal, and in the days between her visit to Baginton and the young man's coming to her home, she had, as noted by Cara, suffered "dreadful headaches . . . and can find no relief but in leeches—sweet little creatures, as she calls them."

After she had made her rejection final, she was assailed by another onslaught of miserable feelings, this time of guilt, as she at last realized she had given him unfair encouragement. Cara wrote to Sara about this new stage:

> This affair of M.A.'s is much on our minds; although it is given up irrevocably, she is so extremely wretched about it, and we know, wants it to come on again—not that she cares much for him, but she is so grieved to have wounded his feelings, and he has behaved so well and unselfishly that he deserves pity. But we can do nothing in the matter—indeed she entreats us not to meddle, and the Hootons are the only parties who could—they being the friends of both. She says it shall not interfere with the M.S. [the Strauss translation], but poor girl, everything seems against the grain with her.

George Eliot also wrote to Sara on the same day, April 6, in much the same vein:

> I have never yet half thanked you for taking an interest in my little personal matters. My unfortunate "affaire" did not become one "du coeur," but it has been anything but a comfortable one for my conscience. If the circumstances could be repeated with the added condition of my experience I should act very differently. As it is I have now dismissed it from my mind, and only keep it recorded in my book of reference, article "*Precipitancy, ill effects*

of." So now dear Sara, I am once more your true Gemahlinn, which being interpreted, means that I have no loves but those that you can share with me—intellectual and religious loves.

But she had not dismissed the affair as decisively as she implied to Sara, for a week later Cara wrote Sara that "she expects to see the innamorato again soon *as a friend*; but do not mention the matter to her any more." Was it only Sara with whom she was averse to discussing the matter? Obviously she had talked freely about it to Cara, and still later, on the twenty-first, she wrote provocatively to her old school-fellow Martha Jackson:

> What should you say to my becoming a wife? Should you think it a duty to ascertain the name of the rash man that you might warn him from putting on such a matrimonial hair-shirt as he would have with me? I did meditate an engagement, but I have determined, whether wisely or not I cannot tell, to defer it, at least for the present.

As it is unlikely Martha resisted this coyly indirect appeal for further discussion, the now long-lost name probably appeared in a subsequent letter. Unfortunately most of the letters exchanged between George Eliot and Martha have vanished. (Martha refused Cross's request to incorporate extracts from them in the *Life*, and although she asserted that she would publish them herself, she never did so.)

Also in this 21 April letter to Martha, she gives—although cryptically if the reader does not know something of the background—what was no doubt a part of the complex motive for her first impulsiveness with the young man, as well as an indication of what the experience had cost her emotionally:

> Nay, the experience of a week, of a day, may make one grey in wisdom or in sadness as well as in hair. Perhaps you would find some symptoms of age creeping over me if you were with me now, and you would accuse me of being too old for five-and-twenty, which is a sufficiently venerable sum of years in the calendar of young ladies generally. But I can laugh and love and fall into a fit of enthusiasm still, so there is some of the youthful sap left. . . .

Added to the stigma of spinsterhood according to the social standards of her time, there would have been the nagging reminder in her mind of Isaac's hint that by staying unmarried she was a drain on the family income. Yet these reasons do not explain the dramatic suddenness of her change in attitude toward the man; as reasons they are, in fact, too realistic to account for the bizarre climax and anticlimax. The lack of any mention of her father in the surviving record is also unrealistic. He was increasingly dependent upon her as companion and practical nurse, and she considered her fulfillment of those roles a sacred trust of her own choice. Her marriage would surely have jeopardized such a relationship with him. This perhaps occurred to her belatedly, for in the 21 April letter to Martha, she wrote: "I and father go on living and loving together as usual, and it is my chief source of happiness to know that I form one item of his."

Rather than realistic or even romantic, the affair seems to have been a futile attempt to prove something to herself—and perhaps to others. It is possible that she wished to convince Dr. Brabant she needed no one of his age or learning to adore. This is suggested by her hyperbolic description of the young picture restorer, and also by the fact that when the time for decision came and she could not meet her own challenge, the most coherent charge levied against him (according to Cara) was his youth. Perhaps too she wished to show Brabant that she, as well as his own daughter, could toss aside the Strauss translation for love and marriage. Still more deeply, she may have been urged on by a need to prove—as she had to strive to prove throughout her life —her essential femininity. With significant qualifications, she had already done so with the doctor. With him, probably for the first time since her childhood, her whole being had gone forward harmoniously to an external love object, but as a second daughter. The love object had been clearly defined as ineligible for any other kind of amatory role. The picture restorer, on the other hand, was all too surely available—unattached, the proper age, and even eagerly willing.

She could not yet meet this test for, aside from Brabant, her real emotional attachment during this time was to a woman. When still perplexed over her final decision about the young man, she often said to Cara, "How I wish Sara were here, for she knows what would be for my good!" Sara's presence might well have snuffed out the "precipitancy," for she, like Maria Lewis, frowned upon her young friend's free manner with men. ("Poor little Miss Hennell," noted Edith Simcox in 1885, "apparently always disapproved of Marian for depending so much on the arm of man. . . .") Sara was destined to be the second and last Maria Lewis in George Eliot's life, although probably no one at the time realized this, for even to George Eliot there must have appeared to be essential differences between the two young women. Sara, the enviable sister of Charles Hennell, had attractive attributes of her own. Seven years George Eliot's senior, she was both young enough to seem a contemporary and old enough to be a source of counsel and to provide a stable base for the emotional sallies with men. Furthermore, she was at this time George Eliot's equal in intellectual equipment and achievement and, inspired by her brother, had traveled the same path toward the New Rationalism. Although different in kind, her sensitivity was as intense as George Eliot's, and overflowed into her work. According to Elizabeth Haldane, who met her in her later years, she was "highly strung and nervous, and brought all the ardour of feeling into her metaphysical speculations." She lived with her mother and was otherwise unattached. It was inevitable that an emotionally charged relationship should have quickly developed between the two women—for Sara perhaps, aside from that with her brother, the most meaningful one in her life.

Their language of affection went beyond flower imagery. Beginning in the fall of 1843, George Eliot salutes Sara as "Lieber Gemahl," "Beloved Spouse," "Beloved Achates," etc. At first, neither woman consistently assumed the male or female role; but as time went on, George Eliot, despite her comparative youth, became more regularly the husband, and such passages as this are not infrequent in her letters: "I have saved till last my conjugal gratitude for your affectionate wish to have me with you. It would be a real delight to me to be with my bright-eyed and klarsprechende beloved. . . ." As late as April 1849, she wrote Sara: "I have given you a sad excuse for flirtation [exactly what is meant is not known], but I have not been beyond seas long enough to make it lawful for you to take a new husband—therefore I come back to you with all a husband's privileges and command you to love me. . . . I sometimes talk to you in my soul as lovingly as Solomon's Song." (Cross silently deleted such passages.) But by 1849 several warning signals that she was moving away from Sara both emotionally and intellectually had occurred (it was, one remembers, when she was beginning to feel the need to be free of Maria Lewis that she wrote the most extravagant protestations of her love).

Throughout the translating of Strauss, however, the relationship was intimate and unclouded. Sara resumed her critical supervision of the translation, although she recalled half a century later that she thought her role superfluous now the work had "passed over into hands that were in every way competent for it." Nonetheless, she gave the growing manuscript a close reading and thus had the pleasure of seeing "with what delicacy the meaning was being made to transfuse itself. . . ." In the margins of the copy sent her, she penciled in suggestions of her own which, to her gratification, George Eliot "usually adopted at once with only the remark that to have any failure in accuracy would be intolerable to her."

Although friendship flourished under this arrangement, George Eliot applied herself to her almost overwhelming task with diminishing zeal. Despite Sara's faithful reading, she felt that she had been deserted by everyone originally involved in the project. Charles and Rufa were understandably self-absorbed, and she began to hear rumors that the financial backing for the publication of her translation was not nearly so secure as she had been led to believe. It would seem that "in the first blush of their enthusiasm," Joseph Parkes and his friends had agreed to raise the necessary sum, but then conveniently forgot their promise. By cruel coincidence, in the spring of 1841, just when the financial affairs looked their worst, the Brays and Sara planned a trip to Hastings. She felt desperate. "I am alarmed," she wrote Sara, "to hear that you are all going to the coast without my having any intimation that Mr. Parkes has fulfilled his promise. I begin utterly to despair that Strauss will ever be published unless I . . . print it myself. I have no confidence in Mr. Parkes and shall not be surprised if he fail in his engagement altogether. . . ." She was wrong about Mr. Parkes: he came through magnanimously, personally making the publication financially possible.

Even had she been sent encouraging news by Charles Hennell, who was in London investigating the actual circumstances, she probably would not have believed it. For once again she was caught in a dilemma that emanated as much from herself as from external factors. She felt the need to rationalize her concern over the worldly matter of publication. "It is very laughable," she wrote Sara, "that I should be irritated about a thing in itself so trifling as a translation." It was, she claimed, the "very triviality of the thing" that exasperated her. Had the difficulties been those "that attend a really grand undertaking," they could be borne; "but things should run smoothly and fast when they are not important enough to demand the sacrifice of one's whole soul." Yet when she came to be engaged in "a really grand undertaking"—as the writing of her novels might justly be called—she was to fall equal prey to anxiety over publication arrangements, often for reasons far less realistic than those that concerned her for Strauss. And when the Strauss publication, which she had bitterly prophesied would never occur, did materialize, her anxiety merely shifted. Did Sara think—she could not resist asking— "Mr. Chapman [the publisher] is advertising sufficiently? I hope he is not so penny wise as to economize in that particular." Years later she was to exhaust herself with the same worry that the impeccable and efficient John Blackwood could not adequately take care of his own business.

Harassed though she was over the ambiguous financial situation, there was another reason for her growing distaste for her work, one which eventually swallowed up every other concern. The deeper she went into Strauss, the less sympathy she found for his ideas and method of analysis. It was not that she had become uneasy over his premise or his aim; she was, in fact, never to be openly critical of either. But as she worked on, beating out the meaning from the "leathery" German, she grew convinced that Strauss was belaboring a small portion of objective truth as if it were a whole truth. "I am never pained when I think Strauss right," she wrote Sara at the end of 1845, "but in many cases I think him wrong, as every man must be in working out

into detail an idea which has general truth, but is only one element in
a perfect theory, not a perfect theory in itself."

In his critical examination of the life of Jesus, Strauss's chief objective—the "one element" George Eliot felt needed a larger context
—is to show that the life as recorded in the four Gospels is the result
of an aggregate of Evangelical mythi. By "mythus" in general, Strauss
means "the creation of a fact out of an idea"; and an Evangelical
mythus is a "narrative relating directly or indirectly to Jesus, which
may be considered not as the expression of a fact, but as the product
of an idea of his earliest followers." The two great sources of Evangelical mythi were, according to Strauss, the "Messianic ideas existing in
the Jewish mind before Jesus and independently of him," and the
"particular impression which was left by the personal character, actions, and fate of Jesus, and which modified the Messianic ideas."
Hence, Strauss's real examination is of the Gospels. Although he everywhere tacitly assumes Hume's position on miracles (they are violations
of natural law, and natural law is never violated), he makes only a
casual attempt to explain them away as he proceeds with his analysis.
Nor is he especially intent upon reconstructing the historical life of
Jesus. Always it is the Gospels themselves which are his target, and
he turns upon them not only the light of logical criticism but also the
more relentless light of what he calls "our approved canon, that in
glorifying narratives, such as our gospels, where various statements
are confronted, that is the least probable which best subserves the
object of glorification."

It was this concentrated dissection of the Gospels, not the implication inherent in Strauss's work that Jesus had been only human, which
George Eliot found repugnant. She had gone beyond even the Hennells
in accepting Jesus as a great but wholly human teacher—a "Jewish
philosopher," so she described him to Sara after her translation was
finished and published. She admitted dissatisfaction with that description, yet she thought it the truest one possible, although she was aware
that her conception was different "from the one you seem inclined to
form." The topic had come up because she had given Charles's *Inquiry*
a third reading, and her "delight and high admiration" now surpassed
even what she had earlier felt for it. Strauss is not mentioned by name,
but her new enthusiasm for the *Inquiry* is in direct contrast to the
increasing dislike she felt for *Das Leben Jesu* while translating it. She
had reached the conclusion—she told Sara—that the *Inquiry* "fur-
nishes the utmost that can be done towards obtaining a *real* view of
the life and character of Jesus by rejecting as little as possible from
the Gospels." Her wording is careful, the adjective *"real"* modifying,
not "life and character," but "view." And that "view," with all its
hope, promise, and consolation for humanity, can be gained only from

the Gospels. Take away from them all that Strauss had designated as Evangelical mythi, or—as she put it to Sara—"Subtract from the N[ew] T[estament] the miraculous and highly improbable and what will be the remainder?"

It is clear that George Eliot's estrangement from Evangelicalism had not lessened the hold of the Bible upon her. But then she had never read the Bible merely for the sake of her religion. Her letters to Maria Lewis reveal that she had responded to it as if it were an allegory of the struggle, the failures, and the triumphs of what passed in her own soul. So intermixed was it with her own thinking that she had probably never mentally stepped back to survey it and its significance to her until the involvement with Strauss. The further she went with the translation, the more she felt a traitor to that part of her self which she most valued, so that by the time she reached his analysis of the death and transfiguration of Jesus (the greatest of the "glorifying narratives"), she found it almost impossible to continue. Adding to her personal struggle to keep her thoughts sufficiently in harmony with Strauss to translate him fairly was her recognition that he himself was on the most tenuous ground here that he had yet encountered. Even according to his own "approved canon," he had to conclude that there "is in the Old Testament no doctrine of a suffering and dying Messiah. Also there is no evidence in the New Testament that the Jews in general had the idea of this kind of Messiah." Thus he had to conjecture, rather lamely, that "Jesus Himself may have reached the conclusion of the necessity of his death . . . or the whole idea might have been added *after* his death."

Such reasoning repelled, rather than persuaded, his translator; when only a final spurt of energy was needed to bring her work to an end, she could not stick with it. "We have seen more of M.A. than usual this week," Cara wrote Sara in the middle of February, 1846. "She said she was Strauss-sick—it made her ill dissecting the beautiful story of the crucifixion, and only the sight of her Christ-image and picture made her endure it." The image was, according to Cross, "a cast, 20 inches high, of Thorwaldsen's grand figure of the risen Christ, which was placed in view in her study . . . a little room on the first floor, with a charming view over the country." The picture was an engraving of Christ, "which she considered using as a frontispiece for the Strauss." She seems to have given up this idea. Perhaps fortunately, for Strauss, had he known of it, could hardly have condoned the plan.

Yet he would have felt some sympathy for her anguished reaction to his own work. In the Preface to the first German edition, Strauss had written that he was "aware that the essence of the Christian faith is perfectly independent of [my] criticism. The supernatural birth of Christ, his miracles, his resurrection and ascension, remain eternal

truths, whatever doubts may be cast on their reality as historical facts."
And in his final section—"The Dogmatic Import of the Life of Jesus"
—he becomes almost mystical: "the key to the whole of Christology
[is] that, as subject of the predicate which the Church assigns to Christ,
we place, instead of an individual, an idea"—a real idea, not an
illusion, lying within "the race. . . . Humanity is the union of the two
natures—God become man, the infinite manifesting itself. in the
finite . . . it is the child of the visible Mother and the invisible Father,
Nature and Spirit. . . ." Whether or not George Eliot agreed with that,
she could not forgive him the fact that lying between the Preface and
the "Dogmatic Import" was a long and weighty volume of devastating
criticism in which "the essence of the Christian faith" was entirely
forgotten. That was why, when finally she had thrown off the restraining bonds of the translation, she went quickly back to "thinking of
that most beautiful passage in Luke's Gospel—the appearance of Jesus
to the disciples at Emmaus. How universal in its significance!" she
wrote Sara.

> The soul that has hopefully followed its form—its impersonation
> of the highest and best—all in despondency—its thoughts all re-
> futed, its dreams all dissipated. Then comes another Jesus . . . the
> same highest and best, only chastened, crucified instead of tri-
> umphant—and the soul learns that this is the true way to conquest
> and glory. . . .

Then, as if anticipating Sara's astonishment, she added: "But I am not
become a Methodist, dear Sara."
That was why when she came to Ludwig Feuerbach's *Das Wesen
des Christentums* (*The Essence of Christianity*) she felt the thrill of
confirmation which she could never feel for *Das Leben Jesu*. Feuerbach's theme, "the essence of Christianity is the essence of human
feeling," is actually more unsettling to orthodoxy than Strauss's ponderous critique. But he has reverence for religious symbols because
they *are* of human origin, and it was exactly this which she had found
lacking in Strauss. Jesus was the highest, the ultimate symbol. "Hence,
only in Christ is the last wish of religion realized, the mystery of
religious feeling solved:—solved however in the language of imagery
proper to religion," wrote Feuerbach (as translated by George Eliot).
And ". . . for what God is in essence, that Christ is in actual appearance.
That God, who in himself is nothing else than the nature of man,
should also have a real existence as such, should be as man an object
to the consciousness—this is the goal of religion. . . ." "With the ideas
of Feuerbach," she was to write to the somewhat less enthusiastic Sara
in the spring of 1854, "I everywhere agree. . . ." This was a rare admission of her total consent to another's ideas.

Yet she never lost respect for the impressive qualifications which allowed Strauss to move at ease (and with a dignity she thought Feuerbach did not always command) in his labyrinthine subject—for his scholarly familiarity with medieval and modern theological theory, as well as biblical exegesis, and for his power of close reasoning. Once she had mastered and passed the death-and-transfiguration passage, she gradually recovered from her "Strauss-sickness," so that by the time she had reached the end of her work except for making a few changes in the proofs, she could write Sara: "I do really like reading our Strauss —he is so Klar and Ideenvoll. . . . Next week and we will be merry and sad, wise and nonsensical, devout and wicked together!" With a great sense of release from her long-extended ordeal, she went off to visit Sara at Clapton in the late spring of 1846.

The translation was published that June, yet she felt no jubilation. She was unconvinced that any reviewer—or anyone else, for that matter —would read the huge work all the way through, or that any critic would know both Strauss and the German language adequately to evaluate her own contribution as a translator. Cara, who knew how much suffering had gone into the translation, was determined that the translator find some pleasure in her achievement, and wrote her sister Harriet concerning a late but flattering review: "Mary Ann and I have been so happy this morning reading the review of Strauss." A few days later, however, George Eliot wrote to Sara about the same review in a very different tone:

> The review of Strauss contains some very just remarks, though, on the whole I think it shallow and in many cases unfair. The praise it gives to the translation is just what I should have wished—indeed I cannot imagine anything more gratifying in the way of laudation. Is it not droll that Wicksted should have chosen one of my interpolations or rather paraphrases to dilate on? The expression "granite," applied to the sayings of Jesus is nowhere used by Strauss, but is an impudent addition of mine to eke out his metaphor.

Aside from the personal connotation of this passage, it reveals a little of George Eliot's mode of translating. Although intent upon rendering the original as accurately as possible, she was evidently not adverse to substituting English words, phrases, and idioms where literal translation would have been misleading to the English-reading public. Judging from the letters to Sara during the first part of 1854, when the Feuerbach translation was well under way and Sara, once again, was reading the manuscript as she composed it, she apparently took still more liberty with Feuerbach, whose style occasionally annoyed her and whose ideas she thought needed delicate rendering for English readers. In at least one instance she sent Sara a portion which she called "the *raw* Feuerbach—not any of my own cooking." The implication is that when Sara returned the manuscript she would rewrite what she had translated rapidly and literally and, in her own words, "alter the phraseology considerably." More importantly, she wanted Sara to read this rough draft in order to tell her what she "*must* leave out." A week later she wrote Sara: ". . . I shrink from omission"; and in her final version, the translation of the section under consideration (the Appendix) follows the original closely.

We can only conjecture as to how she dealt with Spinoza in translation, for whatever work she did in Coventry has apparently disappeared, and her completed translation of the *Ethics* is lodged unpublished in the Beinecke Library at Yale University. Probably her intention was to render him as literally as possible, as is suggested by Cara's early remark, "I am sure I could understand his Latin better than her English . . ." and supported by her own statement when she withdrew from a tentative arrangement to translate the whole of the *Tractatus Theologico-Politicus*: "For those who read the very words Spinoza wrote, there is the same sort of interest in his style as in the conversation of a person of great capacity who has led a solitary life, and who says from his own soul what all the world is saying by rote, but this interest hardly belongs to a translation."

Except for snatches such as these in letters written while she was translating Strauss, Feuerbach, and Spinoza, there is no clue as to what her guiding theory of translation was. By the time she finished Spinoza's *Ethics* early in 1856 she surely must have had one, for by then she had done enough substantial work in this medium to have it considered "a life's-work" (as she called Charles Hennell's one book, the *Inquiry*, when she read it for the third time). But she had no desire that her translations be considered as such, and the only public statement she made on the matter of translation is the provocatively brief and inconclusive essay-review of two translations from the German written for the 20 October 1855 issue of the *Leader*. She ends this hurriedly, but not without revealing the reason for her relatively casual attitude toward the work which had consumed much of her adult life:

> Though a good translator is infinitely below the man who produces *good* original works, he is infinitely above the man who produces *feeble* original works. We had meant to say something of the moral qualities especially demanded in the translator—the patience, the rigid fidelity, and the sense of responsibility in interpreting another man's mind. But we have gossiped on this subject long enough.

This was written out of seasoned experience, and one wishes that she had "gossiped" further. What little she says is authoritative and shows how seriously she approached the work of translating despite the fact that such work was for her a private sign of defeat. She longed to be on the other side of the fence with the original writer, and when she did arrive there she did no translating other than for her own reading and occasional use in the novels. Yet she owed a significant debt to the discipline of translating, for the three moral qualities she lists as demanded of the translator were to serve her well in novel writing.

More specifically, she owed this and other debts to *The Life of Jesus*, in which she first acquired the discipline. She often justly accused herself of being a procrastinator and had neglected at least one past project —the "Chart of Ecclesiastical History"—until it was no longer needed. But unless she were to fail those depending upon her Strauss translation, she did not dare allow herself the freedom of working on it only when the spirit moved her. So she forged a pattern for work, although her working hours were, as Bray recorded, "never more than from 9 a.m. till 1 p.m."—her temperament being (he explains phrenologically) "nervous lymphatic," so that it was "active without endurance." When she came to write fiction, her power of endurance was often to be as sorely tested as it had been by the Strauss, although for different reasons, and she instinctively revived this working schedule almost to the minute.

Of even greater importance was Strauss's challenge to her own conception of the fundamental meaning in religion. This had been growing tentatively within her ever since her parting from Evangelicalism, but she needed the decisive push from Strauss to clarify it to herself. By negative means, he had renewed her faith in the symbolic value of the Scriptures, and to keep this value intact, she disassociated it from all doctrine. This gave her the freedom (usually spoken of as her "tolerance," or as Bray called it, the "exceeding fairness, for which she is noted, towards all parties . . . sects and denominations") to penetrate with sympathetic insight the symbolic value of the doctrinal expressions of the great Western faiths—Protestantism, Catholicism, Judaism. Ironically, Bray, again appealing to phrenology, ascribed this fairness to "her little feeling on the subject,—at least not enough to interfere with her judgment." She had extraordinary feeling on the subject. It was the friction between this feeling and her work on Strauss which led her to reaffirm what she had already realized as the result of the one open conflict with her father—the importance of the truth of feeling underlying belief.

She was to be indebted to Strauss on yet another level, for her translation, even though her name was not on the title page, eventually rescued her from provincial life. *The Life of Jesus* appeared under the aegis of the Chapman Brothers, Newgate Street, London. One of the two brothers soon withdrew as an active partner in the publishing and bookselling business. John Chapman was to stay with it and, despite eccentric and entangled methods, to make secure the firm's growing reputation as the most important London outlet for books of liberal thought. At the time of publication of the translation, George Eliot knew him only slightly and had no way of detecting the intricate strands emanating from Strauss which would lead her out of Coventry to London and hence to a totally new life. All she knew was that she had completed a grueling and perhaps thankless task.

A̲T THIS TIME SOMETHING MORE THAN MERE RELIEF WAS astir within George Eliot. When the struggle to keep her thoughts in harmony with Strauss's was at last no longer necessary, she felt a sense of liberation as decisive and dynamic as that from Evangelicalism. The immediate consequence was a surge of creativity. In September of 1846 Sara wrote her mother: "M.A. looks very brilliant just now —we fancy she must be writing her novel." She still was not ready for this, and the attempt was fated to be an abortive one, although it may well be that this was the fragment of fiction she valued enough to keep among her papers and read aloud to Lewes during their first Continental sojourn. Despite this failure, she did not—until three years later—take refuge in more translating. If she could not yet produce creative work, she could at least write about it. In several issues ranging from December 1846 to February 1847 of the *Coventry Herald and Observer* (which Bray had purchased), she published a series of supposed extracts under the general title "Poetry and Prose, from the Notebook of an Eccentric" (although no poetry is included). These are of the same form (what Pinney calls "moralia") to which she was to return in *The Impressions of Theophrastus Such*. A portion of the contents is somewhat similar too, but in the 1846-7 work, the tone is lighter and less world-weary although, on the whole, no more optimistic. These early sketches reveal her new interest in the artist as distinguished by temperament from his fellow man, and the non-didactic importance of art to its creator as a haven against the vicissitudes of life. The second sketch—significantly titled "How to Avoid Disappointment"—ends: "Who would not have some purpose in life as independent in its value as art is to the artist?"

The "Introductory" opens in a sentimental style reminiscent of

Mackenzie's *Man of Feeling*. The narrator has been mourning at the grave of his friend Macarthy, a writer whose alien and hypersensitive spirit had made him unfit to live in the world.

> His soul was a lyre of exquisite structure, but men knew not how to play on it: it was a bird endowed with rich and varied notes, which it was ready to bestow on human hearers; but their coarse fondling or brutal harshness scared it away, and the poor bird ceased to sing, save in the depths of the forest or the silence of night.

His feeling for beauty was most unusual and could be compared to

> those alleged states of mesmeric lucidity, in which the patient obtains an unenviable cognizance of irregularities, happily imperceptible to us in the ordinary state of our consciousness. His ideal was not, as with most men, an enshrined object of worship, but a beautiful shadow which was ever floating before him, importunately presenting itself as a twin object with all realities, whether external or mental, and turning all their charms into mockery.

His "preternaturally sharpened vision" forced him to see blemishes "where all was smoothness to others." The poverty and ignorance of the masses, the distorting conventionalities of the upper classes, and "the absence of artistic harmony and beauty in the details of outward existence" were as "sharp iron entering into his soul." Had he been less noble and benevolent, "he would have been a misanthropist, all compact of bitter sarcasm, and therefore no poet." Over thirty years later, Macarthy was to re-emerge in the tougher (because more misanthropic) Theophrastus Such. Both characters—the one standing at the threshold of her writing career and the other at the very end of it—are reminders that their creator had to struggle against being "all compact of bitter sarcasm, and therefore no poet." As a matter of fact, the fourth and final (also the longest) extract from Macarthy's manuscripts is the sarcastic and un-Macarthy-like "Hints on Snubbing," reminiscent not of *The Man of Feeling* but of Swift and Fielding.

Like the *Clerical Scenes* in 1857, ten years later, "Poetry and Prose, from the Notebook of an Eccentric" came to an abrupt and unplanned close, although both works had a framework which seemed to promise a much longer series than appeared. There, however, the similarity ends. Aside from content, the great difference between them is that the *Scenes* were followed by the novels, whereas only a dearth of creativity came after the Macarthy extracts. Nonetheless, George Eliot was seeing—and feeling—life more creatively than ever before, even though she was not yet molding what she saw and felt into fiction. The heightened perceptiveness which seems to have come to her as the result of her physical and mental release from Strauss remained with her, and she was beginning to find elements of high drama in even the

mildest and most colorless of lives (such as Amos Barton's was to be).
"I have just had lent me," she wrote John Sibree, Jr., in 1848, "the
journal of a person who died some years ago. When I was less vener-
able I should have felt the reading of such a thing insupportable—now
it interests me, though it is the simplest record of events and feelings."

Indeed, she appears to have caught the spirit of revolution that was
spreading over the Continent although not, to her dismay, in England.
Delighted to learn that Sibree was enthusiastic about the French
Revolution, she praised him for not being "one of those sages whose
reason keeps so tight a rein on their emotions that they are too
constantly occupied in calculating consequences to rejoice in any great
manifestation of the forces that underlie our everyday existence." The
French mind was "highly electrified" by "ideas on social subjects,"
and the people were willing to act according to those ideas. "But
we English are slow crawlers" (a complaint she was to repeat six years
later when writing to Sara from London: "People here are as slow to
be set on fire as a stomach"). All "decayed monarchs," she wrote
Sibree, "should be pensioned off: we should have a hospital for them,
or a sort of Zoological Garden, where these worn-out humbugs may
be preserved." They deserved their keep, "since we have spoiled them
for any honest trade." And at home? "Our little humbug of a queen
is more endurable than the rest of her race because she calls forth a
chivalrous feeling. . . ."

But the undercurrent of stimulated thought and expression which
runs through these 1848 letters to the young John Sibree stems from
more than external revolution: she was looking inward with newly
gained vision. As she was always to write to men with more candor
than to women, she made an attempt to express to him what she had
never attempted in letters even to Sara—her personal philosophy
(really a metapsychology) of life. This is an exploratory, rather than a
finished, statement, and hence not wholly lucid in that her verbal
symbols could not possibly connote to everyone else the specific meanings she attached to them. She begins with an admission of continued
unhappiness, for which she blames the old bugbear that had tortured
and mocked her as far back as the earliest Evangelical days, "my own
egotism." But this is no renewed attempt to cast it out by confession,
or even to restrain or suppress it. Instead, she gropes toward a new
idea, that of preserving but transforming its energy. "The passions and
the senses decompose . . ." she told the perhaps startled Sibree. "The
intellect by its analytic power, restrains the fury with which they rush
to their own destruction, the moral nature purifies beautifies and at
length transmutes them." Earlier in the letter she had implicitly
defined the moral nature as "sympathy, all-embracing love. . . ." Here
she is unconsciously anticipating herself as others would see her years

later—a woman of great but effortlessly controlled feeling, with a rare power of sympathy and love. And she also inadvertently clarifies why when her genius was finally freed for creative expression, it was to be restricted by her need to analyze. As her own psychic life had led her to believe, the passions and the senses, in their natural, un-hampered state, were furiously destructive; and if unrestrained by the analytic intellect could lead only to utter decomposition, death.

Although much of the thinking represented in this passage reflects her lingering fear of the forces within herself, it also shows that in her solitary thoughts (much too private to pass on to Sibree) about her own inability to write fiction, she had come to understand the vital difference between the talented productive artist and the equally talented but nonproductive neurotic. She herself, in 1848, was still hovering between these two poles; it was probably with a pathos which Sibree would have missed that she wrote him: "It is necessary to me, not simply to *be* but to *utter*. . . ." She could not yet *utter*, except in letters. Thus it is not surprising that early in 1849 she had returned to translating, despite the fact that in 1844 she had vowed, "I will never translate again if I live to correct the sheets for Strauss."

This time it was Spinoza again, the *Tractatus Theologico-Politicus*, which possibly she had started to translate in 1843. Her interest in Spinoza was sincere and she even made an unofficial arrangement with John Chapman for the publication of this translation, although later she was to cancel it. Cara had written Sara in March of 1849: "I suppose M.A. writes to you, and tells you her great desire to undertake Spinoza. She can find time now, and the occupation is just what she longs for." And in the middle of April, Cara wrote again to Sara: "M.A. is happy now with this Spinoza to do; she says it is such a rest to her mind."

But no one said that she was looking "brilliant." There is little doubt that she would have eagerly exchanged this "rest to her mind" for the stimulation of the creativity she felt surging, although still imprisoned, within herself. She was, however, finding a vicarious ex-tension of her creative self in a new kind of reading that supplied the deficiency of which she had been painfully conscious in Strauss— depiction of the subjective side of truth. When she was almost ready to resume translating, she wrote to Sara, not about Spinoza, but rhapsodically about Rousseau and George Sand as the two writers "who have rolled away the waters from their bed raised new mountains and spread delicious valleys for me."

Sometime during her London days she told William Hale White "that it was worth while to undertake all the labour of learning French if it resulted in nothing more than reading one book—Rous-seau's 'Confessions.'" Exactly when she first read this tumultuous autobiography (the title alone would have pleased her greatly) is not known. Perhaps it was very soon after her release from Strauss, for the first reference to Rousseau in her writing, including letters, is in the second Macarthy extract. This is called "The Wisdom of the Child" and opens with a statement which suggests both her own new view of the world and what it was she found in Rousseau that so appealed to her:

> It may not be an original idea, but never mind, if it be a true one, that the proper result of intellectual cultivation is to restore the mind to that state of wonder and interest with which it looks on everything in childhood. Thus, Jean Jacques Rousseau, couched on the grass by the side of a plant, that he might examine its structure and appearance at his ease, would have seemed to a little child so like itself in taste and feeling, that it would have lain down by him, in full confidence of entire sympathy between them, in spite of his wizard-like Armenian attire.

It was later, 14 July 1848, that she made her well-known declaration to Ralph Waldo Emerson (who had stayed the night at Rosehill) that it was the *Confessions* that "had first awakened her to deep reflection. . . ."

To Sara she wrote with far less restraint, and also in a defiant tone, as if well aware that Sara did not approve of her new taste in literature: "I wish you thoroughly to understand that the writers who have most profoundly influenced me . . . are not in the least oracles to me. . . . For instance it would signify nothing to me if a very wise person were to stun me with proofs that Rousseau's view of life, religion, and government are miserably erroneous. . . ." Convince her even that "he was guilty of the worst basenesses that have degraded civilized man," and it would still be true that it was his genius that "has sent that electric thrill through my intellectual and moral frame which has awakened me to new perceptions, which has made man and nature a fresh world of thought and feeling to me—and this not by teaching me any new belief." She was not blind to the contradictions and wishful thinking in the *Confessions*, yet they seemed not to matter. It was this which fascinated her. What was Rousseau's mysterious power, which reduced inaccuracy to unimportance whereas in another writer it might appear to be a moral blemish? She gave an answer to this question as late as *Theophrastus Such*, where in the chapter "Looking Inward" she admits that no one more than Rousseau has sinned against the "duteous reticences" which should be observed in autobiography, but then concludes: "Yet half our impressions of his character come not from what he means to convey, but from what he unconsciously enables us to discern."

Her response to Rousseau had the forceful quality of genuine insight. Through his eyes, she saw the old world aglow with fresh beauty, and for this she was never to lose her feeling of reverent gratitude toward him. In the summer of 1876, she and Lewes "went to Chambery," she wrote John Blackwood, "just to make a pilgrimage to Les Charmettes," where Rousseau had lived with Mme de Warens in 1736. And as Lewes noted in his Journal during this time, they read Rousseau aloud in French all summer—*Les Confessions, Émile,* and *La nouvelle Héloïse.* Still later, in May 1880, she made the same pilgrimage with Cross, and wrote to her sister-in-law with undimmed enthusiasm: "Chambery, paradisiacal walk to Les Charmettes! Roses gathered in Jean Jacques' garden!"

Her reaction to George Sand was as vibrant as that to Rousseau, and for similar reasons. "I should never dream," she told Sara in the same letter in which she explains her feeling for Rousseau, "of going to her writings as a moral code or text-book." Nor would it matter if she were proved to be not a great literary artist—that, for example, "she had no precise design at all but began to write as the spirit moved her and trusted to Providence for the catastrophe, which I think the more probable case. . . ." Transcending those considerations was the simple fact,

> sufficient for me as a reason for bowing before her in eternal gratitude to that "great power of God" manifest in her—that I cannot read six pages of hers without feeling that it is given to her to delineate human passion and its results—(and I must say in spite of your judgment) some of the moral instincts and their tendencies —with such truthfulness . . . that one might live a century with nothing but one's own dull faculties and not know so much as those six pages will suggest.

Through these two French writers she had made the discovery, perhaps a surprise to herself, that what she most valued in creative literature had little to do with intellectual power or even literary artistry. Her search for delineations of human passion with which she could empathize was to cause her to form several literary judgments not in harmony with the accepted taste of the day. Meaning it as praise, for example, she said she could see in Charlotte Brontë an English George Sand ("only the clothing is less voluptuous") at a time when even the free-thinking Harriet Martineau, although personally fond of Charlotte, shuddered away from what she considered to be the vulgar passion in *Villette.* Unconventional too was the importance she attached to Benjamin Constant's *Adolphe,* "a novel"—as Oscar Browning rightly describes it—"of the minutest self-inspection." He tells how she herself showed him from her own library a copy of *Adolphe* which was "interlined and marked by her in every page, and thumbed so as almost to fall to pieces." Browning perhaps goes too far in suggesting that she deliberately studied this and similar works in preparation for her own analysis of character and that from "such elements were those tales produced which shook so rapidly the heart of England." It is highly doubtful whether any of her fiction resulted from literary inspiration alone. Yet Browning is less wide of the mark than those biographers who persist in tracing her work to some philosopher or philosophical system.

THE 1849 LETTER TO SARA CONCERNING ROUSSEAU AND George Sand, with its strong argumentative undertone, is the first clear indication that George Eliot was at least partially aware she had begun to travel a path Sara could not follow. These writers were the first she had encountered who kept pace with her emancipated feelings, as shortly Feuerbach was to do with her ideas. But Sara had not experienced such a private revolution; there was no compelling reason why either her ideas or her feelings should have changed significantly from when she first met George Eliot. For the first time in their association, Sara could offer neither total agreement nor understanding, and although there was never to be a decisive break in the relationship, from 1849 on, signs that it had lost its vital meaning were to multiply. Sara, however, was to learn of the inevitable separation with painful belatedness.

When later in the same year—1849—George Eliot was in Switzerland after the death of her father, she was quick to reveal her growing impatience with Sara's maternalistic criticism of her actions (although once she had very much wanted just that). In response to Sara's apparent disapproval of her desire "to raise a little extra money" for cultural pursuits, she wrote the Brays:

> I hope Sara's fears are supererogatory—a proof of a too nervous solicitude about me for which I am grateful, though it does me no good to hear of it. I want encouraging rather than warning and checking. I believe I am so constituted that I shall never be cured of any faults except by God's discipline—if human beings would but believe it, they do me most good by saying to me the kindest things truth will permit. . . .

She did give up her plan for raising the money "since you think my scheme impracticable," but it is clear that she had been both hurt and annoyed by Sara—hurt because she looked to her for total trust as to the rightness of her motives, especially when they had to do with giving herself some enjoyment; and annoyed because the rebuke, perhaps more imagined than real, seemed a gesture of possessiveness. By habit, she had come to expect from Sara loving and unqualified acceptance, yet also complete freedom. She had earlier made this unreasonable demand upon Maria Lewis.

Circumstances, as well as her own continued inner growth, were soon to lead her still farther away from Sara. Once in London after the Switzerland interlude she was quickly preoccupied, both emotionally and intellectually, with new experiences and people. It would seem that Charles Bray—who made fairly frequent trips to London, and who had never been overly fond of his sister-in-law—told Sara that George Eliot's feeling for her had altered. (Or did Sara conjure up this complication to force a special response from George Eliot?) Whatever the actual background, George Eliot promptly wrote Sara:

> I am lost in amazement at your letter and cannot rest without writing. . . .
>
> It is perhaps vain to inquire what fancied foundation Mr. Bray may have had for his assertion about me. I hope it is enough to say that he was never more completely in error. If there is any change in my affection for you, it is that I love you more than ever, not less. . . . I have confidence that this friendship can never be shaken —that it must last while I last, and that the supposition of its ever being weakened by a momentary irritation is too contemptibly absurd for me to take the trouble to deny it. I am not conscious of having felt even that transient irritation towards you for a long, long time on my own account. I have admitted to Mr. Bray that I perceived what it was in you that frequently repelled him and chilled his affection for you, but . . . I have chiefly to repent of having been too severe upon *him* rather than upon you in relation to this matter.
>
> . . . It is impossible that I should ever love two women better than I love you and Cara—indeed it seems to me that I can never love any so well, and it is certain that I can never have any friend— not even a husband—who would supply the loss of those associations with the past which belong to you.
>
> . . . dear Sara, do believe in my love for you and that it will remain as long as I have my senses, because it is interwoven with my best nature and is dependent, not on any accidents of manner but on long experience which has confirmed the instinctive attraction of earlier days.

Obviously this was meant to be a reassuring letter, and in most respects, it is. Yet the contents of the second paragraph, no matter how true, must have cast a chill over Sara had she been hoping for

a revival of the "conjugal" letters. It is little wonder that she fell victim to the common cold, as a reference in George Eliot's next extant
letter to her, which is brief and casual, discloses.

Even after her intimacy with Lewes had begun in London (presumably unknown to Sara), George Eliot turned to her for help with the
Feuerbach translation; or possibly Sara volunteered her services.
Surprised though she was when Sara claimed enthusiasm for *Das
Wesen des Christentums*, George Eliot was grateful for her offer to
read her manuscript. Lewes was ailing, she was, in fact, doing much
of his work as well as her own for the *Westminster Review*, and she
was beginning to feel drearily alone with an additional work which
she was (as usual) convinced no one wanted. Probably Sara's real
enthusiasm was over the prospect of reassuming her role as critic-
reader, for there appears to have been little rapport between her mind
and Feuerbach's ideas. "There are some passages," George Eliot wrote
her a few months after the reading had been undertaken, "which you
disappoint me very much by not understanding and I should like to
write to you about them, but I haven't strength or spirit to do it."
Nonetheless, Sara continued the reading and there are no further complaints until the translation was published in July 1854, when Sara
wrote a review of it for the *Coventry Herald*, devoting half of it to
praise of the translator: "Miss Evans stands unrivalled in her power
of dealing with the tough metaphysical German. . . ." If Sara expected
thanks for this, she was once again sorely disappointed. "It seems very
ungracious to say so," George Eliot wrote her three days after the
review had appeared, "but it is the fact, that I am vexed Feuerbach
has been noticed in the Herald, and especially that anything had been
said about me." What Sara did not know was that George Eliot and
Lewes were about to leave for the Continent, so that their intimacy
—for some months kept a relative secret—would become the object
of common gossip. With courage and perhaps some audacity, George
Eliot had allowed her name (Marian Evans) to appear in *The Essence
of Christianity* as its translator, but she had no wish to have further
attention called to it even in a flattering review of her work.

There is no sign in the extant record that Sara resented the un-
graciousness, and she weathered the shock of the elopement. In
fact, she seems to have lived for several years in blissful ignorance of
the ever-widening gap between herself and George Eliot. But some
kind of climax to the relationship was inevitable, and it came in late
June of 1859, when she with the Brays visited the Leweses in London,
seeing them for the first time since their return from the Continent.
Again Sara had no way of knowing an important factor which, had
she been aware of it, might have changed the tenor of the meeting.
George Eliot had resolved to reveal to her Coventry friends her iden-

tity as the author of the *Clerical Scenes* and *Adam Bede*. As usual with her, however, the situation was more complex than outsiders could realize. She wanted her closest friends to know of her authorship, but because of her relationship with Lewes she wished to retain anonymity to the rest of the world (although this was an unrealistic hope). It was therefore with unintentional ill-timing that Sara brought along her own most recent manuscript upon some topic pertaining to Christianity—all Sara's now forgotten writings stayed within this ken—about which she and George Eliot might have conversed congenially ten years earlier. She handed her essay over to her friend, secure in the expectation of a sympathetic critical response.

But her work was temporarily forgotten as George Eliot made her startling revelation, swearing her audience to secrecy. By the next day, Sara had written a sonnet to celebrate the momentous occasion. George Eliot, in her turn, was perhaps unreasonably hurt that her news should have seemed so startling to all three of her friends: "This experience," she noted in her Journal after they had parted for the night, "has enlightened me a good deal as to the ignorance in which we all live of each other." Yet she had gone out of her way to steer them away from even making an intelligent guess that she might be the "Adam Bede Lady."

Sara's manuscript had still to be returned to her, and it was on the last day of the visit—23 June—that Lewes rather than George Eliot took on what he confided in his Journal was "the disagreeable office of conveying to Sara(h) our decided disapprobation of her m.s.— which made her very unhappy." Lewes's last clause appears to have been an understatement, for on the twenty-sixth Charles Bray wrote George Eliot from Coventry: "We had Sara in strong stericks all the way home, because she had missed her final chance of explanation and advice from you." Just why the chance was missed is not made clear, but Bray adds with some tact for George Eliot and brutal frankness concerning Sara's work: " . . . I know you would not have grudged the half hour she wanted, although I am quite of opinion, no good could have come of it. *I don't believe she can do better* and if she likes to amuse herself and spend her money in publishing, she can afford it and she does no one any harm and it may attract some *half-doz* congenial minds."

Even before she received this letter from Bray, George Eliot was feeling compunction and had written Sara an apology. Although sincere in tone, this also contained traces of the annoyance and condescension that were to become more marked in many of her later letters to Sara. (Sara's unhappiness was, after all, an implicit criticism of her own conduct.) Having reminded Sara that theirs was now perforce an "interrupted intercourse," she acknowledged "that the blundering efforts we have made towards mutual understanding have only made a new veil between us. . . ." But this was perhaps inevitable when separation must occur after a brief meeting. "We are quite unable to represent ourselves truly—why should we complain that our friends see a false image?" Then follows the familiar admission that her own failure to respond adequately was "from too much egoism and too little sympathy." She concludes:

> . . . and yet, I can't help wanting to assure you that, if I am too imperfect to do and feel the right thing at the right moment, I am not without the slower sympathy that becomes all the stronger from a sense of previous mistake.
>
> Dear Sara, believe that I shall think of you and your work much, and that my ear and heart are more open for the future because I feel I have not done what a better spirit would have made me do in the past.

Although it was probably news to Sara that there had been a veil between them, she was soothed "to find your sweet letter awaiting me here—full of the tenderness of heart and conscience that comes with happiness!" She responded to it bravely, insisting that the visit had been to "a little world of Elysium" and that the trouble had been caused by *her* egoism. But she could not help revealing, with characteristic emotionalism, the depth with which she was feeling this now openly acknowledged "separation."

> I have been fancying you, as ten years ago, still interested in what we then conversed together upon—I was not sure that the writing that now occupied you was not the "Idea of a Future Life" that was then in nubilas—that perhaps your thoughts had not been flowing in a parallel tract to my own—I see now that I have lost the only reader in whom I felt confident in having secure sympathy with the *subject* (not with *me*) whom I most gratefully believe—believed in —that she has floated beyond me in another sphere, and I remain gazing at the glory into which she has departed, wistfully and very lonely.

She recognized irrevocable change: "How for ever remote we should have felt if you had made a pretence of being quite unchanged from your former self, and tried to converse as of former times!"

It was costly to Sara's emotions to write this long letter. Halfway through it she figuratively pauses with a sentence which would have been wholly clear only to George Eliot and herself: "My head is getting so tired I cannot say all I want to say—but *they* will write about this part of our thought." The second half of the letter is calmer, giving a detailed report of a conversation about the "mystery" author of *Adam Bede* that she and the Brays had had with a fellow passenger on their train home to Coventry. (Thus far, they were keeping their secret well.) The letter is signed "Farewell, meine liebe und beruhmte / Sara."

Having survived this crisis, the friendship was to endure to the end of George Eliot's life. If at times the relationship seemed carried on in a perfunctory way by George Eliot, Sara remained the one personal friend who could most easily ruffle the benign and tranquil spirit that the world came to know as George Eliot, novelist. Perhaps the latter's occasional impatience with her old friend stemmed from Sara's reminding her of an especially unhappy time in her life, a decade during which she only half successfully struggled against a burden she did not then wholly understand. Perhaps too Sara continued to remind her of "the instinctive attraction of earlier days," which not all the years of being "Mrs. Lewes" could wholly allay.

FOUR

A Self That
Self Restrains

ALL OF THE STRAUSS TRANSLATION HAD BEEN DONE UNDER considerable varied pressures pertaining to the work itself, and additional anxiety concerning her father's health. When in 1846 Cara Bray wrote Sara about M.A.'s "Strauss-sickness," she added: "Poor thing, I do pity her sometimes, with her pale, sickly face and dreadful headaches, and anxiety, too, about her father. This illness of his has tried her so much, for all the time she had for rest and fresh air she had to read to him." As Robert Evans declined physically, he became increasingly demanding of her companionship and resentful of the time she spent with the Brays. No doubt he also resented the hours she shut herself up in her study to work at Strauss and was suspicious too, for it is unlikely that he knew enough about what she was doing even to voice disapproval of it. She ignored his occasional ill-temper and inconsiderateness, and attended him devotedly, often (according to the observant Brays) at the expense of her own health. Despite the emotional and physical drain upon her, she was at peace in her mind concerning him. The strength gained from her private triumph over the Holy War was still within her, making her almost invulnerable to external happenings between them. Only during the very last year of his life did she find it necessary to make a conscious effort to sustain "the poetry of duty," without which she felt herself to be "nothing more than miserable agglomerations of atoms—poor tentative efforts of the Natur Princip to mould a personality."

She confessed this temporary lapse to her three Coventry friends in the summer of 1848 when writing to them from St. Leonard's in Sussex, where she had taken her father in the hope that a change of air and scene would do him good. An earlier trip to the Isle of Wight made for the same reason had been fairly successful, but this one was a dismal failure. Although when they had arrived he looked and acted so well that she was "almost ashamed of having introduced [him] as an invalid," he made "not the slightest attempt to amuse himself, so that I scarcely feel easy in following my own bent even for an hour." The days were filled with "very trivial doings . . . spread over a large space," so that at the end of each she could say only "the evening and the morning were the eighth or ninth day." She could have endured her own boredom had her father's physical condition not worsened, thus making the monotonous sojourn seem not only futile but a mistake. It was inevitable that she should fall into one of the old moods of morbid introspection: "I feel a sort of madness growing upon me. . . . It seems to me as if I were shrinking into that mathematical abstraction, a point—so entirely am I destitute of contact. . . ." However, she recovered with a quickness and a wholeness which would have been impossible in earlier days. To be sure, her friends had diligently sent her cheering notes, but these could not have lifted her out of depression had she not been able to prepare an inward receptiveness to them: "The kind words and thoughts of my beloved ones are so many little gauze wings which were of no avail to me when I had not inward strength to fly withal—but now my native vigour is come again I flutter them joyously and soar with them into the Empyrean 'in spite of sorrow.' "

Robert Evans was using his ill health as a means of keeping her at least physically near to him. At this late date in his life his doing so is understandable, but he had done so for a number of years, beginning shortly after the Holy War, when he was still in at least adequate health. Perhaps he sensed that, in some mysterious way, she had been the real victor in that daughter-father skirmish. Perhaps too, even without realizing it, he was deeply hurt to be so decisively shut out of the most meaningful part of her life—the Brays and the Hennells, the Strauss. To assume a father's right and request her close attention and care was his way of ignoring and thereby closing the real distance between them. Almost always his requests for her time and help—even when only tacit—produced effective results. He did not thank or praise her for her response to his demands, as she was, in his eyes, merely what she should be—a dutiful daughter (not realizing that she had her own unorthodox concept of duty). Yet there were a few occasions when although obediently awaiting his permission, she seemed to want to be away from him. Puzzled, hurt, and angry, he at least once acted in blind desperation. And Isaac entered the scene, adding to its tension.

The incident occurred in the fall of 1845, when she was working on that part of Das Leben Jesu which she found most repugnant to her. Recognizing her serious need for a vacation from Strauss, the Brays and Sara invited her to join them on a tour of the Scottish Highlands. She very much wanted to accompany them, but had to decline, so Sara reported to her mother, because of "the bankruptcy of her brother-in-law, which brings upon her the charge of her sister and family for the present. She is much disappointed." This seems a strange reason. Why should the charge have divulged upon her rather than upon Isaac, or, for that matter, upon Robert Evans himself, who was still active in managing business affairs? One suspects that the father dictated the reasons, for it was to him that Charles Bray then appealed personally. "After all," Sara wrote in her next letter to her mother, "to our great delight, M.A. is of our party. She looked so miserable at our going without her, that CB persuaded her father it was most desirable for the good of her health." One can be fairly sure that if George Eliot really thought she alone could care for Chrissey and her family in this emergency (not unusual for the Clarkes), she never would have tolerated Bray's interceding.

On 14 October the four set off in high spirits. That very night Robert Evans, experienced rider that he was, fell off his horse and broke his leg. Fortunately, his daughter did not learn of the accident until almost two weeks later, when Isaac's urgent letter finally reached her at Edinburgh, where—so Sara wrote her mother—"We were all in ecstasies, but Mary Ann's were beyond everything. . . ." Needless to say, the letter "begging her to come home as soon as possible" was "a sad damper" to everyone's pleasure. She of course was frantic and insisted that she immediately set out on the trip back home. Understandably, her friends "could not let her travel 300 miles alone, as she wished, and after much difficulty in contriving, CB. persuaded her to be easy and stay with us over another day, as the letter said her father was going on well." It is clear that Isaac's message considerably shortened the trip from what had been originally planned, for Bray describes the episode by saying that "at Edinburgh we were called home suddenly by the tidings that her father had met with an accident, and required her immediate presence."

Possibly even Cross sensed that the fall off the horse was not wholly an "accident" and that Isaac's recalling her home when she was three hundred miles away was as cruel as it was futile, for although Cross refers to the tour as a "misty vision" that "took palpable shape" and summarizes the itinerary, he makes no reference to the injury or the letter, but concludes his account simply: "They were away from the 14th to the 28th, and on returning to Coventry Strauss was taken up again."

Was it the father's insistence or Isaac's own compulsion which dictated the unsettling letter? Why could not Isaac and his wife have cared for Robert during this temporary invalidism? Apparently Isaac had established during the upheaval of the Holy War a pattern of relationship with his sister which he was unwilling to relinquish; he stood between her and her father even when a mediator was not needed, as if to make certain that she considered herself responsible directly to him for her acts and decisions. Later, when the father was gone, he was to stand in the same way between her and Chrissey; and still later, even between her and the payment of her inheritance from her father. From one point of view, Isaac was properly fulfilling the Victorian role of the older brother, who by social sanction succeeded the father as dictator to the family. Yet there is something about his emphatic persistence in this role until the estrangement caused by her living with Lewes which suggests that he was attempting to prove himself, aside from merely acting out an accepted filial function. In the early years, he had been indifferent to her adoring attachment to him; now, although as incapable of entering her world as his father, he felt the need to keep control over those matters in her life which he could understand—or at least thought he could.

Occasionally, his intervention was genuinely needed and helpful. One such recorded time came during their father's last illness, although the service he then rendered was more lugubrious than generous. George Eliot had carried the entire burden of nursing her father; years later Mrs. Richard Congreve—whose eventual adoration for George Eliot was almost to match Edith Simcox's and whose father, Dr. Bury, had attended Robert Evans—related to Cross "that her father told her at the time, that he never saw a patient more admirably and thoroughly cared for." But Isaac spared her the difficult task of informing their father of the fatal nature of his condition and that he was likely to die at any moment. "It is a great comfort," Cara wrote Sara,

> that he is now quite aware of his situation, and was not in the least discomposed when Isaac told him he might die suddenly. It was quite a pleasure to see him sitting in his chair looking so calm just after he had known this; and he takes opportunities now of saying kind things to M.A., contrary to his wont. Poor girl, it shows how rare they are by the gratitude with which she repeats the commonest expressions of kindness.

It is to be hoped that his new effort to say kind things to his daughter-nurse (who "keeps up wonderfully mentally," Cara had reported in the same letter, "but looks like a ghost") did not wear off with the first shock of reaction. For he lingered beyond eight months, long enough to give rise to the fear that "he might last for years, in a state of imbecility."

When the end did come, it was her half brother Robert, not Isaac, who was comfortingly on hand. "My Brother," George Eliot wrote the Brays on the morning of 30 May 1849, "slept here last night and will be here again tonight." Her father died before the next dawn.

Oscar Browning writes that when George Eliot's father died that night of the thirtieth, she cried out: "What shall I be without my father! It will seem as if a part of my moral nature were gone." Browning here dramatizes a bit. She did not literally cry out these words, but wrote them in the 30 May letter to Charles and Cara, ending the first of the two sentences with the usual mark of interrogation, not an exclamation point. Yet Browning's version does not distort the essential truth, for those words read even in the proper context of her letter do impress one as an anguished cry. To them she added a still more revealing sentence (too much so for Cross, who deleted it): "I had a horrid vision of myself last night becoming earthly sensual and devilish for want of that purifying restraining influence." The forced realization that her father was actually to die reactivated the old fear of self (as was to happen essentially thirty years later when George Henry Lewes died). Where now could she turn for that external bond of discipline which would save her from the threatening forces within? Evangelicalism had failed, work had failed, and now the self-imposed bond of devotion to her father was ending with the awesome finality of death.

Her fear was not a wholly irrational one. Through suffering and continued introspection, she had gained an unusual amount of self-knowledge, and she had progressed in her ability to objectify this subjective knowledge. "I can take myself up by the ears," she had written Sara in 1847, "and inspect myself, like any other queer monster on a small scale." This was no idle boast, although couched in self-depreciatory expression. She was well aware, as she had indirectly admitted in her 1848 letter to John Sibree, Jr., that the strong passions within her would eventually destroy her if not somehow redirected into constructive channels. And she was equally aware that she had as yet only the insight, not the demonstrable proof of her ability to achieve such transformation. Chronological age—she would be thirty in the November following her father's death—was irrelevant; psychologically, she did not feel ready for the coming test.

Anxiety, combined with natural grief, prostrated her; once again the Brays came to her rescue. Finding her "exceedingly depressed"—Charles Bray recalled—"we took her abroad to France, Italy, Switzerland, etc. . . . We left [her] at Geneva for the winter. . . ." Mathilde Blind, who talked with the Brays and Sara in search of primary material for her 1883 biography, has this to add:

> So they started on their travels, going to Switzerland and Italy by the approved route, which in those days was not so hackneyed as it now is. To so penetrating an observer as Miss Evans there must have been an infinite interest in this first sight of the Continent. But the journey did not seem to dispel her grief, and she continued in such very low spirits that Mrs. Bray almost regretted having taken her abroad so soon after her bereavement. Her terror, too, at the giddy passes which they had to cross, with precipices yawning on either hand—so that it seemed as if a false step must send them rolling into the abyss—was so overpowering that the sublime spectacle of the snow-clad Alps seemed comparatively to produce but little impression on her. Her moral triumph over this constitutional timidity, when any special occasion arose, was all the more remarkable. One day when crossing the Col de Balme from Martigny to Chamounix, one of the side-saddles was found to be badly fitted, and would keep turning around, to the risk of the rider, if not very careful, slipping off at any moment. Marian, however, insisted on having this defective saddle in spite of the protest of Mrs. Bray, who felt quite guilty whenever they came to any perilous places.

George Eliot would have been hurt by Mathilde Blind's subsequent unfavorable comparison between the one writer's timidity and her beloved George Sand's stalwart hardiness in effecting the same passage while encumbered with two young children, as recounted in the *Lettres d'un Voyageur*. But Miss Blind adds that "Miss Evans was just then in a peculiarly nervous and excitable condition, and her frequent fits of weeping were a source of pain to her anxious fellow-travellers. . . . Under these circumstances an immediate return to England seemed unadvisable . . . it was decided that Marian should remain behind at Geneva."

She was to conquer both her physical timidity and her terror over being alone and at the mercy of her own clamoring emotions. The day would come when she would not feel it necessary to take the defective saddle. But in Switzerland she was still unsure of herself. As recently as 1848 she had told the young Sibree that she thought it would be bliss to have a year alone "in a romantic continental town, such as Geneva," perhaps because of its association with Rousseau. But when the reality came, she could not make herself stay beyond eight months. Despite new friends, scenes, and interests, she was unhappy over the lack of letters from her family and felt dependent upon the faithful Rosehill group to relieve her "anxiety to hear of my relations."

Rightly or wrongly, she was waiting to hear from them before *she* wrote. "I shall be very ready to write to every one," she told the Brays in a late August letter, "when every one has written to me, but I require *warming up* by letters first." She was especially irked to learn that Fanny Houghton had told the Brays that she, Fanny, felt no need to write as "she trusts to Isaac's writing. . . ." There is no indication that Isaac had written at all, although his wife, Sarah, had done so, but then only to send the sad news of the death of Chrissey's little girl Clara—the second child that Chrissey had now lost. Presumably Isaac, not unlike many husbands, felt himself adequately represented by a letter from his wife.

Within the first week of September, George Eliot broke her resolve not to write first with an almost desperate letter to Fanny: "Have I confided too much in your generosity in supposing that you would write to me first? or is there some other reason for your silence? I suffer greatly from it. . . . I have not spirit to write of myself until I have heard from you, and have an assurance from yourself that you yet care about me." Fanny must have responded satisfactorily, for a month later George Eliot wrote back to her: "The blessed compensation there is in all things made your letter doubly precious for having been waited for. . . ." However, whether in a retaliating mood or not, she had made Fanny in turn wait for *her* letter, excusing the delay: " . . . it [Fanny's letter] would have inspired me to write to you again much sooner, but that I have been in uncertainty about settling myself for the winter, and I wished to send you my future address."

She did make a move and found herself in an atmosphere so congenial that as the months went on, she grew less tense over hearing or not hearing from home. Her new lodgings were with M. and Mme D'Albert-Durade, who were "evangelical and conservative, b[ut] one finds these views in company with more breadth of cultu[re] here than one can ever augur from them in England." No doubt she did find culture in this home. But the real reason why she could easily be tolerant of their conservative views was that both husband and wife surrounded her with the affection and sympathetic concern she had failed to find within her own family. "I feel that they are my *friends*—" she wrote pointedly to Fanny, "without entering into or even knowing the greater part of my views, they understand my character, and have a real interest in me. . . ." Mme D'Albert quickly became "Maman": "She kisses me like a mother, and I am baby enough"— she confessed to the Brays—"to find that a great addition to my happiness."

No matter how much she luxuriated in the warmth of Maman's care, it was to M. D'Albert that she was drawn in a more serious way. He was an artist by temperament and profession, and had genius, whereas Maman had "less of genius and more of cleverness. . . ." She wrote the Brays: "You will be amused to hear that I am sitting for my portrait," adding, "—at M. d'Albert's request—not mine." The sittings must have provided time and privacy for intimate talk, much as the sessions in Dr. Brabant's library had done. Even earlier she had told the Brays that she loved D'Albert "as if he were father and brother both." That sounds innocent enough; yet it is doubtful that a father-brother figure (D'Albert was fifteen years her senior) could have appeared within her ken and left her unmoved. As if feeling the need to reassure the Brays that this was not another Brabant episode, she follows her statement of love with: "You must know he is not more than 4 feet high with a deformed spine—the result of an accident in his boyhood—but on this little body is placed a finely formed head, full in every direction." A grave obstacle to emotional attraction, to be sure. Maman however had found him attractive enough to marry and bear him two sons.

" . . . I am too much indulged," she wrote Fanny, "and shall go back to England as undisciplined as ever." One wonders to what extent she also was indulging herself by impulsively following her feelings, as she had done with the doctor and as she was to do with yet another man very shortly after her return to England. D'Albert had come into her life at a peculiarly opportune time for love— comparable to that of Philip Wakem's entry into Maggie Tulliver's life. In fact, Mathilde Blind reported of D'Albert, "it is whispered that he suggested some of the traits in the character of the delicate-minded Philip Wakem." "Whispered" is a suggestive word here, especially as Mathilde Blind gathered much of her most intimate information from Cara Bray. Cara had been in a position not only to hear of D'Albert through George Eliot's letters, but to judge of him herself when he stayed at Rosehill—a visit, incidentally, to which Charles Bray makes no allusion in his autobiography.

The occasion for this visit came when D'Albert somewhat surprisingly escorted George Eliot on her sudden return to England. Early in February 1850, she had told Fanny that she intended to come back "as soon as the Jura is passable without sledges—probably the end of March or the beginning of April." A few days later, she wrote the Brays that there was some talk "of M. D'Albert's accompanying me to Paris, but I am afraid he cannot afford the journey. . . ." As it happened, she did not wait until the end of March, but left Geneva on the eighteenth of that month, and D'Albert went with her not only to Paris but all the way to England. They had to go by sledge over the Jura, as is clear from a letter George Eliot wrote him in another March twenty-five years later: "Your words . . . are very sweet to me and rouse vivid pictures of that long past time when I made my first severe acquaintance with sledge travelling. . . ." Neither the reason for the precipitous leavetaking nor what passed between her and D'Albert by letter after his return home is known. They corresponded, mainly in French, but D'Albert destroyed most of her letters because —so he told Cross—"George Eliot having received Mme D'Albert's permission to *tutoyer* him, he was afraid that people might attach some malevolent significance to them after his death." Later, however, he copied out for Cross (who used them in the New Edition of the *Life*) several of the letters that she had written him in English when she was secure in her life with Lewes and in her fame. It was also in the midst of this security that she saw D'Albert once again, in the summer of 1860, when she revisited Geneva with Lewes, who noted in his Journal that it had been a great delight to him to see how truly the D'Alberts "loved and prized Polly and we spent an exciting evening with them." D'Albert rounded out this rare relationship by translating four of her novels and the *Scenes of Clerical Life* into French, the last appearing several years after both George Eliot and Maman had died.

Although D'Albert must have been a disappointment as far as letter-collecting was concerned, Cross was uncritical and loved him because he and Maman had brought George Eliot happiness. Having heard about it from George Eliot herself, Cross was convinced that the Switzerland sojourn was the happiest period in her life before her union with Lewes. The remarks with which he draws together her letters from there are almost as nostalgic as if he had literally lived through that time with her. He had, in fact, made a pilgrimage to Geneva when he was recuperating from both the shock of her death and anxiety over his decision to do the *Life*. At the Campagne Plongeon (where she had first lodged) he admired the avenue of fine chestnut trees she had admired, and then moved on to examine her second lodging and meet D'Albert, who he found was "carrying well the weight of eighty winters." All that he saw affirmed his impression that to be in Geneva had been for her "a delightful, soothing change after the long illness and the painful death of her father—after the monotonous dullness, too, of an English provincial town like Coventry, where there is little beauty of any sort to gladden the soul." To this he adds, perhaps with himself as well as George Eliot in mind:

> In the first months following a great loss it is good to be alone for a time—alone, especially amidst beautiful scenes—and alone in the sense of being removed from habitual associations, but yet constantly in the society of new acquaintances, who are sufficiently interesting, but not too intimate.

For a time, yes. But all her life George Eliot was to need and demand intimacy with a force which not even the death of George Henry Lewes was to extinguish; and it is probable that one underlying reason for her changing lodgings was that at the Campagne Plongeon she had found no one with whom she even wished to form an intimate relationship. Be that as it may, Cross reluctantly concludes this chapter of the *Life*:

> It is with a feeling of regret that we take leave of the pleasant town of Geneva, its lake and mountains, and its agreeable little circle of acquaintance. It was a peacefully happy episode in George Eliot's life, and one she was always fond of recurring to, in our talk, up to the end of her life.

This closing is curiously similar to much in Cross's memoir of her still earlier life, in which it is unintentionally made clear that she reminisced to him about her childhood out of a transformed memory which could enlarge the little happinesses and ignore the anguish she had suffered. For her letters from Switzerland even as presented by Cross are not particularly happy ones other than in the descriptions of the people and events in her new life, which she was well aware was only a temporary one. When she could live in the moment, she was happy enough. But she had little ability for such living: the "moment" for her at this time was usually split between painful memory of the past and dread of the future. The great memory which was to be such a powerful element in the making of the novels was at this time only a powerful instrument of torture; and the letters reveal that although she could bask in it, the affectionate attention given her by D'Albert and Maman also aroused and quickened her recollection of past deprivations. As for the future, she was always—even in the secure days of love and fame—to have more than normal apprehension of it. In 1849–50, the totally unplanned future lay before her like a circular desert, at best a return to the seemingly sterile past.

Certainly her Rosehill friends had not found her Switzerland letters cheerful. It was Sara who let her know this and, for Sara, in a strangely unfeeling way. In response, George Eliot wrote the Brays on 20 September 1849:

> I am quite timid about writing to you because Sara tells me that Mr. Hennell says "there is much that is morbid in your character (his observations were upon your letters only) with a dwelling on yourself and a loving to think yourself unhappy." Nothing can be truer than the observation, but I am distressed and surprised that this is so very evident from letters in which I have really tried to avoid everything which could give you pain and have only told you

of agreeables except the last, which I hope you understood to be playful in its grumbling. I am ashamed to fill sheets about myself, but I imagined that this was precisely what you wished. Pray correct my mistake if it be one. . . .

Despite George Eliot's seemingly meek acceptance, this implied rebuke from one whom she perhaps more than admired distressed her enough to make her ill, as is suggested by the opening of this letter: "I began to write to you on Sunday immediately after reading your letters but a headache came on and sent me to bed where I lay till Wednesday morning." A month later she rallied to a counterattack and accused Sara of too much "self-humiliation" in her relations with her brother: "I share your respect for Mr. Hennell's admirable judgment and feeling but from all that both you and Cara have told me for the last 2 or 3 years I am convinced that both have been *intensified* and *narrowed* in their action to a morbid degree, and that you are doing yourself wrong when you bow to his dicta as a vox Dei." At this time she was evidently not beyond giving pain for pain, for she knew well that Sara idolized her brother; and even after his death in 1850, she was to show increasing impatience for Sara's dedicated efforts to preserve his memory for posterity.

Hennell's rebuke, coming when it did, was unfair in that she then had unusual justification for expressions of unhappiness. Yet she could not help recognizing—and this was another reason why it hurt so much—that it carried some truth independent of external factors. Had she not in past years frequently accused herself of the same fault, self-centered morbidity? She had also learned during those years that self-accusation and self-confession, although making her a little wiser in self-knowledge, left her essential nature untouched. Now, however, to hear the same criticism from someone else was painfully effective—especially when it came from Charles Hennell, whose uncritical admiration she had assumed existed for herself in return for that she had given him.

The rebuke seems to have acted upon her in the manner of the old superstition concerning medicine: the worse it tastes, the better it is for one. She silently increased her efforts to omit her depressive thoughts in her letters to Coventry and to write less about herself and more about her surroundings, and this new note of objectivity was to continue and grow in her later letters from London. Needless to say, control over one's moods in letter writing does not mean that one has equal control over them when not writing letters; yet inevitably, if slowly, the self is affected by its own verbal expression, whether to friends or in creative writing. Inadvertently, Charles Hennell's remark had at least helped to start the important psychic process of reviving the restraints and necessary ego defenses which had been growing but had collapsed when her father died. She was one small step nearer to "the self that self restrains."

She would not backstep again. The return to England which she had yearned for but also feared advanced her further, without anyone's intervention or help other than her own. For once her fears had not outdone reality: she was bitterly reawakened to the fact that she had no real home. The sharp contrast between what she felt when once again in the midst of her real family and what she had enjoyed with the D'Alberts no doubt explains why she later reminisced to Cross about her stay in Switzerland as an idyllic interlude in her life. Even Cross felt it necessary to prepare his readers for the terrible letdown she experienced after coming back to what she considered "home":

> It will have been seen that she had set her hopes high on the delights of home-coming, and with her too sensitive, impressionable nature, it is not difficult to understand, without attributing blame to any one, that she was pretty sure to be laying up disappointment for herself.

Once again, Cross attributes the cause of any unhappiness which he could not ignore to her own hypersensitive nature (an idea no doubt lodged in his mind by George Eliot herself) and not to those people upon whom she was at this time of her life actually dependent, emotionally if not wholly physically. He safely switches to an impersonal interpretation of her new despair when back in England: "All who have had the experience of returning from a bright, sunny climate to England in March will recognize in the next letters the actual presence of the east wind, the leaden sky, the gritty dust, and *le spleen.*" But after a relatively short inward battle, George Eliot was able to make decisions which were to determine her future life. Fortunately, the need for such decisions was thrust upon her by the simple fact that in the "past" to which she had figuratively returned there was no place for her.

After arriving in England with D'Albert on 23 March, she apparently spent a day in London with him and then went on to Rosehill, where she stayed a few days before starting a round of family visits. It was from Griff, on 30 March, that she wrote Fanny she felt more of an outcast in her own country "than at Geneva." Over a week later, still from Griff, she wrote Sara: "O the dismal weather and the dismal country and the dismal people. It was some envious demon that drove me across the Jura to come and see people who don't want me." By May she was in Meriden with Chrissey, and in her own mind at least had reached the point of terminating her efforts to find a place for herself within her family. "Dear Chrissey," she wrote Cara Bray, "is much kinder than any one else in the family and I am happiest with her. She is generous and sympathizing and really cares for my happiness. But I am delighted to feel that I am of no importance to any of them, and have no motive for living amongst them." To this she adds with seeming lightness: "I have often told you I thought Melchisedec [in Hebrews 7:3 he is described as "without father, without mother, without descent. . . ."] the only happy man, and I think so more than ever." But one senses that this was not a flippant remark; she herself had become a symbolic Melchisedec. Heartfelt memories of the past would stay vividly with her always and would largely dictate the course of her fiction. As far as the present was concerned, whether she wished it or not she had gained emotional independence of her family, although her frustrated wish for Isaac's approval would never leave her.

G EORGE ELIOT MADE ROSEHILL HER HOME THAT SUMMER, and her Strauss translation began to bear unexpected results. Its publisher, John Chapman, visited Rosehill, perhaps coming purposely to see her. She thus had the opportunity to readjust her impression of him. She had not cared much for him at their first meeting, which probably occurred during her visit to Sara in May 1846. Several months after the translation appeared, she wrote Sara that she hoped Chapman would "not misbehave," by which she meant that she doubted whether he would be scrupulous in adhering to the pre-publication financial agreement. He was "always too much of the *interesting* gentleman" to please her: "Men must not attempt to be interesting on any lower terms than a fine poetical genius." She was right in not perceiving "fine poetical genius" in his manner; but he appears to have been honest enough in intention, although he had no mind for business. It took him only a short time to plunge the *Westminster Review*, which he purchased in 1851, into debt and a labyrinth of financial entanglements exceeded in complication only by his personal life of domestic chaos and amorous adventure.

In 1846–7, George Eliot's wary attitude was probably based upon nothing more than an instinctive distrust of Chapman's strikingly handsome appearance and charm with women. With reason, some of his friends called him "Byron." By 1850, however, she was inclined to find beneath the interesting gentleman a man of disarming candor and at least verbal moral earnestness. His championship of advanced and free thought was sincerely motivated, and he went straight to her heart with his candid confessions that he could not realize the moral improvement of the self he so earnestly desired. His life was cluttered with business and uninspiring domestic details, so that he lacked the time and solitude necessary for meditative self-probing. Otherwise, what pained him most—so he confided in his Diary— was that his wife, Susanna, who was an inefficient manager of their lodging house in the Strand, had done nothing whatever to improve herself intellectually or morally since their marriage in 1843. In all likelihood he also confided these matters to George Eliot as they walked and talked intimately in the garden at Rosehill; she would have understood very well the pattern of heroic aspiration and non-heroic frustration unfolded before her.

Chapman's charm was surely far more substantial than the flirtation she might once have thought it. He had, after all, gained the loyal friendship of the unromantic but rigorously exacting Harriet Martineau, and the enlightened thinkers who frequented 142 Strand—men such as Spencer, Lewes, Mackay, Froude, and Brabant—regarded him with friendly respect. As for the physical attractiveness which had perhaps first aroused her suspicion, it might have proved an unacknowledged relief after her close companionship with the deformed D'Albert. In addition, Chapman had the rare ability to admire a woman's mental power without a trace of insulting astonishment, condescension, or envy. He was becomingly humble before her scholarly attainments and linguistic proficiency. He himself should like nothing better than to be tutored in German by her.

Most importantly, he had reappeared in her life when she was totally adrift, without home or work, and so forged a link between an otherwise pointless past and an unknown future. Also—he insisted —she could be of great intellectual help to him and his publishing business if she would come to London and settle in his lodging house; at the same time she would have the chance to try her luck as a free-lance writer. She began to find it easy to let herself be persuaded. Chapman was the first person to urge her toward an independent career which was worthy of her talent, and he had asked her to be his workmate. His proposal might be the answer to the prayer-like wish she had confided to Charles and Cara from Switzerland: ". . . the only ardent hope I have for my future life is to have given to me some woman's duty, some possibility of devoting myself where I may see a daily result of pure calm blessedness in the life of another." Besides, rather than a father figure Chapman was, at two years her junior, more like a brother. The difference may have disturbed her, for when she finally settled in London she allowed it to be thought that she had been born in 1820 rather than 1819.

Plans were fairly definite by fall. In October, Chapman returned to

Rosehill, bringing with him Robert Mackay, whose book *The Progress of the Intellect* he had just published. It was agreed that she would write a review of it. She did so, but was lodged in London before the article appeared in print. Perhaps as a trial visit, she had stayed at the Chapmans' the last two weeks in November and apparently decided that living there could be pleasant and știmulating. It was probably with some idea of permanence in mind that she returned to 142 Strand on 8 January 1851. Chapman met her at the station and later noted in his Diary that her manner had been "friendly but formal and studied." Possibly she was already aware that she was in love with him but had resolved not to let her feelings show—and Chapman's recording the description suggests that he too may have been aware of this. Her struggle for self-possession and his awareness of the reason for the struggle constituted the kind of emotionally charged situation upon which he thrived, despite his protestations to the contrary.

If she had so resolved, she reckoned without either the demands of her own nature or the bizarre household in which, even if possible, a studied and formal bearing would have been comically incongruous. She was in love with a married man who maintained a mistress—Elisabeth Tilley—in his home ostensibly as governess to his children Ernest and Beatrice. Mrs. Chapman's complacent acceptance of this arrangement came either from her ignorance of or utter resignation to her husband's relations with Elisabeth. One suspects the latter, for there is little evidence that she had any more genuine love for her husband at this time than he for her, whereas he was passionately attached to Elisabeth, although that ardor was to cool within a year. How much George Eliot understood of the entire situation is not revealed in the record. Gordon Haight assumes that "she was certainly ignorant of Elisabeth's position there," but this is hard to believe. In any event, she was shortly initiated into and contributed to episodes such as the one Chapman recorded 22 January 1851, which was presumably not atypical:

> Invited Miss Evans to go out after breakfast, did not get a decisive answer, E. afterwards said if I did go, she should be glad to go,—I then invited Miss Evans again telling her E. would go whereupon she declined rather rudely, Susanna being willing to go out, and neither E. nor S. wishing to walk far I proposed they should go a short distance without me, which E. considered an insult from me and reproached me in no measured terms accordingly, and heaped upon me suspicions and accusations I do not in any way deserve. I was very severe and harsh, said things I was sorry for afterwards, and we became reconciled in the Park.

Miss Evans apologized for her rudeness tonight, which roused all E's jealousy again, and consequent bitterness. S. E. and Miss Evans are gone to spend the evening with Mr. and Mrs. Holland.

It looks as if Susanna and Elisabeth were willing to lay down arms to make certain that Miss Evans did not stay home alone that evening with Chapman.

The forced peace was short-lived. Apparently Elisabeth saw to it that hostilities were reopened, for it was her barrage of jealous remarks (Chapman confided in his Diary) which caused Susanna to adopt the same point of view. One morning they had a long talk, "which resulted in their comparing notes on the subject of my intimacy with Miss Evans, and their arrival at the conclusion that we are completely in love with each other." In the same entry he candidly admits that appearances might seem to justify this conclusion: there was, for example, the incident of Susanna's finding him with his hand in Miss Evans's, and it would seem that he made frequent trips to her room, for "S. said to me that if ever I went to M's room again she will write to Mr. Bray, and say that she dislikes her." (Aside from affording insight into the Chapman household, this entry brings to light Charles Bray's role as older brother in sponsoring George Eliot alone in London, which explains why she frequently confided personal matters to him before disclosing them to Cara and Sara.)

It was inevitable that the two established women should have joined forces against the interloper, much as the two older women in the Brabant household had done. But this affair was to have a far different ending, for Chapman, whether to his credit or not, had none of the doctor's evasiveness. He was in the thick of the emotional fray. Diligently he sought reconciliation on all three sides, and when it was not easily effected, he was as innocently perplexed as any sultan might have been upon finding jealous strife within his harem. He seems to have been incredibly naïve in his expectation that a few judicious words from him would bring unity to his divided establishment—or could it be that in his own mind he was conducting a small-scale commune similar to the far more complex phalanstery in Queen's Road, Bayswater, in which, despite the ideals of the founders, George Henry Lewes was to find himself tawdrily entangled? This would explain the openness of the major participants' discussion of their jealousies and suspicions, as well as the continued respect accorded to Chapman by individuals who could accept nonconventionality but would not have tolerated hypocrisy and deceit, foremost among whom would have been George Eliot herself.

Chapman's one impartial confidant was his Diary, and into this he recorded the minutiae of daily upheavals with such apparent relish that had he suddenly been granted the tranquility he professed to desire, life would have seemed for him without savor. He quickly rescued himself from the threat of such dullness by involving his new assistant in a situation which while nominally passing under the head of business was bound to add to the tensely personal reverberations so common in 142 Strand. At his request, George Eliot took over certain correspondence and negotiation with authors whose manuscripts he was considering for publication, one of which was Eliza Lynn's latest novel, *Realities*. This move could hardly have allayed Susanna's growing belief that Elisabeth was right in her jealous accusations, for such work had hitherto been her own province, and she was already corresponding with Miss Lynn over passages in the novel to which she objected. Chapman's Diary reveals that he vicariously enjoyed the letters exchanged between the two women and that he as often sided with Eliza as with Susanna.

References to this correspondence cease in the Diary after George Eliot's return. Chapman had no sooner brought her back to the Strand from Euston Station than Eliza appeared in person to tell him that she acquiesced to only one of his corrections on her proofs. Chapman noted in his Diary that the following day he talked "about Miss Lynn and her book" to George Eliot, although the latter was "very poorly"—understandably so; Elisabeth as "the results of her groundless suspicions" had already created a characteristic scene by giving "notice at the dinner table that she intended to leave in the Autumn."

On Saturday the eleventh another scene occurred, Chapman perhaps triggering it by going off alone with George Eliot to buy a piano for her use and then taking a long walk with her during which they conversed "much on *general topics* [emphasis Chapman's], and about Miss Lynn and her moral principles." Later in the day he

Received and read through one of Miss L's "proofs" of a love scene which is warmly and vividly depicted, with a tone and tendency which I entirely disapprove. Miss Evans concurs with me, and Elisabeth and Susanna are most anxious I should not publish the work.

Miss E. and Susanna had a long talk on the point, when S. became excited and used language in reference to Miss L. unbecoming and unjust. She also said that I, when conversing with Miss L. in her presence on the subject, had "lowered myself," but she retracted the expression when I told her she did not believe what she herself said.

Was not some of Susanna's "unbecoming" language really directed at George Eliot? It is easy to imagine that Chapman found pleasure in dissecting Eliza's love scene with such impressionable, highly strung womenfolk as audience.

He began Sunday by taking advantage of the new piano and

> sat in Miss E's room while she played one of Mosart's [sic] Masses with much expression. The[n] went with her to call on Miss Lynn in the hope of inducing her to cancel some objectionable passages, and succeeded to the extent of a few lines only. I said that such passages were addressed [to] and excited the sensual nature and were therefore injurious;—and that as I am the publisher of works notable for the[ir] intellectual freedom it behoves me to be exceedingly careful of the *moral* tendency of all I issue.

That evening Susanna, Chapman and a cousin dined out, and still later they "met Miss Lynn at the house of Mrs. Peter Taylor. Had a painful night with S." Had they met Miss Lynn by plan or accident, and did Susanna know that her husband and George Eliot had visited Miss Lynn only that afternoon? Finally, which of these happenings caused Susanna to give Chapman a painful night?

Eliza had boarded with the Chapmans in Clapton before they moved to the Strand in 1847. Three years George Eliot's junior, she had come to London before she was twenty to try her success at writing. At first she took lodgings near the old Reading Room of the British Museum so that she could spend her days doing research for her first novel, *Azeth, the Egyptian*, which she had begun at home. It must have been when she had managed to publish this at her own expense in 1846 that she went to the Chapmans', for Sara Hennell met her on a visit there during the fall of that year and sent back to Coventry an apparently unfavorable impression. "Do not judge too harshly of the L.L. [Literary Lady] on a first interview," George Eliot returned. "I am quite glad to hear of prettiness associated with learning and heresy. Is there genius too? If so, the gods are getting kinder to mortals." The word "heresy" suggests that Eliza was already an outspoken "advanced" thinker, as indeed she was to remain throughout her long pioneering career as a woman journalist. Later she was to declare war on the "freewoman" issue in her reactionary *Girl of the Period*, 1868; but in 1846 she herself was a young freewoman and her agnosticism and philosophical materialism would have been enough to draw her to Chapman. Even so, Cara Bray's somewhat arch response to her sister Sara's letter indicates that Chapman already was sufficiently Byronic in reputation to make questionable the motives of an attractive young woman who chose to take lodgings with him: "Very peculiar of Miss Sennacherib to take lodgings at Mr. Chapman's; how many more young ladies is he going to have?"

Eliza's second novel, *Anymone, A Romance of the Days of Pericles*, was more financially successful than her first, but the reviews made it clear that she was beginning to be typed as a novelist who did her writing in the British Museum without regard for the contemporary scene. The title of her third novel, *Realities*, signaled her determination to prove that, when she chose, she could be as nonacademic and realistic as anyone else then writing. Chapman's expressed willingness to publish the novel apparently without having seen much, if any, of it in manuscript form must have seemed quite natural to Eliza. From her knowledge of his publications and his own beliefs, not to mention his home life, she had reason to assume that his unorthodoxy extended into all avenues of life. There may even have been a more personal relationship and commitment from him than has entered into the surviving records. Certainly she had the power to distress Susanna. Be that as it may, he was to surprise her with his disapproval of her novel.

Eliza would have been working upon *Realities* when George Eliot first met her during her stay at the Chapmans' near the end of 1850. "Miss Lynn was here last night," she wrote the Brays on 30 November. "She says she was 'never so attracted to a woman before as to me'—I am 'such a loveable person.' She is so different from all I had imagined her that I was quite startled. Spectacles! and altogether an L.L. looking person." Eliza's memory of her first reaction to George Eliot was to be harshly different. As late as 1885 she wrote Herbert Spencer that gossip (which she does not specify) had early prejudiced her "against Miss Evans as a girl of infinitely bad taste" and that upon meeting her at the Strand she found no reason to change her opinion: "When I saw her two or three days I did not like her." Eliza's antagonism toward George Eliot was to be lifelong. It was nourished by the events of later years, but its roots were in the Strand days, when Eliza was a not wholly objective spectator as George Eliot swiftly ascended to the position of star boarder and the center of John Chapman's deferential attention.

At the time, George Eliot appeared unaware that she was either the object of Eliza's resentment or the target of unpleasant gossip. References to Eliza in her letters back to Coventry are infrequent and matter-of-fact. On 28 January 1851, she wrote the Brays amidst more interesting news, "Mr. Chapman's feud with Miss Lynn about her novel is not yet terminated." And when the feud was terminated, on 10 February 1851, after Eliza had called in legal help and Chapman had promised to pay her £5 to cover such help, she wrote simply but with a terminal exclamation point: "Miss Lynn's affair with Mr. C.

is closed by her accepting of £5 as compensation!" Eliza eventually had *Realities* published by Saunders and Otley in May 1851; ironically, the reviews criticized it for being too unrealistic.

Meanwhile, George Eliot became increasingly nonplussed by her ill-defined work as Chapman's assistant. Although always kept busy, she had no sense of contributing to any one solid project. True, Chapman was planning and interesting her in an analytical catalogue of what he had so far published, which would serve (and this was not an immodest claim) as an index to most of the advanced thinking of the age that had appeared in English and in translated works from the Continent, such as her own Strauss. But the peace needed for working out this plan was checkered by outbursts from Susanna and Elisabeth. Refraining from mentioning her personal involvement, she made light of her situation to the Brays: "There is really no time to do anything here I am a poor never-having-time-to-clean-myself potter's wessel." Once again she was on a treadmill: her emotional energy was being sapped, she had no chance to do any writing for herself, and she had no clear conviction that she was being of constructive help to Chapman.

Chapman's actual conduct with her when they were alone is a matter of pure conjecture. The otherwise intimate Diary reveals little about it. Yet a few of the later entries—made after she had gone and come again—indicate that he had somehow committed himself to her in a way he did not care to remember. On her side, although she was repeating her pattern of emotional precipitancy, a new factor does appear in her outward conduct—one that certainly was not present in the Brabant affair. On several occasions she made, or attempted to make, apologies to Susanna. But if Susanna was temporarily mollified by these overtures, Elisabeth, who appears to have had no object in her life other than indulging her feelings for Chapman, was constantly upset. George Eliot perhaps began to comprehend and even pity her, and perhaps too she was beginning to have a more objective view of Chapman. In Chapman's own version, she "accorded me some justice and told me she would help me to be what I wish to be to E. and would sustain me in the right as a 'second self' if E " (Unfortunately, Chapman made the ending of this interesting passage illegible.)

After only a little more than three months of such futile expenditure of strength and feeling, George Eliot brought her stay to a close and returned to Coventry. For this new departure, Chapman "accompanied her to the railway. She was very sad, and hence made me feel so." As he recorded it, she pressed him for some intimation of the state of his feelings: "I told her that I felt great affection for her, but that I loved E. and S. also, though each in a different way." At this, "she burst into tears. I tried to comfort her, and reminded [her] of the dear friends and pleasant home she was returning to,—but the train whirled her away very very sad."

A day later, Susanna took herself off on a visit. One would think that Chapman might have looked forward to this rare day of peace and the chance to be alone with his Elisabeth; but after taking Susanna to the train, he noted in his Diary: "On returning home found the house quite empty and felt a sense of extreme loneliness." For a week and a half after that, the Diary entries are meager and uninspired. He managed to keep life interesting only by sending to Coventry the letters that Susanna wrote him. Upon first reading these letters, George Eliot wrote him that she was no longer interested in working on his analytical catalogue. Then she changed her mind and wrote him a second note to say that she would continue with the work, "on condition that you state or rather, I should hope, *re*state to Mrs. C. the fact that I am doing it, not because I 'like,' but in compliance with your request." She made it clear also that she would continue the work "with the utmost repugnance, and only on the understanding that I shall accept no remuneration." This, then, was to be "conscience" work, and her attitude about payment is drastically different from a few years hence, when she was most zealous in making certain that she gained every possible shilling from her novel writing. Chapman of course immediately sent both notes on to Susanna. Two weeks later, a friendlier letter from Coventry arrived: George Eliot was beginning to enjoy the catalogue work, and she agreed to his proposal that she abridge her Strauss translation for £100 (a plan that was not in fact carried out). This well-meaning conciliatory letter merely provoked another scene: "Elisabeth left the breakfast table this morning in tears, caused by the sight of M's letter. . . ."

Thus did letters sustain the high tension just as successfully as the actual presence of all three women. The fact that Chapman himself saw to it that they did so offers a clue to his otherwise enigmatic nature. The real force of his feeling for women arose not from physical relationship but from his involvement in the peripheral emotional drama which he kept constantly moving. Much of his passion was probably converted into the verbalism which found expression in the Diary, intimate talk, and letters, especially those he was to write to Barbara Leigh Smith. By 1854 Barbara had supplanted Elisabeth in Chapman's affections, but not all was clear romance, for Barbara was suffering from a nervous ailment and Chapman (later to become a medical doctor) proposed that they form an extramarital union for the benefit of her health. They did so, and he embellished the affair with letters described by Gordon Haight as "a most singular mélange of love-making, petty economies, and quite unprintable clinical details." It is not improbable that the writing of these letters was more exciting to Chapman than the physical experiences which prompted them.

Before Barbara's appearance, however, he felt a lull in his amorous life. "For my own part," he admitted in his Diary in the spring of 1851, "I do not feel in raptures with any woman now, and my passionate moods are exceptional and transient and are rather *permitted* as a means of according the strongest evidence of *affection* than storms wh: I cannot controul." Far more than passion, it was "benificent affection, and pleasure of social intercourse," that interested him, and these were "equally distributed towards Susanna E and M, but in regard to *passionate enthusiasm*, my 'first love' will I believe also be my last." (Four weeks earlier, he had admitted that even this first love—for Elisabeth—was "no longer so dazzling as it once was. . . .")

The tenor of these observations suggests that they came from a man past his prime who was looking forward to the serene compensations of old age; yet Chapman was only thirty when he made them. True, even Barbara Leigh Smith was by no means his last passion, but each of the later affairs of which there is any knowledge was to be surrounded by essentially the same pattern of petty strife and complexities. He perhaps came nearest to his peculiar heaven in later life when he practiced medicine, specializing in "treating certain functional diseases of women by means of heat and cold applied along the spine." By then he had also taken another wife. One preserved entry from an otherwise lost Diary re-creates a scene in Paris, where he by then lived, closely resembling the daily tempests of 142 Strand. He and his wife, whom he called Pres, were riding in a cab when they fell into violent argument because he had confused the identity of two women. Pres reviled him violently for such stupidity, and "when I attempted to defend myself by remarking that if I were to use like language to her she would not tolerate it for a moment, or words to that effect, she became still more excited, stopped the cab, got out . . ." etc.

He would have felt cheated had Pres listened with reason and been reconciled without enacting the melodramatic climax. Similarly, he would have been disappointed had he been able to put down the domestic storm which brewed around him in 1851—or, more accurately, had he been temperamentally able to allow it to blow itself out. The natural opportunity for this had come when George Eliot went back to Coventry in March. Left to herself, she would not have returned; but Chapman pursued her by letter and then in person. Granted that her value to him as co-worker was great, especially now that he had begun negotiations to purchase the *Westminster Review*, another man might have hesitated to retain her help at the risk of losing family, mistress, and peace of mind. And so might have Chapman, had his desire to draw her back within his domain been motivated only by consideration of her worth as a worker. There were deeper unprofessed motives, such as his need to exercise his power to generate an exquisite kind of mutual torture. If this strange side of his nature is not recognized, George Eliot's ultimate triumph over her own feelings for him cannot be fully estimated. Hers was not the clear-cut problem of unrequited love or even that of being in love with a man who had intimated that he might love her were he free, for Chapman demonstrably considered himself free to follow his emotions wherever they led.

All the potentially dangerous forces of her powerful nature were being tested: her need for love at any cost; her need to be needed by the person she loved; and her lingering sense of unworthiness, which caused her to accept compromises that actually were indignities against herself. These compromises, once accepted, could only stir up inner conflict, for as Cross observes, her "absolute" need was of "some one person who should be all in all to her, and to whom she should be all in all," and she was "very jealous in her affections." Yet she was emotionally bound to a man who had made it diabolically clear that he saw no reason why he should not simultaneously distribute his various kinds of love among three women, who was not averse to stimulating jealousy to add spice to his life, and who tightened the bond around her by emphasizing his great need for her.

Perhaps while at Rosehill, after her somewhat humiliating departure from the Strand, she had won a tenuous victory over her feelings. If so, this was quickly turned to defeat when Chapman appeared in late May to urge her return to London to help him with the editing of the *Westminster Review*. Upon arrival, he found her "shy calm and affectionate" (this Diary entry is incomplete, as two words originally underscored he later made illegible). Both the calmness and the shyness soon evaporated. Within two days, during a walk before breakfast, he "told her the exact condition of things in regard to E. whom on every account I wish to stay at the Strand." Apparently his version pointed to her as the cause of Elisabeth's troubles; for she expressed herself "much grieved and . . . prepared to atone in any way she could for the pain she has caused. . . ."

He was punishing her in several different ways, and it would seem that this treatment evoked a positive response from the masochistic streak in her. Had he come merely begging her to return, she might well have refused him. But Chapman could not proceed with such directness. Besides, it is as if he had divined the nature of her vulnerability. The next day he took her to Leamington, where she visited Fanny (perhaps to ask her advice); and on the way back, while they rested on the grass near Kenilworth Castle, he expounded "on the wonderful and mysterious embodiment of all the elements characteristics and beauties of nature which man and woman jointly present. I dwelt also," he added, "on the incomprehensible mystery and witchery of beauty." His words—so he complacently records—"jarred upon her and put an end to her enjoyment. Was it from a consciousness of her own want of beauty? She wept bitterly."

He saw to it also that they talked business and reached decisions. It was agreed that she would become "an active cooperator" in editing the periodical, and that to do so she would have to live near him for much of the time. She offered no resistance to his planning, but "put herself in my hands prepared to accept any arrangement I may make either for her return to the Strand or to any house in London I may think suitable in October." She was aware that ominous clouds had to be cleared from 142 Strand before she could resume lodgings there, but she was willing to be patient.

Meanwhile, she began to help him in two different ways while he was still in Coventry. To encourage his desire for inward peace and spiritual progress, she loaned him her copy of *De Imitatione Christi*, by Thomas à Kempis—a book which had great meaning for her, as it later was to have for Maggie Tulliver. Her second method of help was more certain of success: she began to work on the prospectus for the *Westminster*, which, it was hoped, would elicit financial contributions. On 2 June, after a righteous quotation from à Kempis and then a reference to "intense suffering" caused by a tooth extraction, Chapman noted: "M. is going without dinner in order to progress rapidly with the Prospectus." She finished writing it that night, and read it to him. "I liked it extremely as a whole," he recorded the next day, "and after some alterations at my suggestion I sent it to press." This, incidentally, is a preview of how their collaboration in editing the *Westminster* worked out. She was to do the spade work and he would make minor suggestions after it was done.

Although pleased with the finished prospectus, Chapman was uneasier over the atmosphere at 142 Strand than he had led her to believe. Two days after she put herself in his hands and had agreed to accept any plan of his for her residence at 142 or some other house in London, he recorded in his guilt-absorbent Diary:

> I find it a matter of great difficulty to determine what can be done in regard to M's return to Town. Both Susanna and Elisabeth oppose her return to the Strand, and I suspect they would be equally opposed to her residence elsewhere in London, and yet as an active cooperator with me in Editing the Westminster Review I regret that any cause for distrust should ever have been given. I must and will recover the confidence I once possessed. I will act

consistently with my own fairer thought and thus raise my own self respect and diffuse peace.

The would-be distiller of peace was made even more uncomfortable when the same morning the prospectus had been sent to press he received a letter from Susanna saying that Elisabeth was "wasting away," apparently because of his absence. This made him "deeply anxious and sad." He was still willing to "do anything [in reason] to restore her [Elisabeth], for I love her, and grieve over her intensely." (He later crossed out "in reason.") Later that evening (ignominiously for George Eliot), he wrote to both Elisabeth and Susanna "and offered to defer to them the decision about Miss E's return to the strand, or do anything they wish." Susanna's answering letter was unkind "regarding M.," so of course he immediately related its contents to M. and inquired if she would prefer to stay on at Rosehill or come to town. For once, indeed for the first time since his uninvited presence, she became "extremely excited and indignant"—as earlier they had agreed that she would have to be in London if she were to work with him. But finally—as he recorded—she became "calm and regretful," and later in the evening, during yet another walk, "we made a solemn and holy vow which henceforth will bind us to the right." To this he felt compelled to add: "She is a noble being. Wrote a chiding letter to Susanna."

This solemn and holy vow (although unclear, for it is not known if or how they had deviated from the "right") appears to have had some serious and binding meaning for both of them. However, the path ahead was by no means immediately smooth. On 9 June Chapman reached home to be immediately engulfed in a familiar scene: "Elisabeth received me, and burst into tears, which frightened me, but I found they were tears of joy. I never saw her in such a rapture, which continued all day. / Susanna received me affectionately but soon got into disagreeable talk about M. / Rec'd, a long half sarcastic letter from J. S. Mill containing severe animadversions on the Prospectus."

His womenfolk did not give Chapman time to be very much concerned over John Stuart Mill's criticism of the prospectus: the latter might have been expected, in any event, for the *Westminster* had been founded in 1824 by his father, James Mill, with financial aid from Jeremy Bentham. After initial success and then decline, it had been revitalized by the brilliant editorship of John Stuart from 1837 until 1840, when the proprietorship was transferred to William Hickson, from whom Chapman had purchased it. From 1840, the periodical had again lost prestige and influence, yet its potential power remained great, if only because of its illustrious background. Chapman was shrewd enough to know this. He also had the wisdom to recognize his own limitations: he was no John Stuart Mill and he needed help, desperately. Through a strange chain of events, he had found in Coventry what was probably the best available help in England. But forces that ostensibly had nothing to do with intellectual progress were against him. On 16 June, which happened to be his birthday, he was "made wretched by Elisabeth's positive assurance that she will not live in the Strand after Miss Evans comes to London."

From then on, the pertinent references in his Diary are decidedly in favor of Miss Evans, with sympathy for Elisabeth and her claims clearly on the wane. Susanna appears to have maintained a fairly neutral position, perhaps feeling more secure in her legal rights as Chapman's wife than could his mistress. On 21 June he received a "little note" from Coventry and found it "inexpressibly charming, so quick, intelligent and overflowing with love and sweetness!" Gordon Haight finds nothing in the extant letter of 20 June from George Eliot to Chapman to warrant this effusion from him, and so concludes that the "little note" was a separate enclosure which he detached and destroyed. This might well have been so. Considering the circumstances—Chapman's belatedly troubled conscience, as well as the daily reminders and threats from Susanna and Elisabeth—one can however imagine that the short surviving letter, beginning "My dear Friend," and filled with impersonal but sympathetic interest for him and his affairs, could indeed have seemed to him "overflowing with love and sweetness." The concluding sentence to the Diary entry he made upon receipt of it shows he was especially affected by the impersonal yet friendly tone of her letter: "I feel her to be the living torment to my soul." She was no longer clinging to him emotionally, but she had not withdrawn her offer to help. And a few days later, no doubt by painful contrast, he complained to his faithful Diary about the "wretchedness which Elisabeth diffuses by her intense and morbid egoism. . . ." It is likely that he had picked up the phrase "morbid egoism" from George Eliot.

Then Elisabeth rose above her egoism and on 14 August "acquiesced in Miss Evans' return to the Strand for residence during the winter. . . ." This was but a day after George Eliot had arrived in London with the Brays, ostensibly to see the Great Exhibition. Clearly there was another, more important purpose for this visit. On the fifteenth, Chapman recorded that after having spent most of the day at the Exhibition with the Coventry group, he brought "the ladies" home with him "in order that Miss E. might 'make a call' on Susanna. . . ." To his mind the evening was a success, as it also afforded "the opportunity of a long Editorial Conference, in which after coffee was accomplished much." Possibly the women of the household did not view it so cheerily, for he added: "Susanna is very poorly with bad headache,—and Elisabeth is far from well. She was sad and in tears this evening."

Although it was understood that George Eliot would return to the Strand, Chapman felt restless with her gone; and in late September, having to go to Birmingham, he decided to travel by way of Coventry and stop over at Rosehill. To give him credit, he never lied to his womenfolk when he knew that his next move would upset them. So when he told Susanna of his itinerary, she reproached him for not having asked her to accompany him, until he felt "constrained" to invite her to come along with him.

It was an ill-timed visit and therefore brief. They found Cara ill and expecting Edward Noel and his children as house guests. Chapman had anticipated this possibility, perhaps because he had learned from both George Eliot and Rufa Hennell at separate times (each source admonishing him that it was a great secret) that Cara was in love with Edward Noel; that Charles Bray knew of Cara's passion for Noel, who was related somewhat unconventionally to Byron's family; and that he encouraged Noel's visits to Rosehill. Cara in her turn did her best "to promote [Charles's] happiness in any way that his wishes tend." Chapman, being Chapman, would have been titillated by this newly afforded insight into the Brays' most private life, and alert to the new light it shed upon the close relationship which obviously existed between Charles Bray and George Eliot without seeming to arouse the jealousy of Cara—at least not in the blatantly open way that he experienced from both Susanna and Elisabeth. Rufa's apparently well-founded gossip, including that about George Eliot's 1843 stay at Devizes, intrigued him enough to make a vivid summary of it "on three blank pages at the beginning of the Diary." But when he arrived with Susanna at Rosehill on Saturday 20 September and found his guess about Noel's expected visit to be accurate, he was perturbed and insisted upon finding lodgings elsewhere. Noel and his family did not in fact materialize that night, so Chapman and Susanna were able to remain at Rosehill through an enjoyable Sunday marred only by Cara's continued illness.

During that Sunday he disclosed to George Eliot his ambition not only to edit but to write for the *Westminster Review*. George Eliot had never admired his writing style. Her advice to him at this time amounts to brilliant strategy, revealing that she was in firm control of such professional matters, if not yet of her emotional relationship to him. He recorded: "Miss Evans thinks I should lose power and influence by becoming a writer in the Westminster Review, and could not then maintain that dignified relation with the various contributors that she thinks I may do otherwise." This suggests that Chapman was at least temporarily pleased and satisfied with her argument and may have thought the difficult stay at Rosehill well worth the effort. If so, back home a few days later he had reason to think differently, for he was embroiled in new outbursts from both Susanna and Elisabeth. He complained in his Diary that "in proximity with women a man cannot command his own peace!" As he might have prophesied earlier, the Rosehill visit had only raised further psychological obstacles to George Eliot's return.

Nonetheless, in October she was re-established at 142 Strand, now as subeditor of the *Westminster*. For the two-year period that she was to stay there, she was to be, next to his Diary, Chapman's most loyal and unrecriminating friend. The Diary itself yields only a fragment of the crucial readjustment which had occurred in their relationship, for the extant portions of it jump from the end of 1851 to the opening of 1860. The references to her for the remaining few months of 1851 are relatively impersonal, although they do reveal that Chapman spent considerable time with her and became increasingly dependent upon her judgment concerning plans for the *Westminster* and various other aspects of his publishing business. She appears to have become an island of serenity in his turbulent life. Not that she had quickly and easily transformed her love for him into the calmer feeling of friendship. There are signs that at the Strand she underwent a prolonged inward struggle which—even while exacting its toll in the form of depressions and psychosomatic disturbances—aroused psychic strengths that began to give her the inner poise her later friends assumed she had enjoyed all her life.

At first she may have drawn courage from the solemn and holy vow that she and Chapman had taken together, for to her this would have placed a moral value upon her struggle and hence have made it meaningful. Even that vow, however, could not alleviate the strain of living under the same roof with him. As early as January 1852, she wrote Charles Bray: "I have declared my resolution to leave at the end of this quarter—*but say nothing about it*. Mrs. Chapman is increasingly polite and attentive, and I have many comforts here that I could hardly expect elsewhere, but—" Both the request for secrecy (which, incidentally, Bray ignored) and the unfinished sentence suggest that her reason for desiring to leave 142 Strand was a decidedly personal one. Yet perhaps she was not so firmly resolved as she had written to Bray, for when he told Eliza Lynn of her wish to move, and Eliza, perhaps delighted, informed her of two rooms available in Cavendish Square, George Eliot promptly declared them to be not at all what she wanted. She had decided, she explained to Cara, that it was "undesirable to fix on a London residence at present as I want to go to Brighton for a month or two next quarter." This was plausible as an excuse, but no doubt Chapman had been instrumental in the altering of her plans. He could still successfully appeal to her compassion because she was still fond of him and because she, more than any other person in his life, understood the harassment he felt in both his personal life and business affairs. Her concern for his health and happiness remained constant, and in the January letter to Bray she had written that Chapman looked "horribly ghastly and wants change. . . ."

She took a change for herself by going to Broadstairs instead of Brighton in the late summer and staying essentially the two months she had anticipated. Being away from the hectic lodging house and all that it meant to her was so vast a relief that she wrote Cara she had begun to wonder "whether it would not be wise to retire from the world and live here for the rest of my days." However, she felt guilty because she knew Chapman was figuratively chained to a hot and dusty London, and in a letter to him from Broadstairs she refers to herself as "a wretched helpmate." The first part of this rather long letter is filled with suggestions concerning the *Westminster* that belie her assertion. The second half is given over to her advice—some half-joking, but much of which Chapman might well have taken to heart —about his finding a new editor, one who might have all the glory of the name as well as of the work. She was not at all snide in these remarks, as she never was to be with Chapman on this topic. When away during this respite, she wanted release from both the Strand and the *Westminster*. Yet in late August she returned without having made plans for either new lodgings or new work; she had convinced herself that to leave Chapman at this time would be an act of disloyalty, for the magazine was in an alarming financial state. "But ever since I came back," she wrote Sara a week later, "I have felt something like the madness which imagines that the four walls are contracting and going to crush one."

In January 1853, she made another resolve and wrote Bray: "At last I have determined to leave this house and get another home for myself." Then she added the usual qualification: "I suppose I must stay here, however, until the April number is out of our hands." And in March she wrote him: "Instead of changing my street, I have changed my room only, and am now installed in Mr. Chapman's. It is very light and pleasant, and I suppose I must be content for a few months longer." As her old room had been an unattractively dark one at the back of the house, this move was no doubt maneuvered by Chapman as a bribe to retain her. By this time she was staying only because of lassitude and indifference. "Indeed," she admitted to Bray, "I think I shall never have the energy to move—it seems to be of so little consequence where I am or what I do." Fortunately, during the next few months a new relationship began to give consequence to her daily life and to offer the first real challenge to Chapman's hold upon her. What had been a light friendship with George Henry Lewes had rapidly deepened as she learned the facts of his broken home and broken life; his need for her sympathetic understanding was an appeal she could not long resist. At last she had a positive reason for leaving 142 Strand. She wanted to be where Lewes could visit her freely and privately, and on 17 October she took rooms at 21 Cambridge Street, Hyde Park. "It was this change of lodgings," according to Oscar Browning, "and not the journey to Weimar, as is generally supposed, which marked the commencement of the union with Mr. Lewes."

Shortly after this move she also became more decisive about resigning her position on the *Westminster*. "I told Mr. Chapman yesterday," she reported to Sara in November,

> that I wished to give up any connection with the editorship of the Westminster. He wishes me to continue the present state of things until April, but admits that he is so straitened for money and for *assistance* in the mechanical part of his business that he feels unable to afford an expense on the less tangible services which I render. I shall be much more satisfied on many accounts to have done with that affair—

For once there is no evidence that she did "continue the present state of things." Had she not been worn out from the unpleasant suspense of not knowing if the magazine would remain solvent from one issue to the next, it is doubtful whether she would have remained firm in her decision. Chapman spared her none of the dismal details about the financial condition, as he had spared her none about his divided affection. Although he himself agonized—looking ghastly—over money matters, he had the same sanguine expectation that they would somehow right themselves as he had that his household would miraculously become a peaceful haven. Oddly enough, his optimism was proved justified; over and again he was saved in the nick of time by unexpected loans. However, his indebtedness mounted so high that the worldly-wise Joseph Parkes wrote his daughter, Bessie (by then George Eliot's closest younger friend): "The way he [Chapman] is behaving is, between ourselves, generally the prelude to bankruptcy. . . ." A less fortunate and more reasonable man would have been forced to bow down to such a fate. Chapman was rescued by a strange juncture of circumstances, and eventually managed to rid himself of the proprietorship (and hence the financial problems) of both his publishing business and the *Westminster*. He retained the editorship of the latter until his death in 1894. (Afterwards, Mrs. Chapman—Pres—continued on with it until 1907.)

But in 1853, George Eliot could not know that the magazine was headed toward anything other than stark failure. Her own financial prospects were bleak, for although money enough was to be scraped together to pay contributors, there was little left over that could have gone to her. In any event, she would have terminated her connection with it except as a contributor when she left for Germany with Lewes. Yet she must have relinquished her editorial position with some regret. True, much about it had been a liability to her: from the beginning her feeling for Chapman had drained her energy, she had been underpaid, and she had done a prodigious amount of work, much of which was sheer drudgery and should have been turned over to apprentices. On the other hand, through this work and the associations it brought her with men close to the heart of London's intellectual life, she had led an unrestricted and even exciting existence normally denied to women of the time. She took naturally to both the work and the unconventional atmosphere. "I can see her now," William Hale White recollected in 1885, "with her hair over her shoulders, the easy chair half sideways to the fire, her feet over the arms, and a proof in her hands, in that dark room at the back of No. 142. . . ."

Though she had been inexperienced in editorial work when she first came from Coventry to London, no one had occasion to remind her of that fact. She took command of the *Westminster*—without affronting its nominal editor, Chapman—and guided it to a position of eminence it had not held since the editorship of John Stuart Mill. As early as June 1852, George Combe had given her unqualified praise, which she could not resist repeating to the Brays: "he says, he thinks the Westminster, under *my* management the most important means of enlightenment of a literary nature in existence—the Edinburgh, under Jeffrey, nothing to it etc. etc!!!"

After the appearance of her first number in January 1852, the *Leader* (a radical weekly largely run by George Henry Lewes and Thornton Hunt) gave it faint praise. This notice commended Mr. Chapman for having avoided "heaviness and exclusiveness," but added: "We miss the positive convictions of which it should be the organ. That Mr. Chapman will not allow it to fall into vague routinary orthodoxy his position in the publishing world assures us: it will be fatal if he *do*, for the orthodox *have* their organs already." But in response to the October issue, the *Leader* notice, written by Lewes (himself a contributor to this number with "Goethe as a Man of Science"), was as unqualified in its approval as Combe had been:

> It is a matter of general remark, that the *Westminster Review*, since it passed into Mr. Chapman's hands, has recovered the former importance it acquired when under the editorship of JOHN STAURT MILL. It is now a Review that people talk about, ask for at the

clubs, and read with respect. The variety and general excellence of its articles are not surpassed by any Review.

From Lewes, a great admirer of Mill, this was deeply felt praise; and by this time he would have been aware that "Mr. Chapman's hands" meant Miss Evans's. She had every right to be proud of her achievement. Despite its shaky financial foundation, the *Westminster* had become England's foremost organ of liberal thought and might well have been a truly avant-garde journal had she been able to have her own way completely, without the need to take into consideration the wishes of her employer, the financial backers, and the subscribers.

Although her editing might have proved a creditable life's work and she probably could have prevented the *Westminster*'s gradual decline into conservatism and nondistinction, it is unlikely that she would have remained with it indefinitely. She had written for the magazine sporadically and anonymously, but the editorial work, like her translating, had preoccupied her primarily with other people's thought. It was therefore somewhat daring of her, as she needed an income other than her inheritance, to decide to withdraw from the *Westminster* and devote her time to making an English version of Feuerbach and also to undertaking an original work to be called "The Idea of a Future Life." She was not cutting herself off from Chapman in this plan, for in June 1853, despite his tottering business, he had "launched a new publishing scheme—the Quarterly Series—to consist of works 'by learned and profound thinkers, embracing the subjects of theology, philosophy, Biblical criticism, and the history of opinion.' " And in the original advertisement of this project, he had announced, among other works, the Feuerbach translation and "The Idea of a Future Life" by "The Translator of 'Strauss's Life of Jesus.' "

This new arrangement was once again to strain the otherwise malleable association to almost the breaking point. The Quarterly Series was backed by little else than Chapman's unwarranted optimism. Depressed by the sparse subscriptions, he early expressed his doubt of the practical wisdom of including the controversial Feuerbach. " . . . I shall find the question of supplies rather a difficult one this year," George Eliot wrote Sara in the same letter in which she announced her intention of quitting the *Westminster*, "as I am not likely to get any money either for Feuerbach, which, after all, Mr. Chapman I think will be afraid of publishing in his Series, or for 'The Idea of a Future Life,' for which I am to have 'half profits' = o/o!" Shortly after this letter to Sara, she had a further talk with Chapman about her part in the Quarterly Series, during which he apparently reiterated his fear of including Feuerbach and failed even to mention "The Idea of a Future Life." The following day—2 December 1853

—she wrote him a severe "business" letter to cover matters not brought up or clarified in their conversation: "Friendship is not to be depended on, but business has rather more guarantees. You seem to be oblivious just now of the fact that you have pledged yourself as well as me to the publication of another work besides Feuerbach in your Series." She reminded him of the "ignominy of advertising things, especially as part of a subscription series, which never appear." And she summarized succinctly: "The two requests then which I have to make are first, that you will let me know whether you can, *as a matter of business*, undertake to supply me with the necessary books [for "The Idea of a Future Life," which, it would seem, was to be classified under the "history of opinion" of the proposed series], and secondly, that you will consider the question of Feuerbach as one which concerns our *honour* first and our pockets after." In the concluding sentence, however, she relented, reverting to the affectionately scolding tone which dominates her few extant letters to him: "I have been making a desk of my knee so I fear some of my words may be illegible, which will be a pity because of course you can't substitute any half as good."

The Feuerbach translation was completed and published. "The Idea of a Future Life" did not materialize, but whether because Chapman failed to furnish the necessary books or because new and more forceful plans prompted George Eliot to abandon it, is not wholly clear. Probably the latter, for she and Lewes left for Germany in the same month—July 1854—that the Feuerbach appeared. (But it was "The Idea of a Future Life" which Sara understandably assumed George Eliot to be busily engaged upon when actually she was writing the *Clerical Scenes* and *Adam Bede*.) Her own admission to Charles Bray, written from Weimar, shows that there was no serious disagreement between George Eliot and Chapman over the Quarterly Series: "Mr. and Mrs. Chapman are the only persons to whom I have ever spoken of [Lewes's] private position and of my relation to him. . . ."

The friendship for Chapman remained unbroken; while she was on the Continent and for a time after her return to England, she found in him a very much needed source of income. At his invitation, she wrote for the *Westminster* her notable series of essays beginning with "Woman in France: Madame de Sablé," which appeared in October 1854, and concluding with "Worldliness and Other-Worldliness: The Poet Young" (January 1857, that is, after the writing of "Amos Barton"). When she and Lewes returned to England in March 1855, she wrote Chapman to let him know that she was back, and he responded by asking her to write the "Belles Lettres" section of contemporary reviews for the *Westminster*. She did this, starting with the July number and continuing until January 1857, when she was becoming increasingly engrossed in writing the *Clerical Scenes*.

Apparently Chapman was their first visitor at East Sheen, where they had settled in May—"a charming village close to Richmond Park," as she described it to Charles Bray. He came to dinner on 24 June, bringing with him for her criticism a manuscript of his own, "The Position of Woman in Barbarism and Among the Ancients," part of which was already in type for the July number of the *Westminster*. This was a brave or overly sanguine act on Chapman's part, for from the beginning of their association no amount of compassion for his personal and business problems could overrule her severity toward his writing. "The dreariness," she had lamented to Sara while working with Feuerbach, "of giving such a translation to Mr. Chapman who neither knows what is in itself good English nor what is the difficulty of truly representing German!" As long as he confined his writing to letters, she could be sympathetically tolerant, even equating his bad writing with some undesirable trait in her own character. "The sentence you quote," she had written Cara in 1852,

> is a good specimen of Mr. Chapman's skill in "the art of sinking," not in poetry, but in letter-writing. But it is nothing worse than bungling. He feels better than he writes, just as some other acquaintances of ours write better than they feel. I am sure I ought to have sympathy enough with people who mean well and do ill, for the grand occupation of my life has been contributing to hell-paving.

But Chapman was not content to write letters only; he still aspired to appear in print in his own magazine. As long as George Eliot remained his assistant, she successfully dissuaded him from doing so; in 1855 it was no longer within her rightful province to voice an opinion on this matter. However, he had asked for her criticism of his article, and in a letter written the day after he came to dinner, she gave it to him. After one favorable comment, she quickly switched to the inevitable but's: " . . . but whenever you pass from narrative to dissertation, certain old faults reappear—inexactness of expression, triads and duads of verbs and adjectives, mixed metaphors and a sort of watery volume that requires to be reduced by evaporation." Brusquely, she then specified examples of these characteristics and blue-penciled others in the manuscript. No doubt to remove some of the sting, she concluded: "I have written as unceremoniously as I used to do in the old days, believing that you will like that best."

George Eliot had neither commended nor disapproved of Chapman's sober topic, which might have been discussed in general over dinner the night before she wrote her critical letter, and which he might have chosen with her in mind, for she of all women he knew had achieved the kind of freedom he meant when in the final version of his essay he added: "We must remember that it is *in spite* of English laws that English women have now virtually attained a degree of social freedom and dignity worthy of comparison with that of their Roman predecessors. . . ." Temporarily dejected by her criticism, he withdrew his essay from July publication and asked her by letter if it was worth publishing at all. She replied: "Assuredly your article is worth publishing. I think it very valuable and interesting; indeed I thought I had said so in my letter [she had not]. It is for that very reason that I dwelt on certain defects of style which you can remedy by giving a little more trouble." To this she added a critical suggestion by Lewes and her own summary concerning his writing, which any person but Chapman would have found insufferably condescending:

> There is no reason for you to be desponding about your writing. You have made immense progress during the last few years, and you have so much force of mind and sincerity of purpose that you may work your way to a style which is free from vices, though perhaps you will never attain felicity—indeed, that is a free gift of Nature rather than a reward of labour.

Chapman accepted all this in the spirit of deference which had first endeared him to her. He worked hard at revising his article, using almost all of her suggestions as a guide, and finally had the pleasure of seeing it in the October number of the *Westminster*. Despite the Spartan treatment he knew he was sure to receive, he continued to bring his articles to her for criticism. As late as 11 October 1858, she wrote to Sara what she might have written six years earlier:

> Dr. Chapman [he had received his M.D. from St. Andrews on 6 May 1857] came yesterday, in spite of the weather, and in spite of a bad headache, poor man! . . . I felt deep compassion for him. His health seems to be threatening again, and the load of anxieties he has to carry about his neck, while he is making efforts so strenuous and in many respects so disagreeable that few men would have the courage for them!

At this time she was within a month of completing *Adam Bede*. The relationship between her and Chapman had remained peaceful; although early in that year he had been given reason to wonder why she found it impossible to write the essay on Francis W. Newman's books she had promised him for the *Westminster*. "Alas!" she wrote him on 12 January, "I have not done a stroke towards the article on Newman. . . . It is almost needless to say that I don't neglect the opportunity of working for the W R in order to do work for any other review, and that I have no ground for my negations but inability." Knowing her, he was not convinced by her confession of simple "inability." Although accepting her word that she was not writing for another review, he strongly suspected that she was engaged in some other kind of writing which had brought to a halt her contributions to the *Westminster*. And his successful attempt to allay his suspicion caused (probably to his surprise) the often tested friendship to come to an irrevocable end.

Having rightly guessed that she had taken Herbert Spencer into her confidence about the nature of her new writing, Chapman asked him point-blank if, as rumored, she had written the *Clerical Scenes*. Spencer somehow managed an evasive answer, but he felt duty-bound to report the matter to the Leweses when next he dined with them. Noting this "unpleasant news" in her Journal on 5 November, she added: "I wrote at once to [Chapman] to check further gossip on the subject." She was both indignant and hurt, for Chapman, of all people, knew very well why she desired anonymity as long as possible; and her letter to him was correspondingly curt. When three weeks had lapsed and he had not responded, she noted in her Journal under 30 November "by way of dating the conclusion of an acquaintance extending over eight years, that I have received no answer from Dr. Chapman to my letter of the 5th, and have learned from Mr. Spencer that the circumstances attending this silence are not more excusable than I had imagined them to be. I shall not correspond with him or willingly see him again."

When finally he did write in late December, she relented and wrote him on New Year's Day, 1859, although her brief note was cool in tone and made it clear that she was unimpressed by whatever reasons he had given to justify his "leaving unanswered my letter written two months ago." Apparently it was enough, however, to encourage him to ask leave to visit her and Lewes, for a few days later she wrote him that they were busy making ready to move, "and I think we must deny ourselves the pleasure of seeing any visitors until we are fairly at ease in our new home." But her conclusion indicated she had relented further: "Till then, I remain, as of old, / Your sincere friend / Marian Lewes." She had softened too soon, for the worst was yet to come.

They did move to Holly Lodge, in Wandsworth, on February 11, just ten days after the publication of *Adam Bede*, which was quickly and sensationally successful. Chapman again cornered Spencer, this time with subtler strategy. He said that a Mrs. Dunn had told him Miss Evans was the author of *Adam Bede*: was that true? For a few minutes Spencer was able to fence by asking where Mrs. Dunn had heard any such thing, and so on, but "Chapman soon returned to the question—'Is it true?' To this question"—so Spencer recalled many years later—"I made no answer; and of course my silence amounted to an admission. / When next I went over to Wandsworth, I told them what had occurred, and was blamed for not giving a denial: the case of Scott being named as justifying such a course." At the time, he was hurt that they assumed he should tell an outright lie to preserve the secret. Besides, "a denial from me would have been futile. . . . I have so little control over my features that a vocal 'No' would have been inevitably accompanied by a facial 'Yes.' " Characteristically, Spencer draws a moral: "The lesson which the incident teaches is that a secret cannot safely be committed even to one in whom perfect confidence may be reposed. . . ." Also, he minimizes the effect of the incident: "I may add that fortunately no harm was done. The secret was leaking out; and, moreover, the reason for keeping the secret had no longer much weight."

To the Leweses, however, the effect seemed catastrophic enough to cause a temporary rift between them and Spencer, although Spencer tactfully makes no reference to this in his *Autobiography*. Lewes resolved to take a firm stand: " . . . if the thing is to be denied at all," he wrote in his Journal for 12 February, "I am for distinct, effective denial rather than equivocation." Earlier that day he had written Chapman a terse letter that was indeed unequivocal:

> After the previous correspondence, your continuing to impute those works to Mrs. Lewes may be *meant* as a compliment, but *is* an offence against delicacy and friendship. As you seem so very slow in appreciating her feelings on this point, she authorizes me to state, as distinctly as language can do so, that she is not the author of "Adam Bede."

Even this was stretching the truth, for in his Journal entry he admitted that George Eliot was "reluctant" to have him write the letter. Very probably she would have preferred silence. It must have crossed her mind to wonder what Chapman, who she knew admired and respected her for her scrupulous honesty, would think when he discovered that the unequivocal statement was actually a brazen lie. Mainly, however, she was too deeply hurt to want to pursue the matter further; somewhat unreasonably, she felt that she had been betrayed by Chapman and Spencer, and both men—especially Chapman—had a meaning in her life which not even her near-perfect companionship with Lewes could wholly supplant.

The hurt was not quickly extinguished. Over five months later, in July, when John Blackwood presented her with a pug dog in tribute of the phenomenal success of *Adam Bede*, she made at least three written references to the dog as taking the place of lost friends. To Cara she wrote about "our excitement in the expectation of a real pug dog! . . . He comes a substitute for lost friends." The next day she wrote Barbara

Leigh Smith, now Mme Bodichon, who was planning to visit: "I shall not lose the sense that you are coming . . . in spite of a real *pug*, who is coming too—a present to the Author of A.B. in compensation for lost friends." And to Blackwood upon the pug's arrival: "Pug is come!—come to fill up the void left by false and narrow-hearted friends. I see already that he is without envy, hatred, or malice—that he will betray no secrets, and feel neither pain at my success nor pleasure in my chagrin."

The nameless "lost" friends are of course Spencer and Chapman. The phrase "pain at my success" perhaps referred to Spencer, whose manner seemed changed to her. "Spencer came to spend the day with us," Lewes recorded on 24 March. "But his coming was only pain and disappointment to Polly on account of his coolness." Both she and Lewes attributed his coolness to jealousy of her growing fame; more likely it was Spencer's natural reaction to her thinking that he had deliberately revealed her secret. With more justification, "pleasure in my chagrin" might have referred to Chapman, for earlier there had been some degree of sadism in his treatment of her.

Eventually Spencer was reinstated in her good grace although one senses not wholly in her affection. Not so Chapman. Undaunted by Lewes's insulting letter of unequivocal denial, he continued to write to her, as her remark to Sara on 21 May 1859 indicates: "Dr. Chapman writes that he saw Mr. Bray the other day looking 'wonderfully well.' . . ." This is the last reference to him in the extant letters. Perhaps significantly it is a nonsarcastic one, whereas most of her allusions to Spencer around this time verge on ridicule, especially of his well-known hypochondria. In an earlier letter she told Sara that his friends "are required now to take *nux vomica* on pain of his contempt—the ground therefor being that he took it himself and got a bad cold by it—also, that he drank an extra cup of coffee in consequence."

We do not know for certain that she had stopped writing to Chapman, for most of her letters to him have disappeared. But when in January 1860 he wrote to propose that he republish her *Westminster* essays in book form, Lewes took over with the same decisiveness that had dictated his letter of denial. He noted the "cool request" in his Journal and added: "Squashed that idea." So the door closed on Dr. John Chapman with a finality that perhaps George Eliot privately regretted.

Although he was out of her life, the effect of her unique relationship with him was to be a lasting one—not to be explained in terms of ordinary influence. Its dynamic source lay first in her love for him; more so, however, in her having faced the futility of that love without retreating into either fury or abject despondency and also without forcing him into a critical quarrel with her. It was important, too, that she had not withdrawn physically: painful as it must have been, her continuing to work for and with him and to live at 142 Strand when her emotional struggle was at its height drew forth sustaining inner strengths which carried on the psychic process begun in a small way in Switzerland under the smart of Charles Hennell's criticism. One small sign that a new pattern of reaction was emerging was that she never once sought to make him appear ridiculous to others (as she had the Reverend Sibree, Dr. Brabant, and even, to a lesser degree, Charles Hennell). Her references to him in the letters to Coventry—with the minor exception of the comments on his style—are uniformly respectful and often defensive, as if to forestall criticism of him. There is little doubt that the physical attraction Chapman had for her was stronger than she was to feel for any other man, despite her genuine love for Lewes. This attraction could be sensed by those who observed them together at 142 Strand (Eliza Lynn, for example); there were others whose gossip gave rise to the rumor that she bore Chapman a son and hid him away in Edinburgh. Factually, this is as improbable as the better-intentioned gossip that she never slept with Lewes.

There is usually a germ of truth in all persistent gossip. The truth here appears to have been of a subterranean kind; the kind that so largely shaped her life. She was drawn to Chapman by a force that could have created a child had her desire been allowed physical manifestation. Her physical desire for Lewes, on the other hand, was but one part of an overarching need to give and receive, which also included the feelings of respect, equality, and comradeship, all based in shared confessions of weaknesses, mistakes, and aspirations. The very limitations of her love for Chapman made it, in its single-ness, cut into her psyche almost as deeply as her earlier rejected love for her mother and brother. Even without demonstrable knowledge to prove the point, Chapman appears in many guises in her novels, and especially where a woman is compulsively drawn toward a conventionally nonavailable man—Tina for Anthony Wybrow in the second *Clerical Scene* and, still more notably, Maggie for Stephen Guest in the *Mill*.

But her feeling for Chapman held something in addition to physical attraction. She gave little heed to the eccentric surface of his life and took him seriously, believing in his sincerity when he professed a desire for moral improvement and proudly using his rightful title after he had taken his degree in medicine. In some way or other, he had earned her respect, and she was to give him the same compassion-ate understanding that she gave to Tertius Lydgate of *Middlemarch*, whose essential nature is an admixture of courageous idealism and

human vulnerability. George Eliot did extensive research for Lydgate's medical knowledge and theories, but none of it can explain the
intimacy of the inside-out portrait that resulted. Although no longer
in her external life when she created Lydgate (1869–72), Chapman
was still a part of her inner life. In much the same way, he is in and
yet not in *Middlemarch*; one senses his presence without actually seeing him. Surely he directly inspired at least this sentence describing
Lydgate: "He cared not only for 'cases,' but for John and Elizabeth,
especially Elizabeth" (Book II, chapter 15). George Eliot meant these
names as generic terms, but they may be more specifically applicable
than the reader is meant to realize.

Had John Chapman not chosen to pry into the secret of her authorship, it is probable that she would have remained his friend throughout her life. One suspects that her undue severity toward Herbert
Spencer for his part in the "betrayal" was largely motivated by the
fact that Spencer thought it necessary to inform her that it was Chapman who had been making the impertinent inquiries. Lewes somewhat unfairly noted when he recorded the unhappy day spent with
Spencer: "He always tells us the disagreeable things he hears or reads
of us and never the agreeable things."

Yet it was Spencer who unknowingly provided the most
revealing evidence of the change being effected within her by her ordeal at the Strand. Nostalgic recollections of her—as the translator of
Strauss, as Miss Evans, as Mrs. Lewes, as George Eliot—weave in and
out of his huge *Autobiography* like a persistent motif. They make it
clear that by the time he knew her, she had undergone (or was undergoing) an important personality modulation and that he had never
known the outwardly emotional woman that Chapman had known, the
impetuous and uneven-tempered young woman best known by the
Brays and Hennells, or the unhappy and frustrated girl beloved by
Maria Lewis. Significantly, Spencer's relationship with her was at its
closest during 1852, the year when she was struggling to free herself
of the bondage of unwanted love. They first met during her August
1851 visit, when she was seeing the Great Exhibition and also making
arrangements with the Chapmans for her return. It was not until her
return to the Strand in October (hence after the binding vow taken
with Chapman) that the acquaintance soon ripened into friendship.
Their relationship naturally developed into a close one: they were of
the same age essentially (he was five months younger), both loved the
theater, and music, and each found the other intellectually invigorat-

ing. He respected her translation of Strauss, and she admired his first book, *Social Statics* (published by Chapman in late 1850 and already bringing Spencer some fame), as well as his other versatile accomplishments. He was a civil engineer, inventor, essayist on political and social topics, and, when she first knew him, subeditor of *The Economist*, which had its office in the Strand across the street from the Chapmans. As he lived in rooms above his office, it was easy for him to drop in at 142, and these casual visits increased in number and length after her arrival. There is a light gaiety in their early companionship which is too easily thrust out of sight as a result of the retrospective shadow cast over it by later, less happy circumstances. One of the first references to George Eliot in Spencer's letters to his friend Edward Lott reveals that she regarded him with a half-amused, half-teasing attitude, which (although unbeknownst to him) she never wholly relinquished: "I doubt not you would have greatly enjoyed being a party to the *badinage* that has been carried on at my expense by Chapman and Miss Evans (the translatress of Strauss) for these two months past. They have taken upon themselves to choose me a wife; and the various arrangements and delays in effecting an introduction have afforded subject matter for much mirth."

As Spencer goes on to record with apparent relish (and it must be remembered that he chose to print this letter in his *Autobiography*), Chapman and George Eliot had set their hopes for his marriage upon a young woman who had expressed admiration for *Social Statics* and inquired whether *Herbert Spencer* "was a real or assumed name, &c., &c." Finally an introduction was maneuvered, but nothing came of it. Although Spencer admitted to having found the lady to be "sufficiently good-looking, young, extremely open, a poetess and an heiress," he had several decisive objections. She was "morbidly intellectual. A small brain in a state of intense activity, is the best description. Moreover she seems pretty nearly as combative as I am; and has, I fancy, almost as much self-esteem. Moreover, she did not seem as if she could laugh." Nor had the lady been favorably impressed, as he learned afterwards. "Probably," he speculated,

> she came with high anticipations and was disappointed: looking for intellectual coruscations and meeting with nothing but commonplace remarks. Most people frame very untrue, and often very absurd conceptions of those who write books. . . . One may say that as a rule no man is equal to his book. . . . It would be about as reasonable to suppose that the fermented wort of the distiller will be found of like quality with the spirit distilled from it.

Although only half serious, this episode as recounted by Spencer is helpful in interpreting his relationship with George Eliot before it was to be clouded by less disinterested interpretations. George Eliot, along with other of Spencer's friends, thought that he should marry, but was also aware that someone would have to find him a bride. She was quite willing that this bride be other than herself; but Spencer was to prove ultra-critical of any suggested candidate, whether physically attractive or not. And finally, according to his own account, he recognized that he infused the most vital part of himself into his work rather than into human relationships (George Eliot was to come to realize this also).

By April 1852 Spencer had written his more serious letter to Lott about Miss Evans "as the most admirable woman, mentally, I ever met. We have been for some time past on very intimate terms. I am very frequently at Chapman's and the greatness of her intellect conjoined with her womanly qualities and manner, generally keep me by her side most of the evening." They were now enjoying a remarkably free and happy companionship. Spencer himself remembered:

> The occasions of meeting had been multiplied by the opportunities I had for taking her to places of amusement. My free admissions for two, to the theatres and to the Royal Italian Opera, were, during these early months of 1852, much more used than they would otherwise have been, because I had frequently—indeed nearly always—the pleasure of her companionship in addition to the pleasure afforded by the performance.

When good weather permitted, they had a quiet and private promenade, for the rear of Chapman's house abutted upon Somerset House, the basement of which then rose directly out of the Thames and was surmounted by a long terrace with a balustrade. Chapman had a key to a gate that opened onto this terrace, and on fine afternoons in the spring and summer of 1852, having borrowed the key, "we made our way on to the terrace, where we paced backwards and forwards for an hour or so, discussing many things."

One topic must have been the gossip which inevitably arose around their frequent meetings, all the more perplexing to Victorian society because not clandestine. Writing many years after this momentous one of 1852, Spencer recollected that "people drew their inferences" from their being together so often, and although he complains that the world needs very slight evidence for "positive conclusion," he admits that "here the evidence seemed strong. Naturally, therefore, quite definite statements became current. There were reports that I was in love with her, and that we were about to be married. But neither of these reports was true." It seems probable that these quite definite statements forced both Spencer and George Eliot to confront their feelings for each other; they had drifted into the habit of enjoying one another in a solitude for two, a condition that was to become George Eliot's ideal for a human relationship. She had never before known the luxury of companionship with a man without the threatening background of angrily possessive relatives. Spencer had come from an originally large family, but his eight brothers and sisters had died while he was yet a boy; from thirteen on, he had been reared by an uncle, although he did not sever relations with his mother and father. In fact, Spencer brought his father to visit George Eliot in June 1852, and she reported to the Brays that she found him "altogether very pleasing." But this was two months after she had written them concerning herself and Spencer: "We have agreed that we are not in love with each other and that there is no reason why we should not have as much of each other's society as we like. He is a good, delightful creature and I always feel better for being with him."

Both of them remained sensitive to the suggestive rumors in the air, which were potent enough to destroy their friendship. Thus when in June, Charles Bray invited her to bring Spencer with her on a visit to Rosehill, she quickly responded that although she was pleased Spencer had been asked and he had accepted,

> I think it would be better for him to go down when I am with you. We certainly could not go together, for all the world is setting us down as engaged—a most disagreeable thing if one chose to make oneself uncomfortable. "Tell it not in Gath" however—that is to say, please to avoid mentioning our names together, and pray burn this note, that it may not lie on the chimney piece for general inspection.

This and the earlier letter dealing with her and Spencer's agreement that they were not in love seem written with a sense of liberation from the compulsive feeling that she had to be in love with whatever man circumstances brought close to her. It is quite possible that much later she transferred her own feeling of relief to Sir James Chettam of *Middlemarch,* who discovered "the delight there is in frank kindness and companionship between a man and a woman who have no passion to hide or confess" (Book I, chapter 8). Spencer may or may not have felt such delight; at this time he was probably less experienced in matters of the heart than she.

This is as far as the extant record allows us to go in reconstructing the relationship. Admittedly there are gaps in the record, but what emerges is a fairly convincing account of a man and woman who were fortuitously granted ample opportunity to become lovers but who chose, rather, to remain friends. Had George Henry Lewes not entered and quickly dominated the scene, the record might well have retained its simple outline. But when George Eliot's preference for a

dual solitude noticeably shifted from Spencer to Lewes, the already
flourishing gossip took a similar turn: she had—so the rumor now
went—jilted Spencer for Lewes. Her actually going off with Lewes
ignited a new scandal powerful enough to smother the less sensational
one generated by her relationship with Spencer, who, after all, had
been respectably eligible for such a romantic attachment. However,
that earlier gossip linking him and George Eliot was never wholly
extinguished. It smoldered on and flared forth anew immediately after
George Eliot's death—Spencer had been in love with her, they had
planned marriage, and she had jilted him for Lewes. Always extremely
vulnerable before the slightest threat to his ego, Spencer was ready to
go to incredible lengths to have this gossip repudiated. Only the intervention of close friends prevented him from making imprudent public
statements which would have given rise to talk still less favorable to
himself. He is even reported to have said with ungallant bluntness
when he heard that it was thought she spurned his offer of marriage:
"I did not propose to her; she proposed to me."

No one who has come face to face with the real George Eliot can
be shocked or even surprised at the idea of her proposing marriage to
some man of her choosing. But for various reasons, it is unlikely
that either she *or* Spencer made a decisive proposal. One of the major
reasons for Spencer's reluctance was dictated by his own nature: the
Autobiography reveals indirectly (including his own account of Chapman and George Eliot's teasing offer to find him a bride) that he
feared sexual union with a woman and was, consequently, a confirmed
bachelor long before he was consciously aware of the fact. Later on in
life, he quite knowingly confessed to having given up marriage for his
work, despite the psychosomatic payment he made in exchange:
"Habitually," he lamented (or was he boasting?), "before I have yet
finished rejoicing over my emancipation from a work which has long
played the tyrant over me, I make myself the slave of another. The
truth is, I suppose, that in the absence of wife and children to care for,
the carrying out of my undertakings is the one thing that makes
life worth living—even though, by it, life is continually perturbed."

The subject of marriage—more specifically, of his *not* marrying—
comes up many times throughout the *Autobiography*. It definitely
was in Spencer's mind during his long bachelorhood, or at least came
to the fore as he composed over long years the carefully constructed
and reconstructed version of his life which became the *Autobiography*,
an impressive if sometimes unintentionally funny work. In a digressive
but nonetheless careful way, he records a visit to Auguste Comte in
Paris to discuss philosophy, but admits that of this conversation he
remembered only that when Comte heard of his nervous disorders,
he advised Spencer to marry as a curative measure. "This, by the way,"

Spencer adds, "was a point of agreement between him and one who differed from him in most things—Professor Huxley; who in after years suggested that I should try what he facetiously termed gyneopathy: admitting, however, that the remedy had the serious inconvenience that it could not be left off if it proved unsuitable." One can well imagine with what mixed feelings Spencer listened to George Eliot and Lewes when the same topic came up, although in a somewhat different context. He recalls their response when once, not long before the death of Lewes, Spencer confessed to them that he valued life but little, save for the purpose of finishing his work: "they both of them ascribed my state of feeling to lack of the domestic affections, and simultaneously exclaimed that their great sorrow was that the time would soon come when death would part them."

There is a pathetic note in these reminiscences. They reveal that in Spencer's own mind his lack of a wife was equated with both his tormenting nervous system and occasional melancholy. Probably he rationalized the lack as a necessary sacrifice to his work; hence his somewhat bitter enjoyment when diverse friends called attention to it and solicitously advised him to marry. It is also probable that he deeply yearned to take a wife and no doubt had ample opportunity to do so; that he did not was indeed a sacrifice, but one demanded by his psyche, not his work. Aware that he had remained single for reasons that were private and of the utmost importance to himself, he understandably came near to hysteria when gossip had it that he had been rejected by George Eliot in favor of Lewes and that he had never married because of unrequited love for her.

Spencer gave Cross a bad time. Upon learning that Cross was to do the *Life*, he wrote simply to ask that the rumor that he had been in love with her be negated in some general way. He relaxed for three years—perhaps hoping that Cross would not go through with the difficult project—but then, hearing that it had been resumed, he wrote again, expressing special concern over the we-are-not-in-love letter. (Had Cross shown him this letter, or had it been discussed openly by the Brays, himself, and George Eliot?) Spencer's urgent suggestion to Cross was that he should append to the letter a note worded by Spencer himself to disclaim the still floating rumor that he had been in love with her. Cross did not like the note and quite sensibly thought that the continued intimacy between Spencer and George Eliot after the letter had been written was in itself evidence enough of what Spencer wanted to emphasize. Spencer, however, was dissatisfied and composed yet another note, which also met with Cross's disapproval.

In a desperate effort to come to amicable terms with Spencer, Cross experimented with a note of his own. Spencer rejected this and wrote back: "Much better no note at all than the one you propose." The belabored Cross took him at his word but was still troubled by the words in the letter which he realized had aroused great anxiety in Spencer. Finally he decided to delete them (although Harper's American edition [1885], apparently printed from earlier proofs, contains the original sentence in its entirety). The result was the innocuous remainder: "We have agreed that there is no reason why we should not have as much of each other's society as we like." Seeing this when the English *Life* appeared, Spencer wrote petulantly to Cross:

> As the account now stands it is not only consistent with the report that I was jilted for Lewes, but tends to confirm it. Such a fact as that I was anxious to visit the Brays when she was there, and such a fact as that my name quietly drops out as a companion while Lewes' comes in, gives colour to the statement, and there is nothing I can see to negative it. I cannot say that I have been fairly used.

He was mollified by the friends he again consulted, who assured him that the omitted words might have caused further misinterpretation and that it was also best to have allowed Cross's version of the letter to stand without any explanatory note. Spencer had the good grace to tell Cross of his changed view.

Cross's attitude to both Chapman and Spencer as he worked on the *Life* is highly indicative of how he viewed each man's relationship with George Eliot. He refused to call upon the willing Chapman for information or letters, and he made it clear that he would have welcomed letters from Spencer had they been proffered. Obviously he had qualms about Chapman's association with George Eliot, yet none whatever about Spencer's. It was Spencer alone who confused that relationship, and Cross was of course the first biographer who had to meet head-on the baffling problem created, whereas Oscar Browning was the first who inherited the compromise effected by Cross. Literally, Mathilde Blind wrote the first full-length biography of George Eliot, published in 1883. But as she did not have access to Cross's *Life*, and as, presumably, she had no wish to record unsubstantiated rumors, she was free to summarize the relationship as an acquaintance that "had ripened into a cordial friendship."

Oscar Browning was in a much more difficult position. Writing in 1890—after the *Life* had appeared and while Cross and Spencer were still living—he had little choice but to quote the emasculated version of the we-are-not-in-love letter and to refrain from coloring his account of the *Westminster* days with his own speculations. On the other hand, he refused to pass over the admittedly important friendship in silence (as Leslie Stephen was to do in 1902). After quoting George Eliot's statement that she and Spencer saw each other every

day, Cross adds pointedly: "Mr. Spencer is thus the best living repository of the traditions of that period, which some day he may perhaps
give to the world." Spencer took no heed of this dignified plea; his
only subsequent gesture was to select a half-dozen or more letters from
George Eliot to him, apparently destroying all the others. These few
preserved letters are to be released (presumably for publication),
according to his will, in 1985. Haight predicts that they will "hardly
alter the picture of an ardent, generous nature offering herself to an
egoist who could love nothing but his 'image.' "

Haight's comment comes within the conclusion of his account of
the George Eliot–Spencer relationship, which is the fullest and most
verifiable one given so far. Yet Haight's version is highly interpretive
in that it is based on two related assumptions: first, that the preserved
letters are from the *Westminster* days; and, second, that during those
days, George Eliot offered her love to Spencer only to have it rejected.
Of the first assumption, one wonders why there would be letters from
the time when she and Spencer were seeing each other every day. But
the second assumption, although closely allied with the first, is of
greater significance. Is it really known that George Eliot was in love
with Spencer and was, figuratively, turned away by him? By now, the
biographer inherits a tradition more complex than that bequeathed to
Oscar Browning, for Spencer's efforts to deny that he had been in love
with George Eliot gave rise (consciously or not on his part) to the
counter-rumor that she had been in love with him but obviously
had not been asked by him to be his wife. By attempting to fit the two-
sided gossip into the sparse primary record, it is easy to assume that
one of the principals jilted the other. And as there is no certain proof
in either direction, biographers have been free to speculate on who
jilted whom. Most biographers have settled on George Eliot as the
victim, largely because of Spencer's often-quoted remark, made at a
late date—perhaps even after the appearance of Cross's *Life*—which
appears in his *Autobiography*: "Physical beauty is a *sine qua non* with
me; as was once unhappily proved where the intellectual traits and
the emotional traits were of the highest." This has been accepted
without question as referring to George Eliot, although there is no
direct evidence for such an assumption. It is possible, of course, that
by insinuation rather than direct statement Spencer allowed it to be
thought among his associates that he had her in mind, so that the idea
was sufficiently established to be picked up by biographers less
reverent toward their subject than Cross and Browning.

The echo has lingered, and even Haight—although pertinently
commenting that lack of beauty did not deter Spencer from keeping
a photograph of George Eliot in his bedroom until the day he died—
introduces the we-are-not-in-love letter with: "But to Marian, Spencer

seems very soon to have made it clear that his admiration was of her mental qualities only. . . ." This interpretation, like all the earlier and still more slanted ones, ignores the depth of George Eliot's emotional involvement with Chapman. There is also the fact that in the fall of 1853 she was to begin her alliance with Lewes. It is unlikely that even she, highly emotional and unconventional as she was, could have swung with such quick intensity from man to man to man. It is possible that, recognizing she had come to an emotional impasse with Chapman (and before she was attracted to Lewes), she might have considered marriage with Spencer, especially if she had at first been led to believe that she might find in him, as Haight suggests in an earlier study, "the ideal she had once imagined in Dr. Brabant and later in Chapman . . . a man whom she could dedicate her life to helping with a great work. . . ."

But if she had really thought that for a while, she could not have long sustained the illusion. She had come far since her days of Brabant-worship. Experience had added worldliness to her intellectual sophistication, and by 1852 she was a shrewd judge of people, her own wisdom being augmented daily by *Westminster* traffic. It would have taken her only a short while to discern that although perhaps a stronger character than Chapman, Spencer was certainly a more rigid one. If his *Autobiography* reveals a mild sense of humor, which he could at times turn upon himself, it was the kind that bolstered rather than fissured his self-engrossment. George Eliot always had unstinted admiration for his mental powers. However, she was never to accept any of his ideas with wholehearted approval, and in his *Autobiography* Spencer is both truthful and generous in his disavowal that he had been a significant influence in her "education," affirming, rather, that when he first met her, "she was already distinguished by that breadth of culture and universality of power which have since made her known to all the world." His ideas intrigued her and stimulated her mind, but they seemed too "neat." From the beginning of their association, what disturbed her most was his predilection for ignoring the stubborn facts which did not fit into his preconceived theories. She made light of this in a letter (2 June 1852) to Sara. Describing a "scientific expedition" to Kew with Spencer, "who has all sorts of theories about plants," she added: "I should have said a *proof*-hunting expedition. Of course, if the flowers didn't correspond to the theories, we said, '*tant pis pour les fleurs.*' " But she was serious in her doubts of the validity of his method. Years later, after listening to a story he told her and Lewes about experimenting with "heterodox flies" in fishing for salmon and trout, she said, "Yes, you have such a passion for generalizing, you even fish with a generalization."

Further, she would have found Spencer a pallid individual when set

against Chapman, who had the spark of daring and adventure—
even in his weird handling of the *Westminster,* as well as in his personal life—to which she responded positively because she herself
shared it. Although often beaten down, and certainly almost obliterated by the George Eliot legend, the same spark had from the
earliest years motivated her, starting with tomboyish games with her
brother, taking her over the Jura in a sledge, and bringing her to
142 Strand. Spencer was everything that she admired. Yet she sensed
his lack of something which had become increasingly important to her
—a freedom to swerve from the expected path and to give unstintingly, even if unwisely, to others. "If ever Chapman's history is written
fully and accurately,' said Sir W. Robertson Nicoll, 'it would form a
romance of the most extraordinary kind.'" But Spencer's? In July
1854 she wrote out for Sara a mock-biographical sketch of him: "He
will stand in the Biographical Dictionaries of 1954 as 'Spencer,
Herbert, an original and profound philosophical writer, especially
known by his great work x x x which gave a new impulse to psychology. . . . The life of this philosopher, like that of the great Kant,
offers little material for the narrator. Born in the year 1820 etc.'"

It had not taken her much time to realize that Spencer's work was
to be his life. Although she could, with reservations, commend
Spencer's dedication, she realized too that in his household there
would be no place for a second person who was equally dedicated
to different work. His hypothetical wife would be either a listener-
secretary or a nurse-housekeeper. Once she had thought that her
ultimate desire was to be given "a woman's work" and bring "pure
calm blessedness" into the life of a man engaged in a great work; but
her *Westminster* career had taught her that what she really wanted
was to work *with* a man, not merely to serve him. Besides, Spencer
already enjoyed "pure calm blessedness," even though his psyche
demanded a huge payment for this in the form of the debilitating
nervous upsets which plagued him for most of his long life. By coincidence or not, the most serious onslaught of these began in 1854, the
year George Eliot went off with Lewes. Spencer himself records that
between 1854 and 1855 he was interrupted in synthesizing the major
ideas that were then in his mind because "eighteen months of ill health
here intervened."

There are biographers who think that it was a grave misfortune
for George Eliot that she did not marry Herbert Spencer, Anne
Fremantle being one of the most emphatic on this matter:

It was very unfortunate for George Eliot that Spencer did not
propose, for she would have written far more simply, less de-
fensively, if she could have "attained tradition" by marriage. It

is never good for anyone to feel an outcast, to be always on the defensive, justifying their lives to their fellow men, and George Eliot's implacable theory of retribution, her constant visiting of the sins of the children upon themselves, was in a large measure due to her unfortunate status in society. Had she married Spencer she would have had no such barriers set up against her: she would not have had to punish herself in the person of her heroines for what she had done. . . .

This is a somewhat grim description for what might be called George Eliot's "philosophy of necessity"—to borrow the title of Charles Bray's book, which she of course had read and assented to long before she became an "outcast." And although the idea that she meted out vicarious punishment to herself in the person of her heroines is a demonstrably sound one, surely her need to do so had its origin in some source deeper than her "status in society." But the most serious question provoked by this statement is its underlying assumption that she was destined to be a novelist and that no matter what the circumstances of her life, eventually (as Henry James also believed) "her novels would have got themselves written. . . ." Unless one holds a metaphysical belief in destiny, this position is difficult to accept. On the basis of the indirect evidence available, the George Eliot novels would not have come into existence had she married Spencer.

But Spencer was to stay in her life until its very end as a kind of *deus ex machina.* Although it was Chapman who literally first introduced her to Lewes, it was Spencer (according to his own account in his *Autobiography*) who first allowed Lewes to accompany him on his visits to her at 142 and thus gave him access to her intimate companionship. And it was also Spencer who introduced Lewes to the Cross family and so, indirectly, George Eliot to her second husband. She remained fond of Spencer, if not without a tinge of irony after what she considered his betrayal of her trust concerning the authorship of the *Clerical Scenes* and *Adam Bede*; and both she and Lewes made him feel a welcome guest at the Priory. "There arose," as Spencer recounts, "a standing engagement to go and lunch with them whenever I found it convenient. The motive for the arrangement was in part that we might have opportunities for conversations, enjoyed on both sides, which were impracticable during their Sunday-afternoon assemblies."

Again according to his own account (and fittingly he wrote this to Edward Lott, to whom he had written his first impressions of George Eliot), Spencer visited her "on the very afternoon of the day on which she was taken ill—being impelled to go in response to a note I had received the preceding day, and by the consciousness that I was leaving town and could not otherwise expect to see her for three weeks." On that day no one close to her had the slightest idea that an apparent cold with sore throat would lead to her death only three days later. But what about George Eliot herself—did she have a presentiment that her life, arrow-like, had reached its final mark? Even a few days before her final illness had made itself manifest, she had sent out other notes like Spencer's to Edith Simcox and the Congreves—asking them to come and see her. It is significant that Spencer was included in this short list of very close friends, and certainly he was the oldest of these friends. Whether because he thrust himself forward into her life after their most vital association had ended, or whether because of her own not wholly acknowledged reaction to him from that earliest time onward, Spencer was firmly lodged in her consciousness. Indubitably he appears in her fiction in many guises, but as character creation is the most elusive aspect of the fiction writer's art, he can best be detected in the commentary in which many of her characters are swathed. Possibly his confiding words to her and Lewes about life having little meaning to him other than as a means of completing his work helped to solidify her total impression of him. This impression extended over many years and dictated her to add, somewhat unnecessarily, to her description of Silas Marner's restricted existence:

> His life had reduced itself to the functions of weaving and hoarding, without any contemplation of an end towards which the functions tended. The same sort of process has perhaps been undergone by wiser men, when they havé been cut off from faith and love,—only, instead of a loss and a heap of guineas, they have had some erudite research, some ingenious project, or some well-knit theory. [Part I, chapter 2]

The opening of *The Impressions of Theophrastus Such,* her last published work, is surely animated by the spirit of Spencer (perhaps she had even seen some of the privately printed parts of the *Autobiography*):

> It is my habit to give an account to myself of the characters I meet with; can I give any true account of my own? I am a bachelor, without domestic distractions of any sort, and have all my life been an attentive companion to myself, flattering my nature agreeably on plausible occasions, reviling it rather bitterly when it mortified me; and in general remembering its doings and sufferings with a tenacity which is too apt to raise surprise, if not disgust, at the careless inaccuracy of my acquaintances, who impute to me opinions I never held, express their desire to convert me to my favourite ideas, forget whether I have ever been to the East, and are capable of being three several times astonished at my never

having told them before of my accident in the Alps, causing me the nervous shock which has ever since notably diminished my digestive powers.

Interestingly enough, this description fits George Eliot herself as well as Spencer. True, she had never traveled to the East (Spencer visited Egypt in late 1879); but although she never made much of it, she had a nerve-wracking experience in crossing the Alps in 1850, just as three years later Spencer's self-imposed Alpine climbing was to produce a cardiac condition from which he never recovered. Furthermore, as he had well-meaning friends who annoyed him by insisting that his findings and intellectual system were akin to Darwin's and Comte's, she had equally well-meaning friends—the Brays and the Hennells—who possessively persisted in telling her that her own hard-earned thought was but an echo of Charles Bray's *Philosophy of Necessity* and Charles Hennell's *Inquiry,* and later friends who insisted that she was a Comtist.

Possibly in the next few lines she moves nearer not only to Spencer but to Spencer in relationship to herself:

> Yet I have often been forced into the reflection that even the acquaintances who are as forgetful of my biography and tenets as they would be if I were a dead philosopher, are probably aware of certain points in me which may not be included in my most active suspicion. We sing an exquisite passage out of tune, and innocently repeat it for the greater pleasure of our hearers. . . . And how can a man be conscious of that dull perception which causes him to mistake altogether what will make him agreeable to a particular woman, and to persevere eagerly in a behavior which she is privately recording against him? . . . I must still come under the common fatality of mankind, and share the liability to be absurd without knowing that I am absurd.

Surely she herself is behind the mask of Theophrastus when she opens the second paragraph:

> Thus, if I laugh at you, O fellow-men! if I trace with curious interest your labyrinthine self-delusions, note the inconsistencies in your zealous adhesions, and smile at your helpless endeavours in a rashly chosen part, it is not that I feel myself aloof from you: the more intimately I seem to discern your weaknesses, the stronger to me is the proof that I share them.

This is, in one sense, George Eliot's farewell to her readers, and it is most interesting that Spencer appears to have comprised a part of it. There is little doubt that their relationship had evolved into a complex one, and certainly, as it progressed, there came to be a tincture of ambivalence on both sides. Perhaps both privately regretted that their companionship could not have remained throughout their lives as it was at its height in the spring of 1852, uncomplicated by each one's deep inner commitment to inevitably separate paths.

But in the spring of 1852, both were mercifully unaware of the convolutions of the future, and both were eager to preserve their friendship in spirited independence of the growing gossip which attempted to make it what they knew it was not. Only a month after she had written the Brays her we-are-not-in-love letter, she wrote Cara in the same happy vein, a new one for her: "My brightest spot next to my love of *old* friends, is the deliciously calm *new* friendship that Herbert Spencer gives me. We see each other every day and have a delightful *camaraderie* in everything." This kind of relationship could not have occurred to the same woman even a few years earlier. She had never before in her life had a *calm* human relationship of significance, and that she could have it at this particular time with Spencer is another indication that 1852 marked an important change in her.

Spencer, even seeing her every day, was given no reason to suspect that the calmness in their relationship was a novelty to her; it was in keeping with his own character and he assumed it to be equally natural to hers. "Calmness," he observed of her with confidence, "was an habitual trait." And he was almost as much impressed by her self-control and restraint as by her intellect. "Her self-control, leading to evenness of temper was marked." He could remember only one occasion (which he does not specify) when he saw in her "irritation, not unjustified, a little too much manifested." He was also favorably impressed by the fact that when forced to express a difference of opinion, she did so "in a half apologetic manner." She was so "little given to argument" that once when they were in a discussion of Comte and she discovered that his view was antagonistic to hers, "she forthwith dropped the subject. . . ."

He was, however, vaguely aware (probably through conversation with her Coventry friends) that she was somewhat different from what she had been: "In early days she was, I believe, sometimes vivacious; but she was not so when I first knew her, nor afterwards." But the loss of vivacity cannot explain the drastic contrast between Bray's recollection of the two sides of her "temperament of genius" and Spencer's of her "self-control." Nor does Spencer's account contain any suggestion of her "vehemence of tone" when she had argued with Mary Sibree's father. As late as 1851 Chapman was noting in his Diary instances in which she broke into sobs and others in which she showed extreme agitation and anger. It would seem, then, that by the time Spencer came to know her well, she had achieved considerable control over exhibiting her feelings.

SHE PRODUCED A SIMILAR AND LASTING IMPRESSION UPON THE hypersensitive William Hale White (his pseudonym was Mark Rutherford), who came to work for Chapman and to lodge in 142 Strand sometime in the fall of 1852. Very much like George Eliot herself, although twelve years her junior, White had experienced the painful change from orthodox belief to a kind of spiritualized agnosticism which cannot easily be summed up in words, but which essentially places the traditional responsibility of God upon the shoulders of living human beings. White too was to be a novelist. Not destined to become as well known as she, he was in his writing, again like George Eliot, to draw the line between subjectively determined personal beliefs and the inexorable nonpersonal laws of nature (including psychological ones). Also by coincidence or not, he was to follow her in translating Spinoza. Possibly he sensed his own future and more cohesive self in her. For whatever reason, he was magnetically attracted to her from, so it seems, his first sight of and faltering talk with her.

When White came to the Strand, he was more adrift than she was by then. In fact his position was, in a figurative way, not unlike what hers had been in 1849 after the death of her father. Only a few months before coming to Chapman, he had been expelled from New College, London,

> a Noncomformist theological school—on a charge of heresy. This experience marked the great spiritual watershed of his life. On the one side of the event lay his early life in the Calvinistic Dissenting society of Bedford and Chestnut College; on the other lay an uncharted country he was to spend the rest of his life exploring.

In search of employment, White was led to Chapman, not only because of the latter's general reputation for supporting free thought but because he had published the translation of Strauss's *Life of Jesus*, which White, along with many others older and more sophisticated in the New Rationalism, thought the most significant, controversial book of the mid-century (only the *Origin of the Species* in 1859 could be said to supplant it). Chapman accepted White as a publisher's canvasser, but only after subjecting him to a rigorous catechism concerning his belief in miracles. To this White responded much as George Eliot might have done, saying, in effect, that although he did not believe in the literal truth of so-called miracles, he did believe in their symbolic value. Chapman was only partially satisfied, as White records: "This reply was allowed to pass, although my scepticism would have been more satisfactory and more useful if it had been a little more thorough." This is some indication of Chapman's personal and staunch espousal of the atheistic literature that he published—a fact which has since been overshadowed by the more sensational details of his relationships with women.

White was soon disenchanted by what he considered the "cold negativism" of Chapman's publications, although there is no evidence that he lost respect for Chapman as an individual. Very soon after his arrival at the Strand, he wrote his father about his reawakened appreciation of the Gospels:

> No literary world here full of attempts at book and sentence making, no writing for the sake of writing, no thought of publishing here, no vain empty cleverness. . . . Oh, after all the soul rests only in calm satisfaction *on* the *soul* nothing short of this—and if you feel in a book that the writer's *heart*, his own real truest thought is not present, there is no rest but a vague dis-satisfaction and disquiet.

George Eliot might well have written this herself after her struggle with Strauss. In fact, there might be an echo of the real George Eliot in White's words, for very soon after meeting her as a fellow lodger at the Strand, he was "entirely overcome with unhesitating absorbing love for her." She played for him on the piano that Chapman had bought for her use, and they exchanged confessions, he describing a mild but compulsive wine-drinking habit of which he had by then cured himself through rigorous self-discipline. She showed sympathetic interest in his most trifling remarks, and in her presence White cast off his excessive shyness and felt release from the morbid anxiety that tormented him when he was left to himself. In fervent tribute he was to say of her: "Blessed are they who heal us of self-despisings."

In White's many direct and indirect references to George Eliot, there is little if any indication that he was aware of an emotionally tinged relationship between her and Chapman. However, it may be significant that in the *Autobiography of Mark Rutherford*—White's thinly disguised fictional account of his earliest years, including his stay at the Strand—Chapman (as Wollaston) and George Eliot (as Theresa) are presented as uncle and niece, thus rendering their physical and intellectual closeness a family relationship. Certainly he gives no evidence (as Eliza Lynn appears to have done) of being repulsed by any word, tone, or gesture he may have observed in either Chapman or George Eliot. To the contrary, his love for her remained with him throughout his long life. Assuredly this was an idealistic love, for at the time he was also (much to his perplexity) still in love with the young woman who was to become his first wife. Unlike Prufrock, he dared to ask the question but, according to his own admission, not to the right woman: "Oh! when I look back now over my life and call to mind what I might have had simply for taking and did not take, my heart is like to break. The curse for me has not been pluck-ing forbidden fruit, but the refusal of divine fruit offered me by heavenly angels." Although he did not accept the proffered love ac-cording to his own account, and one can only guess to what extent George Eliot actually offered it, Wilfred Stone points out that "throughout his writings we are shown middle-aged men who in second marriages find the opportunity to rectify their earlier mistakes, to marry their George Eliots, and to find the real happiness their youthful inhibitions had lost for them."

The extant records disclose only two attempts on White's part to communicate with George Eliot after their separate departures from the Strand. Almost a quarter of a century later, he wrote to ask her help in finding remunerative work as a translator for William Maccall, whom both had known at the Chapmans'. If he had hoped that his letter would elicit a personal reply he was disappointed, for as she was then (in May 1876) under the exhausting strain of finishing *Daniel Deronda,* Lewes had taken over all correspondence except that to her most personal friends. Lewes did fulfill his promise to do what he could for Maccall by talking to Chapman about him. Ap-parently his talk led to something substantial, for White wrote to thank Lewes. In acknowledging this, Lewes in turn thanked White for "the very acceptable present you have sent Mrs. Lewes, with the graceful letter which preceded it. She is much touched at your having thought of gratifying her by the portrait of her old favorite. . . ." (Presumably the acceptable present was a portrait of Maccall, although "her old favorite" is a somewhat mystifying description. However, she had thought highly enough of Maccall to observe in March 1852 that he was "too good a man to write otherwise than sincerely. . . .") So again White was cheated of a message from her own hand. She and Lewes had found his letter waiting when they returned from a pleasant but tiring trip to France and Switzerland. A more drastic strain for her was the fact that although the final part of *Daniel Deronda* had at last appeared in print, the sale of the novel had decreased. Or was it that she was reluctant to risk reopening what had been, although long ago, a very personal relationship?

There is no way of knowing how much White understood of the possible reasons for her not writing to him herself. If he was hurt by her avoidance of a direct exchange of letters with him, he gave no outward sign, nor did his references to her diminish in respect or ardor. The letter he sent to the *Athenaeum* on the publication of Cross's *Life* in 1885 could have served, had it been more widely read and heeded, as a very much needed corrective to the unfortunate legend about to be perpetrated by George Eliot's best-meaning friends. On the whole, these friends were younger people, intimate with her only during the last years of her life; White too was younger than she, but old enough to have known her best before she had become an image which belonged more to the literate public than to herself. He remembered and valued her as a person who was avant-garde in her thinking and perhaps in her actions too. Even more important to White personally was the memory of her physical appearance, which—so one senses—had merged in his mind with the lingering recollection of the spell cast upon him by her presence. Thus in his later years he reminisced about the marvel of her intellectual attainments, and also her "particularly beautiful" hair and the "curiously shifting light" of her gray eyes—eyes which were "generally soft and tender, but convertible into the keenest flash." White's second wife noted: "Of George Eliot he spoke with such devotion, such humility, such peace. He said she was a sweet, gentle creature; he said: 'I could worship that woman.' "

Unknowingly, White was testifying to the existence of the woman Herbert Spencer had discovered. She was, despite an appealing unconventionality, dignified, calm, self-possessed, and compassionately interested in others to the extent of effacing the more aggressive elements of her personality. Conventionally determined beauty had little to do with her appeal to the men who came within her emotional ken. White had been so receptive to that powerful yet gently persuasive personality perhaps because he was younger than Spencer, less warily accepting of a proffered strength outside himself directed toward his own ego. Spencer was well aware of this peculiar strength but backed away from it, feeling it a threat to his own carefully constructed inner defenses. Chapman too knew that strength and came to rely upon it, but could not resist discovering its vulnerability and toying with it. The Brays and Hennells had also experienced the impact of the power that was within her, but by 1852 they had become accustomed to it, taking it for granted until it exploded once more in their midst when she eloped with Lewes.

White's testimony makes it clear that the forces which had long brought havoc to George Eliot's inner life were at last being manifested in an outward way constructive both for herself and the recipients. White could also have testified to what was to be felt by almost everyone who knew her during her days of fame—that the novels, no matter how impressive, seemed insignificant when set against her living presence.

I N 1852 SHE WAS YET TO BE TESTED IN WHAT WAS STILL, DESPITE her increasingly varied and cosmopolitan experiences, the most threatening area of her life. If Edward Clarke, Chrissey's husband, had not died in December of that year, she probably would never have resumed relationships with her family again. However, Isaac's behavior at the time suggests that he had no idea she had mentally relinquished family ties—unless, of course, someone should need her. As it seemed Chrissey might need her now, she planned to go to Meriden for the funeral and to stay with her as long as necessary. How long that would be she could not know, so she wrote Charles Bray, "until I have been on the spot and seen my brother," perhaps because Isaac was taking charge of Chrissey's unsettled financial affairs. On arrival she found that the general situation was not as hopeless as she had anticipated, and reported to the Brays: "Chrissey bears her trouble much better than I expected. Money matters are not in the *very* worst state. . . . I am satisfied now that my duties do not lie here—though the dear creatures here will be a constant motive for work and economy."

So she planned to return to London as quickly as possible, for she had much work awaiting her there. Chrissey agreed that, "all things considered, it was wiser for me to return to town—that I could do her no substantial good by staying another week, while I should be losing time as to other matters." But they had made this plan between themselves without conferring with Isaac. He, as she wrote the Brays when she was back in London,

> was very indignant to find that I had arranged to leave without consulting him and thereupon flew into a violent passion with me, winding up by saying that he desired I would never "apply to him for anything whatever"—which, seeing that I never have done so, was almost as superfluous as if I had said I would never receive a kindness from him.

Before, there had been argument, misunderstanding, and hostile tension between them but probably never an actual outburst, and although he had blustered into the offensive, Isaac was perhaps more hurt than she. He was unprepared for her new outer imperviousness to his opinion. She for her part had spent most of her life in trying to gain it, so that the unpleasant episode must have seemed anticlimactic to her. No longer could the threat or even the actuality of her brother's anger make all her soul a quivering fear. Far from being shattered by his explosion of feelings, she wrote calmly to the Brays: "But he is better than he shewed himself to me and I have no doubt that he will be kind to Chrissey, though not in a very large way."

Unfortunately, he was not to satisfy her in regards to Chrissey even in a small way. His main contribution to her sister's material welfare seems to have been allowing her and her six children to live rent-free in an unattractive, very small Attleborough house owned by him. (Ironically, this house had once belonged to Chrissey, having been left her by an uncle, but her husband had been forced to sell it to Robert Evans, Sr., in 1842, so that Isaac had fallen heir to it in 1849.) At first George Eliot considered this arrangement "a great help" but by spring she wanted desperately to get Chrissey out of the house. "Think of her," she wrote Cara, "in that ugly small house with six children who are inevitably made naughty by being thrown close together from morning till night." She even considered a plan to emigrate temporarily with the Clarkes: "What do you think," she asked Cara, "of my going to Australia with Chrissey and all her family?—to settle them and then come back." That idea was dropped; next, she had to persuade herself that it would be a futile sacrifice for her to give up her literary work and move in with Chrissey. "To live with her," she wrote in her next letter to Cara, "in that hideous neighbourhood amongst ignorant bigots is impossible to me. It would be moral asphyxia and I had better take the other kind—charcoal myself and leave my money, perhaps more acceptable than my labour and affection."

Finally she was forced to decide that she "dare not incur the *material* responsibility of taking [Chrissey] away from Isaac's house and its attendant pecuniary advantages. My health might fail and other things might happen to make her, as well as me, regret the change." (As this letter was written in April 1853, the reference might well have been to her slow-growing resolution to live with Lewes.) At least she could offer moral support when Chrissey, usually mild and submissive, decided to take a stand against Isaac in his plans for her three boys; for in December 1853, George Eliot wrote Fanny Houghton: "I go to Chrissey for a week on the 2d of January. She is anxious about the placing of the boys, and Isaac's ideas on the subject seem to be rather at variance with her hopes." There is no way of knowing who emerged triumphant from the heated family discussion which probably ensued, but it can be assumed that she tolerated the minimum of truckling to Isaac.

Almost four years later she was still worried over Chrissey's being

confined to the ugly house, especially now that her sister's health was
in a deplorable state. She arranged with Isaac to have £15 taken out
of the income from her inheritance from her father (the receipt of
which was still controlled by Isaac) to enable Chrissey to have a very
much needed change of air. Overcome by the fear that Isaac would
presume to have the money spent on some cause deemed by him
more practical, she wrote Fanny Houghton: "Pray do something, if
you can to urge that the money should be so applied. I don't mean
that you should do it *obviously* or directly, or that you should
appear to know anything about that sum, but simply that you should
insist on the importance of leaving that hotbed of fever for a time."
If Chrissey now were to have an influential mediator on the spot, it
would have to be Fanny. There could be no more hurried trips from
London to Attleborough for George Eliot, who had at last gained the
husband Isaac had years earlier so tactlessly admonished her to find.
That her marriage could not be sanctioned by law or therefore by
Isaac himself was but the final irony in the relationship between the
brother and sister.

IN THE LONDON DAYS, UNTIL HER INTIMACY WITH LEWES, SHE
had neither husband nor what she could consider a life's work in
which to find solace. Yet she had come to possess herself as never before, and although still far removed from personal happiness, she
alluded to that lack seldom and then with some positive connotation,
as in an August 1852 letter to Cara. "I am very well . . . and 'plucky,'
a word which I propose to substitute for happy, as more truthful." Not
even Charles Hennell could have accused her of displaying either self-
centeredness or morbidity in the London letters, and they are the
liveliest she was ever to write. Dashed off under the pressure of time
and work, many of them are little more than unstudied notes; but
flashing out of them is the incisive irony of her impressionistic sketches
of people and events. For example, from a June 1852 letter to her
"Dear Trio": "We went to Miss Swanwick's for a stupid evening
on Saturday—12 women and 2½ men!" One of the women was "that
odious Mrs. Richard Greaves. . . . She is fearful—her whole organization seems made for the sake of her teeth—if indeed they are not
false." And a short time after that evening, "good Mr. Mackay" called
upon her: "He looked more miserable and ashamed of presuming to
exist than I ever saw him. I asked him how they liked Weymouth
[where he and his bride had gone for their honeymoon]. 'Not at all,
not at all, but it was not the fault of the place'!" In October of the

same year she had a refreshing trip to Edinburgh, "hardly recognizing myself for the same person as the damozel who left it by the coach with a heavy heart some six years ago," and from there reported an evening of conversation with the phrenologist George Combe and others: "The talk last night was pleasant enough, though of course all the interlocutors besides Mr. Combe have little to do but shape elegant modes of negation and affirmation like the people who are talked to by Socrates in Plato's dialogues—'Certainly, that I firmly believe' etc." Later she agreed with Sara, who perhaps was not certain that Mr. Combe was being taken seriously enough, that he was an apostle: "An apostle, it is true, with a back and front drawing-room. . . ." The same irony was to appear in the novels, but in expanded form and surrounded by detail which in many instances threatens to engulf it.

Despite the new spirit of release conveyed by the London letters, novel writing was still closed to her. It is apparent that as energy-consuming as her life at this time was, she was still thinking yearningly of it, for she talked of her frustrated wish to write creatively to her closest friends. Bessie Parkes, for one, remembered such talks, referring to them when in 1859 she wrote to congratulate George Eliot on the sweeping success of *Adam Bede*: "Dearest Marian, remembering as I do, day after day, in which you used to say with a sort of despair, 'I have no creative power,' it is with an amused delight that I see you take all England by storm. . . ." Perhaps she talked also to Herbert Spencer in greater detail. In fact, he claimed the honor of being the first to suggest "that she should write novels. I thought I saw in her many, if not all, of the needful qualifications in high degrees. . . ." (It would seem that she did not interrupt to tell him that she had thought of it herself years earlier.) It was, he presumed, "her lack of self-confidence which led her, in those days, to resist my suggestion. . . ."

To Spencer, who had once seriously explained to George Eliot that he himself never frowned because he was never puzzled, this lack of confidence in her own obviously great talents was a matter of amazement. But he thought he knew the explanation: "She complained of being troubled by double consciousness—a current of self-criticism being an habitual accompaniment of anything she was saying or doing; and this naturally tended toward self-depreciation and self-distrust." Spencer was both right and wrong: that second and critical consciousness did indeed hamper creative work, yet its presence signified the clamoring growth of the internalized audience so important to the writer—the same audience which was to torment Theophrastus Such so much that he had to make certain all the faces in it remained pale blurs. Neither Spencer nor she herself could know that her very awareness of this disturbing onlooker was a significant phase in her emergence as a writer. No doubt it had developed in proportion to her acquisition of self-control. Truly "the self that self restrains," this control eventually would motivate her writing by demanding a confessional dialogue between it and the other self.

Although she was not yet writing as she wished, she had during this crucial year of 1852 made a great advance in self-realization and hence self-command. There was now a relatively harmonious inter-action between her feelings and the external forces which impinged upon them. She was no longer victimized by fear of her own passions as self-destructive agents. Having been released by sympathy, they had become rather than isolated and warring forces, a part of the moral nature that "purifies beautifies and at length transmutes them." This she had written to John Sibree, Jr., only a few years earlier, when she had thought it impossible that she would ever achieve her implied goal.

FIVE

A Strange New Light

"HAD A LONG WALK WITH MISS EVANS IN HYDE PARK," Chapman noted in his Diary under Monday, 6 October 1851; "called on Jeffes [sic] the French-Bookseller who agreed to lend us books for the purpose of Review." The walk had no doubt been a calmly enjoyable one. This was only four months after Chapman and George Eliot had made their "solemn. and holy vow" to bind them to the right, and only a few days after she had returned, for the final time, to 142 Strand, where at least temporary truce had been established. She had neither happiness nor security, but she was learning to accept what each day brought, although despairingly aware that her life had no more direction than when the death of her father had shattered her moorings. At Jeffs's on that Monday she was introduced to the man who was to lead her into a far more meaningful future than she could have envisioned even in a dream that was wholly subservient to her wishes.

She of course had been aware of George Henry Lewes before actually meeting him. Two days earlier, she had written Bray that Lewes had pronounced Spencer's *Social Statics* "the best book he has seen on the subject," her tone suggesting that she thought this high praise for Spencer's work. Even on the fringe of literary London one could not stay unaware of Lewes. At thirty-four (two and a half years George Eliot's senior), he had made his presence felt in manifold ways—as versatile journalist, literary and drama critic, author of the astonishingly influential *Biographical History of Philosophy*, novelist, and adapter of foreign plays to the English stage. Since 1850, he had also been one of the most dynamic voices in the *Leader*, the liberal, often revolutionary, critical weekly he had helped found. Basically, he was a journalist, even when writing on philosophy. He had developed a supple, lucid prose that could be bent in almost any direction, whether toward melodrama, cogent analysis, or biting criticism. He was unashamed of his adaptability; at twenty-three, free-lancing in London, he had ushered in his own career with the justified boast that he could supply any kind of article to any editor he wished to cultivate. His restless, facile mind was never to be curbed, although in his last years, its remarkable energy was channeled into his determined pursuit of the elusive relationship between body and mind. Even this search would draw him into bypaths of fascinating, if largely futile, experimentation and speculation.

The relationship between these two levels or functions of his own being—the mental and the physical—was an unusually harmonious one. Never robust, Lewes was nonetheless as tireless, adventuresome, and unpredictable in bodily as in intellectual activity. According to Mathilde Blind, "Mr. Thackeray was once heard to say that it would not surprise him to meet Lewes in Piccadilly, riding on a white elephant; whilst another wit likened him to the Wandering Jew, as you could never tell where he was going to turn up, or what he was going to do next." The pulse of the city was within him. He knew and loved his London as Defoe, Fielding, and Johnson had known and loved their London, perhaps sorrowing over but accepting its sordidness, and glorying in its hustling workaday world as well as in its rare beauty. This was one of the few loves that he would not be able to share equally with George Eliot. In London—at least after 1854—she felt entrapped and longed for the sweep of unsullied air and the sight of uncluttered landscape; Lewes, although London had not dealt gently with him, was at his most zestful self only at its hub. Certainly there is more of the feel of London in his novel *Ranthorpe,* for example, than in all of her writing put together. Even in the pieces of his that have no direct bearing upon London, one can catch the sounds of the counterpoint worlds of the metropolis. But he generously conceded to her wish for frequent retreats to the country. Once when she was at work upon *Middlemarch* and he himself was accomplishing a great deal of writing in the peaceful setting that was always to seem alien to him, he admitted to a friend: ". . . I sometimes marvel how it is I have contrived to get through so much work living in London." But to this he added, with a touch of wistfulness: "It's true I'm a London child."

He was also a born cosmopolitan, one who could quickly adapt to the native way in any Continental city. This is only one of the several intriguing paradoxes about Lewes: he was an Englishman and apparently proud of it, but he was also foreign in manner and appearance. The man recorded by this discerning observer was no typical

Englishman: "He was a lightly built, fragile man, with bushy curly hair, and a general shagginess of beard and eyebrow not unsuggestive of a Skye terrier. For the rest, he had a prominent mouth and gray, deeply set eyes under an ample, finely proportioned forehead." Although Lewes was very much a man of his own time, with a unique sense of being so, the broad spectrum of his interests, as well as the spiritedness with which he surrendered his attention to them, recalls the more sophisticated aspects of eighteenth-century intellectual life. A substantial portion of his thought (if not all his conclusions) touched the future, but perhaps with a nudge so gentle that it went unnoticed. It was, after all, the same fascinated interest in the body-mind enigma that gave impetus to researches in physiological psychology and also propelled Freud into psychoanalysis. Aside from the question of his actual influence, Lewes was certainly thinking beyond his own age, often in directions which were to yield productive and lasting results by others who may or may not have heard of him.

But Lewes was to pay a considerable and long-lasting price for these paradoxes which emanated from his very nature. Even the least important of them—his foreign appearance—robbed him of a certain dignity in the eyes of others. The typical Englishman was still inclined to view non-English features with uncharitable suspicion; and as his fame grew, he was referred to with callous jocularity as one of the ugliest men in London, rivaled only by Douglas Jerrold, whose appearance frightened children and the chimpanzee in the zoological gardens (indeed, Jane Welsh Carlyle had dubbed him "The Ape"). Lewes may or may not have been vulnerable before these barbs. It was fortunate that he had become adept at concealing both personal hurt and sorrow, for there was little he could do to bring a halt to a practice tolerated under the guise of wit. Nor did he have any power to fend off the more serious damage done to his reputation as literary man and thinker that came about because of his versatility and the refreshing lightness with which he often approached the designated solemn topics of his age.

Many Victorians thought and wrote as if the English Renaissance had never occurred. To them, writing had a legitimate raison d'être only as an instrument of didacticism; to subserve this purpose, the writer must be, above all, sincere. Such sincerity could only be measured—so it seemed tacitly agreed—by the degree of gravity that surfaced in a given writing style. Whether or not he ever consciously thought of the matter, Lewes was incapable of smothering his sparkling sense of humor. It was easy to equate his facileness with insincerity, especially by ignoring the fact that although he turned from topic to topic, his stated convictions on the nature of reality did not shift.

His reverence for the totality of life and his essentially democratic stance before it remained unwavering and recognized only one kind of aristocracy—that of the intellect.

Very few of Lewes's contemporaries were impartial or sharp-sighted enough to detect this kind of sincerity, let alone respect it. Besides, as Lewes had married in 1841 and soon had need to support a growing family (and to make the evidence still more damning, a not very natural family), he could be accused of making a bread-winning game of writing. His critics of course ignored the fact that almost all other writers of the time, sincere or not, were playing the same game if less openly. Unfortunately, this aspect of Lewes's earliest reputation—that he was a mere dilettante in literature, and a mercenary one at that—was to cling to him all his life. John Chapman was, with ironic significance, one of the first to eye Lewes with righteous disapproval. During the end of August 1851, Chapman dicsussed with Lewes the prospect of an article by the latter on "Modern Novelists for the *Jany No* of the Westminster." Apparently Lewes did not react positively to Chapman's suggestion

> that he should give the characteristics of each of the leading Novelists, describe their relative and intrinsic merits, erect a standard of Criticism whereby to judge them with a view of elevating the productions of the Novelists as works of Art and as refining and moral influences. If more were claimed from the Novelist the best of them would accord more.

When Lewes remained unenthusiastic, Chapman concluded: "But Lewes is a 'bread scholar' and lacks the enthusiasm of thought and earnest purpose which I must alone seek for in Contributors to the Westminster." (No such article by Lewes or anyone else appeared in the *Westminster*.)

It is therefore quite possible that when George Eliot was first brought face to face with Lewes, she saw him through the eyes of Chapman, whose somewhat pathetic affectations she had not yet wholly divined. Did she know that Lewes had called at the Strand "to express his high opinion of Miss Evans' Article [a review of Greg's *The Creed of Christendom*] in the Leader"? Whether or not she was aware of this friendly gesture on Lewes's part, she was not particularly impressed by him during this first brief meeting in the autumn of 1851, perhaps because she was preoccupied with the new phase of her relationship with Chapman and also with her new duties as subeditor of the *Westminster*. Perhaps too Lewes said something that she found distasteful, for he could be brashly flippant if he so desired, and quite possibly the presence of the sententiously grave and handsome Chapman in Jeffs's made him so desire. Despite her grudging respect for his criticism, if only because it carried surprising weight in London, George Eliot was still enough under Chapman's spell to regard Lewes as a sporadically brilliant eccentric whom it was wisest not to take very seriously. But his appearance intrigued her. Seeing him at close hand she could not help observing that the rumor of his ugliness, according to English standards, was justified. Not long before this, Chapman had made her painfully aware of her own lack of beauty, and Lewes's features could have afforded her some compensation, particularly as he was a celebrity. For whatever reason, she reported the meeting briefly to Bray, commenting only that Lewes had seemed to her "a sort of miniature Mirabeau in appearance." Years later, after her life with Lewes, Cross was moved to footnote this seeming irreverence: "This was a merely formal and casual introduction. That George Eliot was ever brought into close relations with Mr. Lewes was due to Mr. Herbert Spencer having taken him to call on her in the Strand later in this year."

Lewes himself bears out Cross's assertion in a retrospective Journal entry of 28 January 1859 (written only two months before he thought he had cause to attribute Spencer's "coolness" to jealousy of both himself and George Eliot). After acknowledging his "debt of gratitude" for Spencer's friendship—"the brightest ray in a very dreary, *wasted* period of my life"—he added: "I owe Spencer another and a deeper debt. It was through him that I learned to know Marian—to know her was to love her—and since then my life has been a new birth." However, in the autumn of 1851, George Eliot had no way of knowing that underneath his bright gaiety, Lewes's mood was amazingly like her own, that he considered his past life a waste, and that he had "given up all ambition whatever, lived from hand to mouth, and thought the evil of each day sufficient."

He would have been feeling this acutely on 6 October 1851, for in two weeks Agnes, his wife of ten years, was to give birth to her second child by Thornton Leigh Hunt, Lewes's co-worker on the *Leader*. Lewes had implicitly condoned the birth of the first child by Hunt, and so had shut himself off from divorce. But he was close-mouthed about his personal unhappiness and determined to conceal it from the world. Even Spencer, by 1851 his intimate friend, later admitted that he "knew nothing in those days of his domestic life, or, indeed, of anything concerning him beyond that which our conversations disclosed."

Spencer had first met Lewes in the spring of 1850, when they happened to leave 142 Strand together; soon after this accidental meeting they were frequently together, walking and talking, always animatedly. Yet in March of that year, Lewes had lost an infant son (although there is some question as to whether even this son was his), and in April,

Agnes had borne her first child by Hunt. Neither the walks nor the talks were interrupted, and Spencer found Lewes as a companion "extremely attractive. Interested in, and well informed upon, a variety of subjects; full of various anecdote; and an admirable mimic; it was impossible to be dull in his company."

Although during these crucial years Lewes's gaiety was in part simulated, it wore well. Others besides Spencer who were often with him bear witness to the charm of his presence. Even Eliza Lynn Linton, whose feelings for him became increasingly ambivalent, recalled how Lewes carried with him a unique atmosphere: "In work and in idleness, in the *sans façon* of Bohemianism and in the more orderly amusements of conventional society—in scientific discussions and empty persiflage, he was equally at home; and wherever he went there was a patch of intellectual sunshine in the room." To be sure, serious-minded people meeting him only once were likely to be more repelled than attracted by his effervescence, as perhaps George Eliot was at first. Margaret Fuller, for instance, met him at a dinner party at the Carlyles' and described him as a "witty, French, flippant sort of man, author of a History of Philosophy, and now writing a Life of Goethe, a task for which he must be as unfit as irreligion and sparkling shallowness can make him. But he told stories admirably and was allowed sometimes to interrupt Carlyle a little, of which one was glad." One can only guess what was going on inside Lewes during these times of outward animation, but there is some evidence that he, like George Eliot, had early been alerted to the danger of indulging the self in the bitter-sweet contemplation of its own wounds. By the time he was writing *Ranthorpe*—which was first published in 1847, but essentially written in 1842 and then drastically revised, as Lewes's Preface indicates—he had developed what might be called a psycho-philosophical concept of grief:

> The "luxury of grief" is a curious paradox; but it is an incontestable fact. The morbid dwelling on some hateful matter is a diseased delight; but it is a delight. . . . When we have real cause for grief, we are too apt to accept of the excuse it affords for the indulgence of this morbid feeling; and hence the profound advice of Jean Paul, that the first thing to be conquered in grief, is the *pleasure we feel in indulging it*.

Indeed, Lewes was ready to arm his reader with practical rules from mental hygiene as defense against the insidious allurement of grief:

> If you find yourself haunted by any ideas which you would fain shake off, remember that the only effectual way to rid yourself of them is one somewhat analogous to that practiced for inflammation of the body. You must draw the current of your thoughts else-

where. You must actively, healthily, employ your mind and your affections. You must create associations with such things as have a tendency to recall the thoughts you would evade. Let the mind recover its elasticity by various activity, and you are safe.

This advice is meant for the ordinary person who realizes that he cannot escape the great common sorrows of the human lot but wants at least a fighting chance to meet them head-on and wrest from them a peculiar strength as well as pain. However, there was—so Lewes thought—another possibility, open only to the artist or genius: the miracle of art is its power to transform the commonest but individually felt sorrow, and even failure, into a beauty and meaning that defy analysis but add a new dimension to the directly perceived world:

> Genius is the happiest, as it is the greatest, of human faculties. It has no immunity from the common sorrows of humanity; but it has one glorious privilege, which it alone possesses; the privilege of turning its sorrows into beauty, and brooding delighted over them!

Despite the arrogance of which he was sometimes accused, Lewes was inherently modest before greatness; it is probable that he had a shrewd opinion of himself as a person of high intelligence and marketable talent, not in the rank of genius. But he refused to grovel before it or to consider himself shut off from it, for by temperament, if not capability, he felt a kinship with genius. And he assumed as his own the right to study and understand it, to detect its fallibilities and approach it in familiar, comradely fashion—as he was notably to do in his biographical study of Goethe with a lasting success that must have astonished, or perhaps appalled, Margaret Fuller. He was thus unusually well equipped to recognize that genius was unfolding as George Eliot created novel after novel. When he was initiated into the autobiographical nature of her work—intricately concealed except in the *Mill*—he would have recognized further that she had at last earned the glorious privilege of turning her sorrows into beauty and brooding delighted over them.

APPARENTLY LEWES HIMSELF PRACTICED WHAT HE ADVOcated, for according to Spencer and others, he seemed neither morbid nor withdrawn when his family problems were at their height. Of course one cannot be sure how much in his manner was concealment and how much represented real conquest over anguish. When he desired, he could be an adroit pretender, for acting was in his blood. His grandfather was Charles Lee Lewes, a well-known comic actor, and his father, John Lee (nicknamed "Dandy Lewes"), also had acted and for a while had managed the Theatre Royal in Liverpool. No doubt his paternal inheritance guided George Henry to the theater, to which he gave an absorbing love and service as actor, playwright, and critic. Yet his mother, Elizabeth Ashweek Lewes, was to constitute his only family tie, one that stretched into the last decade of his own life. She had borne John Lee two sons before George Henry. The first, Edgar, died in 1836; and the next, Edward, died at sea in 1855, George Henry giving financial help to his widow and son, although there does not appear to have been any especially close relationship between the two brothers. In fact, the original family had little chance to become strongly knit, for John Lee died not long before 1825. His widow, then thirty-eight, married John Willim, about ten years her senior and already a retired captain from the infantry in Bengal.

It was perhaps as a result of this marriage and the subsequent disruption of whatever family pattern had been established that George Henry, then only eight, was thrust forward into a most unconventional early education. He seems to have attended no one school long, but studied in London, Jersey, Brittany, and Greenwich, reappearing in London at sixteen to embark upon an adventuresome quest of fortune gained by his wits. It is not known when or for how long he was home during these years, but there is no sign that Willim was ever more than a nominal father surrogate to him; his stepfather appears to have floated across the surface of his life as "the Captain" until his death in 1864, at which time George Henry spent two busy weeks taking care of the funeral arrangements and settling Willim's estate. Although circumstances had forced this chore upon him as a natural responsibility, George Henry accepted it willingly, perhaps even with a sense of relief, for he had reason to know that his mother had not found life with the Captain easy or pleasant during the last few years.

Lewes appears to have been genuinely fond of his mother. Although quite capable of making a life independent of her, he did take his bride, Agnes, to live with her (and, presumably, the Captain) in Kensington until after the birth of their first son, Charles Lee, in 1842. By the time of the birth of the second son in 1844, he had moved his small family to separate living quarters, and there is no evidence that he ever again lived with his mother. He no doubt remained in close touch with her, but as there is no extant diary before 1856, the record of his contacts with her begins only after he was back near London with George Eliot, when he resumed short visits to his mother, Agnes occasionally being present also.

George Eliot thus found herself in the midst of another strange family situation. And as she was once again in the unenviable position of being the usurper, she must have awaited some sign of acceptance by Mrs. Willim with an anxiety that had long been undergirt by her old fear of maternal rejection. Mrs. Willim comes through the scant records as intelligent and noninterfering. No meeting between her and George Eliot occurred before the Leweses moved to Blandford Square very near the end of 1860, by which time George Eliot was steadily growing more famous than infamous. There are several possible reasons for this long postponement, but one suspects that the decisive one was dictated by the irascible Captain, until either even he was sufficiently impressed by George Eliot's prestige or his wife finally defied him.

Other visits soon followed this obviously successful one. Late in March 1861, a few days before the official publication date of *Silas Marner*, George Eliot ordered only one presentation copy of that novel and requested that it be sent to Mrs. Willim. As George Eliot was not one to make an empty gesture, one can assume that she had felt affection and respect for Mrs. Willim without effort. No matter what the potential for it, spontaneous and unwary love on her part may have been out of the question, for the pattern which had drawn herself, George Henry, and his mother together was only a slight distortion of the earlier one which had enfolded herself. Isaac, and their mother. Mrs. Willim could not possibly have had an inkling of the undercurrent from the past that might have produced some constraint in George Eliot's manner toward her, and if any did exist, she seems not to have been aware of it. In fact, meeting George Eliot in person seems to have made her realize that her son at last had a home, no matter how unconventional, to which she might turn as a haven if need be. She quickly manifested a new freedom in applying to her son on her own behalf:

> One day she sent word that she was coming to consult Lewes about the Captain's treatment of her. "He won't let any one come to the house, and is so irritable that she can't sit in the room with him," Lewes wrote in his Journal. "I told her to tell him that unless he could treat her better she should come and live with us. She stayed all day and seemed to pick up wonderfully."

Whether Mrs. Willim had been merely testing her welcome, and whether Lewes had made her his promise feeling quite certain that she would not take advantage of it, this crisis fortunately resolved itself. Lewes's son Charles was already living with them, and it is unlikely that George Eliot could have endured a further intrusion into her precious dual solitude with George Henry. Mrs. Willim valiantly maintained an independent existence even after the Captain's death and as, under the handicap of mounting infirmities, she entered her eighth decade, George Eliot visited her devotedly. Since Mrs. Willim had several times proved herself remarkably resilient physically, George Eliot did show some irritation when George Henry quickly responded to his mother's increasingly anxious wishes that he never be far away from her. This curtailed a few of the Leweses' excursions, especially a vaguely projected trip to Egypt. "Mr. Lewes's mother is 83 and is likely enough to outlive us," George Eliot wrote Cara Bray somewhat testily on 12 September 1870. But by 10 December of that same year she had occasion to write in her Journal, underlining the passage to emphasize its significance and perhaps also to symbolize some contrition on her part: "George's Mother died this morning, quite peacefully as she sat in her chair."

IF IN HIS MATURE YEARS LEWES WAS PROTECTIVELY ACTIVE IN all family affairs that touched his mother, he does not even then give the impression of seriously considering himself a flesh-and-blood member of that family. Perhaps the Captain's domineering presence and non-Lewesian temperament had early made him feel and desire to be an alien. Perhaps his own nomadic nature demanded at least a semblance of rootlessness. Even in 1833, although apparently living with his mother and brothers, he arrived on the London scene splendidly unattached. The glimpses of Lewes during this exploratory period are few and indistinct, although one fairly full view is provided by William Bell Scott, artist and poet, who became one of Lewes's earliest and best London friends. With his insatiable quest for knowledge, Lewes had gone to sit at the feet of a triad of informal but brilliant teachers—Leigh Hunt, Thomas Carlyle, and John Stuart Mill. For several reasons, the greatest impact upon Lewes's personal life was to come from the Hunt circle, to which Scott also belonged. Having been assured by Hunt that they were "cordial natures," Lewes addressed the six-year-older Scott by letter in 1837 as "the shortest and easiest way I can think of for our better acquaintance," although he was aware that in "this most artificial of worlds" such a gesture would be considered an impertinence by most people. He described himself as "a student living a quiet life, but with a great gusto for intellectual acquaintance, with which I am sorry to say, I am not over burdened." Scott not only responded affirmatively, but valued Lewes's letter enough to preserve it and have it reproduced in his two-volume *Auto-*

biographical Notes (published in 1892, two years after his death), as was also his etching showing himself, Lewes, and Vincent Hunt listening in rapt attention to Leigh Hunt.

Reviewing Scott's *Chorea Sancti Viti* for the *Leader* in 1851, Lewes was moved to reminisce:

> Some thirteen years were pushed aside and once more I was sitting beside the grave and high-minded Scott, in his low-roofed study, crammed with books, casts, woodblocks, sketches and papers. . . . He was at that time a wood engraver by profession, but a poet, a philosopher and artist by ambition. . . . I had then the two-fold ambition of philosopher and poet. We read together, argued together, told each other all our magnificent schemes, and admired each other with unfeigned sincerity, were sure of each other's success!
>
> Among our plans was one to this effect: Scott had conceived a series of designs of the great typical events of life. I was filled with thoughts as he unfolded the scheme to me, and proposed to write a poem illustrative of the designs.
>
> Our fortunes lay apart. I left England and solaced many long winter nights by the composition of my *Life-Journey of Prince Legion*. I have the fragment still and read it not a year ago: it is detestable!

Apparently the friendship was not resumed with intimacy when Lewes returned to England, but Scott remained an interested onlooker as Lewes married and then separated from his wife, Agnes. And, unmoved by the most malicious of the gossip that circulated when Lewes and George Eliot left England together, he stayed in Lewes's good graces enough to be invited to dinner to "get acquainted with his [Lewes's] new wife, whom I found the most bland and amiable of plain women, and most excellent in conversation, not finding it necessary to be always saying fine things." George Eliot in her turn was charmed "by his simplicity and genuine talk." In return for the hospitality, Scott sent a drawing that must have been meant as a memento of days long before George Eliot had entered Lewes's life, for Lewes wrote back with a certain formality combined with friendly appreciation: "It was very kind of you to send us that spirited sketch—though the 'old times' remain indelible and need no souvenir. I am often in that study of yours in Edwards Street where we passed the night 'talking of lovely things that conquer death.'" Scott's final view of Lewes surveyed the latter's entire life of intellectual achievement:

> He is nearly the only man among all my friends who has never ceased to advance. At first he was only the clever fellow, but at a very early time he became the literary adept, then the able investigator and lastly the scientific thinker and philosopher, one of

the most trenchant and advanced minds in the science of this country.

Scott does not mention Lewes's absorbing and long-lived interest in the theater. No doubt during his most impoverished early days in London, Lewes managed, by hook or crook, to see plays and himself acted with whatever groups were open to him; for during the 1840's he performed with various companies, including the amateur one headed by Dickens, in a way that suggests he was already well practiced. It was not until 1849 that he relinquished the idea of becoming a professional actor. In November of that year, after completing a series of lectures on philosophy in Edinburgh, he immediately played the role of Shylock there—a combination that his friend Spencer found "droll," adding that Lewes's "dramatic quality" justified a stage career, but that "his figure was not sufficiently impressive for many parts; and his voice was not effective." Lewes himself seems to have reached the same sensible conclusion and regretfully withdrew from the stage except as playwright and critic. However, he was to remain something of an offstage showman all his life although, when detected, this role was to be eyed with as much suspicion and envy as his brilliant versatility. When, for example, he was moved to avert ever-threatening dullness at the later austere Sunday afternoon receptions at the Priory, George Meredith stood aside to observe and then with cool contempt recorded the antics of that "mercurial little showman." Lewes's very last piece of showmanship was to allay George Eliot's anxiety by concealing his pain and playing the gay companion to her and Johnnie Cross when he well knew that he was dying.

EVEN WHILE UNDER THE INFLUENCE OF STAGE AND LITERATURE, the young Lewes did not neglect to investigate other means of livelihood. He experimented with various kinds of work almost as if he were dutifully checking off the possibilities of becoming a doctor, a lawyer, or a merchant, although not quite in that order. For a brief while he served as a clerk in a notary's office and then in the counting room of a Russian merchant. More seriously, he applied himself to the study of anatomy, thinking vaguely of pursuing medicine. In 1836 or so he joined a small but heterogeneous students' club that met in Red Lion Square, and reminiscing thirty years later in the *Fortnightly Review* about the members, wrote of himself: "A sixth studied anatomy and many other things with vast aspirations and no very definite career before him." He tried to make medicine a definite career, but a short experience in walking the London hospitals convinced him that it was not for him, as he could not tolerate the nauseating scenes he was forced to witness in the operating rooms. His enthusiasm for the study of anatomy had been real and did not subside; its influence can be traced throughout the varied career he finally chose for himself, leading him into pioneering research in the newly opened area of physiological psychology, to which he was to devote himself with uncharacteristic exclusiveness during the last decade of his life.

Lewes felt he had mounted the highest peak in his life's endeavors when he could record in his Journal on 31 October 1876: *"Discovered the psychological explanation of the relation of Body and Mind*—the form of the function." The thought and investigations which led to this discovery culminated in the ambitious *Problems of Life and Mind*, the Third Series of which George Eliot completed from Lewes's notes and saw through the press after his death in 1878. For Lewes the writing of these somewhat rambling but always stimulating volumes marked the exciting end of a quest that had beckoned to him even while he was exploring so many other modes of thought during those first five independent years in London. This work—so he wrote in his first Preface, datelined from the Priory, September 1873—"has been many years in preparation; indeed, its origin may be said to go so far back as 1836, when with the rashness of ambitious youth I planned a treatise on the Philosophy of the Mind. . . ." Since its naïve inception, his study had undergone several significant changes in direction, the last of which had caused it to grow "into a systematic introduction to the philosophy of Science; and what was intended merely as a preparation for a Psychology discloses itself as the *Foundations of a Creed*."

Although the course of Lewes's long study may have altered with time, interruptions, and intriguing digressions, his idea of what constituted the only legitimate basis of belief remained unchanged. It would seem that from his first immersion in philosophy he came up an unyielding empiricist. In 1873, as a result of many years of thinking, he said: "Deeply as we may feel the mystery of this universe and the limitations of our faculties, the *Foundations of a Creed* can only rest upon the Known and Knowable." Perhaps because this hope-inspiring phrase—"The Foundations of a Creed"—stood as its subtitle, the first volume of the *Problems* sold fast and well. Many post-Strauss and post-Darwin minds were anxiously awaiting guidelines to a creed that might bridge the newly created chasm of despair. However, the subsequent volumes were little read. Even the most earnest and energetic seeker of guidance must have been intimidated by the array of data offered as volume after volume appeared in print.

There were other reasons, too. The most justifiable, although only a few of Lewes's contemporaries would have been in a position to comprehend it, was that the work as a whole is not the satisfactorily inclusive introduction to the philosophy of science that Lewes had with proud sincerity announced it to be. If his full-fledged concept of empiricism gave him a triumphant grasp upon the fragmented world of sense experience, he was at the same time too much its victim to envision a methodology which could carry man beyond observation of the sensible world. He was aware of the great revolutionary spirit sweeping over mathematics, giving rise to the construction of non-Euclidean and four-dimensional geometries. His own adventuresome spirit responded, but not sufficiently to take him out of the confines of his chosen point of reference. He could issue only one verdict upon what was to be the pioneering trail (although, to be sure, not a straight one) leading to Einstein: ". . . to suppose that a manipulation of symbols without regard to sensible experience can lead to anything *more* than symbolic results, is like supposing that the imaginary creations of poets have a real existence in the sensible world."

Because of his firmly entrenched predilections, Lewes was not to be a prophet of the Nuclear Space Age; nor would he, except fitfully, point the way to depth psychology. (George Eliot, with her intuitive awareness of the large unmapped countries of the human psyche, was to do this with quiet effectiveness.) However, he extended his premise to include several aspects of life apparently incapable of being represented by, or transformed into, the linguistic and arithmetic inductions upon which it was commonly thought empiricism had to stand or fall. One such aspect was, of course, Lewes's own doctrine of Emergence, and even he had to grant that the emergent quality in organisms could be described only artificially, "as if the parts were separable." But there were at least two other aspects, both of which were important to George Eliot before she met Lewes and are implicit in her novels— the immediately felt inner life of the individual; and its relationship to the larger life beyond the individual, that is, by nature, not felt with the same immediacy. Of the first, Lewes wrote: "None but shrivelled souls with narrow vision of the facts of life can entertain the notion that Philosophy ought to be restricted within the limits of the Logic of Signs; it has roots in the Logic of Feeling, and many of its products which cannot emerge into the air of exact science nevertheless give impulse to theories, and regulate conducts." Inevitably, one is reminded of George Eliot's early insistence upon "the truth of feeling" as being more meaningful than intellectual debate. It is quite possible that she was responsible for bringing this idea to fruition in Lewes, who had only to substitute the term "logic" for "truth" to fit it into the scheme of the *Problems*. But if by any chance this is what happened, all it means is that George Eliot, in one of their conversations, happened to express an idea she had gleaned from costly experience but which was already astir, although only nebulously, in Lewes's mind. For neither George Eliot nor Lewes had the power to implant totally new ideas in the other's mind. The bond between them became stronger and clarified as the years went on because each mind carried in potential form a nearly total reflection of the other.

Lewes was on fairly firm ground when he assumed that everyone was aware of an inner life that could not be expressed in the "logic of signs." He stepped onto very vulnerable terrain, however, when he brought "evidence" of the existence of a life force larger than that of the individual. Significantly, he temporarily switches from the indicative to the subjunctive mode in describing the varying degrees of awareness by which men sense this presence beyond themselves:

> If a man is insensible to the mystery of the universe; if his soul, like that of an animal, is unvisited by any suggestions of a life larger than his own, and of any existence where his feelings have no home; if he is blind to the visible facts of evolution manifest in the history of the world and the progress of his race, deaf to the cries of pain and struggle which deeply move his feelings, dead to the stirring impulses of pity which move others to remedy the sorrow and enlarge the pleasures of mankind,—by what barrage of argument could we hope to make him feel what his nature does not feel? Happily there is no such man. There are only men who feel less vividly than others. . . .

Related to this emphatic statement is the explanation which occurs much later in the *Problems* of why every phenomenon known to man has two aspects: "Because it is the product of two factors, an organism that feels, and an external that is felt." Lewes calls the "external that is felt" a "Notself acting on the Self; but all we know of this is what we feel." Sensitiveness to the presence of the Notself is of supreme importance in the development of the moral sense; some people never feel this.

> But in a mind where the educated tracing of hurtful consequences to others is associated with a sympathetic imagination of their suffering, Remorse has no relation to an external source of punishment for the wrong committed: it is the agonised sense, the contrite contemplation, of the wound inflicted on another. . . . The sanction which was once the outside whip has become the inward sympathetic pang.

Arranging these pieces into a mosaic, one can begin to hear George Eliot speaking of any one of her several heroines who, after the purgation of self-bound suffering, is enabled to struggle toward awareness of the Notself. In fact, George Eliot went far beyond what Lewes has here suggested. Several of her heroines, beginning as early as Caterina

Sarti in "Mr. Gilfil's Love Story" and ending as late as Gwendolen Harleth in *Daniel Deronda*—and in between there is at least one heroine, Maggie Tulliver, whose destiny might be questioned—internalized "the outside whip" in order to relieve guilt over crimes internally conceived in varying degrees of consciousness but never literally committed.

Perhaps this latter portion of the *Problems* seems especially close to George Eliot's thought because it was she who edited it for the press, so that even some of the wording may be hers. However, one can believe that she performed this task with complete fidelity to Lewes's stated and implied intentions. As late as it occurs, this is only another instance of the congenital similarities in their views. And the mature views of each had been arrived at in amazingly similar fashion. Each had independently spoken a thoughtfully honest farewell to inherited faith. The farther they had strayed separately from typical mid-Victorian orthodoxy, the more each felt a renewal of the significance of life, even when it did not bring personal happiness. It was this enriched meaning that they could share when finally they came together.

Lewes's departure from accepted creeds antedated George Eliot's by only a few years. Again in his *Fortnightly* reminiscence of 1836—apparently a seminal year for him—he speaks of his introduction to Spinoza through the Jew watchmaker Cohn, who had written a book in German on that unorthodox philosopher and who often joined the students' club in Red Lion Square to discuss Spinozism (then little known in England, although Coleridge had touched upon it during the course of his philosophical lectures delivered between December 1818 and March 1819). By 1836 Lewes was already anti-mystic and anti-metaphysical. But Cohn's allusions to the great Hebrew philosopher, who had been branded a heretic by the majority of his own race, stirred Lewes's empathetic interest "partly"—he remembered—"because [Spinoza] was an outcast, for as I was then suffering the social persecution which embitters all departure from accepted creeds, I had a rebellious sympathy with all outcasts." He sought to learn more of Spinoza. The most obvious source, Cohn's book, was closed to him, for although he was then proficient in classical Greek and Latin, he had not yet mastered German. In a dingy secondhand bookstore he found a copy of the *Ethics* in its original Latin, which he carried home with excitement and impetuously began to translate. But impatience, at times his most serious enemy, overtook his enthusiasm and he put the work aside without (one suspects) having gone far into it, although he kept it within reach and used portions of it in his *Biographical History of Philosophy.*

Perhaps at about the same time that he was beginning to plan this unique account of the wayward growth of philosophy, Lewes was motivated by his early study of Spinoza to write an essay on that philosopher's life and work, which was published in the *Westminster Review,* May 1843. It was at the beginning of this same year that George Eliot commenced translating Spinoza. There is no evidence as to whether she read Lewes's article. The topic would have beckoned to her because of her own newly aroused interest in Spinoza, but as this was during the decade when the *Westminster* was floundering in search of strong leadership after the withdrawal of John Stuart Mill, she may not have been paying much attention to the magazine. She might have seen the essay outside the *Westminster,* for shortly after publication there it was reprinted with a special title page bearing Lewes's name. Whenever she read it (and it is implicitly clear that she did so at some time before the summer of 1855), she may not have been wholly satisfied with it. At least she did not take advantage of a ready-made occasion to confirm a high opinion of Lewes's essay when in July 1855 she responded negatively to Sara Hennell, who had read J. A. Froude's recent *Westminster* article on Spinoza and compared it unfavorably with Lewes's, no doubt hoping to win approval from George Eliot. The latter's response may have surprised Sara: "You hardly do justice to Froude's article on Spinoza. I don't at all agree with Froude's own views, but I think his account of Spinoza's doctrines admirable." By this time she was in a better position to evaluate a presentation of Spinoza's ideas, for she was within six months of completing her own translation of the *Ethics.* During this correspondence with Sara she was working on Part IV ("Of Human Bondage; or of the Strength of the Emotions"), which contains the analysis of human nature that led A. A. Brill to say Spinoza "anticipated many of the truths that Freud later discovered and elaborated on the basis of clinical experience."

But Lewes is silent upon this aspect of the *Ethics.* His concentration is almost exclusively with the metaphysics set forth in Part I ("Of God"), and his primary objection to Spinoza is that the latter had adopted Descartes's assumption that "the mind is a mirror reflecting things as they are." Nonetheless, Lewes accredits Spinoza with having demonstrated this assumption and its implications irrefutably, in the manner of Euclid. And he admits that one can escape Spinozism only "by denying the possibility of metaphysical science. . . ." This is exactly what Lewes was most determined to deny—and his preoccupation with so doing perhaps explains his seeming indifference to the remarkable psychology of the *Ethics.* His was a lasting conviction "that the mind is not a passive mirror reflecting the nature of things, but the partial creator of its own forms—that in perception there is nothing but certain changes in the percipient. . . ."

This view is actively present throughout George Eliot's novels, but the creative power she allows in perception is even more profound than that suggested by Lewes. Perhaps her most skillfully integrated presentation of the dynamic relationship between percipient and what is perceived is in the unfolding characterization of Dorothea Brooke as she moves through her relatively uneventful life in the provincial town of Middlemarch. The evidence of Dorothea's gradual and painful liberation from inadequate (in Spinoza's sense) ideas concerning her own nature, as well as from restrictive emotions, appears in subtly unified images and symbols which stay embedded in the flow of narrative. Consciously or not, George Eliot was more faithful to the total spirit of Spinoza than Lewes. It is quite possible that their first discussions of this philosopher, whom each had independently studied with pioneering interest, were argumentative; if so, it would have been in a provocative way which made each carefully measure the other during these increasingly intimate talks in 1852 and 1853. They soon would have discovered that they shared something of far greater importance than agreement or disagreement over Spinoza's ideas. Their separate departures from religious orthodoxy had not left them stranded in remorse (as had happened to many of their contemporaries), but by freeing them from the need to deny man-structured views of reality had rendered them free also to affirm and feel reverence for things that are as they are. Spinoza, the archtypical outcast, would have approved: not wholly extinguished in the austere *Ethics* is a paean of joy which rises in tribute to the nature of things; and what Lewes wrote of Spinoza might well have been said of himself and George Eliot: "The ribald Atheist turns out, on nearer acquaintance, to be a 'God-intoxicated man.' "

WE DO NOT KNOW EXACTLY WHAT ACCEPTED CREED LEWES dissented from. Perhaps it was his stepfather's (whatever that may have been), or perhaps it was simply that loosely ascribed to the Establishment. Whatever its form, it was probably less self-nurtured than George Eliot's Evangelicalism. In varying ways and degrees, his earliest surviving writings reflect his break from some undefined authority which appears to have demanded belief in a supra-sensible force. Whether or not Lewes's rebellion was ever confined to religion proper, by the time of his *Biographical History of Philosophy* (published in separate volumes during 1854–6), his weapons of attack are aimed at philosophy alone. In this work, Lewes lives up to the objective implied in his title. Although he gives some attention to the actual biographies of philosophers, his steadiest focus is upon the life history of philosophy itself, with special emphasis upon "how and by what steps Philosophy became Positive Science; in other words, by what Methods the Human Mind was enabled to conquer for itself, in the long struggle of centuries, its present modicum of certain knowledge." Consequently, metaphysics is the villain of the work, and Bacon and Comte ("the Bacon of the nineteenth century") its heroes.

Slanted and overgeneralized as are many of its discussions, this book fulfilled a real need, especially for those of the rising generation who had become distrustful of the verbalized ideals of their elders. As early as 1853, George Eliot wrote Sara that Lewes, visiting Cambridge, had found "a knot of devotees there who make his history of Philosophy a private text-book." And as late as the 1930's, Anna Kitchel had a difficult time finding a copy in London because—so a book dealer told her—London University students had exhausted the supply: "You see, Madam, they can understand *Lewes.*"

Just as the *Biographical History of Philosophy* made a good private textbook for many years, so its author might have made a good teacher. Certainly the voice of the teacher runs throughout Lewes's work, including the novels, in which his addresses to the reader are more pedagogical than George Eliot's in her novels. It came naturally to Lewes to lecture on whatever was engrossing him at the moment: in the Preface to the *Problems* he mentions having given a series of lectures in 1837 on the issues that were to form the basis of that work; and during the forties he gave occasional lectures on philosophy, such as the one in Edinburgh preceding his enacting the role of Shylock. While abroad during these years, once in 1838 and then again in early 1840, he supported himself by giving English lessons. Haight reasonably suggests that it was as a tutor that he was introduced into the home of Swynfen Jervis, M.P., of Darlaston Hall, Staffordshire, whose eldest daughter, Agnes, Lewes married in 1841.

Agnes was nineteen (only four years Lewes's junior), when William Bell Scott, who with his wife called on the Leweses shortly after their marriage, described her as a "child-wife," and "one of the loveliest creatures in the world," as charming as she was beautiful. Intelligent also, she had responded positively to the liberal upbringing provided by her father, a man of artistic tastes, a devotee of Shelley, and a free-thinker concerning relations between the sexes: "Feelings could not be trammelled by legal bonds or religious sanctions; love would not be constrained; no one was to blame if his affections changed." Thus Agnes's views may well have been in tune with Lewes's own nonconventional ones without any proselytizing on his part. If so, Lewes can be exonerated from the charge of having willfully led his "child-wife" into temptations beyond her understanding. One bit of evidence supporting this interpretation is that in the later (admittedly incomplete) records, Agnes never appears as the forsaken and aggrieved wife. She accepts her lot (as George Eliot would have put it), gives Lewes her blessing when he has found a meaningful life away from her, and exacts of him merely the financial aid to which she was no doubt entitled. At the time of their wedding, neither she nor Lewes could have foreseen that the very ideas they thought would safeguard their marriage by permitting temporary and approved emotional adventures would carry them so far apart that reconciliation would become impossible.

Certainly the Leweses appear to have been very happy during the first years of their marriage. They had august witnesses to that early happiness. Both the Carlyles—Thomas and Jane—seem to have been almost possessively interested in the young couple and gave informal testimony to first the happiness and then the earliest observable signs of trouble between them. Carlyle recalled how "They used to come down of an evening to us through the lanes from Kensington, and were as merry as two birds." But by spring 1849, Mrs. Carlyle noticed a change in their attitude toward one another: "I used to think these Leweses a perfect pair of love-birds . . . but the female love-bird appears to have hopped off to some distance and to be now taking a somewhat critical view of her little shaggy mate." Perhaps even shrewd Jane Carlyle was late in noticing such things, for although her wording does not strongly indicate awareness of a cause for a rift between them other than Agnes's growing dissatisfaction with Lewes, it is probable that Agnes was already embarked on the emotional adventure which was to take her to the point of no return. Exactly when cannot now be said, but she fell in love with Thornton Hunt seriously enough to accept nonlegal separation from Lewes and to bear at least four children by Hunt while he maintained a wife and family of his own.

Perhaps even before he had sat at the feet of the Sage of Chelsea, Lewes had been one of the youngest and most enthusiastic members of the group which clustered around Leigh Hunt. An older sage than Carlyle, Hunt was not destined to have Carlyle's influence in the new age which was to become known as that of Victoria. But some of his ideas were perpetuated in a private channel not open to either Carlyle or John Stuart Mill, for Hunt had produced a family which, for the most part, respected his less vagrant thought and attempted to test it in practical living. One such son was Thornton Hunt and it was inevitable that Lewes should have formed an acquaintance with him.

Lewes was possibly then too young to be taken seriously by Thornton, who was seven years his senior, but the two men eventually were to become close colleagues on the *Leader*. Long before that, however, the young Leweses were intimately associated with the Hunt-Gliddon circle which had come about by two marriages uniting the two families: Thornton Hunt had married Katharine (Kate) Gliddon, whose brother John married Jacintha, Thornton's sister. These people—and others who were to be drawn to them—were also bound together in the ideas they sought to live by. Their initial inspiration came from the real and symbolic father, Leigh Hunt. Perhaps through his firsthand knowledge, they were sensitively receptive to both the ideas and the exempla from the lives of Godwin and his son-in-law, Shelley, as well as the more systematic proposals of F. M. C. Fourier, the French socialist (only recently dead, in 1837), who advocated small cooperative groups in an effort to achieve economic, social, and individual harmony. (It is not known to what extent, if any, the plan followed by the Hunts and Gliddons included the sharing of wives.) Possibly some of the original Hunt-Gliddon group were experimenting in cooperative living on a small scale as early as 1841, for William Bell Scott "says that about this time . . . 'Thornton Hunt, Smith Williams and somebody else with all their wives and families'—were living in a united household in Church Street, Kensington, and that there he saw Lewes, 'joining in the playing and singing as if music was as easy to him as writing dramas.' " It may have been here, or perhaps at the Leweses' home in Campden Hill Terrace, that in 1844 Thackeray made his impressionistic pencil sketch of Agnes at the piano, with Lewes by her side, apparently singing, and Thornton Hunt standing alone rather behind them, not singing but with his eyes on Agnes. That same year she was to bear a son, Thornton Arnott. Whether intentionally or not, this casual sketch is grimly prophetic in depicting Lewes as so absorbed in Agnes and his own singing that he is oblivious to the detached scrutiny of Hunt, whose wife, Kate, is conspicuously absent.

It is possible that this modest beginning of a communal establishment in Church Street was the forerunner of the larger phalanstery in the Queen's Road, Bayswater, where other members were admitted, notably the artist Samuel Laurence and his wife, Anastasia (nee Gliddon, cousin to Kate Hunt). Traditionally, it has been accepted that the communal household in Bayswater did exist and that at some time of unspecified year and length, Agnes and George Henry Lewes lived in this house. But Gordon Haight is factually convincing in his claim that the Leweses never actually lived in the Bayswater establishment, and also he indirectly throws some doubt on the existence of the phalanstery itself. After listing the Leweses' addresses from the time of their marriage to 1855, by which year Lewes was openly living with George Eliot, he adds:

> I list these addresses because so much nonsense has been written about the "Phalanstery" at Royal Hill House, Queen's Road, Bayswater, where the Leweses are incorrectly said to have lived in a co-operative household on Fourieresque principles with the Thornton Hunts, the Gliddons, and the Samuel Laurences. Actually, the house, a very large one, later a girls' school, was occupied by Anastasia Laurence's parents, the Arthur Gliddons. Thornton Hunt and his wife Katharine, niece of Mr. Gliddon, lived there with them 1845–9, when they went to live with her father John Gliddon at Broadway House, Hammersmith. So far as I can discover, the Hunts and the Leweses, though they undoubtedly spent much time together, never lived under the same roof.

The mild implication that communal living among sets of younger people would not be likely to occur in a home dominated by parental figures may be a legitimate one. But to be certain on this score, we would have to know more about the viewpoint and sympathy of the Arthur Gliddons. A surprising number of older Victorian families were not only at one with but in advance of their offspring in ideas concerning social life as well as government, two interesting examples being the Charles Brays and the parents of Barbara Leigh Smith Bodichon, George Eliot's closest woman friend after Sara Hennell.

Whether or not the Leweses ever lived under the same roof that sheltered the Hunts and the Gliddons is an incidental matter; by temperament and intellectual interests, they certainly belonged to the Hunt-Gliddon circle. Furthermore, it is difficult to eradicate the idea of an actual phalanstery existing in the Queen's Road, Bayswater, for Eliza Lynn Linton claimed that she was introduced to it shortly after her arrival in London from the country in 1840, when she was eighteen. Unfortunately, she did not describe her impressions of this unusual household until many years later, when her first reactions were no longer fresh in her mind and had been somewhat distorted by her growing animosity toward Lewes and George Eliot, as well as her obsessive desire to cleanse Thornton Hunt's posthumous reputation of scandal.

Yet Eliza Linton's reminiscences are persuasive in detail in some instances, although exasperatingly ambiguous in others. Her fullest account of this tragi-comedy of family life and abuse is in *The Autobiography of Christopher Kirkland* (published in 1885, when of the principals most deeply involved only Agnes Lewes was still living). This is really Mrs. Linton's autobiography, but "in an unfortunate moment she conceived the idea of reversing her own sex and that of many of her characters for their better disguise." (Fortunately, the characters of most concern here suffer no such conversion.) Her opening leaves little doubt that her intention is to crown Hunt with martyrdom and vitiate Lewes's claim to greater fame:

> Among others, I fell in with that notorious group of Free-lovers, whose ultimate transaction was the most notable example of matrimony void of contract of our day. But though those who floated on the crest of the wave and whose informal union came to be regarded as a moral merit even by the strait-laced had the more genius and the better luck, he who made personal ship-wreck and from whose permitted trespass the whole thing started, had the nobler nature, the more faithful heart, the more constant mind, and was in every way the braver and truer man. The one whom society set itself to honor partly because of the transcendent genius of his companion, partly because of his own brilliancy and facility, was less solid than specious. The other whom all men not knowing him reviled was a moral hero. The former betrayed his own principles when he made capital out of his "desecrated hearth" and bewildered society by setting afloat ingenious stories of impossible ceremonies which had made his informal union in a certain sense sacramental, so that he might fill his rooms with "names" and make his Sundays days of illustrious reception.

If there were other sources besides Eliza for the "impossible ceremonies" undertaken to sanctify the "informal union" between Lewes and George Eliot, they have been either lost or successfully stifled; as have possible ones touching upon the more important matter of Lewes's role as a "Free-lover," about which, again, Eliza appears to be the sole source:

> It must never be forgotten, too, that he who afterward posed as the good husband betrayed by the trusted friend, was, in the days when I first knew them all, the most pronounced Free-lover of the group, and openly took for himself the liberty he expressly sanctioned in his wife. As little as he could go into the Divorce Court for his personal relief because of that condonation and his own unclean hands, so little did he deserve the sympathy of society for the transfer which afterwards he put forward as his own justification and that friend's condemnation.

Mrs. Linton concludes with relative calmness, ending on the expected note of eulogy for Hunt:

> At the time I first knew these people they were living in a kind of family communion that was very remarkable. Sisters and cousins and brothers—some of the women married, and with yearly increasing families to which they devoted themselves; others single and of general domestic utility all round—clubbed together their individually thin resources and made a kind of family Agapemone which had its charm and its romance. Among them were some who

practiced no divergence in their own lives and allowed of none in theory, such as Samuel Lawrence [Laurence] and that handsome Egyptologist, George Gliddon. But also there were certain Free-lovers mingled with the orthodox rest and of these the most remarkable was that faithful and loving man, that loyal and devoted friend, Thornton Hunt.

Still later, in an essay included in *My Literary Life*, published posthumously, Mrs. Linton returned to the subject which so obviously engrossed her. Here she describes Agnes Lewes as " 'that pretty rose-bud-like woman, whose *dona fatale di bellezza* worked its usual tale of woe to all concerned.' Mrs. Hunt she terms 'one of the sweetest and best women that ever lived,' which"—as Elizabeth Haldane adds—"certainly does not make Hunt's desertion of her the less culpable." Eliza Linton admits that Hunt was unconcerned over the legal obligation of marriage, and that he had been "irregular" in his loves but not "licentious." And although she does not outrightly call Lewes licentious, she implies that to him life "meant love and pleasure." She ignores the fact that life for Lewes also had come to mean a great deal of hard work, not all of it pleasant, and the shouldering of responsibilities which, had he been as amoral as Eliza suggests, he might easily have evaded. Nor does she mention that Hunt's acknowledged "divergence" created more than the traditional triangle: he fathered two children by his legal wife, Kate, each born within weeks of his first and second children by Agnes.

Briefly considering Eliza's strange championship of Hunt, Gordon Haight concludes that she "could hardly have known" that Hunt had sired children by both Kate and Agnes at approximately the same time. This is unlikely, however, for there is no reason to think that she was out of touch with these people after her introduction to them. Indeed, her later reminiscences indicate that she had followed their lives with avidity. It is more probable that her defense of Hunt had over the years become a necessary appendage to her unhealthily fixed idea that George Eliot had deliberately got the better of her. She conveyed something of this to her sympathetic biographer, as well as her attempt to appease justified guilt feelings:

> What really touched her to the quick was the difference of treatment meted out by society to "the upholder of the sanctity of marriage, while living as the wife of a married man," and to her own law-abiding self, of whom nothing worse could be suggested than that her marriage [to William Linton, engraver and erstwhile *Leader* man] had been ill-considered and unsuccessful. But, bitterly and often though she has spoken to me of the injustice which she then suffered, she was ever ready to pay to George Eliot the homage which her intellectual superiority demanded.

Even with—or in spite of—Eliza Linton's account, the surviving data stubbornly resist a convincing reconstruction of what actually occurred between the Hunts and the Leweses. Did they among themselves agree to exchange sexual partners? Certainly Eliza bluntly indicates that Lewes, as well as Agnes, had sallied forth beyond the marital limit, but she does not insinuate that he did so with Kate Hunt. In any event, Lewes assumed a seemingly complacent attitude when Agnes bore Hunt's son in April 1850, only two weeks after the appearance of the first number of the *Leader*. Lewes and Hunt were working amicably together on the journal, and were to continue to do so until Lewes left with George Eliot for the Continent in the summer of 1854—although by then the amicability may have been more apparent than real. Lewes had this alleged first son by Hunt and Agnes (her fifth boy) duly registered as Edmund Alfred Lewes. Only a few weeks earlier he would have had to report the death of his son St. Vincent Arthy Lewes, who died on 23 March after a three-week onslaught of whooping cough and measles. In June of the same year, Lewes announced in the *Leader* that his family consisted of "four boys and a human Rose in the shape of their mother." One wonders what provoked Lewes to make this unnecessarily definitive statement concerning his family.

Most biographers have assumed that Lewes's acceptance of the situation and all that it implied stemmed from the fact that he was a man of progressive ideas, tolerance, and compassion. This view is probably essentially correct, and one can believe that Lewes would have agreed with what Thornton Hunt wrote in the *Leader*, July 1852: "Human beings are born with passions; you will not discipline those passions by ignoring them, and nature always avenges herself by retorting upon the false moralist some depravity as the result of his handiwork." But for whatever reason Lewes was quiescent over the paternity of Edmund, he felt that a meaningful life with Agnes had come to an end when she became pregnant with her second child by Hunt (born on 21 October 1851 and named Rose Agnes, hence a double reminder of the woman he had once loved).

Did he still love Agnes? It is impossible to know. In Lewes's masterly dissection of Sir Frederick Hawbucke's ambivalent feelings toward his wife in *Ranthorpe* a suggestive passage occurs to the effect that the cessation of love does not in itself remove the torments of jealousy:

> It is mostly pride that feels jealousy, seldom love. A lover may be jealous, but it is almost always his pride that suffers. When a husband ceases to love his wife, he does not cease to feel the pangs occasioned by the suspicion of her preference for another. . . .

Although this novel was published three years before the birth of Edmund and is dedicated "To Her who has lightened the burden of an anxious life," it was in the making during the years when the Leweses and the Hunts were in close relationship, and often served as a receptacle for Lewes's observations when he was warding off moods of depression. The ambivalent use made of the name Thornton in the novel is particularly interesting. It is the surname of the middle-aged benevolent figure who discourses wisely on Goethe and prevents the hero—the morbid genius, Percy Ranthorpe—from committing suicide; and it is also the surname of this Mr. Thornton's nephew, Oliver, the villain of the piece, who murders his uncle in such a way as deliberately to throw all suspicion onto Percy. Although Percy is rescued in the nick of time, both Thorntons meanwhile have come to violent ends, the good one by the destructive power of the evil one. Also, it is in connection with Oliver's growing resolve to kill his uncle that Lewes offers his advice (already quoted) on how to safeguard the mind against nurturing obsessions: form fresh associations, he urges, with those very objects that experience has conditioned to evoke the thoughts you wish to avoid. But Oliver was beyond such counsel. The thought of doing away with his uncle "had become a fixed idea. He must either become a murderer or a monomaniac!" Tenuous though the evidence may be, *Ranthorpe* suggests that the name Thornton had early come to signify to Lewes the polar extremes of character: nobility and duplicity, benevolence and destructiveness, philosophical wisdom and licentiousness; and that he recognized his own need to fight against dejection, jealousy, and, perhaps most seriously of all, the desire to strike out in violence against the source of his torment.

There are reasons besides *Ranthorpe* to believe that the Leweses' marriage was in perilous balance several years before 1850. Blanche Colton Williams—a conservative biographer, although uncritical in her admiration of Lewes and George Eliot—states without qualification:

> Of three sons, Charles Lee, Thornton Arnott, and Herbert Arthur, the first was rightly named Lewes. About the paternity of Thornton and Herbert, opinions differ; they were acknowledged and remembered as his own in Lewes's will; and there were two younger boys who were Thornton Hunt's.

According to this, Lewes was father to no child by Agnes after their first year of marriage (Charles Lee was born in 1842). The two younger sons belonging to Hunt would have included St. Vincent Arthy as well as Edmund, for the three other children that Agnes bore Hunt were girls. Also Dr. William's statement introduces an element which is rarely considered: the possibility that Agnes had engaged in extra-marital relationships with some man or men other than Thornton Hunt. But one can do little more than call attention to these remarks by a scholar of irreproachable integrity. As Dr. Williams is regrettably silent about the source of her statement, one must assume that documentary proof to support it is no longer available. Probably she received her information by word of mouth from one or several of the living relatives of both George Eliot and Lewes with whom she visited as she was collecting material and whom she lists in her Foreword. There is no doubt, however, that she herself considered her source reliable and her information of a status far above unfounded rumor or personal opinion.

No matter what the boys' paternity, Lewes and George Eliot assumed responsibility for Charles, Thornton, and Herbert, although Agnes kept them at home with her until they were old enough to be sent to school in Switzerland. After their Swiss schooling, Charles was the only one of the three whose life became intimately bound with the joint one of his father and George Eliot. He found his career in the Post Office and lived with them until his marriage in 1865 to Gertrude Hill, by whom he had three daughters.

After a few years of farming in Natal, Thornton came home to them fatally ill and died at the age of twenty-five, leaving no family. Herbert had joined Thornton in Africa, where he died in 1875, six years after his brother's death in London. Herbert's widow and their two children—Marian and George—came to England in 1879. One of the first social gestures George Eliot forced herself to make after Lewes's death only a few months earlier was to invite them to lunch, after which she had soon arranged for their support by setting up a generous trust fund for them in her will.

Neither Thornton nor Herbert had prospered in Natal. Lewes and George Eliot contributed substantially to their income, which they could then afford to do, for both were becoming wealthy on George Eliot's royalties. Yet they gave these young men more than material sustenance, and Thornton (Thornie) came "home" to be cared for by them when he sensed that he was soon to die. George Eliot considerately spent an occasional afternoon away from the Priory so that Agnes could visit him, but it was she who nursed Thornie devotedly—making him as comfortable as possible, sitting and talking with him, playing for him. In short, she re-established the routine she had followed in caring for her father almost exactly twenty years earlier, and, without fully realizing it, she also vested in it the same feelings. Hers was now a far more controlled and finely integrated self than at the time of her father's death. Yet when Thornie's expected death occurred and his need for her was suddenly withdrawn, an old fear temporarily reasserted itself: that if there was no longer an external demand on her selfless love, her moral nature would succumb to the released passions of destruction. Thornie's death immediately became a prefiguration of death for herself and for George Henry. On 19 October 1869, the day he died, she wrote in her Journal, "This death seems to me the beginning of our own." Her inner achievement and outward fame dissolved into nothingness as far as these feelings were concerned. Three days after Thornie's death she wrote briefly of it to Barbara Bodichon, who had sent her words of sympathy: "Thanks for your tender words. It has cut deeper than I expected—that he is gone and I can never make him feel my love any more. Just now all else seems trivial compared with the powers of delighting and soothing a heart that is in need."

George Eliot of course soon regained her perspective and resumed normal living, which at this point for her meant continuing with *Middlemarch*, on which she had made a beginning in the interval between Thornie's arrival and his death. Her reaction to Thornie's death had been mild in comparison to that evoked by her father's, but it was faint duplicate enough of that earlier intense experience to serve as a warning that she could never endure the death of George Henry and stay alive if left alone.

The knowledge of the death of Herbert (Bertie), which occurred in 1875 when he was twenty-nine and in the midst of his own family in far-away Natal, struck George Eliot as grievous news, to be sure, but without the power to make her aware of an echo of death within herself. (In fact, she was working on what was to be her last novel, *Daniel Deronda*, and Lewes's death was only three years away.) However, Bertie's death provoked a different kind of self-searching. She began to wonder, apparently for the first time, whether George Henry and she had done what was best for Bertie. She expressed her doubts as well as her resolve not to feel guilty to John Walter Cross, by then elevated from the position of friend to that of "Dearest Nephew." The candor of her remarks shows that she already placed great trust in his understanding:

> He [Bertie] was a sweet-natured creature—not clever, but diligent and well-judging about the things of daily life, and we felt ten years ago that a colony with a fine climate, like Natal, offered him the only fair prospect within his reach. What can we do more than try to arrive at the best conclusion from the conditions as they are known to us? The issue, which one could not foresee, must be borne with resignation—is in no case a ground for self-reproach, and in this case, I imagine would hardly have been favourably altered by a choice of life in the old country.

Personally, George Eliot had little, if any, cause to reproach herself. From their boyhood on, she had treated without discrimination the three who bore Lewes's name, and she did her utmost to make what in reality was an awkward relationship seem easy and natural to them. The last time she was "Miss Evans" to them was in the late summer of 1859 when Lewes, bearing interesting gifts from her to them, made an expedition to their school in Hofwyl for the purpose of informing them of the strange facts of their lives: " . . . lying on the moss I unburthened myself about Agnes to them. They were less distressed than I had anticipated and were delighted to hear about Marian." (It is possible that at this time he also added glamour to Marian in their eyes by telling them that she was the author of *Adam Bede*, which was fast gaining an international reputation, so that a few days after seeing the boys, Lewes could write John Blackwood: "Paris is in a fever about Adam Bede. Even at Hofwyl—five miles from Berne —with only half a dozen English boys—I heard of it; for on telling my second son I had brought him a novel all three shouted 'Is it Adam Bede?' "

George Eliot had accompanied Lewes to Switzerland but not, under-standably, to Hofwyl. She remained behind in Lucerne while Lewes spent two more days with the boys, rambling in the woods, listening to Charles show off his new mastery of the piano, and talking to them, "mainly about the domestic changes, and future arrangements." Back in Lucerne, he had a "Long chat with Polly about the boys." The mission was apparently successful on all sides: at first shyly but then with greater self-assurance as they became confident of her sympathetic response, the boys began to write to her, calling her "Mother" and "Mutter." They reserved the more familiar "Mamma" for Agnes, but there is no indication that there was a really close mother-son relationship between Agnes and any one of her sons after they had once left her home. George Eliot in her turn accepted her maternal responsibility with pride, even though aware of its ironic limitations. While she never would have asserted this publicly, she made it clear to her closest London friends that this voluntarily assumed responsibility toward Lewes's sons was an important justification of her being called "Mrs. Lewes." On 1 April 1861 she wrote a considered statement to Mrs. Peter Taylor, who had known her briefly at 142 Strand and had written her a sympathetic letter in 1856, when the gossip about George Eliot's relationship with Lewes had reached an unpleasant height and tone:

For the last six years I have ceased to be "Miss Evans" for any one who has personal relations with me—having held myself under all the responsibilities of a married woman. I wish this to be distinctly understood; and when I tell you that we have a great boy of eighteen at home who calls me "mother," as well as two other boys, almost as tall, who write to me under the same name, you will understand that the point is not one of mere egoism or personal dignity, when I request that any one who has a regard for me will cease to speak of me by my maiden name.

One does wonder why it was only Charles who was at home and why he alone of the three boys was not made to feel the need to emigrate. Even he, living a relatively sheltered and presumably happy life, died in 1891 in Luxor, Egypt, before he was fifty.

Agnes was the indomitable one. She lived out her eighty years with her children by Hunt, especially Edmund, who became a dentist and remained single, and Rose, who also stayed single and became a governess (the two younger daughters, Ethel and Mildred, went to California and married there). Dying in 1902, Agnes survived her first four sons, as well as Thornton Hunt, Lewes, and George Eliot. After separating from her, Lewes gave her an annual allowance of approximately £100, which was often augmented by substantial gifts to her children. After his death, this payment was continued by George Eliot, then by Charles Lewes, and finally by Charles's widow.

Again thanks to George Eliot's increasing royalties, helping Agnes in addition to supplying for the three boys was eventually no great sacrifice; but in 1854 and a few years following, it was a real burden. In a very serious letter written three months after she and Lewes had eloped to the Continent, George Eliot assured Charles Bray that Lewes "has been anxiously waiting restoration to health that he may once more work hard, not only to provide for his children, but to supply his wife's wants so far as that is not done by another." The "another" was of course Hunt, who had trouble meeting his now complex financial obligations, so that, despite substantial funds sent by Lewes, Agnes was seriously in debt by the end of 1856. (With a large household to maintain, she was now pregnant with the last child—born on 21 May 1857—she was to bear Hunt.) Concerned, Lewes wrote heatedly to Hunt, who took offense and challenged Lewes to a duel. Fortunately, after consultation with Edward Pigott and George Redford—both closely associated with the Leader—the matter was dropped within a week, although there is no sign that good relations were restored between the two principals. Whether or not Hunt became more regular in his payments, he at least made Agnes the beneficiary of an insurance policy. But when he died in 1873, it was Lewes who had to secure Kate Hunt's signature before the policy was payable. In keeping up his own contributions, Lewes maintained a friendly correspondence with Agnes, his last letter to her being dated only two months before his death in 1878.

In the pleasant and peaceful atmosphere of Rosehill, George Eliot had unsuspectingly met at least two of the major participants in the drama which was to form the background of her life for many years to come. By early 1851, although the *Westminster Review* had not yet come her way, life in the Strand had already initiated her enough into the excitement and perils of book and periodical publishing to arouse her interest in Hunt and Lewes as they guided the relatively new *Leader* along its financially precarious course. At this time she perhaps had the greater interest in Hunt, the older man, who occasionally came to the Chapmans' but to her vexation without being introduced to her. She was finally to meet Hunt at Rosehill when she was there after her second flight from 142 Strand one weekend in May 1851. By that time he was of course well into his liaison with Agnes, who was to give birth to his daughter Rose in October. His wife, Kate, may or may not have been with him during the May visit to Rosehill, but it is certain that she was there a few weeks later, for on 15 June, George Eliot wrote Chapman from Coventry: "Good Mrs. Hunt has left behind a very pleasant impression. I think she is the most thoroughly unaffected being I ever saw." She relayed no impressions of Hunt, but commented upon the latest news of the *Leader*:

> I am afraid the Leader is not prospering. The names of Thornton Hunt, Lewes, Linton and several more were specified last week in the papers as withdrawing from partnership in the concern—which seems to imply a presentiment of failure. We are all amused at Thornton Hunt's illustration in yesterday's Leader of "boiled mutton chops" ["Politics are as dull as boiled mutton chops."]—that must be a peculiarly Hammersmith dish. [The Hunts were then living with Kate's father in Hammersmith.]

Was she even then familiar with the well-founded gossip that linked together Hunt's and Lewes's personal lives? If so, she seems deliberately to have stayed quiet about it, almost as if she were waiting to hear the true version from Lewes himself, although he was so far only a name in her life. It is less likely that she realized that, intellectually sophisticated though it purported to be, the *Leader* was already split into pro-Hunt and pro-Lewes factions. By 1854 Hunt would leave the magazine for a journalistic position elsewhere. But it was to play a strange and by now blurred part in her life for several years to come, perhaps even proving to be the surreptitious force that made her reveal herself as George Eliot.

By the end of September she was back in the Strand and soon Chapman had introduced her to Lewes, who lost little time in making her aware of his presence and of his desire to be with her. In spite of herself—for she still saw him through the eyes of others as the playboy of the literary world—she began to find his charm irresistible. As the references to him in her letters increase, so does the lightness of their tone. For a while their relationship was but a continuation of what she had enjoyed with Herbert Spencer, but inevitably there came a change as Lewes teasingly but firmly forced Spencer into the background and she permitted this to happen.

Exactly when Spencer began to bring Lewes with him to the Strand to visit her is not known. Only a few weeks after that first meeting in Jeffs's, Lewes, apparently by self-invitation, sat in the same box with her, Chapman, and Spencer "at the 'Merry Wives of Windsor,' " she reported to Cara Bray, "and helped to carry off the dolorousness of the play by such remarks as 'There's the swan preening,' 'The swan comes out now and then,' and 'The play is a farce in five acts. If it were in one act and one didn't see it, it would be very well' etc., etc." Perhaps neither Chapman nor Spencer was as amused as she by Lewes's witticisms—especially Spencer, as he had invited her and Chapman to see the play with him. In fact, Lewes was probably on the scene at 142 Strand when Spencer's invitation was issued. On Monday, 24 November 1851, George Eliot sent Sara Hennell a brief note to apologize for not having written on the twenty-second as was her rarely broken custom (it was her birthday, and Sara's came the day after): "I did not forget and meant to have written, but on Saturday afternoon I was teazed, and then came Mr. Spencer to ask Mr. Chapman and me to go to the theatre—so I ended the day in a godless manner, seeing the Merry Wives of Windsor." Her wording makes it clear that Spencer was not the tease, and it is unlikely that she would have referred to Chapman's attention in so frivolous a way. But her term fits Lewes's manner. If she was making a private reference to Lewes, then he was with her at the Strand before Spencer's coincidental arrival. In that case, he no longer needed Spencer's presence as an excuse to see George Eliot (although this is considerably earlier than Spencer would indicate to Cross). It would seem that having overheard the invitation, Lewes accidentally on purpose came upon them in the theater that evening.

Spencer and Lewes are intertwined for some time in George Eliot's letters to Coventry. Even in the we-are-not-in-love letter, the two appear together somewhat to Spencer's disadvantage: "I went to the opera on Saturday . . . with my 'excellent friend Herbert Spencer,' as Lewes calls him." Soon she no longer wished to be with Spencer and Lewes together. No doubt thinking to please her, the Brays invited both men to Rosehill, sending the invitation directly to Lewes, who passed it on to Spencer. The latter let George Eliot know that he wished to postpone his visit until she would be there too, whereupon she wrote Bray:

> I have assured Herbert Spencer that you will think it a sufficiently formal answer to the invitation you sent him through Mr. Lewes if I tell you that he will prefer waiting for the pleasure of a visit to you until I am with you—if you will have him then. *Entre nous*, if Mr. Lewes should not accept your invitation now, pray don't ask him when I am with you—not that I don't like him—*au contraire* —but I want nothing so Londonish when I go to enjoy the fields and hedgerows and yet more, friends of ten years' growth.

This was clever, but eventually tactics had to become more open. One afternoon when Spencer had taken Lewes with him to visit George Eliot at the Strand (so he wrote Cross in 1884), he himself rose to leave, but "Lewes signified that he would stay. This marked the beginning of [his and George Eliot's] intimacy." Spencer does not specify the month or year of this visit, but by the middle of September 1852, George Eliot writes casually to Bray, with no mention of Spencer: "Lewes called on me the other day and told me of a conversation with Prof. Owen. . . ." A month later she refers to a still more informal visit: " . . . and when I had sat down again thinking I had two clear hours before dinner—rap at the door—Mr. Lewes—who of course sits talking till the second bell rings." From then on, references to Spencer are sparse in the letters to Coventry, and none of them suggests that she was continuing to accompany him to the theater and concert halls as she had done so frequently since her arrival in London. In view of Lewes's shaky personal reputation, as well as of her own anomalous position as an unattached woman of over thirty, Spencer's respectable presence had been for a while indispensable, and it is little wonder that Lewes was moved to record gratitude for it. But Spencer must have been deeply hurt when he came to realize that his personal importance to his two friends had dwindled to that of an unwanted third party. By his own generosity he had unwittingly lost the intimate friendship of a man whom he obviously liked and admired and the companionship of the only woman he had dared come near to loving. The seeds for what Lewes was later to write off as professional jealousy had been sown.

During the spring of 1853, George Eliot's references to Lewes take on a new note of seriousness, presaged by a statement of her final opinion of Thornton Hunt which would have been cryptic to anyone but her Coventry friends. "Dear Mr. Bray—do you remember the 'boiled mutton chops' in the Leader," she wrote in March. "I don't think that dish would suit me." And in April she told Cara: "People are very good to me. Mr. Lewes especially is kind and attentive and has quite won my regard after having a good deal of my vituperation. Like a few other people in the world, he is much better than he seems —[two words crossed out] a man of heart and conscience wearing a mask of flippancy." She had discovered the real Lewes, and probably by this time each had acknowledged his love and need for the other.

This new awareness could not have brought them immediate joy. Seemingly insuperable problems militated against even the thought of their living together. Nonetheless, it was early in this spring that she resolved to leave the Chapmans', but then, as already recounted, vacillated strangely. There were Chapman's pleas to resist, and there must also have been a disturbing question in her mind: to *what* was she going? Merely a borrowing of another woman's husband? For apparently she and Lewes had agreed that he had no moral right to leave Agnes with finality; that if she, his lawful wife, wished or needed him, he would be bound to return. At least some such understanding may be inferred from George Eliot's otherwise enigmatic statement to Bray in a letter from Weimar: "Circumstances, with which I am not concerned, and *which have arisen since [Lewes] left England*, have led him to determine on a separation from Mrs. Lewes. . . ." It would seem then that, for whatever reason, Lewes did not consider himself decisively separated from Agnes even when he was asking George Eliot to share his life. Understandably, George Eliot found it almost impossible to reach a decision. She knew that she wanted to be with Lewes; she had come to trust him; and, aware of her own sincerity as well as the conditions of his domestic life, she was convinced that her decision to live with him would be a moral one and that she had the strength to withstand the social censure and ostracism sure to follow such a choice. She could even feel noble reaching these conclusions.

Ironically, one remaining question must have reminded her that noble resolutions run the danger of being as self-centered as selfishness in its more ordinary guises and are therefore equally unprepared to stand firm against the random forces which do not distinguish between the egoism of the martyr at the stake and that of the court sycophant. In brief, did she have the courage to build a new life that, no matter how justly founded in her own mind, could be shattered by a whimsical wish from Agnes? She had answered the big questions affirmatively, but to this small one whose existence lay outside the realm of predictability, she could give no immediate response.

Yet she did force herself to make a move of some kind, and on 17 October 1853 she left the Strand for 21 Cambridge Street. The date of this move may have some significance. On the ninth of this month, Agnes gave birth to her second daughter by Hunt, and the *Leader* (which seems to have been uncommonly interested in vital statistics whenever they were likely to cause spicy speculation) announced this birth "to the wife of G. H. Lewes, Esq." It is quite possible that Agnes's giving birth to yet another child by Hunt motivated George Eliot to permit herself an intimate life with Lewes. But the clandestine element in this new life did not make for happiness. Verbally she might toss it off lightly, as when next December she wrote Chapman (who of course visited her in Cambridge Street): "How came you to mention to Miss M[artineau] that you saw the proof of Mr. Lewes's book [on Comte] '*in* [*my*—crossed out] *Miss Evans's room*'? I think you must admit that your mention of my name was quite gratuitous. So far you were naughty—but never mind."

And on 14 April 1854, only three months before she and Lewes would try to leave the past behind them and go to the Continent, it may or may not have been subterfuge that caused her to write to Cara Bray, who she had heard might be planning a spring trip to London: "Alas! I can't invite you, for there is not room for two people to turn around in my bedroom." However, her very nature rebelled against pretense of any kind. Here she was in a far different situation from that time when, after much soul-searching, she had resumed going to church in order to bring peace of mind to her father. Here she must seem to pretend for the sake of gaining something which in the eyes of the world was not rightfully hers. Even Lewes—more adept at simulation than she—felt the strain, and in April 1854 his health broke, so that he was ordered to the country for rest. George Eliot took on much of his work for the *Leader*, a not inconsiderable burden on top of her own necessary writing, which by then included the translating of Feuerbach.

In May, when she was very near to her final decision to go off with Lewes, she wrote Sara a letter that seemed to be reminiscent of the despairing ones of earlier times: "I am terribly out of spirits just now and the pleasantest thought I have is that whatever I may feel affects no one else—happens in a little 'island cut off from other lands.' " Her letter to Cara two days later is no happier: "My various aches determined themselves into an attack of rheumatism which sent me to bed yesterday; but I am better this morning. . . . My troubles are purely psychical—self-dissatisfaction and despair of achieving anything worth the doing." Another of the frequent indications that she did not consider either her translations or her *Westminster* duties her "real" work, this also implies that not even Lewes's companionship had lessened her need to find that work.

Apparently Sara, concerned, had passed on to Cara the island metaphor with the suggestion that it implied a return to self-centered morbidity; for George Eliot felt called upon to explain to Cara:

> When I spoke of myself as an island, I did not mean that I was so exceptionally. We are all islands . . . [she here quotes from Keble's *The Christian Year*] and this seclusion is sometimes the most intensely felt at the very moment your friend is caressing you or consoling you. But this gradually becomes a source of satisfaction instead of repining. When we are young we think our troubles a mighty business—that the world is spread out expressly as a stage for the particular drama of our lives and that we have a right to rant and foam at the mouth if we are crossed. I have done enough of that in my time. But we begin at last to understand that these things are important only to one's own consciousness, which is but as a globule of dew on a rose-leaf that at mid-day there will be no trace of. This is no high-flown sentimentality, but a simple reflection which I find useful to me every day.

Aside from the references to the first person, this might be a passage from one of the novels-to-be, spoken by the omniscient voice, neither pessimistic nor optimistic, but somberly resigned to the inexorably impersonal face of reality.

But one also wonders if the forced ambiguity of her life with Lewes had not given rise to the island metaphor. She was with him and yet not with him even when he was closest to her. Whether or not she revealed any such feelings to Lewes, it would seem that both recognized their relationship had reached a cirsis and had to be either salvaged or abandoned. Their plan to leave watchful, suspicious London for the freer Continent was settled upon with relative suddenness. The first sign of their decision, no doubt deliberately vague, was merely her surprisingly late decision not to return to the Chapmans, who having moved from 142 Strand, had asked her to be their lodger in their new home in Blandford Square. "I have finally decided not to live with the Chapmans," she wrote Charles Bray on 27 May. "The consideration that determined me was that I could not feel at liberty to leave them after causing them to make arrangements on my account, and it is quite possible that I may wish to go to the continent or twenty other things. At all events, I like to feel free." Probably when Bray visited her on 11 June she was more explicit, for later, writing from Weimar, she made it clear that only he and Mr. and Mrs. Chapman had known from her of her intimacy with Lewes.

Feuerbach finished, she spent 17–26 June at Rosehill, probably nostalgically aware that this might well be her last visit there (as it was to be). Returning to Cambridge Street, she soon gave intellectual London a daring, if symbolic, farewell. She had meant to have her translation of *The Essence of Christianity* published anonymously, like the Strauss. It was all in type in early June, and preliminary notices in the newspapers read "By the Translator of 'Strauss's Life of Jesus.'" At the last minute, however, she changed her mind, and when the book appeared in July, the title page announced: "By Marian Evans, Translator of 'Strauss's Life of Jesus.'" In the 1 July issue of the *Leader*, Lewes had predicted that this work would "be a bombshell thrown into the camp of orthodoxy." It was not only religious orthodoxy that was being assailed: Feuerbach's basic premise enveloped human relations, hence morals. A passage such as the following illumines George Eliot's decision to dispel the anonymity of the translator:

> But marriage—we mean, of course, marriage as the free bond of love—is sacred in itself, by the very nature of the union which is therein effected. That alone is a religious marriage, which is a true marriage, which corresponds to the essence of marriage—of love. And so it is with all moral relations. Then only are they moral,— then only are they enjoyed in a moral spirit, when they are regarded as sacred in themselves.

And Feuerbach–George Eliot had footnoted "the free bond of love":

> Yes, only as the free bond of love; for a marriage the bond of which is merely an external restriction, not the voluntary, contented self-restriction of love, in short, a marriage which is not spontaneously concluded, spontaneously willed, self-sufficing, is not a true marriage, and therefore not a truly moral marriage.

By affixing her name to this translation, she had come into the open again and was, as always, stimulated by the challenge from the world which she found there. She would invite comparison between the ideas of Feuerbach and her relationship with Lewes, including the background of his legal marriage. If on her part this was a defiant gesture, it was one that could hurt no one and was rooted in sincerity: both she and Lewes had, independently, assented to the essence of Feuerbach's ideas before meeting him in print or one another in reality.

Lewes had been scheduled to review her translation, but, as she wrote Sara Hennell on 10 July, his "head is not likely to be up to the pitch of Feuerbach, so it will fall to the lot of some other non-leading attache of the Leader." The "bad head" was a plausible excuse, for he had suffered from headaches ever since George Eliot had lived at 21 Cambridge Street. But it is unlikely that under normal conditions even a very bad head would have prevented him from doing a laudatory critique of her work. Probably she and he had decided wisely that a review by him, which would have appeared either right before or after their leaving for the Continent, would have done more harm than good to both themselves and Feuerbach. Also in the 10 July letter, George Eliot began to prepare Sara for her departure: "I shall soon send you a good bye, for I am preparing to go to 'Labassecour.'"

Cross did not understand the significance of "Labassecour"; he rendered it "to go abroad," humbly adding a question mark. "Labassecour" was Charlotte Brontë's name for Belgium in *Villette*, which had been published early in 1853; and on 12 March of that year, George Eliot had written enthusiastically to the Brays: "Villette—Villette—have you read it?" In 1847 she had given only lukewarm praise to *Jane Eyre*, expressing dislike of the binding marriage laws: "All sacrifice is good—but one would like it to be in a somewhat nobler cause than that of a diabolical law which chains a man soul and body to a putrefying carcase. However the book *is* interesting—only I wish the characters would talk a little less like the heroes and heroines of police reports." But this was before Lewes had told her about his meeting with Charlotte at Mrs. Gaskell's home (when, incidentally, Charlotte had been deeply moved because Lewes's face reminded her so much of Emily's).

Only a week before urging the Brays to read *Villette*, George Eliot had written them: "Lewes was describing Currer Bell to me yesterday as a little, plain, provincial, sickly-looking old maid. Yet what passion, what fire in her!" Without doubt, Labassecour to George Eliot meant not merely a geographical location (although she and George Henry were to pass through Brussels as they journeyed toward Weimar), but a symbol of deep-hearted love and the beginning of a new life. They may have guessed that Lucy Snowe was in part Charlotte herself and that M. Paul Emmanuel had a prototype in real life. However, perhaps fortunately, they could not have known that the real M. Héger did not drown at sea like his fictional counterpart, but was already married when Charlotte met and fell in love with him, and that the burying of this forbidden love in the depths of her heart was like a long and secret illness. Even when George Eliot and Lewes read Elizabeth Gaskell's *Life of Charlotte Brontë* as soon as it appeared in 1857, they would have learned little more about the background of *Villette*. Mrs. Gaskell, although knowledgeable enough of the episode to have consulted M. Héger himself, handled this phase of her subject's life with a discretion rivaled only by Cross's well-meaning efforts to conceal the "passion and fire" in George Eliot. But Charlotte herself had chosen not to present M. Paul Emmanuel as married, and Mrs. Gaskell's reticence in dealing with Charlotte's love for M. Héger is a reminder that according to Victorian standards, a single woman's love for a married man, no matter how hopeless and virtuous, was judged as harshly as if it had been consummated. It is also a reminder that in leaving England with Lewes, George Eliot was undertaking a greater risk than even she may have realized. Ever since the Brays, the Hennells, and John Chapman had entered her life, she had become so accustomed to being surrounded by atypical Victorians that she was in danger of forgetting the cruelty often disguised as virtue in narrow-mindedness and ignorance.

It is not known whether there was any new factor in Lewes's situation (or George Eliot's) which brought them to the final decision to leave England together. Writing shortly before 1883, when there was still some firsthand gossip afloat, Mathilde Blind says sensibly: "Too little has as yet transpired concerning this important step to indicate more than the bare outline of events. Enough that Mr. Lewes appears to have written a letter in which, after a full explanation of his circumstances, he used all his powers of persuasion to win Miss Evans for his life-long companion. . . ." No such letter or record of it has survived, and it is doubtful whether it was ever written, for surely there was no need unless as a kind of summation of the pros and cons of their planned course of action. Although never in a very peaceful atmosphere, they had been granted time and privacy enough to discover the bonds between them forged unknowingly in the past before they met. The several intellectual bonds were important; of greater meaning to them would have been the more personal bonds which had developed from actual living. Each had earlier loved and suffered profound unhappiness because of it, but neither had become disillusioned with love itself, and each was willing to look to the future without regret or bitterness. For their past sufferings—perhaps even more than for their achievements—each respected the other, with no desire for an ideal image, and each could afford to allow the other independence. "The intense happiness of our union," George Eliot was to write Sara in 1860, "is derived in a high degree from the perfect freedom with which we each follow and declare our impressions." By the summer of 1854, they were thinking of their life together as a collaboration. They had reason to believe that they were ready for what Lewes was to describe Goethe as lacking with Frederika—"the exquisite *companionship* of two souls striving in emulous spirit of loving rivalry to become better, to become wiser, teaching each other to soar."

On 19 July, George Eliot wrote a final farewell to her three Coventry friends: "I have only time to say good bye and God bless you. Poste Restante, Weimar for the next six weeks, and afterwards Berlin. / Ever your loving and grateful / Marian."

A FTER LEAVING WEIMAR, GEORGE ELIOT RECORDED SALIENT impressions and memories of her three months' stay in the first Journal she was not to destroy, the beginning of which Cross renders: "I said a last farewell to Cambridge Street on 20th July, 1854, and found myself on board the *Ravensbourne*, bound for Antwerp. The day was glorious, and our passage perfect. The sunset was lovely, but still lovelier the dawn. . . ." What Cross omits is her own admission of anxiety: she had boarded the ship "about 1/2 an hour earlier than a sensible person would have been aboard, and in consequence I had 20 minutes of terrible fear lest something should have delayed G. But before long I saw his welcome face looking for me over the porter's shoulder and all was well." Even the phrase "and found myself on board" suggests that she was not quite certain whether she was acting under direction of her own will or of some spell cast over her, as in a more pronounced way Maggie Tulliver was to feel when she allowed Stephen Guest to lead her to the small boat that was to carry them into a fateful night.

As George Eliot was taking a premeditated step, she was better fortified than Maggie could be; yet upon her return, she found London to be but a larger and more complex St. Ogg's. Along their Continental route, she and Lewes were to meet a surprising number of individuals who accepted their relationship without a sign of condescending tolerance, thus cushioning their realistic understanding of what awaited them when they recrossed the Channel—unless, of course, they decided to make their real home on the friendlier Continent. There is no indication, however, that they ever seriously considered remaining away from England longer than to secure a respite from Lewes's unresolved problems. They had embarked for a destination which could be described only figuratively—"Labassecour." The embarkation itself was momentous, and as in even the retrospective Journal entry George Eliot describes the shifting, changing light from sunset to sunrise, one assumes that she and Lewes kept to the deck all night.

The first understanding acquaintance they were to meet was a fellow passenger on the *Ravensbourne*—Robert Noel, one of Lady Byron's several cousins and brother to Edward, Cara Bray's special friend. As Noel was worldly-wise and sympathetic, there was no need for concealment from him; they thought him a pleasant companion, especially when he talked about Weimar, which was their realistic destination. Parting from him in Antwerp, where they lingered to do some sight-seeing, they went on to Brussels (doing more sight-seeing, especially in tribute to *Villette*); then to Cologne, where they were briefly joined by Brabant and Strauss; and finally to Frankfurt, twice visiting the house of Goethe's birth. On 2 August they reached Weimar, the little town rich in Goethe lore, and for three months gathered and evaluated data for Lewes's long projected biography of the great German writer. Weimar was enriched for them by the presence of Franz Liszt, then living "with a Russian Princess, who is in fact his wife," so George Eliot wrote to Charles Bray somewhat precipitously on 16 August, for the Princess Wittgenstein was not divorced until the following year. No man on the Continent could have been better equipped than Liszt to understand their position and to make them feel at ease. Lewes's earlier (1839) introduction to Liszt in Vienna may have helped smooth the way to an easy exchange of meetings, and soon, when they were visiting him at the Altenburg, he played the piano for them. George Eliot had been longing for this and managed to sit "near him so that I could see both his hands and face. For the first time in my life I beheld real inspiration—for the first time I heard the true tones of the piano."

On 29 August another sympathetic friend, Arthur Helps, appeared unexpectedly in Weimar after a visit in Spain and the next evening accompanied them on their second drive to Ettersburg. In addition to giving them good companionship, he was "a great comfort"—as George Eliot told John Chapman in a confidential letter of 15 October —because he had known in advance and had approved of their plan to come to the Continent. Possibly it was Helps who suggested that they ease their situation even on the Continent by calling themselves man and wife. They appear to have done this, although it was not until they were back in England that George Eliot began to insist that she be addressed as "Mrs. Lewes" by those who had occasion to write personal letters to her. For whatever reason, Helps's no doubt deliberate stopover in Weimar meant much to her, and she commemorated it in her Journal by writing that she would always associate him with Ettersburg. Temporarily free of all but happy reminders of England, at the end of an idyllic August she could write to Chapman (for whom she was doing an article on Mme de Sablé): "I am happier every day and find my domesticity more and more delightful and beneficial to me. Affection, respect, and intellectual sympathy deepen, and for the first time in my life I can say to the moments 'Verweilen sie, sie sind so schön.' "

It was of course fitting that she should quote from *Faust*; in Weimar, her life with Lewes was inevitably Goethe-oriented. She was assuredly interested but, one suspects, not wholly absorbed. There is little to suggest—as there most certainly is in the case of Spinoza— that Goethe appealed to her especially before she met Lewes. As a matter of fact, one of her longest comments on Goethe in her record of this time abroad concerns his "wonderful observations on Spinoza. Particularly struck with the beautiful modesty of the passage in which he says he cannot presume to say that he thoroughly understands Spinoza." Stripped of Goethe associations, Weimar itself was but a provincial small town such as she had known all too well in England. "One's first feeling," she was to confess in "Three Months in Weimar," "was—how could Goethe live here in this dull, lifeless village?" In the essay, this initial impression is quickly dispelled, although she maintains that it is "worth recording, because it is true as a sort of back view." After over a month of daily re-creating Goethe's Weimar life, she wrote Bessie Parkes on 10 September:

> My life here is full of quiet happiness—a little island of repose between the fortnight's journeying which was full of more exciting pleasure, and the stay at Dresden and Berlin to which I am looking forward. Liszt is here, as you know, and has been particularly friendly. He is a glorious creature in every way—a bright genius. . . . Soon, I hope we shall be having some of Wagner's operas performed under his (Liszt's) superintendance and perhaps that will tempt us to linger here; otherwise I think we shall leave Weimar at the end of this month.

When the theater opened in the middle of September, she and Lewes went to see *Ernani* conducted by Liszt, who looked splendid as the stage lamps threw into dark relief the "grand outline of his face and floating hair." As Wagner would not be produced until a month or so later, they lingered on. But when on 22 October they finally saw *Lohengrin*, they felt unrewarded for having postponed leaving Weimar for the more exciting Berlin. Lewes could not sit out more than two acts of the opera, and George Eliot, also wearied, presumably left with him. Both were to wrestle valiantly with Wagner in an attempt to reconcile their own concept of great music and great drama with his, and—aside from the timeless problem of what constitutes great music and great drama—they had well-considered reasons for their criticism. But what they could not acknowledge in their public writings on the subject was that they had first heard Wagner's powerful and to them discordant music as an echo of their own disturbed emotional state induced by recent news from London.

B Y OCTOBER, MALICIOUS GOSSIP ABOUT THEM HAD REACHED A peak in London, although they were—so they thought—safely removed from it. And from a large part of it, they were. For instance, they probably never learned that the sculptor Thomas Woolner (himself unaware that he was addressing one of Lewes's best friends of earlier days) wrote to William Bell Scott:

> By the way—have you heard of . . . two blackguard literary fellows, Lewes and Thornton Hunt? They seem to have used wives on the ancient Briton practice of having them in common: now blackguard Lewes has bolted with a —— and is living in Germany with her. I believe it dangerous to write facts of anyone nowadays so I will not further lift the mantle and display the filthy contaminations of these hideous satyrs and smirking moralists—these workers in the Agepemone—these Mormonities in another name—stink pots of humanity.

Whether converted by Scott or by George Eliot's growing prestige, Woolner later came to be on friendly terms with the Leweses: he visited at the Priory, explained "certain technical excellencies of the statues" as he guided them through the sculpture room at the Louvre, and was identified by the newspapers as one of the "distinguished men" among the mourners at George Eliot's burial in Highgate Cemetery.

But even in their "island of repose" there was no escaping the mail from people intent upon pursuing them. On 11 October, George Eliot noted in her Journal: "A painful letter from London caused us both a bad night." Apparently the letter was from Carlyle, for it was to him (and also to Helps—but why should that have been necessary after having seen Helps so recently in person?) that Lewes wrote the next day "explaining his position."

Judging from the subsequent correspondence, one can assume that Lewes was answering at least two pointed accusations leveled against George Eliot: that she had willfully taken Lewes away from his wife and family; and that she had written some kind of insulting letter to Harriet Martineau. Lewes's answering letter no longer exists, but the envelope in which it was sent, now at Princeton, bears Carlyle's notation: "G. H. Lewes and 'Strong minded Woman.'" In any case, Carlyle responded promptly with what George Eliot described as "a letter of noble sympathy." Lewes was so overjoyed that he was moved to write a second letter to Carlyle:

> I sat at your feet when my mind was first awakening; I have honoured and loved you ever since both as teacher and friend, and *now* to find that you judge me rightly, and are not estranged by what has estranged so many from me, gives me strength to bear what yet must be borne!
>
> So much in gratitude. Now for justice: On my *word of honor* there is no foundation for the scandal as it runs. My separation was in nowise caused by the lady named, nor by any other lady.

Well aware that Carlyle had once held great affection for Harriet Martineau, Lewes emphatically pronounced the alleged letter to her to be "a pure, or impure, fabrication—the letter, the purport, the language, all fiction." But Carlyle was not satisfied with this letter and added a half-sarcastic note at the end of it:

> Alas, alas!—I had (at his request) approved unequivocally of parting *such a marriage*; and advised to contradict, if he could, on his word of honour, the bad rumours circulating about a certain "strong minded woman" and him. He assures me, on his word of honour, the strong minded did not *write* etc.: as well assure me her stockings are both of one colour; that is a very insignificant point!—No answer to this second letter.

It appears from this that Carlyle's suspicious ire, perhaps tinted with some jealousy, was aimed at George Eliot and that, short of declaring that he had discovered her to be the scheming female Carlyle thought her, Lewes could have said nothing which would have placated him. As Carlyle admits in his addendum to Lewes's letter that he himself had advised "parting" the marriage with Agnes, it could hardly have been concern over Agnes which aroused his indignation. Possibly he was responding to the moral problem in general. More likely, his intense feeling stemmed from his proprietary interest in Goethe, to which he had some right: he had been ahead of his countrymen in his knowledge and appreciation of the German poet-philosopher as much as Coleridge and Hallam had been in their recognition of Spinoza. When he delivered his lectures on "Heroes and Hero Worship" in 1832—the year of Goethe's death—Carlyle had made it almost insultingly clear that had his audience been capable of knowing whom he was talking about, he would have chosen Goethe, rather than Burns, to illumine the Hero as Poet. It is probable that Lewes's own early introduction to Goethe came through Carlyle, who may have looked upon the projected biography as the fruition of an ardent disciple of Carlyle himself as well as Goethe. If Lewes had gone off to Germany alone, even though broken in health and spirit, Carlyle would have wished him well, for he was not even potentially envious of what Lewes might do with Goethe. But he was painfully sensitive to the fact that there was with Lewes a woman of large mind (even the most malicious rumor did not deny her mental capacity) and with a fine command of German who would work closely with Lewes as he went onward into more and more sanctified Goethe grounds. She was an interloper of a far worse kind than the ones who broke up physical families, and against the enormity of her existence Lewes himself, Agnes, and her children were but straws in the wind.

And so, in a strange way, was Harriet Martineau. As his note makes clear, Carlyle thought it a matter of insignificance whether or not George Eliot had written the letter of which she had been accused. Earlier—in the thirties—he would have been highly incensed over even the slightest suggestion of an insult meant for Harriet. But his fondness for her had been cooled by her growing radicalism, as well as personal eccentricity, and then her leap into the public arena as a strident atheist with the publication in 1851 of *Letters on the Laws of Man's Nature and Development* (which gave rise to Douglas Jerrold's witticism: "There is no God, and Harriet is his prophet"). Because of her notoriety and Carlyle's more solid fame, he was asked sometime in the fifties to give an estimate of Harriet as a person, to which he responded enigmatically: " 'Miss Martineau had been extremely kind to me'; then he paused and continued slowly: 'Well, she is the sort of woman that would have made a good matron in an hospital.' "

Yet it was in the middle of the same decade that Carlyle was willing to use Harriet's name as a means of intruding into Lewes's temporary refuge—as he sought to piece together the fragments of his own life as well as Goethe's—and to force him into open defensiveness. This is not to suggest that Harriet had not gone to Carlyle with a letter—or some kind of "message"—which purported to be from George Eliot. Carlyle would not have fabricated its existence or at least Harriet's word that it, or something comparable, did exist. But at this time Harriet was not always capable of distinguishing between delusion and reality.

Harriet Martineau was often a noble and brilliant woman who at times showed pathological strains in both her actions and attitudes. Certainly there was a pathological element in her conduct toward George Eliot. The most intimate part of the relationship appears to have started in October two years earlier when, at Harriet's urgent invitation, George Eliot visited her at the Knoll, Ambleside, as she was returning from a trip to Edinburgh. At this time Harriet was more than cordial, as George Eliot reported in writing to the Brays: "Miss M. is charming in her own home—quite handsome from her animation and intelligence. She came behind me, put her hands round me and kissed me in the prettiest way this evening, telling me she was so glad she had got me here." Soon after this promising beginning, the friendship between these two outstanding Victorian women came to an abortive end, largely, one presumes, because of George Eliot's increasingly intimate association with Lewes. Lewes had not been complimentary to Harriet in the *Leader* and had rivaled her in bringing Comte to English readers in 1853. One suspects, however, that it was George Eliot's going off with Lewes which turned Harriet decisively against both of them, just as her friendship with Elizabeth

Barrett did not survive the latter's elopement with Robert Browning. Rightly or wrongly she felt betrayed, not by a personal friend, but by Womanhood. When her dear friend Charlotte Brontë wrote *Villette*, she felt it marred by the author's

> incessant . . . tendency to describe the need of being loved. . . . It is not thus in real life. There are substantial, heartfelt interests for women of all ages, and under ordinary circumstances, quite apart from love: there is an absence of introspection, an unconsciousness, a repose in women's lives—unless under peculiarly unfortunate circumstances—of which we find no admission in this book; and to the absence of it, may be attributed some of the criticism which the book will meet from readers who are not prudes, but whose reason and taste will reject the assumption that events and characters are to be regarded through the medium of one passion only.

On learning when she went to London in the summer of 1854 that George Eliot and Lewes had gone off together to the Continent, Harriet became an avowed enemy of both of them, although not so vocal a one as Eliza Linton. She recognized the signs of literary genius in *Adam Bede* and like Mrs. Gaskell fervently hoped it was not written by Miss Evans as rumor had it. Even when the rumor was confirmed, she praised the novel although it hurt her to do so. *Middlemarch*, however, moved her so profoundly that as she read it, her disgust over the personal life of the author was temporarily obliterated. It was revived when she heard news which forcibly reminded her of the open liaison and which evoked in her, along with many other Victorians, that strange mixture of indignation and jealousy. "Almost the only deliberately nasty thing I have found in a Martineau letter," states one of her most astute biographers, "was about George Eliot: 'Do you know that Lewes is likely to die? . . . What will she do? Take a successor, I shd expect.'"

In fact, Harriet died shortly before Lewes. She had expected to die twenty years earlier, when with a heart condition which had been pronounced fatal she took to her bed and wrote her message to posterity in the form of an autobiography in which fact and fantasy are blended together much as she lived them simultaneously in real life. By then—1856—George Eliot was sufficiently removed from Harriet to see (perhaps with more clarity than anyone else in the century was to do) how the pathological elements in her nature threatened to outweigh in people's minds the positive nature of her contribution. And, with reason, she was concerned about the memoir that Harriet was preparing. "I feel for her terrible bodily suffering"—she wrote Sara Hennell, who had informed her of Harriet's "incurable disease" —"and think of her with deep respect and admiration. Whatever may have been her mistakes and weaknesses, the great and good things she has done far outweigh them, and I should be grieved if anything in her memoir should cast a momentary shadow over the agreeable image of her that the world will ultimately keep in its memory." With the same concern in mind, she wrote John Chapman on 20 July 1856: "I am going to make rather an odd request. When Harriet Martineau dies—if I outlive her—and her memoirs are published, I should like to write an article upon her. I need hardly say that mine would be an admiring appreciation of her."

But when Harriet did not die as predicted, George Eliot had to struggle a bit to keep her perspective, especially when in 1859 Sara let it be known that she had served as an intermediary in a correspondence between Harriet and Mrs. Gaskell concerning the authorship of *Adam Bede*: "Don't, please," she wrote Sara,

> tell me more *at any time*, of what Miss Martineau or any one else has said or done about me. . . . As to Miss Martineau, I respect her so much as an authoress, and have so pleasant a recollection of her as a hostess for three days, that I wish that distant impression from herself and her writing to be disturbed as little as possible by more personal details.

Seventeen more years elapsed before Harriet's death, and George Eliot lost her sense of urgency about writing an essay to correct what she had correctly surmised would be the tenor of Harriet's own memoirs. She and Lewes read the *Autobiography,* published posthumously in 1877, which fulfilled her early fear that in giving an uninhibited account of herself Harriet would do more harm than good to her memory, and strengthened George Eliot's resolve to leave behind no autobiography of her own. As she wrote John Blackwood, she found Harriet's version of her childhood and youth "pathetic and interesting." But, she continues, when Harriet "has to tell about her writings and what others said and did concerning them, the impression on me was one of shuddering vexation with myself that I had ever said a word to anybody about either compliments or injuries in relation to my own doings. But assuredly I shall not write such things down to be published after my death."

Two months afterward she wrote Sara, who, apparently unable to avoid a touchy subject, had asked if she had read Maria Weston Chapman's highly eulogistic *Memorials,* which had appeared with the *Autobiography*. George Eliot said that she had not read the book and did not intend to but, thus prodded, she had further words to say about the *Autobiography*:

> . . . I confess, that the more I think of the book and all connected with it, the more it deepens my repugnance—or rather creates a

new repugnance in me—to autobiography, unless it can be so written as to involve neither self-glorification nor impeachment of others. I like that "He, being dead, yet speaketh," should have quite another meaning than that.

And then George Eliot turns to a matter which is relatively unimportant in the *Autobiography* as a whole but obviously loomed large in her own mind, and that was Harriet's involved relationship with her brother James, who had collaborated in a contemptuous review of her *Letters on the Laws.* George Eliot admits that he had been "deplorably in the wrong" in doing this, but that had been a public matter, whereas

> What his sister thought of his motives was no public concern. [three words deleted] You must be quite right in your conclusion that she was the causer of her imputation being made public, for the statement that he was from the very beginning of her success continually moved by jealousy and envy towards her must have come readily to her lips, since she made it to a person so far from intimate with her as I was.

George Eliot was no doubt thinking back to 1852, when as a guest of Harriet's she had received confidences from her concerning James, which she might have honored had Harriet permitted the promised friendship to develop. George Eliot herself for years had lived tight-lipped with her most personal and often hostile memories of and feelings about Isaac. Admittedly she had let a few of them slip out to the Brays and (no doubt) eventually to Lewes, but she would never have entrusted them to what amounted to an overnight guest. George Eliot had no personal reason to be incensed by the *Autobiography,* for it is severely and, one suspects, deliberately silent about her. But it annoyed her far more than Harriet in life had been able to do, for it put into fixed and lasting form Harriet's distorted views of her relations with others. It is pardonable, George Eliot said to Sara, to write a cruel letter in a rage. "But I have no pity to spare for the rancour that corrects its proofs and revises and lays it by, chuckling with the sense of its future publicity."

That is why she found it easier to be tolerant of Harriet even during the unpleasant episode of 1854 than she did after the appearance of the *Autobiography.* She had no illusions about Harriet's readiness to hold and perpetuate flagrantly biased opinions that could harm reputations. Even when she was a victim of this, she accepted it as a personality trait which, although unfortunate, did not necessarily detract from the considerable good Harriet effected through her work. In a letter to Chapman from Weimar dated 30 October 1854, George Eliot was more outspoken than usual in writing about people:

I hope you have contradicted the story of my writing to Miss Martineau. I cannot understand how it originated except in some communication of yours to Miss M. which you intended to be serviceable to me. You must have made the communication in a moment of hallucination as to Miss M's character. Amongst her good qualities we certainly cannot reckon zeal for other people's reputation. She is sure to caricature any information for the amusement of the next person to whom she turns her ear-trumpet.

She was probably correct in suspecting that Chapman had somehow been involved in whatever it was that had sent Harriet off into her private realm of imagined insults. She wrote him only four days after recording the receipt of the "painful letter from London":

We have been told of a silly story about a "message" sent by me "in a letter to Miss Martineau" which letter has been shown at the Reform Club. It is hardly necessary to tell you that I have had no communication with Miss Martineau, and that if I had, she is one of the last persons to whom I should speak as to a confidante. The phrase "run away" as applied to me is simply amusing—I wonder what I had to run away from. But as applied to Mr. Lewes it is more serious, and I have thought it right to explain to you how utterly false it is. You are in possession of the broad facts of the case, but there are very many particulars which you do *not* know and which are perhaps necessary to set his character and conduct in their true light. Such particulars cannot be given in a letter.

This letter to Chapman brings us as close as is now possible to the original source of trouble which reminded the Leweses that not even the Channel could secure them against the censure of London. Lewes, unaware that Carlyle was not satisfied by his second letter, did not write him again. Yet George Eliot was moved to write seriously on 23 October to Charles Bray to assure him that the "report prevalent in London that Mr. Lewes has 'run away' from his wife and family" is false and that "his conduct as a husband has been not only irreproachable, but generous and self-sacrificing to a degree far beyond any standard fixed by the world." And concerning herself:

Of course many silly myths are already afloat about me, in addition to the truth, which of itself would be thought matter for scandal. I am quite unconcerned about them except as they may cause pain to my real friends. If you hear of anything that I have said, done, or written in relation to Mr. Lewes beyond the simple fact that I am attached to him and that I am living with him, do me the justice to believe that it is false.

The last sentence would of course be hilarious in any Victorian context other than what George Eliot could provide. Even in her instance, it is a measure of her concern that she should be exonerated from at least the charge that she had lured Lewes away from his family. As this is the same letter in which she told Bray that new circumstances in England had led Lewes "to determine upon a separation from Mrs. Lewes," one can assume it was the fresh outburst of London gossip, this time viciously pointed at George Eliot, that made Lewes realize the importance of decisiveness in sundering the relationship with Agnes, even though the separation could not be legal. Gordon Haight speculates that since George Eliot says in this letter she herself was not concerned in the new circumstances, the cause for Lewes's sudden firmness must have been some direct word from Agnes, such as a miscarriage as a result of pregnancy by Hunt. But as Agnes had been giving birth to children by Hunt with almost monotonous regularity, it is difficult to see why such news would have altered Lewes's perspective on his home life. As for George Eliot's dismissing the circumstance as having nothing to do with her, that might have been said in the same spirit which moved her to say to Chapman, after chiding him for having blundered in communicating with Harriet Martineau: "*Au reste,* the thing is done and it is useless to dwell on it." The gossip had occurred, but she was not in any way responsible for it.

She was beginning to feel relatively sure of herself because she had become increasingly certain of Lewes's integrity toward both herself and his family. "I have been long enough with Mr. Lewes," she had written Bray in the 23 October letter, "to judge of his character on adequate grounds, and there is therefore no absurdity in offering my opinion as evidence that he is worthy of high respect." It is quite possible that she and Lewes had agreed privately to live together as man and wife away from London long enough to give themselves a chance to decide if they could live together irrevocably.

This kind of private agreement could explain why George Eliot did not confide in either Cara or Sara when she made her plan to go abroad with Lewes, although she had told Charles Bray, as well as the Chapmans, of her plans. On the other hand, she needed no special reason for withholding her confidences from Cara and Sara, for she had long turned to men, rather than women, with her secrets (and perhaps her somewhat mystifying encounters with complicated women such as Eliza Lynn and Harriet Martineau had given her a reasonable basis for what might have been an instinctive distrust of women). In this letter to Bray she somewhat belatedly acknowledged being "ignorant how far Cara and Sara may be acquainted with the state of things, and how they may feel towards me." This was excuse enough for Sara to write back what must have been an explosive letter asking why George Eliot had not told her and Cara about her intention to live with Lewes. George Eliot responded, but in a way which Sara would not have been happy to read:

> The reason why I wrote to Mr. Bray and not to you and Cara is simply this. Before I left England, I communicated by Mr. Lewes's desire, certain facts in strict confidence to Mr. Bray and Mr. Chapman and I did so for special reasons which would not apply to any female friend. After your kind letters came to me, we heard much painful news from London as to reports which were partly a perversion of the truth, partly pure falsehood. . . . There is now no longer any secrecy to be preserved about Mr. Lewes's affairs or mine, and whatever I have written to Mr. Bray, I have written to you. I am under no foolish hallucinations about either the present or the future and am standing on no stilts of any kind.

The letter closes with a statement of the fear already justified by experience—that written attempts to untangle misunderstandings and soothe hurt feelings were more likely than not to add to the confusion. She also reiterates her love for Sara and Cara, even while making it decisively clear that this now comes second in her life: " . . . I love Cara and you with unchanged and unchangeable affection and while I retain your friendship I retain the best that life has given me next to that which is the deepest and gravest joy in all human experience." Accepting this explanation, Sara could not help adding: "—but I have a strange sort of feeling that I am writing to some one in a book, and not to the Marian that we have known and loved so many years. Do not mistake me, I mean nothing unkind." Sara was destined to be one of the first readers of the George Eliot novels who would know with certainty that the truth of the whole life and thought of their creator was indeed stranger than the fiction which comprised her books.

Sara's answer is dated 15 November, a full month after that first painful letter from London had arrived, so that the island of repose had been considerably disrupted by a continuous spate of angry correspondence. It did finally diminish, and although unpleasant, had realistically prepared George Eliot and Lewes for what would confront them when they returned to England. Perhaps too it brought them closer together, for in reading and discussing these letters, they could hardly have left untouched any foreseeable aspect of their future life.

THROUGHOUT THE ORDEAL, GEORGE ELIOT AND LEWES WERE secure in their own companionship and in their work. Although she might not of her own choosing have devoted so much time to Goethe,

Lewes's interest in him was contagious because empathetic. Goethe's versatility and manifold avocations resembled his own, and he was able to interpret some of Goethe's emotional experiences against his. This is most apparent in his discussion of Goethe's much-censured withdrawal from the relationship with Frederika. Although Lewes is here describing a broken engagement, not a marriage, much of his explanation applies to himself and Agnes:

> We may regret that [Goethe] did not feel the serious affection which would have claimed [Frederika] as a wife; we may upbraid him for the thoughtlessness with which he encouraged the senti-mental relation; but he was perfectly right to draw back from an engagement which he felt his love was not strong enough prop-erly to fulfil. It seems to me that he acted a more moral part in relinquishing her, than if he had swamped this lesser in a greater wrong, and escaped one breach of faith by a still greater breach of faith—a reluctant, because unloving marriage. The thoughtlessness of youth, and the headlong impetus of passion, frequently throw people into rash engagements; and in these cases the *formal* morality of the world, more careful of externals than of truth, declares it to be nobler for such rash engagements to be kept . . . than that a man's honour should be stained by a withdrawal. The letter thus takes precedence of the spirit. To satisfy this prejudice a life is sacrificed. . . . I am not forgetting the necessity of being stringent against the common thoughtlessness of youth in forming such relations . . . but I say that . . . the pain which a separation may bring had better be endured, than evaded by an unholy mar-riage, which cannot come to good.
>
> Frederika herself must have felt so too, for never did a word of blame escape her; and we shall see how affectionately she welcomed him, when they met after the lapse of years.

One can only surmise about such passages, of course, but there is much in them and others throughout the finished work which suggests that the renewal of life Lewes felt with George Eliot had inspired the confident intimacy with which he now approached Goethe. George Eliot's long held wish that she be important to a man's signifi-cant work was being fulfilled. Her unseen presence was being felt in the pages of the *Goethe*, and she had become the unidentified "accomplished German translator" referred to in a footnote. Early in the work, Lewes promises to translate from the German "every word cited" for the benefit of those readers "whose want of leisure or inclination has prevented their acquiring the language." It was with George Eliot's considerable help that he stayed relatively faithful to this promise. In fact, Lewes's still important biography of Goethe might be considered, as Gordon Haight remarks, "a composite pro-duction with George Eliot as silent collaborator."

Although Lewes's task at hand was to re-create eighteenth-century Weimar as Goethe had known it, the shared impressions of contemporary Weimar were bound to enter into his writing as well as hers. There are striking similarities between her essay "Three Months in Weimar" and his description of the little town in the *Goethe*. Both pieces are redolent with memories of their many walks in the lovely park, which was largely Goethe's own creation. It "would be remarkably beautiful even among English parks," she wrote, "and it has one advantage over all these, namely, that it is without a fence. It runs up to the houses, and far out into the corn fields and meadows, as if it had a 'sweet will' of its own. . . ." "Southwards from the palace [the park] begins," he wrote, "with no obstacle of wall or iron gate. . . . In the dew of morning, and in the silence of moonlight, we may wander undisturbed as if in our own grounds. The land stretches for miles away without barrier; park and yellow cornlands forming one friendly expanse."

Still more remarkable and involved examples of sharing and borrowing are found in "Liszt, Wagner, and Weimar," which George Eliot wrote as a companion piece to "Three Months in Weimar." Their association with Liszt had given them an intimate introduction to Wagnerian opera, and although they had been more bored than inspired by this "music of the future" (as it was then called, usually in a derogatory sense), they were impressed by Liszt's great faith in it, as well as by the innovating dramatic power which Wagner had brought to opera. Her essay opens with a consideration of Liszt himself: Would his ultimate reputation be that of a great instrumentalist and conductor, or would posterity judge him as a composer? She then contrasts the quickly extinguished fame of the performing artist— which, she admits, somewhat justifies "the apparently excessive tribute of adoration paid to a great actor, a great singer, or a great instrumentalist"—with the more lasting fame of "the genius who can leave permanent creations behind him," even though in his own lifetime "his Paradise Lost will fetch only five pounds, and his symphony is received with contemptuous laughter. . . ."

Lewes had drawn a very similar distinction in his 1851 essay on Macready:

> It is thought a hardship that great actors in quitting the stage can leave no monument more solid than a name. The painter leaves behind him pictures to attest his power; the author leaves behind him books; the actor leaves only a tradition. . . . Succeeding generations may be told of his genius; none can test it.
>
> All this I take to be a most misplaced sorrow. With the best wishes in the world I cannot bring myself to place the actor on a level with the painter or the author . . . while, at the same time,

I am forced to remember that, with inferior abilities, he secures far greater reward, both of pudding and praise.

Turning to Wagner, George Eliot is critical, particularly of what seems to her to be his "exclusion of melody." But she concedes:

> As to melody—who knows? It is just possible that melody, as we conceive it, is only a transitory phase of music, and that the musicians of the future may read the airs of Mozart and Beethoven and Rossini as scholars read the *Stabreim* and assonance of early poetry. We are but in "the morning of the times". . . .

Thus she suspends final judgment, making it clear that her own failure to respond positively was "only accidentally in agreement with the judgment of anti-Wagner critics, who are certainly in the majority at present." The history of music amply illustrates that these critics might well be proved ridiculous in the future: "A man of high standing, both as a composer and executant, told a friend of mine, that when a symphony of Beethoven's was first played at the Philharmonic, there was a general titter among the musicians in the orchestra, of whom he was one, at the idea of sitting seriously to execute such music!" Years later, in 1867, Lewes was to express similar forbearance in the brief discussion of Wagner with which he concludes his essay "The Drama in Germany":

> I may confess that the music rarely charms me, and that, as far as my ear in its present state of musical education determines what is exquisite for it, the Wagner music wants both form and melody. But then a little reflection suffices to remind one how such *negative* judgments, even from far more competent critics, are liable to complete reversal. It is not many years since Beethoven was laughed at. . . .

By then, as Lewes mentions in his essay, the number of people enthusiastic about Wagner was steadily increasing and of course was to go on doing so. This is perhaps why when revising a selection of her essays for posthumous appearance, George Eliot made one essay out of "Three Months in Weimar" and "Liszt, Wagner, and Weimar," using the title and content of the former (with a few slight changes and omissions), but deleting from the latter all the Liszt-Wagner material and retaining only the seven paragraphs which had concluded the original. In these she resumes describing Weimar—as, for example:

> Among the quieter every-day pleasures of the Weimarians, perhaps the most delightful is a stroll on a bright afternoon or evening to Belvedere, one of the Duke's summer residences, about two miles from Weimar. A glorious avenue of chestnut trees leads all the way from the town to the entrance of the grounds, which are open to

all the world as much as to the Duke himself. . . . A sort of pavilion stands on a spot commanding a lovely view of Weimar and its valley, and here the Weimarians constantly come on summer and autumn evenings to smoke a cigar, or drink a cup of coffee.

This is rendered by Lewes:

If we pass into [the park] from the palace gates, a winding path to the right conducts us into the Belvedere Allee,—a magnificent avenue of chestnut trees, two miles long, stretching from the new street to the summer palace of Belvedere. This affords a shaded promenade along the park, in summer grateful for its coolness, in autumn looking like an avenue of golden trees. It terminates in the gardens of the Belvedere, which has its park also beautifully disposed. Here the Weimarians resort, to enjoy the fresh air after their fashion, namely, with accompaniments of bad beer, questionable coffee, and detestable tobacco.

George Eliot concludes the original essay (and she kept it also as an ending to the revised "Three Months in Weimar") with the short lyric Goethe had written on the wall of his little wooden house at Ilmenau—"perhaps the finest expression yet given to the sense of resignation inspired by the sublime calm of Nature":

> Ueber allen Gipfeln
> Ist Ruh,
> In allen Wipfeln
> Spürest du
> Kaum einen Hauch;
> Die Vögelein schweigen im Walde.
> Warte nur, balde
> Ruhest du auch.*

Both she and Lewes had been profoundly moved by these lines. They added their own names to the wall, she copied the poem down in her Journal, and he quoted it twice in the *Goethe*; in none of these instances does either he or she intrude with a translation, except for the last two lines rendered by Lewes as he imagined Goethe repeating them to himself—"Yes, wait but a little, thou too soon wilt be at rest."

---

* My own literal translation of Goethe's poem:

> Over the mountain tops
> Is quiet,
> In all the treetops
> You perceive
> Scarcely a trace of breeze;
> The little birds are silent in the woods.
> Wait only, soon
> You will rest too.

GEORGE ELIOT'S ISLAND METAPHOR, USED ONLY A FEW months earlier to connote the inevitable isolation of the single self, had been converted (as the 10 September letter to Bessie Parkes indicates) to signify a peaceful lull for two selves, united by choice and work against the attacking forces which lay in wait outside the island. As these two selves thought and discussed, there was such a fine intermingling of their ideas that by now it is impossible—and unimportant —to say which expressed or wrote down each thought first. Because George Eliot has become known as the greater writer, it is tempting to pronounce her the initiator, as Mathilde Blind suggests when she calls attention to the undeniable similarities in the "views concerning fundamental laws of Art" found in George Eliot's 1856 essay "Silly Novels by Lady Novelists" and Lewes's 1858 essay "Realism in Art: Recent German Fiction." Either might have served as a manifesto of the kind of realism—as opposed not so much to idealism as to what Lewes calls "Falsism"—which was to make its first well-planned appearance in *Adam Bede*, being written while Lewes composed his essay for the *Westminster*. In this instance at least the sequence is clear, so that perhaps Mathilde Blind was intuitively correct in her statement: "It seems probable that Lewes, with his flexible adaptiveness, had come under the influence of George Eliot's powerful intellect, and that many of the views he expresses here at the same time render George Eliot's, as they frequently appear, identical with hers."

Although this may have become true by 1858, it seems quite clear that in 1854—at least while they were abroad—George Eliot looked upon Lewes as the greater master in both writing and criticism. This was a sincere and also an essential stance on her part. It justified her being with him, and it fulfilled her old need of being a helpmate to a man whose work she could respect. A short while back she had not particularly admired his periodical writings; in July of 1852, two years—almost to the day—before she was to sail away from England with him, she had advised Chapman to sound Lewes out concerning his willingness to produce an article for the *Westminster* on Lamarck or something similar, adding: "Defective as his articles are, they are the best we can get *of the kind*." (Lewes did come up with an article, not on Lamarck but on "Goethe as a Man of Science," of which he was to make substantial use in the chapter "The Poet as a Man of Science" in the *Goethe*.)

But that high-handed attitude toward his work had been largely dictated by Lewes's reputation as a journalist who would write almost anything to accommodate a paying editor. Coming to know him better, she found cause to revise her opinion of his writing as she did of his character, although probably her changed estimate of the man influenced her judgment of his work. Starting in Weimar (if not in London during their earliest intimacy), Lewes read her articles before she sent them out for publication, and she submitted to his dicta with a docility which is surprising when one remembers her haughty independence in dealing with Chapman. She was proud of Lewes's active interest in her work, and no doubt she took some malicious pleasure in writing Chapman the reason for the delay in sending him her essay on Mme de Sablé. She thought she could "make it more satisfactory by rendering the introductory part fuller. . . . I have just read the part to which I refer to Mr. Lewes, and he thinks the ideas are crowded and would impress the reader if they were diluted a little. . . ." Perhaps Chapman resented Lewes's participation in work that she was doing for him; to her disappointment, he sent her no word of approval or disapproval of the essay even after it appeared in print. Or was it that Chapman was silenced by surprise (and readers today are still surprised) over her handling of what he had supposed would be a unified review of three French books on French women, the featured one being Victor Cousin's *Madame de Sablé*?

Her essay, entitled "Woman in France," is indeed a review, but one in the grand old manner in which a theme dwarfs the books presumably under scrutiny. She asserts with an emphasis which may have startled masculine-oriented English readers that "in France alone the mind of woman has passed like an electric current through the language, making crisp and definite what is elsewhere heavy and blurred; in France alone, if the writings of women were swept away, a serious gap would be made in the national history." Several reasons are given for the supremacy of French women writers; the major one stems from the simple fact that there *is* sex in literature, and French women have had the courage to write like women, "without any intention to prove that women could write as well as men, without affecting manly views or suppressing womanly ones." Their English counterparts have either lacked this courage, or perhaps (as the conclusion of the essay suggests) have not been given a fair opportunity to identify themselves as women:

> With a few remarkable exceptions, our own feminine literature is made up of books which could have been better written by men; books which have the same relation to literature in general, as academic prize poems have to poetry: when not a feeble imitation, they are usually an absurd exaggeration of the masculine style, like the swaggering gait of a bad actress in male attire.

Perhaps it was with half-hearted conviction that George Eliot suggests that the primary reason for the "more abundant manifestation" of feminine intellect in France

> lies in the physiological characteristics of the Gallic race: the small brain and vivacious temperament which permit the fragile system of woman to sustain the superlative activity requisite for intellectual creativeness; while, on the other hand, the larger brain and slower temperament of the English and Germans are, in the womanly organization, generally dreamy and passive. The type of humanity in the latter may be grander, but it requires a larger sum of conditions to produce a perfect specimen.

Lewes may have had a hand in this "physiological" idea, although the last clause of the last sentence is peculiarly applicable to George Eliot herself, possibly more so than she was wholly aware when writing it.

She proceeds in her argument with more vigor and daring:

> A secondary cause was probably the laxity of opinion and practice with regard to the marriage-tie. Heaven forbid that we should enter on a defence of French morals, most of all in relation to marriage! But it is undeniable, that unions formed in the maturity of thought and feeling, and grounded only on inherent fitness and mutual attraction, tended to bring women into more intelligent sympathy with men. . . . The quiescence and security of the conjugal relation, are doubtless favourable to the manifestation of the highest qualities by persons who have already attained a high standard of culture, but rarely foster a passion sufficient to rouse all the faculties to aid in winning or retaining its beloved object— to convert indolence into activity, indifference into ardent partisanship, dulness into perspicuity. Gallantry and intrigue are sorry enough things in themselves, but they certainly serve better to arouse the dormant faculties of woman than embroidery and domestic drudgery. . . .

These motifs are woven into a symphonic opening, after which come the intermediate movements that consider the specific books under review (or, rather, the women therein), and then the coda, a subdued and generalized restatement of the dominant theme:

> Women become superior in France by being admitted to a common fund of ideas, to common objects of interest with men: and this must ever be the essential condition at once of true womanly culture and of true social well-being. . . . Let the whole field of reality be laid open to woman as well as to man, and then that which is peculiar in her mental modification, instead of being, as it is now, a source of discord and repulsion between the sexes, will be found to be a necessary complement to the truth and beauty of

life. Then we shall have that marriage of minds which alone can
blend all the hues of thought and feeling in one lovely rainbow
of promise for the harvest of human happiness.

"Woman in France" is a stimulating essay, in part as a result of
the intriguing contradictions which are present because George Eliot
still contained within herself the same contradictions. At this early
stage of her life with Lewes she was feeling very womanly—and gratefully so. But there were within her still unresolved masculine demands
(they had plagued her for much of her life) which would need and
seek outlet, other than that provided by marriage, even of the most
unconventional kind. It is possible that Chapman, who, after all, knew
her quite well, recognized she was not wholly at one with her real
self in this essay. And he may too have remembered Lewes's July
1852 article for the *Westminster* (only six months after he had acquired the magazine) in which Lewes, writing about "The Lady
Novelists," had said: "Woman, by her greater affectionateness, her
greater range and depth of emotional experience, is well fitted to give
expression to the emotional facts of life, and demands a place in
literature corresponding with that she occupies in society." Chapman
could justifiably have wondered who had really written "Woman in
France"—the Marian Evans he had known at the end of her stay with
him, or the Marian Evans he had known when she first came to the
Strand, almost abject in her eagerness to prove that she was a woman
who desired above all else to help a noble man with his noble work.

IN BERLIN, HAVING EXHAUSTED GOETHE LORE AND WAGNERIAN
opera in Weimar and leaving there on 4 November, George Eliot
showed Lewes the introductory chapter to a novel she had long ago
planned. He was impressed enough with the concrete description to
think that she could write a novel, but—so she was to record later—
"he distrusted—indeed disbelieved in, my possession of any dramatic
power. Still, he began to think that I might as well try, some time,
what I could do in fiction. . . ." The "some time" was of unfortunate
significance, for it was also in Berlin that she undertook the translation of Spinoza's *Ethics*, despite the fact that she had earlier vowed
to be done with translating. No doubt she was spurred on by talk with
Lewes about Spinoza and his own abortive translation, as well as by
their ever-increasing need for funds because of Lewes's responsibility
to his family; and as Lewes had already committed himself to Bohn
to provide a translation, publication seemed a certainty. On 22

November, George Eliot wrote in the usual birthday letter to Sara that although there were "plenty of subjects suggested by new German books which would be fresh and instructive in an English Review," she could not afford to take the time out to write such articles. ". . . I cannot bring myself to run the risk of a refusal from an editor. . . . So I am working at what will ultimately yield something which is secured by agreement with Bohn." If a part of her rebelled against returning to translating, another part was looking forward to further collaboration with Lewes. For, as he was to announce in the published *Goethe*, he would be at her side to give editorial assistance (although it is doubtful that she needed this): "It may interest some readers to learn, that Spinoza will ere long appear in English, edited by the writer of these lines."

She was to finish the translation in England, to which they returned in March 1855, steeling themselves to confront what she called the "bigotry of exclusiveness." The transition was not an easy one. The first five weeks especially were difficult and must have revived tormenting doubts and fears, for she spent them alone in Dover while Lewes rediscussed financial arrangements with Agnes and then visited Arthur Helps at Vernon Hill. Alone again, she must have looked back upon the Continental sojourn as an unreal interlude. Also, she was perhaps forcibly reminded of her earlier March return to England from Switzerland five years ago, almost to the day, when she discovered that although she had numerous relatives, she had no real home of her own. She trusted Lewes, but the possessive jealousy which was admittedly inherent in her nature had not yet been quelled and it was not helped by her sensing (without need of direct words) that neither Chapman nor the Brays thought Lewes would remain constant.

What Chapman and the Brays could not have understood was that she was not an ordinary woman anxious over the faithfulness of her lover; she was also a child reawaiting the return of the mother-brother who had once abandoned her. Lewes had imperceptibly slipped into this role with her, the first side of it having begun in London early in their acquaintance when they gave no thought to the potential seriousness of their relationship; then his lighthearted companionship had revived in her the sense of fun which had been dormant ever since she lost Isaac as playfellow. Although their games were never to be childish, their ability to play took them without bitterness through their days of poverty and outside malice; and it survived into the affluent days and the solemnity of George Eliot's fame. This aspect of their life was of course a most private one, so that very little of it overflowed into the letters and journals. When an outsider was afforded a glimpse into it, he usually carried away an impression without insight or understanding—as when Lewes was overheard to call George Eliot "Madonna" and their Sunday receptions "religious services" because they were then living in a house called the Priory, a fact that amused them both. The public thought this a sign of insufferable adulation on Lewes's part, although there was one exception, Edith Simcox, who strove to equal, if not outdo Lewes's reverential attitude and so quite seriously began to refer to George Eliot as "the Madonna" and "Our Lady."

After their relationship had deepened into love and they were still in London, it was Lewes, ill and riddled by indecision, who needed the strong sympathy and help George Eliot willingly gave him. But when they were alone together on the Continent, she aroused his feeling of protectiveness, because he felt responsible for her difficult position, and also because he gradually discovered in her an unexpected need to be dependent and hence an intriguing paradox in her nature. She was the strong-minded woman Carlyle had rightfully judged her to be; but she was also a woman who required someone, not to dominate, but to look up to for guidance. In a practical way, she could do without such help; yet for her it was a necessary proof that there was someone who would proffer it to her with love. Not all men could have met this complex demand; in Lewes, however, it evoked a peculiar kind of tenderness usually designated as "feminine." To some extent Agnes may have called forth this trait in him, probably in the natural way a beautiful and very feminine woman calls upon manliness for protection as her rightful due. George Eliot's tacit demand, however, had the strange allure of that of a strong man who had suddenly shown a vulnerable side to his nature that needed shielding. Had George Eliot been an *obviously* masculine woman and Lewes an obviously feminine man, the attraction which flamed up between them would never have come into being.

What psychic intermingling did occur can be expressed in many different ways; Lewes put the beginning of it very well when he explored the effect upon Goethe of his rejection of Frederika. It will be remembered that Lewes had approved of this, but only, as he subsequently makes it clear, because Goethe's love had not been complete enough to warrant other than a wretched marriage:

> Had he loved her enough to share a life with her, his experience of women might have been less extensive, but it would assuredly have gained an element it wanted. It would have been deepened. He had experienced, and he could paint (no one better), the exquisite devotion of woman to man; but he had scarcely ever felt the peculiar tenderness of man for woman, when that tenderness takes the form of vigilant protecting fondness.

This "protecting fondness" was to grow in Lewes as his life with George Eliot went on. It was to be remarked upon, usually jestingly by observers. As Mathilde Blind expressed it: "Indeed, [Lewes] was more than a husband: he was, as an intimate friend once pithily remarked, a very mother to her."

Like many of their intellectual interests, the personal bond between them had been growing, unknown to either, in their past lives, so that it was more deeply rooted than even the closest of their friends could have realized. Although it is not clear why Lewes had to leave her alone in Dover for so long, he did come back to her—as he was always to do. But not because she was doing her best to make herself as feminine as possible: she had declared in print that women did best in literature when they remembered that they were women as they wrote, and on one lonely night in Dover, she had even taken up sewing. Fortunately, when Lewes returned, she had to make few minor adjustments to become again the woman he was beginning to know. She dropped her sewing, went on with the Spinoza translation (which indeed she had never stopped), and ceased to pretend that she wished to be known as a woman writing as a woman. Both George Eliot and Lewes may have realized that it was the masculine element in her complementing the feminine element in him which gave their union a more secure basis than if it had rested upon physical attraction alone.

After the Dover ordeal, Lewes found them lodgings in Bayswater. They stayed there only two weeks, moving on 2 May to East Sheen, Richmond, where there were a very few brave visitors (Rufa Hennell, Chapman, Bessie Parkes), who understandably were uncertain as to how to address her when writing to her, and at first she appeared hesitant to instruct them. After Bessie had come to see her, George Eliot sent her a hurried note the next day to say that if she wrote, she should "enclose the letter to G. H. Lewes, Esq.," and in directing Bray where to write, she added: "As to the rest of the address, I leave it to your judgment." But in March 1856 Bessie was told in no uncertain terms:

> Your address to me as *Miss Evans* was unfortunate, as I am not known under that name here. We find it indispensable to our comfort that I should bear Mr. Lewes's name while we occupy lodgings, and we are now with so excellent a woman that any cause of removal would be a misfortune. If you have occasion to write to me again, please to bear this in mind.

She and Lewes were by this time living at 8 Park Shot, Richmond, their first real home together, for they were to remain there until 1859. It was neither too far from nor too close to London, and Bessie was probably not that surprised to read in the same letter: "You will be surprized to hear that I have not been to town more than twice since last spring—once to call on Mr. Chapman, and once to call on the Molluscs in the Zool[ogical] Gardens. I have no other visits to pay and I shudder at shopping so there has been no motive for rushing into the smoke. Mr. Lewes goes to town once a week, and he does any errands for me."

It was here that the *Scenes of Clerical Life* and almost the whole of *Adam Bede* were to be written—something of a miracle, for in their small lodgings she and Lewes had to do their writing in the same room, and years later she told Cross "that the scratching of another pen used to affect her nerves to such an extent that it nearly drove her wild." When she wrote Bessie the March letter she was only a few months away from actually beginning "Amos Barton," although in frame of mind she was still years removed from fiction writing. Lewes had not ceased to urge her to try a story, and many of the old blocks to writing had been resolved. In assuming the title "Mrs. Lewes" and in accepting her life with Lewes as permanent, she had gained happiness, of course, but also a growing sense of security and self-identity. She need no longer feel, as she had written Bray when delaying her move from the Strand, that it was of little consequence where she was or what she did. Furthermore, she had what she had always psychologically demanded, a clear-cut duty, that of earning as much money as possible.

But it is also clear that she clung to the conviction that fiction writing was a mode of self-indulgence; her duty thus lay in essay writing and translating. Lewes would have disagreed, and it was probably with a thought to their potential income that he became more and more insistent she should begin a story at once. "I deferred it, however," she later admitted, "after my usual fashion, with work that does not present itself as an absolute duty." The old guilt feeling which had led her to denounce fiction in her Evangelical days was still active, although in subtler disguise. Not until an unexpected circumstance forced her to consider fiction as a source of necessary income would she be able to give herself up to writing it.

Meanwhile, Lewes had seen to it that she turn even her Journal writing to account. Shortly after their return to England, she wrote Bray:

If in the next or the subsequent number of Frazer [*sic*] you should see an article called "Three Months in Weimar" perhaps it will interest you to know a little about what we saw there. The article is merely a sketch which I wrote at the wrong end of my journal and is worth little. But when I read it to Mr. Lewes he was so pleased with it that he would have me offer it to Frazer, and as this was a mode of turning it into guineas I could have no objection.

By "the wrong end" of her Journal, she apparently meant the fact that she had written her recollections of Weimar in Berlin, not on the spot. She used this retrospective method in almost all of her most significant Journal entries, such as the "Berlin Recollections," "Ilfracombe Recollections," "How I Came to Write Fiction," and her occasional summary of a given year near its end or at the beginning of a new one. Her daily entries—at least, those which have thus far been published—are brief and factual. Apparently she was most at ease when looking back and recalling impressions, a factor which was to have considerable importance in her technique as a novelist.

She was self-conscious about the long Weimar essay's being almost wholly descriptive. She asked Bray, if he should see it, not to "say anything about it, for to people who do not enjoy description of scenery it will seem very tame and stupid, and I really think a taste for descriptive writing is the rarest of all tastes among ordinary people." The somewhat snobbish last clause suggests defensiveness; she was still smarting under Lewes's backhanded praise of the fragment of the novel she had shown him in Berlin, which he had thought good as concrete description but which had also led him to disbelieve in her ability to write narrative of dramatic power. His remarks were bound to have disturbed her deeply, not only because whatever he said about her writing was important to her but because she would have instinctively shared his disbelief without fully understanding why. Her fear of exhibitionism had long been one of the most stubborn of her inner resistances to writing fiction. It seemed safe enough to discuss books and ideas in anonymous articles, but psychologically, it was quite a different matter to present a directly dramatic scene in writing. Ironically, she herself was now living dramatically, for her unconventional union with Lewes'had made her life a public spectacle. That she could, with relative serenity, live this new life is a measure of her sincerity in adapting to it. She was not acting a part —she *was* Mrs. Lewes. However, she was not yet George Eliot.

The Weimar essays did appear in the June and July 1855 numbers of *Fraser's Magazine*. They had been shrewdly placed and timed by Lewes. From his long association with this periodical, he knew that it welcomed articles on German topics; and although then almost totally unknown in England as a composer, Wagner was guest conductor with the London Philharmonic from 12 March to 25 June of that year. It is probable that certain readers found the articles less "tame" than she had feared. "Three Months in Weimar" opens in the first-person singular, but quickly shifts into the plural and personal "we" (not the editorial one which appears in her other essays); surely some readers either knew or guessed at the identity of that "we," thus mildly anticipating the "Who-is-George Eliot?" guessing game which was soon to spread throughout literary England. Those of her readers in *Fraser's* who by means of gossip or otherwise knew she had been in Germany with Lewes would have no trouble in making the identification. Even without that knowledge, an astute reader who read both the essays and *The Life and Works of Goethe* (which appeared that year on 30 October and for which she wrote an announcement in the *Leader*) could not have missed making it.

This openness, as well as the naturalness with which she called Bray's attention to the Weimar essay, suggests that neither she nor Lewes was yet fully aware of the danger involved in having her writing identified. True, she had requested that Bray not speak of it, but the reason had nothing to do with concealing herself as the author. Realization was soon to come, however, and the first sign of it occurred with the appearance of her "Evangelical Teaching: Dr. Cumming" in the October 1855 issue of the *Westminster*. The new vigor in style of this essay clearly indicated that her writing ability was not suffering from the relative ostracism in which she was forced to live. Indeed, according to Cross (who heard it from Charles Lewes), it was this article which convinced Lewes that she had not merely talent but genius. Long familiar with her ideas on Evangelicalism, Charles Bray had little trouble in detecting her authorship and wrote to tell her so. "Since you have found out the 'Cumming,'" she responded,

> I write by to-day's post just to say, that it *is* mine, but also to beg that you will not mention it as such to any one likely to transmit the information to London, as we are keeping the authorship a secret. The article appears to have produced a strong impression, and that impression would be a little counteracted if the author were known to be a *woman*. [Six words deleted]

Despite her ingenious argument to the contrary in the Mme de Sablé essay, this was not a new stand for her. From the time when she had dreaded Strauss's discovery that his work was being translated by a transla*tress*, she had not altered her opinion that the effect of any writing was lessened when it was known to be a woman's. Her life now was even more complex than in the Strauss days: she was not only a woman writer, but that particular one who lived with George Henry Lewes.

This problem was to be ever present during the early years of her novel writing. Even before then, concern over it grew steadily in her mind, especially in relation to her translation of Spinoza's *Ethics*. The

Journal extracts published by Cross show that she worked diligently at this, along with the essay writing and the prodigious amount of reading she did in preparation for the essays, as well as that done by her and Lewes together for pleasure. This entry for 13 June 1855 appears to describe a fairly typical day:

> Began Part IV. of Spinoza's "Ethics." Began to read Cumming, for article in the *Westminster*. We are reading in the evenings now Sydney Smith's letters, Boswell, Whewell's "History of Inductive Science," "The Odyssey," and occasionally Heine's "Reisebilder." I began the second book of the "Iliad," in Greek, this morning.

She completed the translation on 19 February 1856, and a month later wrote Bray: "By the way, when Spinoza comes out, be so good as not to mention *my* name in connection with it. I particularly wish not to be known as the translator of the Ethics, for reasons which it would be 'too tedious to mention.'" There is at least a double meaning here. Part refers to her belated recognition that it was necessary she conceal her identity as the translator; the other part was in reference to Lewes's complex arrangement for the appearance of the *Ethics* (of which Bray may or may not have been aware, although her words suggest that he was). It is evident that she thought publication assured, and in the very next paragraph in this letter to Bray, she turns to the subject of money: "You don't know what a severely practical person I am become, and what a sharp eye I have to the main chance. I keep the purse and dole out sovereigns with all the pangs of a miser." Money was understandably uppermost in her mind: in a few months, Charles and Thornton Lewes were to be placed in school in Switzerland, and Lewes had recently begun to contribute to the support of his brother's widow and son. As far as she could see, publication of the *Ethics* was her "main chance."

But something went wrong. Lewes had negotiated with Bohn, who had published his Comte book in 1853, for a translation of Spinoza's *Ethics* and the *Tractatus Theologico-Politicus* to be done by one Kelly, with Lewes providing the editing and annotations. Kelly backed out of the assignment. However Lewes, before leaving for the Continent, made another arrangement with Bohn's son, to the effect that he would receive the combined payment for both translation and editorial work if he would supply a translation of the *Ethics* and excerpts from the *Tractatus*. But the elder Bohn was dissatisfied with the agreement made with his son (of which there appears to have been no written copy) and also had become less enthusiastic about issuing any translation of Spinoza. To add to his disinclination to honor the dubious contract, he thought the price agreed upon by his son too high; nonetheless, he wrote Lewes that he wished to see him with the manuscript, "and we will enter into a proper agreement." Perhaps because (unknown to Bohn) George Eliot was so intimately involved, Lewes considered this letter insulting and wrote in response a still more insulting one: "I altogether decline to have transactions with a man who shows such wonderful facility in forgetting. I beg you will send back my M.S. and consider the whole business at an end between us." Lewes's letter did indeed end all negotiations with Bohn for George Eliot's translation of the *Ethics* (and how easily she could have supplied passages from the *Tractatus!*). In 1859 Lewes attempted to place the translation with another publisher, A. and C. Black, but he met with no success.

There is no way of knowing what George Eliot thought or felt about Lewes's handling of the situation with Bohn; her Journal and letters are silent on the matter. Did it pass through her mind that he had been unnecessarily hotheaded and impetuous, especially as the long, hard work thus made useless had been hers, not his? Possibly she realized that the intensity of his action stemmed from the fact that it *was* her work, rather than his, that he felt was being so capriciously considered. At best, the recall of her translation must have appeared a bad omen for the start of a new life which had seemed bright with the promise that sincere and diligent work would be justly, if modestly, rewarded. Furthermore the return of her manuscript, even though Lewes had ordered it, meant a rejection—actually her first in the publishing world. As such it no doubt seemed an insidious justification of her own natural fear of rejection when she sent out her first fiction.

In reality, however, the fiasco with Bohn was good fortune in the guise of miserable luck. Had her translation of the *Ethics* appeared in 1859 or later during her lifetime, it would have posed no serious threat to her novel writing, for from *Adam Bede* on, she was writing fiction almost compulsively. But if the *Ethics* had appeared in 1856, as she expected it to, it is doubtful that she would have found the courage or incentive to strike out in an entirely different direction to find "the main chance." As it happened, Lewes had concluded his exchange of letters with Bohn by the middle of June; within a month she was noting in her Journal: "Mr. Chapman invites me to contribute to the *Westminster* for this quarter. I am anxious to begin my fiction-writing, and so am not inclined to undertake an article that will give me much trouble, but, at all events, I will finish my article on Young."

There is some poetic justice in the fact that Lewes was instrumental in ruining the chance for publication of her Spinoza. For as the cancellation of his agreement with Bohn urged her on to write fiction, so was it good for her personal life with Lewes. Allowed to settle into a routine of periodical writing and translating with him, she would eventually have again been haunted by the really important work which had eluded her. Although she had almost convinced herself to the contrary, not even her near-perfect relationship with him would for many years have satisfied all the demands of her complex and powerful nature.

SIX

My Present Past

In August 1859 George Eliot declined Barbara Bodi-chon's invitation to visit her in Hastings and meet a few of her special friends, if ever she "should want to see any more life." Her explanation was significant: "I *do* wish to see more of human life—how can one see enough in the short years one has to stay in this world? But . . . at present my mind works with the most freedom and the keenest sense of poetry in my remotest past, and there are many strata to be worked through before I can begin to use *artistically* any material I may gather in the present." She was then at work on *The Mill on the Floss*, the writing of which was to toss her into the ruthless current of the creative process almost as fatally as Maggie and Tom were to be swept down the flood-swollen river. It had taken three years of fiction writing for the full impact of the creative force to reach her and release memory from its practical duty of ordinary recall. It could then plunge downward in its relentless search for origins and set in motion the tantalizing dialectic of artistic creation—the need to find, to defend, but also to disguise the house of self that is buried under layers of time and feeling. The earliest writing, the three *Clerical Scenes*, had been discerned and captured with relative ease under the first stratum. Even these tales were not so near the surface as they at first seem, for each had roots in the unhappy past which she was at last free to explore. This is one reason why George Eliot retained a fondness for the *Scenes* throughout her life and refused to look upon them as mere preliminaries to a great career. She alone knew their personal basis, so that when Barbara commented, along with her invitation, that she had been certain the whole of *Adam Bede* had sprung directly out of its creator's life, George Eliot responded: "Curiously enough, a propos of your remark about 'Adam

Bede' there is much less 'out of my own life' in that book—i.e. the
materials are much more a combination from imperfectly known and
widely sundered elements than the 'Clerical Scenes.' "

Although the writing of the *Scenes* did not alone ensure the emergence of the greater novels, one can share Cross's feeling when in the
Life he heralds 23 September 1856, the day she commenced "The Sad
Fortunes of the Reverend Amos Barton": "We have now arrived at
the period of the new birth. . . ." In looking back, George Eliot herself recalled: "September 1856 made a new era in my life, for it was
then I began to write Fiction." She had been ready to start this story
at least two months earlier, for the dream-vision of her writing about
Amos Barton had come to her one morning while she was lying in
bed at Tenby, on the coast of South Wales, where she and Lewes had
gone from Ilfracombe on 26 June. They were in search of health, especially for Lewes, who was plagued by a singing in his ears; but they
were also seriously studying molluscs, zoophytes, and annelids. Perhaps spurred on by Thomas Henry Huxley's derisive criticism of him
as a "book scientist," Lewes was intent upon producing a reputable
work in natural science. So with the seaside as their laboratory, he
and she once again collaborated, this time in a pursuit that was a
refreshing change from the sedentary one of literature and philosophy
—although their usual reading schedule was only slightly diminished.
The completed project was to involve trips to the Scilly Isles and
Jersey, but it took definite enough shape at Tenby to enable Lewes
to publish the first of his "Sea-side" essays in the August 1856 issue
of *Blackwood's Edinburgh Magazine.* The long series was completed
in the issue of October 1857, some of it thus coinciding with the appearance of *Scenes of Clerical Life* in the same periodical; and in 1858
(the year that George Eliot completed *Adam Bede*) it was made into
what was to be one of Lewes's most popular and readable books. As
he had done for the *Goethe,* he borrowed from her Journal to fill out
the descriptions, having—so he claims in the book, seriously or not—
no "descriptive power" of his own. Possibly this was one of their
private jokes, for as he doubted her dramatic power and she did not
easily, if ever, forget this implied criticism, he may have publicly
announced his own deficiency in descriptive power, in which he had
acknowledged she excelled, as a kind of teasing appeasement. They
worked together in Tenby as closely as they had in Weimar, she
entering into the "zoophyte hunt" with great zest.

The leisurely stay at Tenby afforded the needed respite from London and its environs. Yet there were intrusions which must have made
the past jostle against the present in George Eliot's mind. Thirteen
years earlier—in July 1843—she had spent ten days there with the
Brays, Sara and Charles Hennell, and Rufa Brabant. According to

Cross, this vacation trip had been "chiefly memorable from the fact that it was indirectly responsible for Miss Evans undertaking the translation of Strauss's 'Leben Jesu.' For Miss Brabant . . . became engaged to be married to Mr. Charles Hennell; and shortly after her marriage she handed the work over to Miss Evans." It is unlikely that George Eliot could have forgotten this momentous time. Even had she, Sara was jealously quick in reminding her of it, and it was to her prompting that George Eliot responded: "Yes, indeed; I do remember old Tenby days, and had set my heart on being in the very same house again. We saw a ticket in the window and turned in, but alas! it had just been let." Possibly she had been relieved at this; she was, after all, doing her best to start a wholly new life. But she felt kindly disposed toward Sara and was beginning also to feel a tender protectiveness about old memories, even the sad ones, especially when they could be matched against happier moments gleaned from the present. "To me there is the additional pleasure," she went on to Sara, "—half melancholy—of recalling all the old impressions and comparing them with the new."

Also while they were at Tenby two friends closely associated with the turbulent recent years past—Barbara Leigh Smith and Edward S. F. Pigott—came to see them. One is first inclined to regard these people as intruders into the dual solitude so zealously guarded by the Leweses. Yet their visits seem to have been planned and welcomed by the Leweses themselves, who by this time may have been wondering what English friends they could trust. Barbara came first, perhaps self-invited; if so, the invitation was soon seconded by George Eliot, who wrote her on 13 June: "I wish I could drink in the sight of you among other pleasant things; and perhaps if the weather will have the goodness to clear up, you can make a little expedition to Ilfracombe before we leave." Before Barbara could manage the trip, the persistently uncongenial weather had driven the Leweses from the coast of Devon to that of Wales, George Eliot writing Sara that by this move they lost "the pleasure of having Miss Barbara Smith for a week sketching the rocks and putting our love of them into the tangible form of a picture." However, Barbara came to them at Tenby, arriving on 12 July and staying four days.

This visit was a success on both sides, Barbara leaving with new respect for Lewes (rumor had led her to believe him too sensual for Marian). After talking frankly with George Eliot, she wrote to their mutual friend Bessie Parkes:

> I do wish, my dear, that you would revise your view of Lewes. I have quite revised mine. Like you, I thought him an extremely sensual man. Marian tells me that in their intimate marital re-

lationship he is unsensual, extremely considerate. His manner to
her is delightful. It is plain to me that he makes her extremely
happy.

Assuming that this account is essentially true, it provides an insight
into the relationship between George Eliot and Lewes that accords
with other evidence. They did indeed live together as man and wife,
but without great passion. Each had given that to someone else; their
basic relationship was comradely, a sharing of interests, joys, and
tribulations.

Aside from her natural curiosity about Lewes, Barbara was eager
to discuss John Chapman with someone who knew him better than
even she. Beginning in the previous summer, and referring to "Lewes
and M.E." as happy examples of what he proposed, Chapman had
urged Barbara to live with him. By the time she came to Tenby,
Barbara was fairly firm in her own mind that she did not love Chapman enough to risk this arrangement; and presumably when she
departed from Tenby, she had resolved to free herself from emotional
entanglement with him. In any event, almost exactly a year later
in London she married Dr. Eugène Bodichon, whom she had met in
Algiers, where her parents had taken her in the hope of helping her
over her infatuation for Chapman. This seems not to have been a
remarkably happy marriage, but it endured. Barbara found satisfaction in her painting and her stalwart championship of women's
rights as well as of the underprivileged children of London. She was
to have a unique relationship with George Eliot, who after the
Tenby visit accepted her warmly proffered friendship. Although eight
years younger than George Eliot, Barbara had entered her life too
early to be one of the "daughters" who were later to cluster around
the famous novelist. It would be inaccurate to say that she supplanted
Sara, for Lewes had already done that; but she did replace Sara as
second to Lewes, and she was to give steadily and generously of that
affirming faith in her as person and artist which, justifiably or not,
George Eliot felt was no longer forthcoming from Sara.

Sara was still an important link with the past, however, as a member of the Rosehill group and also as an acquaintance of the few
Londoners with whom the Leweses wished to keep in touch. It was
to her that George Eliot had written on 29 June when they were
"looking out now for Mr. Pigott in his yacht, and his amiable face
will make an agreeable variety on the sands." Earlier that month
Pigott had been cruising with Herbert Spencer, their chief destination Guernsey (one of the Channel Islands), where Victor Hugo was
living in political exile. Carrying a letter of introduction from Louis
Blanc, they dined with Hugo, probably in Hauteville House which

Hugo had purchased only a month before with the proceeds from the unexpectedly successful *Les Contemplations*—a long poem which George Eliot lamented having to review for the July 1856 number of the *Westminster*. Interestingly, Spencer made no attempt to join the Leweses at Tenby, but went to Rosehill for the last part of June and the first of July. Apparently he had abstained from corresponding also, for in the 29 June letter to Sara, George Eliot wrote: "I suppose [Spencer] is with you now. If so, give him my very evil regards, and tell him that because he has not written to us, we will diligently *not* tell him a great many things he would have liked to know." Perhaps, as Blanche Colton Williams suggests, he made an effort while at Rosehill to convert Cara to George Eliot's new way of life. But one suspects he was guided by a very different motive as he roamed around George Eliot's once favorite haunt. She was merely piqued by his not writing. He was already suffering seriously from the psychosomatic disturbances which he was to describe with meticulous and loving care in his *Autobiography* and which coincide in time so suggestively with her living with Lewes.

For whatever reason, Pigott did not arrive at Tenby until 28 July, uncomfortably near the time when the Leweses were thinking that they should pack up the results of their maritime experiments and return to Richmond, as Lewes had plans to take his boys to Hofwyl. But once again Tenby proved to be a happy meeting place. By the time Pigott sailed away on 1 August, the Leweses felt that they had gained a lifelong friend, as indeed the future was to confirm. Being uncritical as well as sensitively understanding, he had a rare talent for friendship—Margaret Oliphant was to write of him: "He is the only man I have ever met, I think, from whom I never heard an unkind word of any one." As a dedicated *Leader* man (in fact, that spirited periodical may have owed its inception to him alone), he was of course on intimate terms with both Lewes and Thornton Hunt. It is not improbable that Lewes had purposely invited him to Tenby to give him the chance to know George Eliot outside the hectic and prejudiced London context. He immediately accepted her as "Mrs. Lewes" and obviously felt drawn to her as a person in her own right. However, subsequent developments were at least twice to make precarious his relationship to both her and Lewes. Only five months after his Tenby visit, Pigott was asked to be an intermediary in the threatened duel between Hunt and Lewes, an unpleasant request which he accepted as a duty and discharged without incurring the animosity of either of the two principals. Still later (and apparently without malice), he helped spread the word that George Eliot was Marian Evans Lewes at a time when the Leweses were unrealistically clinging to the hope that they could keep this fact a secret.

Although Pigott claimed Spencer as his informant in this matter, he seems to have added speculative evidence of his own. Even when the Leweses were told of this, however, they were steadfast in regarding Spencer as the only real culprit, so that, deservedly or not, Pigott remained innocent in their eyes. Having what George Eliot described as "a delicious tenor voice," he was to be one of the most regular participants in the informal musicales the Leweses began to hold on Saturday evenings as soon as they had space enough and a piano. He was to take a special interest in Charles Lewes (perhaps a remnant of his liking for Agnes in the pre–George Eliot days); and, along with Barbara, he was sympathetic with George Eliot's late marriage, being almost the only one of Lewes's old friends to send Cross a congratulatory note. Finally, with symbolic appropriateness, at George Eliot's funeral he rode with Herbert Spencer in the third carriage (which was also occupied by Richard Congreve and Robert Browning).

WHEN THE LEWESES ARRIVED HOME ON 9 AUGUST, THEY must have felt renewed confidence in the possibility of their sharing a meaningful life *in England,* which was what each deeply desired. As if in token of this revival of hope, Lewes had on 24 July at Tenby begun the first Journal he was not to destroy (whereas the less hesitant George Eliot had begun hers two years earlier when leaving England with him). As planned, Lewes soon set out to Hofwyl with Charles and Thornton, returning to Richmond on 4 September. George Eliot was supposed to have spent this interval in writing the article on "Silly Women's Novels" that she had promised Chapman. But as so often happened when left alone, she suffered physical discomfort which prevented her from working, this time from the aching of a wisdom tooth that had to be removed. This enforced pause from work perhaps served a good purpose, for the candid talks with Barbara and Pigott would have stirred up conflicting (because not yet harmonized) levels of memory, whereas the first story she had envisioned demanded a relatively simple fusion of present and past.

After Lewes came back to her at Richmond, it took her only slightly more than a week to complete the writing of "Silly Novels by Lady Novelists," which was wanted for the October *Westminster.* She had yet to do the "Belles Lettres" section for the same issue, which involved a considerable amount of reading, for several of the novels she was to review were strictly contemporary. But she worked with industrious speed, so that the entire obligation to Chapman was completed by 19 September. Exasperating though this delay in meeting "Amos Barton" face to face must have been, this work brought her, although by detour, near to what awaited her. By way of contrast, the lush settings, the melodramatic plots, and the extravagantly drawn characters of the "silly novels" sharpened her inward vision of what and how *she* wished to write. Much of the acrid criticism which she put into this essay was to spill over into her story as scornful addresses to the imaginary lady reader "who prefers the ideal in fiction; to whom tragedy means ermine tippets, adultery, and murder; and comedy, the adventures of some personage who is quite a 'character' " (Chapter 5). She could, however, give admiring respect to Harriet Beecher Stowe's *Dred,* which she reviewed for "Belles Lettres"; and in her essay on the silly novels she expressed her own ripening intention in the guise of a question: "Why can we not have pictures of religious life among the industrial classes in England, as interesting as Mrs. Stowe's pictures of religious life among the negroes?"

The *Westminster* articles at last completed and sent off, she was free to begin "Amos." And the remarkable thing, in view of her past procrastination, is that within a few days she did so, completing it in about six weeks of fairly steady work, apparently not seriously interrupted by moods of despair. Even more impressive, she was not at this time thinking of "Amos" so much as a separate story as the opening scene of what even on 18 August she had considered her "novel." The first vision of herself writing "The Sad Fortunes of the Reverend Amos Barton" had expanded to include the larger image of herself writing a series of loosely connected episodes (the germ of *Adam Bede* being one of them) to be called "Scenes from Clerical Life," a plan that Lewes had approved as being "fresh and striking." The word "Scenes" in this overall title is perhaps a sign of both Lewes's and her own fear that she lacked dramatic power and should not commit herself to telling *stories.* Neither she nor Lewes could anticipate how this seeming limitation of her talent would be obliterated by the emergence of new elements which originated in the dynamics of the writing process itself. So, as her first idea of the kind of novel that she could execute without fear of failure was a series of interrelated scenes, she carefully studded "Amos" with anticipatory references to the Oldinports, Milby, and especially to the Reverend Mr. Gilfil, who was to be the mild but catalytic hero of her second *Scene.*

Although still hampered by her restricted view of her own narrative power, George Eliot clearly had embarked upon a project far more ambitious than completing a single short story. And the fact that she had done so unhesitatingly is proof that the hard surface at least of her long-standing fear of writing fiction had crumbled. Resistance had been converted into propelling motivation, the nature of which she herself makes explicit in a letter to Sara Hennell: "Writing is part of my religion, and I can write no word that [words crossed out] is not prompted from within. At the same time I believe that almost all the best books in the world have been written with the hope of getting money for them." As she had by then completed the three *Clerical Scenes* and was pondering *Adam Bede,* fiction writing obviously no longer carried in her mind the stigma of self-indulgence. Rather, it had been transformed into both a religion and a strict duty (the latter, as always necessary for her, a self-imposed one): that of earning money, the moral pressure for doing so being in direct proportion to the unorthodoxy of her union with Lewes.

Perhaps the worldly Lewes had helped convince her that good fiction could be both a beneficent influence upon readers and an honorable source of income for the author. Indeed, it may have been for her that he had prepared the arguments he later presented in his review of Renan's *Essais de Morale et de Critique,* in which he takes sensible umbrage with the author's dismal view of the spread of industrialism, especially in relation to the arts. In answer to Renan's objection that payment for a work of art somehow sullies both the art and its creator, Lewes makes a clear distinction:

> The creation of art is not industrialism. The disposal of a work of art is. All the gold of California would be insufficient to buy a single poem, or a single picture, unless the poet and the painter had seen and suffered what their art expressed. All that industrialism can do to favour art, is by stimulating the artist to labour more; and all that it can do to deteriorate art, is by seducing the artist to become a rapid manufacturer.

And then he points to illustrious examples of artists whose work had not been degraded by material reward:

> Shakespeare, Goethe, Michael Angelo, Raphael, and Rubens managed to secure their share of the good things of this life, without missing the reward of glory. In fact . . . the artist produces his work because he is an artist; whether or not that work will be rewarded in hard cash and present renown, depends upon a variety of conditions; but paid and applauded, or unpaid and neglected, he will work on, if the noble impulse lives within him.

This review was published in December 1859, so that Lewes had already been given stunning opportunity to witness justification of his point of view. By then *Adam Bede,* published in February of that year, had alone brought in £1,705. Far from having been seduced into "manufacturing" literature, George Eliot had been stimulated to go on to *The Mill on the Floss,* the novel which came most directly and spontaneously from within herself. But in 1856—before "Amos Barton" and hence before she had earned money except from periodicals—even Lewes could not have anticipated how deeply she was to respond to his pragmatic reasoning, for soon her concern over the income from her fiction was to exceed the demands of practical necessity. Nor could he have foreseen the "variety of conditions" that would lead to both the hard cash and renown.

In the beginning, the rewards would have seemed unlikely: an author who with reason was determined to conceal her identity could hardly expect renown in any satisfactory personal sense; and "Amos Barton" was not the kind of story to promise much hard cash, even if some courageous publisher decided to risk publishing it. In its plotlessness, "Amos" might be considered a premature Chekhovian story. And if the character Amos possessed something of the morbid self-consciousness of Dostoevsky's Underground Man (who came into being about eight years later), he might be considered the first of the anti-heroes who were to invade modern literature. The fact is, this first *Clerical Scene* is not so much a story as a somewhat belligerent illustration of what its author thought realistic fiction should be.

Amos himself came directly out of her past, impinging upon her memory with force enough to make her feel the need to re-create him. His undeniable prototype was the Rev. John Gwyther, who in 1831 arrived full of Evangelical zeal to be curate at Chilvers Coton, where he was to stay until 1841. While at home on vacations, she no doubt listened to his sermons with her father, who on 12 February 1832 recorded in his Journal that the parson had "stopd the Singers" very much as Amos is reported to have done in Chapter 1 of his story—and, incidentally, not unlike her own hysterical stopping of the dancing at Mrs. Thomas Bull's party in 1840. Also Gwyther officiated at her mother's funeral and at Chrissey's wedding (there may be something of Chrissey in the long-suffering Milly Barton, who willingly sacrifices herself to her obtuse husband and childbearing). As the first six or seven years of his residence at Chilvers Coton coincided with George Eliot's period of Evangelical fervor, she might well have felt some kinship with him, approving of his clumsy efforts to bring order into the Coton Workhouse and overlooking his uncertain grammar.

He was still present when doubt began to eat at her faith, and may have been one of the clergymen who rushed to save her soul as it hovered tentatively on the borderline of orthodox belief. At the time, secretly hoping to be persuaded to re-enter the fold, she was disillusioned by their well-meaning but ineffectual efforts. It is possible that she felt a particular sense of betrayal by the Rev. Gwyther because by then his reputation was beclouded with gossip over his ambiguous relationship with a mysterious countess, who in turn had an equally ambiguous living arrangement with a man who passed as her father (in the story these are the Countess Czerlaski and Mr. Bridmain, her half brother). There was still bitterness in George Eliot over the worldly weaknesses of those who considered themselves the special representatives of other-worldliness. Some of this is reflected in her depiction of Amos, whom she created in between her verbal castigation of the fashionable Evangelical preacher Dr. John Cumming and her relentless dissection of Edward Young (although his *Night Thoughts* had inspired and comforted her in her own Evangelical days).

Yet there is interesting proof that Amos was a more vibrant reflection of real life than of a theme that lingered in George Eliot's mind. When the Rev. Gwyther, whom she had somewhat thoughtlessly presumed dead, came upon the story in *Blackwood's* he immediately recognized himself in Amos and "much perplexed," showed the first instalment to his daughter, who exclaimed, " 'Who in the world could have written this—have you Papa?' " He stayed silent for over two years, when he was prompted to write to the Blackwoods, not so much to complain as to explain his innocent involvement in the curious Liggins affair. It was fortunate that Gwyther delayed this letter as long as he did, for already fearful of her own creative power, George Eliot might not earlier have withstood the shock felt by most writers when they first learn that their living models have identified themselves in the writers' creation. As it happened, when her publishers, thinking it deserved some kind of acknowledgment, forwarded the letter to her, she was able to respond to it the very day she received it—15 June 1859. She did so with a cool aplomb which could hardly have afforded the good gentleman much consolation for his involuntary contribution to English literature, but which does testify to George Eliot's new poise and consciousness of herself as a writer of fiction. Her note (copied and addressed by her publisher) assured Gwyther that "Amos Barton" had been written

> under the impression that the clergyman whose long past trial suggested the groundwork of the story was no longer living, and that the incidents, not only through the license and necessities of artistic writing, but in consequence of the writer's imperfect knowledge, must have been so varied from the actual facts, that any one who discerned the core of truth must also recognize the large amount of arbitrary, imaginative addition.

> But for any annoyance, even though it may have been brief and not well-founded, which the appearance of the story may have caused Mr. Gwyther, the writer is sincerely sorry.

It was the "arbitrary, imaginative addition" that Lewes had watched carefully as the story came from George Eliot's pen, for keen and sophisticated literary critic that he was, he would have realized that the germinal idea held little promise of narrative value and would need stiff bolstering. From her own account, it would seem that he took her through the stages of a course in Creative Writing and that she loved every minute of it. The scene at Cross Farm convinced him that she could write good dialogue. There remained a crucial question: Could she command pathos? Since this was supposed to be the dominant effect of Milly Barton's death, he went off to town to give her an evening of quiet in which to write that scene. She had it ready for him to hear when he returned, and, as she was to record, it was a great success: "We both cried over it, and then he came up to me and kissed me, saying 'I think your pathos is better than your fun.'" This was no doubt the highlight of the writing experience. Perhaps it was this scene that decided Lewes the story had marketability, although before "Amos" was actually written, he had thought it probable her first attempt at fiction would have to be put aside and a new try made.

Or perhaps George Eliot herself made the decision, for from its beginning, she was far more assertive on behalf of her career than those whose opinion was formed by Cross's *Life* were to think. On the very day she finished "Amos," 5 November 1856, she wrote Sara Hennell (referring to Sara's trouble over publishing her latest effort to reconcile science and religion): "But don't let your determination to publish depend on him [George Baillie, the publisher who was now causing difficulties]. Work honestly done must not be shut up in a drawer. Some good will come of it." She may well have been convincing herself that "Amos" should not be relegated to a drawer for even a brief time. Both she and Lewes were experienced enough to know that no self-respecting editor would be likely to commit himself to a series of sketches upon seeing only the first one. Yet her impatience would have been heightened by the realization that between the completed "Amos" and the second *Scene* lay the writing of almost eighty pages for the *Westminster*, primary of which was perforce the long-dreaded and postponed essay on Edward Young.

However prompted, Lewes mailed the story the next day—6 November—to John Blackwood, publisher and editor of *Blackwood's Edinburgh Magazine* (or Maga, as it was, and still is, familiarly called). Even before "Amos" had materialized, they had agreed upon this

monthly periodical as a safe home for the projected *Scenes*. It was
a natural choice, for Lewes's "Sea-side Studies" was currently running
in it, and he had been "a kind of dropping contributor" to it since
1843, when he came to know John Blackwood, then managing the
London branch of the family's publishing firm. It is probable, however, that the Leweses had more serious reasons for turning to Maga.
Although its political conservatism would not have appealed to them,
its reputation for dignified fiction and nonfiction would have. After
a sensational, even scandalous beginning nearly forty years earlier
under John's father, William Blackwood, Maga had become highly
respectable and respected. Also, John Blackwood had demonstrated
his genuine interest in discovering new talent; and—perhaps in the
eyes of the Leweses at this time, its most pertinent asset—Maga had
a long-standing policy of anonymous publication. What they could
not have realized in the fall of 1856 and perhaps never did fully appreciate was that their choice proved a brilliant one because of the
nature of John Blackwood himself.

His patience, good humor, and sincerity as an editor were put to
the test almost immediately. To accompany the manuscript, Lewes
had prepared a strategic letter, opening it with the pretext that he was
writing about himself:

> Did you get my last letter proposing an article on Sea Anemones?
> and did your "silence give consent"?
> Meanwhile I trouble you with a m.s. of "Sketches of Clerical
> Life" which was submitted to me by a friend who desired my good
> offices with you. It goes by this post.

The plural "Sketches" (had Lewes on his own substituted this for
"Scenes"?) glosses over the fact that only one was included, although
he does refer to the proposed series as consisting "of tales and sketches
illustrative of the actual life of our country clergy about a quarter
of a century ago." Then, refraining from passing judgment upon
"Amos" as a story, he comments on its special qualities:

> I confess that before reading the m.s. I had considerable doubts
> of my friend's power as a writer of fiction; but after reading it those
> doubts were changed into a very high admiration. I don't know
> what you will think of the story, but according to my judgment
> such humour, pathos, vivid presentation and nice observation have
> not been exhibited (in this style) since the "Vicar of Wakefield"
> and in consequence of that opinion I feel quite pleased in negoti-
> ating the matter with you.

Blackwood's friendly but frank reply came within the week. He
was sure "Amos" showed "a happy turn of expression throughout,

also much humor and pathos." But he was not fired with enough enthusiasm to accept it unconditionally and commit himself to a series without first seeing further sketches (he had assumed that at least several others were completed and awaiting inspection). He had objections to "Amos," some soundly critical, others merely personal. He thought the author explained his characters too much "by descriptions instead of allowing them to evolve in the action of the story"; and although he had detected no sneer at "real religious feeling," he found the author's clergymen, with one exception, "not very attractive specimens of the body." To George Eliot, the most rewarding of his remarks must have been: "The death of Milly is powerfully done and affected me much." But he diluted even that praise by adding: "I am not sure whether he does not spoil it a little by specifying so minutely the different children and their names."

Blackwood thought the "Conclusion" had the same defect: "The windup is perhaps the lamest part of the story. . . ." However, he added—and he was not an editor to say this lightly: "If the author is a new writer I beg to congratulate him on being worthy of the honours of print and pay. I shall be very glad to hear from you or him soon." He had reserved until last Lewes's opening gambit: "I do not recollect your note proposing a short paper on the anemones but you may take the unintentional silence as consent." He may or may not have believed in the existence of such a note: he would not have been surprised at strategy from Lewes, whom he had long thought "a monstrous clever fellow," thoroughly experienced in dealing with editors. In fact, the essay on sea anemones did materialize in time to appear in the same issue of Maga that published the first instalment of "Amos."

As Blackwood had begun his letter with the affirmative statement, "I am happy to say that I think your friend's reminiscences of Clerical Life will do," he was dismayed and perplexed when by return mail Lewes wrote him that his "clerical friend" had been "somewhat discouraged" by the letter but would, upon his advice, submit a second story as soon as it was written. That would not be before three weeks or more as he was very busy with "avocations" (the *Westminster* work). Having no new material to submit, Lewes could only reaffirm his faith in the first *Scene* "as exhibiting in a high degree that faculty which I find to be the rarest of all, viz. the dramatic ventriloquism." To this he added a politic note: ". . . I told him that I perfectly understood your editorial caution in not accepting from an unknown hand a series on the strength of one specimen." And then, perhaps partly to divert attention from his special interest in the *Clerical Scenes*, he enlarged his role as dispatcher of manuscripts by clerical writers: "I have another paper sent to me by another friend—the Rev. George

Tugwell [the young curate they had met and liked at Ilfracombe, and who shared their zoological interests]. . . ."

Blackwood's response was prompt and gratifying. He had not meant to sound discouraging, he liked "Amos" very much indeed but had not yet had time to give it a second reading, and although he could not commit himself to the publishing of a series until he had seen more of the sketches, he would be happy to run "Amos" in the January and February numbers of Maga if that would "stimulate the author to go on with the other Tales with more spirit." He was also "glad to hear that your friend is as I supposed a Clergyman. Such a subject is best in clerical hands. . . ." Not only did this sensitively reassuring letter set the tone for almost the whole of Blackwood's future correspondence with George Eliot. Without doubt it saved an astonishingly successful literary career from ending before it had begun. It is unlikely that her newly found courage to write fiction would have survived even one rejection. She had the "noble impulse" that Lewes was to say carries the artist on in his work despite worldly neglect, but militating against this were still her old fear of personal rejection and sense of unworthiness. From "Amos" on, her writing was to stand as a symbol of herself, her *whole* self, not merely her intellectual views as in the nonfiction. Inevitably, acceptance or rejection was to have a private connotation for her which could not be wholly understood, let alone felt, by anyone outside herself. Not only had this pattern been painfully established in very early years, but it had been reactivated by seriously deflating experiences through the course of her life until she met Lewes, and was even now being reinforced by the social disapproval she had brought upon herself in living with him.

Lewes alone had opportunity to understand something of the emotional basis for her excessive fear of failure and her equally powerful desire for success. In writing to thank Blackwood for his promise to publish "Amos," he attempted to provide some insight into the complex nature of Maga's new contributor:

> Your letter has greatly restored the shaken confidence of my friend, who is unusually sensitive, and unlike most writers is more anxious about *excellence* than about appearing in print—as his waiting so long before taking the venture proves. He is consequently afraid of failure though not afraid of obscurity; and by failure he would understand that which I suspect most writers would be apt to consider as success—so high is his ambition.
>
> I tell you this that you may understand the sort of shy, shrinking, ambitious nature you have to deal with.

The remainder of the letter should have signified to Blackwood what he was to learn through less happy experience in the future—that the author of "Amos," although sensitive to the point of morbidity, was also astute and ambitious in a more worldly sense than Lewes was suggesting. His clerical friend—so Lewes explained—had questioned why Blackwood felt it necessary to hesitate over "Amos" for fear of committing himself to a series, "as he never contemplated binding you to the publication of any portion of the series to which you might object. . . ." Although this calmly ignored the fact that no portion of the series existed beyond "Amos," the clerical friend then asked, through Lewes, that Blackwood commit himself to publish at least one further story not yet written:

> He will be gratified if you publish Amos Barton in January, as it will give him ample time to get the second story ready, so as to appear when Barton is finished, should you wish it. He is anxious, however, that you should publish the general title of "Scenes of Clerical Life"—and I think you may do this with perfect safety, since it is quite clear that the writer of Amos Barton is capable of writing at least one more story suitable to Maga, and two would suffice to justify the general title.

A less genial and more suspicious publisher might have resented this attempted coercion, but Blackwood did not withdraw. Probably he assumed that Lewes had initiated the plan, and he could be fairly sure Lewes would not stake his own reputation as literary critic on anyone likely to prove only an ordinary or flash-in-the-pan writer. Besides, his curiosity as to the identity of the anonymous contributor had been whetted, for Lewes had now had the good grace to correct the impression that the author of "Amos" was a clergyman:

> Let me not forget to add that when I referred to "my clerical friend" I meant to designate the writer of the clerical stories, not that he was a clericus. I am not at liberty to remove the veil of anonymity—even as regards social position. Be pleased therefore to keep the whole secret—and not even mention *my* negotiation or in any way lead guessers—(should any one trouble himself with such a guess—*not very likely*) to jump from me to my friend.

This amounted to an invitation to Blackwood to make a knowing guess of his own. He was necessarily familiar with the gossip of literary London, if not through his own occasional presence there, then through his London agent, William Langford, who had succeeded him as manager of the Pall Mall branch. But if John Blackwood made the correct inference, he kept it to himself and at least outwardly acquiesced to the unrealistic proposal that his new writer remain ostensibly unknown even to his mystified but cooperative publisher.

In letters, Blackwood could salute the shadowy figure as "My dear Amos." When Part I of the story opened the January 1857 number of Maga and it was time to send the first check, however, Blackwood had no recourse but to make it payable to Lewes. "Amos" accepted the check without reference to the payee, and what must have been still more disconcerting to John Blackwood, sent an acknowledgment of its receipt not to him, but to his brother Major William Blackwood, although George Eliot's letter is a point-by-point answer to the one John had written to accompany the check. This is an unexpected twist to the correspondence, one that Cross was to conceal by publishing portions of this letter as being to John Blackwood. Cross probably interpreted her writing to the major as a deliberate slight to John; in as genteel way as possible, she was punishing Blackwood for his first frank criticism of "Amos."

However, John Blackwood showed no signs of taking offense—and William's business mail was of course essentially his also. The two brothers had worked well and closely together since 1848, when the major had cut short his military career in India to help his younger brother with the management of both the publishing house and Maga. He was not a man of letters, but John often consulted him and usually abided by his opinions on literary matters. He had, in fact, done just this with "Amos," asking the major if he did not agree that the author should remove the individualization of the children in Milly Barton's death scene. And in the letter which he sent with payment for the story, he had with his usual candidness (soon to be modified by Lewes's vehement promptings, although this time it served its intended good purpose) reported the major's reaction: "My brother says no—'Do not advise the author to touch anything so exquisite'—Of course you are the best judge."

After John Blackwood's unwittingly reckless criticism of that all-important scene, William's words must have seemed to George Eliot like well-deserved balm. She was even moved to concede to a small part of John's criticism, explaining to the no doubt surprised major (who had not hitherto been involved in the correspondence) that although she wished the particularization of the children to remain in the deathbed scene, she had removed their names from the "Conclusion," except those of Patty and Dickey. She also told him that she hoped to send him "the second story by the beginning of February." This, her first letter to her publishers, was written 4 January 1857 and signed "The Author of Amos Barton."

Lewes would probably have continued the "Amos" correspondence with John Blackwood, but he was away on his customary Christmas–New Year's visit to Arthur Helps at Vernon Hill. The previous year, George Eliot had taken a lonely journey to Chrissey's and back, returning to Richmond a week earlier than he. This year, however, she planned to stay alone in Richmond, and in anticipation of this she wrote Sara Hennell on 17 December: "I am looking forward with some pleasure to having a week of quiet solitude, for which I have not lost an occasional relish." But she may have written this with some bravado; and she had underestimated the time of her quiet solitude, for Lewes was gone from 24 December 1856 to 7 January 1857. She celebrated Christmas Day by beginning "Mr. Gilfil's Love Story," and perhaps felt some relief to be able to plunge into a new work out of earshot of the scratching of Lewes's ever-busy pen. Even so, she might well have wished for a different kind of celebration this particular year, for she had in hand the first concrete evidence that an old dream had come true—Part I of "Amos" in print in Maga's January number, and proofs for the remainder of the story, which would appear in the February issue. With these had come John Blackwood's letter and check for the whole of "Amos"—£52 10s. (In words he had added "Fifty Guineas.") With Lewes away, there was no one to be glad with and for her over this momentous communication; she did not dare mention the happy news even to her Coventry friends when she sent them her season's greetings (if Charles Bray knew her great secret, she could not address him separately without arousing the suspicion of both Cara and Sara).

So she must have begun working upon "Gilfil" with mixed feelings, Lewes's presence at Vernon Hill perhaps uppermost in her mind. He had early introduced her to Arthur Helps, and she had dined with him on 28 December 1853 at Sir James Clark's: "Very snug—only he and myself," she reported to Cara. "He is a sleek man with close-snipped hair—has a quiet, humorous way of talking, like his books." She and Lewes had also had the pleasant meeting with Helps in Weimar, where he had been without family and temporarily outside the pale of Victorian England. But now, in 1856 and living unmarried with Lewes, she could no more have been invited to accompany Lewes to Vernon Hill than she could, at that time, have expected to be asked to take tea with Queen Victoria. (Time works magnificent changes. When Sir Arthur Helps died, the Leweses sent their condolences to Alice, his eldest daughter and a friend of theirs, and Alice tore off the double signatures because the Queen had requested them.) But it was with a more immediate sense of irony that George Eliot might have contemplated her position while she sat at home in Richmond as Lewes at Vernon Hill read aloud Part I of "Amos," which charmed everyone, especially his feminine audience. It was these same women—figuratively speaking, of course—who were closing their doors to her, although in fairness to them it should be said that they did so at the command of their menfolk. Even Alice Helps, who had early joined the adulating chorus around George Eliot, did not visit the Priory freely until after her father's death.

The double standard would prevail: Lewes would be little affected, except by those who already disliked him for one reason or another. But she would be as thoroughly ostracized as possible in a presumably civilized society—except by the few pre-Lewes friends who could regard her way of life without moral indignation or frustrated envy. It is very difficult now to recapture the paralyzing effect of the powerful system of rigid, if tacit, laws of propriety in which George Eliot was caught. And it is also easy to minimize what she personally endured as a result of her position; what a serious threat it was to her career, especially during the first few years; and what a determining influence it was to be upon the very nature of her work. Her own frequent reiteration of the great value she placed on the dual solitude she enjoyed with Lewes was largely genuine. At least in small part, however, it was also defensive. All other evidence points to the fact that she was by nature a social being, who loved to share lively times and talk with many acquaintances, not merely the most intimate of them. That aspect of her naure had early been thwarted by circumstances within her family. Then, starting with the Coventry days, she had made friends quickly and without effort wherever she happened to be. When her life with Lewes began, she was again forced into an asocial mold. Acutely aware of having been unjustly cut off from a normal source of human interaction, she did not fight (except, perhaps, obliquely in her writing) against the restrictions imposed upon her. Rather, she quietly built a meaningful life around them, yet there was neither masochistic pleasure nor abject humility in her acceptance of the punishment meted out by society. With the breadth and depth of vision which was to characterize her fiction, she had perceived that both she and society were right, although upon different levels of existence—the individual and the general—so that there was no common ground upon which they could reach any single or lasting agreement.

In the early spring of 1856, not long before she and Lewes went off to Ilfracombe, she had written a brief but cogent essay for the *Leader* to bring to attention the fact that a new edition of Sophocles' *Antigone* had been issued by Oxford with English notes. This could have been a routine notice. Instead, it was one of the most personal statements she was ever to make, although the personal element was skillfully hidden under an objective style and the seeming remoteness of the subject matter. She had found a classic counterpart to her own situation in the *Antigone*, a baffling play because its context does not yield a decisive answer as to who is right and who wrong in the essential conflict between Antigone and Creon. Antigone is a lone person with an inner commitment to the unwritten law of unseen gods; King Creon, justly or not, represents the state and hence conventionalized opinion, which takes a deadly stand against the individual who dares defy its conditioned view of right and wrong. What initially may have drawn George Eliot to this play is that Antigone's defiant stance against Creon is prompted by her determination to give her brother Polynices the honorable burial refused because he has been declared a traitor. If Isaac was in her thoughts as she wrote "The Antigone and its Moral" (as he most probably was), she found him in Creon rather than Polynices—a transformation that was to persist in *The Mill on the Floss*, in which the adult Tom Tulliver uses Creon-like arguments to criticize and finally accuse Maggie, although in the end of that novel he also becomes Polynices .in that he goes to his underwater death firmly locked in his sister's embrace. The *Leader* essay is the first sign that in her mind Isaac's essentially critical attitude was beginning to merge with the disapproving voice of society as a whole; thus she pays little heed to the brother-sister relationship, but concentrates on the struggle between Antigone and Creon, which (as she saw it)

> represents that struggle between elemental tendencies and established laws by which the outer life of man is gradually and painfully being brought into harmony with his inward needs. Until this harmony is perfected, we shall never be able to attain a great right without also doing a wrong. Reformers, martyrs, revolutionists, are never fighting against evil only; they are also placing themselves in opposition to a good—to a valid principle which cannot be infringed upon without harm. Resist the payment of ship-money, you bring on civil war; preach against false doctrines, you disturb feeble minds and send them adrift on a sea of doubt. . . . Wherever the strength of a man's intellect, or moral sense, or affection brings him into opposition with the rules which society has sanctioned, *there* is renewed the conflict between Antigone and Creon; such a man must not only dare to be right, he must also dare to be wrong—to shake faith, to wound friendship, perhaps, to hem in his own powers.

She could not forever stay on the altitude of Sophoclean tragedy. On the more personal level, she quite humanly allowed herself some bitterness. Although there are few explicit references to her private life with Lewes in her extant letters, one of 1860—when she had lived through five years of English ostracism—is revealing enough to serve as many. It is written to Barbara Bodichon, who, with a friend, had apparently been urging the Leweses to investigate the possibility of a Continental divorce.

> By the way, we have consulted a barrister, very accomplished in foreign and English law, about that matter broached by your friend Mrs. Brodie. He pronounces it *impossible*. I am not sorry. I think the boys will not suffer, and for myself I prefer excommunication. I have no earthly thing that I care for, to gain by being brought within the pale of people's personal attention, and I have many things to care for that I should lose—my freedom from petty worldly torments, commonly called pleasure, and that isolation which really keeps my charity warm instead of chilling it, as much contact with frivolous women would do.

This was defensive camouflage. Realistically, she could not afford to be as indifferent to social acceptance as she wished others to think—not if she wanted a reading public, and she certainly did.

But a deeper reason had flung up her defense: the old familiar hurt over rejection had been uncovered and was in danger of being exposed. As J. C. Flugel has written, the desire for public approval is "to a very large extent a continuation into adolescent and adult life of the young child's need for the approval of his parents, while the anxiety and despondency caused by the sense of being outcasts from society corresponds similarly to the infant's distress at losing their love and support." The irony was that she had been forced into this new area of rejection as a result of living with Lewes, the one important person in her life who had accepted her wholly and unquestioningly. Lewes's total acceptance of her might easily have compensated for society's disapproval had the latter not vigorously reinforced her earliest feeling of alienation from her family, which had come to be centralized in Isaac's essentially critical attitude toward her.

THERE ARE BOTH SURFACE AND DEEP SIGNS THAT ISAAC WAS very much in her mind as she wrote her second *Clerical Scene*, "Mr. Gilfil's Love Story." She had a practical need to correspond with him about financial matters and Chrissey's health. Further, she was guiltily aware that she had not yet informed him of her changed mode of living. As she had by then been with Lewes two and a half years, Isaac no doubt knew of this through the inevitable grapevine. But such roundabout knowledge could not take the place of an announcement from her, which—so she both hoped and feared—would elicit some kind of personal response from him. With this in mind, as well as the thoughts aroused by Lewes's absence, it is not surprising that she produced a story which welds together emotionally charged aspects of her childhood and near-present, a premature *Mill on the Floss,* in which she was to present much of the same material with far less tortuous concealment.

In "Gilfil" she ceased to copy only the outer sphere of reality as she had done in "Amos." Both her characters and their actions were inner-propelled but superimposed upon a recognizable historical background, that of the Newdigate-Newdegate family, with which she had been intimately familiar through anecdote and firsthand experience from infancy onward. She was at ease enough with this material to manipulate it to suit her purposes, converting Arbury Hall into Cheverel Manor with a sureness of touch and hardly a trace of change, but for the most part rejecting the personalities (and the dates) of the real people who had figured against this background. However, she used enough of the actual configuration of these people to cause her first Warwickshire readers to track down the prototypes of all "Gilfil's" characters with joyous zeal. One of the most illustrious and careful readers of the story was Charles Newdigate-Newdegate, son of Maria Boucherett Newdegate, who had encouraged George Eliot to use the library of Arbury Hall for help in compiling the uncompleted "Chart of Ecclesiastical History." Knowing John Blackwood and seeing him at Epsom Downs on Derby Day in the spring of 1858, Charles Newdegate told him that he recognized "Gilfil" to be about his family and could provide a key for all the characters. By then Blackwood was understandably uneasy over his new writer's seeming penchant for drawing portraits from life. He had received a number of letters from both irate and flattered readers of Maga who claimed to have identified prototypes for all of the characters in the three *Clerical Scenes,* and so, although in a light vein, he passed the gist of his conversation with Newdegate on to Lewes. At this time the Leweses were in Munich, where George Eliot was engrossed in writing *Adam Bede* and no doubt wished to forget, at least temporarily, the *Clerical Scenes.* She answered Blackwood with a considered statement which suggests she now had greater mastery over the story than she had had while writing it:

Certain vague traditions about Sir Roger Newdegate . . . which I heard when I was a child are woven into the character of Sir Christopher Cheverel, and the house he improved into a charming

Gothic place with beautiful cielings [*sic*], I knew from actual vision
—but the rest of "Mr. Gilfil's Love Story" is spun out of the
subtlest web of minute observation and inward experience, from
my first childish recollections up to recent years.

Because "Gilfil" sprang from a much deeper stratum of self than
had "Amos," George Eliot was no longer interested in tracing individual lives with historical accuracy. Thus her memory was free to
assume greater creativity than that involved in simple recall. As a
result, autobiographical fragments float through this story in sur-
realist fashion, but always centered in Caterina (Tina) Sarti, who
is as much an alien in Cheverel Manor as George Eliot had felt herself
to be in her own home. At the death of her impoverished father,
a singer and copier of music, Tina is taken charge of by Sir Christopher and Lady Cheverel. With a child's natural charm she overcomes
the servants' prejudice against her foreign blood and becomes "the
pet of the household, thrusting Sir Christopher's favourite blood-
hound of that day, Mrs. Bellamy's two canaries, and Mr. Bates's
largest Dorking hen, into a merely secondary position." Lacking,
however, are love and respect for her as a human being. Sir Christopher is fond of her but in an absent-minded way; and as a mother-
surrogate, Lady Cheverel is remote, hers being the "kindness that
never melts into caresses, and is severely but uniformly benificent."
Tina marks the beginning of George Eliot's deeply rooted reluctance
to provide a satisfactory mother for any of her heroines with whom
she identifies in an important way. Tina's experiences during the
summers of her childhood are remarkably similar to those of Maggie
Tulliver and her brother, and of the younger sister and brother of
the sonnet sequence, the significant difference being that in "Gilfil"
the feelings of the girl and boy are reversed: Tina accepts adoration
as her natural due and without fear of its being withdrawn. She has
no brother, but Maynard Gilfil, Sir Christopher's ward, quickly becomes one in spirit when as a lad of fifteen, he

began to spend his vacations at Cheverel Manor, and found there
no playfellow so much to his mind as Caterina. Maynard was an
affectionate lad, who retained a propensity to white rabbits, pet
squirrels, and guinea-pigs, perhaps a little beyond the age at which
young gentlemen usually look down on such pleasures as puerile.
He was also much given to fishing, and to carpentry, considered as
a fine art, without any base view to utility. And in all these
pleasures it was his delight to have Caterina as his companion, to
call her little pet names, answer her wondering questions, and have
her toddling after him as you may have seen a Blenheim spaniel
trotting after a large setter. [Chapter 4]

It is almost as if George Eliot had constructed Tina's childhood out of Maggie's wishful daydreaming: for "Maggie's was a troublous life, and . . . the form in which she took her opium" after Tom had vented his anger on her, was "to sit down by the hollow, or wander by the hedgerow and fancy it was all different, refashioning her little world into just what she should like it to be" (Book I, chapter 5). It is possible, too, that George Eliot made special note of Maynard's clinging to such interests as pet rabbits, squirrels, and guinea pigs in soothing contrast to Isaac's early relinquishing them—and hence her companionship—in favor of a pony (as Cross relates). According to the final sonnet of the series, school first parts the brother and sister, as it does Tom and Maggie, and also Maynard and Tina. But unlike her sister counterparts, Tina feels no anguish over this parting, for Maynard is the anxious one who creates a "little scene" each fall when it comes time for him to leave: "You won't forget me, Tina, before I come back again? I shall leave you all the whipcord we've made; and don't you let Guinea die. Come, give me a kiss, and promise not to forget me" (Chapter 4).

The reader is not told whether Tina let Guinea die, but one is reminded of the episode in which Maggie does allow Tom's rabbits to die, so that despite admission, apology, and plea for forgiveness, she must bear her brother's unrelenting anger and the worst of all his threats—that he will not take her fishing the next day (Book I, chapter 5). Fishing is mentioned only cursorily in the account of the summer activities that drew Maynard and Tina together; but years later, when both are adults and confronted with separate yet related emotional crises, Maynard reminds Tina of their fishing expeditions and also for the first time refers to himself as her "brother": "I speak to you as a brother,—the old Maynard that used to scold you for getting your fishing-line tangled ten years ago" (Chapter 9). Obviously, his scolding had never been the inflexible, righteous kind that left the sting of remorse in Tina's heart as Tom's did in Maggie's. Yet Gilfil's gently indulgent attitude may have been Tina's great misfortune, for it is he rather than she who finds in the memory of those happy summers the strong root of piety which leads to "the self that self restrains."

As he watched "Mr. Gilfil's Love Story" unfold, John Blackwood in Edinburgh became increasingly perturbed. It was very different from what he had expected from the author of "Amos Barton." He had been forced to read it piecemeal and even to begin to set it in type before he had seen the ending, but the first few chapters were enough to alarm him. Although he was too considerate to ask the question directly, he might well have wondered how the story could be called a *Clerical Scene*. True, Maynard Gilfil had become the family chaplain at the Manor and had an independent living awaiting him in Shepperton; and certainly he was a more favorable representative of the clergy than Amos. But fine as the author insisted he was, he seemed stunted in character, showing little other than his unwavering and protective love for Tina. Tina herself was a most improper heroine, who needed a rigorous wash at the age of two and a half (Chapter 3), and more seriously, persisted in loving a cad (Anthony Wybrow) she very well knew intended to marry another woman. Like Gilfil she seemed to be all feeling, but, unlike Gilfil, she harbored destructive feelings as well as simple, outgoing love—and even that was not directed wisely. Her one redeeming feature as a heroine—her artistry in song—merely emphasized her turbulent nature, for

> her emotion, instead of being a hindrance to her singing, gave additional power. Her singing was what she could do best; it was her one point of superiority, in which it was probable she would excel the high-born beauty whom Anthony was to woo; and her love, her jealousy, her pride, her rebellion against her destiny, made one stream of passion which welled forth in the deep rich tones of her voice. [Chapter 2]

What bothered Blackwood most was the scene in the long gallery where Sir Christopher housed his heterogeneous collection of relics from several dead civilizations. It was here that Tina had clandestine meetings with Anthony Wybrow, but on this particular evening she went to the gallery hoping to be alone with her final, shattering realization that Wybrow would never marry her. However, Wybrow had followed her, and she sensed his presence before she heard or saw him, for suddenly

> a breath of warmth and roses seemed to float towards her, and an arm stole gently round her waist, while a soft hand took up her tiny fingers. Caterina felt an electric thrill, and was motionless for one long moment; then she pushed away the arm and hand, and turning round, lifted up to the face that hung over her, eyes full of tenderness and reproach. The fawnlike unconsciousness was gone, and in that one look were the ground tones of poor little Caterina's nature,—intense love and fierce jealousy. [Chapter 2]

Blackwood must have paused over "electric," which in 1857 was a most original, even bizarre, adjective to be used in connection with human emotions. So was "intoxication," used in a later scene Blackwood disliked still more. By this time in the story, Beatrice (Anthony's betrothed) is at the Manor with her mother; nevertheless when he is near to Tina, Wybrow feels "the fascination of old habit returning on him" so that, alone with her for a moment, he quite naturally "put his arm round her waist, and leaned his cheek down to hers. The lips couldn't help meeting after that . . ." (Chapter 6). Tina no doubt earned Blackwood's approval by rushing away from Wybrow the next moment, but at the beginning of the next chapter he learned Tina had torn herself from Wybrow "with the desperate effort of one who had just self-recollection enough left to be conscious that the fumes of charcoal will master his senses unless he bursts a way for himself to the fresh air"; even "when she reached her own room, she was still too intoxicated with that momentary revival of old emotions . . . to know whether pain or pleasure predominated." Blackwood was puzzled and disturbed, for in all probability he himself had not experienced such compulsive and self-devouring emotions as Tina's, which are recounted with an immediacy that causes the reader to forget the historical setting of the story.

When he came to write the letter to accompany the first batch of proof to the author, Blackwood held his misgivings in check and began with characteristically politic and encouraging remarks: "The first eight pages in particular are bright, lifelike, and witty as may be. . . . I think Mr. Gilfil is likely to be more generally popular than Amos and I have no qualms in starting him without seeing the conclusion." Then he concentrated on Gilfil and Tina, bringing in Wybrow (the conventional villain, as Blackwood would have seen him, who should be hissed off the stage) only as he affected the other two:

> It is not a pleasant picture to see a good fellow loving on when the lady's heart is *openly* devoted to a Jackanapes, and I am a little puzzled as to how you are to bring the excellent Gilfil out . . . without making him too abjectly devoted a lover for a man of character. I think the objection would be readily met by making Caterina a little less openly devoted to Wybrow and giving a little more dignity to her character. . . . I look with great anxiety for the picture of her half-broken heart turning to Gilfil. I hope she finally rejects the insufferable Wybrow—but . . . if I am wrong in my opinions about the demeanour of Caterina with Wybrow recollect that I write to some extent in the dark.

At the end of his letter, he delicately hinted that his "critical censorship" might be moved by "the allusion to dirt in common with your heroine and the cool proceeding of Wybrow." He closed with "many congratulations on your success," meaning the run of "Amos Barton" in Maga.

In responding, George Eliot was also politic, amiably conceding that

Blackwood was right in questioning (on the proofs) the fitness of the French phrases she had used in the first part of "Gilfil." Ignoring his implied criticism of the association of the child Tina and dirt, she next turned with firmness to what she rightly sensed was his major concern:

> But I am unable to alter anything in relation to the delineation of development of character, as my stories always grow out of my psychological conception of the dramatis personae. For example the behaviour of a Caterina in the gallery is essential to my conception of her nature and to the development of that nature in the plot. My artistic bent is directed not at all to the presentation of eminently irreproachable characters, but to the presentation of mixed human beings in such a way as to call forth tolerant judgment, pity, and sympathy. And I cannot stir a step aside from what I *feel* to be *true* in character. If anything strikes you as untrue to human nature in my delineations, I shall be very glad if you will point it out to me, that I may reconsider the matter. But alas! inconsistencies and weaknesses are not untrue.
>
> I hope that your doubts about the plot will be removed by the further development of the story.

It is unlikely that Blackwood was convinced, but he recognized the adamantine quality of her own conviction. In his reply he charitably refrained from reminding her that as she had written only one and a half stories, she was perhaps over-hasty in using "always" to describe her method of developing plot. Nor did he risk pointing out any discrepancy that he might have felt existed between her characters and human nature as he knew it. Rather, he offered an implicit apology for having formed his first opinion rashly: "When I first read the M.S. the night was so far advanced that my eyes as I drew towards the end were beginning to get weary, and although I arrived substantially at the same opinion of the merits of Part 2 as I now entertain, I do not know that I fully appreciated all the excellences and beauties of this portion of the Story."

However, when he later read for the first time the scene in which Tina deliberately secures a knife with which she intends to murder Wybrow, he could no longer pretend or stay silent. The crime, if perpetrated, could not have been written off as wholly an act of passion, for the context makes it clear that it had been partially premeditated. Having been instructed still to send George Eliot's earned money from Maga to Lewes, Blackwood took the opportunity to accompany the check for the second and third parts of "Gilfil" with a letter in which he expressed his renewed concern with more frankness than if he had been writing directly to George Eliot—although knowing that she would see the letter, he softened his criticism accordingly.

I have grave doubt about the dagger, beautifully as the impossibility of her using it is indicated. I daresay George Eliot will kick furiously at the base idea of altering a syllable at this point, but I am pretty sure that his dear little heroine would be more sure of universal sympathy if she only dreamed or felt as if she could stab the cur to the heart and I think it would be more consistent with her character than the active step of getting hold of the lethal weapon. I may be wrong however and I daresay many will prefer the *dadger*.

Had George Eliot been less emotionally involved in her story, she would have reacted to Blackwood's last quoted sentence as a sly thrust which he probably hoped would jolt her back to the Dutch type of realism in painting that she had already professed to emulate in writing. There is little doubt that by the "many" Blackwood meant those readers who were addicted to cloak-and-dagger fiction. She was also immune to the sarcasm inherent in his suggestion that she would kick furiously at the idea of altering a syllable of what she had already sent him. Even this early she was proving to be the kind of writer who considered that once her work had passed her own censorship it was irrevocable. Besides, at the time of Blackwood's letter, she had her eye trained on an inward vision, and it seems never to have occcurred to her that the external form she gave it might appear sheer melodrama to an outsider. Shortly after "Gilfil" had appeared in Maga, many readers attributed it to that master of melodrama, Bulwer-Lytton, and Blackwood admitted that there were "some touches in Mr. Gilfil which look a little like Sir Edward." Although George Eliot was never to remove all traces of melodrama from her fiction, further experience in writing—not the mechanical aspect of it solely but the new control gained each time she successfully objectified subjective material—was to reduce such elements drastically. Her ability to bring together the inner and outer worlds without sacrificing the one to the other was consequently strengthened.

In 1857, however, criticism of "Gilfil" amounted to blunt intrusion into a world so private that not even Lewes could share the whole of it. Exactly what Lewes thought of "Gilfil" is not clear. He naturally spoke enthusiastically of it to Blackwood, insisting that it was superior to "Amos" as he mailed him the succeeding parts of the story, commenting especially on the third part (which contains the dagger scene): "The interest of the story becomes exciting; and the subtle truth in delineation of complex motives is better than anything he [the author] has yet done in that way." When he sent in the remainder of "Gilfil," he said without adornment: "By this post I forward the last part of Eliot's story, as he requests." The date of this letter—16 April—is arresting, for according to her Journal, George Eliot had finished her story a week earlier. She rarely allowed that much time to elapse between finishing a specific portion of a work and sending it on to Blackwood. As far as extant evidence reveals, Lewes had not been nearly so close to the actual writing of "Gilfil" as he had to that of "Amos." It is possible that after she had completed the manuscript, he raised questions about it, perhaps even asking her to reconsider Blackwood's criticism of the dagger scene. Lewes, aware that Blackwood was speaking as an editor and not merely as an individual reader, would have taken his reluctance to endorse the scene quite seriously. If so, George Eliot was not persuaded to make a change that went contrary to her earliest conception of Tina, which she had expressed in response to Blackwood's first criticism, and which she had reiterated in reply to the more explicit disapproval he had expressed of the dagger scene in his letter to Lewes:

> I am glad you retain a doubt in favour of the "dadger," and wish I could convert you to entire approval, for I am much more satisfied when your feeling is thoroughly with me. But it would be the death of my story to substitute a dream for the real scene. Dreams usually play an important part in fiction, but rarely, I think in actual life.
>
> So many of us have reason to know that criminal impulses may be felt by a nature which is nevertheless guarded by its entire constitution from the commission of crime, that I can't help hoping my Caterina will not forfeit the sympathy of all my readers.

An equivocal answer to Blackwood's real question, this ignores the way in which much of the story emphasizes how Tina's nature had never been safeguarded against the unrestrained expression of itself and that alongside her great need to love and be loved had grown up the equally strong forces of vindictiveness, anger, and jealousy. Tina had to die as a result of that complex of passion just as surely as George Eliot would have been destroyed (in her own mind, at least) by her passionate self had she not had the power, denied Tina, to transform it into the liberating self-knowledge which brings with it self-control. When George Eliot told Blackwood that to make the dagger scene a dream would be the death of her story, she was really saying that such a change would eliminate the necessity of Tina's death. This in turn would nullify the story's purpose. For it is this scene which provides the decisive step toward Tina's death. Tina's tragedy is, in effect, a dramatic statement of the conviction George Eliot had expressed to the young John Sibree in 1848: "The intellect by its analytic power, restrains the fury with which [the passions] rush to their own destruction, the moral nature purifies beautifies and at length transmutes them." Tina's nature is neither moral nor immoral; it is amoral.

Maggie Tulliver was not to be granted much more life than Tina, but she at least was permitted to gain some awareness of the illusory nature of her childhood dream that she could find entire harmony with circumstances in any mode of living. Although only dimly, she came to realize that she was caught midway in the inexorable struggle George Eliot had found at the heart of the conflict in *Antigone*—that "between elemental tendencies and established laws by which the outer life of man is gradually and painfully being brought into harmony with his inward needs." Almost all of George Eliot's subsequent major characters—men and women both—were to achieve this same realization with varying degrees of comprehension. But even the beginning of such understanding was outside Tina's scope, as was the inner adjustment which might accompany it—the "self-amelioration," as George Eliot in her letter to Sibree had termed the still little known psycho-physical phenomenon of genuine insight.

It is not surprising that Anthony Wybrow's death is as fated as Tina's, for his very presence in the story is determined by what is to happen to her. As a functional character, he is similar to Stephen Guest in *The Mill on the Floss*, whose presence is also needed to bring about the climax of that novel. What *is* surprising is the persuasiveness of George Eliot's portrayal of the passionate attachment felt by Tina and Maggie Tulliver for these two scantily characterized young men, neither of whom is rendered noble or distinguished in any way. Readers from her own time on have argued that these two heroines *should* not have fallen in love with these men, but no one can argue that they *did* not. Maggie, as the justly better known heroine, has received the greater attention in this respect. But as an editor, John Blackwood perforce gave Tina as much critical thought as later he would to Maggie—perhaps more so, because by then he was inclined to grant George Eliot the benefit of any doubts he might hold concerning characterization. Never wholly reconciled to the realistic nature of the dagger scene, he touched upon it only lightly when writing to Lewes to say with apparent conviction: "Any one really reading the last part of Gilfil will I think be affected by the cry of love pervading it."

What Blackwood had unknowingly heard in the story was an echo of George Eliot's experiences at 142 Strand, where she had begun the painful process of remolding the self that Tina represents. Wybrow is assuredly no John Chapman; he could not survive the demands of two jealous women, let alone three. Yet he is reminiscent of the more resilient Chapman in furthering the drama at Cheverel Manor with himself at its center when he could have brought it to an end by decisive action. It is possible that Chapman made his entry into this story simply because George Eliot was not yet far enough removed in time from her experience with him to write about a woman's passionate love for a man without making him the man, no matter how camouflaged. This does not mean that she was still in love with Chapman when she wrote "Gilfil"; it does, however, suggest that the conflicting forces evoked by the diabolical situation at the Strand were still alive and working themselves out into a safe daydream which obediently fulfilled the demands of vicarious punishment for both herself and Chapman. Blackwood was nearer to the spirit of this aspect of the story than he could have realized when he urged that the dagger scene be converted into a dream, especially as he later explained that he had not meant one in sleep "but a passing dream or thought in the mind not carried the length of actually getting hold of the dagger." Much in the story needed no conversion to be exactly that.

Not all of the story is on the elementary level of wishful daydreaming. At times it is impossible to say which level is the consciously intended one and which the unbidden intruder—the daydream or the past reflected in identifiable form. After what Blackwood had described as Wybrow's "cool" conduct in the gallery, Tina holds an interior debate in which she accuses him of having encouraged her love, but in the midst of her accusations admits to herself: "He was led on by the feeling of the moment, as you have been, Caterina; and now you ought to help him to do what is right" (Chapter 2). Since Tina's infatuation for Wybrow had made her as blindly self-centered as his congenital egotism makes him, this sudden enlargement of her vision to include him as a person existing independently outside her own feeling is uncharacteristic and soon appropriately forgotten by both Tina and the reader. Yet it remains in the story as a relic of the real George Eliot's acceptance of the challenge to renounce, or conquer, her feeling for Chapman and to help him do what was right. The climax of this movement in relation to Chapman came, it will be remembered, during his June 1851 Coventry visit, when he and she made a holy vow to bind them to the right. This was of course to mark a crucial turning point in her life and personality, as well as the great depth of difference between herself and Tina.

Also perhaps she had been saddened by a renewed awareness of all that had been lost between Tina and Wybrow. For their story was surely that part of "Gilfil" spun out of "the subtlest web of minute observation and inward experience" of her recent years, whereas the Tina-Gilfil relationship had been more happily (but with less regard to reality) spun out of earliest years. Significantly, she could not write this first personal story without juxtaposing Isaac and Chapman. The relationships are curiously intertwined in the story: Gilfil, originally the brother figure, becomes Tina's husband; and Wybrow, the object of her passion, says to Beatrice, " 'One has a brotherly affection for such a woman as Tina; but it is another sort of woman that one loves' "

(Chapter 8). Even though Wybrow is obviously seeking to allay Beatrice's jealousy with these words, this is, interestingly, the only time in the story that Tina is convincingly referred to as a woman.

As this subtly suggests, Wybrow, along with the other major characters, does not stay fixed in one identity, but slips from one into another. Finally the multiple identities converge, so that as he stands in the Rookery unknowingly awaiting his death he is suddenly the essence of Chapman, Isaac, perhaps even the mother hiding in the shadows behind these two men—and anyone else who had been miserly in returning love with love. Maynard Gilfil also is fluid; he glides from Isaac into Lewes, a transition which is most noticeable when the maternal aspect of Gilfil's love for Tina is stressed, as when after Wybrow's death he races toward her on horseback, planning how he will cherish her to the end of his days: "In the love of a brave and faithful man there is always a strain of maternal tenderness; he gives out again those beams of protecting fondness which were shed on him as he lay on his mother's knee" (Chapter 19). Gilfil's shift was perhaps the most necessary one in the story, for even a ghost of a brother could not marry his sister. On a more realistic level, as Gilfil rescued Tina from the aftermath of loving Wybrow so did Lewes, in a sense, rescue George Eliot from the aftermath of having loved Chapman.

Containing as it does protean characters and clashing levels of being, "Gilfil" was not easy to write. After two months of working on it, George Eliot wrote John Blackwood that she needed more time and space than she had anticipated to reach its climax and that the finished piece would need more pages in Maga than had "Amos." This suggests (as does internal evidence) that the story was shaping itself with a will of its own and also that, once she perceived its direction, she was unconsciously putting distance between herself and the climactic goal —the dagger scene. Privately, Blackwood may have felt that the story did not merit more time and pages. But without demur he gave it space in four issues of Maga (March, April, May, June 1857), whereas "Amos" had required only the January and February issues.

Despite its unexpected length, George Eliot was still not satisfied when she came to the end of the story proper. Two weeks after she had sent Blackwood the manuscript of the final section (and when she was already at work on the third *Clerical Scene*), she informed him of her decision to do a short epilogue to "Gilfil." She seems to have enjoyed writing this while sitting on Fortification Hill at St. Mary's, the largest of the Scilly Isles, where she and Lewes had gone to further his "Sea-side Studies," and where also she had written the concluding portion of the story. She twice recorded writing this three-paragraph Epilogue—in her Journal at hand and then six months later in her retrospective account of how she came to write fiction—and both times she recalled particularly the May sunshine that had enveloped her and her work. It gave her pleasure to create the pervasive calmness of the Epilogue, which, although not providing a happy ending, serves to relieve the starkness of the tragedy brought about by a young girl's overwhelming need for love.

IT IS POSSIBLE THAT THE PROJECTION OF TINA'S FEELINGS INTO the context of the story had caused George Eliot to suffer the first of the attacks of vaguely defined illness which were to occur intermittently throughout her writing career. She herself came to note the association between her work and seizures of physical discomfort, and she seemed resigned to these as just payment for the guilt that writing aroused in her. No doubt she felt a share of the universal guilt which almost all human beings experience when thrust into the godlike role of creator on whatever level of existence. In her, this would have been augmented by the residue of the fears that had long prevented her from creating fiction. In late life she could speak lightly of ill health as an inevitable accompaniment to her writing, as in an 1877 letter to Cross to thank him for his gift of a badminton set, which, however, she thought too lavish for her meager skill and energy:

> Still—which would you choose? An aunt who lost headaches and gained flesh by spending her time on tennis and Badminton, or an aunt who remained sickly and beckoned death by writing more books? Behold yourself in a dilemma! If you choose the plump and idle aunt, she will declare that you don't mind about her writing. If you choose the pallid and productive aunt she will declare that you have no real affection for her. It is impossible to satisfy an author.

Apparently startled by the idea that to her writing beckoned death, Cross deleted the whole of this paragraph from his published version of the letter. Twenty years earlier, while working upon "Gilfil," George Eliot herself was startled by her initial experience of reacting physically to the effects of her own writing. She was as yet unprepared for the fact that no matter how fragile the connection between Tina and herself, it was still an identification of the psyche's making, so that Tina's passion and guilt would necessarily reverberate in her in some form or other. The form that it took was a bilious attack. "Unable to work for four days from bilious headache," she recorded in her Journal, the entry covering 19–23 January; and as she had finished Chapter 2 on 17 January, this means that she fell ill between setting the stage for the final portion of her drama and plunging into the origin and childhood of Tina. She duly lamented this illness, yet it preoccupied her in a way that suggests she was also a bit proud of it. Several days after the attack had subsided, she opened a letter to Sara with a reference to it. And still later, on 4 February, she wrote Major Blackwood that she had been delayed in sending the second *Clerical Scene* "by a bilious attack—surely one of the worst among the 'calamities of authors.'" It is almost as if the illness had helped to convince her that she was really an author.

Significantly, it was in this same letter that she announced her intention of taking on the pseudonym "George Eliot." While writing "Amos," and having no clear idea of what would follow, she had thought complete anonymity desirable. Then when it became fairly certain that the *Clerical Scenes* could continue in Maga as long as she wished to produce them, both she and Lewes began to realize that they needed to provide Blackwood with a name. They were aware also that if "Gilfil" sustained even the mild interest accorded "Amos," Blackwood would be plied with inquiries concerning its author; they decided that a pseudonym would provide greater security than total namelessness, which once broken through, could reveal no one but Marian Evans Lewes. So she submitted the name that she and Lewes had agreed would fulfill the immediate need:

> Whatever may be the success of my stories, I shall be resolute in preserving my incognito, having observed that a *nom de plume* secures all the advantages without the disagreeables of reputation. Perhaps, therefore, it will be well to give you my prospective name, as a tub to throw to the whale in case of curious inquiries, and accordingly I subscribe myself, best and most sympathizing of editors, / Yours very truly, / George Eliot.

As this letter is of some importance in the history of English literature, it is regrettable that for the second time she ignored John Blackwood and addressed it to his brother William. The reason was similar to that of her first bypassing him. His letter accompanying the February number of Maga was (like his very first letter in response to "Amos") more honest than politic; and his second sentence, although probably meant as prodding encouragement, would have been to George Eliot but a reminder of his initial criticism of her first-draft conclusion of this story: "A good many people will be disappointed at finding his history so speedily wound up, but I trust that you will quickly do away with any such regrets by sending me down an assistant and successor who shall eclipse the worthy Curate of Shepperton." John Blackwood was not yet, despite the cues provided by Lewes, fully alerted to the danger area surrounding the sensitivity of the author of the Clerical Scenes-in-Progress. Instead of congratulating her without qualification, he told her frankly that both critics and some of his personal friends were divided in their opinion of Amos as a character, and he worsened this by adding: "With one of them, Colonel Hamley, I do not recollect of ever differing in opinion before. He thought the Author very possibly a *man of Science* but not a practised writer."

She responded to the first part of this as if he had attacked the very foundations of the concept of literary realism which had gone into the making of Amos; and to the second part as if he and Colonel Hamley had been intent upon personally insulting her:

> In reference to artistic presentation, much adverse opinion will of course arise from a dislike to the order of *art* rather than from a critical estimate of the execution. Any one who detests the Dutch school in general will hardly appreciate fairly the merits of a particular Dutch painting. And against this sort of condemnation, one must steel oneself as one best can. . . . I suppose my scientific illustrations must be a fault, since they seem to have obtruded themselves disagreeably on . . . one of my readers. But if it be a sin to be at once a man of science and a writer of fiction, I can declare my perfect innocence on that head, my scientific knowledge being as superficial as that of the most "practised writers."

Although he had not expected a point-by-point defense, John Blackwood amiably accepted this retort, the pseudonym, and the three-cornered correspondence. His first letter to "My Dear George Eliot," that of 10 February 1857, was a conciliatory one that went far beyond the call of duty. He was somewhat alarmed not to have received even the beginning of the second *Clerical Scene*, which had been promised him so that the story could start in the March number of Maga. Yet he couched his concern in terms of sympathetic understanding of the vagaries of the creative process: "It would be a monstrous pity not to come to time with No. 2 of the series and I hope the M.S. is either on the way or will be dispatched in response to this. Do not of course hurry yourself to the detriment of the story; the perfecting of that must always be the first consideration, but it would be a serious disadvantage to baulk the public expectation now fairly raised." From then on, his letter was designed to allay the distress he now realized he had unintentionally induced: "Amos" was showing "unmistakeable" signs of popularity, most of his immediate friends were "loud in praise" of it, and although they had the impression that the author was "new to writing fiction," they meant this "as a compliment implying not rawness but that invaluable quality *freshness*. In regard to scientific illustrations neither Hamley nor I meant that you used them too much. We merely alluded to a sort of precision of expression or illustration which gave us the idea that the writer was accustomed to scientific definitions."

He was obviously intrigued by the pseudonym and seemed to accept it as a sure indicator that his mysterious author was really a man. Having heard from Albert Smith that "the luminaries of the Garrick generally seem to have mingled their tears with their tumblers over the death bed of Milly," he imagines what great fun it would be "if you are a member of that society and hear yourself discussed." But this is followed by a more serious remark: "I sympathize with your desire for the incognito, although I hope to break through it erelong as far as myself." It is possible that he here meant "sympathize" in a deeper and more comprehensive sense than the Leweses were to interpret it, and that he went along with their guessing game as an assurance to them that he intended to keep their secret. For as early as 27 January, William Langford had addressed an anxious query to him: "Who wrote Amos Barton? Can you tell me? I have heard a hint that I dare not entertain and from no bad judge." The dire wording made the mention of a name unnecessary, for no one in literary London at that moment occupied a more notorious position than Marian Evans Lewes, and only a publisher who intended to exploit the sensationalism of that identity would wish to disclose that it belonged to one of his writers. John Blackwood was not such a publisher, but he accepted the possibility calmly and neither demanded the truth from the Leweses nor hinted that he was aware that speculation was already well under way in London. Rather, as if to re-emphasize his willingness to follow their lead, he returned to the *nom de plume* near the end of his letter, telling them how the handwriting of "George Eliot" had so reminded him of a Captain George Warburton (who had a brother named "Eliot") that he had asked his clerk to turn up ten-year-old letters in order to compare them: "I found a remarkable resemblance but not identity nor does Amos seem to me anything like what the good artillery man would or could write."

No doubt the Leweses smiled with superior amusement over this, for they alone knew the deeply personal origin of the pseudonym. "George" was borrowed directly from Lewes; and "Eliot," besides being "a good, mouth-filling, easily pronounced word" (so she told Cross), is, according to another family tradition, to be decoded as "To L—I owe it." One can imagine that they had conjured up the name in a spirit of fun, thinking of it as an expediency and little anticipating either the first troublesome or the later solemnly majestic consequences that were to follow. No matter how ludicrously Blackwood seemed off the mark, George Eliot was, as always, gratified to have her work accepted unequivocally as that of a man. And although she was probably happier to be thought a member of the Garrick Club than identified with the artillery captain, she remembered and recorded both guesses evoked by her first use of the pseudonym. (She never did put down in writing, even in summary form, the origin of or reasons for it.)

Otherwise, they were well pleased with Blackwood's letter. Although they underestimated his perspicuity, his disarming candor elicited from George Eliot at least one response which he had hoped for: "Sent off to Edinburgh the first two parts of 'Mr. Gilfil's Love Story' after having a delightful letter from Blackwood"—so ran her Journal entry for the very day she had received it, 11 February. Earlier that same day Lewes had mailed the manuscript and written Blackwood: "By this post you will receive an instalment of Eliot's new story. . . ." It is thus clear that she had been deliberately withholding her new material. If Blackwood had written in a peremptory mood, she might never have completed "Gilfil" or any other fiction. Lewes's casual use of "Eliot" in advising Blackwood that the manuscript was on its way may have been an effort to divert attention from "George" for the same reason that earlier he had begged Blackwood not to jump from him, the negotiator, to his friend, the anonymous clerical writer; or it may have been an implicit sign of appreciation of Blackwood's accepting the pseudonym without question. Without doubt, Blackwood was glad for this active response to his letter. Yet he must also have been disappointed, for besides being a subtle request for promised material, his letter had been an indirect appeal to her to confide in him. He was not allowed to break through the incognito until a year later, when he made a special trip to Richmond to meet George Eliot, although by then he was well aware of her identity.

Already accustomed to thinking of his new writer as a man, Blackwood took easily to using the pseudonym, although always in its full form. The habit of masculine reference persisted even after he knew for certain that George Eliot was a woman, so that for several years to come and without a thought to the ludicrous incongruity of the pronoun, he and his associates often discussed among themselves the unfortunate position "he" had placed "himself" in living with Lewes. Yet the choice of that quickly accepted name had been a daring one —and perhaps a silent tribute on George Eliot's part to George Sand. Anonymity was still usual for English women writers, but wholly masculine pen names certainly were not. Even Charlotte Brontë (by no means a timid soul, no matter how shy she appeared in public) describes how she and her sisters avoided them when planning to publish a selection of their poems: "We veiled our names under those of Currer, Ellis, and Acton Bell; the ambiguous choice being dictated by a sort of conscientious scruple at assuming Christian names positively masculine, while we did not like to declare ourselves women, because we had a vague impression that authoresses were liable to be looked on with prejudice. . . ." George Eliot had the conviction that authoresses were looked on with prejudice, and she certainly had a far more stringent reason for concealment than the Brontës. It may be that she and Lewes thought a decisively masculine name the safest; but it may be too that by some unerring impulse George Eliot herself recognized such a name would be of the greatest service to her.

For the pseudonym was to serve diverse needs, concealment being, ironically, that of shortest duration. One of its most abiding and phenomenal functions was to provide the reading public with an identity mystically distinct from Marian Evans Lewes, of whom that public did not at all approve. The name first appeared in print on the title page of the edition of the three *Clerical Scenes* which the Blackwoods published as a book early in January 1858. Already there was a whiff of scandal attached to the name, but most critics deliberately ignored this. Samuel Lucas, in his review for the *Times*, did his best to turn attention away from the pseudonym to the originality of the writing:

> Of the other recent fictions we have been most impressed with the series of *Scenes from Clerical Life* . . . which are now claimed by Mr. George Eliot—a name unknown to us. It is quite possible that this may be a mere *nom de plume*, and we are not curious to inquire at all upon this point. But we should be greatly surprised to hear that the real writer was previously known under any other appellation, for, like others who have speculated on his identity while these tales were publishing, we cannot assign his peculiarities to any living novelist.

But when the name made its second appearance a year later, this time on the title page of *Adam Bede*, indifference over the identity of George Eliot was no longer possible, for the novel had quickly become a best-seller, whereas the *Clerical Scenes* had enjoyed at best a literary success. In London there was much gossipy speculation that pointed to Marian Evans Lewes, but in the midst of this emerged a loosely organized movement to sponsor one Joseph Liggins, an obscure Warwickshire parson, as the real author of both the novel and the *Scenes*. Interestingly as well as somewhat inconsistently, he was allowed to have written the books, but there was no serious effort to equate him with "George Eliot." It was as if that pseudonym had somehow been detached from the fray and directed to float in the air, immune to pressures from below. The miraculous rescue of the name had been effected by the great mass of the reading public, described by John Blackwood fondly but without illusion as "a very curious animal and those who are most accustomed to feel its pulse know best how difficult it is to tell what will hit the bull's eyes. . . ." These were the readers who were remote from the relatively small but verbally active group of people who for various reasons were intent upon exposing the identity of the author. But the other readers, the majority, did not know enough about the real George Eliot to censor or praise her should she come out of hiding, and the name of Liggins drew only a larger and less interesting blank in their minds.

There was a limit to their leniency once they were informed. When at last it was publicly known that George Eliot was—just as the lowest of the gossip had insinuated—the unmarried wife of George Henry Lewes, the sales of *The Mill on the Floss* wavered, even dipped, but then steadied and climbed again. And from that time on, except to a few detractors who were personally motivated, the name "George Eliot" was virtually inviolate until the woman behind the pseudonym once again attracted public attention by marrying John Cross.

For the author herself the name at first meant nothing more than a convenient shelter which she had assumed was temporary. But circumstances prolonged its necessity so that imperceptibly she, both as writer and person, grew into the name, endowing it with a personality all its own. As a literary technique, it was but a natural extension of that of the male narrator-commentator already used in "Amos" and again being used in "Gilfil" when she adopted the pseudonym. Thus strengthened by having been given a name, the device admirably suited both the power and the limitation of her literary talent. As George Eliot, she could stand aside from her characters and avoid the dramatic confrontation she had always feared. And yet, if and when she wished, she could come forward to mingle with them and even, occasionally, to disappear altogether at strategically planned times. As omniscient storyteller, she was guaranteed (in the tradition firmly established by Fielding) her right to comment, adding scope and depth to the restricted understanding of her characters. It was in this way that "George Eliot" came to perform the function of dramatic irony as in the Greek tragedies; she gives the reader the privilege of knowing more about the inner and outer natures of the characters and their relationship to their world than they could know or articulate themselves. Basically, this need for a dual technique by which to tell a story stemmed from George Eliot herself. It can perhaps be traced back at least to the Strand days, when she "complained" to Spencer "of being troubled by double consciousness—a current of self-criticism being an habitual accompaniment of anything she was saying or doing; and this naturally tended towards self-depreciation and self-distrust." "George Eliot," although only a name, became the critical half of this consciousness, thus converting the force which had undermined self-confidence into the one which critically analyzed characters. In its final form, this force was perhaps the "not herself" which George Eliot told Cross had taken possession of her in all that she considered her best writing, so "that she felt her own personality to be merely the instrument through which this spirit . . . was acting." Unique in combining the critical with creative energy, it is one of the most distinctive characteristics of George Eliot's art.

The pseudonym was a synthesizing agent in her life in yet another respect. Probably no other woman in any age more effectively and with less calculated effort reconciled the opposing demands of her androgynous nature. In a sense, both the masculine name of "George Eliot" and the feminine one of "Mrs. Lewes" were unfounded in reality. Yet both were highly operative symbols of the two spheres of being which constituted her life—her writing and her relationship with Lewes. Her inner self responded to her outward life as signified by the two names, so that the process of self-control which had begun with her ordeal at 142 Strand was carried onward. Very gradually the process brought about a psycho-physical change, one aspect of which was observed by Oscar Browning who, uncritically devoted though he was, admits that when he first met her in 1866, "a certain awkwardness of manner was a salient characteristic of George Eliot, and did not entirely disappear till the last ten years of her life, when it was absorbed in that kindly and majestic grace which has impressed itself on so many who have recorded her appearance." Rather than clumsiness (which, once present, is rarely lost), the awkwardness suggests an unnaturalness which may have arisen from a deeply felt indecision as to where between the opposite poles of passivity and aggressiveness lay the proper manner. Indecision and awkwardness were finally replaced by an inward harmony, which radiated outward to give grace to her bearing and beauty to her heavy and not well-proportioned facial features. Forewarned that he would find a woman with a mannish face, many "a stranger,"—Edith Simcox recalled—"seeing her for the first time, asked why he had never been told she was so beautiful."

Similarly, those who came to the Sunday receptions at the Priory to talk admiringly of her work found the books dwarfed by her personal presence. "She appeared much greater than her books," Browning states simply, and he had the highest opinion of her work. "Her ability seemed to shrink beside her moral grandeur. . . . You never dared to speak to her of her works; her personality was so much more impressive than its product." Writing a few years earlier, Mathilde Blind had reached the same conclusion: "Those who knew George Eliot were even more struck by the force of her entire personality than by her writings." Loving her, and herself ravaged by uncontrollable emotional stresses, Edith Simcox perhaps came nearest to understanding the meaning of what in the vocabulary of the day was called George Eliot's "moral grandeur." "What fascinated one," she wrote in her "Autobiography" two weeks after George Eliot's death, "was the vision of a wholly *natural* nature, full of all manner of primitive passions of irresistible strength, but so beautifully ordered and inspired that her impulses were in fact more righteous than another's laboured resolutions." As Edith had not known the earlier George Eliot, in whom there had been a vast array of *un*ordered primitive passions, she may not have realized that she was describing a great personal triumph.

Although the most vital effects of the pseudonym took considerable time to become evident, there is some indication that even when she thought of it as a casual matter, George Eliot almost immediately gained new confidence in herself as a writer by having it at hand to use in her correspondence with the Blackwoods. The specific name gave her in their eyes what she must have wanted but had not consciously sought—an identity no longer wholly dependent upon Lewes's or even upon his generous role as entrepreneur. Having been born, like Athena, out of the mind and fully endowed, the name had a timeless quality about it. It was probably this, rather than arrogance, which permitted her to tell John Blackwood only two weeks after the pseudonym had been invented that her stories *always* grew out of the psychology of her characters, and to go on responding to his criticisms as if she were a well-seasoned writer of fiction. After the 4 February letter in which the pseudonym was declared, she was never again to take the indirect route of writing to the major what she really meant to say to his brother.

T HE PSEUDONYM COULD HAVE GIVEN HER NO DIRECT HELP IN her troubled relationship with Isaac, yet she may have drawn courage from the mere awareness of its existence. For years Isaac had made her feel that she needed to justify her existence, and the pseudonym stood as a promise of an independent career which was only beginning to unfold. If it was the kind of career that would mean nothing to him, this was one of the ironies she would have to bear. She perceived, too, the irony surrounding her need to report her peculiar marriage to Isaac. He had once predicted that she would never find a man willing to take her on as a wife because of her association with those radical, free-thinking Brays and Hennells; well, she had found a man—far more free-thinking than her old Coventry friends—who wanted to make her his wife, but was powerless to do so in the way approved by the law and society, possibly as a result of his early freethinking about human relationships. So, in a deeply ironic way, Isaac had been more prophetic than his inflexible mind could ever have envisaged.

It was neither sisterly love nor the feeling of obligation toward an older brother which prompted her to tell him of her marriage. Isaac needed to know her whereabouts so that she could receive the income from her inheritance, the semi-annual payments of which were under his control. It was for this reason that she had been sporadically in touch with him from almost the beginning of her life with Lewes, for going abroad in 1854 had necessitated special arrangements by which the money could reach her. Her first solution had been to request Isaac to make the December payment directly to Charles Bray, who of course was fully aware of the complicating conditions. She also asked Isaac to be sure to make the payment on 1 December, when it was due; but his answer to this (sent through Chrissey) was an uncompromising statement that he would pay the money no earlier than he received it. This not only angered her but made her concerned that it might inconvenience Bray, to whom she wrote that she would "take care in future not to involve anyone else in the annoyance resulting from [Isaac's] disinclination to accommodate me." In the same letter she informed Bray that she had also received from Chrissey, Isaac's message "that circumstances render it desirable for the trustees to call in £1,500 of my money, which must consequently be placed in the funds until a new investment can be found for it. So next Midsummer my income will be less than usual."

As Bray would have understood, this was unwelcome news. At the time, she needed money far more than when she had been alone; and indeed the calling in of that sum might drastically have reduced her income, for her father had willed her only £2,000 in trust, neither more nor less than he had given (divided between cash and trust) to Fanny and Chrissey each, although he did also leave her £100 worth of household goods "not already disposed of" (which, fortunately, by codicil to his will he substituted with that amount in cash). Perhaps this was material repayment in his mind for her dedicated nursing. Although he was fairly generous with Robert, Jr., he left the bulk of his estate to Isaac; it is possible that he envisioned his spinster daughter living her life out in the midst of Isaac's household as governess, ambiguous companion, even housekeeper (just as Fanny would have lived in Robert's household had she not married Henry Houghton). Her father's will was no more unfair to her than many another Victorian father's to an unmarried daughter. Certainly, there is no surviving indication that George Eliot thought herself unfairly treated as far as the sum of her inheritance was concerned; but she did resent the humiliating strings attached to her collecting what was lawfully hers. Robert, Isaac, and Vincent Holbeche (the family solicitor) had been appointed the trustees of all moneys; it would seem, however, that Isaac took it upon himself alone to supervise the payments to her.

Back in England by the spring of 1855, she realized that she had to make yet another plan, and while waiting alone in Dover for Lewes's return, she wrote Isaac again, asking him to pay her income into the Coventry and Warwickshire Bank. No longer believing that he would comply with any request from her, she confided her misgivings to Bray: ". . . as he is not precise in answering letters (mine at least) it is difficult to know what he will do." Apparently he did the right thing, for on 17 June she told Bray: "My brother has sent me an order on Jones, Lloyd and Co. for my half year's income, with a kind letter saying that he hopes to find a good investment for the money which has been called in." If this payment was due on the first of the month—as the December one was—she evidently was forced to wait at least two weeks for the order on the bank; in her mind, however, the kind letter from Isaac would have more than offset any trouble which might have been caused by the delay. The mere fact that he had written directly to her as her wording suggests, although the letter has not survived, would have been enough to have made a terse explanation of the financial situation seem a loving message to her; his niggardliness in writing had hurt her ever since she had been in Switzerland awaiting some kind of consoling letter from him that never did arrive. One assumes from the lack of reference to them in the extant correspondence that for the next two years Isaac handled the subsequent payments satisfactorily. But it is clear that he retreated into his old habit of having his wife, Sarah, carry on the meager communication, for in George Eliot's first letter to him since 1855—that of 16 April 1857, written at St. Mary's—she begs more news of Chrissey, about whose serious illness she had heard from Sarah Evans, and asks him to withhold £15 from her midsummer payment to use toward a change of air for her sister. She admits that she is telling him of this plan "rather prematurely," and gives as her ostensible reason "to save multiplying letters, which I know you are not fond of. . . ."

This letter led indirectly to the seemingly final divorce—as she was to call it in the "Brother and Sister" sonnets—between her and Isaac. When neither he nor Sarah answered her, she felt compelled to write again, and this time she not only repeated her questions and instruction concerning Chrissey but added:

> You will be surprised, I dare say, but I hope not sorry, to learn that I have changed my name, and have someone to take care of me in the world. The event is not at all a sudden one, though it

may appear sudden in its announcement to you. My husband has been known to me for several years. . . .

Even so, she had waited a full five weeks before writing this second letter, mailed on 26 May from the Channel Island of Jersey, for which she and Lewes had quitted the Scillies on 11 May. On that same day she had received via Blackwood (who had enclosed it in a note to Lewes) a sincere fan letter from Archer Gurney—a writer about her own age whose work included a translation of Part II of *Faust*. After some heady compliments on what had thus far been published of the *Clerical Scenes*, Gurney asked her certain questions that she was beginning to ask herself:

> Will you always remain equally natural? That is the doubt. Will the fear of the critic, or the public, or the literary world, which spoils almost every one, never master you? Will you always write to please yourself, and preserve the true independence which seems to mark a real supremacy of intellect?

This was a new milestone, as Cross noted with fitting reverence:

> I subjoin this letter, as it is the first she received in her character of a creative author, and it still bears a pencil memorandum in her writing: "This letter [Lewes] brought up to me at Jersey after reading it, saying, with intense joy, 'Her fame is beginning.'"

Six months later this episode was still vividly in her mind, for she describes it in "How I Came to Write Fiction" in even greater detail. Obviously Gurney's letter meant much to her, and its arrival may have buoyed her up enough to overcome almost three years' procrastination in telling her brother that she had changed her name to Lewes, enclosing in his letter one for Fanny to give her the same news. But there remained the old problem of devising a method by which she could receive the payments from her trust fund, especially as one would be due her on 1 June and she and Lewes did not plan to end their happy stay at Gorey, Jersey, until near the end of July. The suggestion she makes to Isaac would have re-emphasized to him how totally she and Lewes were sharing their lives:

> We shall remain at the coast here, or in Brittany for some months, on account of my health, which has for some time been very frail, and which is benefited by the sea air. [This seems a pathetic—and an unheeded—bid for sympathy, as there is no other indication that the sojourn at Scilly and Jersey was for any reason besides zoological research, and the extant letters are remarkably free of references to physical complaints.] The winter we shall probably spend in Germany. But an inconvenience about money payments to me may, I suppose, be avoided if you will be kind enough to

pay my income to the account of Mr. G. H. Lewes, into the Union
Bank of London, Charing Cross Branch, 4, Pall Mall East, Mr.
Lewes having an account there.

Lewes had only recently opened this bank account, the first he had
ever had, as in the past he had chosen to invest whatever money was
left after meeting his immediate expenses. One of the major functions
of his account was to serve as a repository for George Eliot's new
literary earnings, for as a measure of securing anonymity even with
bankers, she had instructed Blackwood to make all payments due her
to Lewes's account. Now the account stood ready to receive also the
interest from her inheritance. Perhaps to make certain that they had
a record of the method of payment which she had specified to Isaac,
as well as to preserve what he rightly sensed to be a momentous docu-
ment, Lewes copied her letter, as he would also her next letter meant
for Isaac but not addressed directly to him.

George Eliot was immensely relieved to have written the dreaded
letter. The very next day she wrote happily to John Chapman to tell
him he no longer need serve as her post office for her family, as she
had taken the step she had "long been meditating—that of telling
my brother and sister that I am married. I wrote for that purpose
on Monday, so now I shall not need to trouble you further with the
transmission of letters, and you must henceforth remember that I am
Mrs. Lewes to all my relatives. . . ." By 2 June she was responding to
Fanny with "a thousand thanks" for what must have been a friendly
and understanding answer to her letter, and saying that she had just
written to Chrissey, having heard—apparently from Fanny, although
she had asked Isaac the question—that her sister could receive such a
letter without being dangerously agitated. On 5 June she told Sara
Hennell about Fanny's "very kind letter" but mentioned that she had
not yet heard from either her brother or Chrissey. At this time, no
word from Chrissey signified to her only that her sister was too ill to
write, and with unwarranted confidence she stated to Sara: "I do not
think that Chrissey will give up correspondence with me in any case,
and that is the point I most care about, as I shall still be able to help
her as far as my means will allow." Surely by this time she could not
have been so sanguine in her expectations of a reply from Isaac.

Yet one senses that she was shocked when Isaac delegated the obligation of answering her to Vincent Holbeche, who, writing on 9 June
put to her the crucial question: "Permit me to ask when and where
you were married. . . ." He prefaced this by explaining that Isaac was
"so much hurt at your not having previously made some communication to him as to your intention and prospects that he cannot
make up his mind to write, feeling that he could not do so in a

Brotherly Spirit." This was probably quite true, absurd as it seems in the context of the total situation. Just as Isaac had been angered and hurt by her plan to leave Chrissey's after the funeral of Edward Clarke without first consulting him, so now he was offended because she was telling him about an important event in her life only after it had transpired, even though he could not have approved of it under any circumstance. Holbeche seems to have been well aware of his delicately balanced role as intermediary between two violently opposed temperaments and ways of life. His letter to her, addressed to "Dear Mrs. Lewes," is as kindly as such a letter could be; and his concluding wish, that the result of further explanation from her "may be that of your Brother corresponding directly with you," was no doubt sincere.

Although at last convinced that there could be no direct communication—confrontation, rather—between herself and her brother, she did not shrink from replying to Holbeche. She felt no rancor toward him, for she recognized that he had been forced into a difficult position, and also she gratefully remembered—as she tells him in this letter of 13 June—that it was through his intercession she had been left cash instead of household goods and hence granted a modicum of independence during that terrible and aimless year following her father's death. But she could not resist inserting a barb for Isaac, who she knew would be impatiently awaiting her answer:

> My brother has judged wisely in begging you to communicate with me. If his feelings towards me are unfriendly, there is no necessity for his paining himself by any direct intercourse with me, indeed, if he had written to me in a tone which I could not recognize (since I am not conscious of having done him any injury) I must myself have employed a third person as a correspondent.

She then describes Lewes as "a well-known writer," and admits that although to them their marriage is "a sacred bond," it is not a legal one "because, though long deprived of his first wife by her misconduct, [Lewes] is not legally divorced." The reason she gives for withholding the fact of her living with Lewes from the members of her own family is that, knowing their views of life differed from hers, she "wished not to give them unnecessary pain." Then she refers to her writing:

> It may be desirable to mention to you that I am not dependent on any one, the larger part of my income for several years having been derived from my own constant labour as a writer. You will perceive, therefore, that in my conduct towards my own family I have not been guided by any motives of self-interest, since I have been neither in the reception nor the expectation of the slightest favour from them.

Four days after she had sent her letter to Holbeche, she wrote Sara Hennell about it, concluding: "I dare say I shall never have any further correspondence with my brother, which will be a great relief to me. So now there is nothing to be concealed from any one. . . ." She was right about Isaac. There was to be no further correspondence between them for twenty-three years; and she was sincere—not bitterly defiant, as she might have been only a few years earlier—in claiming that it was a relief to have him out of her life. But in an unhappily negative way, he continued to make his presence felt through his hold over Chrissey, who obeyed his command not to write to their wayward sister, although she was finally to do so late in February 1859, with sad apology for having "ceased to write and neglected one who under all circumstances was kind to me and mine."

Chrissey perhaps gained the courage to defy Isaac through her awareness that the time was drawing near when the expression of regrets would be impossible. She died only three weeks after writing her letter, although within that time George Eliot responded, offering to come to her, and Chrissey wrote back through her daughter Emily and also with a few penciled words of her own that she thought seeing her sister would be too much excitement for her. Despite her genuine grief over Chrissey's condition, George Eliot could not help feeling that by her sister's wise decision she had been granted a reprieve from impending doom, for she could hardly have traveled back to see Chrissey without also seeing Isaac. For this she was not ready; both her personal peace and her writing (she had only recently begun *The Mill on the Floss*) demanded that he stay out of her life.

WHEN, AFTER HER LETTER TO HOLBECHE, GEORGE ELIOT HAD written to Sara that "now there is nothing to be concealed from any one," she seems to have temporarily forgotten that her new writing had committed her to a concealment far more extensive than the one determined by her living with Lewes, although of course the reason for the second subterfuge was inextricably bound with that of the first. But she had the need for caution in mind as she wrote to Isaac and then to Holbeche, for she must have yearned to specify the kind of writing she was doing and yet held herself severely in check, making it sound in her letter to Holbeche like sheer drudgery. She was well aware that one unguarded hint from her would shatter the scaffolding of the anonymity which she and Lewes were carefully constructing around her true identity. As it was, Fanny Houghton (the one reader in the remaining family circle) came dangerously near the secret when, in her letter acknowledging George Eliot's change of name, she remarked upon the two published *Clerical Scenes*, which had been written—so she had been told—by a Mr. Liggins. George Eliot's response is ingenious and shows signs of Lewes's fine touch:

> You are wrong about Mr. Liggins or rather your informants are wrong. We too have been struck with the "Clerical Sketches," and I have recognized some figures and traditions connected with our old neighbourhood. But Blackwood informs Mr. Lewes that the author is a Mr. Eliot, a clergyman, I presume. *Au reste*, he may be a relation of Mr. Liggins's or some other "Mr." who knows Coton stories.

George Eliot disliked deviousness, but with Lewes's help she was coming to see it as a game that must be played for a short while. Liggins was a freak who would gain no one's serious attention, and "Mr. Eliot" a comic phantom who would disappear with a puff when no longer needed. Yet one wonders how she might have answered had Fanny asked her real question—Did *you* write these two *Clerical Scenes*? Left to herself, without asking Lewes's advice, George Eliot might not have resisted the temptation to admit that she had written them. For she was already caught in the first of the several dilemmas which were to beset her early career: she yearned for those people whose approbation she most desired to detect her authorship (and was irrationally hurt when they did not); at the same time, she lived in dread that they would do just that.

Obviously Fanny had decided to explore tentatively at first, perhaps offering up the earliest rumors of Liggins's authorship of the *Scenes* as a kind of bait. As George Eliot's response was successfully evasive in all directions, she may have thought it best to cease probing. But without doubt she had called the *Scenes* to the attention of Isaac, who probably was neither a subscriber nor a regular reader of Maga, and they agreed that the only person in England who could have written them was their unpredictable sister. What evidence exists—admittedly scant and intermittent—indicates that Isaac, with Fanny's help, kept close watch on George Eliot's career. He assuredly did not do so out of literary interest or pride in her rapid advance to fame, but in fear that she would disgrace him and the family in print as she had done—according to his way of thinking—in real life. Sara Hennell reported to George Eliot that Isaac had "been heard to say after reading Adam Bede—'No one but his Sister could write the book'—'there are things in it about his Father that she must have written'—and his impression has been the same for 'Clerical Sketches.' "

George Eliot may have been surprised to learn that her brother had actually read these works. She knew from childhood on that he was not a natural reader: his element was the earth, his delight to be active upon it, and his life purpose to own a portion of it and control it, he being, "in the words of his granddaughter Alison . . . the archetype of the Englishman who loves land for the sake of land. . . ." But she would have been prepared for his reaction to what he read, as described by Mathilde Blind, who talked with Isaac himself and many of his old neighbors, and whose findings support Sara's version of his anxious interest in his sister's earliest writing:

> While the public had been trying to discover who the mysterious George Eliot could possibly be, one person there was who immediately penetrated the disguise, and felt positive as to the identity of the author. He recognized incidents, touches, a saying here or there, just the things that no one outside his own home could by any chance have come upon. But George Eliot's brother kept this discovery closely locked within his own breast. He trembled lest any one else should discover the secret, fearing the outcry of neighbors who might not always feel that the author had represented them in colors sufficiently flattering.

With the hindsight now possible, one realizes that just as Isaac was certain only his sister could have written these works, so he—and he alone—had the power at his command to put a stop to the Liggins affair before it was elevated from the realm of not very amusing farce to that of ugly menace. He need not have stepped into the arena to have done this; even a small authenticated notice to the *Times* would have turned the tide and saved George Eliot from many months of harrowing anxiety. But of course his overriding fear that she would be identified with him prevented him from taking any action whatever.

Isaac and Fanny kept their attention trained on what came from George Eliot's pen, although the surviving record skips to *Felix Holt*. As soon as Fanny had spotted an announcement of the publication of this new work, she wrote Isaac: "I am on the tip-toe of expectation to see the forthcoming novel by Mary Ann. It is too much to hope that no member of her own family will figure in it." Her curiosity was not so restricted as this might suggest, for she commented (and the majority of contemporary readers were to agree) that the subject of Felix "is one of general interest and will be much more to the taste of the ordinary novel reader than Romola was." Six months later, after having read *Felix*, she wrote again to Isaac in a way that suggests he too was still reading the novels: "I cannot expect you to join in my admiration of her last work. 'Felix' is a Radical, and I know radicals find no favour in your sight. But all the same the Book is marvellously clever; that you *must* confess." Apparently Fanny found nothing in this novel likely to arouse family indignation, and perhaps the record ends here because the easily recognizable autobiographical elements fade out of the later novels (not without leaving tantalizing traces).

Most conspicuously lacking in this brief record is reference of any kind to *The Mill on the Floss*, which must have given the family—especially Isaac—a severe shock. When Isaac recovered, he probably looked upon the book as autobiography twisted to vindicate the writer and to point accusingly at himself. It would not have been within the range of his perceptiveness to realize that the novel was an act of confession, not one of mere retaliation.

I F ISAAC HAD REMAINED IN HER LIFE, GEORGE ELIOT COULD not have written *The Mill on the Floss*. She never would have been free of the inhibiting awareness of his constant disapproval and the attendant, uneasy doubt that she alone was to blame for the deep trouble between them. Negative as it was in itself, Isaac's deliberate shutting himself off from her may have been the final step needed to liberate the full force of her creative power. She had early introjected her brother's demanding and yet indifferent attitude into her own consciousness and his was probably the fatal physiognomy which late in life she described as ever threatening the literary productivity of Theophrastus Such, who attempted to guard himself against it by blissfully imagining

> a far-off, hazy multitudinous assemblage, as in a picture of Paradise, making an approving chorus to the sentences and paragraphs of which I myself particularly enjoy the writing. The haze is a necessary condition. If any physiognomy becomes distinct in the foreground, it is fatal. The countenance is sure to be one bent on discountenancing my innocent intentions: it is pale-eyed, incapable of being amused when I am amused, or indignant at what makes me indignant; it stares at my presumption, pities my ignorance, or is manifestly preparing to expose the various instances in which I unconsciously disgrace myself. I shudder at this too corporeal auditor, and turn toward another point of the compass where the haze is unbroken. ["Looking Inward"]

This specter of an auditor was too deeply engrained within her to be eradicated at one stroke by Isaac's withdrawal; even when its control over her had lessened, she needed reassurance from friendly but discriminating critics who could stand between it and the hazy multitude. Nonetheless, her desire to explore the past—to confess yet defend herself—had been sharpened with new urgency and direction; and eventually, as in the *Mill*, she was to be able to do so with far fewer bizarre disguises and circumlocutions than she had found necessary in "Gilfil." But the transition did not occur painlessly. At the time it was beginning, she was writing "Janet's Repentance," which even she had hoped to make a happier story than "Gilfil." "I am longing to be a little merrier again," she wrote John Blackwood while finishing what she by then was admitting to be the "very melancholy story" of Tina. Blackwood was delighted to hear this, for he was shamelessly open about his preference for "happy" stories to whatever his new and most provocative contributor was sending him. He was very much disappointed when he received the first part of "Janet" (Chapters 1 through 4), which seemed to him "rather harsh for a sketch of English County Town life only 25 years ago."

She received this letter from Blackwood at almost the same time as Holbeche's response to her 26 May letter to Isaac. Plagued on all sides, she nonetheless answered her editor as if she had nothing else on her mind and showed more understanding of his role than she had in the correspondence over "Gilfil": "I am able, I think, to enter into an editor's doubts and difficulties, and to see my stories in some degree from your point of view as well as my own." But to his "I feel certain that I am right in advising you to *soften* your picture as much as you can," she wrote with a certainty which surpassed even his:

> Everything is softened from the fact, so far as art is permitted to soften and yet to remain essentially true. The real town was more vicious than my Milby; the real Dempster was far more disgusting than mine; the real Janet alas! had a far sadder end than mine, who will melt away from the reader's sight in purity, happiness and beauty.

She had allowed herself some irony in her last clause, a sign that she was more self-assured in arguing with Blackwood than during their disagreements over "Gilfil." She even went so far as to suggest that he not publish "Janet" in Maga but, significantly, in book form with the first two *Scenes*, an idea he had not yet broached. By now she was not easily to be deterred as a writer. After agreeing to make some alterations to meet his "marginal objections," she stated firmly:

> There is nothing to be done with the story, but either to let Dempster and Janet and the rest be as I *see* them, or to renounce it as too painful. I am keenly alive at once to the scruples and alarms an editor may feel, and to my own utter inability to write under any cramping influence, and on this double ground I should like you to consider whether it will not be better to close the series for

the Magazine *now*. I daresay you will feel no difficulty about publishing a volume containing the story of Janet's Repentance,
though you may not like to hazard its insertion in the Magazine,
and I shall accept that plan with no other feeling than that you
have been to me the most liberal and agreeable of editors and are
the man of all others I would choose for a publisher.

Three days later Lewes followed up this letter with one of his own,
which legitimately covered his returning the proof of a section of the
"Sea-side Studies," but which was also rhapsodic about "Janet" and
expressed bewilderment over Blackwood's negative reaction to the
story. However, Blackwood—perhaps goaded by her mild taunt that
he was afraid to publish the story, as well as by his genuine concern
that he lose this stimulating, if difficult, writer as a contributor to
Maga—had not waited for this letter from Lewes to write back to
the author herself:

I do not fall in with George Eliots every day and the idea of stopping the Series as suggested in your letter gave me "quite a turn"
to use one of Thackeray's favourite phrases. There is nothing in
the part that can make me "afraid" to publish it. . . . I only
wished to convey my fear that you are wasting power in sketching
in so many figures who would not help on or add to the popularity
of your story.

She was grateful for Blackwood's response and wrote back promptly:
"Thanks for your kind letter. It shows that you have understood me,
and will give me confidence for the future."

Possibly the pain caused by Isaac's cold way of sundering their
relationship may have added to the harshness of her depiction of
Milby, as it may have made her unduly sensitive to Blackwood's
criticism. At the same time, this released the urge to thrust the
dynamic process of confession up onto the surface of her writing,
where it had already appeared tentatively in the form of Tina's
"broken confessions" to Maynard Gilfil. In "Janet," confession
emerges as a major and redemptive theme, as well as a structurally
important element in this story of regeneration. It is told with the
help of sustained imagery derived from wine and water, each of which
serves as both destructive and regenerative symbol.

Janet Dempster is a beautiful woman of thirty-five who has become
a compulsive wine-drinker in an effort to make her indifferent to the
brutality of her alcoholic husband. Her own resolutions to abstain
from drinking having failed, Janet recognizes that she needs outside
help and for it turns to the Reverend Edgar Tryan, an Evangelical
curate of about her own age in whom she has sensed a deep sadness
which convinces her he has known some personal sorrow as profound

as hers. It was the remembrance of this that "seemed to promise her an untried spring, where the waters might be sweet. . . . If she could pour out her heart to him! If she could for the first time in her life unlock all the chambers of her soul!" (Chapter 16). After listening attentively to her confession of misery and weakness, Tryan assures her that God has not forsaken her. His words are sincerely meant, but she has heard them many times before without their having dented her anguish. Tryan, watching her closely, is aware of her disappointment and realizes that what she most needs now is the assurance of *human* sympathy:

> She must be made to feel that her anguish was not strange to him; that he entered into the only half-expressed secrets of her spiritual weakness before any other message of consolation could find its way to her heart. . . . And Janet's anguish was not strange to Mr. Tryan. He had never been in the presence of a sorrow and a self-despair that had sent so strong a thrill through all the recesses of his saddest experience; and it is because sympathy is but a living again through our own past in a new form, that confession often prompts a response of confession. [Chapter 18]

Tryan then recognizes that he must find the sympathy which would have the power to penetrate Janet's numbness in the depths of his own experience, as she has become immune not only to the coarseness in her husband but to life itself. "Yet [Tryan] hesitated: as we tremble to let in the daylight on a chamber of relics which we have never visited except in curtained silence. But the first impulse triumphed, and he went on" (Chapter 18). His going on is salvation for Janet, not because his confidential story has any significant meaning for her, but because he has allowed her to look into a hitherto secret chamber of his heart. Janet's ordeal has reached its climax, but it is not quite over. Her husband dies as a result of his intemperate drinking, thus removing the only external excuse for her own drinking; yet she feels a new surge of temptation when she accidentally comes upon a half decanter of brandy that her husband had hidden for his own use. Successfully withstanding the first "paroxysm of temptation," she dashes the bottle to the floor. Then shaken with fright, she wisely rushes to Tryan, whose heartfelt welcome and penetrative words of consolation and encouragement offered generously, despite his own tiredness and mortal illness, make her feel that "the water-floods that had threatened to overwhelm her rolled back again, and life once more spread its heaven-covered space before her" (Chapter 25). Not long after this, it can be seen by all that "Janet Dempster was a changed woman,—changed as the dusty, bruised, and sun-withered plant is changed when the soft rains of heaven have fallen on it . . ." (Chapter 26). As if in exchange for the life which has been restored to Janet, Tryan dies; and in the brief description of his burial, in which are juxtaposed the pagan and Christian symbols of death and regeneration, one is reminded that he has been both a human sinner and a Christ-like figure. When Janet leaves his grave, she goes to her home in Orchard Street, where her mother awaits her. Together they walk around the garden in silence with hands clasped, "looking at the golden crocuses bright in the spring sunshine. Janet felt a deep stillness within. She thirsted for no pleasure . . ." (Chapter 18).

This patterned imagery was new in George Eliot's writing, and was to reappear with unobtrusive effectiveness in all her novels. In "Janet's Repentance" it is already so harmoniously embedded within the narrative that even Lewes seems not to have detected it. If he had, he probably would not have made a punlike reference to Janet's drinking when admitting to Blackwood that although he found her story "singularly powerful and pathetic," his "sympathies [were] not easily enlisted on the side of an Evangelical curate and woman with 'spiritual' weaknesses. . . ." Blackwood was never won over to Janet as a suitable heroine, although after reading the concluding section of the story he tried valiantly to appear to be so, revealing at the same time that he, like Lewes, saw nothing in the story other than its surface realism:

> The pathetic interest is very great and gathers strong round Janet in spite of the unpoetic nature of her weakness and temptation. It was a bold choice of a plot and some will object to such a feature in a heroine, but there is no more common agent of human misery and trial than drunkenness, and consequently there can be no more legitimate material "for the writer of Fiction."

Janet was to be an embarrassment to most readers of the time, but there were a few exceptions. One was James Anthony Froude, who, little realizing that he was addressing the "Translator of Strauss" he had made a special effort to meet ten years earlier, wrote George Eliot through the Blackwoods to thank her for the complimentary copy of *Adam Bede* which had been sent him: "Yet you will understand my feeling when I tell you that to me Janet is the greatest character which you have drawn, and I should say the healthiest. . . . Janet abides with me, and will abide while I live. . . ." George Eliot responded appreciatively: ". . . so far as I am aware, you are only the *second* person who has shared my own satisfaction in Janet. I think she is the least popular of my characters. You will judge from that, that it was worth your while to tell me what you felt about her."

Months later, on 10 November 1859, when she had finally established the real identity of the author of the *Scenes* and *Adam Bede*, Elizabeth Gaskell wrote directly to George Eliot thanking her "most gratefully for having written all—Janet's Repentance perhaps most especially of all. . . ." Worrying that the *Scenes* would fade out of the public's mind, George Eliot wrote Blackwood on 29 February 1860: "I looked into them the other day, and felt that I had done nothing better than the writing in many parts of 'Janet.'"

She seems to have realized that in this third *Scene*, she had come of age as a writer. It is the one *Scene* which a reader knowing her only through her novels could easily identify as being George Eliot's. Maturity had come rapidly, all three *Scenes* having been written in slightly less than thirteen months. "Janet" alone had taken essentially six of these months; she began it on 18 April 1857 (Lewes's fortieth birthday) and finished it on 9 October. During this time she had proved that her writing need not be seriously interrupted by change of location or personal sorrow. At St. Mary's and then at Jersey, she demonstrated what was always to be her remarkable ability to resume whatever she was working on wherever the Leweses' wanderlust took them—perhaps because her writing was safely sealed in her own mind against the fluctuations of the immediate present; or perhaps because, as Oscar Browning thought, she was happiest and therefore most productive when off the mainland of England. Also during this time she had been forced to absorb Isaac's expected break with her and Chrissey's unexpected one, both of which happened to coincide with the most serious criticism of her writing she had thus far received from her publisher. These problems drained joy out of her daily life, yet her deepest reaction to them was somehow transformed into an energy that added itself to the strength now flowing freely into her writing. And, too, she had become more conscious of the forces controlling her writing; it was by no accident of time that in analyzing what Blackwood described as "the community of feeling between Tryan and Janet," she had also externalized the three components of the creative process which were already determining the course of her writing—confession, sympathy, and memory. The first of these had been with Isaac's unknowing help converted into the motivating force which was to lead her from novel to novel.

She was ready for a new beginning, and in October 1857 she commenced *Adam Bede*. But she was not wholly convinced that this was the result of her own free choice. She was inclined to blame Blackwood for bringing to an end the *Clerical Scenes*, for his obvious dislike of "Janet" had penetrated more deeply than had their major difference over the dagger scene in "Gilfil." Some time in August when back in Richmond and still very much absorbed in writing "Janet," she must have talked over with Lewes her growing fear that

Blackwood's criticism might curtail her freedom in writing. They apparently agreed that once "Janet" had appeared in Maga, the *Scenes* should come to a halt. Lewes began to prepare Blackwood when he sent back the next batch of corrected proof: "One feels the want of a larger canvas so as to bring out [in "Janet"] those admirable figures, Old Mr. Jerome—the Linnets—and the rest; but that is the drawback in all short stories." A few days later, 5 September, George Eliot wrote Blackwood: "Unless there be any strong reason to the contrary, I should like to close the series with this story. . . . I have a subject in my mind which will not come under the limitations of the title 'Clerical Life,' and I am inclined to take a large canvas for it, and write a novel." On 9 October, when she had finished "Janet," she wrote in her Journal: "I had meant to carry on the series, and especially I longed to tell the story of the 'Clerical Tutor,' but my annoyance at Blackwood's want of sympathy in the first part [of "Janet"] determined me to close the series and republish them in two volumes." Two months later, she was to repeat this entry word for word in her summary account of how she came to write fiction. She would forestall John Blackwood's attempt to control her writing. Without fully realizing it, she was perhaps beginning to shunt off onto him feelings meant for Isaac.

By the close of 1857, she was in love with her novel-in-progress and almost willing to think that she had turned to the longer form as a result of her own free decision. The year had not been an easy one, yet for the first time in her life she felt refreshed and hopefully ready for the future; her growing sense of security with Lewes and the dynamics of her writing had brought both new tranquility and new energy. As if in recognition that there were special reasons for celebration, Lewes postponed his seasonal visit to Vernon Hill at least long enough to spend Christmas Day with her, and her Journal entry reflects her gratitude: "George and I spent this lovely day together— lovely as a clear spring day. . . . We ate our turkey together in a happy *solitude à deux*." On the last night of the year, however, she was alone and in an introspective mood:

> The dear old year is gone with all its *Weben* and *Streben*. Yet not gone either; for what I have suffered and enjoyed in it remains to me an everlasting possession while my soul's life remains. This time last year I was alone, as I am now. . . . I was writing the introduction to "Mr. Gilfil's Love-Story." What a world of thought and feelings since then! My life has deepened unspeakably during the last year: I feel a greater capacity for moral and intellectual enjoyment, a more acute sense of my deficiencies in the past, a more solemn desire to be faithful to coming duties, than I remember at any former period of my life. And my happiness has deepened too;

the blessedness of a perfect love and union grows daily. I have had some severe suffering this year from anxiety about my sister, and what will probably be a final separation from her—there has been no other real trouble. Few women, I fear, have had such reason as I have to think the long, sad years of youth were worth living for the sake of middle age.

The lack of reference to Isaac indicates how decisively she intended to put him outside her present life. Also missing is any mention of the pseudonym which was to appear before the public only a few days later in the two-volume edition of the *Clerical Scenes*. She still had not disclosed her identity to the Blackwoods, although on 10 December, the major had descended on the Leweses at Richmond, ostensibly to do business with Lewes but probably most intent upon seeing George Eliot in person. She, however, "did not show"—so he wrote back to John, no doubt the instigator of the visit—"he is such a timid fellow, L. said. . . . I saw *a* Mrs. Lewes." George Eliot noted in her Journal, "Major Blackwood called—an unaffected agreeable man. It was evident to us when he had only been in the room a few minutes that he knew I was George Eliot." Perhaps belatedly feeling some compunction for having ignored John Blackwood in her earliest correspondence with the firm, she was reserving for him the right to be the first to meet her under the pseudonym he had long honored without bothersome questions. If so, the gesture was a fitting one, for he was to be the only person to enter her life after Lewes who was to have a profound effect upon herself and her work.

WHEN BLACKWOOD DID ARRIVE AT RICHMOND ON THE LAST Sunday in February 1858, a scene (described in her Journal) was enacted which might have been startlingly dramatic had not the guest been so able to predict its climax:

> He talked a good deal about the "Clerical Scenes" and George Eliot, and at last asked, "Well, am I to see George Eliot this time?" G. said, "Do you wish to see him?" "As he likes—I wish it to be quite spontaneous." I left the room, and G. following me a moment, I told him he might reveal me. Blackwood was kind. . . .

He enjoyed himself so much that he missed the train he had intended to take back to London. When at last in his hotel, he immediately wrote his wife, Julia, that he had found George Eliot to be "a woman (the Mrs. Lewes whom we suspected). This is to be kept a profound secret. . . . She is a most intelligent pleasant woman, with a face like a man, but a good expression." The following Friday he returned for a second visit, this time taking away with him what she had so far written of *Adam Bede*.

She was as favorably impressed with him as he with her. His letters had prepared her for his considerateness and good humor, and when she saw him, she found him personable. Also, being but a year older than she, he was within the age range of the men who had meant the most to her—Isaac, Chapman, Spencer, Lewes. Yet there were obstacles that she and John Blackwood each had to overcome before their relationship could become more than purely functional. In fact, to have made it even that, Blackwood had already surmounted what to him was the most forbidding of the obstacles, her living with Lewes; otherwise he would not have come to Richmond, nor would he have continued the *Clerical Scenes* through "Janet." Perhaps at the beginning he had been attracted to "Amos" because he really did believe that it was, as Lewes had intimated, a story by a clericus who was shyly attempting to break into print relatively late in life and without much literary background. It may have crossed his mind that this was hardly the kind of writer Lewes would sponsor. But he was a busy man and unwilling to give up his comfortable assumptions concerning the author of "Amos" until they were contradicted by reports from London which he could not ignore. To make the situation more difficult, he had been given a pseudonym rather than confidence. However, the pseudonym proved to be a shock absorber (as it was for the large reading public) and gave him time to readjust his original conception of the author whose three stories he had carried in Maga.

The readjustment was not easily made, but once achieved, Blackwood never wavered from it. He was a moral man who moved comfortably within the standards of his own times, but he had not thereby suffered atrophy of vision. He could recognize legitimate exceptions to convention, and George Eliot's obvious sincerity in her writing and manner when he met her convinced him that she possessed the necessary reverence for life and people to live as a law unto herself. Of course he regretted that she had to do so, and occasionally he had to curb his impulse to blame Lewes for her plight, although for the most part he willingly conspired with Lewes to protect and please her as much as possible. Privately he continued to wish that she was living more acceptably in the eyes of society, and early in 1861, when she was writing her novel about another outcast from society, Silas Marner, he wrote Langford: "She is a very fine creature I am certain, and I never can think of her position without positive pain."

George Eliot would have realized that by coming to Richmond, Blackwood had decided to accept her as Mrs. Lewes as well as George Eliot. She was grateful for this and no doubt had it in mind when she noted in her Journal that he had been "kind." Yet this also would have stiffened her pride as a writer. She was aware that he sought to publish in Maga not only material that was good in itself but also "what was, for the occasion, good enough." As an editor, she herself had frequently used material from the latter category (and had once seen even Lewes's articles as belonging in it). As a writer, however, she could not consider herself "occasional"; nor was she stimulated by writing for readers whose concept of a heroine was so restricted that they could not bear the thought that even as a child she might have had a dirty face, or to whom (as Blackwood reprovingly reminded Lewes) the clinical "analysis of the faeces of the Actiniae . . . could not be otherwise than distasteful. . . ." Such matters would have been in her mind, for when Blackwood came to Richmond, both he and she were assuming that *Adam Bede* would run as a serial in Maga.

Actually, she had already discovered that when she wished she could safely ignore his purely editorial criticism without his insisting that she comply. What was beginning to trouble her far more were his personal opinions, which increasingly revealed his congenital preference for happy stories and an aversion to melancholy and tragic ones. His obvious dislike for what he considered the harsh and unpleasant elements in her writing had begun to seem like an expression of disapproval of herself. She sensed that there was a gulf of temperament between them not unlike that which separated her and Isaac, and there is little doubt that the latter's withdrawal while she was at work upon "Janet" intensified her reactions to Blackwood's unenthusiastic reception of the story. Perhaps what hurt her more than any specific criticism he had given it was his frank statement after reading the first four chapters. "I greatly regret not being able to give applause altogether unqualified. . . ." His concluding sentence to this letter left her untouched as a mere bit of sophistry: "If my comments upon Janet disappoint you, consider that I am wrong and attribute my want of appreciation to a fortnight of hot weather and hotter dinners in London."

Although Blackwood had early learned from Lewes and her own few letters that she was extremely sensitive about her writing, he could not possibly know that by the simple act of becoming her editor-publisher, with the necessary right to approve or disapprove of her work, he had also entered into the most dangerously personal orbit of her life. Despite other intentions, she was compelled to regard him with wariness and distrust even while yearning for his approval, until finally she was to test him almost beyond the breaking point. Yet to a remarkable degree Blackwood seems to have understood that her writing was an extension of herself and therefore as independent of the ordinary criteria as her own life was of conventional morality. "Certainly," he wrote late in her career to his nephew William (the major's son), "she does seem to feel that in producing her books she is producing a living thing, and no doubt her books will live longer than is given to children of the flesh." Almost as if receptive to a telepathetic plea from her, he soon began to refrain from being openly critical of her manuscripts as he read them; and along with the praise which he took pains to make specific, he expressed confidence that whatever doubts he might have would be resolved when he could read the work as a whole. At times those doubts were grave ones, as over the Jewish element in *Daniel Deronda*: "But the simple fact is," he wrote to Langford, whose misgivings on the matter were even greater, "she is so great a giant that there is nothing for it but to accept her inspirations and leave criticism alone." It was not until the publication of this novel, her final one, that George Eliot came to the full realization of Blackwood's undeviating loyalty and importance to her.

During the intervening years she was more often than not convinced of his good will, but the moment some disagreement arose between him and her concerning the practical problems of publication, her confidence crumbled. Then she reverted to her suspicion that he was an undeclared enemy awaiting the chance to take advantage of her and refuse her what she had rightfully earned. Admittedly, he had proved over and over that although they were indeed temperamentally unlike, his nature was free of the self-centered narrowness and obstinacy which had oppressed her in Isaac's. Yet she remained uneasily aware that if he and she were to engage in rigorous intellectual debate (which apparently they never did), they would end up on opposing sides of every major issue as surely as would she and Isaac. She knew that Blackwood sympathized with none of the counter-movements of the age which had once strongly appealed to her and in which she still had hope as meliorating agents leading into the future. By family tradition he was born into political conservatism and he remained in it because he liked it. After his marriage (which took place in the same year in which the Leweses had united their lives), he always had a dog named Tory. And in Maga, although unlike his father (who had founded the magazine to combat Whigism) in separating politics from literature, he rarely lost an opportunity to have "fun" with the radicals. This, however, caused no rift between him and George Eliot. Not that she had lost all the revolutionary ardor which had led her in 1848 to write the young John Sibree that Europe's monarchs were worn-out humbugs and, after being pensioned off, should be preserved in a kind of zoological garden. But she had become increasingly convinced of what she had expressed in this same letter to Sibree, that the English working classes were as yet too unenlightened to bring about anything other than destruction by a revolutionary movement. Thus, despite its alarming title, *Felix Holt, the Radical* pleased Blackwood, while disappointing those readers who had hoped for something more militantly progressive.

Conservative in religious and metaphysical thought as he was in politics, Blackwood was still no naïve conformist. There was a tinge of pessimism, a Swiftian element, in his distrust of human reason when it invaded areas that he considered to belong to faith or common sense. With some irony he admitted, "I know I am a sad unbeliever in human wisdom, and if I could speak and write, which fortunately I cannot, I should be hooted off any platform in these enlightened days." His religious faith was, in his own words, "very simple"; he felt no need to rebel against any existing creed because he thought creeds in themselves, as well as the differences and disputes among them, relatively unimportant. But he intensely disliked the New Rationalism (of which Strauss was a prophet), which had become an instrument of religious skepticism, especially when applied to the dissecting of the biblical miracles. He thought the attempt to explain these miracles away wantonly destructive and arrogant, "when our whole existence, the whole world, and all we see above us, is a miracle which God alone understands"; and he also thought that the so-called Higher Criticism was a movement which might well lead to "a pretty general throwing up of creeds . . . when it was far wiser to leave people to believe as much as they can." In 1864 he wrote heatedly to Margaret Oliphant about his refusal to publish a proposed article on Renan's *Vie de Jesus*: "My feeling is always to let the heathen rage and say nothing about them. . . . Has not every poor devil doubts enough of his own without a posing ass of an essayist or reviewer trying to suggest other than them?"

George Eliot's response to Renan and the Higher Criticism in general was of course far more sophisticated than Blackwood's; yet she too had decided not to stir up winds of doctrine which might, as she had said in her *Antigone* essay, "disturb feeble minds and send them adrift on a sea of doubt." Starting from vastly different premises, she and Blackwood had arrived at similar conclusions. If there was some patronizing condescension in their attitude, it came from their serious acceptance of responsibility toward the readers who made possible their respective positions of influence. There is no indication that she and he ever discussed either her translations of Strauss and Feuerbach or her work on the *Westminster*, almost all of which would have been objectionable to him. But it seems clear that at least one phase of her unorthodoxy was well known to the Blackwood circle, for upon hearing of George Eliot's death, Margaret Oliphant wrote young William Blackwood (who by then had succeeded John as publisher and editor): "There is something very solemn in the thought of a great spirit like hers entering the spiritual world which she did not believe in. If we are right in our faith, what a blessed surprise to her!"

In the novels George Eliot remained, as she had long been, an avant-garde thinker. Had she wished, she could have blazed a track of defiant thought but she chose, rather, to move among all the great religions of Western civilization with compassionate understanding not so much for their creeds and doctrines, as for the people who are succored by them. Blackwood, at heart no more provincial than she, appreciated this, although he probably never realized how much of her own belief she refrained from expressing. She stayed silent even in 1873, when at the last minute Blackwood felt compelled to reject Lewes's *Problems of Life and Mind* for publication, although some of it was already in proof. He had worriedly procrastinated in making this decision because he realized the views expressed by Lewes in his work were also George Eliot's. However, to his great relief, Lewes reacted generously and quickly found another publisher. George Eliot had wisely intervened in no way, and thus the final occasion which might have provoked an intellectual confrontation between herself and Blackwood slipped quietly into the past.

Aⁿᵒᵗʰᵉʳ ᴘᴏᴛᴇɴᴛɪᴀʟʟʏ ᴅɪsʀᴜᴘᴛɪᴠᴇ ᴘʀᴏʙʟᴇᴍ ɪɴ Bʟᴀᴄᴋwood's relationship with George Eliot was neatly averted when by her own decision she stayed on the fringe of the growing women's rights movement. He was convinced that John Stuart Mill and other male champions of the feminist cause would in the long run do women more harm than service. Two sticks or two stones might be almost identical and so might be said to be equal; but to Blackwood's way of thinking, the innate differences between man and woman made that kind of equality an impossibility, no matter how many legal rights women might win. With candor he held the opinion—as his daughter says—that man "was the stronger in every way, and likelier to make his mark in the world, as history has shown us, and this not entirely on account of his superior schooling, as some would maintain."

By the same reasoning, he was unusually alert to superior work from women, which when found he accepted without prejudice, admiring it all the more because it was by a woman but at the same time judging it only on its intrinsic merits. There was pride in his acknowledgment that two of his best writers were women, Margaret Oliphant and George Eliot, who as novelists were "able to hold their own against all male competitors." He observed further (probably with some relief) that they and the other accomplished women he knew were the "least distressed about the Rights of Women." What he ignored was that George Eliot was automatically out of the struggle; her unique position as George Eliot and Mrs. Lewes made her so exceptional that the whole complex issue lost its relevancy when applied to her. She was sadly aware of this, as she showed in 1867, when she said to John Morley, who had asked her opinion of Mill's amendment to Gladstone's Reform Bill to give women the vote, "The peculiarities of my own lot have caused me to have idiosyncrasies rather than an average judgment."

Like Blackwood, she was annoyed by the bad writing that women were producing as propaganda to further their movement. However, she could not completely turn away from the scene of their special literary activity, for her good friends Bessie Parkes and Barbara Bodichon were ardent, although not fanatical, feminists. Barbara did some writing but mainly collected signatures for petitions relating to more equitable marriage laws. Bessie canvassed too, but her main contribution was the thankless one of editing pioneer feminist periodicals. Despite her fondness for Bessie, George Eliot was dismayed by the writing that she sponsored. In September 1857, when she was engrossed in bringing "Janet" to a conclusion, she urged Bessie to concentrate upon *business* in the *Waverley Journal*: ". . . the more statements of philanthropic movements and social facts, and the *less literature*, the better. Not because I like philanthropy and hate literature, but because I want to *know* about philanthropy and don't care for second-rate literature." Early in 1858, when invited to contribute to Bessie's second venture in editing, the *English Woman's Journal*, she was happy to have a legitimate excuse for declining (all her energy was going into the writing of *Adam Bede*), but as she could not say this openly, she told Bessie she had turned to writing books rather than articles and hoped that her negative response would not be misunderstood: "It is a question whether I shall give up building my own house to go and help in the building of my neighbour's garden wall." She had no desire to add to the potpourri she was sure would be assembled for the next— or any future—issue of the magazine. After meeting the attractive Matilda Hays, an indifferent writer who had been named Bessie's co-editor of the *Journal*, she wrote Sara Hennell that Miss Hays must have "been chosen on the charitable ground that she had nothing else to do in the world. There is something more piteous almost than soapless poverty in this application of feminine incapacity to literature." In a sense, George Eliot was the greatest feminist of them all, for what she detested was the possibility that mediocre writing should be praised simply because it was by a woman espousing a woman's cause.

Also she would have assented to John Blackwood's belief that no amount of external equality would nullify the inherent disparity between women and men that resulted from their physical differences. Unlike Blackwood, however, she did not thereby bring her thought about women's position to a halt in a glow of sentimental rationalization. In *Felix Holt*, Mrs. Transome states flatly, "God was cruel when he made women" (Chapter 39). In the story, personal tragedy lay behind this statement: when young she had been trapped by nature to bear an illegitimate son sired by a man she came to loathe. Several months after the publication of this novel, George Eliot said something similar in her 1867 letter to John Morley, although with softening qualifications: "I mean," she explained (continuing a discussion begun earlier in the evening), "that as a fact of mere zoological evolution, woman seems to me to have the worse share in existence." Her physical make-up is a harsh fatality, a non-moral fact, which at present can be mitigated only by "love in the largest sense." However, the present is but one transitional stage, the goal being "a more clearly discerned distinction of function (allowing always for exceptional cases of individual organization) with as near an approach to equivalence of good for woman and man as can be secured by the effort of growing moral force to lighten the pressure of hard non-moral outward conditions." Mrs. Transome is not one of the "exceptional cases of individual organization"; she allows her fate to be shaped, and she crumbles before it. Preceding the depiction of Mrs. Transome's wasted life had been other portraits of women victimized by both man and nature: the Lucy (although seen only through Tryan's words) of "Janet"; the tragically naïve Hetty of *Adam Bede*; and Molly Farran (Eppie's mother) of *Silas Marner*. Finally in *Daniel Deronda* comes Lydia Glasher, mistress to Grandcourt, for whom she had left her husband and child and by whom, after bearing four of his children, she is pushed aside as he marries Gwendolen Harleth. During Gwendolen's first encounter with Lydia, Gwendolen feels "a sort of terror: it was as if some ghastly vision had come to her in a dream and said, 'I am a woman's life' " (Book II, chapter 4).

This novel also contains the only woman character—the Princess Halm-Eberstein, Daniel's mother—who possesses without question that exceptional "individual organization" that allows her to defy the pre-established limitations into which she had been born as a Jewish woman. Since her rebellion comes from the depths of her nature, it transcends the specific restrictions of her Jewishness and lashes out at the man-made code of submissiveness to familial duties imposed upon all women. Unlike Mrs. Transome, the Princess has no illegitimate child to conceal. Daniel is born of the marriage she had entered into only when she had extracted from the man his promise that he would not in any way thwart her desire to become a great dramatic artist (a desire which she fulfills). For the same reason, and without compunction, she eliminates Daniel from her life, contriving that he be reared as an English gentleman in comfortable circumstances and in ignorance of his Jewish heritage. She bids him come to her only when she realizes that she is dying and he has attained young manhood. Somewhat appalled, he listens as she discloses the unwomanly motives that had directed her life:

> Every woman is supposed to have the same set of motives, or else to be a monster. I am not a monster, but I have not felt exactly what other women feel—or say they feel, for fear of being thought unlike others. When you reproach me in your heart for sending you away from me, you mean that I ought to say I felt about you as other women say they feel about their children. I did *not* feel that. I was glad to be freed from you. [Book VII, chapter 2]

Near the end of her second and final interview with Daniel, she thrusts upon him a jeweled miniature of herself "in all the fire of youth," and as he looks at it "with admiring sadness," she demands:

> Had I not a rightful claim to be something more than a mere daughter and mother? The voice and the genius matched the face. Whatever else was wrong, acknowledge that I had a right to be an artist. . . . My nature gave me a charter. [Book VII, chapter 4]

Daniel departs convinced that his mother has missed happiness because of her inability to love in a personal sense. George Eliot neither agrees nor disagrees with him, and she does not indicate to the reader that the Princess *should* have sacrificed her passion for art to being a loving wife and mother.

Assuredly, the Princess is not presented as a happy woman, but her unhappiness, as well as her pride, stems from having a man's genius imprisoned in her woman's body. "You may try—" she had said to her son during their first meeting, "but you can never imagine what it is to have a man's force of genius in you, and yet to suffer the slavery of being a girl" (Book VII, chapter 2). This is the sentence which Cross quotes as applicable to George Eliot herself while keeping house for her father and Isaac at Griff. Cross admits: "This is a point of view that must be distinctly recognized by any one attempting to follow the development of George Eliot's character," but then continues with one of his abrupt switches: "and it will always be corrected by the other point of view which she has made so prominent in all her own writing—the soothing, strengthening, sacred influences of the home life, the home loves, the home duties." Yet in the whole range of her fiction, George Eliot depicts at most two intact and happy families, the Poysers in *Adam Bede* and the Garths in *Middlemarch*. Admittedly each of the novels (except *Romola* and *The Spanish Gypsy*) ends with a marriage which holds the hope of leading to a happier and more meaningful family life than had preceded it. What she seems to be saying implicitly is that the nuclear family is the most efficient means of holding together men and women related by blood and marriage, but as its mere existence is in itself neither a virtue nor an assurance of the felicitous lives of its members, young people should be impressed with "the immense possibilities of making a small home circle brighter and better. Few are born to do the great work of the world, but all are born to this." These are (as one might guess) Cross's words attempting to summarize George Eliot's attitude toward both the Family and Woman, and they are words that helped create a design in the George Eliot legend which he was carefully weaving into the *Life* as he composed it. In his eyes, as in Blackwood's, the women who solicited equality from men were unpleasantly masculine, and he wanted above all else to secure George Eliot against the charge of masculinity:

> She was keenly anxious to redress injustices to women, and to raise their general status in the community. This, she thought, could best be effected by women improving their work—ceasing to be amateurs. But it was one of the most distinctly marked traits in her character that she particularly disliked everything generally associated with the idea of a "masculine woman." She was, and as a woman wished to be, above all things, feminine. . . . Nothing offended her more than the idea that because a woman had exceptional intellectual powers therefore it was right that she should absolve herself, or be absolved, from her ordinary household duties.

In fact, Cross was not wholly wide of the mark. He was saying what he thought George Eliot would have wished him to say, and probably a part was a fairly literal reproduction of what she actually had expressed to him. Her consciousness that her fame was being achieved under a masculine pseudonym may have led her to over-protest both her own femininity and the traditionally sanctioned roles of women.

However, it was not this alone which determined her cautious approach to what was thought of as "the problem of higher education for women." With all the objectivity at her command, she believed that both women and education were integral parts of the fabric of civilization, and that to isolate the one in relation to the other was to move away from the ideal goal of harmonizing the sexes by making it possible for them to complement one another. What George Eliot really wanted was an educational plan for both men and women which would give to each an equal chance to read the classics and study the sciences, and further, an opportunity to know themselves and hence their true vocations. Her own experience had taught her reverence for "vocation" in its most literal sense—a call heard from God or (as in her instance) from within; and her first fictional character, Amos Barton, brought tragedy upon himself and others because he had become a clergyman without having heard the call. Yet she felt constrained in expressing herself. Not only was there her peculiar position as Mrs. Lewes–George Eliot, but her own genuinely followed vocation had brought fame and fortune, whereas (she was well aware) few other vocations were then open to women which could offer such status-pleasing careers. She did not dare suggest outright that a woman should make certain within herself that she was drawn to a particular kind of work rather than to the hope of the prestige it might bring; but in 1868 she did write to Barbara Bodichon that she was afraid women, in the excitement of the movement which promised to take care of all their grievances, would forget "the great amount of social unproductive labour which needs to be done by women, and which is now either not done at all or done wretchedly." She knew that this was not the clarion call wanted, yet she went doggedly on. Most women, given new rights, would be likely to think themselves ready to aim

> at doing the highest kind of work, which ought rather to be held in sanctity as what only the few can do well. I believe—and I want it to be well shown—that a more thorough education will tend to do away with the odious vulgarity of our notions about functions and employment, and to propagate the true gospel that the deepest disgrace is to insist on doing work for which we are unfit—to do work of any sort badly. There are many points of this kind that want being urged, but they do not come well from me, and I never like to be quoted in any way on this subject. But I will talk to you some day, and ask you to prevail on Miss Davies to write a little book which is much wanted.

Emily Davies did not write that "little book" but she worked tirelessly to bring about the founding of Girton College at Hitchin (not far from Cambridge) in October 1869. When in that month George Eliot was queried about her part in this venture, she made it clear that she was essentially uninvolved:

> I have no . . . practical connexion with the proposed college, beyond subscribing to it, and occasionally answering questions which Miss Davies has put to me about the curriculum which would be desirable. I feel too deeply the difficult complications that beset every measure likely to affect the position of women and also I feel too imperfect a sympathy with many women who have put themselves forward in connexion with such measures, to give

any practical adhesion to them. There is no subject on which I am more inclined to hold my peace and learn, than on the "Women Question." It seems to me to overhang abysses, of which even prostitution is not the worst. . . .

But on one point I have a strong conviction, and I feel bound to act on it, so far as my retired way of life allows of public action. And that is, that women ought to have the same fund of truth placed within their reach as men have; that their lives (i.e. the lives of men and women) ought to be passed together under the hallowing influence of a common faith as to their duty and its basis. . . . It is not likely that any perfect plan for educating women can soon be found, for we are very far from having found a perfect plan for educating men. But it will not do to wait for perfection.

Although lacking its sweeping and joyous optimism, this letter is not significantly different in thought from the conclusion to her "Woman in France" essay written fifteen years earlier.

The experience of being so well known that her simplest statement might be considered a news item, as well as the necessity of thinking in terms of a planned curriculum rather than "the whole field of reality," had sobered her. She would have been a wonderful teacher within the tutorial system, never a happy educational administrator. However, she put forth effort to maintain a more than perfunctory interest in Girton College, if only to please Barbara Bodichon, who was one of its founders. In the late spring of 1877, she and Lewes made the last of their several festive trips to Cambridge. Their main object was Trinity College but they did, upon invitation, visit Girton, which had by then moved from Hitchin to the outskirts of Cambridge, and also Newnham Hall, another women's college, initiated by Jemima Clough two years after the founding of Girton and soon settled in the old suburb of Newnham on the west bank of the Cam. Lewes's brief Journal entry suggests that the women's colleges were swallowed up by the magnificence of the entertainment proffered at Trinity: "Our stay at Cambridge one uninterrupted excitement—guests at breakfast, lunch and dinner. Very delightful. We visited Girton and Newnham Hall." Unfortunately, George Eliot's retrospective reference of five months later is still more sparse, merely mentioning "a delightful visit to Cambridge." To Oscar Browning, a Cambridge man, this visit was one of the several highlights in his memory of George Eliot:

I remember the occasion well. . . . The authoress was more tender, more dignified, and more impressive than ever. . . . I remember the interest she showed in an American typewriting machine, expressing at the same time . . . the fear lest the type-writer should not only reveal its utterances in print, but should multiply them after the manner of a printing-press, thus adding to the number of

worthless books. . . . A rather large party had been asked to meet
them, and as most of the guests had never met George Lewes and
his wife before, there was some excitement to hear the words which
might fall from their lips. The silence was broken by Lewes saying
to her, "Why, my dear, you surely don't like that heavy black
Bavarian beer, do you?" an unexpected beginning of memorable
table-talk.

Fifty-one years later, in October 1928, another great novelist made
the same visits to deliver two lectures on "Women and Fiction," one
at Newnham Hall and the other as Girton College, lectures that were
later reworked into the long, sinuous essay *A Room of One's Own*. It
is in this work that Virginia Woolf with disarming candor exposes the
disparity between the opulent furnishings and food for the men at
Cambridge and the Spartan frugality of what she found at the
women's dormitories of both Newnham and Girton. For evidence as
to how these women were respected as students, she draws upon
Mr. Oscar Browning,

> because Mr. Oscar Browning was a great figure in Cambridge
> at one time, and used to examine the students at Girton and
> Newnham. Mr. Oscar Browning was wont to declare "that the im-
> pression left on his mind, after looking over any set of examination
> papers, was that, irrespective of the marks he might give, the best
> woman was intellectually the inferior of the worst man."

Although intent upon laying bare the unfairnesses at Newnham
and Girton, including masculine snobbery, Virginia Woolf did not
approve of those well-meaning reformers of either sex who had
brought about segregated colleges and movements which induced in
women an unhealthy consciousness of their own sex. With relief she
thinks of

> that happy age, before Miss Davies and Miss Clough were born,
> when the writer used both sides of his mind equally. One must turn
> back to Shakespeare then, for Shakespeare was androgynous. . . .
> It is fatal to be a man or woman pure and simple; one must be
> woman-manly or man-womanly. It is fatal for a woman to lay the
> least stress on any grievance; to plead even with justice any cause;
> in any way to speak consciously as a woman.

George Eliot would have agreed wholeheartedly. Surely in 1877 the
dismal difference between the appointments of the women's colleges
and those of the men at Cambridge would have been observed by
her. She may even have been astute enough to realize that the young
Oscar Browning—whose loyal and deferential friendship she sin-

cerely appreciated—would evolve into a Cambridge don who gave
generous marks to women students' papers and then in private dole-
fully shook his head over their hopeless inadequacy. But she did not
have the spirit to remonstrate; these were problems (perhaps the very
ones she thought worse than prostitution) which would have to be
resolved in a future beyond her lifetime. She chose not to risk expressing her deep distrust of this early form of apartheid for fear of
seeming too unwomanly, in the new sense, and a traitor to her own
sex.

Earlier she had expressed the hope that those who subjected themselves to this experiment of higher education for women would be
"girls or young women whose natures are large and rich enough not
to be used up in their efforts after knowledge." She was afraid that
in their competition with men in pursuing higher education, women
would sacrifice so much of themselves that they would emerge less
whole human beings than they had begun. She herself had acquired immense learning without stultifying the spirit in her which desired
and thrived upon human intercourse and activity little connected
with erudition. This side of her, however, is almost lost in the George
Eliot legend, some of which was begun before Cross had a chance
to compile and publish the *Life*. Because of her extraordinary
empathy, she could appear to be what anyone talking with her wished
her to be. Serious young men of a poetic, philosophic cast especially
saw in her what they wished to find within themselves. One such
subjectively recorded conversation was the "momentous" one (as
Oscar Browning calls it) between her and Frederic (F. W. H.) Myers
during her 1873 visit to Cambridge:

> I remember how . . . I walked with her once in the Fellows' Garden
> of Trinity, on an evening of rainy May; and she, stirred somewhat
> beyond her wont, and taking as her text the three words which
> have been used so often as the inspiring trumpet-call of men—the
> words God, Immortality, Duty—pronounced with terrible earnest-
> ness how inconceivable was the first, how unbelievable the second,
> and yet how peremptory and absolute the third. Never, perhaps,
> have sterner accents affirmed the sovereignty of impersonal and
> unrecompensing Law. I listened, and night fell, her grave, majestic
> countenance turned towards me like a sibyl's in the gloom. . . .

Myers, who was then thirty, did not publish this account until after
her death, so she was spared the knowledge of how solemnly she had
impressed him. Her own commemoration of this happy stay at
Cambridge was "A College Breakfast Party," written almost a year
later. In this poem—very similar in concept and verse form to Edna

St. Vincent Millay's greater *Conversation at Midnight*—she presents
a metaphysical discussion carried on by "Young Hamlet, not the
hesitating Dane, / But one named after him, who lately strove / For
honours at our English Wittenberg," and several of his friends.

> Small words held mighty meanings: Matter, Force,
> Self, Not-self, Being, Seeming, Space and Time—
> Plebian toilers on the dusty road
> Of daily traffic, turned to Genii
> And cloudy giants darkening sun and moon.
> Creation was reversed in human talk;
> None said, "Let Darkness be," but Darkness was.

The poem is sympathetic and without mockery, for she herself had
known well the Hamlet-road of quest and questioning. But its pervasive tone of benevolent amusement is a much-needed corrective to
Myers's testimony, which obliterates her sense of humor and fluidity
of conversational manner.

Other accounts support the idea that her power of empathy made
her chameleon-like as she talked with individuals. When she was
with someone who wanted and deserved intellectual discourse, she
was glad to provide her share of it. When that no longer fitted the
occasion, she could effortlessly and unaffectedly move into anecdotal
and general talk. She seems to have done this successfully with the
Burne-Joneses. Georgiana relates that Edward had admired George
Eliot's novels before meeting her, and

> he was astonished by her intellectual power when he came to know
> her personally [in 1868]. "There is no one living better to talk to
> . . . for she speaks carefully, so that nothing has to be taken back or
> qualified in any way. Her knowledge is really deep, and her heart
> one of the most sympathetic to me I ever knew." . . . Occasionally
> we dined [at the Priory], or [she and George Henry] drove over to
> the Grange on a weekday afternoon—they never dined out—and
> the general conversation that went on at such times, I am bound to
> own, was chiefly very funny, with much laughter and many anec-
> dotes.

This suggests that George Eliot smoothly shifted the whole tenor of
her talk from what it had been while conversing alone with the
intense Burne-Jones to something more appropriate in the presence
of his lovely wife and the always witty table-talker Lewes.

Another aspect of the fluid nature of George Eliot's conversation
and manner as she moved from person to person was caught by Mary
Blackwood, John's daughter, who as a young woman was occasionally
taken by her parents to visit at the Priory. Over two decades later,
when Mary had assumed the compiling and annotating of the Black-

woods' history (begun by Margaret Oliphant but interrupted by her death in 1897), she remembered that on all occasions when she saw George Eliot,

> the impression was that of a person beyond all things kindly and sympathetic, ever ready to be amused and interested in all that concerned her friends. Her sense of humour too, was extremely keen, and my father, I remember, always made her laugh. The ponderosity of her conversation and the difficulty of making any way with her, of which some visitors have complained, must . . . have been caused by their selecting topics not really congenial to themselves simply because they were talking to George Eliot, scaling heights that were beyond them, and as a result getting crushed by a solid avalanche of learning. But if one talked with her upon music, which she loved, pictures, the play, a flower-show, or equally a horse-show, she was with you—we were all talking upon what we equally understood.

JOHN BLACKWOOD WOULD HAVE APPRECIATED GEORGE ELIOT'S allowing him to make her laugh, her natural charm in including his wife and daughter in the talk, and her releasing the avalanche of learning on some head other than his own. He must have quickly discovered that she was a profoundly learned woman with no desire to impress him with that fact. Next to those who campaigned for women's rights, he disliked women who made an ostentatious display of their learning so that he was made to feel that he had to stay—as he described the uneasy feeling to his daughter—"on his altitudes."

George Eliot put him at his ease, so much so that he felt drawn to her with a force he probably never stopped to analyze other than to say to himself that she was, after all, one of his most interesting writers. Julia, his wife, may have come to wonder whether it was genius alone that caused her husband to regard George Eliot in a light so different from other women. She had read (probably at her husband's request) the manuscript of "Amos Barton" and perhaps had helped decide him to publish it; also she had been convinced that it was by a man, an opinion which delighted George Eliot when Blackwood relayed it to her. Julia may have had a shock when it was revealed that George Eliot was not only a woman but one living in circumstances which ordinarily her husband would not tolerate. If she felt any jealousy, she sensibly did not express it; she always remained the ideal of the kind of woman John Blackwood most admired. In fact, Julia was largely responsible for the harmony which pervaded John Blackwood's life. This, added to his cheerfully optimistic nature, made him that rarity of all times, a happy man—happy in his marriage and family, happy in his work. There would seem to have been nothing lacking in his life.

Yet there was something about George Eliot which drew him toward *her* life, made him wish to be considered by her a more vital part of that life than she would permit. Even though she grew fond of him and even though she learned by experience that he would never allow his own opinion to stand in the way of her writing as she wished, she remained wary of him because he still had control of the publication and hence the financial end of her writing. Subtly she continued to reject any overture from him which suggested he would have liked a more personal tone to their relationship. She did accept his gift of Pug, which he secured and transported at considerable expense and with the cooperation of several friends. She welcomed the dog as a symbolic compensation for her loss of trust in Spencer and Chapman, yet wrote him a not very enthusiastic thanks: "I am too lazy a lover of dogs and all earthly things to like them when they give me much trouble, preferring to describe the pleasure other people have in taking trouble." Pug did not thrive on being merely a symbol, and he came to an untimely, unrecorded end only a year and a half after his heralded arrival on 30 July 1859. Undaunted, Blackwood sent her a china pug, which she acknowledged in "memory of my poor black-nosed pet, and the kindness of the Friend who gratified my too extravagant desires."

In June 1860 he asked for a photograph of her, which he would "treasure very much." He added hopefully (the Leweses were then abroad) that there were "beautiful coloured ones done in Paris and you would be safe from the illustrated papers in a place where you were not known." She wrote back that it "would be a pleasure to me to meet a slight wish of yours," but said that both she and Lewes were too dissatisfied with the 1858 photograph taken in London by Mayall to send him a print, and she expressed no intention of having a new one taken in Paris or elsewhere. She did mention that she had promised to sit to Samuel Laurence for a chalk portrait upon her return, and it was more or less understood that if he wished, Blackwood might see about having a copy made for himself when the work was completed, Lewes apparently meaning to keep the original.

In August she gave Laurence nine sittings, which she appeared to enjoy, and also she seemed happy enough with the finished portrait. But Lewes and Laurence had a strange falling out over it when Lewes refused his permission to have it exhibited in the Royal Academy and finally made it clear that he had no interest in owning it. (Lewes may have resented those nine sittings; whether jealous or not, he might have wondered to what extent Laurence had talked to George Eliot about the past, for as Anastasia Gliddon's husband he had been an intimate member of the Hunt-Gliddon circle when George Henry and Agnes Lewes were also a part of it.) In any event, when Blackwood negotiated through Langford to have a copy of the portrait made, Laurence told him he was free, to purchase the original. This Blackwood did, hanging it in his Edinburgh office at 45 George Street, no doubt downstairs in the "old saloon," where in earlier years, he would "point out the portraits and describe them to us [Mary and her brother] so that they became as familiar to us as those of our own kindred." Four years later Lewes was consoled by the softer, but less exciting, portrait in chalk done by Sir Frederick Burton. He was in raptures with it and hung it over the mantel in his Priory study; George Eliot for her part wrote Barbara Bodichon "I don't know myself whether it is good or not."

Slightly over a decade after the Laurence portrait was hung in his Edinburgh office, John Blackwood sent George Eliot two photographs of himself. She accepted them of course and acknowledged her appreciation; at the same time, in the skillful way she had cultivated with him, she drew his attention to the fact that their basic relationship was one between writer and publisher: "This likeness will always carry me back to the first time I saw you, in our little Richmond lodging, when I was thinking anxiously of 'Adam Bede,' as I now am of 'Middlemarch.'" Still later, in the spring of 1875, when she was beginning her last novel, it was Blackwood who remembered that first meeting and his carrying off what was written of *Adam Bede*. He, perhaps more than she, was poignantly aware of the difference time and repeated success had made in her reputation. "I was walking about with Theodore Martin yesterday," he wrote,

> when talking about you and Lewes; he mentioned how devoted the Queen was to your works, especially Adam Bede. So I told him how you had given me the M.S. of the first volume of Adam Bede with strict injunctions not to read it until I could do so quietly at home and how I utterly disobeyed orders by peeping into the first pages on the top of the omnibus where Lewes deposited me at Kew and fastening upon it the moment I left King's Cross next morning until I finished my reading with delight before I reached Newcastle when night was setting in.

In reality, about a week after his second visit to Richmond, Blackwood had written from Edinburgh to Lewes: "In spite of all injunctions I began Adam Bede on the Railway and felt very savage when the waning light stopped me as we neared the Scottish border." He also said to tell George Eliot that he thought what he had read "all right, most lifelike and real," but wished "to read the MS quietly over again before writing in detail about it. . . . Is there much more written or is it merely blocked out?" He repeated this question more specifically and directly when he wrote on 31 March to give his considered and very favorable opinion of the manuscript. Much as he liked this, he recognized it as quite different from anything which had appeared in Maga, so that before he could decide whether it should be published there or not, he needed to know what was to come and requested "a sketch of the rest of the story." She sent him a decisive refusal in a letter which has been lost but can be reconstructed by Blackwood's delighted, rather than annoyed, reaction to it expressed to Lewes:

> I have an admirable letter from George Eliot today. I knew that he would fear to give me a sketch of the rest of the Story lest he should give me a wrong impression and I very nearly said so when I made the request. On the whole I think he is right. What he says of the treatment of a subject being the essence of art is very true and a more elegant rendering of my constant reply to fellows sending lists of subjects for articles, "that any subject being suitable entirely depends upon how it is handled." I shall steal his expression the next time I wish to choke off any anxious enquirer as to the probable acceptability of his proposed "little paper."

Blackwood would always savor whatever George Eliot chose to tell him of her methods of bringing nascent novels into being. In this instance he also had a protective eye on Maga, for which, as Margaret Oliphant noted, he was inclined to think nothing good enough. Having already published two of George Eliot's shorter stories without knowing the outcome of either before it began its run in Maga, he decided that he would not risk starting a novel-length work under the same uncertain conditions.

There was no clash of wills over this matter, for George Eliot was aware that to have her new work published directly in book form without being serialized in Maga would release her from thinking of her story in segments and meeting instalment deadlines. Although she was no doubt sincere in giving aesthetics as the basic reason for denying Blackwood a synopsis of her story, there was also the more prosaic fact that the essential elements did not yet exist clearly enough in her own mind for her to determine their relationship or how to lead them toward what she had early fixed on as her climax—Hetty's prison scene. When she had first conceived her story as one of the *Clerical Scenes*, she knew that she wished to blend Hetty's tragedy (a modification of an anecdote from real life told her by her Methodist aunt, Mrs. Samuel Evans) with other recollections of her aunt, who had been a preacher, and also with some stories she had heard about her father's early life and character. With these scattered elements, she recognized that the "problem of construction that remained was to make the unhappy girl [Hetty] one of the chief *dramatis personae* and connect her with the hero." By the time she was doing the writing that she handed over to Blackwood at Richmond, she had her major characters set—Dinah, Adam, Arthur, and Hetty—and was relatively clear in her mind about the mutual relationship of Adam and Arthur to Hetty. But Dinah and Adam had no planned relationship. Later, she was to become adept at bringing unlikely characters together in seemingly natural relationships—*Middlemarch* perhaps being the supreme example. *Adam Bede* was her first real challenge of this nature, and she may have asked for suggestions from Lewes. Whether she did or not, he gave one which she accepted without hesitation:

> Dinah's ultimate relation to Adam was suggested by George, when I had read to him the first part of the first volume: he was so delighted with the presentation of Dinah and so convinced that the readers' interest would centre in her, that he wanted her to be the principal figure at the last. I accepted the idea at once, and from the end of the third chapter worked with it constantly in view.

This is the first instance for which there is evidence that Lewes literally contributed to the structuring of her narrative as she wrote. There is one other: it was he again who decided that Adam should be brought into "direct collision" with Arthur Donnithorne, and although George Eliot had not thought so, once Lewes had suggested it, "doubt haunted me, and out of it grew the scene in the Wood between Arthur and Adam: the fight came to me as a *necessity* on a night at the Munich opera when I was listening to William Tell." She makes it clear that after she had done the actual writing, Lewes's suggestions were few and of a less fundamental nature: "Throughout the book I have altered little, and the only cases, I think in which George [has] suggested more than a verbal alteration, when I [have] read the M.S. aloud to him, [have been] . . . the first scene at the Farm and the scene in the Wood between Arthur and Adam, both of which he recommended me to 'space out' a little, which I did." The bracketed words are those she first wrote and then struck out, thus effecting a consistent shift from the present perfect to the simple past, a strange change to bother with in a record which was (as far as she knew) for herself alone. It is almost as if, now that the novel was awaiting publication, she had begun to see Lewes's help as a form of intrusion.

Perhaps alerted by the obvious compulsion with which she accepted his ideas (most pronounced in that of the fight between Adam and Arthur, which ran counter to her own belief), Lewes began to realize that she was still too unsure of the rightness of her creative vision to withstand the influence of someone so close to her. He knew that once the vision was encased in writing, it was relatively safe against external demands. But he had now learned that the period of gestation was for her the most dangerously vulnerable time. He was also growing aware of the deeply personal motivation of her writing and recognized that even he had no right to enter the private domain of its origin. As a result, because of his love for George Eliot and his sincere belief in the autocracy of creativity wherever it was found, he withdrew as participant in the actual composition of her work, although by no means depriving her of his stimulating encouragement. He was rarely given credit for the sensitive perceptiveness which determined this attitude toward her writing. As early as 1883, Mathilde Blind—with an unusual understanding of the kind of fiction George Eliot had brought into being —did her best to halt the fast-growing idea that he had detrimentally interfered with it:

> There is an impression abroad that Mr. Lewes . . . did some injury to George Eliot from a literary point of view; that the nature of his pursuits led her to adopt too technical and pedantic a phraseology in her novels. But this idea is unjust to both. In comparing her earliest with her latest style, it is clear that from the first she was apt to cull her illustrations from the physical sciences, thereby showing how much these studies had become part of herself. Indeed, she was far more liable to introduce these scientific modes of expression than Mr. Lewes, as may be easily seen by comparing his "Life of Goethe," . . . with some of her essays of the same date. As to her matter, it is curious how much of it was drawn from the earliest sources of memory. . . . Most of her works might, indeed, not inaptly be called "Looking Backward." . . . No one, however intimate, could really intermeddle with the workings of a genius drawing its happiest inspiration from the earliest experiences of its own individual past.

It was inevitable that in describing the prevalent characteristic of George Eliot's writing, Mathilde Blind should have referred to the "Looking Backward" chapter of *The Impressions of Theophrastus Such*. Here, in this and its complementary chapter "Looking Inward," George Eliot analyzes the two aspects of the creative process as she had experienced them—the calm, retrospective journey into the past, and the futile attempts to free herself from the cruelly indifferent auditor within her. The tonal difference between these two chapters is marked: "Looking Backward" is gently nostalgic, whereas "Looking Inward" is starkly bitter. Only Lewes could have been instrumental in bringing the two aspects together into what was at first a kind of perilous compromise, but finally became a foundation with only the slightest crack running through it. Lewes could not have used *Theophrastus Such* as a guide, for the completed manuscript of that work did not go to the Blackwoods' until nine days before his death. With unerring intuition he worked to save her from the forces which prevented Theophrastus, not from writing, but from having his writing made public. If Lewes could not expell or replace the introjected influence of Isaac, he could at least stand between her and the externalized physiognomy of that unwanted auditor. His self-appointed task came to mean that he had to keep her writing, and writing with some constructive plan of publication always in view. He spurred her on by enthusiastically affirming whatever she read him from her work-in-progress and by shielding her—especially as her fame grew—from all criticism that threatened to reach her from the outside world, favorable as well as unfavorable.

Each critical report seemed to George Eliot to carry with it a visage distinct enough to destroy the illusion of the hazy, multitudinous assemblage which was as necessary to her as it was to Theophrastus. Fortunately, Lewes was richly endowed with the talent for strategy that this task necessitated. He had to confront her closest friends and risk alienating them as he tried to convince them that it was not their prerogative to bestow upon her even their most undiluted praise. And he had also to confront himself when he needed to convince her that each of her works was superior to the preceding ones, which (as his Journal entries reveal) he did not always believe to be true. Finally, he helped as tactfully as possible with the financial arrangements of her publications, although he did far less of this than legend purported, but just enough to make some of the Blackwood circle lay the cause to him whenever there was the slightest hesitation on George Eliot's part in accepting John Blackwood's terms. By others, especially those who were envious and thought that success had come too easily to her, Lewes was accused of being overprotective. "Should I have done better if I had been kept, like her, in a mental greenhouse and taken care of?" asks Margaret Oliphant at the start of her *Autobiography*, which she admits was prompted by Cross's *Life*. She had the honesty to add: "This is one of the things it is perfectly impossible to tell."

George Eliot, of course, had no consciousness of living in a mental greenhouse. Her mind was her own and free; she knew that with more certainty than she knew anything else about herself, and Lewes knew it too. She was to be forever grateful to him for taking upon his shoulders the one problem in connection with her writing which she could not confront alone—that of deciding whether or not what she wrote was worthy of presentation to the public. This is the same question which is to torment Theophrastus Such and nullify what writing he does, and Theophrastus's solution to it is a drastic one:

> I leave my manuscripts to a judgment outside my imagination; but I will not ask to hear it, or request my friend to pronounce before I have been buried decently, what he really thinks of my parts, and to state candidly whether my papers would be most usefully applied in lighting the cheerful domestic fire. ["Looking Inward"]

George Eliot was far more fortunate: in Lewes she had a critic who was outside her imagination and yet sympathetically near enough to understand and trust her sincerity in writing. At first she looked to him for corroboration of her own judgment of her work. "He is the prime blessing that has made all the rest possible to me," she wrote Barbara Bodichon in May 1859, "—giving me a response to everything I have written, a response that I could confide in as proof that I had not mistaken my work." By then *Adam Bede* had been published and *The Mill on the Floss* was under way.

Repeated success only augmented her distrust of her creative power, so that by November 1873—when all her novels through *Middlemarch* had been published—she was much nearer to Theophrastus's desperate need to find a judgment of his work outside himself. Underneath her light tone there is a note of seriousness as she writes Dr. Thomas Clifford Allbutt (who contributed to the medical background of *Middlemarch*) in response to his suggestions as to how to make herself physically comfortable while writing:

> It is in vain to get one's back and knees in the right attitude if one's mind is superannuated. Some time or other, if death does not come to silence one, there ought to be deliberate abstinence from writing—self-judgment which decides that one has no more to say. . . . Happily for me, I have a critic at hand whom I can trust to tell me when I write what ought to be put behind the fire.

Still later, in January 1875 when at work on *Daniel Deronda*, she wrote to a relative stranger, Charles Ritter, who had made his admiration of her work known by letter in 1872:

> I suffer always increasingly from doubt as to the quality of what I am actually doing. Just now I am writing a new novel . . . but if it were not for his [Lewes's] firmness of opinion as to the worth of what is already written I could not carry out my intention. In this way he has always supported me—by his unreserved sympathy and the independence of his judgment.

Writing to someone whom she respected but had not met personally, she could casually yet succinctly summarize Lewes's indispensable help in sustaining her career. It was essential for her to believe that his critical judgment of her work was independent of his sympathy for her as a person; and it is a tribute to Lewes's subtlety and awareness of what should come first in importance that he never gave her cause to doubt that this was so.

BUT WHILE SHE WAS WRITING *Adam Bede*—IN THE PRE-FAME days—her reliance upon Lewes was the simple one it had been during the writing of the three *Scenes*; it was he alone who took note of and precaution against its potential complexity. The *Bedesman*—so Lewes early called the novel as it progressed, and Blackwood soon took up the name—was to be a much-traveled manuscript. She started it at Richmond on 22 October 1857, and then in early April carried it to the Continent, where as a change from English coasts and islands the Leweses had decided to spend their annual busman's holiday. They stayed in Munich three months, which should have made possible her establishing a temporarily stable working schedule, especially as Lewes was writing too. But museums lured them both forth from their rooms, and she was eager to accompany him on his visits to local philosophers and scientists whose projects coincided with his own manifold interests. For a while she was able to maintain the old routine: she wrote, and read him what she had written. Then on 17 June came an especially disruptive event. She recorded: "This evening G. left me to set out on his journey to Hofwyl to see his boys." The next day she kept herself busy revisiting people whom she had met with Lewes, but for the three following days she apparently tried valiantly to engross herself in her writing. She seems not to have been successful, for her 22 June entry is an abrupt one which suggests defeat: "Tired of loneliness, I went to the Frau von Siebold, chatted with her over tea, and then heard some music." She was perhaps drawn back to the Siebolds, with whom she had also spent some time on 18 June, because when they had entertained her and Lewes in their home, she thought she had witnessed "the prettiest little picture of married life—

> the great comparative anatomist (von Siebold) seated at the piano in his spectacles playing the difficult accompaniments to Schubert's songs, while his little round-faced wife sang them with much taste and feeling. They are not young—von Siebold is grey, and probably more than fifty, his wife perhaps nearly forty, and it is all the prettier to see their admiration of each other.

In their admiration for each other, the Siebolds may have reminded her of herself and Lewes; and she was right in thinking that they would appreciate her loneliness. Frau von Siebold appeared the next morning with roses and an invitation to go with them to see a new comedy that evening. This George Eliot did, and the following night, a week after his departure, she noted in her Journal: "G. came in the evening, at 10 o'clock—after I had suffered a great deal in thinking of the possibilities that might prevent him from coming." By the next day there was a return to normalcy: "This morning I have read to G. all I have written during his absence, and he approves it more than I expected." Then she was ill for a week, although that seemed "almost a luxury, because of the love that tended me." She regretted parting from "the dear, charming Siebolds," but otherwise she was glad to say a final good-bye on 7 July to "the general languor and sense of depression produced by Munich air and the way of life."

Lewes, however, had been stimulated by the stay and he wrote John Chapman, for whom he was doing an article on recent German fiction: "Polly, although very popular, did not enjoy Munich; but I learned so much there from Liebig, Von Siebold, Bischoff, Harless, and others that the place will be ever memorable to me." He also mentioned that "Polly saw Strauss the day before we left," and of that meeting she wrote Sara Hennell that it had been an improvement over seeing him "in that dumb way at Cologne" in 1854. Lewes's boys in Switzerland, Strauss, Chapman—the past had revived itself in Munich with a vengeance that even new friends and the *Bedesman* could not allay.

After a ten-day "exquisite journey," in Lewes's words, "through the Tyrol, down the Danube, a stay of three days at Vienna and one day at Prag," they settled in Dresden for six weeks. Both were enchanted with this city, and George Eliot began to recover from the languor induced by Munich. Raphael's Madonna di San Sisto drew them to the Picture Gallery at least three times a week, but otherwise they were resolute in devoting themselves to quiet work uninterrupted by visits and visitors. They had found excellent lodgings, an apartment of six rooms all to themselves, which somewhat later George Eliot recalled with pleasure:

> We were as happy as princes—are not—George writing at the far corner of the great *salon*, I at my *Schrank* in my own private room, with closed doors. Here I wrote the latter half of the second volume of "Adam Bede" in the long mornings that our early hours—rising at six o'clock—secured us.

Lewes had good reason to write Blackwood from Dresden: "Bedesman is in training, and will make a splendid run if he does not win the

Derby. I have faith in that horse and will back him to any reasonable amount."

Even so, George Eliot felt "behindhand" in her writing when they returned to Richmond on 2 September, after having been gone five months. She resumed writing immediately, and despite the usual vexations of daily living and the additional worry of the accelerated Liggins imposture, she had by 29 October enough new manuscript ready ("to the end of the love scene at the Farm, between Adam and Dinah") to expect Blackwood to make a financial offer. On 4 November she admitted in her Journal: "This is a moment of suspense, for I am awaiting Blackwood's opinion and proposals concerning 'Adam Bede.' " The wait was mercifully short, and under 4 November she entered: "Received a letter from Blackwood containing warm praise of my third volume, and offering £800 for the copyright of 'Adam Bede' for four years. I wrote to accept." Finally, on 16 November she was able to record: "Wrote the last word of 'Adam Bede' and sent it to Mr. Langford. *Jubilate.*" The novel had required thirteen months, almost exactly the same amount of time that she had needed to produce the three *Clerical Scenes*.

Adam Bede shows little trace of having been largely composed during a not always happy Continental sojourn; once again she had demonstrated that she could keep whatever she was working upon insulated against the intrusion of the immediate present. There are signs in the novel that she was conscious of making a fresh beginning in her fiction writing. She luxuriated in the new spatial element at her command, and the novel reflects this, although, interestingly, not in the expected matter of length (it is slightly shorter than either she or Blackwood had thought it would be), but in the many scenes which take place in the unhampered out-of-doors, ranging from Dinah's preaching to Hetty's childbearing. She had in part anticipated this, for a week before she began to write it, she had told Blackwood that her new story would "be a country story—full of the breath of cows and the scent of hay." She may have been motivated by a desire to have a vicarious release from the cramped Richmond lodgings, or—and this is far more likely—she was prompted by some force of memory set free by the writing of the *Clerical Scenes,* and which had begun its miraculous transformation of originally disagreeable events that lay like blemishes on the surface of her remembered past.

This was the force that transformed the Michaelmas (Harvest Home) festivities. In real life when she was managing Griff for her father and Isaac, George Eliot hated these occasions: it meant much extra work for her, a vigilant watch of the servants, and a tolerant absorption (of which she was not then capable) of the men's drinking songs and crude talk. "Remember," she had written Maria Lewis in September 1839, "Michaelmas is coming and I shall be engaged in matters so nauseating to me that it will be a charity to console me. . . ." By the time she came to present Michaelmas in *Adam Bede* (Book VI, chapter 5), she saw it as an autumnal festival complementing the spring one she had already celebrated in "Janet's Repentance." She creates a Brueghel-like scene, although underlying it is a tone of gravity (but perhaps this is in Brueghel too), which serves as a reminder that man and the earth he cultivates and reaps will ultimately be one and the same. This peculiar transformation sprang from the tension between the love and hate evoked by her memory; and it is this which gives to her novel its remarkable sense of place, conveying with inevitability the atmosphere of the rural English Midlands. Hers was the same kind of dynamic ambivalence which aided in the re-creation of other notably vivid places in literature—for example, Balzac's Paris, Dickens's London, or Joyce's Dublin.

Although *Adam Bede* is highly original even within the context of George Eliot's own writing, it bears comparison with the product of her first beginning in fiction, "Amos Barton." In both the novel and the *Scene*, she assumes a defensive position toward a clergyman who in some way does not measure up to the conventional image. There is, to be sure, a vast difference between the two men themselves: the Rev. Mr. Irwine of the novel is a far more attractive character than Amos and, although important, he is not the central character of the narrative. Book II of *Adam Bede* opens in a style that is reminiscent of "Amos Barton," but which was not to reappear in either "Gilfil" or "Janet," where indeed it would have been conspicuously inappropriate. In the novel, it reasserted itself naturally, for she had returned to the somewhat defiant projection of homely realism which had preoccupied her in her first *Scene*:

> "This Rector of Broxton [Irwine] is little better than a pagan!"
> I hear one of my readers exclaim. "How much more edifying it
> would have been if you had made him give Arthur some truly
> spiritual advice! You might have put into his mouth the most
> beautiful things,—quite as good as reading a sermon."
> Certainly I could, if I held it the highest vocation of the novelist
> to represent things as they never have been and never will be. . . .
> But it happens, on the contrary, that my strongest effort is . . . to
> give a faithful account of men and things as they have mirrored
> themselves in my mind.

She admits that the mirror might be defective—a qualification not in the earlier story. Yet it is still her best guide to truth, the kind of truth that finds beauty in the object as it is: "It is for this rare, precious quality of truthfulness that I delight in many Dutch paintings, which lofty-minded people despise." This analogy, which she expands, may have been prompted by her memory of her statement to Major Blackwood when she thought "Amos Barton" was being adversely criticized because of its unenhanced realism. However, this chapter in *Adam Bede* was to be the last of her manifestos upholding such realism. She was beginning to realize, and had already demonstrated in the second and third *Clerical Scenes,* that this type of realistic treatment was too simple to cover adequately what was proving her natural bent in portraying the inner and outer lives of people as they related to others and to the consequences of their own actions.

A more important similarity between *Adam Bede* and "Amos Barton" is that both had arisen out of substance which had come to her secondhand, although in the novel her power to transmute such material into the immediacy of direct experience is immeasurably greater than its somewhat halting manifestation in "Amos." One of the reasons for this increased power (aside from further practice in writing) was that the primary matter of the novel was associated with her father, and that as children she and Isaac together had been eager listeners when, in his genial moods, he related anecdotes of his early life. It may be sheer coincidence that the initials of Adam Bede are the same as those of Amos Barton, but it is hardly happenstance that "Adam" and "Bede" both suggest symbolic fathers and new beginnings—Adam, the father of Man; and Bede, the first English scholar-historian. *Adam Bede* was George Eliot's Book of the Father, homage to the Robert Evans she had never known, a tribute purified of the impatience and annoyance she had felt toward him over a decade before he went out of her life forever.

But she could not yet write even remotely about her family without introducing elements of her own anguish and hostility caused by her forced exile from them. These drift like flotsam over the surface of the novel, as in the chapter entitled "Home and Its Sorrows":

> Family likeness has often a deep sadness in it. Nature, that great tragic dramatist, knits us together by bone and muscle, and divides us by the subtler web of our brains; blends yearning and repulsion, and ties us by our heart-strings to the beings that jar us at every movement. We hear a voice with the very cadence of our own uttering the thoughts we despise; we see eyes—ah! so like our mother's—averted from us in cold alienation; and our last darling child startles us with the air and gestures of the sister we parted from in bitterness long years ago. The father to whom we owe our best heritage—the mechanical instinct, the keen sensibility to harmony, the unconscious skill of the modelling hand—galls us, and puts us to shame by his daily errors; the long-lost mother, whose face we

begin to see in the glass as our own wrinkles come, once fretted our young souls with her anxious humours and irrational persistence. [Book I, chapter 4]

This passage is noteworthy as an objectively disciplined résumé of her troubled relationship with the four principals of her family. However, it is not clearly relevant to the story that she is telling, and, as she might have anticipated, John Blackwood wrote her; " . . . some of the remarks about relations are most beautiful and true, but part of the reflections might be softened with advantage." She did not answer him on this point and made no changes in the manuscript.

There is not much, but enough of this personal flotsam to intimate that, as "Amos Barton" had unknowingly prepared her for the inward plunge into "Mr. Gilfil," *Adam Bede* was similarly preparing her for *The Mill on the Floss*. For the most part she stayed uninvolved as she wrote, except for the joyous emotion which accompanies creation, so that the novel emerges an essentially happy one, despite the tragedy it contains. On the last day of November 1858, two weeks after she had completed it, she recorded what she was to say about no other novel of hers: "I love it very much and am deeply thankful to have written it, whatever the public may say to it—a result which is still in darkness, for I have at present had only four sheets of the proof." The second half of her statement indicates that there was already cause for her elation to ebb. Publication was being, it seemed to the Leweses, unjustifiably delayed, and they were anxiously concerned, for it had been early the same month that Chapman had cleverly extracted from Spencer his great secret that Marian Lewes was writing fiction. Also they had heard rumors that someone in Warwickshire was making embarrassingly accurate guesses about the authorship of the *Clerical Scenes*.

The reason Blackwood first gave the Leweses for holding up the printing of *Adam Bede* was that he was committed to bringing out Bulwer-Lytton's *What Will He Do with It?* in book form immediately after completing its run in Maga in January, and he thought that the simultaneous appearance of the two novels might injure sales of both. Lewes argued that it would be far more injurious for *Adam Bede* to appear when there was no longer any mystery surrounding the identity of George Eliot; but Blackwood held fast to his view. On 22 December, George Eliot wrote Blackwood, "At Mr. Lewes's suggestion, I have written the enclosed 'Remonstrance,' which he recommends me to prefix to 'Adam Bede.' " She adds, "I confess, I have written it rather against the grain. . . " Whatever was in the "Remonstrance," Blackwood curtly informed Lewes of his disapproval of it: "It is not like so knowing a party as you to suggest so dangerous a preface as that proposed for G.E." In responding to George Eliot he was less abrupt: "What you say by way of Preface is excellent in itself and I cordially sympathise with your feelings, but I decidedly advise against the publication of such a preface. It might raise a nest of hornets about you." As he was not certain how she would take his going over Lewes's head on the matter, he was gently politic: "Lewes is almost as knowing and experienced about such things as I am, so that I attach great weight to his suggestion, but I am sure I am right." He was sorry to think that she had troubled to write her Preface for nothing: "Do you ever think of reviewing or writing miscellaneous papers. Your preface would come in capitally in a review." Was he at this time really ignorant of her extensive periodical writing, or was he curious to know how she would answer? If the latter, he must have smiled as he read her response (as she must have smiled when she wrote it): "I have left off writing articles of late, but my hand is not quite untried in that sort of work, and if you think the doctrine in my 'Remonstrance' is one desirable to be enforced . . . I would willingly do that service to my future self and my fellow novelists." Unless it is somehow embedded in *The Impressions of Theophrastus Such,* she was not to make use of the "Remonstrance," so that one can only surmise what Lewes advocated which aroused Blackwood's indignation.

Meanwhile, the Leweses had learned from Blackwood the real cause of the delay in publication: Bulwer had failed to return proof of his novel, thus locking up a ton and a half of type of the same kind needed for the printing of *Adam Bede*. Blackwood was apologetic, but Bulwer was an old friend of his whom he genuinely admired, and he had no intention of disengaging the type simply because the veteran author had procrastinated in his proof-reading. In the face of this obdurate circumstance, the Leweses had little choice but to sit back and try to relax. So ended a mild skirmish that was but a prologue to similar more serious problems which lay ahead in the near future.

George Eliot was annoyed with both Bulwer and Blackwood, but years later she was to have reason to be grateful for John Blackwood's leniency in holding up type to accommodate an old author-friend. She was in the midst of reading proofs for *Theophrastus Such* when Lewes died in 1878, and it was over a month before she could bring herself to offer to go on with the reading of them and to express concern over having monopolized the type that long. Blackwood's response was, as always, reassuring: "Do not allow the proofs of 'Theophrastus Such' to concern you in the least, the type can wait your perfect convenience. I had it set up that the proofs might be ready to your hand when you were able to turn your thoughts that way."

But at the end of 1858 all she could feel was that time was being wasted. A letter from Blackwood on 9 December was consoling, even if it did not possess the magic to take the *Bedesman* over the last hurdle and appear in print the next day: "I have been quite vexed about the delay in the printing, but it was one of those unexpected fixes which will arise in the best regulated establishments. I am thankful to say that we have now got a release of Type and your Bedes or rather pearls will be strung as fast as you could wish now. I expect to have the whole in Type by the end of the year. . . ." He was able to keep his implied promise, and *Adam Bede* was ready to be subscribed to on 1 February 1859, thus appearing to the public only three days short of the second anniversary of the George Eliot pseudonym. On 29 January, Blackwood had sent her the check agreed upon (£400 at this time; the second £400 to be paid nine months after the date of publication), and with it these words:

> Whatever the subscription may be I am confident of success, great success. The book is so novel and so true. The whole story remains in my mind like a succession of incidents in the lives of people whom I know. Adam Bede can certainly never come under the class of popular agreeable stories, but those who love power, real humour and true natural description will stand by the sturdy Carpenter and the living groups you have painted in and about Hayslope.

To this George Eliot answered with explicit truthfulness, anticipating the dilemma that was to be one of the last contributory forces to the shaping of her art: "I perceive that I have not the characteristics of the 'popular author,' and yet I am much in need of the warmly expressed sympathy which only popularity can win."

SIX WEEKS AFTER THE APPEARANCE OF *Adam Bede*, A SECond edition was needed. On 16 March, Blackwood wrote to tell her this good news, beginning his letter: "I think I may now fairly congratulate you upon being a *popular* as well as a great author." As she had heard of Chrissey's death only the day before, she felt no exultation and merely noted in her Journal the gist of Blackwood's letter. However, when sales continued their steady crescendo, astonishing even Blackwood, she could not remain so detached; she began to keep an account of the various signs of this unexpected popularity, but as early as 17 April had to give it up: "I have left off recording the history of 'Adam Bede' and the pleasant letters and words that came to me— the success has been so triumphantly beyond anything I had dreamed of that it would be tiresome to put down particulars." A special triumph came when Charles Edward Mudie, who had paid scant attention to the *Scenes of Clerical Life,* doubled his original subscription of five hundred copies for his Select Library. There were other exciting surprises: less than two months after publication, Herbert Spencer brought word to the Leweses "that 'Adam Bede' had been quoted by Mr. Charles Buxton in the House of Commons"; and on 19 May she made this Journal entry: "A letter from Blackwood, in which he proposes to give me another £400 at the end of the year, making in all £1200, as an acknowledgement of 'Adam Bede's' success." By the end of July there had been a fifth edition.

There was bitter-sweet irony in the warm acceptance accorded her novel by the same society which had ostracized her; and there was further irony in that she could neither celebrate by rejoicing with friends nor enjoy the fame that rested upon public identification of her as the author of *Adam Bede.* Nonetheless, she was grateful for the popular success, which had to come to her before she realized how deeply she desired it. Having received through Blackwood several laudatory letters from readers, as well as good news about sales that were fast cleaning out all the stock on hand, she had written him:

> I sing my "Magnificat" in a quiet way, and have a great deal of deep, silent joy, but few authors, I suppose, who have had a real success, have known less of the flush and the sensations of triumph that are talked of as the accompaniments of success.

Although George Eliot was soon to write Barbara Bodichon that she was indifferent about Lewes's chance of obtaining a divorce because she herself preferred excommunication, she was being more defiant than truthful. She could (and did) accept excommunication as far as her personal life was concerned, but it was not within her nature to become a total excommunicant. She could not permit herself to be a Spinoza. The latter, unembittered and in solitude, had pursued his inexorable analysis of human nature. She revered him and had given many hours of her life to the study and translating of his works. But she had early perceived that as a result of his forced solitude he had forged a language so individual that even when his work was faithfully translated, the reader was forced to make yet another translation for himself. Her own analysis of human nature was to be, in its own way, as thorough and relentless as his, yet always concretely rendered within the human framework and in language unhampered by abstractions culled from the logic of mathematics. Nor could she afford to be the uncompromising avant-garde writer she might easily have become had she wished. The phenomenal success of *Adam Bede* had awakened her to the fact that it was through her writing that she was to find re-entry into the society which had rejected her, a chance that never would have opened up had she lived out her life as an ordinary citizen. She had no wish either to speak in a language that this society would not understand or to shock it. She desired, rather, to reach its heart and thereby enlarge its sympathy and tolerance by painlessly removing the blinders which too often accompanied English provincialism. This was the peculiar challenge that was to determine the boundary line of her art.

She was caught between two opposing pressures: the artist's inherent suspicion of popularity, and her own driving need to reach and be favorably accepted by as large a reading audience as possible without prostituting her art. When the latter need was unexpectedly met by *Adam Bede,* which she had written without even a thought of popular success, she felt justified in looking to sales, rather than only to reviews, as a sign of the worth of her writing. She became hawklike in watching the advertising that the Blackwoods did for her works and was almost always morbidly convinced it was inadequate. The slightest dip in sales threw her into such a fit of depression that both John Blackwood and Lewes took to concealing this event from her with the same care that they guarded her against seeing or hearing adverse criticism. Margaret Oliphant read the whole of the George Eliot–Blackwood correspondence in preparing to write her history of the firm, and was thus the first to be made aware of these unexpected traits in George Eliot. Commenting upon the latter's well-known idealism, sensitivity, and tendency to disbelieve in her own genius, Mrs. Oliphant continues:

> At the same time, we find that she was an admirable woman of business, alert and observant of every fluctuation of the book-market, and determined that in every way her works should have the fullest justice done them. There is no commoner subject of mourning and indignation on the part of authors whose works do not sell sufficiently to please them, than that of inadequate advertisement and the perverse inclination of publishers . . . to keep their works behind backs. . . . But it is less usual to find a very popular and successful writer taking up the same complaint.

Mrs. Oliphant had no way of knowing that to George Eliot popular success was in its own way as anxiety-arousing as failure, for it raised doubts about the future. In April, after noting in her Journal that the signs of her first novel's fame had become too numerous to record in detail, she added: "Shall I ever write another book as true as 'Adam Bede'? The weight of the future presses on me, and makes itself felt even more than the deep satisfaction of the past and present." Also, there was the terrifying possibility that her readers were finding nothing different from what they were accustomed to in the usual popular novel. The first press reviews of *Adam Bede* suggested this, for they were laudatory without being discriminating; even Lewes was disheartened by one in which the reviewer echoed the hackneyed tribute, " 'One of the best novels we have read for a long time.' The nincompoop"—Lewes wrote in his Journal—"couldn't see the distinction between Adam and the mass of novels he had been reading." When Blackwood sent George Eliot a packet of such reviews and Lewes read portions of them to her, she hurriedly sent back to Blackwood her advice on advertising:

> I have not ventured to look into the folio myself, but I learn that there are certain threatening marks in ink by the side of such sentences as "best novel of the season" or "best novel we have read for a long while" . . . as if these sentences were to be selected for reprint in the form of advertisement. I shudder at the suggestion. Am I taking a liberty in intreating you to keep a sharp watch over the advertisements that no hackneyed puffing phrase of this kind may be tacked to my book?

Blackwood of course knew his business. He had no intention of making an issue of the matter, and replied calmly to Lewes that the "reviews in the papers, although not good in themselves, will do good to the book."

It was of supreme importance to George Eliot that her work should not be confused with the typical popular novel. This attitude did not stem from mere egoism, any more than did her conflicting desire for popularity. She wanted to prove to herself and to the world that her Antigone stand in living with Lewes would lead to a greater *social good* than if she had stayed within the bounds of convention. As she wrote Sara Hennell in June of 1857 (when she was working upon "Gilfil," although Sara did not know this), "If I live five years longer, the positive result of my existence on the side of truth and goodness will outweigh the small negative good that would have consisted in my not doing anything to shock others. . . ." Within those five years, she had completed and published the *Clerical Scenes, Adam Bede, The Mill on the Floss,* and *Silas Marner,* and was at work on *Romola.* This is an impressive achievement, and her literary reputation was secure, even exalted. Yet she had been more anxious over the acceptance of each new book than the preceding one. Proof that her writing was a positive contribution to society had to occur over and over; the slightest backsliding, the smallest falling off of sales, meant that she had somehow failed. If sales stayed steady or climbed, she was immediately seized by the equally tormenting fear that readers bought her books only for their surface entertainment value. As late as December 1871—by which time she had added (not counting minor poems) the completed *Romola, Felix Holt, The Spanish Gypsy,* and Book I of *Middlemarch* to her list of publications—Lewes saw fit to write one of his customary warnings to the growing number of readers (this one the young Alexander Main) who were not content to worship from afar but sought to describe to her the minutiae of their personal reactions to her work:

> I don't know whether I told you that she does not read criticism on her works, favorable or unfavorable,—not because she is less sensitive than others but because she is more, and does not think it right to occupy her mind with such necessarily distracting details. But she is proportionately delighted at all such evidences of influence as your letters have conveyed—and these have reached her from all parts of the world, so that now in spite of her extraordinary diffidence and self-questioning, she begins to feel that her life has indeed not been unavailing. Unhappily the habitual tone of her mind is distrust of herself, and no sympathy, no praise, can do more than lift her out of it for a day or two; but by repetition the curing influences *tell*, for they become *massed*, and as we psychologists say they enable her to *apperceive* the fact that her books are something more than mere amusements.

Circumstances—her exile from conventional society and her own nature—had structured a pattern of requisites her writing had to fulfill: it had to satisfy her sense of social responsibility, her artistic integrity, and her need for popularity. Artistic integrity occupied the most vulnerable position, and although it may have left itself open for a few compromises, it is a miracle that it did not suffer a total collapse in the midst of the conflicting demands of the other two requirements. Sometime between 1872 and 1878 George Eliot jotted down random thoughts in a notebook which served as a quarry for *Theophrastus Such*. It is improbable that she intended any of the unused portions of this notebook to see the light of day, but as she did not destroy it, Charles Lewes reverentially gathered up its contents and, under the title "Leaves from a Note-Book," included them in the first authorized edition of her essays in 1884. The longest note is headed "Authorship"; it is humorless and formidably impersonal, yet in it she brings together as nowhere else the three requisites which had commandeered her own writing; also it is such a fitting objective complement to her subjective analysis of Theophrastus as a writer that one wonders why she did not incorporate it into the book. Perhaps it seemed to her *too* personal—or perhaps too arrogantly didactic; but in this carefully developed note these two characteristics come together, for her starting point is that authorship is among "those callings which have not yet acquired anything near a full-grown conscience in the public mind," and her unexpressed aim is to construct for that incipient conscience a guide drawn from her own experience and thoughts.

By the mere act of publishing, whether it be a trifle or an epic, the writer has become involved in a social activity. And next: "Let it be taken as admitted that all legitimate social activity must be beneficial to others besides the agent." Those who write only for their own satisfaction are not socially irresponsible as long as their writing does not cause them to neglect their proper business or make them so silly as to injure society in a roundabout way.

> But man or woman who publishes writings inevitably assumes the office of teacher or influencer of the public mind. Let him protest as he will that he only seeks to amuse . . . he can no more escape influencing the moral taste, and with it the action of the intelligence, than a setter of fashions in furniture and dress can fill the shops with his designs and leave the garniture of persons and houses unaffected by his industry.

"Teacher" here has a special meaning; George Eliot herself was very much concerned that the charge of didacticism did not come near her writing. She resisted working with material that might tempt her into a more utilitarian type of instruction than she could manage artistically.

It was for this reason that she did not succumb to Frederic Harrison's flattering suggestion in 1866 that she and she alone had the talent necessary to bring into reality "an ever present" dream of his "that the grand features of Comte's world might be sketched in fiction in their normal relations though under the forms of our familiar life." She rewarded him with a long letter which contains the most complete statement of her mature aim in her art:

> That is a tremendously difficult problem which you have laid before me, and I think you see its difficulties, though they can hardly press upon you as they do on me, who have gone through again and again the severe effort of trying to make certain ideas thoroughly incarnate, as if they had revealed themselves to me first in the flesh and not in the spirit. I think aesthetic teaching is the highest of all teaching because it deals with life in its highest complexity. But if it ceases to be purely aesthetic—if it lapses anywhere from the picture to the diagram—it becomes the most offensive of all teaching.

She briefly describes her "unspeakable pains in preparing to write Romola," which by then she had persuaded herself was an ideal clothed in flesh and blood. Then she adds (no doubt rightly assuming that Harrison meant his inspired idea to emerge as a "happy" novel; otherwise why delineate the "grand features" of Comtism?): "And again, it is my way, (rather too much so perhaps) to teach [then she crossed out "teach"; obviously she was afraid of this word yet unable to avoid it] urge the human sanctities through tragedy—through pity and terror as well as admiration and delights." She has told him all this "to show the tenfold arduousness of such a work" as he has requested. Yet her "whole soul" was with his desire that it should be done, and she promised at least to "keep the great possibility (or impossibility) perpetually in my mind, as something towards which I must strive, though it may be that I can do so only in a fragmentary way."

A related aesthetic problem arose over Alexander Main's abstracting wise, witty, and tender sayings from her novels, published in December 1871 as the *Wit and Wisdom of George Eliot*. She liked Main, recognized that he had undertaken the project as an affectionate tribute to her, and thought that he had shown "a very fine instinct in his extracts and mode of arrangement." But she remained uneasy because he was necessarily breaking each novel down into segments of a few sentences which would stand alone, perhaps with misleading emphasis, especially to one who had not read the whole story. Blackwood privately called Main "the Gusher" and disliked the idea from the beginning. Somewhat slyly, he suggested that in a new preface written for the second edition, "our friend puts the case rather too strong in favour of his compilation as compared with the Works." She wrote in response:

> Unless my readers are more moved towards the ends I seek by my works as wholes than by an assemblage of extracts, my writings are a mistake. I have always exercised a severe watch against anything that could be called preaching, and if I have ever allowed myself in dissertation or in dialogue [anything] which is not part of the structure of my books, I have there sinned against my own laws.
>
> I am particularly susceptible on this point, because it touches deeply my conviction of what art should be, and because a great deal of foolish stuff has been written in this relation.
>
> Unless I am condemned by my own principles, my books are not properly separable into "direct" and "indirect" teaching. My chief doubt as to the desirability of the "Sayings" has always turned on the possibility that the volume might encourage such a view of my writings.

George Eliot's wrestle with this peculiar problem forms an ironic footnote to literary history, for the "foolish stuff" which she had already observed being written about the seemingly didactic element in her writing was to multiply until her art was smothered under the heavy accusation of moral preaching. She would be appalled by what would seem to her a misreading of her novels. But she would remain convinced that some kind of aesthetic teaching is absorbed by the reader of a book as surely as he perceives physical reality when it impinges upon his senses, the main difference being that it is his senses which organize the scattered data outside himself, whereas the book to which he reacts is an environmental field that has already been selected, unified, and controlled by its author. This is why (to return to her original point) any writer who makes his work available to readers beyond himself is inevitably a teacher; and also why only his talent and integrity will determine whether his teaching is muddled or coherent, for good or for evil. It was in this sense that Freud used the term "teacher" when discussing the neurosis which caused Dostoevsky to end up,

> retrograde fashion, with submission both to the temporal and the spiritual authorities, with veneration for the Tsar and the God of the Christians, and a narrow Russian nationalism, a position which lesser minds have reached with less effort. This is the weak point of the great personality. Dostoevsky threw away the chance of becoming a teacher and liberator of humanity; instead, he appointed himself its jailer.

As in Dostoevsky, there is a strong tendency toward masochism in several of George Eliot's novels, particularly noticeable in heroines such as Maggie Tulliver, Romola, and Gwendolen Harleth. The masochistic strain is not so compelling as it is in Dostoevsky because there is always a control behind it, the George Eliot presence. This technical aspect of her novel writing—forged by her double consciousness—defrauds readers not only of undiluted sensationalism but of encountering a character commensurate to George Eliot herself. One of the most serious losses to George Eliot's posterity is the result of the dialectics of her chosen technique: if George Eliot had created another George Eliot, who would have been in the background overseeing and directing that creation?

However, that same posterity can be grateful for an equally natural source of restraint: George Eliot could not indoctrinate. As a teacher in the sense in which she meant the term, she removes (or at least attempts to remove) blinders; she does not inculcate. When forced to hear reactions to her work, those she could best tolerate were the ones which indicated a moral awakening—an awareness of other-than-self, a new breadth of vision. Such individual tributes were especially welcome after the disappointingly passive public acceptance of *Daniel Deronda*, which she had thought would stir up controversy. She wrote Blackwood on 3 November 1876:

> A statesman who shall be nameless has said that I first opened to him a vision of Italian life, then of Spanish, and now I have kindled in him a quite new understanding of the Jewish people. This is what I wanted to do—to widen the English vision a little in that

direction and let in a little conscience and refinement. I expected to
excite more resistance of feeling than I have seen the signs of,
but I did what I chose to do—not as well as I should have liked
to do it, but as well as I could.

It is fitting that she made this comment about her last novel for, with
little revision, it could stand as an observation upon her total work.

If the ideal author—as she severely outlines him in "Leaves from
a Note-Book"—discovers that his writing perhaps unfortunately has
whatever it takes to be popular, then his relationships with both society
and himself have doubled in complexity. In a way that is faintly
reminiscent of Lewes's 1859 review of Renan's *Essais*, she draws the
necessary contrast between the rules of production which govern an
honest manufacturer and those which apply to an equally honest
author. A wise calico manufacturer, for example, turns his capital into
more and more calico of essentially the same quality: "the sameness is
desirable. . . ." But the author who says, "I will make the most of it
while the public likes my wares—as long as the market is open and I
am able to supply it at a money profit—such profit being the sign
of liking" is carrying "on authorship on the principle of the gin-
palace. . . .

A writer capable of being popular can only escape this social
culpability by first of all getting a profound sense that literature
is good-for-nothing, if it is not admirably good: he must detest bad
literature too heartily to be indifferent about producing it if only
other people don't detest it. And if he has this sign of the divine
afflatus within him, he must make up his mind that he must not
pursue authorship as a vocation with a trading determination to
get rich by it. It is in the highest sense lawful for him to get as
good a price as he honourably can for the best work he is capable
of; but not for him to force or hurry his production, or even do
over again what has already been done, either by himself or others,
so as to render his work no real contribution, for the sake of bringing up his income to the fancy pitch. An author who would keep a
pure and noble conscience, and with that a developing instead of
degenerating intellect and taste, must cast out of his aims the aim
to be rich.

By the time George Eliot wrote this, she had several times over
proved herself a "writer capable of being popular," she had honorably
become wealthy through her writing, and she had remained a writer
with "a pure and noble conscience." Most troubling had been the second element, perhaps because it stood as the balance between the other
two, which were not unlike the opposite ends of a seesaw. Ideally,
money earned from writing should have been equal acknowledgment

of both the popular consumption and the artistic worth of that writing, but she herself was quickly suspicious whenever the board tipped in the direction of popularity. It was then that she was likely to move away from the style and content proved popular, but at the same time, somewhat paradoxically, was also moved to seek greater compensation for the new work. She was to do this most conspicuously with *Romola*, over which she left John Blackwood as publisher to go elsewhere for more money than he was willing to offer, despite her own conviction that this novel—if only because of its alien setting in both country and time—would have less popular appeal than any of her preceding works.

Even without such intricate motivation, she had produced in her first fiction writing three markedly different stories. The *Clerical Scenes* had too few readers for this difference to be noted. *Adam Bede*, however, put an end to ambiguity in the expectations of her readers. It not only attracted a great number of readers but homogenized them into a single audience primed to expect another *Adam Bede*. There is some evidence that she almost succumbed to the temptation to give them just this. It was not solely that the monetary value of another best-seller was attractive; she had grown attached to the characters she had created, so that she was loath to cast them out of her mind to make place for new ones. In December 1858, after she had completed the novel but before it had appeared in print, she wrote Blackwood that she was delighted he liked her Mrs. Poyser: "I'm very sorry to part with her and some of my other characters—there seems to be so much more to be done with them. . . . Even in our imaginary worlds there is the sorrow of parting." Apparently she did quite seriously consider what more could be done with these characters, for six months later William Blackwood writes to John about a projected sequel to *Adam Bede*:

> With regard to the Poysers at the Seaside Simpson [the Blackwoods' printing manager] . . . does not think favourably of it commercially. I have rather the feeling that the Poysers are so good as they stand in Adam Bede that it would be a pity to weaken the effect of that unique work by extending as it were one section of it. Altogether I doubt whether such a thing will be for the author's advantage in the end; at the same time there is no doubt it would take, and if the author is bent on it we would be wrong not to go into it heartily, but I certainly would not press it in any way. . . .

As nothing further is heard of the idea (although in October a fraudulent sequel was advertised), she seems to have allowed it to fade away; perhaps because the *Mill*, which had earlier given her trouble, had suddenly sprinted forward. When she was beginning the *Mill*, she told

Blackwood that it would be "as long as AB, and a sort of companion picture of provincial life." By the time it was irrevocably under way, intentionally or not, she had injected into it the peculiar bitterness which many of the first readers disapprovingly noted distinguished it from *Adam Bede*.

THE BITTERNESS IS NOT SURPRISING. *The Mill on the Floss* springs from some of George Eliot's unhappiest memories. Furthermore, the events leading to its publication, and hence occurring during the writing of the novel, formed a crucible in her writing career although the experience had begun pleasantly enough. "I half venture to think that before I leave London," John Blackwood wrote his brother on 24 June 1859, "I should do something decisive about the new Novel. I have very little doubt that at present a new work by George Eliot might affect the sale of the Mag. most materially. . . ." His wording—indeed, his reasoning—suggests that at this time he had every intention of appending the name "George Eliot" to the work whenever it appeared. This point (later to become crucial) may or may not have been discussed when he spent the better part of the next day with the Leweses at Holly Lodge, Wandsworth, where they had moved from Richmond in February 1859. Blackwood reported favorably to his brother:

> I have just returned from a long day with George Eliot and Lewes. It is impossible not to like her excessively. She gives irresistibly the impression of a real good woman. It is impossible not to like him too. It is most melancholy that their relations cannot be put straight. They have been receiving fresh letters about Liggins who it seems is showing a M.S. and nothing will satisfy them but her writing another letter which I am disinclined for. It does not much matter however and of course the letter is a good one.
>
> She honestly confesses to a most deep seated anxiety to get a large price for the new Tale and I think we will be well able to afford to give it. It should be a little fortune to her. You would have been pleased with the way she spoke about it. You will need to go up to see them.

Blackwood proved far too complacent. He had underestimated the Leweses' disappointment over his failure to make decisive efforts to curb the Liggins imposture.

Actually, the Blackwoods were as seriously concerned over the Liggins affair as the Leweses, but thanks to the clever maneuvering by the perpetrators of a hoax which was meant to be more than a practical joke, they felt constrained in responding to its implicit challenge. Writing to Lewes on 18 April, John Blackwood had succinctly summarized the stance the firm had taken on the matter and meant to maintain as long as possible: "My objection to a point blank denial from us is that if any one stumbles on the real name a less decided denial from us would be an admission." However, at the time, the Leweses were too much in the thick of the fray to realize that the Blackwoods' concern to preserve the anonymity of "George Eliot" went beyond even their own. Feeling deserted by John Blackwood and the resources they assumed he had at hand to quash the Liggins myth whenever he chose, the Leweses had taken a step of their own. Under the signature of "George Eliot," Lewes wrote a letter to the *Times* (where it was printed on 16 April) in which he curtly denied Liggins's authorship and added:

> Allow me to ask whether the act of publishing a book deprives a man of all claim to the courtesies usual among gentlemen? If not, the attempt to pry into what is obviously meant to be withheld— my name—and to publish the rumours which such prying may give rise to, seems to me quite indefensible. . . .

Unnoticed by the Leweses, this letter elicited, in London at least, a different strategy in the assault upon George Eliot's identity. The Liggins case was cast into limbo, and militant attention was trained upon the letter's demand that an author's right to privacy be honored. Also abandoned was the pawn in this queer game, Joseph Liggins, the dissolute Warwickshire clergyman who was perhaps bribed to sustain silence while his fraudulent claim to the authorship of the *Clerical Scenes* and *Adam Bede* was being advertised. If bribery occurred, it was skillfully concealed, for to this day there is no rational explanation of why Joseph Liggins was catapulted into a brief moment of vicarious fame. Yet it is easy to imagine a person (or persons) proffering a bribe to this Liggins so that Lewes and George Eliot could be smoked out into the open. The most likely suspects are enemies of Lewes from his last *Leader* days, when his co-workers thought it necessary to take sides on the issue between him and Thornton Hunt. A few well-meaning but deluded champions of Liggins stayed loyal to his cause, even taking up a subscription for him because they assumed that the Blackwoods had cheated him out of money due him from the highly profitable *Adam Bede*. Eventually even the staunchest of his supporters left him to himself, and apparently nothing so good came his way again, for he died destitute in the Nuneaton workhouse in May 1872, just fifteen years after he had first been presented to the reading public as "the great unknown."

By then, George Eliot had only a hazy memory of the almost daily torment he had caused her in 1859.

The Blackwoods had made no move to endorse the 16 April letter to the *Times*, for they recognized that rather than forestall, this would invite an invasion of George Eliot's privacy and anonymity. Although it arose from the same source, their dilemma was somewhat different from George Eliot's. Perhaps feeling it indelicate to emphasize that difference, John Blackwood wrote to Lewes about the letter with ill-timed levity: "George Eliot's contradiction in the Times is exceedingly well put and made me laugh considerably. It will stop all the better class papers from publishing rumours as to the authorship." Even Margaret Oliphant (pro-Blackwood to the extent of being anti–George Eliot) acknowledged that "the laugh of the Blackwoods over what [George Eliot] felt to be an insult and wrong scarcely to be borne should seem to her almost unfeeling. . . ."

However, when on 20 April, George Eliot and Lewes each wrote to urge John Blackwood to reconsider and insert a statement in the *Times* which would bolster their letter, he answered immediately and straightforwardly:

> We did not write to the Times about the Liggins delusion, as we thought our doing so might be misinterpreted as a publishing dodge to reraise the discussion and stimulate curiosity. Also we did not think it wise, as some of the myrmidons of the press do not seem disposed to admit an author's right to privacy, and a sharp protest from us without any immediate call for it might further tempt the fellows to make your case the battle field of the question. That there is such a tendency you may see from the last number of the Leader and the Critic. I think I see Lewes' astonishment and indignation when he read the Leader.

The reference to the *Leader* and *Critic* articles did not disturb the Leweses as much as Blackwood had probably wished. Lewes quickly wrote back that Blackwood was far off in his "wildly chimerical supposition, that we see such papers as the 'Critic' and 'Leader' (the very name of the last, has long been a sore to me)." George Eliot had already written Blackwood that she was wholly in agreement with his abstaining "from the remotest appearance of a 'dodge,' " and asked for more information about the articles, although her thinking was proceeding in a different direction from Blackwood's major concern:

> What have they been saying? I am anxious to know of any *positive* rumour that may get abroad, for while I would willingly, if it were possible—which it clearly is not—retain my incognito as long as I live, I can suffer no one to bear my arms on his shield.

In response to her request, Major Blackwood answered her a few days later:

> I have tried to recover the numbers of the "Leader" and "Critic" which contained the remarks about the secret of authorship, but unsuccessfully. They were foolish and impertinent; attempting to prove that the public had a right to know who was the author of any book. . . . The articles were contemptible and any notice of such things would only gratify the creatures who had written them.

For the first and perhaps the only time in her life, George Eliot's anxiety was more easily quelled than the objective situation warranted. She responded simply: "Thank you for telling me the drift of the 'Leader' folly. I feared it might be something demanding a denial." One suspects that these articles arose out of the very source of the Liggins myth, so that what was needed was not another denial but a trenchant and sophisticated reply to those who persisted in carrying on the undeclared war even after they had forsaken their proclaimed cause, Joseph Liggins.

The Leweses, however, had begun to think that the attempted fraud could be brought to a decisive end only by means of George Eliot's open revelation of her identity. Sensing this intention, the Blackwoods were alarmed, and John Blackwood decided that it was again time to talk in person with them. His main objective was so uppermost in his mind that he ended his letter announcing his plan to come to Wandsworth with emphatic capitals: "KEEP YOUR SECRET." He reiterated this imperative when he visited with them on 27 May, Lewes noting in his Journal: "Blackwood urged that the secret should stedfastly [*sic*] be kept, at least until after the next book."

The Leweses agreed to continue to safeguard the secret as long as possible. In return, Blackwood offered to submit a notice to the *Times* in response to a new letter printed there requesting that the mystery of the authorship be cleared up in the interest of those who were contributing to Liggins's financial support. To this the *Times* editor, John Thadeus Delane (often called "the Thunderer" and a long-time personal friend of John Blackwood) had added what was perhaps the most effective statement thus far made: "We have no knowledge of Mr. Liggins, and have no desire to penetrate a secret which the author of *Adam Bede* has a perfect right to preserve; but we have the best authority for stating that he is entirely satisfied with the treatment he has received from his publishers, whose liberality, indeed, seems to have been almost beyond all literary precedent." Wishing to reassure the Leweses that he now meant to be actively helpful, Blackwood returned to Wandsworth on 5 June and together they drafted a double letter for the *Times*, where it appeared the next day. The first part was a statement by William Blackwood and Sons to the editor denying Liggins's authorship of either the *Scenes* or *Adam Bede*. Subjoined to this was a letter from George Eliot to John Blackwood, ending: "If those benevolent persons who persist in attributing the authorship . . . to Mr. Liggins, will induce Mr. Liggins to write one chapter of a story, that chapter may possibly do what my denial has failed to do." John Blackwood had especially enjoyed this visit and wrote his brother: "G.E. was full of fun yesterday, and gave me more the idea of the creator of her humorous characters than I have yet seen." But Lewes was unimpressed with what he considered the Blackwoods' belated gesture and wrote flatly about it to the major:

> Your brother was with us yesterday and will tell you of the letter concocted. I am surprised at . . . the equanimity with which you have both sat down under the absurd imputation. As to the secret, that can be kept in spite of rumours, since only one person knows it as a matter of fact.

The "one person" meant by Lewes was of course Herbert Spencer, and it was unwittingly he, as well as Liggins, who forced the veil of anonymity to be lifted. The catalytic agent seems to have been Barbara Bodichon. As early as 26 April she had written George Eliot from Algiers that she had detected her as author of *Adam Bede* through reading excerpts from it in a newspaper. This may have been the truth, or she may have fabricated a little after having heard the truth (or an intelligent guess) from John Chapman. In any event, George Eliot had been pathetically happy to be identified by a friend who admired the work without having any reason to threaten disclosure:

> God bless you, dearest Barbara, for your love and sympathy. You are the first friend who has given any symptom of knowing me—the first heart that has recognized me in a book which has come from my heart of hearts. But keep the secret solemnly till I give you leave to tell it, and give way to no impulses of triumphant affection. You have sense enough to know how important the *incognito* has been, and we are anxious to keep it up a few months longer.

Soon Barbara was visiting England, and on 19 June she came to Wandsworth, where, as Lewes recorded in his Journal, "The talk almost all day hovered round 'Adam Bede' and the deep impression it made on people. We showed her the m.s. and some letters." Whether or not anything was said during this visit to help the Leweses decide to confide in George Eliot's other closest friends—Sara Hennell and the Brays—they did so the very next evening. Having so recently talked in person with Barbara, George Eliot was sadly disappointed that her Coventry friends had not only failed to guess the truth but had been taken in by the claims of the Liggins party.

Barbara returned to Wandsworth a week after her first visit, on Sunday, 26 June, when there was no doubt more talk about the novel and the problem of its author's identity. Perhaps this was not so uninhibited as the earlier visit, for this time Barbara had brought with her Dr. Elizabeth Blackwell, the first English woman physician. Obviously Barbara's semi-exile in Algiers had not daunted her zeal in espousing women's rights. Not only was she "exhibiting" Dr. Blackwell as the embodiment of supreme feminine achievement; she was also immediately engrossed in investigating the justice and injustice being done her woman-novelist friend. Unerringly she went straight to the source of the most pertinent gossip concerning the authorship and the pseudonym. Only two days after her second visit to Wandsworth, she sent George Eliot a letter in which she had set down in spontaneous fashion what news she had collected:

I am going to tell you exactly what I heard from Mrs. O[wen] Jones last night as it may be of some use to you.

They both (the O J's) attacked me as knowing all about it. I talked *that* off and then asked for their evidence that it was you. . . . "How did Mr. Pigot [*sic*] know." Answer through H. Spencer who said he knows the author*ess* and had seen her lately—etc. Also Mr. P. knew *Mrs.* Lewes was at work on a novel for a long time. Also the Lewes style of living was changed. Also Mr. Lewes talked long ago of Clerical Scenes and Mr. O J said his eyes kindled at any praises of A. B. or C. Scenes. Mrs. O J said also that there is a reason for secrecy great enough to explain the obstinate mystery, for the book could not have succeeded if it had been known as hers; *every newspaper critic would have written against it* (! ! !) Evidently they think when it is know[n] the book will be differently judged.

They assured me all the literary men were certain it was Marian Lewes: ⟨that they should not assert it before they were told by Mr. Lewes but⟩ that they did not much like saying so because it would do so much harm, but *Mr.* O J seemed to have no doubt.

From their way of talking it was evident they thought you would do the book more harm than the book do you good in public opinion.

I tried to make Mrs. O J say she would like to know you (not that you would like to know her) but she seemed to feel fear! I do not think she would call even if she knew you were George Eliot. I said a great deal about my pleasant visits. I was trying experiments on her for my own satisfaction not on your account at all. Oh Marian, Marian, what cowards people are!

Almost all women are jealous of you. From this feeling I fear a ⟨howl⟩ yell mixed with the men's hypocritical howl.

Although the Leweses may have encouraged Barbara to collect and send them this kind of information, the letter must have been a shock to George Eliot. They responded to it jointly on 30 June, but her portion has not survived intact enough to be intelligible. To whatever she had written, Lewes added a postscript which she probably saw and approved:

> . . . we have come to the resolution of no longer concealing the authorship. It makes me angry to think that people should say that the secret has been kept because there was any *fear* of the author's name. You may tell it openly to all who care to hear it that the object of anonymity was to get [*Adam Bede*] judged on its own merits, and not prejudged as the work of a woman, or of a particular woman. It is quite clear that people would have sniffed at it if they had known the writer to be a woman but they can't now unsay their admiration.

Confirming what they had suspected but had not been willing to admit even to themselves, Barbara's letter had an impact which forced Lewes into defensive bravado. Despite his denial, he himself, George Eliot, and certainly the Blackwoods had been afraid of the author's name being known. Mainly, however, he was concerned over George Eliot's reaction to any further reports Barbara might send, so that he attached a private warning:

> P.P.S. *Entre nous.* Please don't write or tell Marian anything *unpleasant* that you hear unless it is important for her to hear it. She is so very sensitive, and has such a tendency to dwell on and believe in unpleasant ideas that I always keep them from her. What other people would disregard or despise sinks into her mind. She knows nothing of this second postscript, of course.

Of the several persons mentioned in Barbara's letter, the Leweses immediately fastened upon Spencer as the arch-betrayer. The gravity of the tone in which George Eliot refers to the matter in her 5 July letter to Charles Bray indicates how seriously she had taken to heart Spencer's seeming perfidy:

> I feel so deeply the duty of doubting everything to the disadvantage of another until demonstration comes, that I beg you not to regard the last thing Mr. Lewes told you about Herbert Spencer, as a thing incapable of being so explained as to make it more consistent with our previous conviction concerning his character. Mr. Lewes and I both hope in the possibility of such an explanation. . . . *We* shall be doubly careful to speak only of what we admire in him to

the world generally. The rest we have told to no one but Mrs. Bodichon, you, and Blackwood. Blackwood we were obliged to tell in order to account for the betrayal of the anonymity.

It was on 29 July, the day after the receipt of Barbara's letter, that Lewes made a special trip into London to tell John and William Blackwood that they had resolved to keep the secret of George Eliot's identity no longer. On the same day, George Eliot wrote John Blackwood that she hoped he and the major would visit them the next Saturday as she wished "very much to talk with you of the new aspect things are wearing."

When the Blackwoods came to lunch at Wandsworth that Saturday, they perhaps carried with them the current issue of the *Athenaeum*, which revealed that the Liggins "party" had suddenly reversed its direction. Liggins was no longer a real claimant, but a fabrication by George Eliot to increase interest in and thus the sale of the books:

> It is time to end this pother about the authorship of "Adam Bede." The writer is in no sense a "great unknown"; the tale, if bright in parts, and such as a clever woman with an observant eye and unschooled moral nature might have written, has no great quality of any kind. Long ago we hinted our impression that Mr. Liggins . . . was a mystification, got up by George Eliot,—as the showman in a country fair sets up a second learned pig to create a division among the penny paying rustics. . . . The elaborate attempt to mystify the reading public, pursued in many articles and letters at the same time, but with the same Roman hand observable in all, is itself decisive of the writer's power. No woman of genius ever condescended to such a *ruse*,—no book was ever permanently helped by such a trick.

Only a few months back, the *Athenaeum* had run a review of *Adam Bede* by Geraldine Jewsbury in which she had said: "It is very seldom we are called on to deal with a book in which there is so little to qualify our praise." Whether George Eliot had read the July *Athenaeum* before, during, or after the Blackwoods' arrival, the luncheon conference apparently went off calmly and even enjoyably, for John Blackwood ended his 8 July letter: "The Major sends his best regards. We frequently talk of our very interesting visit to you." However, by the end of the day she was suffering a reaction that forced her to cut short her letter to Barbara, who had written in the happy, enthusiastic spirit prompted by Lewes's confidential postscript. "Your letter, with its heart-warming words, came just after we had read the Athenaeum!" she explained apologetically. ". . . I [am] very poorly and trembling, and am only fit to sit in a heap with a warm water bottle at my feet. So no more now."

By DISENTANGLING HERSELF FROM THE LIGGINS AFFAIR AND relaxing her hold on anonymity, George Eliot only intensified her problems with the Blackwoods. Signs that her publishers would be wary over using her pseudonym whenever it was given an identity had been present ever since the middle of June, when they refused to agree to affix the name to "The Lifted Veil," the last fiction of hers to appear in Maga. But earlier—just as in the beginning of the talk about her new novel—the privilege of using that name was the major reason for wanting a work from her to follow *Adam Bede* as soon as possible. It was in his letter of 30 March, in which Blackwood said he was returning the MS of *Adam Bede* but keeping that of the *Clerical Scenes* for himself, that he also said: "I want a Tale for the Magazine and I know I can trust to George Eliot." She answered the next day, saying that the new work he had heard about from Lewes would be a novel as long as *Adam Bede* and would require "time and labour," but that she was engaged in writing "a slight story of an outré kind—not a *jeu d'esprit*, but a *jeu de melancolie*," which she could send him in a few days for acceptance or rejection for Maga of one number only. Blackwood was of course eager to have the new short story and told her so on 6 April.

During that month, an illness interrupted her work on the story so that, according to her Journal, she did not complete it until 26 April, even though she had begun it one morning at Richmond before she and Lewes moved to Wandsworth on 11 February. When she sent it to Blackwood three days after completing it, she referred to it apologetically as "the dismal story, which I did not send before because I thought you were already choked with the proofs for Maga, just issued." A few days earlier, Lewes had written Blackwood: "You must prepare for a surprise with the new story G.E. is writing. It is *totally* unlike anything he has written yet. . . . [It] is of an imaginative philosophical kind, quite new and piquant." Had the story reached him from some other source, Blackwood probably would have rejected it. As it was, he delayed acknowledging it for almost three weeks and even then had trouble keeping back from the author his personal dissatisfaction with it:

> I feel quite ashamed of my long silence. . . .
> I inclose proof of the Lifted Veil. It is a very striking story, full of thought and most beautifully written. I wish the theme had been a happier one, and I think you must have been worrying and disturbing yourself about something when you wrote. Still, others are not so fond of sweets as I am, and no judge can read the Lifted

Veil without deep admiration and the feeling that it is the work of
a great writer.

He went on to say that he very much disliked "the revivifying experiment at the end and would strongly advise its deletion." He assumed
that this lurid scene had been suggested by "some of our excellent
scientific friend's experiments on some confounded animalcule."
Clearly he did not wish to accept the story as it stood, and he added:
"The Magazine is still in such a dreadful state of size that it will suit
me better to postpone the Veil for a month so we will have plenty of
time to talk it over." Whether or not it had been talked over, when
the story appeared in the July number of Maga, the revivifying scene
was intact.

Like "Gilfil," "The Lifted Veil" has multiple but fragmented
themes, as well as a number of details which suggest allegorical autobiography. One of the most tantalizingly specific of these is the date
20 September 1850, the time set in the story for the death of the central character, Latimer. Through his remarkable but unenviable
power of prevision, Latimer knows exactly when, where, and how
he will die; he is spending his last remaining month writing an
account of his strange and bitter life. In George Eliot's real life, this
of course had been an extremely trying time for her: temporarily
living at Rosehill, she was indecisively poised between her old life,
which had been ended by the death of her father, and a new one
which was as yet ambiguous. However, the date may have signified
the commencement of her life of creativity, whereas in the story it
marks the passing of a man whose power of creativity has been
paralyzed by the very psychic components which should have ensured
its fruition.

Only a year later—midsummer 1851—Herbert Spencer (according
to his own memory) was urging her to write fiction because he thought
he saw in her many of the needful qualifications, especially that of
"unusual and rapid intuition into others' states of mind." It was at
this time, too, that he noted her self-admitted possession of double
consciousness, which he interpreted to mean "a current of self-
criticism" that would obstruct spontaneous expression. Significantly,
Latimer of "The Lifted Veil" is possessed by, rather than in possession
of, both unusual intuition and double consciousness. In fact, these
two psychic phenomena merge within him in a bizarre manner. Latimer has a poet's sensibility and yearning to express himself, but he
is defeated by a second consciousness that deadens his feelings before
they find an outlet. In his words:

> My self-consciousness was heightened to that pitch of intensity in
> which our own emotions take the form of a drama that urges

> itself imperatively on our contemplation, and we begin to weep, less under the sense of our suffering than at the thought of it. . . .
> I went dumbly through that stage of the poet's suffering, in which he feels the delicious pang of utterance, and makes an image of his sorrows. [Chapter 2]

This no doubt is near to what George Eliot herself had felt and described to Spencer, which he had rightly assumed was then blocking her creativity. Eventually, she had been able to convert the self-reflexive layer of consciousness—that which Spencer calls the "current of self-criticism"—into a voice that could be projected outward. This is the George Eliot voice, which is distinctively present in all of her fiction, including "The Lifted Veil," despite the fact that the first-person narrator is supposedly Latimer at all times. The writing of *Adam Bede* had so solidified that voice as an entity in her own consciousness that she could no longer abandon or disregard it without risking the collapse of the psychic structure which was making creativity possible.

It is made clear that George Eliot had discovered for herself the potentially constructive power, as well as the negative force, of Latimer's first phase of double consciousness by the way in which she qualifies its result when she ascribes it to the Princess Halm-Eberstein, Daniel Deronda's mother—the one character besides Latimer to whom George Eliot grants this phenomenon and who was also among the last of her creations. After the Princess has eloquently disclaimed to her somewhat bewildered son why she had eliminated him from her life when he was an infant, the George Eliot voice intervenes:

> The speech was in fact a piece of what may be called sincere acting: this woman's nature was one in which all feeling . . . immediately became matter of conscious representation: experience immediately passed into drama, and she acted her own emotions. . . . It would not be true to say that she felt less because of this double consciousness; she felt—that is, her mind went through—all the more, but with a difference: each nucleus of pain or pleasure had a deep atmosphere of the excitement or spiritual intoxication which *at once exalts and deadens*. [Book VII, chapter 2; emphasis mine]

The Princess is enabled to experience exalted feelings because double consciousness operates within her in perfect accord with her natural and trained talent for acting. Latimer too was aware that his emotions were enacting a drama, but always under the deadening perception of his second consciousness so that they could never escape into artistic expression or decisive action.

As if erupting from its own pent-up energy, this double consciousness in Latimer expands into a more pathological kind, in which the normally outgoing process of intuition is internalized. He suddenly finds himself unable to ward off the invasion of other people's states of consciousness and even previsions of his own future. At first he is excited, thinking that at last the poet's nature in him is manifesting itself. But when he consciously attempts to produce images of equal vividness, intuition fails him utterly. Also, his visions and previsions are powerless to influence him in any way, for after he has perceived them in a state of "rapt passivity," they undergo the same fate as his feelings. In fact, wherever the veil is lifted upon human nature, Latimer finds meanness, egotism, and banality. Finally, through the revivifying experiment which so dismayed Blackwood, he learns that the dead return to life only to complete their half-uttered curses and intended crimes. In every instance to see beyond the veil arouses his disgust or horror, and his engulfing bitterness is the most consistently present element in the story.

Yet Latimer's bitterness is only a secondary offshoot of his looking beyond the veil: of far greater importance is the underlying psychic paralysis which robs him of the power of artistic creation that alone could have salvaged his life. This Latimer accepts and endures with "passive suffering," almost as if he regarded it as deserved punishment for having seen too much. His remarkable clairvoyance he regards as a disease, not a power. Imprisoned with his unwilled visions, Latimer receives each with a sense of horror even when its content is trivial. He yearns for death, which he envisages as an unending journey into a darkness that will not permit even inward vision. His only remembered happiness in life is of a short period in his earliest years when an eye complaint made him temporarily blind, so that his mother frequently held him on her knee and lovingly caressed him. This brief interlude of blindness in Latimer's life seems highly significant, for advancing from the murky depths of myth into the daylight of recorded time come the great seers who accepted blindness as punishment for having seen too deeply into divine and human nature— Tiresias, Homer, Milton, Joyce. Daringly, Latimer thinks of two of these when for a few moments of wild joy he deems it possible that his meticulously detailed vision of Prague (coming before he has visited that city) signifies the liberation of creative power: "Surely," he thinks in soon deflated triumph, "it was in this way that Homer saw the plain of Troy . . . that Milton saw the earthward flight of the Tempter" (Chapter 1).

Viewed from this aspect, "The Lifted Veil" emerges as a symbolic expression of George Eliot's last serious battle with the dynamics of the creative process. The surface current of Latimer's outspoken bitterness only partially conceals the strong undertow of George

Eliot's own fear and guilt—both of which, singly or together, could have produced paralysis. Much had happened to reawaken the ghosts of old, especially as the writing itself had taken her into uncharted areas. Moreover, she was having second thoughts (as the story suggests) about her right even to pretend to invade other psyches, and her doubt concerning this matter caused her to desire anonymity for reasons deeper than the apparent ones. The letter from Blackwood which reached her in Munich telling her Newdegate claimed he could identify all the characters in the *Clerical Scenes* perhaps aroused more guilt than she herself realized; indeed, it may have been a major cause of the peculiar languor she blamed upon the air and way of life of that city. Still later, her exultation over the writing of *Adam Bede* and then over its triumph when published may have begun to seem to her a kind of hubris. And Chrissey's death, although expected, might have seemed a personal judgment passed on her, for already in re-creating her own childhood (in "Gilfil"), she had denied Chrissey her rightful place in it. These were as yet unassimilated matters from her recent past.

"The Lifted Veil" also reflects the anticipatory anxiety she felt over the major creative task immediately confronting her—the writing of *The Mill on the Floss*. In this novel, which she had unsuccessfully attempted to begin before digressing to the short story, she was to tamper with human relationships and lives more drastically than ever before. It was inevitable that she should ask herself whether she could do so with impunity. Or was she, like Latimer, to be rendered sterile?

Fourteen years after she had written "The Lifted Veil," John Blackwood wrote to ask her permission to use it in the new series of *Tales from Blackwood*. He still thought the story too painful, but time had enabled him to appreciate "the wonderful skill" of the writing. She refused her permission, not desiring the story to go forth "in its dismal loneliness." If ever it reappeared, it should be "in harness" with other works of hers, for "the best effect of writing . . . often depends on circumstances much as pictures depend on light and juxtaposition." Blackwood's letter and request did move her to reconsider the story and write a motto for it, which—so she told him—both expressed its main idea and justified its painfulness:

> Give me no light, great heaven, but such as turns
> To energy of human fellowship;
> No powers save the growing heritage
> That makes completer manhood.

Although this motto does not fit the literal story, as Latimer neither wills nor desires his unnatural light, it is a hymnlike expression of thankfulness for deliverance from the sense of guilt which the story dramatizes and which had almost paralyzed her creativity in 1859. By 1873, when she produced the motto, she had written all of her novels up to *Daniel Deronda* and was England's most respected living novelist. Her own wavering belief in her right to exercise creative power had been gradually strengthened by the accumulation of external testimony bearing witness to the positive value of her work. No longer was there reason to fear punishment for seeing too much. She had looked deeply yet almost always with compassionate understanding; her vision was already a part of "the growing heritage / That makes completer manhood."

I n 1859 THE WRITING OF "THE LIFTED VEIL" WAS GOOD THERapy for George Eliot, but her more objective problems with Blackwood increased in seriousness. His delay in placing "The Lifted Veil" in Maga gave Lewes the opportunity to write him on 13 June: "It has occurred to us that if the name were affixed to 'Lifted Veil' it might effectively put a stop to any rumours. It not being likely that L[iggins] would write on such a subject: or that he would continue to write when not paid. Qu'en dites vous?" Had George Eliot been ready with her story when Blackwood first asked for it, he would have proposed this himself; but by mid-June, the most sensational gossip concerning her identity no longer centered on Liggins. Only two days after Lewes had made the suggestion, Blackwood told the major how he had responded:

> . . . I said I thought it better not to fritter away the prestige which should be kept fresh for the new novel. In this I am sure you will agree with me, although I daresay I am the only editor who would have objected to the name in the present furor. I suppose the other Magazines would give any money for a scrap with George Eliot's name attached.

The major did agree and wrote the next day to say so, adding his hope that the secret would be kept despite his misgivings that it would not. However, when "The Lifted Veil" finally did appear in the July Maga, so did the name "George Eliot," although not affixed to her story. By plan or coincidence, the same issue printed Lewes's essay "The Novels of Jane Austen," into which he adroitly slipped the name while discussing Jane Austen's "sympathy with ordinary life." Quoting a passage from "Amos," he identifies it as from "one of the works of Mr. George Eliot, a writer who seems to us inferior [to Austen] in the art of telling a story, and generally in what we have

called the 'economy of art'; but equal in truthfulness, dramatic ventriloquism, and humour, and greatly superior in culture, reach of
mind, and depth of emotional sensibility." This was a round slyly
won, but it did nothing to dispel the unpleasant question that was
dawning in her mind: was Blackwood rejecting her pseudonym for
essentially the same reason that in icy silence Isaac had refused to
acknowledge "Mrs. Lewes"?

Inwardly alerted, she turned her concentrated attention to money
matters: would John Blackwood prove to be as stinting, noncoopera-
tive, and officious in handling money that was rightfully hers as had
been her brother? Having good reason on her side, as well as inward
prompting, she put Blackwood to the test, writing him in September
1859 to express "without circumlocution" her considered opinion
why it would be to her financial advantage to have the new novel first
appear in book form rather than be serialized in Maga: "I have now
so large and eager a public, that if we were to publish the work without a preliminary appearance in the Magazine, the first sale would
infallibly be large, and a considerable profit would be gained even
though the work might not ultimately impress the public so strongly
as 'Adam' had done." But if the novel were to be serialized, then the
"Magazine edition would be devoured, and would sweep away perhaps 20,000—nay, 40,000—readers who would otherwise demand
copies of the complete work from the libraries." There was one more
possibility: "Again, the book might be in some respects superior to
Adam, and yet not continue in the course of periodical reading to
excite the same interest in the mass of readers, and an impression of
its inferiority might be spread before republication:—another source
of risk." In short, precisely what arrangement did he propose? If she
should consent to publish in Maga, could he promise her terms to
compensate "for the inevitable subtractions from subsequent proceeds"? Her conclusion neatly formulates what probably is the deepest
wish of every artist: "I don't want the world to give me anything for
my books except money enough to save me from the temptation to
write only for money."

Blackwood took a week to answer, obviously composing his letter
with care; he wrote about his intended reply to the major and then
sent him the final version before he posted it to George Eliot. Yet
when his letter reached her, it was at best an oblique response to hers;
he opened it with a remark that totally ignored her arguments against
serialization: "I wish to have your new novel for the Magazine as
from what I read of the story I feel confident that it will be admirably
adapted for publication there. Publishing in that form we will give
you at least as much as we would for it to publish in any other way."
He followed this by announcing the firm's intention to make her the

offer of "Three Thousand Pounds for the right to publish the tale in the Magazine and for the copyright for four years after the completion of its publication there." This in itself would have been a generous offer, but he made no reference to her question of whether such terms would be compensation for the twenty or forty thousand lost sales she had predicted. The closest he came to this touchy matter was to refute, with careful indirectness, her assumption that the huge success of *Adam Bede* automatically ensured an equally large demand for her next novel. "The prospects of the book are great," he admitted to her, "but there is no certainty under the sun. Who would have supposed that Clerical Scenes, admirable as they are, would not have been carried off in thousands by the flood tide of Adam's popularity." She would not have liked this reminder that her first published fiction was not moving off the booksellers' shelves. Blackwood's still more crushing blow came at the end of his letter, when he described in detail the plan for publishing her new novel:

> In the Magazine we would not put any author's name, and it would be great fun to watch the speculation as to the author's life. The style would be to me easily recognisable but no one, especially of the puffing writing and publishing order, would suppose that we would throw away such an advantage as putting the magic words by George Eliot at the head of a series of papers. In the long run however ours is the wisest course, as nothing equals the excitement of uncertainty.

These are uncharacteristically tactless remarks, especially as she was at this very time the victim of merciless speculation concerning her private life. But that was exactly the reason for Blackwood's reaction. Although he did not want to lose George Eliot as a writer, he wanted no scandal for Maga or the firm. As editor and publisher, he knew that he had the power to exploit her pseudonym to the full of its immediate sensational value; yet he was restrained by both his own ethics and his awareness that there was a strong counter-movement to remove the glamour from her as an object of scandal. From London he heard that the puritanical Mudie, having learned her identity, was threatening to boycott her new novel, and that Smith Williams (reader for Smith, Elder & Co.) had told Langford he did not believe a novel like *Adam Bede* could have come from such a polluted source. Another Smith, Elder man, George Smith (who would publish *Romola* a few years hence), was being beseeched by Elizabeth Gaskell: "*Will you please contradict if you can the statement that Miss Evans is the author of Adam Bede. . . .* It is a noble grand book, whoever wrote it, but Miss Evans' life—taken at the best construction, does so jar against the beautiful book that one cannot help hoping against

hope." Blackwood had no desire to offend George Eliot by reproducing this kind of talk, nor did he wish to tell her that both he and his
brother believed once her identity was firmly established, the sale of
any book by her would be unfavorably affected. In holding back what
was really in his mind, he produced a clumsy letter.

It hurt her, and in spirit her response to it was similar to that of
the 1842 letter she wrote her father after Isaac had said that by making public her unorthodox views on religion, she had ruined her
chances of finding a husband, so that her father would have to support
her with money which normally would be distributed among other
members of the family. Very well, she had replied in effect to her
father; I cannot sacrifice my intellectual integrity even for you, but if
by staying with you I am robbing others of what is rightfully theirs,
I will leave home to make my own way—unless you give me a sign
that you wish me to remain. By 1859, circumstances had changed;
but the same emotional pattern was still operative and by analogous
feelings she was drawn into it. Writing (and her pseudonym) had
become an extension of herself, so that money gained from her writing
was a symbol of her own worth and thus no more easily sacrificed
than an abstract quality such as intellectual integrity. She replied
tersely to Blackwood:

> When I wrote to you I felt no disposition to publish in the
> Magazine beyond the inclination to meet your wishes—if they still
> pointed in that direction, and if I could do so without sacrifice.
> Your letter confirms my presupposition that you would not find
> it worth your while to compensate me for the renunciation of the
> unquestionable advantages my book would derive from being
> presented to the public in three volumes with all its freshness
> upon it.
> It was an oversight of mine not to inform you that I do not
> intend to part with the copyright, but only with an edition. As,
> from the nature of your offer, I infer that you think my next book
> will be a speculation attended with risk, I prefer incurring that
> risk myself.

Somewhat hurt in turn, John Blackwood quickly passed the letter
on to his brother, for they were in the midst of deciding how much
they should give her for *Adam Bede* in addition to the £400 already
promised her over the original contractual agreement. The major was
displeased with her letter, but he was of a mind to proceed with the
planned increment, although he thought it might be more tasteful
to wait until negotiations for the new novel were completed—even
if they proved to be with some rival publisher. John concurred, yet
he hesitated almost three weeks before writing her, perhaps hoping
to hear something decisive about the growing rumors that she was

considering offers from other publishers. When he did write, he made no mention of either the rumors or the extra remuneration, but said merely: "The Major and I are very sorry indeed that you cannot entertain our proposal for the new Tale." He added a sentence which he no doubt wished would penetrate the thickening wall of disagreement and misunderstanding being built between them: "I hope Maggie gets on as gloriously as she promised."

George Eliot answered promptly but with annoyance, apparently having expected a quicker and more specific response; perhaps too she had hoped for a denial of the painful assumptions in her letter. She took out her frustration in complaining about the misprints in the most recent edition of *Adam Bede*, as well as about the inconvenience of having him in Edinburgh rather than London. And although by the final paragraph she was able to give him news of Pug in a light and friendly tone, it was with an unmistakable gesture of withdrawal that she signed herself "Marian Evans Lewes" instead of "George Eliot." For some reason her letter went first to the major, who in sending it on to John remarked: "I am rather sorry to see the change of signature." From the time of its origin, the pseudonym had been a bond between her and the Blackwoods, a tacit understanding of good will and trust. In his next letter to her, John had no recourse other than to address her as "My Dear Madam," and although he would have missed writing the familiar "My Dear George Eliot," he had reason to think that this signature was absent only temporarily. He expected his letter to set right their relationship, as it was written to accompany the final payment for *Adam Bede* according to the original terms and to inform her that he and his brother had decided to give her "a further share in the triumph of Adam" to the extent of £800. She acknowledged this news with one sentence of perfunctory thanks, the remainder of her letter being given to reminding him that neither he nor she had anticipated the popularity of the novel, and to deploring the lack of action taken to stop Newby's advertising a sequel to that novel. The signature remained "Marian Evans Lewes."

This letter, written on 28 October 1859, affected John Blackwood more seriously than any other words that had passed between them— although there had been earlier ones which should have concerned him more as a publisher. Obviously he had hoped for a heartfelt expression of gratitude, or at least of appreciation. The meager substitute that he found seemed a personal affront which equaled in depth the personal nature of his feeling for her. He immediately sent her letter on to his brother:

The enclosed *cool* note from George Eliot has given me a fit of disgust and I think I shall notice it distinctly when I get home, which I intend to do upon Tuesday. It is quite as well however, and above all things, except doing what we thought fair and kind, it was desirable that if the most popular author of the day left us we should be able to show that she had been treated with un-exampled liberality. However I do feel savage and am half disposed to write a formal note enclosing one you wrote to me expressing our feelings about the matter.

The long and involved second sentence suggests that John Black-wood's own feelings had overridden his reason, for there was nothing whatever in George Eliot's letter to indicate to him that she was negotiating with another publisher. He read into her avoidance of this topic the thickening rumors that she, prompted by Lewes, was holding out for the highest bidder for her work-in-progress. In reality, nothing of moment had been said about the new novel since George Eliot had put forth her unanswered arguments against serial publica-tion. Perhaps fearing that his feelings would explode on the page, Blackwood did not notice her letter "distinctly" the next Tuesday, but waited until he heard again from her. Thus, as a matter of curious fact, the problem which had caused the rift between them remained dangling for over a month.

Despite the halted correspondence (or perhaps because of it), the Blackwood people soon knew that the firm was in the midst of some kind of crisis over George Eliot. John Blackwood made it clear that he wished to talk to no one about it, even neglecting to let Langford in London know what had and had not happened. This lack of com-munication put Langford at a disadvantage; he suspected that some-thing was wrong, but without knowing what it was, he could not effectively counter the questions and remarks of Lewes, whom he saw in the City with fair regularity. He had already been mystified by George Eliot's having engaged him in a brief but pleasant corre-spondence two weeks after she had written Blackwood that she did not intend to part with the copyright of her new work. What she had requested of Langford was that he introduce her to some "hard-headed lawyer" whom she might consult about the affairs of her "heroes and heroines (and a little also about my own)." Langford must have com-plied to her satisfaction, because a week after her first letter to him, she wrote to thank him for his cooperation and also the lawyer for having supplied answers to the list of questions she had submitted. Apparently, the list of answered questions has not survived. In gen-eral, those concerning her work-in-progress can be guessed, for with the *Mill* she began to inject into her narrative the Daedalian money problems, usually centered in inheritance, which were to be con-spicuously present in all of her novels.

It is less easy to speculate upon her personal need for a lawyer's advice, although several possibilities immediately present themselves. Probably it was the gesture that was important to her—the reaching out to a traditionally unbiased and fixed source of wisdom, which stood its ground firmly against human mutability and irrationality. She was to make the same gesture later, particularly in conjunction with *Felix Holt*, the novel by which she returned to Blackwood after having left him over the publication of *Romola*. Whatever her immediate problem, it could not have been especially intimate or she never would have given it to Langford in written form—unless, by chance, she had hoped he would pass it on to Blackwood. For it is possible that in her mind Langford had become Blackwood's surrogate, and she may have been moved to find out what privileged relationship, if any, existed between herself and the firm after her defiant stand against serial publication for the new novel. If so, Langford was in no position to reassure her one way or another; he knew less than did she herself.

Up in Edinburgh Blackwood's printing manager, George Simpson, was too much on the daily scene not to be confided in, and he surreptitiously forwarded the information to Langford. About George Eliot's acceptance of the £800, he wrote:

> Not a single expression of gratitude or acknowledgment of Mr. B's handsome conduct. The result is that both Mr. John and Major B are utterly disgusted and I do think would now decline the new book if it were offered them. Mr. John has been most thoroughly hood-winked. His enthusiasm about GE was extraordinary, and his feeling of sympathy for his unfortunate position most heartfelt, but I must say the reaction is very great.

Then, slightly over a week later, Simpson wrote hurriedly to Langford: "Pray take no notice of my communication, for in reply to a remark of mine that you should be informed, Mr. John answered very impatiently as if he were disgusted with the affair and did not care to have anything more to say about it or the parties, and this after he had said he would write you." Nonetheless, backstairs gossip remained rife. Both the Leweses were villains, although Lewes was considered the real source of the supposed avarice which guided them—despite Simpson's admission to Langford that he was puzzled that, although writing to Blackwood about other matters, Lewes was saying "nothing about GE. Read me the riddle if you can, but address to my house 5 Lothian Road, when you write about it."

Undeviatingly loyal to the firm and John Blackwood, Simpson probably would have supported him against any opponent. In this instance it is clear that he was not displeased that the guilty one was George Eliot: he may never before have witnessed his genial but proud employer being so dejected by words from someone he had earlier admired with extraordinary enthusiasm. Margaret Oliphant, an equally loyal and dependent writer, would have been even more jealously aware of George Eliot's seeming usurpation of the Black-wood kingdom. Something of her original feeling was revived when many years later she read the Blackwood–George Eliot correspondence and wrote her summary account of why at this time there arose

> a temporary *refroidissement* between writer and publisher, which, I confess for my part, makes rather an interesting break in the applause on one side and acceptance of it on the other, which, however we may join in the applause, makes us after a while desire the interposition of some other human sentiment to vary the pre-vailing note.

At last Lewes broke the silence which had perplexed and annoyed Simpson. On 18 November he wrote Blackwood: "What days these are for furious speculation in the periodical world! My precious time is occupied with declining offers on all sides—every one imagining that he can seduce George Eliot, simply because he (the everyone, not G.E.) *wants* that result!" On the very day this was received at 45 George Street, Simpson wrote Langford:

> There was a very awkward letter from Lewes today. He and his friend are evidently in a fix. I fear L. is not highminded. His con-duct in this matter is most disingenuous. . . . He makes an absurd remark just the sort of thing the Ladies have such a knack of doing. After saying that he is pestered on all hands to contribute to new Magazines etc. he adds that "numerous attempts are also made to seduce George Eliot!" I say no wonder when Mr. Lewes has shown them the way!

Simpson was right in thinking that the Leweses were "in a fix." No realistic discussion had ensued between George Eliot and Blackwood about bringing the new work out in book form, but she had a growing manuscript in dire need of a home. Lewes had no doubt wished to prod Blackwood into remembering this fact. His way of doing so may have been lacking in taste, yet he was not merely bragging. On 27 October, George Smith had approached him to ask his cooperation in the forthcoming *Cornhill Magazine*. Lewes had already been alerted to the new magazine by Thackeray, who was the first editor and who dedicated his 1 November prospectus-letter to Lewes in appreciation of the latter's helpful suggestions and promise of con-tributions. When the first issue appeared in January 1860, Lewes was listed as a staff member and represented by the first of his "Studies in Animal Life." Without doubt, Smith was well aware that through Lewes he was moving close to George Eliot; but he made her no offer, for he had heard that she was averse to serial publication of her latest work. However, he did not forget and was later to come forward at exactly the right time to make a successful bid for *Romola*.

Other representatives of new periodicals were not so reticent. As early as 5 April 1859, Samuel Lucas had urged her to contribute to the first number of *Once a Week*, to be published by Bradbury and Evans with himself as editor. She unhesitatingly declined, telling Blackwood about the proposal when she asked him to forward her brief refusal to Lucas. However, Lucas persisted, writing twice more to beg her to begin a serial in *Once a Week*, or if she could not do that, at least to submit a short article. Whatever she did, he assured her, Bradbury and Evans were "perfectly prepared to meet *any* views you might entertain as to remuneration." On 23 May, she sent all three of Lucas's letters to Blackwood, asking him to put a "definitive conclusion" to the matter by writing in his own name "a brief and civil letter" for her to Lucas. If she had hoped to impress Blackwood with Lucas's flattering offer, she gained little satisfaction, for Blackwood, replying promptly, merely said that he had written Lucas "a civil note yesterday."

By mid-November, a competitive offer was put forth by Charles Dickens, who had quarreled with his former publishers, Bradbury and Evans, and who wished to have a novel from George Eliot to be serialized in *All the Year Round*, in which his own *A Tale of Two Cities* was currently finishing and Wilkie Collins's *The Woman in White* about to begin. With some justification, he thought that if these two novels could be followed by one from George Eliot, the series would "take its place in English Literature." Dickens promised attractive terms, and Lewes recorded in his Journal that he and George Eliot had "turned the matter over and almost think it feasible." Only three days later, 18 November, George Eliot noted in her Journal that they had written Dickens to say that "*Time*" was an "insurmountable obstacle to his proposition"; apparently, Dickens's offer applied to a novel to be written after she had completed her present work-in-progress. Although nothing was to come of this tenuous arrangement with Dickens, word that some kind of agreement between him and George Eliot had occurred was quickly broadcast, so that by 16 November, Simpson could reply to Langford:

> I am sorry to see my suspicions confirmed by your note of yesterday. G.E. has sold herself to the highest bidder. I said very early that he

> [George Eliot] was an avaricious soul, but even with this failing if he had known what dealing with Gentlemen was I think he would have explained the matter to the Messrs. B. before accepting the offer of another party. I have no doubt the tempter is that fallen angel C.D.

Perhaps aware that Dickens had entered the scene, Samuel Lucas reappeared, this time concentrating on Lewes. The day after Dickens's initial offer Lewes went by appointment to see Lucas and Evans (of Bradbury), who pressed him to write a novel for *Once a Week*. Although tempted, Lewes declined after "having agreed with Polly that it was desirable I should not swerve from Science any more, at least just now. . . ." They then asked him to continue to submit articles (which he had begun to do in July) on his own terms; but what they most wanted to know was whether George Eliot's new work was in the market. Lewes answered honestly: "I told them I thought it unlikely that she would publish in 'Once a Week' and that she felt bound to give Blackwood the refusal; but they assured me that *whatever* Blackwood offered they would give more. We parted on that understanding that they were to make an offer."

It was only a few days after this that Lewes wrote to tell Blackwood he was "declining offers on all sides" on behalf of George Eliot. Since his letter elicited no response, and no specific offer had been made by Bradbury and Evans, George Eliot herself wrote abruptly to Blackwood on 26 November:

> As the time for the publication of my next work is not very far removed, and as thorough frankness is the condition of satisfactoriness in all relations, I am induced to ask you whether you still wish to remain my publishers, or whether the removal of my incognito has caused a change in your views on that point.
>
> I have never myself thought of putting an end to a connection which has hitherto not appeared inauspicious to either of us, and I have looked forward to your being my publishers as long as I produced books to be published; but various indications, which I may possibly have misinterpreted, have made me desire a clear understanding in the matter.

Blackwood might well have asked what she meant by "the time for the publication" of her next work, as their discussions had never reached the point of setting even a tentative date for publication. She probably meant that her writing pace had been accelerated as Maggie's story thrust itself through her consciousness—although it was to be four months more before she was able to bring the novel to its conclusion. However, Blackwood was in no mood to question her assumption about publication time. He was happy to have her note and quickly responded with the frankness she proposed. He admitted that he had been hurt by her reply to the terms he had suggested for the new novel, "and also at the very dry way in which our conduct in doubling the purchase money of Adam Bede was acknowledged." Although he "would be the very last man who would wish for a moment to stand in the way of your doing what you thought best for yourself," he did think that he should have been told by her if she had received offers more generous than his. He concluded:

> As to the withdrawal of the incognito, you know how much I have been opposed to it all along. It may prove a disadvantage and in the eyes of many it will, but my opinion of your genius and confidence in the truly good, honest, religious, and moral tone of all you have written or will write is such that I think you will overcome any possible detriment from the withdrawal of the mystery which has so far taken place.

George Eliot was equally responsive, seeing now—so she said—"that there has been a misunderstanding between us." She would try to explain her part in it. She admitted that she too had been hurt, especially by what she called his "stultification" of the letter in which she had argued that serial publication of her next novel would be to her disadvantage. Further, "Your proposition at the same time to publish the story without the name of George Eliot seemed to me (rendered doubly sensitive by the recent withdrawal of my incognito) part of a depreciatory view that ran through your whole letter, in contrast with the usual delicacy and generosity of your tone." There seems to have been a sad result of the interested comments exchanged between Simpson and Langford, for George Eliot claimed she had no idea that Blackwood, even after their disagreement, had given up the plan to publish "Maggie" in three volumes "until Mr. Langford, a short time ago, in conversation with Mr. Lewes, appeared to presuppose that you would *not* publish it." She concluded her long letter with the hope "that we have cleared the air, and that whatever may seem dubious in the future may not be left without an immediate request for explanation."

Although he read her letter immediately upon receiving it in Edinburgh, John Blackwood deliberately held off responding until he had arrived at Arbury Hall, where he was a houseguest of the Newdegates. He had taken care to send her letter to the major, who was pleased with it on the whole but far more cautious than his brother, to whom he wrote at Arbury:

> The dropping of the incognito is the most serious part of the business and will, I feel satisfied, affect the circulation in families of any future work. Then there is the danger of G.E. coming before

the public in his own name from some crotchet or another. I really think we should have some understanding with Lewes about this. Altogether it is a tangled kind of business, and though I feel that we should continue to publish for her as long as we have confidence in her other writings, we shall always, I am afraid, have disagreeables attending it in some shape or another. I think too very strongly that we should not bind ourselves until we have seen the new work.

Thus it was from Arbury Hall that John Blackwood wrote George Eliot the final letter which was to clear the way for rational negotiation over the *Mill*. It is easy to believe that he had been lured to the Gothicized manor with the thought of George Eliot in mind; inevitably as he looked about him, he would have remembered Tina's and Gilfil's experiences, and would have tried to see the place as the young George Eliot had done. "I need not describe," he wrote her during his long weekend there, "this fine quaint old place to you, of all people in the world." He eagerly gathered up what he heard about that earlier George Eliot and passed it on to the major, whose reaction is the only remaining indication of what the talk was like: "The account of G.E. is very curious. It is pleasant to hear that N. has so good an opinion of her." Yet John's long letter to George Eliot from the Hall is by no means sentimental; it gives signs of having been carefully composed and perhaps even edited after he had heard from his brother (it is dated 2–4 December, suggesting that he wrote it over a period of at least two days). Although he said nothing essentially new, he did invite himself to meet her and Lewes early the following week to talk decisively about terms for the still untitled novel usually referred to as "Maggie."

George Eliot was pleased by the prospect of their at last meeting again, and asked him to come to luncheon on Wednesday: "It will be a great comfort to see you, and exchange our 'winged words' in a less blind and ambiguous fashion than by letter." She was of course moved by his having visited Arbury and written her from there; one senses that for a moment all her troubles fell away while the best of the past and present came together harmoniously. She concluded her brief note to him: "I congratulate [you] on having seen that fine old place, Arbury. You must have passed by my brother's house, too—my old, old home." She could not resist signing this note "George Eliot." But she quickly shifted back to "Marian Evans Lewes" and would use "George Eliot" only once again when writing to Blackwood—on 29 February 1860, when she was excited over coming near to the conclusion of the *Mill*. Her use of the signature at this time may have been a gesture of significance, or it may have been a reversion to an old habit. From then on, she was to reserve that signature for letters to readers who wrote her about her books.

Blackwood came to luncheon on Wednesday, 7 December, and essential agreement was reached concerning publication of the new novel in book form, as he had given up asking that it appear first in Maga. On the fourteenth he wrote to make his formal offer of "Two Thousand Pounds for an edition of four thousand copies selling at 31/6 and payment at the same rate for every copy that we may sell beyond the four thousand at the above price." Included also were terms for possible cheaper editions so "that the arrangement should be a permanent one." Although Lewes had obtruded with an alternate scheme of serial publication, George Eliot wrote Blackwood on 20 December: "I think we have fairly dissipated the Nightmare of the Serial by dint of much talking. So we may consider the publication of Maggie settled according to the terms of your letter of the 14th December. . . ." This was a comfortably solid contract, even though (as Lewes had recognized) it was not based on a prediction of sales that the success of *Adam Bede* seemed to warrant. Perhaps George Eliot herself was not convinced that the Blackwoods had done their best for her. For the time being, however, a friendly and relatively frank business relationship had been restored between them.

In her Journal entry for 12 January 1859, three days before she read the final proof sheets for *Adam Bede,* George Eliot wrote that she and Lewes "went into town to-day and looked in the 'Annual Register' for cases of *inundation*." She was already seeking realistic data to support her vision of the cataclysmic flood which she knew must conclude her new novel and take the lives of Maggie and Tom Tulliver as they clung together in a final embrace. It is possible that at this time she also was certain the story would have a natural beginning in the childhood of the brother and sister, although it is unlikely that she was confident about specific contents beyond the all-important personalities of her two major characters. Not until eight months later, in September, did she and Lewes make excursions to study seriously a credible locale for both the flood and the Tulliver mill. George Eliot was finally satisfied with the old town of Gainsborough on the River Trent, which had the Idle as a tributary, so that these became, respectively, St. Ogg's, the Floss, and the Ripple, upon the bank of which stood the physical nucleus of the story, the mill.

She was equally slow in deciding upon a title, a possible indication that she was uncertain as to which element in her story she wished to emphasize—should it be Maggie as a sister, Maggie and Tom together, the Tullivers as a family, or even St. Ogg's as a society, which had through its materialism and hypocritical moral standards demeaned the rich historical legacy of the town? After finishing "The Lifted Veil" near the end of April 1859, she wrote in the Journal that she intended to resume her new novel, which she would call "provisionally 'The Tullivers,' for the sake of a title *quelconque,* or perhaps 'St. Ogg's on the Floss.' " Her own first choice was "Sister Maggie," but Lewes objected that this made the novel sound too much like a children's book, especially as the first portion of it would indeed be about children. When her major disagreement with John Blackwood had been resolved and it was definite that the novel would be published by his firm, she appealed to him for help with the title. Blackwood went to some trouble to cooperate, writing that he and the major still preferred "Sister Maggie." Yet from a sales standpoint, he could see Lewes's more sophisticated criticism of it, and after testing out various possibilities on the people at 45 George Street, he had come up with a suggestion of his own, "The Mill on the Floss," which he thought was conveniently general and had "a sort of poetical sound." George Eliot accepted this, but not without objections to remind Blackwood that he was not wholly returned to her good graces: the title was inaccurate, as the mill was not actually on the Floss but, rather, on its tributary, the Ripple; also she found the phrase "of rather laborious utterance," thus annihilating his somewhat shy remark (for Blackwood was not one to talk easily about poetry in any form) that it had a poetical sound.

As he read further into the unfolding novel, Blackwood himself questioned the choice of title. On 27 February 1860, less than a month before the novel was to be concluded, he wrote George Eliot: "Maggie is an individual character and no mistake. I begin to regret that we did not stick to our own favorite name of Sister Maggie, but no matter. If it was, Lewes and I should have our heads punched." By then, George Eliot was content with the title. From the beginning, she had struggled in the writing against making it a Maggie-centered story, even though Maggie was beating at her consciousness for release. The one guiding motif from which she never swerved was the flood; as Oscar Browning perceived, "She was always apparently writing with a view to the final catastrophe of the inundation." She was propelled toward this ending with the same inevitability that directed the progress of the flood itself. She had willed Tom to die, and so, in recompense, Maggie had to die. It is improbable that George Eliot searched her consciousness for the true causal connection between the two deaths; or that she was aware of either the surge of frustrated but hostile feeling for Isaac which had led her to study inundations or the great need for self-justification which was slowly plotting her story. What she did know was that her brother and sister were to be reunited and made secure against further separation. It was this positive side of her ambivalence that was needed to give to the water symbolism which pervades the novel its life-sustaining, as well as destructive, function, so that after the ravaging flood had come and gone, she could close her story with the promise of II Samuel 1.23: "In their death they were not divided."

There was a dangerous amount of explosive material to cope with before she could reach this regenerative ending, and as she was beleaguered by outer as well as inner problems the novel moved slowly. In August, seven months after she had consulted the "Annual Register," she told Blackwood that it was still "only in the leaf-bud," although she had "faith that the flower will come." At the same time (a month before their serious disagreement over the mode of its publication), she had confided in him her fear that it would not equal *Adam Bede* in popular appeal: "The characters are on a lower level generally, and the environment less romantic." This is a revealing comment, for socially and economically, the major figures of the *Mill* are a cut above those of the earlier novel, and rivers, mill, and an ancient town are as potentially romantic as fields and cottages. She was perhaps projecting her own mood onto her material; perhaps too she was thinking of the "lower level" of moral vision of many of her characters, as well as the unromantic, insular nature of provincial life. Finally, her uneasy awareness that she was exhibiting herself and her family to the world would have been in itself enough to make her subject seem to her low and without romance.

Her mood lightened and her writing pace quickened not long after the resolution of the immediate problem with Blackwood. By mid-January 1860 it seemed time to consider publication date. While she hoped the novel (to appear as a three-decker) would be out by Easter, she assured Blackwood that "no amount of horse-power would make me *hurry* over my book, so as not to do my best. If it is written fast, it will be because I can't help writing it fast." These proved to be prophetic words, for on 29 February she wrote him: "I am rather in a drive of feeling and writing with my third volume: that is in the nature of third volumes, and you will find my writing getting less legible. Pity you can't read it in print first!" Only a few days later, Lewes reported to Blackwood: "Mrs. Lewes is getting her eyes redder and *swollener* every morning as she lives through her tragic story. But there is such a strain of poetry to relieve the tragedy that the more she cries, and the readers cry, the better say I."

Normally, Lewes was the last literary critic alive to assert that the more the writer cried over his creation, the more the readers would cry (a popular assumption of the age). But he was working hard to convince Blackwood that the *Mill* was as great as *Adam Bede*—an opinion he privately did not hold. Despite her almost total absorption in the writing now that she was nearing the catastrophic finale. George Eliot feared Blackwood's reaction, having learned by sad experience of his dislike of tragedy and misery in literature. Temperamentally, Blackwood could empathize only with the earliest portion of the Mill. As he continued to read the instalments sent him, he became increasingly distressed by the somber turn of the narrative, although he had valiantly abstained from being directly critical. But Lewes wanted to risk no last-minute negative reaction from Blackwood; so to his testimony of George Eliot's emotional involvement with her story, he added an implicit plea: "She is anxious to hear your opinion of the part you have got; although she knows you don't like disagreeable and uncomfortable situations."

Blackwood responded at once and in gratifying manner, putting aside whatever reservation he might personally have felt: "I am indeed wearying for the rest and feel the misfortunes impending on Maggie like a personal grief. . . . This third volume will be perfectly fascinating." Within two weeks and after he had read new manuscript that went up to the last chapter, he wrote again: "The Mill on the Floss is safe for immortality." This letter reached her on 21 March, just in time to be read before she set to work to complete the novel, so that the next day she wrote back gratefully: "Your letter yesterday morning helped to inspire me for the last 11 pages—if they have any inspiration in them. They were written in a furor, but I dare say there is not a word different from what it would have been if I had written them at the slowest pace." The real reason for her letter was to send him three corrections which had occurred to her while she was "Lying awake in the night and living through the [final] scene again." The intensity of the feeling which had dominated her while she created this last section of the novel was not easily dissipated.

From Rome, where she and Lewes had fled as soon as she was outwardly free of the writing, she told Blackwood in her first letter to him: "I think Rome will at last chase away Maggie and the Mill from my thoughts: I hope it will, for she and her sorrows have clung to me painfully." Her next remarks, however, reveal that she was already beginning to distinguish between her obsessional empathy with Maggie and her concern for the novel as a whole: "As for the book, I can see nothing in it just now but the absence of things that might have been there. In fact, the third volume has the material of a novel compressed into it. I tremble rather, to hear of its reception. . . ." She was of course anxious, knowing that the novel was scheduled to appear before the public the next day, 4 April; but she felt relatively safe in Italy, with the Channel and a part of the Continent between herself and England, where many had penetrated her identity and a few would even be able to decipher the personal message of her new novel.

In *The Mill on the Floss*, GEORGE ELIOT BOLDLY TACKLED the problem of Isaac in recognizable form, thus producing her most frankly autobiographical novel. There were disguises, of course—some designed by her, such as the change in setting, the simplified family structure, and a fictional father who is conspicuously different from her real one. Then there are others dictated by a transforming force of memory which projected and objectified wishes as if they were real events, such as Maggie's being her father's favorite child. Of the same nature is Maggie's punishing the feared and secretly hated rival, Lucy Deane, which is childishly direct when Maggie pushes her into the mud, but becomes subtly indirect when both are young women and Maggie comes between Lucy and Stephen Guest. On the surface, Maggie is here motivated by an infatuation she is temporarily powerless to resist; but the underlying reason for punishing Lucy remains unchanged, for Tom is in love with his cousin (although this fact is so briefly touched upon and in such dispersed fashion that it is easily forgotten). It is for Tom that the ultimate punishment of death is reserved, and although Maggie goes to her own death with him, she does so in triumph. When first aware of the grave threat of the flood, Maggie felt "an undefined sense of reconcilement with her brother," who had recently turned her away from her home because of her night with Stephen Guest:

> what quarrel, what harshness, what unbelief in each other can subsist in the presence of a great calamity, when all the artificial vesture of our life is gone, and we are all one with each other in primitive mortal needs? Vaguely, Maggie felt this,—in the strong resurgent love towards her brother, that swept away all the later impressions of hard, cruel offence and misunderstanding, and left only the deep, underlying, unshakable memories of early union. [Book VII, chapter 5]

With almost superhuman power, Maggie guides her boat through the turbulent Floss and (the opening of the Ripple being closed to her) through the flooded fields up to the house by the now flood-ravaged mill. Her boat is on a level with an upstairs window, and Tom answers her piercing call from a window in the attic—the same attic in which as a child she had often isolated herself to relieve her anguish by driving nails into the head of her fetish doll. Tom is alone in the house, without boat or other help; astonished to find that it is Maggie alone who has come to his rescue, he steps into the boat and takes the oars from her. But it was not until he had pushed off and they were on the wide water—

> he face to face with Maggie—that the full meaning of what had happened rushed upon his mind. It came with so overpowering a force—it was such a new revelation to his spirit, of the depths in life that had lain beyond his vision, which he had fancied so keen and clear—that he was unable to ask a question. They sat mutely gazing at each other,—Maggie with eyes of intense life looking out from a weary, beaten face; Tom pale with a certain awe and humiliation. [Book VII, chapter 5]

Being Tom, he could not express this feeling verbally, but at last his lips

> found a word they could utter: the old childish—"Magsie!"
> Maggie could make no answer but a long deep sob of that mysterious wondrous happiness that is one with pain.
> As soon as she could speak, she said, "We will go to Lucy, Tom: we'll go and see if she is safe, and then we can help the rest." [Book VII, chapter 5]

To a reader lost in the drama of the flood and concerned over the welfare of Tom and Maggie, this reference to Lucy is both anticlimactic and digressive. It shows, however, that Maggie has forgotten neither Tom's love for Lucy nor her own justified feeling of guilt toward her cousin. She persists in speaking of Lucy once again. Tom, busy with the boat, responds to neither of her remarks, and soon it is clear to him that they cannot escape death from the onrushing pieces of wooden machinery which have broken loose from one of the wharves. Dropping his oars, Tom clasps Maggie to him as the huge mass of inanimate material rolls over them in its senseless passage to nowhere.

> The boat reappeared,—but brother and sister had gone down in an embrace never to be parted: living through again in one supreme moment the days when they had clasped their little hands in love and roamed the daisied fields together. [Book VII, chapter 5]

Thus the real reason for the flood is revealed. Even John Blackwood overcame his distaste of the morbid as he read the ending of the *Mill* and was reconciled to Maggie's death, although he fumbled in finding words to express his feeling to George Eliot: "The greatest lovers of all ending happily must admit that Providence was kind in removing Maggie. She could not have been happy here. . . . I was pretty well prepared for the end but would not have been so knowing had I not been aware that a flood was coming." The last remark touched upon a matter that concerned George Eliot as soon as she could look upon her novel with the objective eye of a writer assaying the craftsmanship of a completed work and ignoring the personal forces which had brought that work into being. She was never to retract her own criticism that, in comparison with the first two volumes, the third one was too compressed. When Bulwer-Lytton submitted (through Blackwood) a similar criticism, she readily agreed that therefore "the tragedy is not adequately prepared. . . . The *'epische Breite'* into what I was beguiled by love of my subject in the two first volumes, caused a want of proportionate fullness in the treatment of the third, which I shall always regret." There is no doubt that she believed this. A more profound truth is that as she had originally conceived it, the flood did not function as tragedy: it was, rather, the agent of vicarious punishment and reward, and it was also the means of reuniting brother and sister. As the latter the flood had tragic connotations in her own mind, for through it she was indirectly expressing her conviction that reconciliation between herself and Isaac was an impossibility in this life. The flood was therefore an attractive yet also a fearful objective to work toward, and it was easy for her to put distance between herself and it by lingering over the first two volumes, for she did indeed love that material.

Even in the nostalgic childhood scenes, Tom and Maggie exist under the burden of their creator's present, specifically that of 1859 or 1860, and in general that of an adulthood which will be denied them. Although George Eliot was adjusting to the idea that Isaac was permanently out of her life, she was not beyond pleading to him to remember their past, not merely as a linear manifestation of time but as a contrast to the harsh present. When ordered by his father to fetch his sister down from the attic, where she had gone in despair after her brother had told her that he would not take her fishing with him the next day because she had allowed his rabbits to die while he was away at school, the thirteen-year-old Tom Tulliver went sullenly up the stairs, bearing a piece of plumcake for himself and the resolve not "to reprieve Maggie's punishment, which was no more than she deserved." For, although undecided about grammar and arithmetic, Tom "was particularly clear and positive on one point,—namely, that he would punish everybody who deserved it: why, he wouldn't have minded being punished himself, if he deserved it; but, then, he never *did* deserve it" (Book I, chapter 5). But when he stood at the top of the stairs, Maggie rushed to him, begging him to forgive her and also to love her, so that his firm intention melted away, although he never could have said for what reason. "We learn," comments George Eliot,

> to restrain ourselves as we get older. We keep apart when we have quarrelled, express ourselves in well-bred phrases, and in this way preserve a dignified alienation, showing much firmness on one

side, and swallowing much grief on the other. We no longer approximate in our behaviour to the mere impulsiveness of the lower
animals, but conduct ourselves in every respect like members of a
highly civilized society. [Book I, chapter 5]

Unless inserted later, this would have been written before her trouble
with Blackwood reached a crisis. But the passage shows how already
familiar she was with the pattern of "dignified alienation" she had
maintained with him; fortunately, when she felt the need to break
the pattern, Blackwood had proved approachable and yielding. A few
years hence, Tom Tulliver would no longer be capable of being either,
for despite his being "one of those lads that grow everywhere in England, and at twelve or thirteen years of age look as much alike as
goslings," Nature had concealed under this "average boyish" appearance "some of her most rigid, inflexible purposes, [and one] of her
most unmodifiable characters" (Book I, chapter 5). But at thirteen,
Tom and the younger Maggie

> were still very much like young animals, and so she could rub her
> cheek against his, and kiss his ear in a random, sobbing way; and
> there were tender fibres in the lad that had been used to answer
> to Maggie's fondling; so that he behaved with a weakness quite
> inconsistent with his resolution to punish her as much as she
> deserved: he actually began to kiss her in return, and say,—
> "Don't cry, then, Magsie—here, eat a bit o' cake!" Maggie's sobs
> began to subside, and she put out her mouth for the cake and bit
> a piece; and then Tom bit a piece, just for company, and they ate
> together and rubbed each other's cheeks and brows and noses
> together, while they ate, with a humiliating resemblance to two
> friendly ponies. [Book I, chapter 5]

Until the intrusion of the ironic "humiliating resemblance," there is
a ritualistic simplicity and repetition in this passage. Despite its surface
childishness, it brings to mind the Communion-like supper of bread
and wine that Bartle Massey shares with Adam Bede on the evening
of the first day of Hetty's trial. For Maggie and Tom, plumcake is
their bread and their wine is happiness.

After this reconciliation, Maggie is of course allowed to go fishing
with Tom the next day. They went to the Round Pool ("that wonderful pool, which the floods had made a long while ago"), into which,
with Tom's help, Maggie cast her line and then sat down, looking
dreamily into the glassy water and forgetful of the fish, until Tom
startles her with a loud whisper and comes running toward her.

> Maggie was frightened lest she had been doing something wrong,
> as usual; but presently Tom drew out her line, and brought a large
> tench bouncing on the grass.

Tom was excited.

"O Magsie, you little duck! . . ."

Maggie was not conscious of unusual merit, but it was enough that Tom called her Magsie, and was pleased with her. [Book I, chapter 5]

This "was one of their happy mornings. They trotted along and sat down together, with no thought that life would ever change much for them. . . ." But as they sat in the grass, blissfully absorbed in the present, George Eliot hovers above and around them: "Life did change for Tom and Maggie; and yet they were not wrong in believing that the thoughts and loves of these first years would always make part of their lives." A few sentences more, and the children are forgotten; it is George Eliot herself who synthesizes the levels of time that have been operating in this deceivingly simple scene: the children's present (her past) and their vaguely adumbrated future (her present).

The wood I walk in on this mild May day, with the young yellow-brown foliage of the oaks between me and the blue sky, the white star-flowers and the blue-eyed speedwell and the ground ivy at my feet. . . . Our delight in the sunshine on the deep-bladed grass to-day might be no more than the faint perception of wearied souls, if it were not for the sunshine and the grass in the far-off years which still live in us, and transform our perception into love. [Book I, chapter 5]

She, with Wordsworth, had rediscovered the cause of the splendor in the grass—what he had called the intimations of immortality, and what she in the "Brother and Sister" sonnets was to describe as her root of piety.

In the third volume, the fictional present and George Eliot's own are often telescoped, as in the Maggie–Stephen Guest relationship. Tom's outburst of verbal brutality when Maggie comes home after her night with Stephen is George Eliot's interpretive rendering of Isaac's cold silence when she told him that she was living with Lewes —with irrefutable reasons precluding marriage, if not in the sexual innocence of Maggie's relationship with Stephen. To Maggie's " 'I am come back home,—for refuge,—to tell you everything,' " Tom responds with "tremulous rage": " 'You will find no home with me. . . . You have disgraced us all. . . . I wash my hands of you for-ever. You don't belong to me.' " While issuing this ultimatum, Tom was "trembling and white with disgust and indignation." Maggie "felt the hatred in his face,—felt it rushing through her fibres . . ." (Book VII, chapter 1). Tom thrusts aside her explanation of what had really happened to her and Stephen during their night together; further, he accuses her of having carried on a clandestine affair with

Stephen and using Philip Wakem as a screen to deceive Lucy Deane. Half-stunned by his terrible anger, Maggie is unable "even to discern any difference between her actual guilt and her brother's accusations, still less to vindicate herself." As head of the household, he has the right to refuse her entry to the house, and he uses it, but words remain his most wounding weapon. He flings them at her:

> You struggled with your feelings, you say. Yes! *I* have had feelings to struggle with; but I conquered them. I have had a harder life than you have had; but I have found *my* comfort in doing my duty. But I will sanction no such character as yours: the world shall know that *I* feel the difference between right and wrong. If you are in want, I will provide for you—let my mother know. But you shall not come under my roof. It is enough that I have to bear the thought of your disgrace: the sight of you is hateful to me. [Book VII, chapter 1]

Unexpectedly, the mother steps forward: "My child! I'll go with you. You've got a mother." This is the same Mrs. Tulliver who at the opening of the novel had complained "I don't like to fly i' the face o' Providence, but it seems hard as I should have but one gell, an' her so comical" (Book I, chapter 2). Slightly later it is said of this mother, if she "had a strong feeling, it was fondness for her boy" (Book I, chapter 5). Finally, in contrast to her reluctant but natural antipathy toward Maggie, she feels drawn to the neat and docile Lucy Deane, who is "such a good child,—you may set her on a stool, and there she'll sit for an hour together, and never offer to get off. I can't help loving the child as if she was my own" (Book I, chapter 6). It is not really Mrs. Tulliver who emerges to protect and shelter Maggie against Tom; it is an imperative created out of the dynamics of the scene, a wish-incarnate. Once they step outside and close the door on Tom, she becomes Mrs. Tulliver again and shrinks into her usual indecisive, fearful self; Maggie must decide where they will go for the night. Mrs. Tulliver is absent from the flood scene, having gone (so Tom tells Maggie) to Garum; nor is she mentioned in the "Conclusion."

For two weeks Maggie lived the scene with Tom over and over. It took the townspeople just this long to reach a conclusion and pass their damning judgment on her, but she

> was too entirely filled with a more agonizing anxiety to spend any thought on the view that was being taken of her conduct by the world of St. Ogg's. . . . If she had thought of rejection and injustice at all, it would have seemed to her that they had done their worst,— that she could hardly feel any stroke from the intolerable since the

words she had heard from her brother's lips. Across all her anxiety for the loved and the injured, those words shot again and again, like a horrible pang that would have brought misery and dread even into a heaven of delights. [Book VII, chapter 2]

The sequence is noteworthy here, suggesting (as evidence supports) that by suffering early divorce from her family, George Eliot had been prepared for social ostracism, so that she was able to face it with courage and at least a convincing pretense of indifference. However, she was still only human, and the plea to Isaac which permeates the *Mill* inevitably crescendoed to an address to society, although not without her first having castigated that society in the form of St. Ogg's:

If Miss Tulliver, after a few months of well-chosen travel, had re-turned as Mrs. Stephen Guest,—with a post-marital *trousseau*, and all the advantages possessed even by the most unwelcome wife of an only son,—public opinion, which at St. Ogg's, as elsewhere, always knew what to think would have judged in strict consistency with those results. Public opinion in these cases is always of the feminine gender,—not the world, but the world's wife. [Book VII, chapter 2]

Had that all-important wedding taken place, the world's wife would have been happy to interpret the incident with humane generosity: "Mr. Stephen Guest had certainly not behaved well; but then, young men were liable to those sudden infatuated attachments; and bad as it might seem in Mrs. Stephen Guest to admit the faintest advances from her cousin's lover . . . still she was very young." True, Philip Wakem had been as good as jilted, but he was "a deformed young man, you know!—and young Guest so very fascinating." Miss Deane was "very pitiable; but then, there was no positive engagement; and the air at the coast will do her good. After all, if young Guest felt no more for her than *that*, it was better for her not to marry him. . . ." George Eliot goes on:

. . . But Maggie returned without a husband, and the world's wife, with that fine instinct which is given her for the preservation of Society, saw at once that Miss Tulliver's conduct had been of the most aggravated kind. Could anything be more detestable? . . . Why her own brother had turned her from his door; he had seen enough, you might be sure, before he would do that. A truly re-spectable young man,—Mr. Tom Tulliver: quite likely to rise in the world! His sister's disgrace was naturally a heavy blow to him. It was to be hoped that she would go out of the neighbourhood,—to America, or anywhere,—so as to purify the air of St. Ogg's from the taint of her presence, extremely dangerous to daughters there!

No good could happen to her: it was only to be hoped she would repent, and that God would have mercy on her: he had not the care of Society on his hands,—as the world's wife had. [Book VII, chapter 2]

The chapter closes with an emphatic but nonironic declaration that moral judgments must remain hypocritical "unless they are checked and enlightened by a perpetual reference to the special circumstances that mark the individual lot.

All people of broad, strong sense have an instinctive repugnance to the men of maxims. . . . And the man of maxims is the popular representative of the minds that are guided in their moral judgment solely by general rules, thinking that these will lead them to justice by a ready-made patent method, without the trouble of exerting patience, discrimination, impartiality,—without any care to assure themselves whether they have the insight that comes from a hardly earned estimate of temptation, or from a life vivid and intense enough to have created a wide fellow-feeling with all that is human. [Book VII, chapter 2]

This premise for an individualistic ethic was too out of tune with contemporary thought to be even noticed by any but a very few readers. Her appeal to Isaac was equally futile; he was a man of maxims.

Nevertheless, in writing *The Mill on the Floss* she had effected a catharsis of destructive emotions, and so was free to move on to other subjects. She had also created a new kind of autobiographical novel which was to be further explored and developed in the twentieth century.

IN ROME, THE LEWESES ANXIOUSLY AWAITED NEWS OF THE sale of the novel, which for a while was disappointingly neutral. One good sign came early from Mudie, who far from banning the book, was "nibbling at a third thousand," Blackwood reported on 24 April. But he could not resist adding a less promising note: "Langford does not say much of the opinion of The Garrick about The Mill but I rather gather that the verdict there is not so universally favourable as about Adam. The knowledge of the secret would make them more critical I daresay." They did not take his remark amiss; in fact Lewes concurred, noting in his Journal:

Received a letter from Blackwood containing checquered news about the "Mill on the Floss." The sale is about 5,600—immense, but I gather that the general talk about the book is less favorable than it was about Adam. The disclosure of the authorship would have much influence in that direction, which would be increased by the fact of the book being a "second book." Moreover I doubt whether it is intrinsically so interesting as "Adam." Neither the story nor the characters take so profound a hold of the sympathies. Mais nous verrons. It is early days yet.

Blackwood remained satisfied with the sales, which perhaps exceeded his expectations; he was far more grateful for the reviews, which—as he wrote the Leweses—"have been very favourable and there has been nothing *offensive* that I have seen." The Blackwoods were fearing vulgar attacks such as had appeared in the *Athenaeum* gossip column almost a year earlier. They may have anticipated the kind of literary criticism practiced by their father, who had countenanced a series of virulent articles on John Keats and other members of the Cockney School of Poetry. Fortunately, four decades had made a difference; literary criticism was now relatively humane, primarily concerned with literature rather than politics and personalities. Even so, Margaret Oliphant implies that among those readers who knew something of George Eliot's personal life there was a considerable amount of talk which was not reflected in the reviews. She states that when the author's identity was revealed, "the foolish part of the public read an equivocal meaning into various portions of a book so spotless, and inspired with a spirit so noble and pure. . . ." In the somewhat contradictory way in which she usually discusses George Eliot, Mrs. Oliphant concludes that *The Mill on the Floss* achieved its contemporary fame as much from its intriguing resemblance to its author's real life as from "its own admirable qualities." If such talk reached George Eliot, she was unperturbed by it—at least according to the extant records; it is quite possible that there were many conversations about the matter with close friends. She surely must have anticipated some such reaction to the *Mill*, for she had written the third volume in full awareness that her incognito was no longer a source of mystery. In making Maggie and Stephen's relationship even remotely similar to that between herself and Lewes she had invited reactions with the same audacious courage with which in 1854 she had signed her real name to her translation of Feuerbach just before going off to the Continent with Lewes.

Yet she was deeply concerned over what readers would think about Tom and Maggie. Most readers assumed that the brother-sister relationship was present as an excuse for the more exciting Maggie-Stephen relationship. Only her Coventry friends, since she was no longer in touch with Maria Lewis, could have guessed that Isaac was the real emotional basis of the book. Apparently she heard little, if any, comment from these intimate friends; they were perhaps embarrassedly silent. But when back in England, she wrote Charles Bray a note which suggests that she was responding to some remark of his:

> I have read no reviews of the Mill on the Floss, except that in the "Times," which Blackwood sent me to Florence. I abstain, not from superciliousness, but on a calm consideration of the probable proportion of benefit on the one hand and waste of thought on the other. It was certain that in the notices of my first book after the removal of my incognito there would be much *ex post facto* wisdom, which could hardly profit me, since *I* certainly knew who I was beforehand, and knew also that no one else knew, who had not been told.

The 19 May review in the *Times* which she had steeled herself to read was by E. S. Dallas. Both John and William Blackwood had been delighted that this crucial review had fallen into the hands of so respected a friend of theirs. When they read it, however, they realized that although a very good kind of notice for the *Mill* to receive, it was one which George Eliot would not particularly appreciate; so each hastened to tell her that he did not wholly agree with all the views expressed by Dallas. The review did shock her, giving her a totally objective view of what she had done without quite knowing that she had done it:

> The reader will at once remember that he could not help liking all the characters in [*Adam Bede*]. . . . The general influence of the book was to reconcile us to human nature. . . . The author, apparently afraid of repeating herself, and determined to avoid the imputation of representing the world as too good and sugary, now introduces us to a very different set of personages. A majority of the characters brought together in these three volumes are unpleasant companions—prosaic, selfish, nasty.

After paying homage to the author's "marvellous powers of delineation," Dallas continues:

> Everybody in this tale is repelling everybody, and life is in the strictest sense a battle. Even the good angel of the story, that little Maggie . . . is first of all introduced to us while she is indulging an unnatural ferocity towards her doll. . . . Her brother Tom . . . is chiefly remarkable for self-assertion and hard-headed resistance of fate—his strong wrestling with adversity, and his anxiety to punish the slightest offence.

Dallas is interested above all in the Dodsons, the maternal aunts and uncles who at times are caricatured; neglecting Tom and Maggie, he returns to them time and again as the mainspring of the narrative. They are the ones from whom emanates the atmosphere conducive to the trouble between Tom and Maggie; they are the ones who live "the sort of life which thousands upon thousands of our countrymen lead —a life that outwardly is most respectable, but inherently is most degraded—so degraded, indeed, that the very virtues which adorn it are scarcely to be distinguished from vices. . . ."

Ignoring the personal element in the novel, Dallas read the *Mill* as a social study in depth, and he valued it as such. George Eliot, however, was concerned only with the implication that she had deliberately portrayed the Dodsons and Tom in an unfavorable light. "Tom is painted with as much love and pity as Maggie," she protested to William Blackwood after reading Dallas's review, "and I am so far from hating the Dodsons myself, that I am rather aghast to find them ticketed with such very ugly adjectives." Yet a year later she was equally disturbed by an opposite view of Tom which she read in *Macmillan's Magazine* of April 1861:

> . . . notwithstanding the author's evident yearning over *Maggie*, and disdain for *Tom*, we cannot but feel that if people are to be judged by the only fair human judgment, of how far they act up to what they believe in, *Tom*, so far as his light goes, is a finer character than his sister. He alone has the self-denial to do what he does not like, for the sake of doing right; he alone has the self-command to smother his hopeless love, and live on, a brave, hard-working life; he, except in his injustice to poor *Maggie*, has at least the merit of having made no one else miserable.

She was torn between appreciating the reviewer's good opinion of Tom and disliking him for it. It was not only that he was against Maggie; if her disdain for Tom was as noticeable as he claimed, then she had failed in her role as objective novelist. Were it not for the encouraging letters that kept coming in about the *Mill*, reassuring her "that where one has a large public, one's words must hit their mark," so she wrote John Blackwood,

> special cases of misinterpretation might paralyze me. For example, when you read McMillan [*sic*], pray notice how my critic attributes to me a disdain for Tom: as if it were not *my* respect for Tom which infused itself into my reader—as if he would have respected Tom, if I had not painted him with respect; the exhibition of the' *right* on both sides being the very soul of my intention in the story. However, I ought to be satisfied if I have roused the feeling that does justice to both sides.

Such reactions to the *Mill*, as well as her own doubts as to what she had achieved in the novel, prevented her from feeling the exhilaration she had experienced upon completing *Adam Bede*. At the end of the year she dutifully recorded in her Journal that 1860 had "been marked by many blessings," but her listing of them is joyless. Charles Lewes was with them, thus disrupting (although she does not say so) the "dual solitude" she treasured with Lewes; and they had moved to 16 Blandford Square in London, where, as usual, her health suffered. Her only reference to the *Mill* is her noting the receipt of £1,000 for its second instalment.

In fact, the *Mill* had proved to be a monetary, if not a popular triumph. As early as 25 May 1860, John Blackwood had written her at Florence in the same letter which enclosed Dallas's review that 6,000 copies had been sold and 550 were being reprinted. He could not resist adding: "This is highly satisfactory and I rejoice to think that there is every prospect of your making as much by our arrangement as the most speculative publisher was likely to have offered you. That it was the best plan for you in the long run I had no doubt, but I thought it very probable there might be an apparent loss in the in-dividual book." This was his first admission that her early arguments for book publication, as against serialization, had been valid. Had the *Mill* sold the 16,000 copies that *Adam Bede* did during its first year, she would have made her fortune then and there. Even as it happened, her own record of her literary earnings shows that she received well over twice as much for the second novel as had come to her from *Adam Bede*.

Of greater importance than the money earned was the fact that the steady sale of the *Mill*, as well as the absence of personally offensive reviews, demonstrated that George Eliot had been tested and accepted by the novel-reading public. But it was a critical time, and in looking back upon it, Margaret Oliphant was too sanguine in thinking that "the faint cloud upon the sky" which originated when George Eliot's identity became known "was of very short duration, and the reputation of the great novelist soon surmounted the temporary shock." Once dispersed, admittedly, the cloud was never to reappear. Yet if she had lived longer, her marriage to John Cross might well have posed a new threat. For in accepting her, the public also tacitly accepted her living with Lewes, even while the world's wife continued to close the door to her. Like her pseudonym, her fame became an entity in itself and was eventually given a crown of respectability; those who stayed critical of her as a woman did so in silence. In the words of Richard Church: "Her seat was set too high for the tide of scandal to lap at it, though amongst some of her family connections she was looked at askance, as the present writer knows, being a distant kinsman, with lifelong memories of a certain hushed legend."

That hushed legend did as much harm to George Eliot's posthumous literary reputation as the legend created by Cross's *Life*, although each projected a different kind of distorted image. For several decades,

parental censorship of her novels operated strictly. Harriet Shaw
Weaver was only one of many young women who felt its pressure.
Discovered reading *Adam Bede*, Harriet was sent to her room to await
the coming of the vicar, who had been summoned by her mother—too
shaken to undertake the task herself—to explain why it was dangerously wrong to read a novel which contained the birth of an illegitimate child and had been written by a woman who had lived for over
twenty years with a man to whom she was not lawfully married. The
episode deeply impressed Harriet Weaver. It was a strong factor giving
rise to her resolve to fight against any tyranny against freedom of
individual thought, which in turn led to her courageous championship
of James Joyce. George Eliot would have been amused over such
ironic diffusion of her influence.

O<small>NCE AGAIN BETWEEN NOVELS</small>, G<small>EORGE</small> E<small>LIOT INDULGED HER</small>-
self by writing her second and final short story, "Brother Jacob," in
August 1860. This served as a prelude to a strange sequence of fiction
which included *Silas Marner* and ended with *Romola*, although the
latter had been conceived first. Money was to be an important motif
in both the short story and *Silas*, and money would lure her away
from Blackwood for the publication of *Romola*.

In Florence where the Leweses were continuing their Italian sojourn, he was inspired that May with the idea that the life and times
of Savonarola afforded "fine material for an historical romance. Polly
at once caught at the idea with enthusiasm." Lewes had probably been
casting about for a relatively impersonal subject which would not
evoke the painful associations he had seen her suffer through while
writing the *Mill*. But her creation of *Romola* was to bring its own
kind of pain. From the first she was fearful of the project, partly because of its magnitude, and also because she realized that such a novel
would be utterly different in scene and time from what her public
now expected of her. She began to guard the idea as if it were a secret
to be divulged only to the Blackwoods, as she wrote the major from
Florence. But in June she wrote John Blackwood from Switzerland,
where they had gone to collect Charles Lewes and visit the D'Albert-
Durades before proceeding home: "I don't think I can venture to tell
you what my great project is by letter, for I am anxious to keep it a
secret. It will require a great deal of study and labour, and I am
athirst to begin."

By the time the Leweses returned to Wandsworth in early July,
Blackwood had concluded his London season and was back in Edin-

burgh, so that there was no opportunity for confidential talk. If he was annoyed at being plunged into another "grand secret" so soon after that. of her identity, he gave no sign, but wrote her good-naturedly: "Recollect that I am a first-rate hand at keeping a secret." It was not until late August that she told him by letter of her plan to write a historical romance based on the life of Savonarola, and whatever he may have felt about this idea alone must have been lost in astonishment over her other revelations:

> But I want first to write another English story, and the plan I should like to carry out is this: to publish my next English novel when my Italian one is advanced enough for us to begin its publication a few months afterwards in Maga. It would appear without a name in the Magazine, and be subsequently reprinted with the name of George Eliot. I need not tell you the wherefore of this plan—you know well enough the received phrases with which a writer is greeted when he does something else than what was expected of him.

Not only was she assuming that he would be happy to publish a new English novel about which he knew nothing. She was also proposing for the Italian novel the selfsame mode of anonymous serialization in Maga which, almost at the expense of an irreparable rift between them, she had rejected for the Mill. He may have sensed that an oddly repetitive chain of events was happening, but in reverse of its original occurrence. It was he who had urged her to keep her secret of identity, and it was he who had urged that she publish the Mill anonymously in Maga. Perhaps he was merely bewildered, being this time preoccupied with the major's serious illness. He replied as best he could: "Your letter communicating the Great Secret is truly refreshing and opens up a famous prospect. . . . I expect that you will return Historical Romance to its ancient popularity." He said also that the major rejoiced with him "in the idea of such a series for the Magazine and also in the prospect of publishing another Story of English Life by you."

By the time of her letter to Blackwood announcing her plans for the two new novels, she either had written or was writing "Brother Jacob." Yet she did not then or ever mention it to him as a possibility for Maga. Although he may have recognized it as hers when it appeared anonymously in the Cornhill for July 1864, he had no direct contact with the story until late 1866, when she thought it and "The Lifted Veil" might be included in the proposed new edition of her novels. He strongly advised against including either story, as each had "a painful want of light," and she acquiesced. In the fable-like "Brother Jacob," the unprincipled David Faux begins his career by tricking his idiot brother Jacob (who always carries a pitchfork, which frightens

David). Jacob is persuaded into exchanging guineas for golden-col-
ored lozenges, which he craves. Eventually Faux changes his name to
Freely and becomes a confectioner, although had he "fallen on the
present times, and enjoyed the advantages of a Mechanics' Institute,
he would certainly have taken to literature and have written reviews;
but his education had not been liberal" (Chapter ,1). As it happened,
Faux and the confectionery business were beautifully matched, so that
soon the making of "the more fanciful viands was fast passing out of
the hands of maids and matrons in private families, and was becoming
the work of a special commercial organ" (Chapter 2). Faux's prosperity
might have endured forever had not fate overtaken him in the form
of Jacob, who, discovering his whereabouts, comes to him in frantic
search for more lozenges. Noting the idiot brother's insatiable desire
for sweets, the townspeople at first assume that he too is a confectioner;
but when they are made aware of the real relationship between David
and Jacob, they drive both out of town with their contempt and
ridicule.

Once the fable is detected, its purport is clear: those publishers
and reviewers who encouraged the production and consumption of
saccharine literature which catered only to the taste of the public
would be attacked by Jacob, who has no real need for the pitchfork
because an idiot is, according to long-lasting superstition, an "innocent." Such people possess the instinct to divine good from evil. George
Eliot had obviously been brooding over the expressed opinion, as in
Dallas's review, that the *Mill* presented a more pessimistic vision of
life than *Adam Bede*. Of more immediate concern to her was Blackwood's negative reaction to whatever she wrote that swerved from the
popular conception of happiness and society's favorable image of itself
as the protector of civilization. By now, Blackwood's reaction was
predictable, so that while she was writing the *Mill*, it hovered over her
as an inhibiting force. After reading "The Lifted Veil," he had written
her that he wished it could have had a happier theme, but then
acknowledged that "others are not so fond of sweets as I am." This
remark may have stayed in her mind and, nourished by the general
reaction to the *Mill*, germinated into "Brother Jacob." Blackwood's
dismissal of it and "The Lifted Veil" as being essentially similar in
their lack of light indicates that he remained unaware of the real
meaning of this story. True, "Brother Jacob" has as much bitterness
as the earlier story, but it is here converted to sardonic comedy. The
allegorical level is more consistently sustained so that, without baffling
digressions, the realistic details support the symbolic narrative. In
this respect—as well as in the appearance of guineas for a purpose
beyond their monetary value—"Brother Jacob" points directly to
Silas Marner.

It would seem that the specific idea for *Silas* did not come to George Eliot until a month after she had told Blackwood that she wished to write and publish an English novel before bringing out the Italian one. Under 28 November 1860, she entered in her Journal: "I am engaged now in writing a story, the idea of which came to me after our arrival in this house, and which has thrust itself between me and the other book I was meditating. It is 'Silas Marner, the Weaver of Raveloe.' " The "other book" may have been another English novel she was contemplating in order to fulfill her plan of publication but which had not taken a firm hold upon her; or it may have been what was to become *Romola*. We know that the Leweses had rented a house, 10 Harewood Square, furnished for six months, as all their efforts to find a suitable house to lease for a longer time had failed. The fact that she started *Silas* on 30 September, only five days after moving into the house, suggests that again living in London quickly forced into her mind the story of a man who had been alienated from his native society by an unjust accusation of theft, as well as by the perfidy of trusted friends. Everything she has to say about the conception of this story stresses the overwhelming power with which it invaded her mind and also the meager external detail upon which it was based. To Blackwood she wrote on 12 January 1861:

> I am writing a story which came *across* my other plans by a sudden inspiration. I don't know at present whether it will resolve itself into a book short enough for me to complete before Easter, or whether it will expand beyond that possibility. It seems to me that nobody will take any interest in it but myself, for it is extremely unlike the popular stories going; but Mr. Lewes declares that I am wrong, and says it is as good as anything I have done. It is a story of old-fashioned village life, which has unfolded itself from the merest millet-seed of thought.

Over a month later she had occasion to write again about the novel to Blackwood, who had by then read over half of it in manuscript form. Characteristically, he was admiring but sorry that the story so far lacked "brighter lights and some characters of whom one can think with pleasure as fellow creatures." He was also at this time skeptical of her prediction that the completed novel would take up only one volume; he had become familiar with her need to develop her characters and setting in a leisurely way that demanded space.

She wrote back on 24 February that she was quite certain about the length and that she was not surprised at his finding the story "rather sombre; indeed, I should not have believed that any one would have been interested in it but myself (since William Wordsworth is dead) if Mr. Lewes had not been strongly arrested by it." Actually, Lewes seems to have been less excited over *Silas* than any of her other novels, although he no doubt hoped that writing it would help restore her equilibrium after the devastating *Mill*. "I am in love with it," he wrote Blackwood when he sent more manuscript; but that is all he said. It is unlikely that Lewes went beyond the not very appealing Silas or the provincial life of Raveloe to the more abstract level of meaning intended by George Eliot. She admitted in her February letter to Blackwood that she had decided to subordinate this level to the realism:

> I have felt all through as if the story would have lent itself best to metrical rather than prose fiction, especially in all that relates to the psychology of Silas; except that, under that treatment, there could not be an equal play of humour. It came to me first of all, quite suddenly, as a sort of legendary tale, suggested by my recollection of having once, in early childhood, seen a linen-weaver with a bag on his back; but, as my mind dwelt on the subject, I became inclined to a more realistic treatment.

Two weeks later she sent more manuscript and a motto from Wordsworth's *Michael* (lines 146–8):

> A child, more than all other gifts
> That earth can offer to declining man,
> Brings hope with it, and forward-looking thoughts.

She was worried that this might indicate "the story too distinctly." When he had read the new manuscript, Blackwood was still in anxious search for happiness and upstanding character. He nonetheless wrote back reassuringly: "The motto giving to some extent the keynote to the story does not I think signify in this case, as whenever the child appears her mission is felt." Thus Blackwood was the first reader of *Silas* to recognize that Eppie—the child—was a force in the novel rather than a character.

When George Eliot had completed the novel and it was ready to appear in print, she answered Charles Bray's inquiry about its nature by commenting once again on its origin: "It was quite a sudden inspiration that came across me in the midst of altogether different meditations." She was still thinking of this even after publication. In a conversation with Blackwood (who reported the talk to his wife), she gave a slightly changed version of the image which had provoked the inspiration: " 'Silas Marner' sprang from her childish recollection of a man with a stoop and expression of face that led her to think that he was an alien from his fellows." In this later vision, the weaver's bag on his back—his burden—has been replaced by features suggesting alienation. As this is an improbable impression to have occurred to a child, it would seem that some force from her present life coincided with that vision from the past (the latter stayed intact to open the book). Thus it was the coming together of these two visions, each charged with its own meaning, which took the form of inspiration and demanded release, not at first as a realistic novel but as a poem and a legend. She checked her impulse toward poetic form, although in her own mind her material remained poetry. Yet the legend persisted in finding expression, perhaps to an extent of which she herself was unaware, for it came forth clothed in the illusion of realism which by now was second nature for her to create.

Silas Marner is her personal myth—a projection of an emotional pattern into a concise image that has the power to unfold into narrative. By mythic (although not realistic) identification, George Eliot, the weaver of tales, is Silas, the linen-weaver, who is unjustly ostracized by his native Lantern Yard. He makes his way to the town of Raveloe, which "lay in the rich central plain of what we are pleased to call Merry England . . . nestled in a snug well-wooded hollow, quite an hour's journey on horseback from any turnpike, where it was never reached by the vibrations of the coach-horn or of public opinion" (Part I, chapter 1). Here he is tolerated, if not warmly welcomed, because of his craft ("the old linen-weaver in the neighbouring parish of Tarley being dead"), and also because of the superstitious fear aroused by his epilepsy, which, like idiocy, was thought to bring its possessor into touch with a source of truth closed to the normal individual. Had Silas not been an honest man, he might have played upon the awe of those who beheld his trances by "the subsequent creation of a vision in the form of resurgent memory; a less sane man might have believed in such a creation; but Silas was both sane and honest . . ." (Part I, chapter 1). In fact, it was a perfidious friend's taking advantage of this affliction that drove Silas out of Lantern Yard. But in Raveloe he was not persecuted because it was seen that he kept to himself and was harmlessly industrious: "he sought no man or woman, save for the purposes of his calling, or in order to supply himself with necessaries . . ." (Part I, chapter 1).

Having been falsely accused of theft at Lantern Yard, Silas becomes a miser at Raveloe, hoarding the golden guineas he rightfully earns from his painstaking labor. These are stolen from him, but eventually there appears a seemingly miraculous substitute—a girl-child whose hair is so much the color of the guineas that Silas at first thinks his gold has been restored to him. For a while, he is understandably dismayed by the child's presence. Then gradually she revives his stunted affections and trust, and it is through her that he regains total entry into society. This is the element of the myth contributed by the present. The transformation of Silas's guineas into the child Eppie justifies George Eliot's seeking and accepting money for her writings because they have a humane value which is beyond measurement. Myths are timeless, so that this one is both a summation of the past and an adumbration of the future.

Myths are also fluid and metamorphic. In this one George Eliot is not only Silas; she is Eppie, who proves to be worth more than money and thus is some vindication of "such an unpromising woman-child" —as George Eliot described herself to Cara Bray in October 1859, after the unexpected fame of *Adam Bede* had reached her but left her untouched because the triumph could not be enjoyed with her own family. Throughout her entire life at home, it seemed to her that her monetary value had been calculated with a shrewd eye. Isaac had made it clear that in his opinion it was her intelligence which had led her into unorthodox ways of thinking and cut off her prospects of finding a husband. Something of this attitude is reflected in the *Mill* when Mr. Tulliver comments that Maggie took after his side of the family and was therefore

> twice as 'cute as Tom. Too 'cute for a woman, I'm afraid. . . . It's no mischief much while she's a little un, but an over-'cute woman's no better nor a long-tailed sheep,—she'll fetch none the bigger price for that. [Book I, chapter 1]

Coming perilously near the surface of the myth Eppie is also, even if only briefly, a sister. When Silas is at last convinced that what he has found on his hearth is not his guineas but a golden-haired child, a question darts across his mind: "Could this be his little sister come back to him in a dream—his little sister whom he had carried about in his arms for a year before she died, when he was a small boy without shoes or stockings?" The mere possibility that this might be so brought him "a vision of the old home and the old streets leading to Lantern Yard,—and within that vision another, of the thoughts which had been present with him in those far-off scenes." Unlike Isaac, and despite his isolation, Silas was still susceptible to the power of memory, which in him (as always in George Eliot) stirred feelings of love with a religious intensity. Led back to the past by thoughts of his sister, he felt the "old quiverings of tenderness,—old impressions of awe at the presentiment of some Power presiding over his life . . ." (Part I, chapter 12). Although soon forced to realize that the child is unknown to him, he reunites himself with his past by naming her Eppie, a shortened form of Hepzibah—the name of both his sister and his mother. Through Eppie he is reunited with his fellow men.

Yet another aspect of the myth has thus appeared, one which is unrelated in content but admirably suited for subtle incorporation into the Silas-Eppie relationship, although Silas ceases to fulfill a significant role. As far as he knows, Eppie has appeared upon his hearth out of nowhere. Actually, having been attracted by the firelight from his cottage, the child had toddled right past him as he stood in a trance by his open door. Regaining his senses, he discovers her and gradually distinguishes her from both his money and his sister, finally accepting her as an unexplained message from his past life: "for his imagination had not yet extricated itself from the sense of mystery in the child's sudden presence, and had formed no conjectures of ordinary natural means by which the event could have been brought about" (Part I, chapter 12). This particular Eppie seems the product of a childhood fantasy which George Eliot had harbored for many years but which was only now coming to light as she worked through the strata of her mind in her writing. It is the not uncommon fantasy indulged in by highly inquisitive and imaginative children who sense their own birth as having been both miraculous and mysterious, so that they can dream freely about a destiny uncircumscribed by the known facts of an ordinary family background. In the narration of the novel, Eppie counters this part of the myth by spurning her revealed identity as the daughter of a wealthy man; but the abortive handling of this mythical element was necessitated by the fact that in a more important portion of the total myth, Eppie is already a symbol that has a value far greater than money. The myth concerning origin was to persist in George Eliot's novels: there is something of it in the story of Esther Lyon in *Felix Holt*; it operates on a grand scale in *The Spanish Gypsy*; and it is a constructive factor in leading Daniel Deronda to his special destiny, which is the founding of a new nation.

But these elements appear to be separate myths in *Silas* only when analyzed. Undergirding the narrative, they function as a single and continuous entity from which radiates an energy not seriously disturbed by the rational explanations given for the key symbols—Silas, Money, Eppie. It is this remarkably harmonious cooperation between myth and realism which gives rise to the balance and unity that pervade the novel and which has led to its being frequently dramatized and pictorially represented. The same reasons, as well as its convenient length, made it seem the ideal "literary" novel to be thrust upon young students. As a sad, but not surprising, result *Silas Marner* now rivals *The Spanish Gypsy* as George Eliot's least-read novel.

O<small>N</small> 25 M<small>ARCH</small> 1861, G<small>EORGE</small> E<small>LIOT</small> <small>RECEIVED THE FIRST</small> printed copy of *Silas*, which was due to come before the public on 2 April. Writing to thank Langford for having sent it, she reiterated her old dilemma, which was now activated by her fear that the volume was too expensively priced: "I am rather uncomfortably constituted; for while I am unable to write a sentence for the sake of pleasing other people, I should be unable to write at all without strong proofs that I had touched them. I confess I shudder a little at the high price of the book. . . ." Her fear was unjustified; within a month after publication, Blackwood had cause to double the original edition of 4,000 copies and to be confident that all of them soon would be sold. The Leweses heard this good news in Florence, where they had gone again so that she could absorb more material and atmosphere for the projected *Romola*.

Back in their London home (16 Blandford Square) by 14 June, George Eliot no longer had any real reason to delay beginning the Italian novel. Yet she procrastinated, afraid that the prodigious information she had amassed would stand between her and the characters and scenes she wished to bring to life. Lewes encouragingly reminded her that most of the English scenes and characters she had already handled so well and fearlessly had been "quite as *historical* to her direct personal experience, as the 15th century of Florence," and that she knew "infinitely more about Savonarola than she knew of Silas, besides having deep personal sympathies with the old reforming priest which she had not with the miser." (He was right in principle although wrong in assuming that she had felt no deep personal tie with Silas.)

John Blackwood came to lunch with the Leweses two days after their return from the Continent. All three were sadly aware of the absence of Major Blackwood, who had died 8 April. Even so the visit was a good one and during it George Eliot confided that although she could now hear her still-unborn characters talking, there was "a weight upon her mind as if Savonarola and friends ought to be speaking Italian instead of English." Blackwood interestedly reported this to his wife. As far as he knew, he was again on excellent terms with both Lewes and George Eliot. Lewes himself strengthened this impression by sending him bits of news about George Eliot's progress which, however, continued to be in study of background rather than in writing. "Mrs. Lewes is buried in old quartos and vellum bound literature," he wrote on 28 June, "which I would rather *not* read; but she extracts nutriment, I have no doubt." And on 9 October: "Mrs. Lewes is very well and buried in musty old antiquities, which she will have to vivify. I am a sort of Italian Jackal, hunting up rare books, and vellum bound unreadabilities in all the second hand book stalls of London."

Yet two days earlier—7 October—George Eliot had entered in her Journal the fact that she had started to write the first chapter of her new novel. This beginning was cut short three days later when a letter arrived from Blackwood offering her £3,000 for the remaining copyright of the *Scenes*, *Adam Bede*, the *Mill*, and *Silas*. Apparently this matter had been pending for some time as Blackwood apologized for having taken so long to write, fearing she would think that all the while he had been puzzling over the proper amount to offer. He was willing to show the calculations to her and Lewes if they wished to see them, and he added in a way which suggested he already had misgivings over her acceptance: "If the sum I have mentioned does not come up to your expectations I shall be sorry, but I am sure you will give me credit for wishing to give as much as any prudent man would."

As she recorded in her Journal, George Eliot was so "excited and perturbed" by the question of selling her copyrights that after reading Blackwood's letter she could not work, but spent the remainder of the morning "at the piano." The grand piano had been purchased by the Leweses and delivered only a week or so earlier, one of the first signs that as a result of her substantially increased income they were feeling more relaxed about money than they had been able to do since living together. Cross happily allows the delivery of the piano to stand intact in a Journal entry, but omits the reason why she played it so assiduously the morning of 12 October, although he does admit her agreeable entry for the later part of that day: "In the evening we had our usual Saturday mixture of visitors, talk, and music. . . ." It seems possible that Cross deleted all allusions to Blackwood's offer because he recognized George Eliot's intense reaction to it as a warning signal that still graver trouble lay ahead in the form of financial arrangements over her works. Everyone involved in this unsuccessful bargaining between her and Blackwood seems to have conspired to becloud the conclusion of the matter, which, according to the extant records, came with George Eliot's Journal entry for 17 October: "In consequence of a letter from Bradbury and Evans, wrote to Blackwood declining to sell my copyrights for which he had offered £3000." Her letter to Blackwood has not been found, and the contents of the letter from Bradbury and Evans are not known. It seems clear that the basic myth of *Silas* was at work, however; money for her work signified an assessment of her personal worth, and it was no time for prudence on the part of the assessor.

Athough the good relationship between the Leweses and John Blackwood did not at this time suffer, *Romola* stood still. The start made on 7 October seems to have been put aside and forgotten. A month later, she noted in her Journal: "So utterly dejected that, in walking with G. in the Park, I almost resolved to give up my Italian novel." A few days later she found temporary relief in thinking about a new English novel, but the very next morning the Italian scenes returned to her

with "fresh attraction." She still evaded writing by clinging to her
Florentine studies, and on 14 November she noted: "Went to the
British Museum reading-room for the first time—looking over costumes." When another month had passed and she still had not begun
writing, even Lewes was concerned and urged Blackwood to visit them:

> Your presence will I hope act like a stimulus to her to make her
> begin. At present she remains immovable in the conviction that
> she *can't* write the romance because she has not knowledge enough.
> Now as a matter of fact I know that she has immensely more knowl-
> edge of the particular period than any other writer who has
> touched it; but her distressing diffidence paralyses her.
>
> This between ourselves. When you see her, mind your care is to
> discountenance the idea of a Romance being the product of an
> Encyclopaedia.

In the same letter, Lewes referred to Maga's one-year-old competitor:
"I am the more pleased that Maga should be in force because the Cornhill has become utterly unreadable. Thackeray is less *mangy* and
therefore more interesting than he was; but his contributions [con-
tributors?] ought to have their posteriors brought into relation with
Mrs. Beecher's toe." At the time Blackwood may have been gratified
by this jocular thrust at his rival; later, if he remembered it, he must
have done so with bitterness.

For the present, however, he was happy to comply with Lewes's wish
that he come to Blandford Square, and he did so on 22 December, the
next day describing his pleasant visit to his nephew William, the
major's eldest son, who was to be made a partner in the firm during
the coming year:

> [Lewes] and I were reproaching her for not fairly beginning to
> write and she defended herself by saying, "Well I have notes for a
> great many scenes." There is a talk of making a start on New Year's
> day. She seems to be studying her subject as subject never was
> studied before.
>
> We are going there this afternoon. . . .

So Blackwood returned to Blandford Square with his wife, this being
the first meeting between Julia and George Eliot. It was also a significant gesture on Blackwood's part, although George Eliot may have
preferred that he not have made it; she barely mentions the occasion
in her Journal. On New Year's Day 1862 she recorded that Blackwood
had sent on to her a letter from Montalembert (author of *The Monks
of the West*) filled with praises of *Silas Marner*, and a few hours later
the Dresden china pug in memory of the real one she had lost about
a year earlier. To this entry she added with emphasis: "*I began my*

Novel of Romola." Wishing to encourage her personally in this momentous undertaking, Blackwood appeared in person on 2 January and yet again on the twelfth.

The conversation on the twelfth was unsettling to George Eliot. She followed it up the same day with a letter to Blackwood which reverted to the injured tone of some of her correspondence with him when they were in the thick of the trouble over the *Mill*. They had discussed the series Blackwood was bringing out under the general title "The Works of George Eliot" at 6s. a volume. *Adam Bede* and *The Mill on the Floss* had appeared so far. The plan was next to publish the *Scenes* and *Silas* together in the same volume, although he had not yet specified a date for this third volume. What was even worse in George Eliot's mind, he had intimated that he thought this new edition of the *Mill* had been brought out too soon for the 1,455 copies to be absorbed (in fact, they lasted until 1866, when 500 more were printed). In her letter she advised him that if he intended to go ahead with the series, the third volume should not be deferred so long that it could not be advertised with the two preceding volumes, thus making the expected three-volume set. And she reminded him that Easter was a good time for publication. She supposed that such details of management "must affect the temporary destiny of books, or publishers would not continue to give so much attention to them." Her real concern was that he thought "too despondingly" of her books "to like incurring the risk of another 6s/ volume"; had she "had any idea that the 6s/ edition could have been considered premature, as you appeared to hint concerning the Mill, I should certainly have been in the highest degree averse to it." She assured him this letter was merely to stress that, "supposing the third volume is not to be given up in despair, it would be for the interest of my books that it should not be deferred." And she concluded: "I fear Mr. Langford has forgotten my existence, for I have not had a copy of the 6s/ 'Mill' sent me."

Her next extant letter to Blackwood is not dated until well over a month later, 22 February. Its purpose was to complain about Simpson's management of the advertising of her books: "I have no doubt Mr. Simpson regulates the advertisements according to the system he regards as best for our common interests; but it would be well that he should have under his consideration a few facts which have come under our experience, and which indicate that to the majority of readers the fact of my books having entered a new edition remains quite a secret." She added (not very convincingly): "I think you have seen enough of me to know that I do not willingly obtrude my opinion on business matters, and you will prefer that I should say at once what I cannot help dwelling on a little mentally rather than retain a sense of puzzled dissatisfaction about it." Simpson, no doubt keeping his thoughts to himself, prepared a meticulous list of the advertisements he had placed, and upon looking this over when it was sent to her, George Eliot found that she had missed a few important ones and could but apologize when she wrote again to Blackwood on 28 February: "Mr. Simpson's list is a sufficient vindication of his advertising energy, and I am sorry to have worried him on the subject." Yet she excused herself by insisting "that the erroneous inferences were but built on the remarks of personal friends, from whom I take care to hear nothing about my books."

Meanwhile, the writing of *Romola* had gone on, but slowly and painfully, and she herself was ill. Her Journal entry for 26 February is significant:

> I have been very ailing all this last week and have worked under impeding discouragement. I have a distrust in myself, in my work, in others' loving acceptance of it which robs my otherwise happy life of all joy. I ask myself, without being able to answer, whether I have ever before felt so chilled and oppressed.

There was a demanding force within her which she did not like and did not understand enough to control. When writing *Silas* she had, figuratively, taken this same force up in her hand and surveyed it objectively. By now that knowledge was lost to her because the force was again disseminated through her entire being. She knew well that she was not a person whose life values were based upon materialism, yet she also was reluctantly aware that she was determined to receive as much money as possible for her work—that is, as much as Christian ethics and her own artistic integrity would permit. There was no transforming Eppie at hand to help her, but there was George Smith—although later she may have thought back upon him as her Nemesis.

Smith reappeared in her and Lewes's life on 23 January, when he called at Blandford Square to consult with Lewes about his "Studies in Animal Life," which Smith had accepted for his *Cornhill Magazine* and then discontinued after six numbers. Now, because the *Cornhill* needed a decided boost, Smith was reconsidering Lewes's contributions in a more favorable light and asked him to begin a new series. Having been incensed by Smith's arbitrary abandonment of the "Animal Studies," Lewes declined. However, because of the terms of his original agreement, he could not refuse Smith the privilege of reprinting in a small volume the numbers which had appeared. Although Smith did not see George Eliot on this visit, he definitely had her on his mind and asked Lewes if she would be open to "a magnificent offer." When Lewes relayed this question to George Eliot, she wrote in her Journal: "This made me think about money—but it is better for me not to be rich." On 27 February, Smith returned with the whole of the proofs of "Animal Studies." Lewes recorded:

> In the course of our chat he made a proposal to purchase Polly's new work for £10,000. This of course includes the entire copyright. It is the most magnificent offer ever yet made for a novel; and Polly, as usual was disinclined to accept it, on the ground that her work would not be worth the sum! Moreover she felt it impossible to begin publication in April or May—the period when Smith wishes it to begin to appear in the "Cornhill Mag." Unless she sees her book nearly completed and such as she considers worthy of publication she objects to begin printing it. I went down to Smith [this suggests Smith still was not conferring with George Eliot in person] to tell him of her difficulties. He was much put out, April or May being the months when the Magazine will stand in need of some reinforcement as Thackeray's story [*The Adventures of Philip*] is quite insufficient to keep up the sale. Smith then proposed to print her story of Brother Jacob . . . if it can be split up into three numbers, and thus tide over the three months; and then to commence in August or September with the new work. She has consented to let him see the story to see if this arrangement will do. If not some other proposal will be made by him.

Three weeks earlier, Lewes had mentioned that "Brother Jacob" was lying at hand, and Smith had offered 250 guineas for it, sight unseen; but George Eliot had made no move to accept his offer. By 1 March, the project seemed off. Apparently having decided that "Brother Jacob" would not do as a filler, Smith announced that he could not wait until August or September to begin the new novel in the *Cornhill*. Yet he still very much wanted to publish it, and he and the Leweses discussed the plan of bringing it out as a sixpenny serial or of waiting until it was completed and publishing it at 6s. Without much enthusiasm for either of these possibilities, Lewes wrote in his Journal that Smith was to make calculations and come up with a new proposal: "Although I regret the loss of such an opportunity of £10,000, I am just as well pleased that Polly should not be hurried or flurried, by being bound to appear at an earlier date than she would like."

George Eliot too assumed that publication in the *Cornhill* was now out of the question. She recorded the supposed fact without an expression of regret, although she, as well as Lewes, had been impressed and flattered by the offer of £10,000 for a work which held little promise of popular appeal and was still largely in embryonic form, only the Proem and two chapters having been written (at this time, Smith had neither seen nor heard even these). She could not have missed the implication that Smith was bidding for the use of her name, which not so long ago Blackwood had thought an embarrassment rather than an advantage. In a different mood she might have resented this. Coming when it did, the proposal overwhelmed her desire to publish the Italian novel anonymously as she had tentatively planned with Blackwood. Neither she nor Lewes was to have occasion to be displeased with George Smith's handling of his financial agreements with them. However, both might have had a different perspective on his "magnificent offer" had they known that he had spent exactly half that sum—£5,000—on preliminary advertisement for the first issue of the *Cornhill*. George Smith offered fancy prices while his eye was shrewdly trained on the main chance.

Smith kept in touch. On 8 April he called with two missions: to propose publishing *Romola* in weekly numbers; and to discuss with Lewes the editorship of the *Cornhill*, from which Thackeray had resigned in early March. Lewes declined even to consider the editorship because it would interfere with his own pursuits, but he did agree to be a consulting editor if the right terms could be reached. Exactly a month later, what Lewes thought "very handsome" terms were agreed upon, so that his official connection with the *Cornhill* was begun. On 17 May, Lewes recorded that one evening during the past week George Eliot had

> read several chapters of *Romola* to George Smith, in order that before finally making any proposals he should know the kind of work it was to be. He dissuaded us from the notion of a serial, believing that it would not *tell* in small portions. He wishes to publish it in the "Cornhill Magazine," but in considerable instalments—of 45 or 40 pages each number, with two illustrations. He is to send a proposal on that basis.

The idea of long instalments had been arrived at with great difficulty and caused another promised £10,000 to dwindle. According to George Smith's own account, he had offered that sum for sixteen parts of about twenty-four pages each. George Eliot found that she could not divide the novel in this way, although she understood that the fewer and longer parts she desired would bring less money, as Smith's calculations had been made "with regard to the Magazine being able to afford a payment of so much a number." Smith remembered that he and even Lewes did their best to persuade her to reconsider her decision: "We pointed out to her that the publication in the Magazine was ephemeral, and that the work would be published in a separate form afterwards and be judged as a whole. However, nothing could move her. . . ." Smith had no recourse but to make new calculations, as a result of which he offered £7,000, which she accepted. By an interesting coincidence, the "lost" £3,000 was the exact amount she had refused from Blackwood for her copyrights.

The agreement with Smith was sealed on 19 May; on that day she wrote Blackwood:

> I fear this letter will seem rather abrupt to you, but the abruptness is unavoidable.
>
> Some time ago I received an offer for my next novel which I suppose was handsomer than almost any terms ever offered to a writer of Fiction. As long as I hesitated on the subject I contemplated writing to you to ascertain your views as to the arrangement you would be inclined to make for the publication of the same work; since I was not willing to exchange my relations with you for any new ones without overpowering reasons. Ultimately I declined the offer (on various grounds) and there was therefore no need to write.
>
> But another offer, removing former objections, has been made, and after further reflection, I felt that, as I was not at liberty to mention the terms to you, and as they were hopelessly beyond your usual estimate of the value of my books to you, there would be an indelicacy in my making an appeal to you before decision. I have consequently accepted the offer, retaining however a power over my copyright at the end of six years so that my new work may then be included in any general edition.
>
> I know quite well from the feeling you have invariably shown, that if the matter were of more importance to you than it is likely to be, you would enter fully into the views of the case as it concerned my interests as well as your own.

Blackwood replied on 20 May, the day he received her letter:

> I am of course sorry that your new Novel is not to come out under the old colours but I am glad to hear that you have made so satisfactory an arrangement.
>
> Hearing of the wild sums that were being offered to writers of much inferior mark to you, I thought it highly probable that offers would be made to you, and I can readily imagine that you are to receive such a price as I could not make remunerative by any machinery that I could resort to.
>
> Rest assured that I feel fully satisfied of the extreme reluctance with which you would decide upon leaving your old friend for any other publisher, however great the pecuniary consideration might be, and it would destroy my pleasure in business if I knew any friend was publishing with me when he thought he could do better for himself by going elsewhere. We have had several most successful enterprises together and much pleasant correspondence and I hope we shall have much more.

On 23 May she noted in her Journal that she had made the important decision to publish *Romola* in the *Cornhill* "for £7000, paid in twelve monthly payments. There has been the regret of leaving Blackwood, who has written me a letter in the most perfect spirit of gentlemanliness and good-feeling."

Blackwood would have been pleased to know that his letter was convincing, but in reality he had neither gentlemanly nor good feelings. He was shocked, not so much over her having left him for a higher price as that she should have kept him totally in the dark about the possibility, especially when it involved an acknowledged rival of his. His staff seemed to know of the defection as soon as he. On 23 May, Langford wrote him:

> I think you should know without delay that Smith and Elder are announcing the new tale by Miss Evans for their July number—they are sending a bill [i.e., advertisement] for Maga to which in the first flirt of temper I thought you should refuse insertion, but it will certainly be more dignified to insert it. I shall have an opportunity of talking over with you this disgusting transaction, which certainly does not surprise me on her part, but does rather on the part of Mr. Smith.

Blackwood responded with as much restraint as he could muster:

> The conduct of our friends in Blandford Square is certainly not pleasing nor in the long run will they find it wise however great the bribe may have been. It is too bad after all the kindness she has experienced but I am sure she would do it against her inclination. The going over to the enemy without giving me any warning and with a story on which from what they both said I was fully intitled to calculate upon, sticks in my throat but I shall not quarrel—quarrels especially literary ones are vulgar.
>
> In reality I do not care about the defection and it has not disturbed me a bit. From the voracity of Lewes I saw that there would be great difficulty in making the arrangement with them and marchanding or bidding against any one else is a thing I could not stand, so "let them go." Besides if the story is the one I suppose, I have no doubt it will be a fine thing but it was doubtful in my mind how far it would bear being given in fragments in the Magazine and certainly it would not suit the readers of the Cornhill. I intended to have decided on the form of publication when I had read the M.S.

As when trouble had arisen over the *Mill*, Blackwood wished to be left alone with his thoughts about George Eliot and was doing his best to persuade himself that Lewes, rather than she, was the cause of this new breach between them. Had the major been available, John Blackwood might have expressed himself more freely. As he could address himself only to the young William Blackwood, he did so with some pretense of indifference when he sent on the advertisement which Langford had forwarded:

> Langford attempted to sour my stomach this morning by the inclosed, but it had no effect. Of course I would never dream of checking the bill. I am sorry for and disappointed in her but with their extortionate views we could not have made an arrangement so all is for the best. She does not know how strongly her desertion and going over to the enemy will tell upon the public estimate of her character and most justly. Literary quarrels are vulgar and I shall not quarrel but I shall make myself much more effectively understood and felt by not doing so.

Blackwood was wrong in thinking the public estimate of her character would be affected by her desertion of him. She had won her battle for public acceptance with the publication of the *Mill*, and no change in publishers was going to register upon the majority of those readers.

While Blackwood was bolstering his view that he was well rid of her, George Eliot was apparently having second thoughts about having left him. Upon invitation, he visited Blandford Square on 17 June, during which time Lewes became ill and had to take to his room, so that Blackwood and George Eliot had a few minutes alone together. Their talk during this brief time (as reported by John Blackwood to his nephew William) was succinctly pertinent enough to suggest that Lewes had deliberately absented himself:

> She said that "under all the circumstances she had felt that she must accept the enormous offer that had been made—that she could never feel to another publisher as she felt towards me—that pleasure to her was gone in the matter and she did not feel sure now whether she had acted right"—whether she meant this last as towards me or as wisely regarding herself I could not tell. She also said that she "hoped another time would arise," apparently meaning that she would then show how strong her feeling was. I did not wish any *confidences* nor in her peculiar circumstances to hit her, so merely looked her full in the face and shaking hands said, "I'm fully satisfied that it must have been a very sharp pang to you" and came away.

Without doubt George Eliot had prepared the way for a return to Blackwood. He could not resist her tacit appeal, nor did he wish to. The only retributive justice he allowed himself was to decline to issue *Romola* in a subsequent inexpensive edition of her works, although the novel was incorporated into all later editions. Other members of the firm did not quickly forget what understandably they thought of as her desertion. As late as July 1877 Langford wrote William Blackwood: "George Eliot's books sell more like Holloway's Pies than like books, and it pays to keep them before the public by advertising. I often think that not one out of a thousand would have kept up this connection as your Uncle did when there was such ground for discontent at her being taken away from us."

WHILE AT WORK ON PART IX OF *Romola*, GEORGE ELIOT decided that she could not complete the novel in only three more instalments. She lengthened it to fourteen, and since she had to delete planned material to stay within this new plan, she might easily have produced the sixteen parts which had been the basis of Smith's offer of £10,000. As it happened, she did the two extra numbers "for nothing." By this time, George Eliot was aware that (as Blackwood could have told her) Smith had been overly optimistic about the attraction *Romola* would have for the *Cornhill* readers. For a while the name "George Eliot" had worked its magic, but then reader interest slackened and was not significantly revived when Smith, Elder brought the novel out in three volumes. As a token of compensation, George Eliot gave Smith outright "Brother Jacob," which he accepted with grace and used in the July 1864 issue of the *Cornhill*. Thus, in every way available to her, George Eliot had proved to her own satisfaction that she was not a mercenary author.

She had feared from the beginning that *Romola* would not be popular, and it was proving to be true. The well-meaning but not always tactful Sara Hennell read the first instalment and wrote to say that although she was entranced by the beginning of the novel, she did not think many other readers would be. To this George Eliot responded:

> Of necessity, the book is addressed to fewer readers than my previous works, and I myself have never expected—I might rather say *intended*—that the book should be as "popular" in the same sense as the others. If one is to have freedom to write out one's unfolding self, and not be a machine always grinding out the same material or spinning the same sort of web, one cannot always write for the same public.

It was letters such as this one from Sara which made Lewes rush to get at the mail first and answer them himself. Yet when the novel was completed and out in book form, there was no need to fear the major reviews. While admitting *Romola*'s lack of popular appeal, they attributed to it greatness. The *Spectator*, for instance, called it "one of the greatest works of modern fiction," and concluded: "It will never be George Eliot's most popular book—it seems to us, however, much the greatest she has yet produced." And the *Westminster*, for which she herself had reviewed so many books, was still more gratifying: "No! *Romola* is not likely to be generally popular; it is too great both in mind and heart."

It is no accident that the one novel in which George Eliot deliberately defied popularity is a historical romance with a foreign setting. Despite the restrictive nature of the scholarship *Romola* had required, its remoteness in time and place proved to be a liberating force. Could Tessa, for example, have appeared in one of the English novels? Pretty, sensual, and childishly vain, she is as natural as one of the elements and in harmony with the onward flow of life. Tito's mistress, she bears his children without a sense of shame or guilt, survives both his marriage to Romola and his death, and at the end of the novel is a happy mother with Romola at her side to help care for the bastard children. Tessa's nearest English counterpart is Hetty Sorrel, of *Adam Bede*, who is also pretty, sensual, and childishly vain. But these attributes entrap her: for a pathetically short time the mistress of Arthur Donnithorne, she bears his child in an agony of guilt and secrecy that forces her into infanticide and leads her within a hairsbreadth of the gallows.

Also in *Romola* is the painter Piero di Cosimo, who exclaims, " '*Va!* your human talk and doings are a tame jest; the only passionate life is in form and colour' " (Book I, chapter 8). To most contemporary readers, Cosimo seemed too minor and eccentric a character to be taken seriously; Alexander Main granted him only one quotation when he culled specimens from the novel for the *Wit and Wisdom of George Eliot*. However, there were those few readers who were eagerly searching for an aesthetic philosophy to supplant Benthamite materialism and Anglican morality. They heard in Cosimo a new voice proclaiming the superiority of art over life, a herald's voice announcing the coming of Pater's *Renaissance* with its explosive Conclusion, which was to be translated from theory into practice by Wilde and other *fin de siècle* thinkers. It is improbable that George Eliot would have given consent to this interpretation of her Cosimo. On 5 November 1873, she wrote Blackwood that she "agreed very warmly with the remarks made by your contributor [unknown to her, Margaret Oliphant] this month on Mr. Pater's book, which seems to me quite poisonous in its false principles of criticism and false conceptions of life." Nonetheless she did create Cosimo, as well as Tessa, with obvious delight and a less burdensome sense of reponsibility toward her reader than usual. She luxuriated also in the right to allude to the Greek and

Roman mythology she loved but felt she could introduce only with inhibiting indirectness in her English novels. She did admit to Frederic Harrison, however, that making certain ideas in *Romola* "thoroughly incarnate" had been "agonizing labour to an English-fed imagination."

Romola herself is the most English character in the novel, a somber anachronism no more at home in fifteenth-century Florence than the young Evangelicalist Mary Ann Evans, with whom Romola shares a few joyless traits, would have been. The first young women of Girton may have felt honored but had little cause to be encouraged in their venture when George Eliot's founding subscription of £50 reached them "from the author of *Romola*." The novel might stand as an illustrative warning of what George Eliot called "the abysses worse than prostitution" that imperil a woman's journey toward liberation through education. Romola is her best-educated heroine, primarily because she is forced into servitude as amanuensis to Bardo, her blind scholar-father, who gives her grudging praise despite her unfortunate sex:

> And even in learning thou art not, according to thy measure, contemptible. . . . thou hast a ready apprehension, and even a wide-glancing intelligence. And thou hast a man's nobility of soul: thou hast never fretted me with thy petty desires as thy mother did. It is true, I have been careful to keep thee aloof from the debasing influences of thy own sex, with their sparrowlike frivolity and their enslaving superstition. . . . But though . . . I cannot boast that thou art entirely lifted out of that lower category to which Nature assigned thee . . . thou art my sweet daughter, and thy voice is as the lower notes of the flute. . . . [Book I, chapter 5]

Yet Romola's learning profits her ill, for it only adds to the unworldliness of her upbringing. She is an easy prey to Tito's charm and diabolic machinations, which lead her into great suffering. Touched by Savonarola's influence, she journeys on into suffering, but now of a selfless kind, in which anguish over lost happiness and a desire for death give way to the caring for others. Her almost superhuman ministrations to a plague-ridden village transform her into the legend of "the blessed Lady who came over the sea" (Book II, chapter 22). In the Epilogue, Romola is still a young woman, although an "eager life" has left its marks upon her physical beauty, and she is without family other than that of Tessa and her children, to which she has attached herself. But she has gained placidity, and the omniscient narrator charitably grants her at least one thing to be grateful for: "It is but once that we can know our worst sorrows, and Romola had known them while life was new."

Small wonder that among its first readers, young men were more enthusiastic over this novel than young women. The curiously sadistic portrait of Romola was a means of self-flagellation for her creator, who was convinced that she had strayed from her earliest goals, the selfless ones she forced her heroine to fulfill. In August 1863, after she had completed reading the novel, the irrepressible Sara Hennell wrote ecstatically yet with the pointedness of one who had known George Eliot well in her most personally troubled days:

> I say Romola is pure idealism—very, very, very beautiful,—because she lies so outside of, so altogether *above* my own experience. . . . [You have made her] one who, feeling intensely that the only salvation from her own inner sins and sorrows was in loving communion with fellow beings, yet felt herself for ever rejected as exactly the nature that is *not* capable of communicating that which really makes her a blessing to others; one whose most earnest efforts to get out of self are always a most desperate flinging back upon self. . . . It is only those who want nothing for themselves, that can really be wanted by others. And therefore I feel, that in Romola you have painted a goddess, and not a woman.

Intentionally or not, Sara had touched upon several matters which privately disturbed George Eliot: she was uneasily aware that the most intense phase of her friendship with Sara had been impetuously self-motivated; that almost all of her efforts to get out of herself had flung her back upon self; and that she had neither attained nor deserved the apotheosis which she had bestowed upon Romola while taking from her all chances of ordinary personal happiness and success. Yet Sara had also given her a comforting explanation of the disparity between herself and her heroine—in creating Romola, she had been breathing life into an ideal. Although there is no indication that George Eliot had planned Romola as such, her response to Sara accepts the idea: "You are right in saying that Romola is ideal—I feel it acutely in the reproof my own soul is constantly getting from the image it has made. My own books scourge me."

The *Mill* had scourged her too, but not with self-reproof. *Romola* surrounded her with it: if she looked into its contents, she found the saintly Romola to remind her of what she was not; and if she looked outside it, she saw George Smith and the *Cornhill*, reminders that she should be with John Blackwood and Maga. Cross vividly remembered her telling him that the writing of *Romola*

> ploughed into her more than any of her other books. She told me she could put her finger on it as marking a well-defined transition in her life. In her own words, "I began it a young woman—I finished it an old woman."

Romola WAS FINISHED ON 9 JUNE 1863. IT WAS APRIL 1866 before George Eliot negotiated with Blackwood over *Felix Holt, the Radical*. First of all, she had taken a year's rest from writing; during this relatively peaceful time the Leweses had obtained a forty-nine-year lease on a pleasant house called the Priory at 21 North Bank, with a rose garden between it and Regent's Canal. This was at last a permanent London home. (George Eliot left it only after her marriage to John Cross to move with him into the house he had provided at 4 Cheyne Walk, where she died within three weeks.) After the flurry of settling into the Priory, the Leweses went again to Italy and then later on made a shorter visit to Paris. On 29 June 1864, George Eliot began *The Spanish Gypsy* as a play; but working upon it aroused so much anxiety in her that Lewes forcibly took it away from her near the end of February 1865 in order to safeguard her health.

By 29 March, according to her Journal, she had begun a new novel, *Felix Holt*. (It is not clear whether this was the same English novel that was in her mind when she conceived *Romola* and which *Silas Marner* temporarily ousted.) The work was leisurely, however, and it was not until 20 June that she read the opening to Lewes. For once there is no mention of his reaction. Within her scheme of the novel, she had become involved in financial intricacies which even Lewes could not unravel, and so on 9 January 1866, she consulted Frederic Harrison, whom she had met about five years earlier and who had recently come to her attention again because of his article on industrial cooperation in the *Fortnightly Review* (of which Lewes was now editor, having given up his connection with the *Cornhill* in 1864). Harrison helped George Eliot with the legal aspect of *Felix* until she had completed the writing on 31 May. He emerged as one of the few readers convinced that it was a great novel. He read and reread it, so he wrote her on 19 July, as if he were taking up "Tennyson or Shelley or Browning and thinking out the sequences of thought suggested by the undertones of the thought and the harmony of the lines." Privately, he may have thought that George Eliot had wasted her fine eye for social detail on a view of society unstructured by Comtism; for it was *Felix* which led him to suggest that she should write a novel showing "the great elements of society and human life" in "relation to the complete ideal of Comte."

According to the extant correspondence, George Eliot was involved almost exclusively in writing to Harrison throughout January. Then during February and March there is a paucity in her letters not unlike those occasional gaps during earlier crucial years in her life. A brief note on 13 March to George Smith is preserved but has nothing to do with her novel-in-progress. Not much more than a month later—20 April—John Blackwood is writing Lewes: "I am delighted to hear that Mrs. Lewes has so nearly finished her Novel and also much pleased that she should think in the first instance of her old friend as the publisher." Lewes had obviously not mentioned to him the fact that a considerable portion of *Felix* had already been submitted to George Smith and rejected by him: "George Eliot offered me her next book, 'Felix Holt,' " Smith wrote, "and Lewes gave me to understand she expected £5,000 for it. I read the MS. to my wife, and we came to the conclusion it would not be a profitable venture and I declined it."

If Blackwood had heard through the grapevine that Smith had rejected the manuscript, he took no note of it and was optimistically certain that he would like the book when he saw some of it (for once he was right). He made a gesture of reminding Lewes that it was against his principle to make a decisive offer before he had seen the manuscript, but he also made it clear that he was prepared to offer between £4,000–£5,000, assuming of course that the completed work would run to the customary length of three volumes. To this he added: "Will you give her my regards and tell her that I have been thinking so much of her Novel since receiving your note that I have found it very difficult to attend to my ordinary work. . . ."

Immediately upon receiving this letter, the Leweses sent off "volumes 1 and 2 of the novel," asking that acknowledgment of its arrival be telegraphed. Blackwood complied with the telegraph, read the manuscript, and, not allowing himself to be wholly uncritical, wrote back: "I am lost in wonder and admiration of Mrs. Lewes' powers. It is not like a Novel and there may be a complaint of want of the ordinary Novel interest, but it is like looking on at a series of panoramas where human beings speak and act before us." Quickly following upon this letter was the formal offer for £5,000, which George Eliot accepted, saying simply, "It is a great pleasure to me to be writing to you again, as in the old days."

This was enough to evoke from Blackwood a long and enthusiastic letter, which began: "I most heartily respond to the feelings expressed in your gratifying note and do rejoice in resuming old relations with you. It quite takes me back to the days when Adam Bede won the Derby." Blackwood continued in a euphoric mood over the novel, partly because of his genuine liking for the book, but also because he was delighted to have George Eliot back with him. "The book is a perfect marvel," he wrote Langford on 26 April:

The time is 1832 just after the passing of the Reform Bill and surely such a picture or rather series of pictures of English Life, manners, and conversation never was drawn. . . . It has been a quick transaction but I have thought well about it and I do not see how I can be mistaken about the merits. . . . Her politics are excellent and will attract all parties. . . . It is a great publishing triumph her returning to us, and she expresses the warmest feeling of gratification in resuming her old relations with me. Lewes too says it has quite cheered her up. Keep the sum strictly a secret.

Two days later he wrote to his old friend and contributor, the Rev. W. Lucas Collins (who eventually wrote a favorable review of *Felix* for Maga):

From the advertisement in the Magazine, you will see that George Eliot has returned to her first friend. The overture did not come from me, and the whole transaction has been of the most gratifying kind. I read the first two MS. volumes before concluding anything, and I am delighted to say that I think the book a marvel.

On 1 June, Lewes noted in his Journal:

Yesterday Polly finished *Felix Holt*. The sense of relief was very great and all day long suffused itself over our thoughts. The continual ill health of the last months, and her dreadful nervousness and depression, made the writing a serious matter. Blackwood (who is overjoyed at her return to him . . .) thinks the book superior to *Adam Bede*. I cannot share that opinion; but the book is a noble book and will I think be more popular than the Mill.

Felix Holt was published quickly and on sale by 15 June. The reactions to it were extremely varied on the parts of both professional critics and independent readers. There were several minority groups, one being those few who, like Harrison and Blackwood, thought *Felix* her finest novel thus far. In fact, Blackwood was to remain more spontaneously drawn to it than to any of the other novels, although he was to have great admiration for *Middlemarch* and never lost his nostalgic feeling for the *Bedesman*. *Felix* was of course haloed in his mind if only because it had (so he thought) brought George Eliot back to him voluntarily. Then there were other reasons for his liking that were strong enough to offset his uneasiness over the situation of Mrs. Transome and the consequences of her illicit love affair. He enjoyed the relative modernity and felt at home with both the characters and the author's point of view. "I had nearly forgot to say," he wrote in a postscript to one of his early letters to George Eliot about the novel, "how good your politics are. As far as I see yet, I suspect

I am a radical of the Felix Holt breed, and so was my father before me."

Blackwood felt that the novel became even more timely with the passing of the Second Reform Bill in 1867. Inspired by Disraeli's "Address to the Working Men" at Edinburgh on 29 October of that year, he urged George Eliot to write her own version of such an address and sign it "Felix Holt." She did so, although reluctantly (she was again tackling *The Spanish Gypsy*), and the essay was printed in the January 1868 number of Maga. This was her first appearance there since "The Lifted Veil"; it was also to be her last one. Rightly interpreting the gesture as a personal favor to him, Blackwood thanked her heartily, but he may have been disappointed that her piece did not speak more directly to the working men: "The Address is excellent. The only fear is that it may be too good. If the mass could appreciate rightly such words and feelings, what a grand nation we would become."

Some readers despised the conservative nature of the radicalism that appealed to Blackwood; and still others were more shocked by the "unpleasant Transome theme," which they thought exceeded the bounds of good taste. A few even put politics and morality aside to concentrate on literary qualities. Reviewing the novel in *The Nation*, 16 August 1866, Henry James was severely critical of Felix as a hero: "We find him a Radical and we leave him what?—only 'utterly married'; which is all very well in its place, but which by itself makes no conclusion." Margaret Oliphant, realizing the importance of this novel to Blackwood, had planned to review it for him. After she had read it, however, she begged off, "for I don't think I could say anything satisfactory about it. It leaves an impression on my mind as of 'Hamlet' played by six sets of gravediggers. Of course it will be a successful book, but I think chiefly because 'Adam Bede' and 'Silas Marner' went before it." Mrs. Oliphant was proved at least partly right. The vast majority of readers ignored the dissenting minority voices and proclaimed *Felix* a success by buying it and enjoying it, delighting especially in the depiction of an England which still lived in the memory of many.

George Eliot had announced her return to an English setting by affixing as a motto to *Felix Holt* seven lines from Drayton's *Polyolbion*, which also served to express her pride in being an English writer:

> Upon the midlands now the industrious muse doth fall,
> The shires which we the heart of England well may call.
> ....
> My native country thou, which so brave spirits hast bred,
> If there be virtues yet remaining in thy earth,

> Or any good of thine thou bred'st into my birth,
> Accept it as thine own, whilst now I sing of thee,
> Of all thy later brood the unworthiest though I be.

No other invocation to a muse could have been more inspirational to her readers than this one; they were happy to have her back in England. The *Edinburgh Review* denounced *Romola* and stated flatly: "One sentence of Tommy Trounsem's in *Felix Holt* is well worth all the pages which are allotted to the Florentine Figaro." This reviewer's major complaint against the Italian novel was George Eliot's fidelity to history, which did not allow her to write out of the fullness of her heart as when revealing "without effort the odd mysteries of custom and character which grow up in some remote Midland village." Her readers were grateful that she had exchanged what she called the "Idiom of Florence" for what Theophrastus Such is to call the "speech of the English landscape."

Before *Felix* appeared in the bookstores, the Leweses had once more crossed the Channel, their destination this time being the German watering places. They were also on a sentimental pilgrimage, for they retraced some of the route that they had taken together twelve years earlier during their first Continental trip. Blackwood's letter carrying good news about reviews and sales reached them on 21 July; and although she wrote back to say that she had awaited information with both "longing and despair," she did so in a light tone and this was the only reference to anxiety in her long letter. It is as if she had at last begun to feel a sense of security—having been warmly welcomed home, first by Blackwood and now by her readers. This homecoming could not take the place of the one that she deeply desired with Isaac, but it was a good one and in harmony with the adult life she had created for herself.

Epilogue

I T IS IMPOSSIBLE TO SAY WHETHER GEORGE ELIOT'S DEATH IN late 1880 was a consequence of the loss of her creative life. An inclusive view, however, does point to a complex of reasons responsible for the cessation of her creativity, some parallel to those which had made creative writing possible for her. The most potent threat to the stable emotional background she required for writing was the death of Lewes on 30 November 1878, only nine days after he had mailed her manuscript of *Theophrastus Such* to Blackwood. She had reason to equate her fiction writing with Lewes's presence; his entry into her life had opened her career, and his leaving may have closed it.

Literally, however, her creative writing came to an end before the death of Lewes. *Theophrastus Such* is not a novel. After the provocatively autobiographical opening chapters of "Looking Inward" and "Looking Backward," the book is a series of only remotely connected essays. Thus *Daniel Deronda* (written 1873–6) was her last work of fiction, and it is quite possible that in the process of writing it she had concluded all the self-exploration that she was willing to translate for the public. Certainly the character Theophrastus was born out of a strong reaction against publication and even writing. The evidence that she was later at work on another novel is inconclusive; in addition there is Cross's assertion that during their brief life together she neither wrote nor talked to him about future writing.

It was the force of memory that had largely dictated the sequence of her fiction. If the workings of that memory could be traced, then the question of whether or not *Daniel Deronda* was a final, personal statement could be answered with some certainty. She herself became aware of the significance of the sequence of her work in 1861, when she found herself writing *Silas Marner* instead of *Romola*. As she knew Blackwood was expecting to bring out the Italian novel next, she wrote him to make sure that he would agree to publish *Silas* in advance of it: "My chief reason for wishing to publish the story now, is, that I like my writings to appear in the order in which they are written, because they belong to successive mental phases, and when they are a year behind me, I can no longer feel that thorough identification with them which gives zest to the sense of authorship." Her phrase "mental phases" suggests states of mind and feeling that are modulated by memory of the past as well as by the impinging present.

She was to make many uses of memory, but rarely did she invoke it to reconstruct a static past. She would have understood Proust's statement in *The Past Recaptured*: "What we call reality is a certain relationship between . . . sensations and the memories which surround us at the same time. . . ." She would also have understood something of Thomas Wolfe's struggle against the "torrential recollectiveness," which he describes in *You Can't Go Home Again* as "a living, million-fibered integument that bound me to the past, not only of my own life, but of the very earth from which I came, so that nothing in the end escaped from its inrooted and all-feeling explorativeness." Although she did not allow herself to submit to the onslaught of memory with the abandon of either Proust or Wolfe, George Eliot too was driven to recapture and explore her total past, her search being directed by her need to confess and to justify. At the end of her life, she might have said (as Goethe said of his work) that all her novels, taken as a whole, were but a fragment of a great confession.

Lewes was not always able to enter into the private life her memory created, yet he was keenly aware that it was the catalytic agent of her writing. When Mrs. John Cash (nee Mary Sibree) visited George Eliot at the Priory after not having seen her for twenty years, she was deeply touched—as she recounted in the memoir she later wrote for Cross—

> to find how much [George Eliot] had retained of her kind interest in all that concerned me and mine, and I remarked on this to Mr. Lewes, who came to the door with my daughter and myself at parting. "Wonderful sympathy," I said. "Is it not?" said he; and when I added, inquiringly, "The power lies there?" "Unquestionably it does," was his answer; "she forgets nothing that has ever come within the curl of her eyelash: above all, she forgets no one who has ever spoken to her one kind word."

In his tacit association of sympathy and memory, Lewes clearly had in mind a kind of memory that went beyond the function of ordinary recall. He described a still more complex kind in the first of a series of essays on the "Principles of Success in Literature," which he contributed to the *Fortnightly Review*, beginning 15 May 1865. In them, not surprisingly, a considerable number of undesignated but identifiable references to George Eliot appear. There is little question but that this is one:

> Genius is rarely able to give any account of its own processes. But those who have had ample opportunities of intimately knowing the growth of works in the minds of artists, will bear me out in saying that a vivid memory supplies the elements from a thousand different sources, most of which are quite beyond the power of localization—the experience of yesterday being strangely intermingled with the dim suggestions of early years, the tones heard in childhood sounding through the diapason of sorrowing maturity; and all these kaleidoscopic fragments are recomposed into images that seem to have a corresponding reality of their own.

The course of such a memory is not easily detected; however, one noteworthy clue supplied by Lewes is that it often brings together the past and the present so that out of the fusion arises a new concept or object. This can be seen in a story as early as "Gilfil," and it is especially apparent in the latter portion of the *Mill*; but the process was no doubt operating in the other novels, although in less observable form. *The Spanish Gypsy*, for example, may have been motivated in part by a lingering trace of the childhood fantasy George Eliot had confessed to Maria Lewis in 1839, that of being the chief actress in scenes of her own imagining. The mere idea of writing a drama may have revived that fantasy enough to lead her to the theme and setting which best fulfilled its demands—demands which had, of course, become more complex with her adult life. That idea had been put into her mind in 1864 as a result of Lewes's interest in writing a play for Helen Faucit, whom he admired as a tragic actress, and whose husband, Theodore Martin, was an old friend of his. Perhaps hoping to urge George Eliot out of the inertia which had followed the completing of *Romola*, Lewes suggested that she use his plot outline and write the play herself. She agreed, and they even made a trip to Glasgow to see Helen Faucit act some of her favorite Shakespearean roles. A friendship developed, but the project was dropped.

The thought of writing a play had by now taken strong hold of George Eliot, however, and in May of that year, three months after Lewes had made his suggestion, she found her subject matter in Venice. Inspiration flashed into her mind as she was contemplating a small painting of the Annunciation said to be by Titian, and at some later but undetermined date she wrote these notes:

> It occurred to me that here was a great dramatic motive of the same class as those used by the Greek dramatists, yet specifically differing from them. A young maiden, believing herself to be on the eve of the chief event of her life,—marriage,—about to share in the ordinary lot of womanhood, full of young hope, has suddenly announced to her that she is chosen to fulfil a great destiny, entailing a terribly different experience from that of ordinary womanhood ... here, I thought, is a subject grander than that of Iphigenia, and it has never been used.

By an association known only to herself, she was led to the surprising conclusion that the most "suitable set of historical and local conditions" in which to clothe the idea was

> that moment in Spanish history when the struggle with the Moors was attaining its climax, and when there was a gypsy race present under such conditions as would enable me to get my heroine and the hereditary claim on her among the gypsies. I required the opposition of race to give the need for renouncing the expectation of marriage.

In the *Mill*, Maggie Tulliver's scene with the gypsies suggests that they were somehow linked with the childhood fantasy of being the chief actress in an imagined drama. Although Maggie's main object in joining the gypsies is to escape home and punishment for having pushed Lucy Deane into the mud, once with them, she finds the experience "just like a story." She enacts her role by offering to become their queen and teach them a great many things; when it seems to her that they are impressed, her eyes begin "to sparkle and her cheeks to flush,—she was really beginning to instruct the gypsies, and gaining great influence over them." Her dream of power is short-lived, being overwhelmed by hunger, fear, and welcome rescue (Book I, Chapter 11). By 1864, the peculiar fascination which George Eliot had felt for the gypsies as a child had become erudite and located in the historical, rather than her personal, past. The gypsy queen is no longer the figment of a child's imagination but the heroic Fedalma, who as queen of the Zincali chooses duty over love, renouncing her womanhood in order to fulfill her hereditary destiny and lead her people toward their promised home in Africa.

George Eliot had seen in the Annunciation the theme of tragic *re*nunciation. On the level of Christian myth, the Annunciation presages motherhood in its most exalted form; but on the human level, it signifies Mary's being deprived of the experiences of ordinary womanhood. The two themes are contrastive but not conflicting, and George Eliot noted that as she pondered it, "the subject had become more and more pregnant to me." "Pregnant" is unintentionally ironic in the general context, for she is considering the tragedy of "the renunciation of marriage, where marriage cannot take place without entailing misery on the children." She lists reasons for deliberate childlessness: "A woman, say, finds herself on the earth with an inherited organization; she may be lame, she may inherit a disease, or what is tantamount to a disease; she may be a negress, or have other marks of race repulsive in the community where she is born, etc." This aspect of her theme would have been deeply personal to George Eliot, whose own position forbade children, if not through heredity then as the result of forces that were equally strong in her society. She was still identifying with the gypsy queen of her (and Maggie's) early daydream; but now she was superimposing upon that queen the sacrificial burden of instructing and liberating her people. George Eliot was forty-five when she conceived her drama and forty-eight when she completed *The Spanish Gypsy* in its present form. These are usually crucial years in a woman's life, a time when she is likely to ask herself whether or not her passion has been well spent. Blanche Colton Williams, in 1936, first called attention to the significance of that age in connection with the prevalence of sexual imagery in the finished poem. It would seem that even as George Eliot consciously exalted renunciation, something in her nature rose up in rebellion against it.

The dramatic form of composition proved too great a challenge. But even after Lewes forced her to put aside her attempt and she had set to work on *Felix Holt*, the desire to write a drama clung to her so that she wrote Barbara Bodichon in April 1866 that she was "in the later acts" of this new novel. Returning to the earlier work in August, she transformed the "Acts" into "Books," giving herself scope for a more analytic presentation of her material, although she retained certain dramatic conventions (such as stage directions and the introduction of speeches by only the names of the characters), as well as the poetic form. She was self-conscious about writing a book-length poem, yet also proud—and proud of Lewes's encouragement, as they both were aware that the project to which she was giving so much effort could not be expected to bring in the money assured by a prose novel. In search of atmosphere, they went to Spain at the end of 1866, and John Blackwood assumed that she was working on a novel with a Spanish setting. She enlightened him on 21 March of the following year: "The work connected with Spain is not a Romance. It is—prepare your fortitude—it is—a poem. . . . Of course, if it is ever finished to my satisfaction, it is not a work for us to get money by, but Mr. Lewes urges and insists that it shall be done."

In July 1867 she wrote similarly to George Smith, who had also heard the rumor that she was engaged in writing a Spanish novel and who had hopes that it might do for the *Cornhill*. She decisively turned down his tentative offer, explaining that what she was writing was *not* a novel and therefore "likely to be dead against the taste of that large public which a publisher is for the most part obligated (rather unhappily) to take into account."

The accommodating if not very eager John Blackwood accepted the poem for publication in book form, and although he shared her own misgivings concerning its reception, managed a final comment which skillfully combined that doubt with tribute: "How far a Poem which requires the reader to pause and dwell so much at every step to feel it aright will be popular with the mass is a thing that no man can tell, but there is no question that it is a grand thing." *The Spanish Gypsy* was not popular, but it sold fairly well because of the name affixed to it. George Eliot was content with the mild success, writing D'Albert-Durade in July 1868 (two months after the poem had been published) that she cared for the unexpectedly good sale

> not in a monetary light (for one does not write poems as the most marketable commodity) [but] because sale means large distribution. We are so happy now as to be independent of all monetary considerations, and Mr. Lewes plunges at his will into the least lucrative of studies, while I on my side follow tastes not much in keeping with those of our noisy, hurrying, ostentatious time.

M*iddlemarch*—NEXT IN THE SEQUENCE OF HER WORKS—WAS the first novel she wrote without anxiety over "monetary considerations." Perhaps this is why she felt free to experiment with beginnings before committing herself to any one plan that would bring together the characters moving around in her mind. On 1 January 1869 she wrote in her Journal that among other projects (all poems) she wished to go on with "a novel called 'Middlemarch.'" However, this is not *Middlemarch* as it now stands; it concerns provincial life and the central character is a physician, but missing are Dorothea Brooke, Edward Casaubon, and Will Ladislaw. She worked at this early version sporadically, but on 2 December 1870 referred in her Journal to another narrative in progress: "I am experimenting in a story ('Miss Brooke') which I began without any very serious intention of carrying it out lengthily. It is a subject which has been recorded among my possible themes ever since I began to write fiction, but will probably take new shapes in the development." By March 1871 and for some reason known only to herself, she had fused these two beginnings with such skill that had the original manuscripts not survived, the fusion might have gone undetected. Retaining the title *Middlemarch*, she then went unfalteringly on until she had completed the novel as we now know it.

This novel is the only one of hers besides *The Mill on the Floss* to bear the name of a place rather than a major character. As in the *Mill*, one hears the indignant and malicious whisperings of provincial society, although the horizon has been broadened to permit glimpses into a larger world lying beyond Middlemarch. Also as in the *Mill*, the reader is aware of the strong affinity between the novelist and her heroine. But George Eliot's compassionate concern for Dorothea Brooke was very different from the possessive protectiveness she had felt toward Maggie Tulliver, who had been born out of her own childhood. George Eliot made Dorothea an orphan, unattached to her past even through memory. Thus her problems are wholly of the present, but they are considerable, for Dorothea is an untimely St. Theresa whose intense nature will lead her, if not into "tragic failure," into "a life of mistakes, the offspring of a certain spiritual grandeur ill-matched with the meanness of opportunity . . ." (Prelude).

Although she brushes against it, Dorothea averts tragedy but not mistakes, the gravest of which is her marriage to the elderly scholar Casaubon. She is freed from this by Casaubon's death, and despite complications, is able to accept the love of Will Ladislaw and later to marry him. Those Middlemarchers who do not know her personally disapprove of her two marriages; they "observed that she could not have been 'a nice woman,' else she would not have married either the one or the other" (Finale). Like Maggie, Dorothea is a target of gossip, but the ugly words are not seared in her consciousness by the voice of a beloved brother. Dorothea's sister, the practical Celia, is occasionally mildly critical of her but never denunciatory.

Celia may have been fashioned after Chrissey (as Cross said George Eliot told him), but her primary purpose in the narrative is to serve as foil to her extraordinary sister, whom she "had been used to think of . . . as the dangerous part of the family machinery" (Book VIII, chapter 13). Dorothea is as unfettered by family as she is by the past. The theme of the importance of family influence is in the novel, but relegated to the Caleb Garths, safely removed from Dorothea. And it is Mary Garth who feels a tie to the past when she chooses to marry her childhood sweetheart, the none too strong Fred Vincy, because she believed that when "a tender affection has been storing itself in us through many of our years, the idea that we could accept any exchange for it seems to be a cheapening of our lives" (Book VI, chapter 57).

Heading this chapter as a motto is the sonnet describing the impact of Sir Walter Scott upon young readers, which George Eliot may have originally intended for the "Brother and Sister" sequence that she composed during 1869, the year of the first version of *Middlemarch*. By this time George Eliot was willing to free her adulthood from her childhood.

She could empathize, even identify, with Dorothea Brooke and yet present her as wholly detached from the forces that led Maggie Tulliver to her death. External happenings, as well as the unplanned therapy of her own writing, had drastically diminished her need for self-justification, of which Maggie, despite her vitality as a character, is an instrument incarnate. This is not to say, however, that the attachment between George Eliot and Dorothea arose out of a less personal basis than did that between her and Maggie. The essential pattern of Dorothea's emotional experience parallels an equally profound one in George Eliot's own life, the nexus of which was her translating *Das Leben Jesu*.

Casaubon, like Strauss, was a killer of myths. In the conclusion of his critical examination of the life of Jesus, Strauss could state with conviction: "This is the key to the whole of Christology, that, as subject of the predicate which the Church assigns to Christ, we place, instead of an individual, an idea. . . ." By the time she translated this statement, George Eliot had grown "Strauss-sick," having learned that to dissect a myth was to rob it of its potency and hence the world of some radiance. But she had begun her work in a far different frame of mind. Casaubon's perennial work-in-progress, the Key to all Mythologies, is a parody of Strauss's explication of the one central myth of Christianity. And Dorothea's first rapt enthusiasm for Casaubon's work and himself is not unlike that of the young George Eliot for Strauss and Brabant. Although Dorothea is finally disillusioned with both her husband and his work, George Eliot preserves Casaubon from caricature; when he goes into death, leaving his Key a still unsolved mystery, he is more pathetic than ludicrous.

Probably there were several nuances of meaning in George Eliot's mind when she responded to a friend who persisted in asking her from whom Casaubon had been drawn: "With a humorous solemnity, which was quite in earnest, she pointed to her own heart." She may have meant that she had put a cast-off part of herself into him—a joylessness and an aridity which might have taken hold of her had she not stopped translating, had she not joined her life with Lewes's, and had she not had the courage and his sustaining help to turn to fiction writing. But it is more likely that she was claiming that Casaubon was her own creation, no matter from what person or persons he had germinated. She had come a long way from the

Clerical Scenes, in which her characters are either identifiable portraits or deliberate distortions of living models. It may well be that all the major characters of *Middlemarch* were suggested by real people, but during the process of creation each evolved into an entity no longer bound to its origin.

The same liberating process entered into the movement of the novel. The sequence of emotion which takes Dorothea from Casaubon to Ladislaw is the same as that experienced by George Eliot as she turned to the nameless young picture-restorer after the deflating ending to her otherwise idyllic visit with Dr. Brabant at Devizes. In the novel, however, the ephemeral picture-restorer becomes substantial and permanent in the form of Ladislaw—as indeed it might be said he did in real life in the form of George Henry Lewes. Also, if George Eliot had been writing about Lydgate with an echo of John Chapman in mind, it is understandable why, shortly after "Miss Brooke" had begun to develop steadily, she was inspired to combine these two segments; for the translating of Strauss had led to Chapman's entry into her life. The magnetic pull that brought Lydgate and Dorothea into the same novel has been sensed if not understood by most of its readers. As Blanche Colton Williams summarizes this reaction: "No reader but must say again and again, 'Too bad Dorothea and Lydgate were not mated, but how like life that men and women apparently destined for each other so seldom are joined.'" In this matter George Eliot chose to follow reality faithfully: Dorothea's final relationship to Lydgate as trustworthy and morally sustaining friend is like George Eliot's to Chapman during her last months at the Strand.

Yet the only truly autobiographical element in the novel is the force of association that determined these sequences and relationships. Mature craftsmanship transformed these into a new world, one that partakes of the universal but also is obedient to a strictly regulated time-setting. The resonant national events which led to the Reform Bill of 1832 are so muted in the narrative that it was to require special study to rediscover *Middlemarch* as an historical novel.

George Eliot herself seemed nonchalant about her achievement in *Middlemarch*. It appeared in eight short volumes—a plan devised by Lewes and accepted by Blackwood—between December 1871 and December 1872. Although it was never to be a popular success in the sense of *Adam Bede*, it took only two numbers to draw to her side even those critics who had looked askance at her preceding work. At about this time she wrote to Alexander Main: "I can't help wondering at the high estimate made of *Middlemarch* in proportion to my other books. I suppose the depressed state of my health makes my writing seem more than usually below the mark of my desires. . . ." After

Middlemarch had completed its appearance in print, even she (despite Lewes's protection) could not help knowing that the critics thought this novel the summit of her career and that anything further would be an inevitable descent.

John Blackwood was well aware of her feelings. When in early November 1873 he received from her the welcome news that she was "simmering towards another big book," he did his best in terms of homely imagery to distract her from her fear that a new work from her would be automatically viewed as anticlimactic: "There are as good fish in the Sea as ever came out of it, and those really studying and loving Middlemarch will feel that the proverb applies to your mind instead of harking back to that great book as a climax." Blackwood went even further and wrote about the prospect of a new George Eliot novel to his friend A. W. Kinglake, who responded as most of her serious readers would have been inclined to do: "Another novel from Mrs. Lewes is really a national blessing! Why don't cities have illuminations for news so grateful, instead of making believe to rejoice at some absurd 'birthday' or the accession of a new Lord Mayor?"

WITH ENCOURAGEMENT FROM BOTH BLACKWOOD AND LEWES, George Eliot went on with *Daniel Deronda*. In fact, these two men—George Eliot's necessary "objective" critics outside herself—came together over this last novel as never before, perhaps because each privately thought the book too strange and innovative to be a popular success, and yet each was dedicated to giving her the assurance that would permit her to complete it. According to Blackwood's account, one day in May 1875 Lewes walked in on him at the Burlington in London while he was in the midst of writing to her about his favorable reactions to the first volume of *Deronda*: "I showed him what I was doing. He said: 'Do go on. You have no idea how much good that will do her. She has more faith in your judgment than in that of any one else.' His own judgment, he says, she naturally enough considers may be biassed, but I must say I have never found him wrong on the subject." Thus sustained, George Eliot finished writing the novel on 8 June 1876. It had actually begun to appear in print on 1 February of that year; publication of the eight monthly parts was completed on 1 September.

No other George Eliot novel more clearly reveals her tendency to bring together two separate themes and groups of characters. Critics had noticed this even in *Felix Holt* (a few unfavorably), but in

Middlemarch she had successfully made the two parts an integrated whole. In *Daniel Deronda*, however, she allowed her two narratives to stand defiantly alone, united only by the uneven relationship between Gwendolen Harleth and Daniel—desperate and confessional on Gwendolen's side, condescending on Daniel's. Curiously, George Eliot herself did not seem to realize the dichotomy within her novel, so that when her first readers were attracted to Gwendolen as the vibrant center of the book, she was dismayed. She had lavished tender and loving care on characterizing Daniel, yet most readers were either bored or appalled by him. Only the exceptional reader sympathized with her daring handling of the Jewish theme, and only later readers could appreciate her remarkable anticipation of Zionism. After the last instalment of the novel had appeared, she began to receive a few letters expressing sympathetic interest in the Deronda portion, and although these presented an incongruous admixture of Christian and Hebraic sentiments, she wrote of them to Barbara Bodichon in early October 1876: "This is better than the laudation of readers who cut the book into scraps and talk of nothing in it but Gwendolen. I meant everything in the book to be related to everything else there."

Perhaps the major reason why George Eliot could not see her novel as her readers were sure to see it was that it had emanated from a single concept in her own mind, but one which had split into two independent yet related entities. The real basis for the relationship remained secreted within her mind rather than effectively incorporated into the novel itself. On one level, Gwendolen embodies the inner forces of egoism, hostility, and aggressiveness that George Eliot had long feared would master her; and Daniel is the incarnation of counteracting ideals. Significantly, Gwendolen was associated in George Eliot's mind with the one human activity for which she had absolutely no tolerance. During the fall of 1872 while she and Lewes were in Homburg (where she wrote the Finale to *Middlemarch*), they looked in upon the gaming tables, after which she expressed her outraged feelings in a letter to John Cross's mother:

> I am not fond of denouncing my fellow-sinners, but gambling being a vice I have no mind to, it stirs my disgust even more than my pity. The sight of the dull faces bending round the gaming tables, the raking-up of the money, and the flinging of the coins towards the winners by the hard-faced croupiers, the hateful, hideous women staring at the board like stupid monomaniacs—all this seems to me the most abject presentation of mortals grasping after something called a good that can be seen on the face of this little earth. Burglary is heroic compared with it. . . . Hell is the only right name for such places.

A few days later she wrote Blackwood:

> The Kursaal is to me a Hell not only for the gambling, but for the
> light and heat of the gas, and we have seen enough of its monoto-
> nous hideousness. There is very little dramatic "Stoff" to be picked
> up by watching or listening. The saddest thing to be witnessed
> is the play of Miss Leigh, Byron's grand niece [actually grand-
> daughter], who is only 26 years old, and is completely in the grasp
> of this mean, money-raking demon.

Lewes too had been moved by the scene and mentioned it in his
Journal as a "painful sight." Although unaware of it at the time,
George Eliot had in fact absorbed a great deal of dramatic "Stoff."
Soon the juxtaposition in her memory of gambling and the living
reminder of Byron's incestuous affair with Augusta Leigh brought
into being Gwendolen Harleth, a symbol of what her creator most
feared and yet with a vitality of her own that takes possession of the
novel. The gambling scene which opens *Deronda* is high among the
most objectively dramatic ones in George Eliot's novels. As Gwendolen
plays roulette, she is uncomfortably aware that Daniel is watching her.
This young woman and man apparently have been brought together
by chance; yet some underlying force in the narrative suggests that the
two are inextricably bound together and will remain so despite the
differences in family and events that sweep them into seemingly
separate currents of life. From the beginning, Deronda is Gwendolen's
source of salvation, but only because there is something within her
capable of responding (and submitting) to his effort to draw her
outside the boundaries of her self. He in turn is strong enough to
accept her confidences and faith in him. It is Daniel who restores the
necklace Gwendolen has been forced to pawn as a result of her loss
at gambling.

The meaning of gambling is made explicit in the course of the
novel. Gwendolen early confesses to Daniel that she should not have
married Grandcourt after she had found out about his mistress, who
had borne his children. Later she returns to this theme after Grandcourt's drowning, for which she blames herself because she knows
that she had wished to be free of her sadistic husband: "I ought not
to have married. . . . I wronged some one else. . . . I wanted to make
my gain out of another's loss . . . it was like roulette—and the money
burnt into me. . . . It was as if I had prayed that another should lose
and I should win. And I had won. I knew it all—I knew I was guilty"
(Book VII, chapter 7). These sentences make one think back to
Maggie Tulliver's frustrated attempt to confide in Tom about her
night with Stephen Guest—and indeed, one might be led still further
back to wonder if George Eliot were not admitting a long-suppressed

doubt about the rightness of living with Lewes when Agnes and her children were alive and in need of support.

Daniel's responses to Gwendolen are stern, yet he never fails to listen to her with his whole being or to assure her that her life is worth salvaging. Although at times reluctantly, he accepts the responsibility created by her reaching out to him for help, so that he and she become brother and sister in a more profound sense than blood relationship might have permitted. As George Eliot comments, Gwendolen's feelings

> had turned this man, only a few years older than herself, into a priest; a sort of trust less rare than the fidelity that guards it. Young reverence for one who is also young is the most coercive of all: there is the same level of temptation, and the higher motive is believed in as a fuller force,—not suspected to be a mere residue from weary experience.
>
> But the coercion is often stronger on the one who takes the reverence. Those who trust us educate us. [Book V, chapter 1]

This was the kind of education that both Tom Tulliver and Isaac Evans had stubbornly rejected.

There is, however, a side to Gwendolen which Daniel does not really know, although he has heard about it from time to time. Throughout the novel she is close to only one person, and that is her mother (thus reversing the facts of George Eliot's early life). Significantly, Gwendolen's relation to her mother is the opposite to that of Daniel's to his, who has rejected him from the time of his infancy. But a common denominator in both relationships is the nullification of men, although both mothers have had two marriages. The Princess Halm-Eberstein describes her marriages as but stepping stones in her own interest, and Daniel is left unimpressed by the account of his own father. He is allowed no intimate relationship with his mother, as she has kept him away from her until she knows she is dying. Gwendolen, in contrast, has early become the mainstay of her mother, although in her life too men have been swept away. Her own father, long since dead, appears to have been little more than a cipher to her, and she is as contemptuous of even the memory of her stepfather, also dead, as she is of his daughters (who are but blurs in the novel, as they are in Gwendolen's mind). Instinctively, she has usurped the man's position in relation to her mother. She feels responsible for providing for the impoverished family, and she protects, succors, and directs her mother, who both fears and adores this brilliant and beautiful daughter. It is for her mother that she subjects herself to marriage to Grandcourt, and love and concern for her mother form a continuous motif throughout her confessions to Daniel. Finally, it is to her mother that she confesses, as she does not to Daniel, her greatest fear about herself. She does this in revulsion against Rex Gascoigne, a promising young man in terms of both immediate wealth and future career. He has been magnetically drawn to Gwendolen, certain that her sensitiveness and excitability of nature would make her "able to love better than other girls" (Book I, chapter 6), and she in turn has enjoyed good times with him. Marriage to him would have resolved her problems, but her reaction to his first attempt at lovemaking startles both herself and him.

> "Pray don't make love to me. I hate it." She looked at him fiercely.
> Rex turned pale and was silent, but could not take his eyes off her, and the impetus was not yet exhausted that made her dart death at him. Gwendolen herself could not have foreseen that she should feel in this way. It was a sudden, new experience to her. . . . But now the life of passion had begun negatively in her. She felt passionately averse to this volunteered love. [Book I, chapter 7]

After Rex has gone, her mother comes upon Gwendolen sobbing bitterly and is as shocked as he had been, for she "had never before seen her darling struck down in this way, and felt something of the alarmed anguish that women feel at the sight of overpowering sorrow in a strong man; for this child had been her ruler." As she attempts to comfort her daughter, Gwendolen does not recoil as she had from Rex, but rests her head against her mother and cries out:

> "Oh, mamma, what can become of my life? there is nothing worth living for!"
> "Why, dear?" said Mrs. Davilow. . . .
> "I shall never love anybody. I can't love people. I hate them."
> "The time will come, dear, the time will come."
> Gwendolen was more and more convulsed with sobbing; but, putting her arms round her mother's neck with an almost painful clinging, she said brokenly, "I can't bear any one to be very near me but you."
> Then the mother began to sob, for this spoiled child had never shown such dependence on her before; and so they clung to each other. [Book I, chapter 7]

At the end of the novel, Gwendolen appears to face a bleak future; yet she has gained what she has most desired from the beginning, for her widowhood has brought her ample money (which Deronda had persuaded her it is right for her to accept) to provide for her mother and the brood of half sisters. *Daniel Deronda* is the only one of George Eliot's novels in which the mother is all-powerful, although not presented as an ideal mother figure. She is split, as is so much else in the novel, into two radically opposing forces—the rejecting mother of Daniel, and the accepting, if dependent, mother of Gwendolen. But in whichever guise, she has at last supplanted both the father and the brother.

George Eliot was in an uncharacteristically relaxed mood after completing this novel, and she wrote Blackwood a long overdue letter of appreciation. Unfortunately the letter has not been found; it can be reconstructed in essence from Blackwood's delighted reaction and his account of it to his nephew William:

> The substance is that she had been looking over my old letters and cannot resist writing to say how much she owes me, in fact pretty much that she could not have gone on without me. You may conceive this in her language. It is the greatest compliment a man in my position could possibly receive, and that and the context about herself brought warm tears to my eyes.

In something of a holiday mood, the Leweses indulged in the luxury of purchasing Witley Heights, in Surrey, as a summer home. Despite their love for the Priory, they (or at least George Eliot) wanted to be out of London for the summer and fall. Oscar Browning tells how he "was more than once employed by them" to find "a retired country spot," but was "never successful in suiting all their requirements." In fairness to Browning, it should be said that he was asked to find a cottage in good condition, whereas the Heights (discovered by John Cross, who lived nearby) was a stately house in sad need of repairs. When they discovered how much work was needed to make the house livable, the Leweses had misgivings, and George Henry began to call it Witley Cross. However, early in June 1877 they valiantly moved in and became "tolerably settled"—as George Eliot wrote Frederic Harrison—in a "camping, experimental fashion." They stayed until near the end of October, rounding out the year, as usual, in the Priory, where on 31 December, George Eliot recorded in her Journal:

> Today I say a final farewell to this little book which is the only record I have made of my personal life for sixteen years and more. I have often been helped by looking back in it to compare former with actual states of despondency from bad health or other apparent causes. . . . But of course as the years advance there is a new rational ground for the expectation that my life may become less fruitful. The difficulty is, to decide how far resolution should set in the direction of activity rather than in the acceptance of a more negative state. Many conceptions of works to be carried out present themselves, but confidence in my own fitness to complete them

worthily is all the more wanting because it is reasonable to argue
that I must have already done my best.

There is resignation but none of the old despair or anxious urgency
in this entry. Probably she recorded some of the conceptions of works
in the "more business-like diary" which she intended to begin, but
no Journal for 1878 has been found; she perhaps destroyed it when
Lewes died.

The next June, she and Lewes returned to Witley Heights, remaining until mid-November. During this stay, she worked on *Theophrastus Such*. They had barely re-established their city routine before
Lewes died, and she was plunged into unspeakable anguish. Blackwood, hearing the news by telegram from Langford, made plans to
come to London to be with her, but had to give them up because of
his own ill health. Isaac's wife, Sarah, wrote a letter of sympathy, as
did the Rev. William Griffiths, husband of Isaac's daughter Edith;
she heard also from Mrs. Robert Evans. Eventually, George Eliot
responded to these letters, but she may have thought with some
justified irony that it had taken no less than Lewes's death to bring
her reminders of home ties she had been asked to forget for a quarter
of a century. She felt half dead—and yet there remained a rebellious
spark of life in her. She expressed this most explicitly to Harriet
Beecher Stowe in April 1879, perhaps because Mrs. Stowe was far
away in America:

> Formerly everything was easy because the supreme human blessing
> of perfect love was always with me. Now everything seems difficult.
> And yet I feel as if I were blaspheming to write that– for the Past
> is not dead, and in all I do, it is a living influence. But I am still
> rebellious—not yet resigned to the cutting short of a full life, while
> so many half empty lives go on in vigorous uselessness. Submission
> will come—but it comes slowly.

She isolated herself by going to Witley Heights as "an experiment,"
so she wrote Barbara Bodichon; and she stayed there from 22 May to
the end of October. It was when she was making ready to leave that
she heard the news of John Blackwood's death. She was deeply affected, of course, but her own grief was still too overwhelming for her
to take in another sorrow. Besides, life was opening up for her again.
She wrote reassuringly to friends who worried about her being alone
at Witley except for servants. Barbara had visited her for a few days
in the fall; Sir James Paget, her physician and a very good friend, had
come to see her; and, most importantly, there was "a devoted friend
who is backwards and forwards continually to see that I lack nothing."
This was John Cross. Evidently the "experiment" of living for a while

at Witley had been to see him almost daily and away from the prying eyes of Londoners. She had fast become dependent upon his presence, and when he made a business trip to London, she wrote him: "Best loved and loving one—the sun it shines so cold, so cold, where there are no eyes to look love on me. I cannot bear to sadden one moment when we are together, but wenn Du bist nicht da I have often a bad time."

Her first and most impulsive reason for desiring to marry John Cross came from a fear of her own not unlike Gwendolen Harleth's: she was afraid of losing her power to love. After the marriage, she wrote Charles Lewes that she would still give up her own life willingly if George Henry could have her new happiness: "But marriage has seemed to restore me to my old self. I was getting hard, and if I had decided differently I think I should have become very selfish." A few weeks later, on 10 June, she wrote Mrs. Richard Congreve from Venice: "But instead of any former affection being displaced in my mind, I seem to have recovered the loving sympathy that I was in danger of losing. I mean that I had been conscious of a certain drying-up of tenderness in me, and that now the spring seems to have risen again."

Edith Simcox may also unwittingly have helped George Eliot toward her decision to marry Cross. As long as Lewes was alive, Edith, although suffering an agony of frustration, had restrained her passion to a harmless form of worship. In the early spring of 1880, however, she became boldly personal and importunate. Without Lewes at her side, George Eliot was peculiarly defenseless, for she herself was then longing for love and although she did not consciously desire it from a woman, she would have been aware that she was not wholly invulnerable. She began to talk firmly to Edith, stressing her own life-long preference for the love and the companionship of men. In her "Autobiography," Edith recorded the following scene as having occurred on 9 March after a discussion of marriage:

> She moved to a low chair opposite the fire to warm her feet and I ventured to kneel by her side. She was a little tired by the discussion and said I had taken it up too seriously, she only spoke in play. . . . I kissed her again and again and murmured broken words of love. She bade me not exaggerate. I said I didn't—nor could, and then scolded her for not being satisfied with letting me love her as I did—as in present reality—and proposing instead that I should save my love for some imaginary he. She said—expressly what she has often before implied to my distress—that the love of men and women for each other must always be more and better than any other and bade me not wish to be wiser than "God who made me"—in pious phrase. I hung over her caressingly and she bade me

not think too much of her—she knew all her own frailty and if I went on, she would have to confess some of it to me. Then she said—perhaps it would shock me—she had never all her life cared very much for women—it must seem monstrous to me—I said I had always known it. She went on to say, what I also knew, that she cared for the womanly ideal, sympathised with women and liked for them to come to her in their troubles, but while feeling near to them in one way, she felt far off in another—the friendship and intimacy of men was more to her. Then she tried to add what I had already imagined in explanation that when she was young, girls and women seemed to look on her as somehow "uncanny" while men were always kind. I kissed her again and said I did not mind—if she did not mind having holes kissed in her cheek—She said I gave her a very beautiful affection—and then again she called me a silly child. . . . I asked her to kiss me—let a trembling lover tell of the intense consciousness of the first deliberate touch of the dear one's lips. I returned the kiss to the lips that gave it and started to go—she waved me a farewell.

Such emotionally charged talk was in itself potentially dangerous. George Eliot must have realized that for Edith's sake, as well as her own, she needed to make some change in her life so decisive that Edith would not dare even hope that their relationship might become still more personal.

Exactly one month later, 9 April, George Eliot made two laconic statements in her Journal: "Sir James Paget came to see me. My marriage decided." She had consulted Paget about a matter other than health: she wanted to know if he thought that marriage to Cross would injure her literary reputation, and he gave her a reassuringly negative answer. But when Charles Lewes told Mrs. Richmond (later Lady) Ritchie of Paget's opinion that the marriage would make no difference to George Eliot's influence, Mrs. Ritchie sharply disagreed "and said of course it would, but it was better to be genuine than to have influence, and that I didn't suppose she imagined herself inspired, though her clique did."

As Thackeray's daughter and a writer herself, Mrs. Ritchie was in a better position than Sir James Paget to predict how readers would be affected. If many of them had reacted as did Alice James—sister to William and Henry—her opinion might have been proved correct. An ardent admirer of George Eliot, especially "as the creator of the immortal *Maggie*," Alice was disturbed by the suggestion of hypocrisy which the marriage conveyed to her. As she wrote in her now famous Diary: "On the subject of her marriage it is of course for an outsider criminal to say anything, but what a shock for her to say she felt as if her life were renewed and for her to express her sense of complacency in the vestry and church! What a betrayal of the much-mentioned 'perfect love' of the past!" Alice James, however, was by no means typical of her readers, a great number of whom would have rejoiced over their favorite author's achievement of respectability. As George Eliot brought out no new book and lived only seven months after her marriage, its effect upon the sale of her works cannot be estimated with enough accuracy to be meaningful. If William Blackwood had misgivings about the possible effect on sales, he kept them to himself. She had written him at the last minute to tell (but not consult) him about the impending marriage. He responded with characteristic Blackwood mildness, saying that her news did surprise him, "but I am very happy to hear it. . . ." His letter was perhaps the last she received with the salutation "My dear Mrs. Lewes," for he had unknowingly written it on her wedding day, 6 May.

Before that date arrived, she had twice reneged on her decision of 9 April because she thought the marriage "impossible." Her wavering was no doubt a reflection of her awareness that the marriage would be painful to those friends who had been equally close to both herself and Lewes and who had looked upon their relationship as a near-perfect union. She was also aware that she was expected always to act with a wisdom that transcended personal feeling. Only a fortnight before her marriage, she called upon the Burne-Joneses, and although she had not confided in them at the time, Georgiana remembered the visit well. It was the last time she saw George Eliot alive.

> Her manner was even gentler and more affectionate than usual, and she looked so unfit to do battle with daily life, that in spite of all her power a protecting feeling towards her rose in my heart. She seemed loth to go, and as if there was something that she would have said, yet did not. I have always remembered, though, the weariness she expressed of the way in which wisdom was attributed to her. "I am so tired of being set on a pedestal and expected to vent wisdom—I am only a poor woman" was the meaning of what she said if not the exact phrase, as I think it was.

Similarly after Cross, at George Eliot's request, had broken the news to Charles Lewes of the coming marriage, she reminded Charles that "if she hadn't been human with feelings and failings like other people, how could she have written her books." Mrs. Ritchie thought Charles "generous about the marriage" when he talked to her after it had taken place. Apparently, he was willing to look upon Cross (but two years his senior) as an elder brother:

> He says he owes everything to her, his Gertrude included, and that his father had no grain of jealousy in him, and only would have wished her happy. . . . He talked about his own mother in confidence, but his eyes all filled up with tears over George Eliot, and

altogether it was the strangest page of life I ever skimmed over. She is an honest woman, and goes in with all her might for what she is about.

Charles even undertook the uncomfortable task of informing Edith Simcox of the marriage, telling her that he "thought it would be well for the world as she might write again now." Edith was pained but not wholly surprised by the news. Not being able to trust herself, she said little to Charles, but later wrote in her "Autobiography" how she "rushed into the streets as soon as he was gone, went fiercely from school to school [she was a member of the London School Board], and through the evening fought off the tears. If I ever write another book I shall dedicate it to the loved memory of George Henry Lewes."

Other friends did not react so drastically, but as George Eliot had feared, several of them thought the marriage shockingly disloyal to the memory of Lewes. Georgiana Burne-Jones, for one, wrote: "Give me time—this was the one 'change' I was unprepared for—but that is my own fault—I have no right to impute to my friends what they do not claim." The faithful Brays and Sara Hennell expressed sympathetic interest, although Cara had to admit that the news was "startling and strange" and that George Eliot seemed to them "as rather in a dream-land." Only Barbara Bodichon responded with unqualified understanding and even enthusiasm: "Tell Johnny Cross I should have done exactly what he has done if you would have let me and I had been a man. / You see I know all love is so different that I do not see it unnatural to love in new ways—not to be unfaithful to any memory."

It is doubtful whether Cross had done much in the way of instigating this marriage, and some of George Eliot's vacillation over it as the set time approached may have resulted from her lack of conviction that it was right for him. He was forty and capable of knowing his own mind. Yet she would have realized that to revere her as a writer and a mother figure (while safely calling her "Aunt") was very different from taking her to be his lawfully wedded wife. He may indeed have been overwhelmed; although reported to be a fever, his illness while they were in Italy may have been a severe mental depression which led him to attempt to take his own life (the evidence for this is not explicit). The relatively few letters that she wrote after her marriage indicate no serious problem which might have disturbed it. But by then she had regained the self-mastery that had temporarily deserted her upon the death of Lewes, and with it she had resumed the obligation of appearing happy. Certainly she remained grateful for Cross's companionship and for her loving acceptance by his family. She had sisters and brothers once again; in signing her personal letters, she reverted to her childhood name of Mary Ann.

Any cause she may have had to regret her marriage would have been instantly obliterated when in Milan she received a letter from Isaac, who had been informed of her new status by Vincent Holbeche, the well-tried family solicitor. Isaac had written promptly "to break the long silence" (twenty-three years) and to congratulate her and Mr. Cross "upon the happy event." From anyone else such a reversal of attitude for so obvious a reason would have evoked her most scathing sarcasm. From her brother it was a matter for gratitude, and in a letter three times as long as his brief note she wrote to tell him that "it was a great joy to me to have your kind words of sympathy, for our long silence has never broken the affection for you which began when we were little ones." She unflinchingly admitted: "The only point to be regretted in our marriage is that I am much older than he, but his affection has made him choose this lot of caring for me rather than any other of the various lots open to him." The letter was signed: "Always your affectionate Sister / Mary Ann Cross." Isaac's approval and re-entry into her life—although she was never to see him—would presumably have lessened her need to explain and justify. This in turn would have weakened her motivation to write. If so, this did not alarm her as it would have earlier; the past had been restored by a means other than through her writing, and she had come home again.

Isaac traveled to London for her funeral on 29 December. To Oscar Browning he was the most noticeable among the mourners, "tall and slightly bent, his features recalling with a striking veracity the lineaments of the dead." At eleven o'clock, eight mourning carriages set out from 4 Cheyne Walk. Isaac was in the first one to follow the four-horse-drawn hearse; with him were John Cross, his brother William, and Charles Lewes. The weather—rain mixed with snow and gusty wind—was an inconvenience but did not detract from the impressiveness of the cortège, which was considerably lengthened as other carriages joined it on its way to Highgate Cemetery.

Isaac may not have known that there had been a movement to bury George Eliot in the Poets' Corner at Westminster Abbey. This was halted by those who—certain permission would be refused because of her relationship with Lewes—feared that the ensuing publicity would result in nothing but the revival of an old scandal. So she was to be put to rest near Lewes, although not in an adjoining grave. If Isaac had been informed of these hasty plans and revisions of plans necessitated by the suddenness of her death, it is unlikely that he was impressed one way or another. As far as he was concerned, he was decently attending the burial of his sister Mary Ann Evans Cross; George Eliot had never been real to him, and Marian Lewes most certainly had never existed.

Everyone else present—and the churchyard was crowded with people awaiting the cortège—was there to pay tribute to George Eliot, a great woman and a great novelist.

Notes

ABBREVIATIONS

Autobiography Herbert Spencer, *An Autobiography*, 2 vols. (New York: D. Appleton and Company, 1904).

Essays *Essays of George Eliot*, ed. Thomas Pinney (New York: Columbia University Press, 1963).

GE George Eliot (in both titles and comments).

GE & JC Gordon S. Haight, *George Eliot & John Chapman*, with Chapman's Diaries (New Haven: Yale University Press, 1940).

Goethe George Henry Lewes, *The Life and Works of Goethe* (London: J. M. Dent & Sons, Ltd., 1908). Reprinted, with an introduction by Victor Lange (New York: G. Ungar, 1974).

Haight, *GE* Gordon S. Haight, *George Eliot, A Biography* (New York and Oxford: Oxford University Press, 1968).

Letters *The George Eliot Letters*, 7 vols., ed. Gordon S. Haight (New Haven: Yale University Press, 1954–5).

Life *George Eliot's Life as Related in Her Letters and Journals*, 3 vols. Arranged and Edited by Her Husband, J. W. Cross (New York: Harper & Brothers, 1885).

Life, New ed. ————. 1 vol. (Edinburgh and London: W. Blackwood & Sons, 1887).

For other works, complete citations are given with the first mention.

PROLOGUE

Page
3 "a tub to throw to the whale" *Letters*, II, 292.
4 "a vague dream of mine" *Letters*, II, 406.
 Henry James "The Life of GE," in *Partial Portraits* (London: Macmillan and Company, 1888), 61.
5 "a Lock-up book" *Letters*, V, 123, n. 4a.
 " 'an increase of bad writing' " *Life*, I, 26.
6 "a miracle-legend" *Letters*, VII, 296.
 "the author of 'Romola' " *Life*, III, 59–60.
7 "kindly and majestic grace" Oscar Browning, *Life of GE* (London and New York: The Walter Scott Publishing Company, 1890, 18.
 "Thornton Lewes died" *Life*, III, 71.
 "could quench that bright flame" *Life*, III, 240.
8 "morning, afternoon, or evening" *Life*, III, 258.
 "Aunt" *Letters*, VII, 138.
 "a renovation of life" *Life*, III, 258–9.
 "as might be found practicable" *Life*, III, 279.
9 "sweet memories of her child-days" *Life*, I, 25.
 "I am stunned" *Letters*, VII, 351.
10 "her intimate converse" *Life*, III, 310.
11 "to wait . . . is moral starvation" Josiah Royce, "GE as a Religious Teacher," in *Fugitive Essays* (Cambridge: Harvard University Press, 1925), 281.
 "But, dear Barbara" *Letters*, III, 65.
 "lessons of my past life" *Letters*, III, 187.
12 "possess the world without belonging to it" *Life*, III, 310–11.
 "by reason of my sins and sorrows" *Letters*, III, 64.
 "that I have lived? I have had" *Life*, II, 78.
 "some one else would" K. A. McKenzie, *Edith Simcox and GE* (London: Oxford University Press, 1961), 116.
 work on the George Eliot *Life* McKenzie, 122.
13 "femininely in love" McKenzie, 7.
 In 1885 she again went McKenzie, 115, 128.
 "at his discretion" McKenzie, 105.
14 "too many letters" McKenzie, 105.
 "self-suppression strangled" McKenzie, 118.
 gave them to Sara Hennell McKenzie, 116.
15 "I entirely differ" *Letters*, III, 163–4.
 is not known *Letters*, III, 376, n. 6.
 only three weeks earlier *Letters*, III, 372.
 "temper of mind" *Letters*, III, 376.
16 "read with hard curiosity" *Letters*, VII, 340–1.
 "this desecrating fate" *Letters*, VII, 341.
17 buried with her *Letters*, VII, 227; Journal entry for 29 November 1879.
 Cross ignored *Letters*, I, xiv.
 as he had known her *Letters*, I, lxxv.
18 "a good likeness" *Life*, I, v, vi.
 "Each letter has been pruned" *Life*, I, vi.
 "fairest flowers of her inspiration" *Life*, I, v.
 "as I am myself" *Life*, I, viii, ix.
 " 'a Reticence' " *Letters*, I, xiv.
 "not so interesting" November 28, 1885 (No. 3031), 702. Also cf. White's "GE as I Knew Her," in *Last Pages from a Journal with Other Papers*, by Mark

Rutherford (London: Oxford University Press, 1915), 131 ff., and *The Auto-biography of Mark Rutherford, Dissenting Minister* (London: Trubner & Company, 1881, Oxford: Oxford University Press, 1936), in which GE is portrayed as Theresa. Throughout his novels there are many echoes of the profound influence GE had exerted upon him.

19 "trials and experiences" Browning, 13.
"a strong, passionate nature" Browning, 39.
"a friendship of fifteen years" Browning, 13.
"the blasphemers" McKenzie, 125.
"is not likely to misuse" McKenzie, 125.

20 "multiform life of man" Henry James, "The Life of GE," in *Partial Portraits*, 62.
"If any admirer" Edwin Percy Whipple, in *Recollections of Eminent Men* (Boston: Ticknor and Company, 1887), 381–2.

21 Blanche Colton Williams *GE* (New York: The Macmillan Company, 1936), xi.

22 "the whole puzzle" *Virginia Woolf & Lytton Strachey: Letters*, eds. Leonard Woolf and James Strachey (New York: Harcourt, Brace and Company, 1956), 112.
"publication of her *Life*" "GE," *The Common Reader*, First and Second Series Combined in One Volume (New York: Harcourt, Brace and Company, 1948), 229.
"erased from the literary mind" Cf. M. G. Devonshire, *The English Novel in France: 1839–1870* (London: University of London Press, Ltd., 1929), 365–75.

o n e—*The Primal Passionate Store*

27 "from his pockets" *Life*, I, 12–13.
28 "inseparable playfellows" *Life*, I, 12.
"a race of yeomen" *Life*, I, 10.
1788 and 1785 *Letters*, I, lxv and 3, n. 4.

29 "giving birth to Mary Ann" According to Haight, *GE*, 3, Christiana Evans also bore twin sons 16 March 1821, who lived only ten days. No source is given for this surprising new information. Is it possible that GE transposes these dead twins to Gritty Moss? (*Mill*, Book I, chapter 8).
"Miss Lathom's at Attleboro" *Life*, I, 10.
"close to Griff gates" *Life*, I, 10.
"his sister Frances" *Life*, I, 2. (It is obvious that by "last child" Cross means Mary Ann. If the twins were a reality, the effect of their brief existence upon Mary Ann and the family in general cannot now be determined.)
"the Arbury estate" *Life*, I, 2.

30 "all my memories" *Letters*, IV, 131.
clarify his meaning Browning, 14.
"no idea" *Letters*, I, 157.

31 slow in learning to read *Life*, I, 10–11.
"a strong family affection" *Life*, I, 22.
"the chief favourite" *Life*, I, 12.
"prototypes of the Dodsons" *Life*, I, 10.

32 "very jealous" *Life*, I, 11.
33 "meek and passive" *Letters*, I, 117.
"her father's" *Life*, I, 12.
"a true history" *Life*, I, 23.
Mary Ann's precocity *Life*, I, 13.

34 "Nov. 22, 1819" *Life*, I, 1.

34 "latent Conservative bias" *Life*, I, 4.
35 "domestic relations" *Life*, I, 9.
George Eliot confirmed this *Letters*, III, 99.
36 "his memory" *Letters*, III, 169.
"several counties" *Letters*, III, 168.
"with the farmers" Charles and Caroline Bray, quoted in Newton Arvin, ed., *The Heart of Hawthorne's Journals* (Boston and New York: Houghton Mifflin Company, 1929), 328.
37 "for my sake" *Life*, I, 13–14.
summer of 1836 *Life*, I, 22.
3 February of that year *Letters*, I, 3, n. 4.
" 'one mother' " *Life*, I, 22.
"before he married my mother" *Letters*, III, 174.
18 August in that year *Letters*, I, 4–5.
38 "the property of the writer" McKenzie, 130.
no account McKenzie, 116.
major gap *Life*, I, 28.
"towards the aged" *Letters*, II, 438.
39 "natural force" *Life*, I, 9.
"thoroughly attached to her" *Life*, I, 10.
"the highest degree" *Life*, I, 11.
40 "religious training of her children" *Life*, New ed., 736.
"Mrs. Poyser vein" *Life*, I, 9–10.
"my own mint" *Letters*, III, 25.
"family tradition" *GE*, 10.
42 "her bedroom" *Life*, I, 15.
"as much as possible" *Letters*, I, 317.
"spoiled child" *Letters*, I, 316.
"by a tempest" *Letters*, I, 329.
43 "most personal utterances" The date of actual writing of this poem is uncertain. It was first submitted to Blackwood in 1878 (nine years after the writing of "Brother and Sister") for inclusion in the Cabinet Edition.
45 "best loved subjects" *Letters*, V, 403.
for £300 Williams, *GE*, 243, and *Life*, III, 63.
46 completed the sonnets *Letters*, V, 53.
"like all of us sinners" *Letters*, V, 54.
"pure, generous feeling" *Letters*, V, 71.
47 "its future publicity" *Letters*, VI, 372.
"the imputed fact" *Letters*, V, 403.
48 "three to five" *Life*, I, 11.
"love for her brother" *Life*, I, 10.
the second and third Williams, *GE*, 246.
50 "the meaning of which is unknown" *Letters*, I, 173.
"Few women, I fear" *Life*, I, 346.
51 "agree not to talk audibly" *Letters*, III, 427–8.
52 "relinquishing her companionship" Williams, *GE*, 22.
"chief actress" *Letters*, I, 22.
54 "anything worth the doing" *Letters*, II, 155–6.
"being meditated" *Letters*, III, 428.
55 "faith in the future" *Letters*, III, 66.
"a mere recipient" McKenzie, 125–6.
"increase her doubts" *Letters*, IV, 58.
57 "liked playing so much better" *Life*, I, 11.
"everything she could lay hands on" *Life*, I, 15.
58 "from Tully Veolan" *Life*, I, 16.

59 "Different though the sexes are"   Virginia Woolf, *Orlando* (New York: New American Library of World Literature, Inc., 1960), 123.
60 "Her imagination"   Anthony Trollope, *An Autobiography* (New York: Dodd, Mead & Company, 1927), 213.
61 "in her childhood"   *Life*, I, 11–12.
   "she was not unhappy"   *Life*, I, 12.
62 "external happiness"   *Letters*, VI, 310.
63 "for your love?"   McKenzie, 102.
   "too much plum cake"   *Letters*, I, 173.
   "images of robbers, wild beasts, ghosts or demons"   George Henry Lewes, *Problems of Life and Mind*, First Series, 2 vols. (Boston: James R. Osgood and Company, 1874–5), II, 221.
   "the subjective factor alone"   *Problems . . .* , First Series, II, 219.
64 "doing and learning"   *Life*, I, 12.
   "with his sister"   *Life*, I, 15.
   "no ordinary child"   *Life*, I, 17.
   "the old home-life"   *Life*, I, 22.
65 "strong High-Church views"   *Life*, I, 23.

т w о—*Root of Piety*

69 "to titter unreproved"   *Letters*, I, 6–7.
   "hunting sketches"   *Life*, I, 29.
   "society was a danger"   *Life*, I, 23.
71 " 'charitable undertaking' "   *Life*, I, 20.
   "exemplary housewife"   *Life*, I, 24.
   "intellectual life of her own"   *Life*, I, 24.
   "very discouraging"   *Life*, I, 24.
   "slavery of being a girl"   *Life*, I, 25; *Daniel Deronda*, Book VII, chapter 1.
   "the home duties"   *Life*, I, 25.
72 "*walled-in* world"   *Letters*, I, 71.
73 religious, philosophical, or social   I realize that this statement will arouse disagreement, especially concerning Positivism. Several eminent George Eliot students have attempted, with varying degrees of success, to show that she accepted this as her own view without major qualifications.
   "all in all"   *Life*, I, 11.
   "by adoption"   *Letters*, I, 46.
   "power of sympathy"   Browning, 39.
74 "easier than moderation"   *Letters*, I, 6.
   " 'watching her elders' "   Browning, 17–18. (He gives no source for his own quotation.)
   "to grown-up people"   *Letters*, I, 41, n. 3.
   "superior to themselves"   *Life*, I, 19.
75 "asunder at every breeze"   *Letters*, I, 6.
   "pursue my way"   *Letters*, I, 112–13.
76 "principal correspondent"   *Life*, I, 15.
   "intimacy she indulged in"   *Life*, I, 17.
   "worldly amusement"   *Letters*, I, lxxii.
77 "leading to a reaction"   McKenzie, 129.
   "aspiring little daughter"   McKenzie, 129.
   "like an elder sister"   McKenzie, 129.
   "as intimately as I once did"   *Letters*, I, lxxiii.
   "any schoolfellow"   McKenzie, 129.
78 Johnsonian English   E.g., *Letters*, I, lxxii.

79 "considerable deal of froth" *Letters*, I, 21.
80 "ask pardon" *Letters*, I, 66.
   "feelings flow" *Letters*, I, 57.
   "in preference to it" *Letters*, I, 17.
   "regularly disgraced myself" *Letters*, I, 41.
   "a dubious character" *Letters*, I, 41.
81 "the occasion of one" *Letters*, I, 27.
   "earth's gifts alone, / Farewell!" *Letters*, I, 28.
   "for heaven's use" *Life*, I, 43.
   "The beautiful heavens" *Letters*, I, 66.
   "the *Christian Observer*" *Life*, I, 42–3.
82 "successively contain" *Letters*, I, 44–5.
   "encouraged to believe" *Letters*, I, 40.
   "slow fingers and slower head" *Letters*, I, 50–1.
83 "engraved on my amulet" *Letters*, I, 51.
   "chronicles of memory" *Letters*, I, 108–9.
   "one epoch of my life to another" *Letters*, II, 406.
84 " 'sober-suited morn' has dissipated" *Letters*, I, 108.
   16 March 1839 *Letters*, I, 21–4.
   " 'Truth is strange' " *Letters*, I, 21–4.
85 "I am I confess" *Letters*, I, 21–4.
   after the essay-letter *Letters*, I, 30.
   "that must be cast down" *Letters*, I, 65–6.
87 "distinguished position" *Life*, I, 10.
   "agony of tears" *Life*, I, 18–19.
   "elevating in its tendency" *Letters*, I, 13.
88 "even against intemperance" *Letters*, I, 9–10.
   "devoid of the capacity" Leslie Stephen, *GE*, 13 and n. 1.
   "especially oratorio" *Life*, I, 32–3.
89 "just been delighted" *Letters*, I, 68.
90 "rarely if ever heard" *Autobiography*, I, 458.
91 "the child's affection" *Life*, I, 10.
   he deleted it *Life*, I, 37.
92 "The self-deceptive practice" *Letters*, I, 24.
   "no corresponding feeling" *Letters*, I, 19.
   "ever struggling ambition" *Letters*, I, 73.
94 "Your letter this morning" *Letters*, I, 84.
   "character of a friend" *Letters*, I, 90.
   "I have a world more to say" *Letters*, I, 92.
   "Write my dear Veronica" *Letters*, I, 94, 95.
95 "a good type of its parent" *Letters*, I, 97.
   "as God approves" *Letters*, I, 99.
   "How should I love" *Letters*, I, 102.
   "details about yourself" *Letters*, I, 105.
96 "congenial to love" *Letters*, I, 108–9.
   "at least at Christmas?" *Letters*, I, 111.
   "more of this trash" *Letters*, I, 111, 112.
   "restore me to Mary Ann" *Letters*, I, 116.
   "my thoughts and feelings" *Letters*, I, 116.
97 "Love and *practically* remember" *Letters*, I, 116–17.
   "confusion in my last letter" *Letters*, I, 119.
   "near a city" *Letters*, I, 120, 121.
   "Went to Trinity Church" *Letters*, I, 124.
   "school at Nuneaton" *Letters*, I, 124.
98 "This was Paul's idea" *Letters*, I, 127.

98 Bray's *Philosophy of Necessity* *Letters*, I, 127, n. 8.
99 "her resurrection" *Letters*, I, 125.
"belong to the Church" *Letters*, I, 156–7.
"the temporary smart" *Letters*, I, 127.
100 own state of mind *Letters*, I, 139–40.
"influencing her for good" McKenzie, 129–30.
"busy at home" *Letters*, I, 230, n. 2.
101 Maria had related it McKenzie, 130.
"Marian always resented this" McKenzie, 131.
"old love still existing" *Letters*, I, lxxiii.
not use it in the *Life* McKenzie, 130.
before her own death *Letters*, VII, 331.
"to pen it all" *Letters*, I, lxxiii.
102 "lasted for some years" *Autobiography*, I, 125.
which ... Chapman accepted *Letters*, II, 258, n. 7.
"the middle and lower classes" *Essays*, 317, 318.

T H R E E—*The Dire Years*

107 "twenty third birthday" *Letters*, I, 24.
108 the entire paragraph *Life*, I, 39.
"animal matter in the universe" *Letters*, I, 50.
"scenery of a Diorama" *Letters*, I, 50.
"will be our situation" *Letters*, I, 60.
"leave the nest" *Letters*, I, 68.
"*grown in* to my affections" *Letters*, I, 71.
109 "again into habit" *Letters*, I, 86.
stormy March day *Letters*, I, 89, n. 1.
"view rather sublime" *Letters*, VI, 45–6.
"a confirmed Londoner" Browning, 40.
"respecting my destination" *Letters*, I, 51.
110 "most important epoch in my life" *Life*, I, 115.
"coming to Coventry" *Life*, I, 114.
" 'more interested in you than ever' " *Life*, I, 114.
111 "does not see any danger" *Life*, New ed., 740.
"or even to religion" *Life*, I, 115.
"opened my heart to her" *Life*, I, 114.
"quite lawful amusements" *Life*, I, 114.
112 "trembled with her agitation" *Life*, New ed., 737.
" 'is himself responsible' " *Life*, New ed., 745–6.
113 "I did not see" *Life*, New ed., 746.
"in favour of orthodox doctrines" *Life*, New ed., 737.
"she had not read" *Life*, New ed., 738.
114 "place in its hands" *Life*, New ed., 739.
" 'found in it' " *Life*, New ed., 739.
"honey from his pages" *Letters*, I, 22.
"ultra-good people" *Letters*, I, 260–1.
115 "final settlement in London" *Life*, New ed., 746.
famous Sunday soirees *Letters*, V, 385, n. 3.
"will not avow it" *Letters*, I, 306.
"impertinent curiosity" *Letters*, I, 306.
"sit down etc." *Letters*, I, 309.
"after having done it" *Letters*, I, 315.
116 "sent up to Rosehill" Charles Bray, *Phases of Opinions and Experience*

during a Long Life: An Autobiography (London: Longmans, Green [1885]), 70.

116 " 'shut that door' " *Life*, I, 116.
"no allusions made to them" Bray, 73.

117 "our heretical minds" Bray, 76.
"cherished home associations" Bray, 48.
"exceedingly uncomfortable" Bray, 48.
"Unitarian stand-points" Bray, 49.

118 "to fall back upon" Bray, 49.
"any place of worship" Bray, 49.
"in heaven or earth" Bray, 73.
"a model of moral excellence" Bray, 76.
"not a requisite to moral excellence" *Letters*, I, 45.
"the most religious person I know" *Life*, I, 115.

119 "well he should perhaps" *Letters*, I, 132.
"*schooled* Mary Ann" *Letters*, I, 129, n. 4.

120 "not belong to the Church" *Letters*, I, 156–7.
"Brothers and Sisters with their children" *Letters*, I, 129.
unintentionally given him pain *Letters*, I, 129.
"even for your sake" *Letters*, I, 128.

121 "I *ought* to do so" *Letters*, I, 129.
"support herself by teaching" *Life*, I, 75.
"back again very soon" *Letters*, I, 132.
went to Griff on 23 March *Letters*, I, 133, n. 5.

122 "how he seems disposed" *Letters*, I, 133–4.
"instead of an integral part" *Letters*, I, 138.
"when writing the 'Inquiry' " *Letters*, I, 138, n. 7.

123 "and Miss Rebecca Franklin" *Life*, I, 82.
"Mary Ann went with me to day" *Letters*, I, 138, n. 7.
"dictates of conscience" *Letters*, I, 127.
"voluntarily leaving you" *Letters*, I, 129.

124 "to the end of her life" Browning, 24.
"avoided with a little management" *Life*, I, 82.

125 "took the form of principles" *Letters*, I, 161–3.
"less credit with it" *Life*, New ed., 745.

126 "in accordance with his own" *Life*, New ed., 741.
"that quite oppressed her" *Life*, New ed., 743.
"a mystery she cannot unravel" *Letters*, I, 308.
"at work collecting material" *Letters*, I, 308, n. 1.

127 "*burning power of sympathy*" Browning, 39. (Emphasis mine.)
"to be invulnerable" *Life*, New ed., 745.
"are still invited to dinner" *Letters*, II, 214.

128 "foolish facility for mastery" *Essays*, 324.
began writing "Amos Barton" on 23 September *Letters*, II, 407, n. 3.
"some one to lean upon" Bray, 75.
"with Charles Bray, 'like lovers' " McKenzie, 131.

129 "withdraw me from myself" *Letters*, I, 136.
"arrange for its publication" *Letters*, I, 136.
"four hundred pages to no purpose" *Letters*, I, 142.

130 "I trust shall not be so again" *Letters*, I, 142.
"linked to your remembrance" *Letters*, I, 154.
"for not returning them before" *Letters*, I, 157–8.

131 "most laconic note that can serve the purpose" *Letters*, I, 158.
to absorb her later Cf. *Letters*, I, 158, n. 8.
"it would disappoint her" *Letters*, I, 158, n. 8.
"under comparison with the original" *Letters*, I, 171, n. 1.

132 "undertake the completion of it" Bray, 77.
before he met George Eliot *GE & JC*, 186 and n. 193. Oddly enough, what Haight literally footnotes has nothing to do with the matter; the following paragraph in his text is more to the point.
"the loss of his only daughter" Bray, 77.

133 "Rather a learned pun" *Letters*, I, 164.
"a longer leave of absence" *Letters*, I, 165.
"yet three weeks" *Letters*, I, 166.
"I hardly know" *Letters*, I, 166-7.

134 "fault lay with her alone" *GE & JC*, p. 186.
"as her permanent home" *GE & JC*, p. 186.
the necessary conventionalisms *GE & JC*, p. 186.
"same tune you are playing" *Letters*, I, 194.
"laughed at him in my sleeve" *Letters*, I, 225.

135 her own expense and sent to him *Letters*, I, 224.
"an anathema maranatha" *Letters*, I, 232. I Cor., 16:22—"If any man love not the Lord Jesus Christ, let him be Anathema Maranatha."
"I really want this" *Letters*, I, 231-2.
impossible to accept *Letters*, I, 236, n. 5.
"exorcised of Dr. Brabant" *Letters*, I, 363.
" 'Overland Route' " *Letters*, I, 364.

136 "better left to imagination" *Letters*, II, 171.
"I must give you some account" *Letters*, I, 183-4.

137 "sweet little creatures, as she calls them" *Letters*, I, 186, n. 7.
"against the grain with her" *Letters*, I, 186.

138 "intellectual and religious loves" *Letters*, I, 185-6.
"she expects to see" *Letters*, I, 187, n. 1.
"at least for the present" *Letters*, I, 188.
she never did so *Letters*, I, l [Roman numeral 50].
"the youthful sap left" *Letters*, I, 189.

139 "one item of his" *Letters*, I, 189.
"the arm of man" McKenzie, 131.

140 "metaphysical speculations" Elizabeth Haldane, *GE and Her Times* (New York: D. Appleton & Company, 1927, 46.
"klarsprechende beloved" *Letters*, I, 240.
"Solomon's Song" *Letters*, I, 279.
"would be intolerable to her" *Letters*, I, 171, n. 1.

141 forgot their promise Mathilde Blind, *GE* (Boston: Little, Brown, and Company, 1904, New ed.), 39, 45.
"fail in his engagement altogether" *Letters*, I, 190-1.
"one's whole soul" *Letters*, I, 191.
"in that particular" *Letters*, I, 213-14.

142 "a perfect theory in itself" *Letters*, I, 203.
"an idea of his earliest followers" David Friedrich Strauss, *The Life of Jesus, Critically Examined*. Tr. from the fourth German ed. (New York: Calvin Blanchard 1855. Reprinted verbatim from the London edition of Chapman Brothers), 39, 69.
"the Messianic ideas" Strauss, 69.
"the object of glorification" Strauss, 299.

143 "will be the remainder?" *Letters*, I, 236-8.
"this kind of Messiah" Strauss, 636.
"*after* his death" Strauss, 636.
"made her endure it" *Letters*, I, 206.
"charming view over the country" *Life*, New ed., 70, n. 1.
"frontispiece for the Strauss" *Letters*, I, 206, n. 8.

144 "historical facts" Strauss, 4.
"Father, Nature and Spirit" Strauss, 895.
"a Methodist, dear Sara" *Letters*, I, 228.
"essence of human feeling" Ludwig Feuerbach, *The Essence of Christianity*, Tr. from the second German ed. by Marian Evans (Boston: Houghton, Mifflin & Company, 2nd ed., 1881), 140. See also the more recent edition with an introductory essay by Karl Barth and a foreword by H. Richard Niebuhr (New York: Harper & Row, 1957).
"the goal of religion" Feuerbach, 145.
"I everywhere agree" *Letters*, II, 153.

145 "devout and wicked together" *Letters*, I, 218.
"review of Strauss" *Letters*, I, 227, n. 4.
"eke out his metaphor" *Letters*, I, 227.

146 "*must* leave out" *Letters*, II, 153.
follows the original closely *Letters*, II, 154; also 153, n. 4.
"belongs to a translation" *Letters*, I, 321.
"subject long enough" *Essays*, 211.

147 "active without endurance" Bray, 74.
"sects and denominations" Bray, 75.
"interfere with her judgment" Bray, 75.

148 "writing her novel" *Letters*, I, 223, n. 4.
first Continental sojourn *Letters*, II, 406–7.
Pinney calls "moralia" *Essays*, 13.
"art is to the artist?" *Essays*, 19.

149 "and therefore no poet" *Essays*, 14–15.
of Swift and Fielding *Essays*, 22–6.

150 "record of events and feelings" *Letters*, I, 252.
"as a stomach" *Letters*, II, 137.
"a chivalrous feeling" *Letters*, I, 253, 254.
"sympathy, all-embracing love" *Letters*, I, 251.

151 "to *be* but to *utter*" *Letters*, I, 255.
"the sheets for Strauss" *Letters*, I, 176.
"a rest to her mind" *Letters*, I, 280, n. 6.
"delicious valleys for me" *Letters*, I, 277.
"one book—Rousseau's 'Confessions'" *Letters*, I, xv.

152 "wizard-like Armenian attire" *Essays*, 19–20.
"to deep reflection" *Life*, New ed., 742–3.
"teaching me any new belief" *Letters*, I, 277.

153 *La nouvelle Héloïse* *Letters*, VI, 265 and n. 3.
"Jean Jacques' garden" *Letters*, VII, 285.
"those six pages will suggest" *Letters*, I, 277–8.
"less voluptuous" *Letters*, II, 91.

154 "the heart of England" Browning, 147.
"truth will permit" *Letters*, I, 312.

155 "I am lost in amazement" *Letters*, II, 19–20.

156 "strength or spirit to do it" *Letters*, II, 152.
"tough metaphysical German" *Letters*, II, 164, n. 8.
"It seems very ungracious" *Letters*, II, 164.

157 "all live of each other" *Letters*, III, 90, n. 4.
"made her very unhappy" *Letters*, III, 90, n. 5.
"*half-doz* congenial minds" *Letters*, II, 94–5.

158 "and yet, I can't help wanting" *Letters*, III, 90.
"wistfully and very lonely" *Letters*, III, 95–6.
"part of our thought" *Letters*, III, 97.

159 "Farewell, meine liebe" *Letters*, III, 98.

FOUR—*A Self That Self Restrains*

163 "to read to him." *Life*, I, 101.
   "to mould a personality" *Letters*, I, 264.
164 "even for an hour" *Letters*, I, 262–3.
   "eighth or ninth day" *Letters*, I, 266–7.
   "destitute of contact" *Letters*, I, 264.
   "The kind words" *Letters*, I, 268.
165 "She is much disappointed" *Letters*, I, 199–200, n. 8.
   "good of her health" *Letters*, I, 100–200, n. 8.
   "father was going on well" *Letters*, I, 201.
   "her immediate presence" Bray, 75.
   "Strauss was taken up again" *Life*, I, 97–8.
166 "thoroughly cared for" *Life*, I, 148.
   "expressions of kindness" *Letters*, I, 272.
   "in a state of imbecility" *Letters*, I, 272, n. 8.
167 "be here again tonight" *Letters*, I, 284 and n. 2.
   "my moral nature were gone" Browning, 30.
   not an exclamation point *Letters*, I, 284.
   Cross, who deleted it *Life*, I, 148.
   "purifying restraining influence" *Letters*, I, 284.
   "queer monster on a small scale" *Letters*, I, 239–40.
168 "at Geneva for the winter" Bray, 75.
   "any perilous places" Mathilde Blind, *GE* (Boston: Roberts Brothers, 1883), 66–7.
   "remain behind at Geneva" Blind, 67–8.
   "in a romantic continental town" *Letters*, I, 261.
   "of my relations" *Letters*, I, 295.
169 "*warming up* by letters first" *Letters*, I, 298.
   "to Isaac's writing" *Letters*, I, 298.
   "yet care about me" *Letters*, I, 303–4.
   "The blessed compensation" *Letters*, I, 313.
   "my future address" *Letters*, I, 313.
   "from them in England" *Letters*, I, 314–15.
   "a real interest in me" *Letters*, I, 328.
   "great addition to my happiness" *Letters*, I, 322.
170 "more of cleverness" *Letters*, I, 317.
   "You will be amused" *Letters*, I, 330.
   "father and brother both" *Letters*, I, 316.
   "undisciplined as ever" *Letters*, I, 328.
   "delicate-minded Philip Wakem" Blind, 70.
   when he stayed at Rosehill *Life*, I, 183.
   "beginning of April" *Letters*, I, 328.
   "cannot afford the journey" *Letters*, I, 330.
171 "with sledge travelling" *Letters*, VI, 129.
   "after his death" *Letters*, I, lxiv and n. 7.
   "loved and prized Polly" *Letters*, III, 308–9.
   "weight of eighty winters" *Life*, I, 151, 167.
   "not too intimate" *Life*, I, 151.
172 "the end of her life" *Life*, I, 180.
173 "my mistake if it be one" *Letters*, I, 307.
   "till Wednesday morning" *Letters*, I, 307.
   "a vox Dei" *Letters*, I, 320.

174 "disappointment for herself" *Life*, I, 181.
"and *le spleen*" *Life*, I, 181.
a round of family visits *Life*, I, 181; *Letters*, I, 332, n. 5.
"than at Geneva" *Letters*, I, 333.
"who don't want me" *Letters*, I, 335.
175 "I think so more than ever" *Letters*, I, 336.
"a fine poetical genius" *Letters*, I, 231.
176 their marriage in 1843 For typical entries on these matters, see *GE & JC*
under 1 Jan. 1851 and 24 July 1860 (123–4, 245–6).
"life of another" *Letters*, I, 322.
rather than 1819 *Letters*, II, 79, n. 9.
177 "but formal and studied" *GE & JC*, 129.
Ernest and Beatrice A third child, Walter, had been deaf and dumb from
birth and was being reared by Susanna's brother, Bellamy Brewitt. (*Letters*,
II, 35, n. 6, 7.)
"Elisabeth's position there" *GE & JC*, 18.
178 "with Mr. and Mrs. Holland" *GE & JC*, 135–6.
"in love with each other" *GE & JC*, 140–2.
"she dislikes her" *GE & JC*, 142.
179 "in the Autumn" *GE & JC*, 129.
"what she herself said" *GE & JC*, 130.
180 "of all I issue" *GE & JC*, 130.
"kinder to mortals" *Letters*, I, 225.
181 "going to have?" *Letters*, I, 225, n. 1.
"L.L. looking person" *Letters*, 1, 337.
"I did not like her" G. S. Layard, *Mrs. Lynn Linton* (London: Methuen,
1901), 251.
"is not yet terminated" *Letters*, I, 344.
182 "£5 as compensation" *Letters*, I, 346; also *GE & JC*, 140.
"potter's wessel" *Letters*, I, 344.
"accorded me some justice" *GE & JC*, 143 and n. 48.
183 "very very sad" *GE & JC*, 147.
"sense of extreme loneliness" *GE & JC*, 148.
"accept no remuneration" *Letters*, I, 348.
"the sight of M's letter" *GE & JC*, 155.
"a most singular mélange of love-making" *GE & JC*, 88–9.
184 "also be my last" *GE & JC*, 173.
"so dazzling as it once was" *GE & JC*, 163.
"applied along the spine" *GE & JC*, 114.
"when I attempted" *GE & JC*, 117.
185 "shy calm and affectionate" *GE & JC*, 171.
"pain she has caused" *GE & JC*, 172.
186 "She wept bitterly" *GE & JC*, 172.
"suitable in October" *GE & JC*, 172.
"with the Prospectus" *GE & JC*, 174.
"I sent it to press" *GE & JC*, 174.
187 "and diffuse peace" *GE & JC*, 173.
"anything they wish" *GE & JC*, 174.
"chiding letter to Susanna" *GE & JC*, 175.
"animadversions on the Prospectus" *GE & JC*, 176.
188 "Miss Evans comes to London" *GE & JC*, 179.
"with love and sweetness" *GE & JC*, 182.
from George Eliot to Chapman *Letters*, I, 253–5.
he detached and destroyed *GE & JC*, 182, n. 180.

188 "living torment to my soul"   *GE & JC*, 182.
"intense and morbid egoism"   *GE & JC*, 183.
"residence during the winter"   *GE & JC*, 201.
189 "in tears this evening"   *GE & JC*, 201–2.
"his wishes tend"   *GE & JC*, 184–5.
"at the beginning of the Diary"   *GE & JC*, 184, n. 189.
"I may do otherwise"   *GE & JC*, 213.
190 "cannot command his own peace"   *GE & JC*, 214.
"hardly expect elsewhere, but—"   *Letters*, II, 6.
"a month or two next quarter"   *Letters*, II, 12.
191 "the rest of my days"   *Letters*, II, 42.
"a wretched helpmate"   *Letters*, II, 48.
"going to crush one"   *Letters*, II, 54.
"out of our hands"   *Letters*, II, 83.
"where I am or what I do"   *Letters*, II, 93.
192 "the union with Mr. Lewes"   Browning, 37.
"have done with that affair"   *Letters*, II, 127–8.
"prelude to bankruptcy"   *Letters*, II, 163.
until 1907 The most complete and interestingly informative account of Chapman's intricate relationship with the *Westminster* is given in *GE & JC*, 3–119.
193 "the back of No. 142"   William Hale White, in *The Athenaeum* (28 Nov. 1885), 702.
"nothing to it etc. etc!!!"   *Letters*, II, 33.
"*have* their organs already"   *GE & JC*, 45.
194 "not surpassed by any Review"   *GE & JC*, 63.
"'the history of opinion'"   *GE & JC*, 71.
"as I am not likely"   *Letters*, II, 128.
195 "any half as good"   *Letters*, II, 130–1.
"my relation to him"   *Letters*, II, 179.
196 writing the *Clerical Scenes*   *GE & JC*, 85.
described it to Charles Bray   *Letters*, II, 199.
"truly representing German"   *Letters*, II, 141.
"contributing to hell-paving"   *Letters*, II, 51.
"reduced by evaporation"   *Letters*, II, 206.
"you will like that best"   *Letters*, II, 207.
197 "their Roman predecessors"   *Letters*, II, 207, n. 2.
worth publishing at all   *GE & JC*, 86.
"a reward of labour"   *Letters*, II, 208.
October number of the *Westminster*   *Letters*, II, 205, n. 9, 207, n. 3.
"the courage for them!"   *Letters*, II, 489.
"no ground for my negations but inability"   *Letters*, II, 420.
198 "further gossip on the subject"   *Letters*, II, 494, n. 7.
correspondingly curt   *Letters*, II, 494.
"not . . . willingly see him again"   *Letters*, II, 505, n. 3.
"written two months ago"   *Letters*, III, 3.
"Till then, I remain"   *Letters*, III, 3–4.
199 "no longer much weight"   *Autobiography*, II, 44–5.
"not the author of 'Adam Bede'"   *Letters*, III, 12, 13.
"substitute for lost friends"   *Letters*, III, 123.
200 "in compensation for lost friends"   *Letters*, III, 123.
"pleasure in my chagrin"   *Letters*, III, 124.
"on account of his coolness"   *Letters*, III, 49, n. 6.
"looking 'wonderfully well'"   *Letters*, III, 71.
"cup of coffee in consequence"   *Letters*, III, 49.

200 "Squashed that idea" *GE& JC*, 196.
201 hid him away in Edinburgh Anne Fremantle, *GE* (New York: The Macmillan Company, 1933), 105.
202 "never the agreeable things" *Letters*, III, 49, n. 6.
203 "the spirit distilled from it" *Autobiography*, I, 422–3. Elizabeth Haldane *GE and Her Times*, (p. 80), for some unexplained reason, assumes that GE herself was the young woman in this jocular affair. But the suggestion fits neither the context of the letter as a whole nor Spencer's itemized description of the young woman.
204 "most of the evening" *Autobiography*, I, 457.
 "afforded by the performance" *Autobiography*, I, 457.
 "discussing many things" *Autobiography*, I, 462.
 "neither . . . was true" *Autobiography*, I, 462.
205 "altogether very pleasing" *Letters*, II, 37.
 "better for being with him" *Letters*, II, 22.
 "the chimney piece for general inspection" *Letters*, II, 35.
206 "she proposed to me" Williams, *GE*, 81.
 "continually perturbed" *Autobiography*, II, 131.
207 "it proved unsuitable" *Autobiography*, I, 578.
 "death would part them" *Autobiography*, II, 375.
208 sentence in its entirety *Life*, I, 200.
 his changed view My summary of Spencer's attempted negotiation with Cross has been drawn from Haight's biography of GE, pp. 121–2. A less full, but nonetheless interesting, account is in Williams, p. 81.
 "into a cordial friendship" Blind, 103. This biography was (and still deserves to be) highly respected. It was included in Little, Brown, and Company's publication of the Foleshill Edition of GE's complete works. The 1904 edition was an attempt to update it by adding material gleaned from Cross's *Life*, Browning's biography, and Leslie Stephen's 1888 article for the *DNB*. The we-are-not-in-love letter is quoted in the Appendix (p. 303) as it had appeared in the first American edition of the *Life*,
209 "give to the world" Browning, 83.
 "nothing but his 'image' " Haight, *GE*, 122.
 "traits were of the highest" *Letters*, II, 520.
210 "her mental qualities only" Haight, *GE*, 113.
 "helping with a great work" *GE & JC*, 50.
 "known to all the world" *Autobiography*, II, 429.
 " 'tant pis pour les fleurs' " *Letters*, II, 40.
 "fish with a generalization" *Autobiography*, II, 236–7.
211 " 'the most extraordinary kind' " *GE & JC*, 119.
 " 'in the year 1820 etc.' " *Letters*, II, 165.
 "ill health here intervened" *Autobiography*, II, 196.
212 "for what she had done" Fremantle, *GE*, 56–7.
 "Sunday-afternoon assemblies" *Autobiography*, II, 236.
213 "not . . . expect to see her for three weeks" *Autobiography*, II, 428.
215 "delightful *camaraderie* in everything" *Letters*, II, 29.
 "forthwith dropped the subject" *Autobiography*, I, 459.
 "nor afterwards" *Autobiography*, I, 459.
216 "rest of his life exploring" Wilfred Stone, *Religion and Art of William Hale White* (Stanford, California: Stanford University Press [1954]), 11.
217 " a little more thorough" Stone, 50.
 "dis-satisfaction and disquiet" Stone, 52.
 "heal us of self-despisings" *Autobiography of Mark Rutherford* (Oxford, 1936), 157.
218 "by heavenly angels" Stone, 193–4.

218 "throughout his writings" Stone, 194.
"had known at the Chapmans' " Stone, 193, n. 4.
her most personal friends *Letters*, VI, 248.
"her old favorite" *Letters*, VI, 278–9.
"otherwise than sincerely" *Letters*, II, 13–14.
the sale of the novel had decreased *Letters*, VI, 279, n. 2.

219 "the keenest flash" Stone, 193.
" 'worship that woman' " Stone, 130.

220 "and seen my brother" *Letters*, II, 73.
"for work and economy" *Letters*, II, 74.
"all things considered" *Letters*, II, 75.
"never receive a kindness from him" *Letters*, II, 75.

221 "not in a very large way" *Letters*, II, 75.
"a great help" *Letters*, II, 75.
"from morning till night" *Letters*, II, 97.
"What do you think" *Letters*, II, 97.
"my labour and affection" *Letters*, II, 97.
"regret the change" *Letters*, II, 97.
"at variance with her hopes" *Letters*, II, 134.

222 "hotbed of fever for a time" *Letters*, II, 336–7.
"as more truthful" *Letters*, II, 51.
"the fault of the place" *Letters*, II, 31–2.

223 " 'I firmly believe' etc." *Letters*, II, 59.
"a back and front drawing-room" *Letters*, II, 61.
"all England by storm" *Letters*, III, 134, n. 3.
"to resist my suggestion" *Autobiography*, I, 459.
"he was never puzzled" *Autobiography*, I, 462.
"self-depreciation and self-distrust" *Autobiography*, I, 459.

F I V E—*A Strange New Light*

227 "purpose of Review" *GE & JC*, 217.
wholly subservient to her wishes *GE & JC*, 217, n. 285.
high praise for Spencer's work *Letters*, I, 364.

228 he wished to cultivate Cf. Anna T. Kitchel, *George Lewes and GE* (New York: John Day, 1933). This excellent study is still the fullest account of Lewes's early life and work.
"what he was going to do next" Blind, *GE*, 112.
"I'm a London child" Blind, 252.

229 "finely proportioned forehead" Blind, 113.
dubbed him "The Ape" Williams, 94.

230 appeared in the *Westminster* *GE & JC*, 203 and n. 246.
"Miss Evans' Article" *GE & JC*, 213 and n. 275.

231 "miniature Mirabeau in appearance" *Letters*, I, 367.
"in the Strand later in this year" *Life*, I, 189, n. 1.
"a new birth" *Life*, II, 55, 56.
"evil of each day sufficient" *Life*, II, 55.
"our conversations disclosed" *Autobiography*, I, 437.
talking, always animatedly *Autobiography*, I, 400.

232 "dull in his company" *Autobiography*, I, 437.
"intellectual sunshine in the room" Haldane *GE and Her Times*, 93, n. †.
"of which one was glad" Kitchel, 61–2.
"The 'luxury of grief' " *Ranthorpe* (New York: Williams S. Gottsberger, 1881), 168–9. A new edition, edited and with an introduction by Barbara Smalley, has been issued by Ohio University Press (Athens: 1974).

232 "If you find yourself" *Ranthorpe*, 191.
233 "Genius is the happiest" *Ranthorpe*, 219.
234 settling William's estate *Letters*, IV, 154, n. 7.
235 more famous than infamous *Letters*, III, 372 and n. 2.
    sent to Mrs. Willim *Letters*, III, 393.
    " 'to pick up wonderfully' " Haight, *GE*, 337.
236 visited her devotedly Cf. *Letters*, V, 109, n. 1.
    testily on 12 September 1870 *Letters*, V, 115.
    "she sat in her chair" *Letters*, V, 125.
237 rapt attention to Leigh Hunt Kitchel, 12–13.
    "it is detestable!" Kitchel, 11–12.
    "simplicity and geniune talk" *Letters*, IV, n. 5 and 494.
    " 'things that conquer death' " *Letters*, IV, 441.
238 "science of this country" Kitchel 298–9.
    already well practiced Kitchel, 59–60, n. 1.
    "voice was not effective" *Autobiography*, I, 437.
    "mercurial little showman" *The Letters of George Meredith* 3 vols., ed. C. L.
    Cline (Oxford, England: Clarendon Press, 1970) III, 1460.
    "career before him" Kitchel, 9.
239 "form of the function" Kitchel, 280.
    "Philosophy of the Mind" *Problems*, First Series, I, v.
    "the *Foundations of a Creed*" *Problems*, First Series, I, viii.
    "the Known and Knowable" *Problems*, First Series, I, lx.
240 "a real existence in the sensible world" *Problems*, First Series, II, 465.
    "the parts were separable" *Problems*, Third Series, 2 vols. (Boston: Hough-
    ton, Osgood and Company, 1879), I, 181.
    "and regulate conducts" *Problems*, First Series, I, 418.
241 "less vividly than others" *Problems*, First Series, I, 420–1.
    "this is what we feel" *Problems*, Third Series, I, 67.
    "the inward sympathetic pang" *Problems*, Third Series, I, 150.
242 December 1818 and March 1819 Kathleen Coburn, ed., *The Philosophical
    Lectures of Samuel Taylor Coleridge* (New York: Philosophical Library,
    1949). Cf. especially Lecture XIII. Coleridge's purpose in these lectures—to
    present "a history of Philosophy as the gradual Evolution of the instinct of
    Man to enquire into the Origin, by the efforts, of his own reason. . . ." (p. 8)—
    is similar to Lewes's intention in his *Biographical History of Philosophy*, al-
    though of course the treatment of the material is significantly different. The
    similarity is coincidental, as verbatim reports of the lectures were not avail-
    able until the twentieth century.
    "sympathy with all outcasts" Kitchel, 10.
243 translating Spinoza *Letters*, I, 158, n. 8.
    bearing Lewes's name *Letters*, IV, 30–1, n. 9. As indicated by his note to
    pp. 436–7 of *A Biographical History of Philosophy* (London: George Rout-
    ledge & Sons, Ltd. [n.d.]), Lewes also had written on Spinoza for the *Penny
    Cyclopaedia*.
    "account of Spinoza's doctrines admirable" *Letters*, II, 211 and n. 3.
    "on the basis of clinical experience" Abraham A. Brill, *Freud's Contribution
    to Psychiatry* (New York: W. W. Norton & Company, Inc., 1944), 37.
    "reflecting things as they are" Lewes, *Biographical History*, 434.
    "possibility of metaphysical science" Lewes, *Biographical History*, 435.
244 "changes in the percipient" Lewes, *Biographical History*, 434.
    flow of narrative Cf. Reva Stump's admirable analysis of *Middlemarch*
    imagery in her *Movement and Vision in GE's Novels* (Seattle: University of
    Washington Press, 1959), especially pp. 136–214.
    "a 'God-intoxicated man' " Lewes, *Biographical History*, 436.

245 "modicum of certain knowledge" Lewes, *Biographical History*, xv–xvi.
"the Bacon of the nineteenth century" Lewes, *Biographical History*, 643.
"a private text-book" *Letters*, II, 126.
"they can understand *Lewes*" Kitchel, 46.
Lewes married in 1841 *Letters*, I, lxviii; also Haight, *GE*, 129.
charming as she was beautiful Kitchel, 15.
"if his affections changed" Haight, *GE*, 130. No source is given for this interesting light on Jervis.
246 "her little shaggy mate" Haight, *GE*, 129–30, 131.
247 " 'as writing dramas' " Kitchel, 15.
his eyes on Agnes Cf. Haight, *GE*, Plate VI, facing 132.
cousin to Kate Hunt Laurence did a now well-known pastel portrait of GE in 1860.
248 "under the same roof" Haight, *GE*, 130.
"for their better disguise" Layard, vii.
249 "days of illustrious reception" Kitchel, 312–13.
"that friend's condemnation" Kitchel, 313.
250 "devoted friend, Thornton Hunt" Kitchel, 313–14.
"the less culpable" Haldane, *GE and Her Times*, 93, n. †.
"love and pleasure" Haldane, 93, n. †.
approximately the same time *Letters*, I, lxx; also Haight, *GE*, 132.
"intellectual superiority demanded" Layard, 134.
251 whooping cough and measles *Letters*, I, lxxi.
"shape of their mother" *Letters*, I, lxix.
"result of his handiwork" Haight, *GE*, 131.
"her preference for another" *Ranthorpe*, 240.
252 "who were Thornton Hunt's" Williams, *GE*, 95.
254 "the beginning of our own" *Letters*, V, 60.
"a heart that is in need" *Letters*, V, 60–1.
"life in the old country" *Letters*, VI, 165.
255 "hear about Marian" *Letters*, III, 116.
" 'Is it Adam Bede?' " *Letters*, III, 117.
"about the boys" *Letters*, III, 116.
256 "by my maiden name" *Letters*, III, 396.
went to California and married there Haight, *GE*, 490–1.
by Charles's widow Haight, *GE*, 460–1, 491.
"not done by another" *Letters*, II, 178.
the two principals Williams, *GE*, 132; Haight, *GE*, 218.
the policy was payable Williams, *GE*, 274.
before his death in 1878 Williams, *GE*, 298.
257 without being introduced to her *Letters*, I, 347.
in Hammersmith *Letters*, I, 352–3 and n. 5.
258 " 'very well' etc., etc." *Letters*, I, 377.
"the Merry Wives of Windsor" *Letters*, I, 376.
"as Lewes calls him" *Letters*, II, 22.
259 "ten years' growth" *Letters*, II, 37.
"Lewes signified" *GE & JC*, 69 and n. 7.
"with Prof. Owen" *Letters*, II, 56.
"the second bell rings" *Letters*, II, 68.
260 "a mask of flippancy" *Letters*, II, 91, 98.
"separation from Mrs. Lewes" *Letters*, II, 178. Emphasis mine.
261 " 'G. H. Lewes, Esq.' " Haight, *GE*, 138.
"but never mind" *Letters*, II, 132.
"in my bedroom" *Letters*, II, 149.
translating of Feuerbach *Letters*, II, 150 and n. 6.

261 " 'from other lands' " *Letters,* II, 154–5.
"anything worth the doing" *Letters,* II, 155–6.
262 "useful to me every day" *Letters,* II, 156.
"I like to feel free" *Letters,* II, 158.
her intimacy with Lewes *Letters,* II, 179.
17–26 June at Rosehill *Letters,* II, 162, n. 2.
263 " 'Strauss's Life of Jesus' " *GE & JC,* 79.
"the camp of orthodoxy" *Letters,* II, 165, n. 3.
"sacred in themselves" Feuerbach *Essence of Christianity,* 271.
"not a truly moral marriage" Feurerbach *Essence of Christianity,* 271, undesignated footnote.
"attache of the Leader" *Letters,* II, 165.
264 both themselves and Feuerbach *Letters,* II, 165, n. 3.
"to go to 'Labassecour' " *Letters,* II, 165.
adding a question mark *Life,* I, 234.
"have you read it?" *Letters,* II, 92.
"heroines of police reports" *Letters,* I, 268.
so much of Emily's *Letters,* II, 91, n. 6.
"what fire in her" *Letters,* II, 91.
appeared in 1857 *Letters,* II, 319.
265 "his life-long companion" Blind, 115–16.
"declare our impressions *Letters,* III, 359.
"teaching each other to soar" George Henry Lewes, *The Life and Works of Goethe* (London: J. M. Dent & Sons Ltd., 1908), 105.
"I have only time" *Letters,* II, 166.
266 "lovelier the dawn" *Life,* I, 239.
"all was well" Haight, *GE,* 148.
their realistic destination Cf. Haight, *GE,* 148–9.
267 the following year *Letters,* II, 171; 169, n. 8.
"true tones of the piano" *Life,* I, 249–50.
come to the Continent Haight, *GE,* 162.
man and wife Browning, 40; Williams, *GE,* 104.
with Ettersburg *Life,* I, 242.
"I am happier" *Letters,* II, 173.
268 "understands Spinoza" *Life,* I, 270.
"sort of back view" *Essays,* 84.
"end of this month" *Letters,* II, 173–4.
"and floating hair" *Life,* I, 243.
left with him *Life,* I, 243; *Letters,* II, 174, n. 6.
269 "stink pots of humanity" *Letters,* II, 175–6.
in Highgate Cemetery *Letters,* IV, 328; Haight, *GE,* 160, 463, 549.
"both a bad night" *Letters,* II, 176, n. 6.
"explaining his position" *Letters,* II, 176, n. 6.
" 'Strong minded Woman' " *Letters,* II, 176, n. 6.
"of noble sympathy" *Letters,* II, 176, n. 6.
270 "the language, all fiction" *Letters,* II, 176–7.
"to this second letter" *Letters,* II, 177, n. 7.
271 "in an hospital" R. K. Webb, *Harriet Martineau* (New York: Columbia University Press, 1960), 15.
"she had got me here" *Letters,* II, 62.
272 "one passion only" Vera Wheatley, *The Life and Work of Harriet Martineau* (London: Secker & Warburg, 1957), 400.
temporarily obliterated Wheatley, 370–1.
" 'I shd expect' " Webb, 14.
273 "in its memory" *Letters,* II, 229–30.

273 "appreciation of her" *Letters*, II, 258.
"more personal details" *Letters*, III, 201.
"after my death" *Letters*, VI, 351–2.
274 "another meaning than that" *Letters*, VI, 371.
"What his sister thought *Letters*, VI, 371.
"its future publicity" *Letters*, VI, 372.
275 "her ear-trumpet" *Letters*, II, 180.
"cannot be given in a letter" Haight, *GE*, 162; not in *Letters*.
"it is false" *Letters*, II, 179.
276 pregnancy by Hunt Haight, *GE*, 163.
"to dwell on it" *Letters*, II, 180–1.
"worthy of high respect" *Letters*, II, 179.
"may feel towards me" *Letters*, II, 179.
277 to live with Lewes Haight, *GE*, 164; but no specific letter is mentioned or documented.
"all human experience" *Letters*, II, 181–2.
"I mean nothing unkind" *Letters*, II, 186.
278 "after the lapse of years" *Goethe*, 104–5.
"accomplished German translator" *Goethe*, 328, n. 2.
"acquiring the language" *Goethe*, 2–3, n. 1.
"silent collaborator" Haight, *GE*, 173.
279 " 'sweet will of its own' " *Essays*, 84–5.
"one friendly expanse" *Goethe*, 199.
"with contemptuous laughter" *Essays*, 98–9.
280 "of pudding and praise" George Henry Lewes, *On Actors and the Art of Acting* (New York: Grove Press, [n.d.]), 49.
" 'the morning of the times' " *Essays*, 102–3.
"to execute such music" *Essays*, 103.
"since Beethoven was laughed at" Lewes, *On Actors and the Art of Acting*, 196.
281 "a cup of coffee" *Essays*, 118.
"detestable tobacco" *Goethe*, 199–200.
"sublime calm of Nature" *Essays*, 122, *Life*, I, 243.
"wilt be at rest" *Goethe*, 293, 574, 575. In the 1872 abridged edition of the *Goethe*, Lewes slightly altered this version to eliminate ambiguity of meaning: "Yes, wait but a little, soon wilt thou too be at rest" (p. 404).
282 "identical with hers" Blind, 89.
"*of the kind*" *Letters*, II, 49.
283 "diluted a little" *Letters*, II, 172.
appeared in print *Letters*, II, 188.
"in the national history" *Essays*, 54.
"suppressing womanly ones" *Essays*, 54.
"in male attire" *Essays*, 53.
284 "a perfect specimen" *Essays*, 55.
"domestic drudgery" *Essays*, 56.
285 "harvest of human happiness" *Essays*, 80–1.
"she occupies in society" *Essays*, 53, n. 2.
leaving there on 4 November *Life*, I, 251.
"I could do in fiction" *Letters*, II, 407.
286 "by agreement with Bohn" *Letters*, II, 189.
"writer of these lines" *Letters*, II, 189, n. 1. This was of course eliminated from subsequent editions of the *Goethe*.
"bigotry of exclusiveness" *Life*, I, 271.
287 "Our Lady" Cf. McKenzie, xv, 112.
"vigilant protecting fondness" *Goethe*, 105.

288 "a very mother to her" Blind, 119.
taken up sewing Haight, *GE*, 178.
"to your judgment" *Letters*, II, 200, 201.
"bear this in mind" *Letters*, II, 232.
289 "does any errands for me" *Letters*, II, 231–2.
"drove her wild" *Life*, I, 277.
"an absolute duty" *Letters*, II, 407.
290 "I could have no objection" *Letters*, II, 201.
"among ordinary people" *Letters*, II, 201.
25 June of that year *Essays*, 96.
291 not merely talent but genius *Life*, I, 277.
"known to be a *woman*" *Letters*, II, 218.
292 "in Greek, this morning" *Life*, I, 275.
" 'too tedious to mention' " *Letters*, II, 233.
"the pangs of a miser" *Letters*, II, 233.
his brother's widow and son *Life*, I, 297; *Letters*, II, 216.
293 "at an end between us" Haight, *GE*, 199–200.
"my article on Young" *Life*, I, 296.

s i x—*My Present Past*

297 "gather in the present" *Letters*, III, 128–9; n. 8.
298 "the 'Clerical Scenes' " *Letters*, III, 129; n. 9.
"to write Fiction" I, 297. Literally, Cross denotes this day as being the
22nd, but cf. *Letters*, II, 407, n. 3, *Letters*, II, 406.
"book scientist" Haight, *GE*, 136.
" 'descriptive power' of his own" Haight, *GE*, 198.
299 "over to Miss Evans" *Life*, I, 85.
"with the new" *Letters*, II, 255, 256.
"before we leave" *Letters*, II, 255.
"tangible form of a picture" *Letters*, II, 257.
300 "makes her extremely happy" Haight, *GE*, 205; but this is not a direct quotation from Barbara Bodichon.
to live with him *GE & JC*, 91.
"variety on the sands" *Letters*, II, 257.
301 1856 number of the *Westminster* Cf. *Letters*, II, 253 and ns. 9, 1; André
Maurois, *Victor Hugo and His World* (New York: The Viking Press, 1966), 89.
"he would have liked to know" *Letters*, II, 256.
new way of life Williams, *GE*, 124.
sailed away on 1 August *Letters*, II, 259, n. 3.
"unkind word of any one" *The Autobiography and Letters of Mrs. M. O. W.
Oliphant*, ed. Mrs. Harry Coghill (New York: Dodd, Mead, 1899), 135.
302 Leweses were told of this *Letters*, III, 103.
Richard Congreve and Robert Browning Cf. *Letters*, IV, 88; III, 415; VII,
278; Williams, *GE*, 314.
first Journal he was not to destroy Williams, *GE*, 123.
"article on 'Silly Women's Novels' " *Letters*, II, 258.
had to be removed *Letters*, II, 261.
for the October *Westminster* *Essays*, 300, 301, n. 3.
completed by 19 September *Essays*, 325 (headnote).
"life among the negroes?" *Essays*, 319.
considered her "novel" *Life*, I, 297.
Adam Bede being one of them *Letters*, II, 502.
"fresh and striking" *Letters*, II, 407–8.

304 "getting money for them" *Letters*, II, 377.

"impulse lives within him" Alice R. Kaminsky, ed., *Literary Criticism of George Henry Lewes* (Lincoln: University of Nebraska Press, 1964), 42. The review ("Another Pleasant French Book") first appeared in *Blackwood's*, LXXXVI (1859), 672–7.

brought in £1,705 *Letters*, VII, Appendix I, 360.

305 "stopd the Singers" Haight, *GE*, 211–12.

306 " 'have you Papa?' " *Letters*, III, 83.

"the writer is sincerely sorry" *Letters*, III, 86.

307 a new try made *Letters*, II, 407–8.

"good will come of it" *Letters*, II, 268–9.

essay on Edward Young *Letters*, II, 274, n. 1.

308 the projected *Scenes* *Letters*, II, 407.

family's publishing firm Margaret Oliphant, *Annals of a Publishing House*, 3 vols. (Edinburgh and London: William Blackwood and Sons, 1897), II, 433. Reprinted (New York: AMS Press, 1974).

"negotiating the matter with you" *Letters*, II, 269.

309 "silence as consent" *Letters*, II, 272–3.

dealing with editors *Letters*, II, 436.

"I have another paper" *Letters*, II, 273, 274.

310 "in clerical hands" *Letters*, II, 275.

"you have to deal with" *Letters*, II, 276–7.

311 "the general title" *Letters*, II, 277.

"from me to my friend" *Letters*, II, 277.

312 payable to Lewes *Letters*, II, 284.

being to John Blackwood *Life*, I, 307–8; cf. *Letters*, II, 288.

"the best judge" *Letters*, II, 283.

"The Author of Amos Barton" *Letters*, II, 288.

313 a week earlier than he *Letters*, II, 223, n. 3; 224, n. 5.

"an occasional relish" *Letters*, II, 281.

"Mr. Gilfil's Love Story" *Life*, I, 305.

"Fifty Guineas" *Letters*, II, 283.

"like his books" *Letters*, II, 135–6.

Alice tore off the double signatures Haight, *GE*, 491.

314 his feminine audience *Letters*, II, 294.

her father's death Haight gives two dates for Help's death: 1873 and 1875; cf. *Letters*, II, 135, n. 6.

with English notes *Essays*, 261 (headnote).

315 "his own powers" *Essays*, 264–5.

316 "frivolous women would do" *Letters*, III, 366–7; cf. n. 5.

"love and support" J. C. Flugel, *Man, Morals and Society* (New York: International Universities Press, 1945), 56.

317 a key for all the characters *Letters*, II, 457.

318 "to recent years" *Letters*, II, 459–60.

321 in Maga *Letters*, II, 297–8.

322 first part of "Gilfil" *Letters*, II, 298–9, n. 9.

"development of the story" *Letters*, II, 299.

"portion of the Story" *Letters*, II, 302–3.

323 "prefer the *dadger*" *Letters*, II, 308.

emulate in writing Cf. *Letters*, II, 292.

"like Sir Edward" *Letters*, II, 322.

"better than anything . . . in that way" *Letters*, II, 307.

"as he requests" *Letters*, II, 316.

324 a week earlier *Letters*, II, 316, n. 9.

"all my readers" *Letters*, II, 309.

324 "transmutes them" *Letters*, I, 251.
325 "love pervading it" *Letters*, II, 334.
326 "hold of the dagger" *Letters*, II, 334.
327 than had "Amos" *Letters*, II, 300.
   epilogue to 'Gilfil' *Letters*, II, 324.
328 "enveloped her and her work" *Life*, I, 319; *Letters*, II, 409.
   "satisfy an author" *Letters*, VI, 415.
   version of the letter *Life*, III, 229.
329 childhood of Tina *Letters*, II, 289, n. 9; 299, n. 8.
   reference to it *Letters*, II, 289.
   "by a bilious attack" *Letters*, II, 292.
   "Whatever may be" *Letters*, II, 292.
   "the worthy Curate of Shepperton" *Letters*, II, 290.
330 "not a practised writer" *Letters*, II, 290–1.
   "most 'practised writers' " *Letters*, II, 291–2.
331 "scientific definitions" *Letters*, II, 293–4.
   "as far as myself" *Letters*, II, 293.
   "from no bad judge" *Letters*, II, 298, n. 8.
   "or could write" *Letters*, II, 294.
   "I owe it" *Life*, I, 310; Williams, *GE*, 131–2.
332 first use of the pseudonym *Letters*, II, 408–9.
   "Eliot's new story" *Letters*, II, 294, n. 2.
   living with Lewes E.g., *Letters*, III, 194.
333 "with prejudice" C. W. Hatfield, ed., *The Complete Poems of Emily Jane Brontë* (New York: Columbia University Press, 1961, 4th printing), 3.
   "any living novelist" John Holmstrom and Laurence Lerner, eds., *GE and Her Readers* (London: The Bodley Head, 1966), 14.
334 "the bull's eyes" *Letters*, II, 290.
335 "was acting" *Life*, III, 306.
   "her appearance" Browning, 18.
   "so beautiful" McKenzie, 120.
   "more impressive than its product" Browning, 90.
   "by her writings" Blind, 277.
336 "laboured resolutions" McKenzie, 116.
337 "less than usual" *Letters*, II, 184.
338 all moneys Williams, *GE*, 11–12.
   "he will do" *Letters*, II, 197.
   "called in" *Letters*, II, 202.
   "not fond of" *Letters*, II, 317.
339 "several years" *Letters*, II, 331.
   "supremacy of intellect?" *Life*, I, 325.
   " 'fame is beginning' " *Life*, I, 324.
   greater detail *Letters*, II, 409.
340 "an account there" *Letters*, II, 332.
   immediate expenses Williams, *GE*, 132.
   Lewes's account *Letters*, II, 336.
   directly to him *Letters*, II, MS identifications preceding letters 331, 349.
   "to all my relatives" Haight, *GE*, 229.
   dangerously agitated *Letters*, II, 336.
   "as far as my means will allow" *Letters*, II, 342.
341 no doubt sincere *Letters*, II, 346.
   "favour from them" *Letters*, II, 349–50.
342 "concealed from any one" *Letters*, II, 364.
   "to me and mine" *Letters*, III, 26.
   excitement for her *Letters*, III, 30.

343 a Mr. Liggins *Letters*, II, 342; Fanny's letter has not survived, but in part
can be reconstructed by GE's response.
"Coton stories" *Letters*, II, 337.
" 'Clerical Sketches' " *Letters*, III, 98.
344 "sake of land" Williams, *GE*, 13.
"colors sufficiently flattering" Blind, 163.
"Romola was" Haight, *GE*, 394. Letter of 13 June 1866.
345 "you *must* confess" Haight, *GE*, 394. Letter of 11 Dec. 1866.
346 "melancholy story" of Tina *Letters*, II, 310.
"25 years ago" *Letters*, II, 344.
347 "for a publisher" *Letters*, II, 347-8.
negative reaction to the story *Letters*, II, 350-1.
"the popularity of your story" *Letters*, II, 352.
"for the future" *Letters*, II, 353.
349 " 'spiritual' weaknesses" *Letters*, II, 378.
" 'writer of Fiction' " *Letters*, II, 386.
"while I live" *Letters*, III, 35, n. 3; cf. II, 285, n. 7.
"felt about her" *Letters*, III, 35.
350 "especially of all" *Letters*, III, 197.
"many parts of 'Janet' " *Letters*, III, 267.
on 9 October *Life*, I, 323; 336.
mainland of England Cf. Browning, 40.
"Tryan and Janet" *Letters*, II, 371.
351 "all short stories" *Letters*, II, 378 (the exact date of this letter is uncertain).
"write a novel" *Letters*, II, 381.
"in two volumes" *Life*, I, 336.
how she came to write fiction *Letters*, II, 409-10.
"*solitude à deux*" *Life*, I, 345.
352 "of middle age" *Life*, I, 345-6.
"*a* Mrs. Lewes" Oliphant, II, 484.
"I was George Eliot" *Letters*, II, 410, n. 1.
"Blackwood was kind" *Letters*, II, 435.
353 "a good expression" Mrs. Gerald Porter, *John Blackwood*. Vol. III of
Annals of a Publishing House (Edinburgh and London: William Blackwood
and Sons, 1898), 46.
Adam Bede *Letters*, II, 435-6.
"positive pain" *Letters*, III, 377, n. 7a.
354 "good enough" Porter, 422. Said by Col. Lockhart in memorial tribute to
John Blackwood.
belonging in it *Letters*, II, 49.
"than distasteful" *Letters*, II, 322.
"altogether unqualified" *Letters*, II, 344.
"dinners in London" *Letters*, II, 345.
355 "given to children of the flesh" Porter, 386.
"leave criticism alone" Porter, 393.
356 revolutionary movement *Letters*, I, 254.
"enlightened days" Porter, 167.
"as much as they can" Porter, 149-50.
"My feeling is . . . to let the heathen rage" Porter, 166-7.
357 "blessed surprise to her!" Oliphant, *Autobiography and Letters*, 292.
"as some would maintain" Porter, 159.
358 "Rights of Women" Porter, 164.
"The peculiarities of my own lot" *Letters*, IV, 364.
"second-rate literature" *Letters*, II, 379.
"my neighbour's garden wall" *Letters*, II, 431.

358 "application of feminine incapacity to literature" *Letters*, II, 439; cf. 438, n. 2.

359 "hard non-moral outward conditions" *Letters*, IV, 364–5. A few sentences in this letter are not easily interpreted; the note was admittedly written in haste to correct a false impression that GE feared she had created in a conversation of which there is no other record.

360 "the home duties" *Life*, I, 25.

361 "are born to this" *Life*, III, 310.
"ordinary household duties" *Life*, III, 308.

362 "much wanted" *Letters*, IV, 425.

363 "for perfection" *Letters*, V, 58.
"Newnham Hall" *Letters*, VI, 380.
"visit to Cambridge" *Life*, III, 230.

364 "memorable table-talk" Browning, 125–6.
"the worst man" Virginia Woolf, *A Room of One's Own* (New York: Harcourt, Brace & World, Inc., A Harbinger Book, 1963), 55.
"as a woman" Woolf, *A Room of One's Own*, 107–8.

365 "after knowledge" *Letters*, V, 406.
"in the gloom" Browning, 115–16. Myer's essay was first published in the *Century Magazine*, 23 (November 1881), 57–64.

366 "many anecdotes" Georgiana Burne-Jones, *Memorials of Edward Burne-Jones* (New York: Benjamin Blom, Inc., 1971, from original London ed., 1904), II, 4.

367 "we equally understood" Porter, 389.
"on his altitudes" Cf. Porter, 161.
relayed it to her *Letters*, II, 291; 435.

368 "in taking trouble" *Letters*, III, 125.
"extravagant desires" *Letters*, IV, 3.
"beautiful colored ones done in Paris" *Letters*, III, 306.
keep the original *Letters*, III, 307–8.

369 "our own kindred" Porter, 169. For the strange history of this portrait cf. *Letters*, III, 401–2, n. 1; Haight, *GE*, 339 and n. 5; Williams, *GE*, facing 186. This portrait is now "lost." Had it not been reproduced by Blanche Colton Williams in her 1936 biography of GE it would be totally unknown to anyone who had not seen it in the Blackwoods' Edinburgh office before 1914 or on one of various tours of exhibition. In 1935 it was acquired by Mr. Jacob Schwartz, of the Ulysses Book Shop, New York. A very interesting sketch by Laurence (quite different from the finished portrait) now hangs in Girton College.
"good or not" Haight, *GE*, 377–8; cf. *Letters*, IV, 167, 174–5. This portrait was given to the National Portrait Gallery after GE's death.
"This likeness" *Letters*, V, 237.
"night was setting in" *Letters*, VI, 137.

370 "blocked out?" *Letters*, II, 439, n. 4.
"rest of the story" *Letters*, II, 445–6.
"his proposed 'little paper'" *Letters*, II, 447.
nothing good enough Oliphant, *Autobiography and Letters*, 7.

371 "with the hero" *Letters*, II, 502.
"constantly in view" *Letters*, II, 503.
"which I did" *Letters*, II, 504.

372 "individual past" Blind, 123–4.

373 "impossible to tell" Oliphant, *Autobiography and Letters*, 5.

374 "had not mistaken my work" *Letters*, III, 64.
"behind the fire" *Letters*, V, 451.
"his judgment" *Letters*, VI, 109; cf. V, 282, n. 8.

375 "some music" *Life*, II, 33.

375 "of each other" *Letters*, II, 454.
376 "I expected" *Life*, II, 33.
"love that tended me" *Life*, II, 34.
on 7 July *Life*, II, 33, 34.
in 1854 *Letters*, II, 470, 472.
for six weeks *Letters*, II, 468.
"secured us" *Life*, II, 42.
377 "any reasonable amount" *Letters*, II, 474.
financial offer *Letters*, II, 504.
"I wrote to accept" *Life*, II, 47.
"*Jubilate*" *Life*, II, 48.
"scent of hay" *Letters*, II, 387.
378 "to console me" *Letters*, I, 31.
380 "with advantage" *Letters*, II, 445.
"four sheets of the proof" *Letters*, II, 504.
the *Clerical Scenes* *Letters*, II, 494, 505.
held fast to his view *Letters*, II, 506.
"against the grain" *Letters*, II, 509.
"It is not like . . . you" *Letters*, II, 513.
381 "in a review" *Letters*, II, 509, 510.
"fellow novelists" *Letters*, II, 512.
"thoughts that way" *Letters*, VII, 94.
382 "end of the year" *Letters*, II, 507.
"about Hayslope" *Letters*, III, 6.
"popularity can win" *Letters*, III, 6.
"great author" *Letters*, III, 33.
Blackwood's letter *Life*, II, 68.
"particulars" *Life*, II, 73.
383 Select Library *Life*, II, 68.
" 'Adam Bede's' success" *Life*, II, 69; 80.
fifth edition *Life*, II, 87-8.
"accompaniments of success" *Letters*, III, 44.
384 "the same complaint" Oliphant, *Annals of a Publishing House*, II, 446-7.
"past and present" *Life*, II, 74.
385 "novels he had been reading" *Letters*, III, 12.
"to my book?" *Letters*, III, 25.
"do good to the book" *Letters*, III, 28.
"shock others" *Letters*, II, 342.
386 "mere amusements" *Letters*, V, 228.
"public mind" *Essays*, 438.
387 "his industry" *Essays*, 439, 440.
"familiar life" *Letters*, IV, 287.
388 "fragmentary way" *Letters*, IV, 300, 301.
"with the Works" *Letters*, V, 456.
"such a view of my writings" *Letters*, V, 458-9.
389 "its jailer" *F. M. Dostoevsky: Stavrogin's Confession*, With a Psychoanalytic Study of the Author by Sigmund Freud (New York: Lear Publishers, 1947), 88.
390 "as well as I could" *Letters*, VI, 304.
"to be rich" *Essays*, 439, 440-1.
391 "sorrow of parting" *Letters*, II, 512.
"not press it in any way" *Letters*, III, 89.
392 "provincial life" *Letters*, III, 41.
"most materially" *Letters*, III, 92.
"to see them" *Letters*, III, 94.
393 "objection to a point blank denial" *Letters*, III, 52.

393 "quite indefensible" *Letters*, III, 50.
394 "rumours as to the authorship" *Letters*, III, 51.
"the laugh of the Blackwoods" Oliphant, *Annals of a Publishing House*, II, 444.
"read the Leader" *Letters*, III, 58.
"a sore to me" *Letters*, III, 61.
"on his shield" *Letters*, III, 60.
395 "the creatures who had written them" *Letters*, III, 65–6.
"demanding a denial" *Letters*, III, 66.
"KEEP YOUR SECRET" *Letters*, III, 68.
"the next book" *Letters*, III, 73.
"literary precedent" *Letters*, III, 75, n. 1.
396 "failed to do" *Letters*, III, 74–5.
"G.E. was full of fun" *Letters*, III, 75, n. 1.
"matter of fact" *Letters*, III, 77.
"a few months longer" *Letters*, III, 63.
"and some letters" *Letters*, III, 102, n. 7.
397 Liggins party *Letters*, 90, n. 4.
398 "hypocritical howl" *Letters*, III, 102–3.
"postscript, of course" *Letters*, III, 106; for GE's extant part of this letter, cf. 105–6.
399 "betrayal of the anonymity" *Letters*, III, 111.
"things are wearing" *Letters*, III, 105, n. 3.
"such a trick" *Letters*, III, 109, n. 1.
"our praise" Holmstrom and Lerner, 21.
"very interesting visit to you" *Letters*, III, 113, n. 8.
"no more now" *Letters*, III, 109.
400 "trust to George Eliot" *Letters*, III, 40; *re*: the MS, ns. 2, 3.
one number only *Letters*, III, 41.
on 6 April *Letters*, III, 42.
on 11 February *Letters*, III, 60, n. 1.
"just issued" *Letters*, III, 60 and n. 1.
"new and piquant" *Letters*, III, 55.
401 "talk it over" *Letters*, III, 67.
spontaneous expression *Autobiography*, I, 459.
404 "the wonderful skill" *Letters*, V, 379–80.
"completer manhood" *Letters*, V, 380; cf. 380, n. 4.
405 "Qu'en dites vous?" *Letters*, III, 83.
misgivings that it would not *Letters*, III, 112, n. 6.
406 "depth of emotional sensibility" *Blackwood's Edinburgh Magazine*, LXXXIX (July 1854), 104.
"*only* for money" *Letters*, III, 151–2.
407 "excitement of uncertainty" *Letters*, III, 160–1.
polluted source *Letters*, III, 209, n. 2.
"*Will you please contradict*" A. B. Hopkins, *Elizabeth Gaskell: Her Life and Work* (London: John Lehmann, 1952), 207.
408 "risk myself" *Letters*, III, 161–2.
rival publisher *Letters*, III, 172–3.
409 "she promised" *Letters*, III, 183.
"instead of 'George Eliot' " *Letters*, III, 184–5.
"change of signature" *Letters*, III, 188.
£800 *Letters*, III, 190.
signature remained "Marian Evans Lewes" *Letters*, III, 191–2.
410 "about the matter" *Letters*, III, 192.
questions she had submitted Cf. *Letters*, III, 173, 180–1, 182.

411 "reaction is very great" *Letters*, III, 194.
"Pray take no notice" *Letters*, III, 200.
"write about it" *Letters*, III, 194.
412 "prevailing note" Oliphant, *Annals of a Publishing House*, II, 443.
"that result!" *Letters*, III, 208.
"shown them the way!" *Letters*, III, 209.
413 "Studies in Animal Life" Spencer L. Eddy, Jr., *The Founding of "The Cornhill Magazine"* (Ball State Monograph Number Nineteen, 1970), 18, 20–2, 43.
"a civil note yesterday" *Letters*, III, 43 and n. 1; 72 and n. 7; 73.
"English Literature" *Letters*, III, 203.
work-in-progress *Letters*, III, 204, 205.
414 "fallen angel C.D." *Letters*, III, 204–5.
"make an offer" *Letters*, III, 204.
"clear understanding in the matter" *Letters*, III, 215.
415 "taken place" *Letters*, III, 216–17.
"for explanation" *Letters*, III, 217–19.
416 "the new work" *Letters*, III, 221.
"opinion of her" *Letters*, III, 223, n. 11.
signing this note "George Eliot" *Letters*, III, 224.
417 "a permanent one" *Letters*, III, 235.
"the 14th December" *Letters*, III, 236.
"*inundation*" *Life*, II, 58.
418 "provisionally" *Life*, II, 75.
"a sort of poetical sound" *Letters*, III, 244.
somewhat shy remark *Letters*, III, 245.
"our heads punched" *Letters*, III, 265.
"catastrophe of the inundation" Browning, 71–2.
419 "less romantic" *Letters*, III, 133.
"writing it fast" *Letters*, III, 249.
"in print first!" *Letters*, III, 267.
420 "disagreeable and uncomfortable situations" *Letters*, III, 269.
"perfectly fascinating" *Letters*, III, 272.
"for immortality" *Letters*, III, 276.
"scene again" *Letters*, III, 278.
"its reception" *Letters*, III, 285.
422 "a flood was coming" *Letters*, III, 277.
423 "always regret" *Letters*, III, 317.
428 "I daresay" *Letters*, III, 289, 290.
429 "early days yet" *Letters*, III, 291–2.
"that I have seen" *Letters*, III, 289.
"admirable qualities" Oliphant, *Annals of a Publishing House*, II, 445, 446.
430 "I have read no reviews" *Letters*, III, 324.
"expressed by Dallas" *Letters*, III, 296, 298.
431 "from vices" Holmstrom and Lerner, 34, 35, 36.
"ugly adjectives" *Letters*, III, 299.
"made no one else miserable" Holmstrom and Lerner, 38.
"to both sides" *Letters*, III, 397.
432 its second instalment *Letters*, III, 368.
"individual book" *Letters*, III, 297–8.
from *Adam Bede* *Letters*, VII, 360.
"temporary shock" Oliphant, *Annals of a Publishing House*, II, 446.
"a certain hushed legend" Richard Church, *The Growth of the English Novel*
(London: Methuen & Company, Ltd., 1951), 163.
433 James Joyce Jane Lidderdale and Mary Nicholson, *Dear Miss Weaver*
(New York: The Viking Press, 1970), 33.

433 "enthusiasm" *Letters*, III, 295.
Florence *Letters*, III, 300.
"athirst to begin" *Letters*, III, 307.
434 "keeping a secret" *Letters*, III, 315.
"expected of him" *Letters*, III, 339.
"Story of English Life by you" *Letters*, III, 340, 341.
and she acquiesced *Letters*, IV, 322.
436 " 'Weaver of Raveloe' " *Letters*, III, 360.
"all their efforts . . . had failed" *Letters*, III, 348–9.
"millet-seed of thought" *Letters*, III, 371.
"leisurely way that demanded space" *Letters*, III, 380.
437 all he said *Letters*, III, 385.
"realistic treatment" *Letters*, III, 382.
"too distinctly" *Letters*, III, 385.
"mission is felt" *Letters*, III, 386.
"altogether different meditations" *Letters*, III, 392.
"alien from his fellows" *Letters*, III, 427.
439 her own family *Letters*, III, 170.
441 "price of the book" *Letters*, III, 410, n. 2.
would be sold *Letters*, III, 410, n. 2.
"the miser" *Letters*, III, 420.
"instead of English" *Letters*, III, 427.
"book stalls of London" *Letters*, III, 430, 457.
her new novel *Life*, II, 230.
442 "prudent man would" *Letters*, III, 458.
"at the piano" *Letters*, III, 458, n. 1.
a week or so earlier *Life*, II, 229.
"talk, and music" *Life*, II, 230.
"£3000" *Letters*, III, 458, n. 1.
443 "costumes" *Life*, II, 231–2.
"Mrs. Beecher's toe" *Letters*, III, 473–4.
"this afternoon" *Letters*, III, 474.
she barely mentions . . . in her Journal Haight, *GE*, 354.
444 "of *Romola*" *Letters*, IV, 3, n. 1.
500 more were printed *Letters*, IV, 7, n. 3.
"6s/ 'Mill' sent me" *Letters*, IV, 6–7.
445 "dissatisfaction about it" *Letters*, IV, 15, 16.
"about my books" *Letters*, IV, 18.
"chilled and oppressed" *Letters*, IV, 17.
numbers which had appeared Cf. Haight, *GE*, 354–5.
446 "not to be rich" *Life*, II, 240.
"made by him" *Letters*, IV, 17–18.
accept his offer *Letters*, IV, 157, n. 4; however, in *GE* (p. 370), Haight
states that Smith had offered £250 for the story.
"an earlier date than she would like" *Letters*, IV, 19–20.
447 first issue of the *Cornhill* Eddy, 40.
"could be reached" *Letters*, IV, 24.
"*Cornhill* was begun" *Letters*, IV, 29.
"on that basis" *Letters*, IV, 33–4.
"nothing could move her" George Smith, "Our Birth and Parentage,"
Cornhill, 83 (January 1901), 10.
448 "my interests as well as your own" *Letters*, IV, 34–5.
"have much more" *Letters*, IV, 35–6.
449 "and good-feeling" *Life*, II, 245–6.
"of Mr. Smith" *Letters*, IV, 38, n. 2.

449 "read the M.S." *Letters*, IV, 38.
450 "by not doing so" *Letters*, IV, 38, n. 3.
"and came away" *Letters*, IV, 44.
451 "taken away from us" *Letters*, VII, 390.
£10,000 Haight, *GE*, 365.
"the same public" *Letters*, IV, 49.
answer them himself E.g., *Letters*, IV, 58–9.
452 "in mind and heart" Holmstrom and Lerner, 64, 65.
"conceptions of life" *Letters*, V, 455 and n. 5.
453 "English-fed imagination" *Letters*, IV, 300.
"author of *Romola*" *Letters*, V, 58, n. 5.
454 "not a woman" *Letters*, IV, 103–4, n. 8.
"scourge me" *Letters*, IV, 103–4.
" 'an old woman' " *Life*, II, 255.
455 a new novel, *Life*, II, 290.
his reaction *Letters*, IV, 195.
"harmony of the lines" *Letters*, IV, 284.
"ideal of Comte" *Letters*, IV, 286; cf. 287–9.
456 "of her old friend as the publisher" *Letters*, IV, 240.
"declined it" *Letters*, IV, 240, n. 9; quoted from Leonard Huxley, ed., *The House of Smith, Elder* (privately printed, 1923), 103.
"my ordinary work" *Letters*, IV, 241.
"act before us" *Letters*, IV, 243.
"the old days" *Letters*, IV, 243.
"won the Derby" *Letters*, IV, 244.
457 "strictly a secret" *Letters*, IV, 247.
"a marvel" Porter, 158.
"more popular than the Mill" *Letters*, IV, 265.
458 "my father before me" *Letters*, IV, 246.
"The Address is excellent" *Letters*, IV, 411.
"went before it" Oliphant, *Autobiography and Letters*, 210.
459 "Midland village" Holmstrom and Lerner, 65.
her long letter *Letters*, IV, 291.

EPILOGUE

463 "evidence . . . is inconclusive" Cf. Spencer, *Autobiography*, II, 430; Williams, *GE*, 290.
464 "sense of authorship" *Letters*, III, 382–3.
" 'one kind word' " *Life*, New ed., 747.
465 "corresponding reality of their own" Kaminsky, ed., 20.
"scenes of her own imagining" *Letters*, I, 22.
the project was dropped Haight, *GE*, 374–5.
466 "expectation of marriage" *Life*, III, 30–1.
467 "pregnant to me" *Life*, III, 31.
"born, etc." *Life*, III, 33–4.
finished poem Williams, *GE*, 238–9.
wrote Barbara Bodichon *Letters*, IV, 236.
"shall be done" *Letters*, IV, 354–5.
468 "take into account" *Letters*, IV, 377.
"a grand thing" *Letters*, IV, 407.
"ostentatious time" *Letters*, IV, 466.
"called 'Middlemarch' " *Life*, III, 55.
469 "take new shapes in the development" *Life*, III, 91.
fusion might have gone undetected Cf. the lucid study by Jerome Beaty,

'*Middlemarch*': *from Notebook to Novel* (Urbana: University of Illinois Press, 1960).
470 "instead of an individual an idea" Strauss, *The Life of Jesus*, 895.
"her own heart" Blind, 243–4.
471 " 'seldom are joined' " Williams, *GE*, 268.
"below the mark of my desires" *Letters*, V, 261.
472 "a climax" *Letters*, V, 456.
"Lord Mayor?" Porter, 114–15.
"on the subject" Porter, 388.
473 "related to everything else there" *Letters*, VI, 290.
"the only right name for such places" *Letters*, V, 312.
474 "money-raking demon" *Letters*, V, 314.
"as a 'painful sight' " *Letters*, V, 314, n. 6.
477 "to my eyes" *Letters*, VI, 293; cf. n. 7.
"their requirements" Browning, 114.
"experimental fashion" *Letters*, VI, 388.
478 "done my best" *Letters*, VI, 439–40; cf. 440, n. 6.
own ill health *Letters*, VII, 85–6.
respónded to these letters *Letters*, VII, 105–6.
"it comes slowly" *Letters*, VII, 132–3.
Barbara Bodichon *Letters*, VII, 128.
"I lack nothing" *Letters*, VII, 174.
479 "wenn Du bist nicht da" *Letters*, VII, 211.
"very selfish" *Letters*, VII, 283.
"risen again" *Letters*, VII, 296.
480 "waved me a farewell" McKenzie, 97.
"marriage decided" *Letters*, VII, 259.
"her clique did" *Letters*, VII, 284.
481 "of the past!" Leon Edel, ed., *The Diary of Alice James* (New York: Dodd, Mead & Company, 1964), 41.
"very happy to hear it" *Letters*, VII, 270.
"impossible" McKenzie, 99.
"I think it was" Burne-Jones, *Memorials of Edward Burne-Jones*, II, 103–4.
482 "for what she is about" *Letters*, VII, 284.
"George Henry Lewes" McKenzie, 99.
"do not claim" *Letters*, VII, 299.
"dream-land" *Letters*, VII, 300.
"any memory" *Letters*, VII, 273.
not explicit Cf. *Letters*, VII, 302, n. 7, and Haight, *GE*, 544.
483 "happy event" *Letters*, VII, 280.
"Mary Ann Cross" *Letters*, VII, 287.
"the lineaments of the dead" Browning, 188–9.

Index

Throughout the index, the abbreviations GE (George Eliot) and Lewes (George Henry Lewes) are used in subentries.

Eliot, George: *Scenes of
Clerical Life (cont'd)*
  authorship question, 156–7, 212,
    305, 306, 311–12, 313, 317, 323,
    329, 330, 331, 332, 334, 342–3,
    349–50, 380, 396, 397, 398–9,
    404; *see also* Liggins, Joseph,
    imposture
  autobiographical elements and
    memory, 297, 298, 306, 317, 377,
    404, 470–1
  Blackwood, John, 307–12 *passim*,
    317, 333, 352, 353, 400;
    correspondence, 351, 404, 441–2,
    448; correspondence with Lewes,
    317, 351
  French translation by D'Albert-
    Durade, 171
  Lewes, 317, 321
  see also "Janet's Repentance";
    "Mr. Gilfil's Love Story"; "Sad
    Fortunes of the Reverend Amos
    Barton" *above*
Scott, Sir Walter, interest in, 58, 470
"Self and Life," 43–4, 48
sexual identification, 59–60, 139,
  140, 287, 288, 335, 361
on Shakespeare, 84, 113–14
and Sibree, John, 110, 111–12, 115,
  116, 201, 215
and Sibree, John, Jr., 110, 114
  correspondence, 114, 115, 150, 151,
    167, 168, 224, 324, 325, 355–6
and Sibree, Mrs. John, 110–11,
  113–14, 115, 116, 118, 129
Silas Marner, 54, 103, 353, 385,
    433–40 *passim*, 444, 445, 464
  autobiographical elements and
    memory, 213, 436, 437–8, 440
  Blackwood, John: correspondence,
    434, 436, 437, 441–2, 448, 464;
    correspondence with Lewes, 437;
    criticism, 436, 437
  characters: Eppie, 437, 438, 439–40;
    Molly Farran, 359; Silas Marner,
    436–41 *passim*; Silas Marner part-
    ly based on Herbert Spencer, 213
  Lewes, 436–7
  money as theme, 433, 435, 436,
    438–9, 440, 442
  motto, 437
  reviews and success, 440, 441
"Silly Novels by Lady Novelists,"
  102, 127–8, 282, 302, 303
  Lewes on, 285

and Simcox, Edith, *see* Simcox,
  Edith, and GE
Simcox, Edith, on, 55, 57–8, 335, 336
and Simpson, George, 391, 444, 445
and sister, Chrissey, *see* Clarke, Mrs.
  Edward, and GE
and sister-in-law, Sarah Evans, 88,
  89, 108, 122, 123
  correspondence, 169, 338, 478
and Smith, George, see *Cornhill
  Magazine*, GE; *Romola*,
  negotiations *above*
Spanish Gypsy, The, 385, 440, 455,
  458, 465–7, 468
  Blackwood, John, correspondence,
    467, 468
and Spencer, Herbert, *see* Spencer,
  Herbert, and GE
Spencer, Herbert, on, 17, 90, 102,
  202, 203, 204, 210, 223
on Spencer, Herbert, 200, 210, 211,
  258
Spinoza, interest in, 267, 268, 383
  Ethics, translation, 131, 146, 243,
    285, 286, 288, 291–3
  Tractatus Theologico-Politicus,
    131, 146, 151, 292, 293
  translation, 130, 131, 146, 216, 243
and Stephen, Sir Leslie, 22
Stephen, Sir Leslie, on, 22, 88, 89,
  208
and Stowe, Harriet Beecher, 46
  correspondence, 46, 47, 479
on Stowe, Harriet Beecher, 46–7, 303
Strauss, David Friedrich: *Leben
  Jesu, Das*, translation, 14, 54,
    131, 132, 134, 135, 136, 137,
    140–9 *passim*, 151, 163, 164–5,
    175, 182, 183, 203, 217, 263, 291,
    299, 356, 470; Sara Hennell as
    critic-reader, 15, 131, 140–5
    passim; parodied in *Middle-
    march*, 470, 471
  meetings with, 135–6, 267, 376
and Taylor, Mrs. Peter, correspondence, 255–6
Theophrastus Such, see *Impressions
  of Theophrastus Such* above
"Three Months in Weimar," 268,
  279, 280, 289–90, 290–1
translations, 129–37 *passim*, 140–9
  passim, 151, 194, 261, 289
  essay on translating, 146
  for Lewes's biography of Goethe,
    278